# THE HUDSON'S BAY COMPANY
## as an Imperial Factor
### 1821–1869

# The
# Hudson's Bay
# Company

## AS AN IMPERIAL FACTOR
## 1821-1869

*By*
JOHN S. GALBRAITH

OCTAGON BOOKS

A DIVISION OF FARRAR, STRAUS AND GIROUX

New York    1977

Reprinted 1977
by special arrangement with the University of California Press

OCTAGON BOOKS
A DIVISION OF FARRAR, STRAUS & GIROUX, INC.
19 Union Square West
New York, N.Y. 10003


Library of Congress Cataloging in Publication Data

Galbraith, John S
    The Hudson's Bay Company as an imperial factor, 1821-1869.

    Reprint of the ed. published by the University of California
    Press, Berkeley.
    Bibliography: p.
    Includes index.
    1. Hudson's Bay Company.  2. Northwest, Canadian—History.
    I. Title.
[F1060.8.G3    1977]                     971.9                     77-326
ISBN 0-374-92974-2


Manufactured by Braun-Brumfield, Inc.
Ann Arbor, Michigan
Printed in the United States of America

*TO LAURA*

# Preface

THE THEME of this narrative is the expansion, consolidation, and decline of the Hudson's Bay Company's fur trade during the period from 1821 to 1869, and the political implications of these developments. The dates mark the beginning and the end of an era. In 1821, by its amalgamation with the North West Company, the Hudson's Bay Company acquired a virtual monopoly of the fur trade of all British North America. In 1869, by the sale of its proprietary rights in Rupert's Land to Canada, the Company recognized that a fur-trade monopoly could not be preserved against the pressure of settlement from the east and south.

I shall analyze the techniques employed by the Hudson's Bay Company along the frontiers of its trade, its attempts to adapt its policies to the changing character of the society in these border areas, and its final recognition that the era of fur-trade monopoly was approaching an end. In prosecuting its policies, the Company became involved in the international relations of three states and a self-governing colony—Great Britain, Russia, the United States, and Canada. I shall attempt to show how the Company contributed, either as an active force or as an obstacle, to the diplomatic negotiations of these governments.

In the preparation of this study I am indebted to numerous persons. I acknowledge with gratitude the courtesy of the governor and committee of the Hudson's Bay Company, who permitted me access to its archives. Miss A. M. Johnson, the Archivist, was of great assistance not only in valuable suggestions but in her criticism of the manuscript, and Miss A. E. Nickson, her assistant, helped me to locate necessary information. Also, I am indebted to the following for reading sections of the manuscript:

Willard E. Ireland, Provincial Archivist of British Columbia; W. L. Morton, University of Manitoba; A. R. M. Lower, Queen's University; Richard W. Van Alstyne, University of Southern California; W. Kaye Lamb, Dominion Archivist of Canada; and my colleagues, John W. Caughey and Bradford Perkins. My thanks to Miss Rita Cassidy for her assistance in editing.

JOHN S. GALBRAITH

*Los Angeles, California*
*January, 1957*

# Contents

PART

I

*Frontier Policies*

# 1

# Prologue

THE EXPANSION of the British Empire has been largely motivated by the energies of the mercantile class. Far more important to the shaping of British Imperial policy than the secretaries and undersecretaries of state often credited with its formulation were hundreds of men in the commercial community, most of them unknown to history, who created the conditions upon which that policy was based.

In North America, west of the narrow strip of land on the St. Lawrence called Canada, "Imperial Britain" throughout most of the period between 1821 and 1869 was the Hudson's Bay Company. At the height of its expansion, the Company ruled an area of more than 3,000,000 square miles, approximately one-fourth of the continent of North America. The core of this domain was "Rupert's Land," a vaguely defined territory of approximately 1,400,000 square miles granted to the Company by Charles II in the charter of 1670. The validity of the grant was frequently challenged and the boundaries claimed by the Company under its provisions were often disputed, notably by the North West Company and by the Canadian government. But until the sale of its privileges to Canada the Company maintained with varying success its rights to monopolize the trade of the area drained by waters flowing toward Hudson Bay.

The responsibility for defending this estate against encroachments by rival traders and for preserving order among the inhabitants rested upon the Company; its tenure during the 200 years after the issue of the charter depended primarily upon its efficiency rather than upon protection afforded it by the charter or by the British government. The destiny of the Hudson's Bay Company was, therefore, determined largely by the wisdom and energy of its directors at the London headquarters. Although the organization of the North American establishment was changed on several occasions, the structure of the London policy-making body remained constant, determined by the terms of the charter, which provided for a governor, a deputy governor, and a committee of seven members. These directors were required to be stockholders of the Company. Their decisions and their tenure in office were subject to control by the entire body of stockholders, which met periodically as the general court of the Company.

During the first century of its existence, the Hudson's Bay Company faced the military and economic opposition of the French from their base on the St. Lawrence. New France could not tolerate the entrenchment of the Company along the bay, for British competition was certain to undermine the price structure of the entire fur trade in addition to diverting into British hands furs that the French would otherwise have collected. The French consequently made repeated efforts to dislodge the English from the bay, and the struggle was not terminated until France was driven from the St. Lawrence in the French and Indian War.

The Treaty of Paris (1763) brought the Hudson's Bay Company no peace. Instead, it was soon confronted by rival British traders, at first petty peddlers whose individual collections were small, but whose combined effect upon the Company's trade was significant.

But the most perilous era in the history of the Hudson's Bay Company began in 1784, when a group of the most efficient and enterprising of these traders formed the North West Company with headquarters at Montreal.[1] After due allowance for the hyperbole of its admirers, some of whom, like Washington Irving, invested its leadership with proportions larger than life, the North West Company remains a most remarkable combination of genius, daring, energy, and business ability. The Mactavishes, McGillivrays, Mackenzies, Frobishers, and other leaders of this enterprise were no ordinary men.

The constitution of the North West Company, by providing the

[1] For notes to chap. 1, see pp. 431–432.

officers in the field with a direct interest in profits through their status as "wintering partners," gave additional energy to its expansion. The Hudson's Bay Company, dependent upon salaried employees and controlled by a more conservative board, moved more ponderously; but, as events were to prove, it had greater strength and endurance than its glamorous Canadian rival.[2]

Increasing restrictions on trade in the United States after the Jay Treaty of 1794 was signed intensified the Nor'Westers' activity in British North America, forcing its traders northward and westward and inaugurating the last, fatal phase of the contest with the Hudson's Bay Company. The focal point of this conflict was the Red River colony, founded by the Earl of Selkirk in 1811. The colony was designed to advance a project dear to Selkirk's heart— the resettlement of landless Scottish farmers in North America. For this purpose, the Hudson's Bay Company granted him 116,000 square miles in the Red River valley, the key point of the Nor'-Westers' communications system. Selkirk thereafter greatly augmented his holdings of Hudson's Bay stock, and he and his friends became dominant in determining the Company's policies. He was aware that the planting of a colony would evoke the opposition of the North West Company with all the power it could muster. He nevertheless accepted the prospect. Thus opened a ten-year period of violent, unrestrained competition.[3]

A private war within British North America could not long be ignored by the governments of Canada and Great Britain. Canada was first involved by the litigation of the contestants in the Canadian courts. In 1816, Governor-General Sir John Sherbrooke appointed Colonel W. B. Coltman to head a commission of inquiry to investigate the causes of the disturbances. Coltman's efforts to promote peace during the next two years were unavailing. Lord Selkirk, with some reason, suspected Coltman of initial bias in favor of the North West Company, but Coltman was by no means a convinced adherent of either side. Examination of the causes and course of the conflict convinced him that the only solution was governmental intervention. The terms of peace, he believed, must end competition in the "Indian territories," for "it appears by the test of experience that the trade with the Indians cannot be well conducted except by the grant of privileges equivalent to a monopoly over tracts of greater or less extent." [4]

Almost simultaneously, perhaps on the basis of Sherbrooke's and Coltman's earlier communications, the Colonial Office reached the same conclusion. On February 13, 1818, Henry Goulburn, permanent undersecretary of state for colonies, suggested to the governor of the Hudson's Bay Company that the two companies unite. By 1818, too, the North West Company, severely wounded by years of ruinous competition, had decided that peace with the Hudson's Bay Company was imperative and had made overtures to Selkirk to renew negotiations.[5] But the Hudson's Bay Company, now imbued with new energy, and carrying the fight into the heart of the North West Company's area of trade in the Athabaska territory, was not enthusiastic. Competition had been costly, but the Company's reserves were large enough to enable it to pay annual dividends of 4 per cent at the height of the struggle.[6] Further, Selkirk's determination to crush the Nor'Westers had hardened as the conflict became more violent, and there was no prospect of a union so long as he and his supporters controlled the Hudson's Bay Company.

The death of Selkirk in 1820 removed an obstacle to amalgamation, and the pressure of the British government could now be exerted on more pliant men.[7] That pressure was greatly intensified at the beginning of 1820. Henry Goulburn began assiduous research into the legality of the Hudson's Bay Company's charter. He pored over the report of the select committee of the House of Commons which in 1749 had investigated the Company's claims.[8] The evidence taken by the committee could be used effectively should the government decide to test the validity of the charter, although a motion to test the Company's rights had been defeated in 1749. The Colonial Office was actively considering such a test in 1820, should the Hudson's Bay Company prove recalcitrant.[9] The knowledge that such proceedings might be instituted undoubtedly influenced the Company's governor and committee to comply with the government's desires, since there was no certainty that the eventual decision of the Privy Council would be favorable to the Company.

The influence of a powerful undersecretary on Lord Bathurst, the colonial secretary, was undoubtedly an important factor in the government's intervention. Goulburn was an official of the same type as James Stephen and Henry Merivale, a subordinate upon whom the politician at the head of the department depended for information and who by his presentation of the facts could make policy. As Richard Croker, an expert on matters of political influence, once said, the most effective way of promoting action by the Colonial Office was to see Mr. Goulburn, who could influence Lord Bathurst, who in turn could issue the necessary instructions.[10]

According to Edward Ellice's account of the amalgamation, given many years later, it was he who performed the feat of merging the interests of the North West and Hudson's Bay companies. Ellice was the London agent for the North West Company. He told a select committee of the British Parliament that Lord Bathurst, "about 1819 or 1820," had requested his assistance in promoting a union, and that he had been instrumental in achieving that objective.[11] Ellice's political influence should not be underestimated, and the interview to which he referred undoubtedly took place, but Ellice's assessment of his part in the merger is an exaggeration.

Clearly, Ellice had been among the first to propose a union of the companies. On December 2, 1818, he had suggested to Andrew Colvile of the Hudson's Bay Company's governing board that the North West Company purchase a controlling interest in the Hudson's Bay Company in order to end the conflict. The proposal was obviously unacceptable to Lord Selkirk, as it was to other shareholders. Ellice undoubtedly pressed Goulburn to use his power to influence the Hudson's Bay Company toward a settlement, and Goulburn, whose partiality toward the Nor'Westers was notorious, was acting in their interests when he put pressure on the Hudson's Bay Company. But an explanation of the union in terms of an Ellice-Goulburn conspiracy is both superficial and distorted.[12]

By 1820, all parties concerned had become aware that they would benefit by amalgamation. At their annual meeting at Fort William, the wintering partners of the North West Company learned that their company was in desperate financial straits. They therefore sent John McLoughlin and Angus Bethune to London to seek a settlement with the Hudson's Bay Company. Simultaneously, William and Simon McGillivray, the agents of the North West Company, went to London with the same objective. [13]

The Hudson's Bay Company also could promote its material interests by eliminating the rivalry that had been so costly to its proprietors. The advantages of union, particularly on terms giving the Hudson's Bay Company dominance over the North West interests, were patent to the directors after the death of Selkirk, and the importunities of the Colonial Office further inclined them to agreement. These were the factors that produced the coalition under the name of the Hudson's Bay Company on March 26, 1821.[14]

As an additional inducement to union, the Imperial government had offered to grant the coalesced companies exclusive trading privileges in British North America west of Rupert's Land. Such a concession was doubly advantageous to the government. Not only did it encourage amalgamation, but it placed upon the fur trade the responsibility for maintaining order in the territory, a function the British government was not willing to assume. Parliament authorized this license of monopoly on July 2, 1821, when it passed "an act for regulating the fur trade" in the territories of the Crown between Rupert's Land and the Pacific Ocean. In the Oregon territory in dispute between the United States and Great Britain, the act forbade any British subject to engage in the fur trade without license of the government.[15]

The license of December 5, 1821, granted the Hudson's Bay Company and the McGillivrays and Ellice exclusive trading privileges for twenty-one years in British North America from Rupert's Land west.[16] The great monopoly formed on March 26 could now with the blessing of government extend its control to the Pacific. Within the tremendous extent of land west of Canada, the Hudson's Bay Company was thereafter to be the British authority.[17]

The organization developed to direct the trade of this imperial domain was a fusion of North West Company and Hudson's Bay Company elements. By the agreement of March, 1821, the capital of the two companies was combined and, for a period of twenty-one years, the trade of the coalesced companies was to be supervised in London by the governor and committee, advised by a board of four members, two selected by each company. The administration in North America was to be supervised by two governors. One, based at York Factory, was to be in charge of the northern department, and the other, with headquarters at Moose, in control of the southern department.

The northern department as first constituted embraced all of

British North America from the Pacific Ocean on the west to the district of Lac la Pluie (Rainy Lake), the posts on the Winnipeg River, and the Severn River district on the east. Included within its borders were the most lucrative fur preserves in North America. The southern department comprised the area to the east, including Fort William, the north shores of Lakes Huron and Superior, the James Bay area, and some of the posts in Upper and Lower Canada. The remainder of the trade in Canada was assigned to the agency of McGillivrays, Thain, and Company.[18] In 1826, after the failure of that concern, the Canada trade was organized under the Montreal department, and the administration of all three departments was placed under a single governor, George Simpson. The North West Company's system of assigning shares in the profits to its officers in the field, the chief factors and chief traders, which had proved to be a strong incentive to energy and efficiency, was introduced into the amalgamated concern. Councils of these officers were to meet annually in both departments and advise the governors on the conduct of the fur trade in the various districts. The councils were modeled to some extent on the meetings of the Nor'Westers at Fort William. The Hudson's Bay Company had established a council in 1815, but it had been subject both to direct control by the governor in North America and to the headquarters in London.[19]

The original agreement remained in effect for only three years. In 1824 it was superseded by another arrangement under which the McGillivrays and Ellice received stock in the Hudson's Bay Company instead of shares of profits, and the joint board established in 1821 to advise the governor and committee was discontinued. The settlement of 1824 confirmed the dominance, only thinly veiled at the coalition, of the Hudson's Bay Company in the new enterprise. But the infusion of old Nor'Westers into the trading operations of the Hudson's Bay Company gave the reorganized Company a greater vitality than it had previously possessed, and the addition of Edward Ellice to the London directorship brought to the Company not only the wisdom of a canny businessman but a valuable liaison with government.

Thus was inaugurated the era of the Great Monopoly, which dominated the fur trade from Canada to the Pacific and from the Arctic Ocean to the American border. The contest between London and Montreal, Hudson Bay and the St. Lawrence, had been settled. London, not Montreal, was to be the entrepôt of the British fur trade.

The territorial expansion of the Hudson's Bay Company after 1821 was not motivated entirely by the value of the areas into which the Company extended its operations. Another important consideration was the destruction of competition that might threaten the profitable fur preserves. The problem may be compared to that faced at the same time by British governors in India and South Africa, who had been forced to cope with turbulent frontiers endangering the areas they had been appointed to control. The usual solution was annexation of border territories to the Empire, either directly as in South Africa, or through the establishment of satellite states, as was frequently done in India. The annexed territories were often valued not for their own sake, but for the protection they afforded to the area regarded as important. But annexations did not eliminate the "turbulent frontier"; rather they brought Imperial administrators into contact with new areas of disturbance and led to further annexations.

The Hudson's Bay Company was faced with a frontier problem of a different character. Its "frontier" was the line where the area of monopoly touched the area of competition. The Company was required to defend its monopoly by its own resources. Employment of troops except to control the population at Red River was out of the question. The patrolling of thousands of miles of frontier would have cost more than any commercial enterprise could afford. The only means of repelling encroachments was a commercial policy that forced the intruders to absorb such large losses on the frontiers that they lost the interest or ability to continue the contest. In the struggle with the North West Company, the Hudson's Bay Company had been able to reduce prices so as to compel its rival to seek peace. The policies established by the governor and committee in the conflict between 1811 and 1821 remained essentially the same thereafter—to drive rivals as far as possible from the area of maximum profit by active trade with the Indians at prices ruinous to opposition. But although these frontier policies had been accepted before the coalition, they were highly systematized after 1821, and they constituted a factor in the territorial expansion of the Hudson's Bay Company which involved it in boundary controversies with Russia and the United States.

In districts remote from competition, profits were high; and, where the fur-bearing animals had been virtually exterminated in competition with the North West Company, trapping could be reduced or terminated. In districts where it had monopoly control, the Hudson's Bay Company could prohibit the use of liquor in trade, a measure demanded by humanitarians and materially beneficial to both Indians and Company. But along the frontier such policies could not be maintained. There prices were regulated by those of the opposition; the Company encouraged the Indians to hunt for every available fur; and liquor was dispensed whenever it was introduced by competitors.

For the formulation of these policies, no single person can be considered responsible. In general outlines they had much in common with monopoly practices everywhere. But their specific application in the various frontier areas was made during the governorship of John Henry Pelly. His successors did not deviate materially from the concepts of his administration. When one of them, Henry Hulse Berens, suggested certain modifications of the frontier concepts, he received a lecture from Sir George Simpson. Simpson's statement, delivered a little over a year before his death, was a clear exposition of the character and foundations of the Company's policies along its frontiers:

> Since I have been connected with the Service the fundamental principle of our business has been to collect *all the Furs* obtainable within the range of our operations. If we are to retain the controul of the Trade, we must prevent other parties getting into it, which can only be done by preventing Furs in any large quantity, falling into their hands. This obliges us to outbid our opponents; and it has always been a maxim with us, that the Compy. are able to pay as high as any other party.
>
> The effect of discontinuing the system on the Canada and United States frontiers would soon be apparent, in the advance of the opposition into the interior, and the transfer of the Chief Seat of the Fur Market from London to New York. In proportion as the Compys. importations to England decreased and those of New York increased, continental Buyers would resort to the latter to make their purchases.[20]

In areas where opposition was present or expected, the Company stationed its most efficient officers and servants. Their duty was to scour the area for furs, to secure, if possible, every fur, and thus to prevent or eliminate competition. The Company officers who have been remembered were usually those stationed in frontier areas. In such positions they encountered conflict, and conflict is the stuff from which history is written. The governor and committee and Simpson chose their most energetic officers for frontier service— McLoughlin, Peter Skene Ogden, James Douglas, and others. Their positions in areas of conflict gave them the opportunity for fame, and they possessed the necessary qualities to insure their being remembered.

The Company was highly successful against rival fur traders. But against competitors who depended for their livelihood on other occupations, and to whom the fur trade was a source of additional income rather than a sole occupation, the Company was much less effective. The fur trade in Canada deteriorated when lumbermen moved into the vicinity of the posts, and it suffered more severely when farmers arrived. Along the international boundary to the south, the threat came, not directly from American fur traders, but from the half-breeds at Red River, who engaged in farming as well as in fur trading. In Oregon, American settlers destroyed the fur trade; and the Company's lucrative districts along the Peace River and the Mackenzie River were first invaded by competitors based upon the gold claims of the Fraser River. James Douglas referred to the Willamette River settlers when he made the following observation, but his words could be applied generally:

> The interests of the Colony and Fur Trade will never harmonize, the farmer can flourish, only, through the protection of equal laws, the influence of free trade, the accession of respectable inhabitants; in short, by establishing a new order of things, while the fur Trade must suffer by each innovation.[21]

Peter Skene Ogden expressed the same view when he wrote to Sir George Simpson:

> You are I presume fully aware that the Fur trade and Civilisation can never blend together and experience teaches us that the former invariably gives way to the latter. Indians and Whites can never amalgamate together, and altho every exertion may be made to secure the trade it seldom or ever proves profitable.[22]

The Company's territorial expansion was not entirely the product of the negative motivation of denying the opposition access to profitable territories. The Company sought profits wherever they could be made, and in pursuit of profits it sent trading parties to California and established an agency in the Hawaiian Islands. Oregon south of 49° continued to be profitable for several years after the treaty of 1846, as New Caledonia [23] was until after the Fraser River gold rush. But even in those areas the motive of eliminating opposition far from the Company's heartland was not absent. Even after the posts in New Caledonia ceased to be profitable, they were maintained to discourage competitors from crossing the Rocky Mountains into the Peace River area.

Although the Company's policies were basically the same along the entire fur-trade frontier, their specific characteristics varied in accordance with the type of opposition. The fur trade in each of the three frontier areas—Canada, the southern border, and the Pacific slope—presented somewhat different problems. An understanding of the Company's various trading policies on these frontiers is essential to the discussion of its role in diplomatic negotiations during the period from 1821 to 1869.

## CHAPTER

## 2

# Personnel of the Monopoly

THE UNION of the North West and Hudson's Bay companies created an enterprise of power unequaled in the history of the fur trade. The resources, experience, and business acumen of the Hudson's Bay Company blended with the energy of the Nor'westers to give unusual vitality to the monopoly that came into being in 1821. Yet the amount of the Company's capital and the number of its personnel were small by the standards of great commercial houses of the twentieth century. Before the coalition, the capital stock of the Hudson's Bay Company was only £103,950. In 1824, after the interests of Ellice and the McGillivrays were converted into shares of stock, the capitalization was increased to £400,000. Capital was increased on three other occasions, finally reaching £500,000 in 1854, at which level it remained until the stockholders sold their interests in 1863.[1]

Control of the Company between 1670 and 1863 was maintained by a small number of families, and the composition of the group changed slowly. There were 18 proprietors when Charles II granted the charter, and by 1822 the total number was only 64. Thereafter the number of proprietors increased relatively rapidly —in 1838 there were 216, and in 1853, 252 [2]—but control remained firmly in the hands of a tight-knit little group bound together by long, intimate association and by intermarriage. The Pelly, Berens, Harrison, Colvile, and Halkett families dominated the Company,

[1] For notes to chap. 2, see pp. 432–435.

and they and their friends virtually monopolized positions on t. governing board.

Meetings of the stockholders between 1821 and 1863 usually were almost identical in personnel with meetings of the directors, and it is therefore not surprising that the proprietors at no time contested the decisions of the governor and committee. This close control of the Company's affairs enabled the directors to maintain a high degree of secrecy which was probably a safeguard against actual and potential competitors. But secrecy was also harmful. Critics could successfully portray the Company to an antimonopoly British society as a sinister enterprise, reaping huge profits from the exploitation of the Indian population, using fraud and debauchery to increase its gains. The directors, victims of a strange delusion that the publication of the facts would stimulate attacks, unwittingly aided their critics.[3] For the Company's success was not derived from exploitation of the innocent savage or from sharp dealings with shoddy merchandise. Its business practices were in no way reprehensible by the moral standards of the century. The most important factors in its success were long experience and intelligent management.

For three decades after the amalgamation the dominant member of the board was John Henry Pelly, and the mark of his influence continued for many years after his death. Pelly's family had become associated with the Company in 1788, when his father, Henry Hind Pelly, had become a proprietor. John Henry, like his father, sailed during his youth in the ships of the East India Company, but in 1806, at the age of twenty-nine, he settled down to the life of a man of business in the City of London. In that year his father transferred to him £1,800 in Hudson's Bay stock to qualify him for membership on the committee, and Pelly was elected a director. His progress thereafter was rapid. He was elected deputy governor in 1812 and governor in 1822. In 1822 he also became a director of the Bank of England, and continued to serve in that capacity until his death. He became deputy governor of the bank in 1839 and served as its governor from 1841 until the end of 1842.[4] In 1840, Queen Victoria elevated Pelly to a baronetcy in recognition of his "acknowledged worth and long and meritorious services as Governor of the Hudson's Bay Company." [5]

These bare biographical details indicate something of the nature of the man. Blessed by birth into a well-to-do and influential family, Pelly had easy access to the community of company directors, as did hundreds of well-born mediocrities. But his subsequent rise to dominant positions in the Hudson's Bay Company and the Bank of England cannot be explained in terms of influence. Stockholders might tolerate nonentities on boards of directors; they would not long accept ineffectuality in their governors, upon whom their profits depended. Pelly's ability to arrive at sound policies founded upon realistic appraisals of the facts was the basis for his election as governor of the Hudson's Bay Company. There is strong evidence that even before the coalition of 1821, while he was deputy governor, Pelly had already become the dominant member of the committee upon whom the titular governor and the other board members primarily relied for advice. His election to the governorship was public recognition of a leadership he was already exercising.[6]

Pelly's influence in the formulation of the Company's policies was less pronounced in the last decade of his life. After suffering a serious illness in the autumn of 1841, he would have resigned as governor had Andrew Colvile not persuaded him to remain.[7] For many weeks the business of the Company was conducted without his participation, and it was not until the autumn of 1842 that he was able to resume his official duties.[8]

Between 1842 and 1850 Pelly devoted himself to the affairs of the Company with apparently undiminished ability, but he suffered increasingly from pain in his head, which he attributed to gout, and was unable to muster the energy he had previously displayed. In December, 1850, the cause of the pain revealed itself when an abscess in his head burst.[9] Although he survived this crisis and was able briefly to return to his work, Pelly did not recover. Before his death on August 13, 1852, from a complication of diseases,[10] actual control of the Company had already passed into other hands. His successors, though capable men, did not reach his stature, and the policies of the Company between 1852 and 1863 were largely those that Pelly had established.

Pelly was one of a quadrumvirate who largely determined the course of Company policy. The others were Andrew Colvile, Edward (nicknamed "Bear") Ellice, and George Simpson.

Colvile, a brother-in-law of the fifth Earl of Selkirk, first became interested in the Company in 1808 through his association with Selkirk. Two years later he was elected to the committee. He served as deputy governor from 1839 to 1852 and became governor upon the death of Pelly, serving until his death in 1856. Through his long association with the Company, his family connection with the Selkirks, and his business ability, Colvile became an influential member of the committee. His patronage made the unknown George Simpson an overseas governor, and his authority in decisions on commercial policy was second only to that of Pelly.[11]

Edward Ellice the Elder was the Company's liaison with the government. Upon his wide and intimate associations with influential British politicians the directors depended either to extract concessions favorable to the Company or to defend its interests against its enemies. The editor of a hostile Canadian newspaper paid Ellice acid tribute when he declared five years after Ellice's death:

> The Hudson's Bay Company has always been a favourite with a good number of the English aristocracy, especially with the Whigs. . . . But for the backstairs influence of Whig magnates, like the late Mr. Ellice, the great monopoly would not have been so tenacious of life; and but for some such underhand dealing and family pecuniary influences involved, the difficulties of arranging the manner in which the country [Rupert's Land] is to become part of our Confederation would not have been so great as they are apparently coming to be.[12]

This assessment of Ellice's power was an exaggeration. The allegation of "family pecuniary influences" had no evident foundation in fact, but the editor was correct in describing Ellice as the liaison between the Company and the government. Except for a brief period in office, Ellice was not a dominant politician, but his acquaintance with those who made policy was wide and often intimate, and he was heard with respect by British statesmen whether they were Whigs, Liberals, or Tories. His political influence was unquestionably at its height in the 1830's, particularly during the prime-ministership of the second Earl Grey, his brother-in-law, when Ellice was a member of the select inner circle of the government. But his value to the Hudson's Bay Company in its political relationships extended to his death in 1863.[13]

Probably second in importance only to Pelly in the commercial operations of the monopoly was George Simpson, the overseas governor from 1826 to 1860. For the first five years after the coalition, he shared power with William Williams, his titular superior, but the division of authority was not successful.[14] When Williams retired, responsibility for the Company's operations from the Arctic to the American border and from the Atlantic to the Pacific was now for the first time vested in one man, and George Simpson was well on his way to becoming the "Little Emperor" of the fur trade.

Simpson's influence in determining Company policies has been variously estimated. He has been described as the virtual dictator of British North America west of Canada, and, on the other hand, as merely the instrument of the London board. Neither of these extreme views is justified. Simpson was always subject not only to the theoretical but to the actual control of the governor and committee. Their periodic dispatches to North America and their instructions to him when he visited London determined the direction of his administration. But, though he was a subordinate, he was an increasingly knowledgeable subordinate whose intimacy with the conditions of trade in North America gave his advice great weight. In the 1840's, at the height of his abilities and with an unmatched background of experience, Simpson was frequently able virtually to write for the governor and committee the dispatch they would send him for the forthcoming year.[15] But even then, in the fullness of his power, he was made to realize that the governing board which had appointed him could remove him and that his authority was circumscribed. In 1846, when he suggested that he be permitted to appoint clerks in the Montreal department, he was chastised by Pelly for "improper interference with the powers of the board." [16] Simpson was no "emperor," as his admirers have dubbed him, although to Company employees in North America he must have appeared an awe-inspiring autocrat. His title might more appropriately have been "viceroy," for he was subject only to the ultimate authority of his employers.

Like the governors of India during the era of slow communications between Great Britain and its overseas dominions, Simpson was given great latitude. He died before the establishment of the trans-Atlantic cable made possible intimate control from London; from his headquarters at Lachine, near Montreal, correspondence to London involved weeks of delay in making decisions, even after mail steamships began regular operations from North America to Europe. In the remote interior of Rupert's Land, months would pass before replies from London could be received.

In his relationships with the commissioned officers of the Company in North America, Simpson's power was virtually absolute. He completely dominated the advisory councils of fur-trade officers by the respect his business ability and his superior grasp of the over-all problems of the trade commanded, by his friendly intimacy with leading members of the council, and by the threat of dire consequences to those who challenged his authority. It was not merely respect for Simpson's judgment which caused members of the councils to follow his recommendations in appointments of chief traders and chief factors, although his judgment was usually excellent. The men of the service believed, and their belief was apparently well founded, that those who evoked the governor's displeasure could expect to be transferred to the least attractive districts in the fur trade.

Simpson possessed some of the qualities of Uriah Heep, unctuously " 'umble" to those who could advance him. But beneath this manner there was a cold, ruthless efficiency in the advancement of his interests and those of the Company. In 1821 a Company employee described Simpson as "a gentlemanly man" who should "not create much alarm" and who could not be deemed as "formidable as an Indian trader." Three years later, the same employee complained that the days of easy discipline were gone and that "the North-west is now beginning to be ruled with an iron rod." [17] Simpson's mind was molded by his preoccupation with the fur trade. His highest ethic was promotion of the interests of the Hudson's Bay Company, and the methods he employed in its service were not overly scrupulous. He was a keen but cynical analyst of human character, and his low estimate of the moral qualities of American and Canadian politicians was reflected in his employment of agents to win government support for the Company's interests by methods ranging from subtle distribution of gifts to outright bribery. The bribe might be a present of buffalo tongues and cigars or the promise of $100,000, but the mentality behind it was that of a man who believed that all politicians—at least those of the American variety—had their price, and that the price was usually low. Canadian politicians whose friendship for the Company was stimulated by the expectation of tangible rewards were officeholders ranging from members of the cabinet [18] to key subordinates. The technique of Simpson and his agent Stuart Derbishire is indicated by the following letter from Derbishire to Simpson on May 12, 1852:

> I would like a box of cheroots for Bouchette. You may send me one or two to spare, & if I do not place them you shall have them back. It is a delicate operation you know—if not well performed does harm, & one cannot make opportunities, but only act when they make themselves. I told Bouchette you wished to shake hands with him & thank him. He said, I like Sir George, everyone does— and his Agent has such an undeniable way with him.[19]

Simpson's estimate of the corruptibility of politicians was un- doubtedly overly cynical since he was frustrated in his efforts to influence governments both in Canada and the United States. But his attitude provides insight into a nature essentially amoral. Simp- son had two loyalties—to his Company and to himself—and he served both with great ability and complete devotion. His service to the Hudson's Bay Company was untainted by the slightest sus- picion of dishonesty. No competitor could have bribed him to desert the enterprise to which he devoted his life. The fortune he acquired in Canada was produced by intelligent investment of his salary.[20]

The hard cynicism of George Simpson may perhaps be par- tially explained by his introduction to life as an illegitimate child. His antecedents were a subject of great sensitivity to him. So ret- icent was he concerning his childhood that the date of his birth is unknown,[21] and the "biography" he contributed to a volume on the aristocracy after his elevation to knighthood in 1841 must be among the shortest recorded.[22]

Differences in the antecedents of Pelly and Simpson and in the ethical standards of London and Montreal perhaps explain the contrast in their characters. Pelly enjoyed the reputation of being a thoroughly honorable businessman who would not contaminate himself and the companies he represented by engaging in any deal- ings which, if exposed, would be condemned as violations of Vic- torian morality. Simpson could not be so characterized by his in- timates. Yet the contrast should not be overdrawn. Despite his evident personal rectitude Pelly at times displayed opaqueness with regard to his associates' deviations from strict ethics. On one occasion he was party to an agreement whose success manifestly depended upon the bribery of American public officials, although the corruption was to be accomplished by others.[23]

In one respect Pelly and Simpson were similar. Both were devoted to the preservation of the fur-trade monopoly, and they were usually in essential agreement as to the policies necessary to safeguard it. At the height of their mental powers they were an effective team.

Under Simpson's control were a corps of commissioned officers —chief factors and chief traders—who received shares in the profits of each year's return. In the coalition of 1821, provision was made for twenty-five chief factors and twenty-eight chief traders. To conduct a trade extending over an area in excess of 3,000,000 square miles, these officers commanded a total of approximately 1,500 contractual employees, including Europeans, half-breeds, Canadians, and Sandwich Islanders.[24] Even this number was considered too high, and after the amalgamation the Company tried to eliminate "excess" manpower. In executing this policy Simpson was perhaps too zealous; the officers in frontier areas were often forced to face competition with inadequate personnel at their disposal. The paucity of manpower resources maintained by the Company is evident in the statistics on its employees in the mid-1830's: [25]

|  | Europeans | Half-breeds | Canadians | Sandwich Islanders |
|---|---|---|---|---|
| Northern Department | 141 | 130 | 157 | — |
| Columbia | 138 | 47 | 218 | 55 |
| Southern Department | 81 | 89 | 51 | — |
| Montreal Department | 38 | 17 | 132 | — |
| Totals | 398 | 283 | 558 | 55 |
|  |  | Grand total |  | 1,294 |

The primary source of European labor was Scotland, in particular the poverty-stricken Orkney Islands. To young men with no prospects for an existence above the level of subsistence, service with the Hudson's Bay Company was attractive despite the reputed rigors of northern American winters, prolonged absence from home, and reports of harsh discipline of recalcitrant employees.[26] Against these liabilities there were overbalancing assets, for laborers employed by the Hudson's Bay Company were provided not only with wages comparable to those paid by other British employers, but with food and lodging. Monetary payments therefore could largely be saved, for in the remote areas of North America there was little opportunity for foolish expenditures. But the appeal of the Company's service lessened as British wages rose and the Company's scale of payments remained relatively constant. Also, the Company faced competition from employers in Canada. As the monetary inducement declined, procurement from Great Britain and from Canada became more difficult, and on one occasion the Company resorted to Norway as a source of labor. The expedient proved unsuccessful because the Norwegians soon became disillusioned with the service. Desertion of contractual employees increased and discipline became more difficult.[27]

The uncertain loyalty of noncommissioned personnel makes more impressive the achievements of the Company's officers during this period. The industry and ability of the supervisory personnel were generally high. The appearance of members of the Pelly, Simpson, or Colvile families in positions of responsibility in the service suggests that nepotism was not entirely absent, and occasionally men selected as officers proved to be worthless, but in general the Company was well served by its "wintering partners." John McLoughlin, James Douglas, Peter Skene Ogden,[28] John Rowand, and many others were men of uncommon talent and unusual power. Without their abilities the policies of Simpson and the directors would have been far less effective.

The organization of the Company remained unchanged until its sale in 1863. The directors of the new Company, subject to increasing pressure from the British government, selected as their governors men of political prominence. Sir Edmund Head, Lord Kimberley, Sir Stafford Northcote, and George Joachim Goschen were leaders in the Liberal and Conservative parties. In contrast, the governors between 1821 and 1863 were virtually unknown to politics. Throughout the earlier period, Edward Ellice the Elder was the only person of political importance who was active in the affairs of the Company. But to ascribe to Ellice's power alone the continued existence of the monopoly in a society devoted to free trade would be a gross exaggeration. The political privileges of the Hudson's Bay Company survived largely because the British government was unwilling to assume the responsibilities and expense that would fall upon it were the privileges to be extinguished.

Until Canada became concerned, there was no practicable alternative to the continuance of Company rule in Rupert's Land. Since the British government was reluctant to exercise direct control, the Company remained the only representative of the British Empire in North America west of Canada. Consequently the policies of the Company created the conditions upon which British statesmen were forced to act in diplomacy involving western North America. To a considerable extent, therefore, British foreign policy in this area was influenced by the decisions of the governor and committee and by the activities of their employees in North America.

# The Canadian Frontier

WHEN THE Hudson's Bay Company acquired the Canadian posts in 1821, the directors realized that they had assumed an unprofitable burden. Two centuries of hunting had drastically reduced the number of fur-bearing animals in the St. Lawrence watershed, and competition was severe. If the Canadian trade had been valued merely as a source of immediate profits, the posts would have been speedily abandoned.

Canada, however, was important because it constituted the most dangerous area on the borders of Rupert's Land. From Canada had come the North West Company; unless the Hudson's Bay Company contested for the trade of Canada, it might again be forced to defend itself against an invasion of the chartered territory. Attacks were most likely to come from three sources. The Ottawa River, traditionally a route of communication into the interior, was in 1821 infested with petty traders. Some of these depended for their livelihood entirely on fur trading. Others dealt in furs as an additional source of income to their primary occupations as lumberers or farmers. A similar condition existed on the River St. Maurice. North of Lake Superior and Lake Huron traders from the United States were active and, if permitted to grow strong, might expand their operations into Rupert's Land.

Nature was the Company's ally in discouraging penetration of Rupert's Land from Canada. The rocky, inhospitable Laurentian shield provided an excellent buffer, and the poverty of the soil

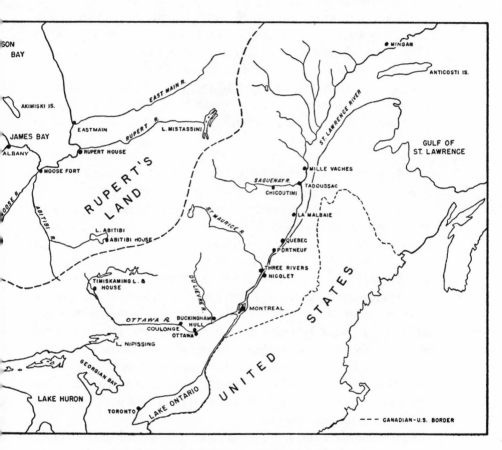

*The Canadian Frontier*

discouraged the westward advance of the farmer beyond Georgian Bay. So effective was this barrier that only experienced canoemen or venturesome spirits essayed voyages through it, and they frequently came to grief through shortage of provisions. The Canadian agricultural frontier was halted until it leaped the barrier into the rich prairies after the sale of the Company's chartered rights. With these advantages, the Company's policy of competitive trade as protection might have seemed unnecessary to some officers, but not to the governor and committee nor to George Simpson. Haunted by the memory of the North West Company, they were determined that another powerful combination should not be allowed to form in Canada.

The most crucial area was the Ottawa, for by that river access into Rupert's Land was relatively easy, and there the Company faced its most dangerous opponents—the "auxiliary fur traders." If petty traders had depended for support on trading with Indians, the Company would easily have been able to eliminate them. But lumbermen and potash makers who dealt with Indians for furs were difficult to drive from the trade, as were general storekeepers who bought furs. All of these were able to trade at less expense than was the Hudson's Bay Company, for the costs of their establishments were virtually the same whether or not they dealt in furs. Also, Iroquois hunters who had previously been employed by the North West Company in the interior trade were now confined to their own hunting grounds in the Ottawa–St. Lawrence area. Deprived of their former employment by the Hudson's Bay Company, they were hostile to the Company and gave preference to the petty traders.

By 1821 settlers and shopkeepers were established in the vicinity of the Hudson's Bay Company's post at Lake of Two Mountains, near Montreal, and some lumbermen had proceeded up the Ottawa River to the vicinity of Fort Coulonge, near the present community of Pembroke. The valley of the Ottawa was, however, not yet heavily populated. The land remained largely in its pristine condition, and the fur trader was able to continue his occupation with little interference.[1]

On the River St. Maurice, the country within approximately 150 miles of Three Rivers was hunted by a tribe of half-breed Abenaki

[1] For notes to chap. 3, see pp. 435–437.

Indians who lived in the village of St. Francis on the St. Lawrence. Like the lumbermen and farmers on the St. Lawrence, the Abenaki did not depend upon furs for their livelihood, but derived their subsistence primarily from the soil. During the hunting season the men purchased outfits from neighboring shopkeepers with cash or produce and, leaving their families at home, traveled up the St. Maurice to hunt and trade. They peddled their furs in communities along the St. Lawrence, receiving higher prices from the Canadian population than were current in either New York or London. In the upper reaches of the St. Maurice another tribe, the Wamontachingues, whom the Company's personnel called the "Montachines," hunted for furs and traded largely with the Hudson's Bay Company's competitors.[2]

Far to the west, on the north shores of Lakes Huron and Superior, the rock-bound, unfriendly shield discouraged the penetration of settlers. When the Company assumed control of the Nor'-Westers' posts, the region was inhabited only by Indians and fur traders. The land above Georgian Bay offered opportunities for lumbering and a little farming, but its use for these purposes awaited further population of the Ontario peninsula. The existence of tremendous mineral resources north of the lakes would not be discovered for almost a century. This was fur-trade territory, though the furs had been depleted by decades of exploitation. Here the Company was initially confronted by the type of opposition against which it was most effective—the petty trader who depended for his livelihood on the sale of furs. Competition on the St. Lawrence watershed thus involved problems different from those in the lakes region.

One of George Simpson's first tasks when he assumed the administration in Canada from the defunct McGillivrays, Thain, and Company was the rectification of a blunder made by the London directors in 1822, when they allowed the lease of the King's Posts to fall into the hands of competitors. These posts had been created by order of the Conseil Souverain de Quebec in 1653 and the territory had been enlarged by subsequent decrees. As defined in 1733 the lease extended along the St. Lawrence from the Saguenay River to Cape Cormorant, about 270 miles; inland it was bounded in general by the height of land between the St. Lawrence and Hudson Bay watersheds. In 1802 it was granted to Simon Mactavish, John Gregory, and their associates, and thus fell under the control of the North West Company. The lease was to run for twenty years at an annual payment of £1,025, Halifax currency;[3] when it passed to the Hudson's Bay Company in 1821 it thus had one year to run. The governor and committee decided that the posts were not worth the rent and agreed to offer only £500 or £600 per year. They were consequently outbid by John Goudie.[4]

After the posts passed from the Company's control, the directors learned a lesson in frontier policy. They soon realized that Goudie and his successors were strategically situated to extend their trade up either the St. Maurice or the Ottawa. The governor and committee belatedly decided that they must regain control of the King's Posts. This proved to be a long and expensive operation.

To squeeze out the lessees, the Company leased Mille Vaches, a seigneury on the St. Lawrence at the southern edge of the King's Posts, at a yearly rental of £300, Halifax currency,[5] and established a trading post at Portneuf. At the same time it renewed the North West Company's lease of the seigneury of Mingan and the Isles and Islets of Mingan to the north, separated from the King's Posts by the Cormorant River. The King's Posts were thus to be caught in a vise and the lessees forced to sell their rights. The nine square miles of Mille Vaches could "scarcely boast the nativity of a single fur."[6] The only source of furs was the King's Posts. Mingan, on the other hand, was a seigneury of great extent and seemed to offer the prospect of profit from furs and fisheries. But here also the primary motive for control was to embarrass the lessees of the King's Posts.

In the ensuing competition, prices rose to levels that made profits impossible. The lessees attempted to counter the Company's competition at Portneuf by employing border guards, but the Indians eluded them by hiding during the day and venturing forth only at night.[7] In desperation, as expenses mounted, the lessees in 1830 sent twenty men into Mille Vaches itself to intercept Indians on their way down the Portneuf River. The result was a collision with a party from the Hudson's Bay Company and suits and countersuits in the Canadian courts.[8]

The competition was ruinous to Goudie's successors, but it was also costly to the Company. In the mid-1820's the lessees had struck back at the Company by establishing two posts on the upper St.

Maurice, demoralizing the trade of that area. Eight years had elapsed since the Company relinquished its lease. It was now involved in court actions that were certain to be prejudicial to its interests. When Curtis M. Lampson, representing the lessees, offered in the summer of 1830 to sell the lease to the Company,[9] the governor and committee did not reject his overture. They instructed James Keith, who was in immediate charge of the Montreal department, to arrange an agreement, since he had superior knowledge of the value of the property, the financial condition of the Lampsons, and other relevant considerations.[10] Keith was aware that the Lampsons were tenacious adversaries who would accept losses rather than give up the contest. Consequently he agreed to pay £25,000 sterling for the transfer of the lease, the Lampsons' establishments on the St. Maurice, and their stock of goods and furs.[11] The Company thus assumed the lease for its remaining twelve years.

Because of their reluctance to pay more than £600 per year at the auction in 1822, the governor and committee had subjected themselves to competition on the St. Maurice, litigation in the Canadian courts, and losses of many thousands of pounds, and had finally been forced to buy out their opponents at a high price and to assume the lease at £1,200 per year. Yet they chastised Keith for having accepted the Lampsons' demands, though later, on sober reconsideration, they decided that he had acted judiciously.[12] In 1830 George Simpson estimated that the Company had lost £2,000 a year by its struggle with the Lampsons.[13] The mistake of 1822 was not repeated.

The Company's policies in opposition to the Lampsons illustrate its general principles of competition. With a petty trader there could be no bargaining, for others would be encouraged to enter the field in the hope of receiving similar treatment. Rather, the small competitor with no capital must be ruined. In competition with firms like the Lampsons, which could cause substantial damage to the Company's interests, the governor and committee were willing to bargain for a settlement under which the opposition would retire from the field at a price—the price being determined by the competitor's powers of resistance. When McGillivrays, Thain, and Company bought out two small competitors on the Ottawa River, George Simpson condemned them for their rashness, since "we do not consider it good policy to buy such people out, who if allowed to contest the trade for one or two years longer would in all probability have been ruined men." [14] Simpson's views were here, as in other respects, a faithful reproduction of those of the governor and committee.

With the withdrawal of the Lampsons from the contest, the Hudson's Bay Company achieved virtual monopoly of the fur trade on the north shore of the St. Lawrence River from its junction with the Saguenay to the Gulf of St. Lawrence. Its only serious competitors were the fishermen who frequented the river and the gulf. On the River St. Maurice the Company enjoyed a temporary respite, since the light sandy soil of the valley had discouraged the entry of farmers.

The conflict had disrupted the trade not only of the St. Maurice but of the Hudson's Bay territory across the height of land. When the Trout Lake Indians, living in the chartered territory, heard that higher prices were being offered on the St. Maurice, they had carried their furs to the Company's post at Ojibuan on that river rather than accept the low monopoly rates offered by the Company's traders in the chartered territory. After tariffs were adjusted to make such journeys less attractive,[15] the Company enjoyed the luxury of monopoly on the upper reaches of the river, adjacent to Rupert's Land.

The trade of the upper St. Maurice did not long remain uncontested. By 1834 Abenaki Indians from St. Francis and Nicolet had appeared at the headwaters of the river and some had even ventured into the chartered territory, where they traded with natives as well as hunted for furs themselves. Since they were not natives of Rupert's Land, they were probably violating the Company's chartered rights, but James Keith was not disposed to order their apprehension. In view of the hostility of reform elements in Lower Canada to the Company, he feared that such action might be used as a basis for further attacks.[16] When repeated warnings failed, Simpson finally decided that the seizure of furs found in possession of the Abenaki in Rupert's Land was the only way to meet their encroachments.[17] But seizures alone could not prevent competition, as Simpson recognized. The only effective protection for the fur trade was to check opposition on the frontier. The Company therefore maintained establishments on the river St.

Maurice even though the returns barely covered expenses. The Indian traders would accept only cash for their furs, and cash prices were more costly to the Company than the equivalent value in goods. It was necessary to pay cash also to the lumbermen and settlers who appeared in the lower reaches of the river in the 1840's.[18] In 1847, the Company suffered a net loss of £100 on the St. Maurice posts,[19] and the district frequently suffered small losses thereafter. But as a result of the maintenance of these posts opposition in the Rupert's River area remained insignificant in the period between 1839 and 1869.

The trade of the Ottawa River, like that of the River St. Maurice, was important to the Company primarily as protection for interior districts. In 1821 there were three main posts on the river. Three hundred miles from its source the Ottawa flows into Lake Timiskaming, a body of water 67 miles long and varying in width from a few hundred yards to almost 10 miles. Upon that lake, located where the river changes its course from its initial westerly to a southeasterly direction, the North West Company had maintained a trading station. Approximately 220 miles below Timiskaming, where the river reunites after diverging into two branches to create Allumette Island, was Fort Coulonge. This post was strategically situated, for it not only controlled the Ottawa River but stood near the outlets of the tributary Black and Coulonge rivers. Another 200 miles downstream and a few miles from Montreal is the widening of the river called Lake of Two Mountains where the Nor'Westers had maintained a post, named for the lake, and two subsidiary establishments.

After the coalition, the governor and committee decided to retain control of Fort Coulonge and Lake of Two Mountains as protection for Timiskaming, which in turn guarded the approach to Rupert's Land. The advance of settlement and lumbering, however, forced the Company to modify its trading operations and gradually to withdraw upstream.

The district of Lake of Two Mountains had become a settled agricultural community by the early 1840's. The county contained a population of over 27,000, double that of three decades before, and the farming population of Canada East had extended up the Ottawa River to the neighborhood of the village of Buckingham, on the Rivière du Lièvre, about twenty-five miles northeast of

Bytown, the present city of Ottawa. On the south bank of the river in Canada West, a similar movement was taking place. In Carleton County, where Bytown was located, there were 10,128 people in 1840, compared with 2,116 in 1824; and in Lanark County, immediately to the west, there were 14,545 inhabitants in 1840, almost double the number in 1824. The lower Ottawa valley as far as Bytown was now dotted with farms, and the fur-trading techniques of the wilderness were no longer practicable. The maintenance of trading posts with their necessary staffs in this altered environment was unduly expensive. In recognition of this fact, Simpson ordered the discontinuance of the posts on the lower reaches of the river and the establishment of a small agency at Buckingham. This was accomplished in 1847. The Company was required to pay only the rent of a house in the village and board and wages for an interpreter and a clerk. The latter made a tour through the surrounding country once or twice a month, collecting furs at the prevailing rate and paying cash for his purchases. The Company discontinued the credit system as well as its previous policy of issuing provisions to half-starved Indians who visited the trading posts of the district.[20]

But even a substantial reduction in expenses could not make the trade profitable, for the Company's agent at Buckingham was forced to pay high prices to keep furs out of the hands of Montreal and New York competitors. In the March, 1858, fur sales in London, for example, buyers paid the Company an average of 5s. 8¼d. per pound for beaver. During that year the agent was paying from 5s. to 7s. 6d. per pound.[21] But if such prices were unprofitable for the Company, they were almost equally so for its opponents, though the New York and Montreal markets usually paid higher prices than London and these higher rates made it possible for petty traders to continue to compete.

The Company could not hope to eliminate all competition on the Ottawa River. At best it could prevent opposition from becoming solidly established and discourage it from expanding into the interior. But the Company could not control the spread of settlement and lumbering up the Ottawa valley; and competition was at least as dependent on the price of lumber as on the price of furs. When lumbering was unprofitable, competition in furs was less severe. Also, as timber resources were reduced in the lower reaches of the valley and the lumbering frontier marched westward, competition in furs was likewise extended. Every shantyman was a potential fur trader, and auxiliary to the lumbermen were publicans who dealt in the most compelling of commodities in the Indian trade—despite the prohibition by the Canadian government of the dispensing of liquor to the Indians. By 1827 the frontier of lumbering had passed Fort Coulonge.[22] In 1831 liquor was being sold in ten or twelve places in the trading area of the post, allegedly to Indians as well as to settlers.[23] Against such competitors the Company was at a disadvantage. Simpson had no moral scruples against the use of liquor in trade when necessary, but he represented a large established company which would suffer much more from the discovery of such dealings than its petty competitors.

By 1840 Fort Coulonge was able to pay its expenses only by selling supplies to lumbermen, as the post at Lake of Two Mountains had earlier been forced to do.[24] This increasing emphasis on retail sales to competitors in the fur trade involved the Company in an anomalous relationship. The coming of the lumberers had disrupted prices, yet the Company was dependent upon their purchases to pay the expenses of the post, and a depression in the timber trade thus meant financial loss for the post. In 1843, for example, a decline in the Canadian timber trade with Great Britain resulted in the withdrawal of nine-tenths of the lumbermen from the vicinity of Fort Coulonge, and the post's slim profits of previous years were replaced by a financial loss.[25]

The farmer followed in the wake of the lumberman. By 1847 the arable land of the Ottawa valley had been settled as far as Fort Coulonge. Every post in the Coulonge district was surrounded with farms and lumbering shanties, a condition of society, as Simpson remarked, "alike destructive to the aboriginal population and the fur-bearing animals." [26] In pursuance of the Company's frontier policies Simpson could not abandon all the establishments in the district, but, as in the Lake of Two Mountains and Buckingham areas, he conceived it necessary drastically to reduce the expenses of trading posts. In 1855 he sold the land and buildings at Fort Coulonge to a farmer for £500 Halifax currency, and concentrated the Company's fur trade in the district at the post of Lac des Allumettes, twenty-seven miles upstream.[27]

In 1860 the frontier of settlement had reached the rapids at

Joachim, forty-two miles above the village of Pembroke and the head of steamboat navigation. The Company's trading post at Fort William, a large establishment of 800 acres on the Quebec side of the river twelve miles above Pembroke, was now surrounded by settlers. Twenty years before it had been in the midst of a wilderness penetrated only by a few enterprising lumberers.[28]

Although the advance of settlement up the Ottawa necessitated reconsideration of the Company's techniques, the basic frontier policy remained the same. George Simpson had attempted to economize by reducing the number of establishments and the number of employees at each post, but he had been unable to divorce himself entirely from the concepts of trade applicable to the Indian country—the maintenance of fixed establishments and the extension of credit to reliable Indians. The officers in charge of these stations were usually men who had formed their habits in the interior of Rupert's Land and were unable to adapt themselves to the requirements of trade in a settled area. After Simpson's death, Alexander G. Dallas, his successor, instituted the policy of abolishing permanent stations when the advance of settlement made them ineffective and of replacing them by small agencies, such as the one Simpson had established at Buckingham. Dallas therefore abandoned Fort William and established in its place a small agency at Pembroke.[29]

The Company's delaying action as it gradually withdrew upstream retarded penetration into the richer fur areas of Timiskaming and eastern Rupert's Land, though it could not entirely remove competition. Timiskaming was a prize worth contending for. In the 1820's the Company annually collected approximately sixty packs (5,400 pounds) of furs of "very superior quality," [30] and the district produced comparable returns for many years thereafter. Yet, surprisingly enough, Timiskaming was not seriously disturbed until the winter of 1838–39, when seven brothers by the name of McConnell, from the village of Hull, began cutting timber on the lake and trading with the Indians. George Simpson attempted to meet this threat from lumbermen–fur traders by ordering his employees to enter the timber trade itself, hewing down the best stands around the lake. From 1840 to 1843 crews employed by the Company cut timber; by 1843 all the trees fit for market within one mile of the lake had been cut down.

The logging experiment involved the Company in financial losses. The timber market was depressed at the time, and the quality of the Company's lumbermen left much to be desired.[31] But more important than the losses, which Simpson estimated at a mere few hundred pounds, was the failure of these efforts to discourage lumbermen. When prices of timber revived in 1844 and 1845, the lumbermen returned, and in the summer of 1845 there were between 200 and 300 in the area.[32]

Until 1869 Timiskaming was exploited almost exclusively by lumbermen and fur traders, although lumber companies maintained small plots in which provisions were grown. The expenses of collecting furs rose steadily because it was necessary to pay competitive prices and to employ runners to watch the opposition. Consequently the district became less lucrative to the Hudson's Bay Company, though at the end of the 1860's it was still sending "large and valuable returns" to London.[33]

But the halcyon days of unchallenged monopoly in the midst of a wilderness would never return. Timiskaming had become part of the Canadian economy. This fact was underlined by a visit of Canadian customs officers to the Company's district headquarters in 1858, which resulted in the Company's being fined for nonpayment of tariff duties on goods imported from Moose Factory.[34] The envelopment of Timiskaming by the frontiers of settlement had been recognized by Simpson in 1851 when he transferred the district from the southern department to the Montreal department and united the Ottawa and Timiskaming districts.[35] By the mid-1850's, the Company had been forced to introduce a cash tariff instead of the barter system previously in effect.[36]

The course of the fur trade in the Ottawa valley amply justified the wisdom the Company's policy of foregoing profits and even accepting losses in frontier areas in order to protect more valuable districts further inland. By its superior organization, resources, control of marketing facilities, and knowledge of the fur business, the Company was usually able to ruin petty competitors and to discourage any formidable opponents from entering the field. By combining the fur trade with retail stores selling to settlers, it was able further to enhance its advantages. The losses suffered in frontier areas were more than compensated by the large profits the Company continued to enjoy in districts thus protected from attack.

To the extent that the tactics of frontier defense conformed to this fundamental strategy, they were usually successful. When they deviated, they usually failed.[37]

Though Simpson may be criticized, with some justification, for errors in judgment in his execution of the Company's frontier policies in the Ottawa valley, the frontier posts performed their function with notable success. In 1869, when Rupert's Land passed into the jurisdiction of Canada and the Company's vested rights came to an end, the chartered territory beyond the Ottawa gateway was still undisturbed by opposition, and the monopoly price structure remained operative. Edward Hopkins, a protégé of Simpson's who after the latter's death had criticized some of his policies in the Montreal department, admitted that the basic philosophy was sound. Said Hopkins:

> This Department was kept up to serve as a protection to the interior; and the most that could reasonably be expected of a business, which was principally that of contending with opposition along an extended frontier, was that it should be so conducted as to be but little burdensome on the rich interior Departments, whose battles were fought here. The success that has attended the efforts to drive back opposition from Canada are well known to you.[38]

The Company paid a price in Canada for pursuing its frontier policy against lumbermen and farmers who sought profits in the fur trade. It became involved in unpleasant controversies, not only with these opponents but with politicians, particularly French Canadians. A serious cause of friction was the Company's lease of the King's Posts, which was increasingly the subject of attacks. The posts attracted the attention of lumbermen in 1837.[39] But even before the arrival of the lumberers, the district had become unproductive. It had been hunted so closely that it contained few fur-bearing animals, and a high proportion of those remaining were collected by fishermen, river pilots, and other petty traders.[40] The competition, although illegal, could be met only by maintaining a larger number of employees than otherwise required for collecting furs, and expenses were consequently higher. The prospect of competition from lumberers led Simpson in 1836 to apply to the Canadian government for permission to cut timber on the king's domains. He had a double purpose: to render the area less attractive to lumbermen, and to provide employment during the off-season for Company employees. The application, made in October, 1836, attracted the notice of Canadian newspapers and drew hostile comment from the followers of Louis Joseph Papineau and other French Canadian members of the Lower Canadian Assembly. Here, they contended, was another example of special privileges to the English; justice demanded that the timber be made available to the inhabitants of the country—the French Canadians. The Company, which had been granted a license and had already cut 6,000 logs when the clamor became insistent early in 1837, concluded that the value of the timber was not worth the odium. Simpson therefore offered to transfer the license to Canadian merchants, but because trade was stagnant in 1837 no lumbermen were interested.[41]

The damage had been done, however, and from 1837 until the Company finally relinquished its lease it was never free from the attacks of French Canadians who believed that by its retention of the King's Posts it had impeded the progress of settlement. The agitation was led by residents of the little community of La Malbaie, at the mouth of the Malbaie River, about fifty miles below the Saguenay. They contended that the banks of the Saguenay were well suited for cultivation and that Canadians should be permitted to exploit the district's resources of agricultural land and timber. To quiet these complaints the colonial secretary, Lord Glenelg, assured the Lower Canadian Assembly that the lease would not be renewed.[42] Also, Simpson agreed to modify the existing lease so that settlers and lumbermen could enter the area.[43]

The outbreak of rebellion in Lower Canada deferred action on the lease, and also terminated the sessions of the Legislative Assembly from which the attacks on the Company had usually emanated. The Executive Council, composed of a British majority, was disposed to be more conciliatory to the Company. On June 26, 1839, the council adopted a report recommending that the Company's lease, limited to hunting and trading, be renewed for another twenty-one years upon its expiration in 1842. The renewal, the council agreed, was justified by the protection the lease afforded the Indian population of the King's Posts, who would thus continue to have employment.[44] After two years of haggling between the Company and the Colonial Office, a new twenty-one-year lease was issued in June, 1841, by which the Company retained the exclusive rights of trading with the Indians and of conducting the seal fisheries for a payment of £600 a year.[45]

The Company's purpose in retaining its trading rights was the protection of the interior, but, as soon became evident, freedom of settlement in the King's Posts rendered exclusive trading rights nugatory. Settlers and lumbermen could be prevented from engaging in the fur trade only by coercion, since no jury or judge in Lower Canada would convict a violator, and the Company did not possess the force necessary to restrain them. By 1844 there were more than 400 families settled on the Saguenay, all hostile to the Company, in addition to the lumberers, "a strong body of robust sturdy men" who were also not inclined to recognize the Company's fur-trade monopoly. Merchants from the south shore of the St. Lawrence, which was then settled below the community of Trois Pistoles, encouraged boatmen to bring them furs from the King's Posts.[46]

By 1847 the directors of the Company desired to relinquish the lease,[47] and after 1848 the Company refused to pay any further rent in protest against the failure of the Canadian government to afford protection against the interlopers. Finally, in 1858, in order to open the fisheries of the King's Posts to the public, the Canadian government, with the consent of the Company, terminated the lease.[48]

Canada's decision to remove the Company from the King's Posts was not based solely upon its desire to open the fisheries. In 1858 hostility toward the Company was general in Canada, and measures that could be interpreted as anti-Company were certain to be popular. Also, there was a widespread belief that the Company reaped handsome profits from the posts and that, if it were ousted, these returns would accrue to Canadians, who could also use the area as a base from which to expand an independent fur trade into the interior. There was some validity in the idea that the possession of the King's Posts by Canadians would facilitate attacks on Rupert's Land; it was to forestall such a possibility that the Company had retained its lease for so long. But reports of profits were fantastically exaggerated. The *Canadian News*, which in 1858 rivaled the Toronto *Globe* in advocating the death of the Hudson's Bay Company, reported that Louis V. Sicotte, commissioner of crown lands, had estimated the profits of the Hudson's Bay Company from the salmon fisheries of the King's Posts alone at £5,000 per year. Consequently, declared the editorialist, the "termination of the lease is hailed with delight by the country." [49] The facts, belatedly presented to Sicotte by Chief Factor Duncan Finlayson of the Montreal department, were that the trade of the King's Posts was of little value.[50] But the ends of political expediency had been served, and the Hudson's Bay Company by its policy of silence had again contributed to the strength of its detractors.

The opposition on the north shores of Lake Huron and Lake Superior was of a different type than that faced by the Company along the St. Lawrence. Here in the shield the opposition came exclusively from petty traders. The land above Georgian Bay offered an opportunity for lumbering and a little farming, but in general nature frowned upon the settler. During the entire period of the Great Monopoly this strip of land between the settled portion of Canada and the eastern boundary of Rupert's Land, approximately 600 miles in length, remained virtually unoccupied, except for a few lumbermen and settlers who first appeared on the north shore of Lake Huron in the mid-1850's.

At Sault Ste. Marie, traders from the United States crossed into Canada and in the 1820's competed with the Company at Michipicoten, 125 miles north of the Sault on the east shore of the lake. Just east of the Sault, on Drummond Island, was another base from which fur traders in the 1820's harassed the Company's post at La Cloche, on Lake Huron north of Manitoulin Island. A third source of opposition was the little frontier community of Newmarket on the Ontario peninsula south of Lake Simcoe, from which traders penetrated as far as Lake Nipissing, approximately sixty miles north of the mouth of the Mississagi River.[51] None of these competitors possessed substantial capital. Many of them were discharged clerks and interpreters of the American Fur Company who attempted to continue as independent traders after their release.[52]

Here as in other frontier districts the Company's policy was to sell goods at prices that would force petty traders to abandon the contest.[53] Yet, as William Williams wrote, "It is astonishing to see the ruined depart annually, but still like the Hydra heads another succeeds." [54] But the constant elimination of competitors prevented their penetration of the frontier zone. By vigorous opposition at Lake Nipissing the Company discouraged them from proceeding further toward Lake Timiskaming, less than 100 miles away and easily reached from the south by rivers, lakes, and short portages. Transportation from the Sault to the Company territory at Brunswick House and north to James Bay was more difficult, and it was also necessary for a trading party to run a gauntlet of frontier posts at the Sault, Batchewana, and Michipicoten, each of which actively opposed any efforts to trade with the Indians either for furs or for provisions.

The Indians of the district were stalked by Company or opposition traders—in much the same way as they themselves hunted game—and were pounced upon when they acquired a few skins. The keenness of competition gave the Indians an opportunity to benefit by the increased value of their furs, and Simpson complained in 1831 that they were no longer "the simple harmless race they originally were," but that unfortunately they too frequently bartered their furs for liquor or for worthless novelties rather than for commodities that would have improved their living conditions.[55]

Despite the necessity of paying high prices, the Company realized small profits in both the Lake Superior and Lake Huron districts, although by 1830 the revenue of the Lake Huron posts was almost balanced by expenses. But in the 1830's more serious opposition appeared on Lake Superior, which contained large numbers of whitefish, trout, and other fish. Fishermen from the Sault, Cleveland, and Detroit established stations along the north shore, and engaged in fur trading with the Indians. This new form of opposition was doubly dangerous, for not only might these competitors force up the price of furs, but by employment of Indians in fishing they might reduce the supply of furs from the district.[56] By the end of the 1830's the governing board decided that the Company should enter the fishery business itself. It would employ the Indians inhabiting the shores to fish in the summers and send them into the interior during the hunting season, when the Company's officers would endeavor to keep them away from the lake and would collect their skins from time to time at their encampments.[57] This policy seemed all the more attractive since the requirements of the American market around the Great Lakes had raised the price of fish to profitable levels.

The Company consequently entered the fishing business in 1840, and for several years the plan seemed to meet expectations. But as fishing in Lake Superior became more extensive, it became evident that the Company's officers were no more competent to conduct such a business than they were to supervise lumbering operations. The Company's employees were not trained in curing fish, and carelessness often rendered shipments unsalable. Had it not been for the motivation of denying good fisheries to rivals, the Company would have retired from the business.[58] But even in this objective the fisheries were not entirely successful, for they provided the Indians with a means of obtaining essential supplies and thus made them better able to bargain for higher prices for their furs.[59] After 1859 the Company's fisheries were reduced in scale.

During the 1840's mining engineers made discoveries that promised to transform the economy of the Lake Superior and Lake Huron districts. They reported evidences of copper in large quantities near the shores of the lakes. The report was circulated that unexploited copper resources on the Canadian side of Lake Superior were more valuable than the copper mines on the American side, and during the summer of 1845 there was a rush of prospectors to the Canadian side of the lake. Almost simultaneously copper was discovered near Lake Huron, and mining was begun in that area.[60] These mines did not justify the optimistic expectations, and by 1848 most of the mining population had departed,[61] but the short-lived boom was coincident with a general quickening of the pace of life in the district. The United States began cutting a ship canal at the Sault to connect Lakes Huron and Superior, which was thrown open to sailing vessels and steamships in 1855. The population of Minnesota pushed up around the western end of Lake Superior, and American competition became more active in the fur trade north of the border. By the mid-1850's the Lake Huron district, which had not been profitable since 1830, had been invaded by lumberers and a few settlers, and steamboats and sailing vessels carried on an increasing business. The district continued to yield fur returns, but the Company was forced to compete with agents of New York and Montreal furriers and to pay for its purchases in cash rather than by barter, and it bought more furs from settlers and petty dealers than from Indians. In recognition of these changed conditions the Company after 1857 supplied the Lake Huron district from Lachine rather than from Moose Factory as before, although its furs continued to be shipped to Moose.[62]

Although the northern rim of Lake Superior, more remote from the rest of Canada and less attractive to the prospective settler, remained sparsely populated,[63] it was evident to Simpson and the local officers of the Company that the proximity of the Lake Superior district to settled society was steadily transforming it. The Canadian government, first displaying interest in the acquisition of southern Rupert's Land as a new area for agricultural expansion in 1857, sent out surveying parties in 1858 to prepare for a road from the settled areas of Canada through the district west of the lake to Red River. The economy of the district was entering a new phase. A symptom of change was the Company's decision, under pressure from the Indians, to end its barter system and to pay for furs in dollars in the Lake Huron district.[64]

Although Simpson recognized that profitable trade in the lake districts could not long continue, he was not without expedients to protect the Company's interests. Since one of the major sources of opposition to the Company's trade was the increasing number of petty traders from Sault Ste. Marie, he prevailed upon the Canadian government to appoint a collector of customs there, who would increase the expenses of American rivals by imposing duties on their goods.[65]

This stroke was followed by a more impressive accomplishment. The Canadian government, in accordance with its treaties with the Indians, annually distributed presents to the tribes at Manitowaning on Manitoulin Island in Lake Huron. The Lake Superior Indians manifested an increasing tendency to travel to the island to receive their gifts, much to the dismay of the Company's officers, one of whom complained, "They never return from these places improved in either morality or honesty." [66] More important than the effect on the Indians' morals, however, was the effect on trade, for the Indians on their trips dealt with petty traders who frequented the island. Obviously the Canadian government could not be prevailed upon to end the distribution of presents at Manitoulin Island because it was harmful to the interests of the Hudson's Bay Company. But there was another approach that might prove effective. In 1845 John Ballenden, the officer in charge at the Sault, wrote Simpson a letter which, if not intended to be read by government officials, was admirably adapted to that purpose. Ballenden stated that with few exceptions the Indians from Lake Superior disposed of their presents for spirits to the petty traders on the island. Also, the contact of Indians from the wilderness with settled communities inevitably caused epidemics when the Indians returned to their homes, since the resistance of wild Indians to "civilized" diseases was low. In 1842, Ballenden said, there had been a "very great" mortality at Fort William from this cause, and at Lake Nipigon, forty-four adults and children died from diseases brought back from Manitoulin Island. Measles were particularly serious.[67] Simpson forwarded Ballenden's letter to Captain J. M. Higginson, of the Canadian Indian Department, and suggested that in the interests of the Indians the Hudson's Bay Company would be willing to undertake the distribution of presents in their home districts. The basis had been laid for a change of policy, although the government did not immediately accept Simpson's offer.[68]

A further opportunity to press the case came as a result of increasing tension between the Indians and the miners, occasionally resulting in violence. Simpson reminded the Canadian government through his friend Francis Hincks that the annual assemblages at Manitoulin Island were not only injurious to the Indians but detrimental to the government, since they gave the Indians an opportunity to discuss imaginary grievances against the government and to see from the hundreds of Indians assembled how strong they were. The meetings also attracted many Indians who had no claims on Canada, since they resided in the United States or the Hudson's Bay territories. If the presents were issued at the Hudson's Bay posts these evils could be avoided.[69]

Simpson did not secure control over the distribution of presents to the Indians, but he was able to promote his objective in a somewhat different manner. In 1850 the Canadian government appointed W. B. Robinson, a Newmarket trader, as commissioner to negotiate a treaty with the Indians from Lake Huron to the borders of Rupert's Land, by which they would cede their rights to the land. Robinson, unacquainted with the Indians, depended on the Hudson's Bay Company's officers to arrange his conferences with the tribesmen, and concluded a treaty in September, 1850. The Indians ceded their rights, except for small reserves for their own use, for £4,000 and an annuity of £1,000 in perpetuity, to be increased from the proceeds of land sales to £1 per year per Indian. Since a large proportion of the Indians lived on the north shore of Lake Superior and frequented the Company's establishments, Robinson gave the Company the responsibility for making the payments to the Indians, and agreed to recommend that the Company distribute presents at Fort William and Michipicoten to the Indians of Lake Superior.[70]

No management, however intelligent, could have made the Montreal department a profitable area of trade. By the 1850's the only district in the department from which profits were realized or expected was Esquimaux Bay, the area around Hamilton Inlet, and appropriately it was detached from the department in 1859 and thereafter received its supplies from and sent its returns to England.[71] The following summary of the trade in Outfit 1862 shows the losses the Company had to absorb in order to retain its frontier posts: [72]

| Source | Returns | Profit | Loss |
|---|---|---|---|
| Lake Huron | $24,979.81 | — | $    490.59 |
| Ottawa | 34,322.71 | — | 7,415.19 |
| Montreal Agency | — | — | 2,887.97 |
| St. Maurice | 12,318.87 | — | 463.02 |
| King's Posts | 16,811.68 | — | 10,336.17 |
| Mingan | 5,122.08 | $1,247.35 | — |
| Servants | — | — | 23.32 |
| General charges | — | — | 780.24 |
| Interest | — | 621.92 | — |
| | $93,555.15 | $1,869.27 | $22,396.50 |
| | | *Net loss:* | $20,527.23 |

The details of the Company's policy varied with changes in the committee and in the conditions of trade, but the basic concept that the way to insure monopoly profits in the interior was to discourage competition on the frontier and to scour the border districts for all valuable furs remained unchanged.[73] In their zeal to carry out the instructions designed to implement this policy, employees sometimes fell victim to the wiles of crafty competitors. The American market offered high prices for skins of superior quality, and inferior furs were almost impossible to sell. Opposition traders from Red River and Canada therefore disposed of their better furs in New York and sent the remainder to Canada, where they were sold to the Hudson's Bay Company for high prices. The Company's returns from Canada thus contained a high proportion of inferior furs. Canadian and American merchants boasted that they could always sell the refuse of their collections to the Hudson's Bay Company, and their statements were to some extent borne out by the evidence.[74] Despite opportunities for such swindling and increasingly large losses in the Montreal department, responsible officers agreed that only by meeting and discouraging competition far from the profitable districts of the fur trade could the Company continue to enjoy substantial profits.

The application of this policy incensed competitors and stimulated attacks in the Canadian legislature. If the Hudson's Bay Company had withdrawn from Canada it might have avoided some criticism, but it would also have withdrawn a measure of protection from the frontiers of Rupert's Land and thereby jeopardized the prosperity of the monopoly. As their land was settled and as their frontier crowded against the shield, Canadians were certain to look longingly at the fertile belt of southern Rupert's Land and to become embittered against the Company as the possessor of thousands of square miles of excellent unoccupied agricultural land in its chartered territory. It is not likely that the Company, short of giving up its chartered rights, could have substantially delayed Canadian attacks upon it as a greedy, grasping monopoly, incompatible with the higher interests of civilization. Under these circumstances, the aggressive-defensive frontier policy, brought to its highest point of perfection in the era of Pelly and Simpson, seems to have achieved its purpose.

CHAPTER

4

# The Southern Frontier

THOUGH CANADA was the source of menace to the Hudson's Bay
Company before 1821, the most vulnerable portion of the Company's frontier after that date lay along the international boundary
from Lake Superior to the neighborhood of the Souris (Mouse)
River, which flows through present-day North Dakota and Manitoba. This section of the border provided access into the interior of
Rupert's Land. By the rivers and lakes that formed a part of the
waterways complex interlacing the district, traders could reach the
Athabaska and the Saskatchewan countries, long rich in furs, as
well as most other sections of southern Rupert's Land. A few portages were necessary, but for hundreds of miles nature imposed no
serious barrier to canoe transportation.

Here was the first point of contact between the Hudson's Bay
Company and the American frontiers of fur trade and of settlement. Here also, around the junction of the Red and Assiniboine
rivers, was established a little colony of Europeans and half-breeds
destined to prove itself the Achilles' heel of the Company.[1] It was
anarchy at Red River which first gave Canada's government occasion to act against the Hudson's Bay Company's chartered rights.
The proximity of American settlement provided the Red River
colonists with opportunities for trade and encouraged their independent tendencies, and increasing intercourse between Red River
and the United States kindled British and Canadian fears that
the area might fall under American influence.

[1] For notes to chap. 4, see pp. 437–441.

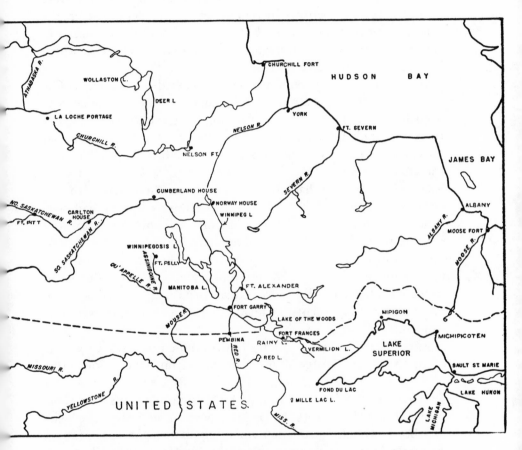

*The Southern Frontier*

At Red River the frontier policies of the Company were put to their most severe test. They could not be as successful against a colony that by the 1860's numbered almost 10,000 inhabitants, hundreds of whom were engaged in fur trading, as they were against a few competitors in remote areas who depended on the fur trade for their livelihood. But the salvation of the Company at Red River proved to be the same techniques of competition which had been effective in other frontier areas.

In 1821 the colony contained several fairly distinct groups. The *métis* or *Boisbrûlés,* half-breed descendants of Indian women and French and British fur traders, had inhabited the Red River valley from the mid-eighteenth century, although their numbers had greatly increased after the appearance of North West Company traders in the area. The colonists brought by Selkirk were mostly Scots whose poverty had driven them from their homes in the Orkney Islands and the Highlands. Selkirk's agents had also brought a group of Swiss to the colony, and the earl had hired soldiers from the De Meuron Regiment for the defense of Red River against the North West Company. The De Meurons were mercenary soldiers from Switzerland, Italy, and other European countries who had fought for Great Britain in the Napoleonic Wars and had been sent to Canada in 1812, where they were disbanded.

Another group in the colony was composed of retired servants of the Company. George Simpson in 1824 estimated that four-fifths of the approximately 2,000 inhabitants of Red River were retired servants, *Boisbrûlés,* and Indians.[2] Of these elements, the most restive in the 1820's were the De Meurons and the Swiss. The Swiss had been brought to the settlement by extravagant promises of overambitious agents, and many of the De Meurons had been demoralized by their careers as mercenary soldiers. But these were not the groups destined to undermine the Company's authority. Disgusted with life in an area swept by floods and scoured by locusts,[3] many of the De Meurons and the Swiss migrated to the United States. None of the other groups in Red River gave much trouble in these years. Simpson considered the Company's retired servants the "most harmless and easily managed people we have to deal with." Even the half-breeds, an increasingly dominant proportion of the population, appeared docile, though Simpson realized that their passionate tendencies might at some time make them dangerous to the vested interests of the Company.[4] A few inhabitants traded furs illegally to the Americans, but in Simpson's estimation these violations of the charter were insignificant.[5]

At this time, when petty competition from settlers was of no consequence, Simpson decided on a change in policy. In 1824 he reorganized the trading system in Assiniboia so that thereafter the Company would trade directly with Indians in the district only in barter transactions at Fort Garry. No advances would be given to Indians within the district. Instead, settlers could secure licenses to collect the hunts of the Indians. They would buy their outfits from the Company for cash and would bring their furs to the Company. This change, Simpson thought, would have two advantages: it would reduce resentment at Red River against the Company's monopoly, and it would sweep up furs along the frontier which might otherwise fall into the hands of the Americans just across the border.[6]

This expedient was highly dangerous, for licensees who had had a taste of profits from the Indian trade might be tempted to increase their activities and thus become a menace to the Company's monopoly. Without a large police force to guard the borders of Assiniboia, there could be no assurance that licensed traders might not carry on clandestine trade with Indians of surrounding districts, and attempts to suppress them would increase the tension with the settlement which Simpson sought to avoid. In view of the semi-nomadic characteristics of the Red River hunters, no policy could maintain harmony between the chartered monopoly and the settlement. A collision between the two was virtually inevitable sooner or later, but the licensing system inaugurated in 1824 probably hastened it.

An early indication of the difficulties created by the policy occurred in the summer of 1826. Chief Factor Donald McKenzie, the officer in charge at Fort Garry, discovered that many of the settlers were carrying on unlicensed trade with the Indians. He served them with notices, but these had no effect. Finally he found it necessary to issue warrants for the arrest of offenders and seized several small parcels of furs. McKenzie sent one of the culprits, Ferdinand Cels, to York Factory to await deportation, but "at his [Cels's] earnest solicitation" Simpson allowed him to return to Red River.[7]

Andrew McDermot, a prominent settler who later came into frequent controversy with the Company, traded with some Red River freemen for furs. When McKenzie ordered the furs seized, McDermot voluntarily delivered them to the Company. He pleaded ignorance of the license regulations and contended that the freemen with whom he had traded had been on their way to sell their furs to the Americans, who offered more than the Company did at Fort Garry.[8] Simpson considered it politic to compensate McDermot for his furs, and the seizure involved no immediate complications. But these incidents reflected the Company's basic problem. Red River traders, whether licensed or unlicensed, would take their furs to the highest bidder, and the only way the Company could retain control of the trade was the same as in other frontier areas—outbidding its opponents.

The wisdom of licensing free traders in the chartered territory was debatable. But Simpson did not content himself with a licensing system restricted to Red River. He turned a blind eye to the extension of the licensees' activities into American territory and, indeed, encouraged them to bring furs from across the border. The governor and committee in approving the licensing system had instructed Simpson that "no person connected with the Company should be permitted to encroach on American territory."[9] But, contended Simpson, these licensees were not "connected with the Company." They were free agents, and the Company could not control them even if it were so inclined. By their excursions across the border, they put the American opposition on the defensive and protected the Hudson's Bay Company's frontier.[10] To their discredit, the governor and committee failed to repudiate Simpson's specious reasoning. By tacitly accepting border violations they helped to undermine their position. Their own moral case rested upon the legality of their trade monopoly and strict observance of their responsibilities. But it became difficult to justify their contentions against illicit trading in Rupert's Land when the Company was accessory to illicit trade in the United States.

The opposition that Simpson's licensing system was designed to embarrass was the American fur trade, in particular the American Fur Company, and the scene of most intensive conflict was the vicinity of Rainy Lake and Rainy River. Here the frontier was most easily penetrated.

The American Fur Company was the closest approximation in the United States to the Hudson's Bay Company. John Jacob Astor had acquired a charter for the company in 1808, and his enterprise grew rapidly to become the giant of the American fur trade. Just before the War of 1812, Astor had forced his way into the trade of the Great Lakes and the upper Mississippi by purchasing a controlling interest in the Mackinaw Company, which had previously dominated the area. By an arrangement with some of the partners of the North West Company, Astor reorganized the Mackinaw Company as the Southwest Company, retaining a two-thirds interest with the Nor'Westers receiving one-third. After the war Astor was instrumental in gaining passage of an act prohibiting foreigners from participating in the American fur trade except in subordinate capacities. By this technique he forced the Nor'-Westers out of the Southwest Company, which in 1817 was merged with the American Fur Company.[11] Ramsay Crooks, a Scot who had served briefly with the North West Company and later with Astor's Pacific Fur Company, was appointed general manager.[12]

The first points of contact between the Hudson's Bay Company and the American Fur Company were near Rainy Lake, where the American company maintained two posts, one on the south side of Rainy River and the other at Vermilion Lake, the source of the Vermilion River.[13] From its outset in 1822 the competition was in marked contrast to the recent conflict betweeen the North West Company and the Hudson's Bay Company. The Hudson's Bay Company now wished to avoid violence, which not only disrupted trade but plunged the participants into political controversy. As Simpson wrote to McLoughlin, "There are 1,000 ways of annoying and harassing our opponents without having recourse to violent measures." [14] Since the American Fur Company entertained similar views, the competition was among the most gentlemanly in the history of the fur trade. Almost from the beginning both sides scrupulously resisted the temptation to cross the frontier, no blows were struck, and Simpson even felt impelled to pay tribute to the good trading manners of his opponents,[15] a compliment he never paid a petty trader.

The Hudson's Bay Company withdrew into its own territory after the appearance of the first American customs officials. When John McLoughlin, appointed to the charge of Lac la Pluie in 1822,

arrived at the post he sent a party under Chief Trader Simon Mc-
Gillivray to oppose rival traders at Lake Vermilion. They found
not only the American traders but a customs agent.[16]

By United States law, any person who traded with the Indians
in American territory without a license was subject to a fine of
$1,000. McLoughlin feared that disaffected employees of the Com-
pany might even offer themselves up to the American authorities
in order to embarrass their erstwhile employers.[17] Encounters with
government officials might be doubly expensive, for they could
cause diplomatic controversy which the Company was anxious
to avoid. In McLoughlin's estimation the stakes were too high to
risk further encroachments on American territory for a trade rapidly being exhausted by intensive competition. Simpson agreed,
and the Company withdrew to the north of the Rainy River,[18]
which was the established international boundary.[19]

The only violations of the boundary occurred in the first winter
of competition, 1822–23, when clerks of both companies occasionally crossed to the other bank of the Rainy River. In order to dissuade the Americans from continuing the practice, McLoughlin
on some pretext enticed two of their clerks to visit the Hudson's
Bay post at Lac la Pluie, where he kept them in custody for about
eight hours, releasing them on their promise that they would make
no further trespasses.[20] No violations were reported thereafter.

Although the border was mutually respected, competition was
severe. Yet the Hudson's Bay Company each year made a profit,
usually a small one, from its trade. Each year, also, Simpson and
the officer in charge declared that the agents of the American Fur
Company must be losing money and must soon retire from the field.
Such pronouncements were not to be taken too seriously. They
were apparently intended to stimulate the Hudson's Bay Company's employees to greater effort rather than to reflect any sober
estimate of the trade of the opposition. Simpson in a moment of
rare frankness admitted that the American Fur Company must at
least be clearing expenses or it would not be continuing the competition.[21]

There is no available evidence to give an insight into the state
of the American Fur Company's trade at this time. Astor himself
is the worst possible source for financial information about his
own company, for he manufactured evidence to support whatever

contention he happened to be advancing. In 1829, when Astor sought legislation against foreign furs, he wrote to his friend Thomas Hart Benton:

> I very much fear, that unless a duty is imposed on foreign furs, the American Fur Company, the only respectable one of any capital now existing in the country will be obliged to suspend their operations. I believe I am safe when I say that all our Indian traders for these 20 years past, with very few exceptions, have been losing time and property in that trade. . . . The American Fur Company have for years past, and do now employ a capital of a million or more of dollars. They have not yet been able to declare a dividend. . . . The Hudson Bay Company divide 10 per cent per annum, and have a large surplus on hand. Their stock is at a premium of 150 per cent above par.[22]

Such statements are of little value in assessing the health of the American Fur Company. Two incidents in 1829, however, suggest that Simpson was not wholly incorrect in his view that the American Fur Company was finding the frontier competition unprofitable and desired to rid itself of the responsibility. In August, 1829, William A. Aitkin, superintendent of the American company's operations at Fond du Lac, visited Chief Factor Angus Bethune, in charge of the Hudson's Bay Company's post at Sault Ste. Marie. Aitkin's ostensible purpose was to protest against infringement of the rights of the American Fur Company by half-breeds from Red River, who were outfitted by the Hudson's Bay Company to trade within the territory of the United States.

But mere complaint was not the primary object of Aitkin's visit, as soon became apparent. He had come to suggest that the two companies end their competition along the entire frontier line. Specifically, his proposal was that the American Fur Company abandon all posts along the frontier west of Lake Superior, with the exception of Vermilion Lake. In exchange, the Hudson's Bay Company would agree not to trade in American territory either directly or through traders outfitted by the Company. The Indians of the vicinity would be allowed full liberty to trade with either company, provided that neither side sought them out in their encampments. Bethune, lacking authority to accede to or reject such a far-reaching arrangement, asked Aitkin to submit his proposals in writing. Aitkin agreed at first, but the next day declined to make so formal a proposition, offering as his reason the imminent reorganization of his company.[23]

At about the same time as Aitkin was indicating the wish to end competition on the border, William B. Astor, president of the American Fur Company and the eldest son of John Jacob, provided additional evidence of this desire. On December 15, 1829, he wrote James Keith, Simpson's lieutenant at Lachine, that his company wanted to eliminate the use of liquor by Indians on the British-American frontier. If the Hudson's Bay Company would pledge itself to end the practice, the American Fur Company promised to do the same. Astor informed Keith that the American Indian agent at Sault Ste. Marie had promised that, if the two companies came to such an agreement, he would not permit competitors to bring liquor into the border area.[24]

The governor and committee were skeptical of Astor's overtures. The Hudson's Bay Company monopolized the trade of the chartered territory and the British side of the Lake Superior frontier. The American Fur Company had not yet demonstrated its ability to maintain the same dominance on the American side of the boundary. The governor and committee therefore told Astor that they were eager to end the liquor trade but that they could not afford to do so until there was evidence of effective prohibition in American territory. When American traders discontinued the use of liquor, the governor and committee wrote Astor, the Hudson's Bay Company would do likewise.[25]

The prospects of an end to liquor, and, more important, of an end to competition on the frontier, were highly attractive to the directors of the Hudson's Bay Company, if the performance of such an arrangement could be guaranteed. But in 1830 they were not satisfied that the American Fur Company possessed such power. Simpson regarded Astor's proposal to discontinue the use of liquor as an evidence of weakness. The Indians of Red, Leech, and Sandy lakes, Simpson told the governor and committee, were so much addicted to the use of liquor that the American Fur Company was forced to maintain large staffs at its posts in those districts in order to protect the establishments against attacks by drunken braves. He believed that Astor's company wanted to prohibit the use of liquor in order to reduce expenses without the risk of the Indians carrying their furs to the Hudson's Bay Company. Such an arrangement could not benefit the Hudson's Bay Company so long as the trade was open to "every desperate worthless adventurer" who chose to enter it.[26] Thus when Aitkin in September, 1830, again proposed that the companies act jointly to control the liquor trade,[27] his suggestion was not favorably received. When Simpson saw John Jacob Astor in New York, he explained that the Hudson's Bay Company could not agree to restricting the use of liquor so long as there were petty competitors in the field. Astor's reply, as Simpson reported it, was: "I now see it is of no use to attempt it, as if we did the Hudson's Bay Company would hold the head of the Cow, the American Fur Company would hold the tail of the Cow, and the Petty traders would come in and milk the Cow." [28]

Competition between the companies therefore continued along the same lines as in the 1820's, with the two sides staying within their respective territories but strenuously trying to attract Indians from across the border. The only exception to this respect for the international boundary was Simpson's practice of advancing supplies to Red River half-breeds whom he encouraged to cross into the United States in the expectation that they would annoy the Company's American competitors. In this objective he was successful, for the activities of the half-breeds, particularly around the American company's post at Pembina on the Red River just south of the boundary, evoked strong protests from the American Fur Company and may have contributed to its desire for agreement. Particularly obnoxious to the Americans was one Nolin, probably the same Augustin Nolin who in 1823 had run afoul of the Hudson's Bay Company for illegal trade in the chartered territory. In the winter of 1830–31 Nolin encamped at Lake Roseau, situated between Pembina and Lake of the Woods. Aitkin rightly contended that the lake was south of the line and threatened to seize Nolin and his property unless he withdrew into British territory. Nolin replied that he had a right to trade regardless of whether the territory was British or American. If it was the former, he had a license from Simpson authorizing him to trade. If it was the latter, he possessed the right as a half-breed native of the soil, who like the Indians was not bound by the restrictions applicable to persons of European descent. Here was an early statement of the doctrine successfully asserted by the half-breeds in opposition to the Hudson's Bay Company's monopoly in the 1840's. In 1830 Simpson viewed its exposition with equanimity, since it contributed to the embarrassment of the Company's competitors.[29]

In the winter of 1830–31, Aitkin renewed his proposal that the two companies end their competition and that neither trade with Indians who normally resided on the other side of the international boundary. Simpson remained unreceptive, since a substantial proportion of the Hudson's Bay Company's returns from the Lac la Pluie district was brought in by Indians from the American territory.[30]

Until this time the American Fur Company had been an eager wooer and the Hudson's Bay Company had been cool to its advances. But certain events now made the Hudson's Bay Company more desirous to end competition. In 1830 Ramsay Crooks dissolved his partnership with the Astors but, as a salaried employee, remained the virtual director of the affairs of the American Fur Company,[31] with even greater authority than he had previously possessed. At the company's annual council in 1831, Crooks, the partners, and the clerks decided upon a change of system in the Rainy Lake district. Instead of the company's maintaining direct responsibility for the trade of the district, as it had previously done, they decided that it should withdraw from direct competition with the Hudson's Bay Company. Two postmasters of the American Fur Company, La Rose [32] and Couttier, agreed to assume entire responsibility for the trade, provided the company outfitted them with goods at reasonable rates and agreed to accept their furs at standard prices.[33]

The news of this change in the technique of opposition alarmed the governor and committee of the Hudson's Bay Company. The American Fur Company had been a responsible competitor; La Rose and Couttier might not be so scrupulous in their observance of the rules of trade. Although the London board had not repudiated Simpson's encouragement of Nolin and other Red River half-breeds to cross into American territory for trade, its members looked askance at the practice. They feared that the half-breeds, having acquired a taste for the profits of the fur trade, might turn upon their erstwhile employers and demoralize the trade of Rupert's Land. Competitors like La Rose and Couttier might contribute to the same eventuality by crossing into British territory, which the American Fur Company had not done. Had these men been the sole competitors, the Hudson's Bay Company undoubtedly would have crushed them as it had other petty opponents. But the governor and committee realized that if these traders were eliminated the American Fur Company would find others to take their place. They therefore authorized Simpson on March 1, 1833, to make overtures to the American Fur Company for an agreement. The board proposed a mutual commitment to end the practices of outfitting independent traders and of supplying arms and ammunition "or other support and encouragement" to the halfbreeds or the petty traders. The Indians on both sides of the border would have the right to trade without restriction with either the American Fur Company or the Hudson's Bay Company.[34]

An agreement on such terms would undoubtedly have been unacceptable to the American Fur Company, since the Indians in American territory would retain their freedom to visit the posts of the Hudson's Bay Company. But before the board's instructions reached Simpson, he had already begun negotiations with Aitkin at the Red River settlement. From these discussions the two reached an agreement by which the American Fur Company would abandon all its frontier posts from Pembina to Lake Superior in exchange for an annual payment of £300 sterling. The agreement was to continue in force for five years, and Aitkin committed his company to prevent opposition to the Hudson's Bay Company on the American side of the frontier.[35] The governor and committee, skeptical of the willingness or ability of the Americans to end opposition on the frontier, were not enthusiastic but deferred to Simpson's superior knowledge of local conditions.[36] The success of the agreement fully justified their confidence in his judgment.

During the first year of the agreement, some petty traders appeared on the Rainy Lake border,[37] but thereafter the American Fur Company almost completely interdicted the border country to competitors, and the Hudson's Bay Company was able to treat the area as one where the practices of monopoly could be maintained. The Hudson's Bay Company began to wean the Indians of the district from the use of liquor by cutting down the supply and to adjust the prices of its goods to those in effect in interior districts.[38] By 1839 the Company felt confident enough in its control of the trade to prohibit entirely the distribution of liquor to the Indians.[39]

This prohibition did not long remain in effect, for the Indians of the Rainy Lake district were not left entirely without expedients to force the hand of the monopoly. On June 3, 1841, when Sir George Simpson visited the post at Lac la Pluie on the first stage of his journey around the world, over 500 Indians from the district were awaiting him. They had not come to do him honor, but rather to inform him that unless a small quantity of liquor was dispensed to them in the autumn of each year the Company could not depend upon them to supply it with wild rice. Since this food was the staple commodity of the district, the threat carried weight. Simpson was warned of their intentions before he met with them in council, and he "made a merit of necessity" by granting them the boon of a supply of liquor before they formally demanded it. In exchange, they made him a present of furs, and the council closed with expressions of satisfaction on both sides. But even with the forced relaxation of the rule against distribution of liquor, the supply was drastically reduced. Before the discontinuance of liquor distribution in 1839, the Lac la Pluie district had received forty-two kegs of rum annually. After Simpson made his concessions in 1841, the supply allotted to the district was only eight kegs, the contents of which were distributed as presents.[40]

With this exception, the practices of the Lac la Pluie district for a few years after 1834 were those of monopoly, not of competition. Prices were reduced to levels that yielded a handsome profit, and when Simpson in 1836, two years before the agreement was scheduled to expire, proposed its extension for an additional three-year period,[41] he had the unqualified support of the governor and committee. They had concluded that £300 sterling was indeed a small price to pay for unchallenged control of the fur trade of the border.

The advantages of the agreement to the Hudson's Bay Company were patent; to the American Fur Company, less so. The American company had been relieved of unprofitable competition, but the amount of payment seems small indeed, since the Americans were responsible for policing the district. The Hudson's Bay Company interpreted the agreement as giving it the right to trade with Indians from either American or British territory, provided that the actual trade was carried on north of the boundary line. In view of such considerations, it is not surprising that Crooks did not respond with alacrity to Simpson's request for a three-year extension of the contract. Instead, he delayed for several months while he consulted with his associates, and then he accepted an extension for only two years. He also demanded and received modifications in the original arrangement. The Hudson's Bay Company agreed to allow the American Fur Company to establish posts for its fisheries on the American side of Lake Superior and to permit fishery employees to sell to the American Fur Company any furs they had acquired by barter. Also, the American company was authorized at these stations to accept furs proffered by needy Indians in exchange for provisions.[42] In 1839 Crooks secured the further concession from Simpson that the Hudson's Bay Company would no longer trade with Indians from American territory.[43] Thereafter, the advantages to the two companies were more nearly balanced. At the end of the two-year extension, the agreement was prolonged by periodic renewals until 1847, when changes in the control of the American fur trade made it impossible for Crooks to offer further protection.[44]

So long as the American Fur Company remained financially sound, trade along the border between Pembina and Lake Superior was kept virtually free of opposition. When William A. Aitkin withdrew from his association with the American Fur Company and prepared to establish a competitive post at Lake Vermilion, Simpson instructed Allan McDonell, in charge of the Lac la Pluie district, to act in concert with the American company to destroy Aitkin's opposition.[45] Aitkin did not carry out his intention,[46] but the close coöperation between the two companies was evident when the American Fur Company's control of the fisheries on Lake Superior was challenged in 1840 by competitors from Detroit and Cleveland. The newcomers did not directly menace the Hudson's Bay Company, and their activities were outside the area of the agreement. Nevertheless, Simpson directed the Company's officers in the Lake Superior district to assist the American Fur Company by making goods available and by entering into direct competition in the fisheries with the Cleveland and Detroit traders.[47] This coöperative venture did not succeed in driving the opposition from the lake, apparently because increasing financial difficulties made the American Fur Company incapable of devoting the necessary energy to the project.

After the Panic of 1837 the financial condition of the American Fur Company became increasingly unstable. In March of that year, Halsey and Company, among the largest stockholders, were forced to close, and the desperate condition of the American Fur Company forced Crooks, who had been president since 1834,[48] to cancel his annual western trip and to remain in New York. Although the company averted liquidation, it did not recover its old vigor. A report current in 1840 that Crooks had gone into bankruptcy was false but not far from the truth.

The decline in his company's fortunes caused Crooks in 1841 to begin negotiations with Pierre Chouteau, Jr., and Company for the sale of the American Fur Company's posts on the upper Mississippi. The dullness of business disposed him to sell the company's interests in the Lake Superior area as well, but no prospective purchaser of sufficient means could be found. The year 1842 was even less profitable, and the sale of the upper Mississippi posts to Chouteau did not provide sufficient revenue to avert catastrophe. The American Fur Company suspended payments in September, 1842, with an indebtedness of approximately $300,000, and went into receivership. The company was not yet dead, for it still retained control of its posts on the Great Lakes,[49] but its usefulness to the Hudson's Bay Company was largely gone. The frontier around the Red River which had previously been protected by the agreement of 1833 was now open to attack, for the Chouteau company was not obligated to respect the arrangement. Competition soon materialized, with disastrous results to the Hudson's Bay Company.

The trader who opened the competition, Norman W. Kittson, was not in himself formidable, but in conjunction with the half-breeds of Red River he helped to undermine the structure of monopoly for hundreds of miles into the interior of Rupert's Land. In 1839 Kittson had opened a small business as fur trader and general merchant near Fort Snelling, Minnesota, and subsequently started a similar business at the mouth of the Minnesota River. But his great opportunity came in 1842. Henry H. Sibley, to whom Chouteau assigned the responsibility for the fur trade of the area, was a long-time friend of Kittson's. He offered Kittson an opportunity to become a "special partner" and allotted him the valleys of the upper Minnesota River and the Red River. This trading area stretched along the international boundary from the Mouse River to Rainy Lake, a distance of about 300 miles.[50]

Kittson established his headquarters at Pembina, the small community of Red River half-breeds just south of the international boundary. The location of his post revealed his intentions. He desired to attract furs from Rupert's Land by encouraging the half-breeds of the Red River settlement to bring him their furs. He provided further evidence of his plans by paying a visit to the settlement in the autumn of 1843. He arrived at a fortunate moment for his interests, since the spirit of free trade had been steadily developing in the colony for the past two decades, and the half-breeds were receptive to a revolt against the Company's trading monopoly.

A detailed account of the growth of the free-trade movement at Red River, of which several excellent studies have been made,[51] is outside the scope of this discussion. But an understanding of the general course of opposition to the Hudson's Bay Company is essential. In the 1820's the Company had allowed licensed settlers to collect the hunts of Indians within the district of Assiniboia. This policy at first seemed to justify the hope that it would provide a safety valve for the more active elements of the settlement. In 1825 Simpson reported that the plan "is found to answer our expectations";[52] in 1828 he reiterated the conviction that the licensing of traders had been a wise action, since the licensees provided protection from American competition and checked other inhabitants of Red River from engaging in illicit trade.[53] But by 1829 a disturbing note had appeared in his correspondence with the governor and committee. Although Simpson continued to express his confidence in the efficacy of the licensing system, he began to take notice of the encroachments of unlicensed settlers who had extended their trade north and west from Assiniboia into the neighboring district of Swan Lake and had compelled the Company to establish outposts at Manitoba Lake and at the source of the Qu'Appelle River. In the latter area some half-breeds and their families had settled and had begun to cultivate the soil in addition to carrying on the fur trade. Simpson had good cause for worry, for the settlement on the Qu'Appelle River was the first impressive evidence of that independent spirit which within two decades was to break the Hudson's Bay Company's monopoly in southern Rupert's Land. Not only had the settlers moved outside the district of Assiniboia without permission, but they had induced the Indians to trade with them rather than with the Company, and delivered their furs not only to Red River but to roving American traders from the upper Missouri River.

Before the 1840's this menace to the Company was largely potential. Two factors contributed to smother the early development of free trade. Until 1843 the Hudson's Bay Company's agreement with the American Fur Company denied the settlers the opportunity to carry furs to a competitor within easy reach of the colony. The population of the nearby territories of the United States was sparse, and there was not yet a satisfactory alternative market for Red River products or source of supplies for the Red River Indian trade. But between 1840 and 1860 the population of Wisconsin increased twenty-five fold, from 30,945 to over 700,000. In 1849, when Minnesota was made a territory, the population was less than 5,000; in 1860 its population was over 172,000.[54] Intercourse between Red River and St. Peter, in southern Minnesota on the Minnesota River, began stirring in the 1830's,[55] but greatly increased during the next decade. At first the Red River colonists traded cattle for horses, but soon the trade was expanded to include furs and supplies for the fur trade.[56]

When Norman Kittson in 1843 accepted Sibley's offer to assume control of the frontier trade, therefore, he did so at a propitious time. Since 1839 traffic on the route along the Red River into the United States had been greatly augmented by settlers driving herds of cattle to St. Peter. This trade was not opposed by the Company. On the contrary, the governor and committee thought it good policy to encourage it, and even instructed Simpson to open negotiations with American officials and persuade them to influence the Sioux, who inhabited the intermediate country, to allow the drovers to pass without molestation.[57]

The expanded trade with the United States enabled Kittson to develop a more intimate intercourse with the settlement, for the carts and herds passed by the post that he established at Pembina in 1844. His most powerful allies at Red River were Alexander McDermot and James Sinclair, prominent merchants in the colony who had been sufficiently influential to obtain contracts to haul the Company's goods from York Factory to Red River. Both had engaged in the fur trade of the frontier under license from the Hudson's Bay Company,[58] and both were in a state of disaffection when Kittson began his competition. The rates paid by the Hudson's Bay Company for haulage of goods were unsatisfactory, and in 1844, at precisely the time that Kittson was establishing his headquarters at Pembina, Simpson decided to cancel all licenses for independent traders on the frontier. He had come to the conclusion that the granting of such authorization might "give the settlers a taste for the fur trade which would become exceedingly inconvenient." [59]

Simultaneously the governor of Assiniboia, Chief Factor Alexander Christie, acting upon instructions from Simpson, issued a proclamation on the subject of illegal trading. The Company would no longer transport the goods of any settler unless he signed a declaration that since December 8, 1844, he had neither "directly nor indirectly trafficked in furs," and that in the future he would neither engage in the illegal fur trade nor give advances of goods or money to anyone who was "generally suspected of trafficking in furs." If by mid-August, 1845, any person who had signed this statement was found to have violated his oath, the Company's officers would be authorized to detain his goods at York Factory or to purchase them at their original cost.[60] The notice was the product of a strange delusion of Sir George Simpson that the Company, without the resources to control the Red River settlement, could by fiat destroy the illicit trade.

Before settlement in Minnesota provided the Red River merchants with an alternative market, Christie's proclamation might have had a chastening effect. But at the time of its issuance the proclamation could only encourage intercourse between Red River and the United States. The initial effect of the order, however, seemed to justify Simpson's judgment. All the importers except McDermot and Sinclair agreed to sign the prescribed oath.[61]

In January, 1845, McDermot and Sinclair complied with Christie's orders to surrender the furs they had collected.[62] McDermot professed penitence, although he secretly continued to trade in furs, but Sinclair defiantly continued to trade and incited others to do likewise. Christie was forced to report to Simpson in

April that "an unprecedented excitement has been kept up in the settlement," and that the impression was widely held that the Company could not prevent trading in furs.[63]

On August 29, 1845, a group of Red River half-breeds, led by Sinclair, presented a list of questions to Governor Christie. They stated that as natives of the country they had the right to hunt for furs anywhere within the Hudson's Bay Company's territories and to sell them to the highest bidder, and the questions involved a detailed exposition of these assumptions. Christie's reply was, of course, that the half-breeds possessed no distinctive rights above those of their fellow citizens not born in the settlement, and that they could not legally engage in the fur trade.[64] But Christie knew that his response had solved no problems and that the assumptions of the half-breeds remained unchanged.

Without a police force to support his authority, Christie had no power. Before 1845 the Company had maintained a constabulary, but it had been reduced to twelve men. When these men themselves were found to be engaged in illicit trade, the force was disbanded.[65] During the spring of 1845 an unusually large number of half-breeds had entered the fur trade.[66] The resulting increase in illegal trade was not entirely the product of Kittson's appearance at Pembina. Another factor may have been the failure of the buffalo hunts in the fall of 1844, which caused the plains hunters to seek another means of providing for themselves.[67] But once the movement became general, it was apparent that the Company was powerless to stop it. Without troops, Christie admitted, the settlement would soon be in a state of anarchy.[68]

It occurred to Simpson that another expedient might be effective. Since the free traders were encouraged by the expectation of higher prices at Kittson's station at Pembina, the destruction of his competition might have a tranquilizing effect upon the settlement. Simpson decided upon a bold stroke. He would send a Hudson's Bay Company clerk into American territory to establish a post near Pembina and ruin Kittson by outbidding him. The Hudson's Bay Company as a foreign enterprise could not legally trade in American territory, but Simpson proposed to circumvent the law by sending Henry Fisher, reputedly an American citizen by virtue of his birth at Prairie du Chien, and by maintaining the fiction that Fisher was an independent trader.[69]

Christie at Fort Garry was dubious as to the wisdom of this action. He believed that such a step would discredit the Hudson's Bay Company and would place it in essentially the same moral position as McDermot and Sinclair, for the Company would be acting as an illicit trader by venturing into American territory.[70] Nevertheless, Simpson proceeded with his plan. He wrote to Dr. Charles W. Borup, agent of the American Fur Company at La Pointe, asking him to secure a license for Fisher to trade in American territory.[71] It was arranged that Fisher, in order to avoid the appearance of being in the employ of the Hudson's Bay Company, would send his returns through the American Fur Company's posts at Red Lake and La Pointe, consigned to Sault Ste. Marie. There they would be delivered to John Ballenden, the officer in charge of the Hudson's Bay post.[72]

Fisher's license was delivered to him in January, 1846, by the still reluctant Alexander Christie.[73] In the spring, equipped with his authorization to trade in American territory, Fisher appeared at Pembina and began to construct a station, much to the discomfiture of Kittson,[74] whose angry protests to his partner Sibley are an indication of the damage done to his trade. Simpson laid plans to augment Fisher's activity by sending other employees of the Hudson's Bay Company into American territory in the guise of servants of the American Fur Company. These men would compete not only against Kittson but against the merchants of St. Peter. During a visit to Montreal, Crooks agreed to allow the American Fur Company to be used for this purpose.[75]

Crooks served the interests of the Hudson's Bay Company in another way. When Simpson asked him to use his influence with the United States government to have Kittson's license revoked, since Kittson was distributing liquor to the Indians, Crooks consented.[76] Simultaneously Kittson, through Sibley, was lodging a similar protest with American officials against the Hudson's Bay Company.[77]

While his agents were harassing Kittson at Pembina, Simpson was attempting to eliminate the American's influence at Red River by pacifying McDermot and Sinclair. Simpson was well aware that these men had been leaders in the illicit trade, that they had sold furs to Kittson, and that they had even made overtures to Crooks during the winter of 1845–46 to unite with them in opposition to

the Hudson's Bay Company. Since this competition was harmful
to the interests of the Hudson's Bay Company, Simpson wanted
to remove it in the most expeditious fashion. He came to an easy
understanding with McDermot. In July, 1846, he paid McDermot
£100 to compensate him for alleged underpayment for his freighting services, and hired his son at a salary of £50 per year.[78]

An accommodation with Sinclair took a little longer than the
reconciliation with McDermot, for, in Simpson's words, "Sinclair
is without exception, the most unprincipled man I ever had any
dealings with in the Company's territories, & has, through misrepresentation & low cunning, very seriously injured the Company's
interests." [79] During a visit to London in the autumn of 1846, Sinclair presented a claim to Pelly for additional payment for his
freighting services. Pelly thought the claim worthless, but since
Simpson had settled similar differences with McDermot for £100,
authorized Simpson to pay Sinclair the same amount.[80] The two
apparently came to a satisfactory understanding, for Simpson made
no further complaints against Sinclair until 1853. In that year
Sinclair again threatened to compete but was induced by Simpson
to join the Company's service as officer in charge at Fort Nez Percés
(Walla Walla), which was judged to be far enough removed from
the Red River settlement.[81]

Simpson did not carry out his plan to send Hudson's Bay employees disguised as servants of the American Fur Company into
the United States, and Henry Fisher was recalled from Pembina.
Possibly the reason for Fisher's recall was the agitation against him
at St. Peter for allegedly using rum in his trade, and the threat
that a military force would be sent from St. Peter to police the
area.[82] It is also possible that the arrival of a detachment of the
Sixth Royal Regiment of Foot in the autumn of 1846 convinced
Simpson that the trade could be protected by less extreme measures.[83] But certainly a factor in the change of policy was Sir John
Henry Pelly's disapproval of unethical methods of meeting opposition.

Pelly's censure was occasioned by an attempt by Simpson and
the council of the northern department to discriminate against the
free traders through manipulation of the currency regulations.
In 1845 Red River possessed no metallic currency aside from British and American coins which were in general circulation. The

local currency consisted of paper notes issued by the Company in denominations of one pound, five shillings, and one shilling sterling, the value of which was based upon the credit of the Company. A trader who wished to purchase goods in England could buy at par bills of exchange which would be honored by the Company's headquarters in London. On the plea that such transactions involved expenses for the Company in loss of interest, the council resolved in the summer of 1844 that all bills of exchange given at Red River in exchange for paper notes should be sold at a premium of 5 per cent. For a bill of £100, £105 Red River currency would be paid.[84] The governor and committee refused to approve the resolution, and Pelly's denunciation of it revealed the difference in basic outlook between the London headquarters and the North American governor. Pelly pointed out to Simpson that, since the Company provided no metallic currency, the notes of the Company had value only as promises to pay in goods. If the Company purchased goods for the settlers, it did not in effect pay for these goods until the settlers used the notes for purchases from the Company. But if the holders of notes preferred money in England to goods at Red River, it was the duty of the Company to provide it without charging the settler a premium.[85]

Pelly was more disturbed by Simpson's opaqueness in ethics than by his lack of understanding of banking and currency. It was beneath the dignity and the honor of the Company, he declared, to tamper with the currency in order to attack free traders. Unless the Company was honest with the settlers, it would arouse further opposition to its rule not only in the settlement but in Great Britain itself. The existence of the settlement was undoubtedly dangerous to the interests of the fur trade, but it was there, and the Company lacked the power even if it had the intent to remove it. The best protection for the fur trade, said Pelly, was "to encourage and direct the industry and adventure of the settlers to objects of more certain profit than they can obtain from attempting an illicit fur trade." [86] If the settlers persisted in the illicit trade, the Company should meet the competition in a straightforward manner, rather than by devious means. Pelly's view was that the time had arrived for a change of policy in trading procedures. If the trade of the settlement and the immediate vicinity were thrown open to any settlers who wished to engage in it, the free traders would not be compelled to smuggle furs to Kittson since they would have a market at Red River. The Company, relieved of the expense of permanent establishments, would be able to pay prices at least as high as its American competitors.[87] The only really effective means to meet opposition in the chartered territory and elsewhere was "by selling as low as you can afford and buying as high." [88]

Pelly had made an important decision. He was now prepared to waive the claims of the Company to its chartered rights of monopoly, at least in the vicinity of the settlement, and to defeat competition from the United States by underselling it in goods and overbidding it for furs. Such a fundamental change was not to be undertaken without long consideration, and Pelly was not yet prepared to insist upon it, but his proposal was evidence of the recognition that a crisis had been reached in the affairs of the settlement and that the prevailing policies were ineffective.

Governor Christie proposed another plan. He recommended that, from Lac la Pluie on the east to Fort Ellice on the west, the settlement be encircled by a chain of well-manned trading posts. Within such a cordon no smuggler could long go unnoticed, and the Company would discourage free traders by seizing their furs. Christie recognized the flaws in his plan. To carry it into execution, the Company would require a large number of men on whose courage and fidelity it could rely, and he admitted that no such body could be drawn from the settlement. The alternative was the employment of a force from outside, perhaps a military unit.[89] Christie's plan suffered from another defect which he did not mention. The maintenance of a permanent force large enough to patrol effectively a line of 400 miles between Lac la Pluie and Fort Ellice, and of an additional body to maintain order in the settlement, would have involved an expense greater than the losses suffered from the competition of Kittson and the Red River traders.[90]

Between Pelly's suggestion of reliance upon competition and Christie's proposals for an adequate force to overawe the settlement and to apprehend smugglers, there could be no feasible middle course. The Company's policy at Red River between 1846 and 1849 fell between two stools. By insisting upon their legal rights and occasionally seizing furs, the Company's officers stimulated antagonism, but they did not possess the force to sustain their actions. When the British government withdrew the Sixth Regiment from Red River in 1848, the Company secured the services of a small corps of pensioners, who soon demonstrated their complete incompetence to perform any useful function. Further, their disregard for discipline and morality contributed to the spread of disaffection in the settlement.[91]

The Company possessed no other power than that of its officers and servants, and the loyalty of the latter was questionable. Demonstration of the Company's weakness by the flouting of its authority was inevitable, and the occasion came with the celebrated trial of Pierre Guillaume Sayer on May 17, 1849. The "trial" rapidly degenerated into a farce. The courthouse was surrounded by an armed mob. This irregular force dominated the proceedings, and though Sayer was found guilty of trading in furs, he escaped without punishment, even confiscation of his furs. The mob was justified in its shouts, *Le commerce est libre!* The Company never again attempted to prevent the free trade of the half-breeds. What Pelly in 1846 proposed to concede voluntarily had been extracted by force.[92]

The competition of Kittson—he was the only significant competitor at this time on the American frontier—thus contributed greatly to the demoralization of the Company's system of trading in southern Rupert's Land. By 1846 he had attracted Indians to the frontier from as far north as Lac Seul,[93] and by 1848 the effects of competition had been felt as far west as Edmonton, where Chief Factor John Rowand reported that "the half-breeds in this district are getting spoiled with all the stories they hear from Red River." [94]

The increase in independent trade at Red River was reflected in an expansion of Kittson's scale of operations. Shortly after he established his headquarters at Pembina, he built a small post at Turtle Mountain and another on the Mouse River. East of Pembina, in wooded country, he maintained another post at Lake Roseau, which was in the midst of some of the best fur preserves of northern Minnesota. By 1848 he had established a post on Lake of the Woods, and by 1850 his operations were extended to Rainy Lake. In that year he employed four clerks, including Joseph Rolette, Jr., son of a famous father, and ten *voyageurs*. Kittson estimated his capital at $12,000.[95]

The Hudson's Bay Company reacted to Kittson's expansion by establishing a post on the British side of the line at Pembina in

1845 [96] and two new posts in 1846, one at Turtle Mountain and the other on Lake of the Woods at the mouth of the Rainy River. Prices at these posts were raised to levels competitive with Kittson's, and *coureurs de bois* went out to Indians in the vicinity to collect their furs.[97] But such measures could not be completely effective so long as half-breeds clandestinely carried furs to Kittson, for the only way they could dispose of their furs was to sell them to him.

So serious had this leakage from British territory become by 1848 that Simpson seriously considered Christie's plan to establish a cordon of posts along the frontier from Fort William on Lake Superior to Fort Ellice on the Assiniboine River, and send large outfits of goods and a strong complement of officers and men to that line.[98] Implementation of these proposals would have created two frontier lines, one at the American boundary and the other between Assiniboia, which was poor in fur resources, and the relatively lucrative fur districts around it.

The fateful decision in the Sayer case altered the course of the Company's policy. After Sayer's release without punishment, no cordon of posts could restrain the free traders. Simpson's recommendation would probably not have been accepted in any event, but the developments of 1849 made it evident that the Company must use other techniques than force to protect its monopoly. Regardless of chartered rights, the Company's only means of defending itself was to trade with the half-breeds. This conclusion the Company, of course, did not publicly announce. But during the trading season in the spring of 1850, the Company raised its prices at Red River and in the Lac la Pluie district to match Kittson's and purchased furs at these prices from all who came to trade, whether Indians or half-breeds. The tacit admission of the half-breeds' right to trade compounded Kittson's difficulties. Since 1845 he had talked of the Company's buying him out. He had been disappointed in this hope, and by 1850 the strain upon his resources of paying high prices was already becoming evident.

The vigor of his competition relaxed in 1851 when he withdrew his posts from the neighborhood of Rainy Lake,[99] and two years later he decided to quit the contest entirely. In 1854 he and Sibley transferred control of the business in the Pembina district to Joseph Rolette, Jr., although Kittson seems to have retained an interest for a few years thereafter.

As late as the spring of 1856, Kittson appeared in the vicinity of Fort Garry to bid for the furs of the half-breeds. Chief Factor John Swanston, then in charge of Fort Garry, immediately raised the prices and continued to raise them until he outbid Kittson. In this way, the bulk of the furs were bought by the Company at prices that produced little, if any, profit.[100] But Kittson did not appear again. He had suffered the same fate as other petty competitors whose resources were exhausted in their efforts to match prices with the Company.[101]

Kittson was gone, but Rolette had replaced him, and if Rolette were forced to retire, another trader would appear at Pembina. The growth of population in Minnesota had made it certain that the Company would continue to face opposition in the Red River area and that the severity of competition would steadily increase as the half-breeds became more active in the trade. Though James Sinclair was bought off, and a few settlers were induced to accompany him on his journey westward, not all the Red River traders could be disposed of in this manner.[102]

Policy could not be founded solely upon the bribery of influential settlers, and the governor and committee could decide upon no method of checking the increasing illicit trade. In the spring of 1853 they wrote Simpson that he should adopt whatever course he thought best to combat the evil.[103] Simpson knew he could not take this instruction too literally, but it was evidence of the bankruptcy of ideas at the London headquarters. Governor Colvile in the autumn of 1854 suggested that free trade might be permitted within the district of Assiniboia, but that all persons who extended their operations beyond its limits should be arrested and their furs seized. Enforcement of such a policy was beyond the resources of the Company. As Simpson pointed out to Colvile, the Company could not muster a force sufficient to prevent the large bodies of Red River traders who each year traveled between Fort Garry and York Factory from liberating a prisoner. Also, such action would not prevent Indians from the outlying districts from carrying their furs to Fort Garry. The lure of high prices to Indians of the interior Simpson considered "the greatest evil that threatens the trade." [104]

While the London headquarters and Sir George Simpson exposed the weaknesses of each other's plans to counteract the Red

River competition, the activities of the free traders steadily expanded, and officers from an ever greater number of posts reported that the Indians of their districts were becoming disaffected. By the winter of 1855–56, westward-moving free traders from Red River were encamped only three days' journey from Fort Carlton.[105] To the north, although the free traders had not proceeded beyond Lake Winnipeg, Indians from the Norway House district were attracted by the high prices at Red River. To prevent them from carrying their furs to the settlement and at the same time to avoid disrupting the monopoly price structure of the interior, the Company in 1855 allowed the Indians at Norway House a gratuity of one "made beaver" for every five they traded. The prices of furs were thus increased by 20 per cent, although they nominally remained unaltered.

By the summer of 1855 the continuing extension of the halfbreeds' competition led Simpson and the officers of the northern department to conclude that they must soon make a stand or the entire fur trade would be wrecked. At the annual meeting of the council of the northern department at Norway House in June, 1855, officers reported the rumored intention of free traders from Red River to send a boatload of trading goods into the Athabaska and Mackenzie River districts, the most lucrative fur districts within the Hudson's Bay Company's area of trade. If such an expedition penetrated these districts and returned with news of the profits to be made, the entire area of the fur trade would be subject to competition. The council therefore decided that the boat and its cargo must be seized on its way inland, regardless of the consequences.[106] The expedition did not appear in 1855, but during the summer of 1856 rumors circulated at Red River that the McGillis family, among the most prominent of the free traders, planned to travel to the Mackenzie River that season.[107]

During the year since the decision to seize the persons and property of any parties that might venture toward the Mackenzie River, Simpson had changed his mind as to the efficacy of such drastic action. Although the Company's officers had the power to seize such parties, repercussions in the settlement might be serious, for the Company's government in Assiniboia existed on the sufferance of the inhabitants. Simpson therefore determined to rely on more subtle measures. The Company's most powerful ally was nature, for the remoteness of the Mackenzie River made a journey from Red River a formidable prospect, particularly to those unacquainted with the intervening terrain. The Company had been trading in the district for decades, yet from five to seven years elapsed from the time goods were shipped from England until the returns on the investment were realized by sale of the furs there. For Red River traders, whose seat of operations was much closer, the time could be much less, provided they could gain the necessary familiarity with the country between the settlement and the Mackenzie. But in 1856 the free traders had reached only the English River district,[108] and over 600 miles of unknown country lay between this furthest point of penetration and the nearest boundary of the Mackenzie River district. A journey through such country was arduous for a well-equipped expedition; for the half-breeds, whose resources were small and who lived largely off the land as they traveled, the difficulties were even greater. Simpson therefore decided that the best means of averting an expedition to the Mackenzie River was to harass free traders on such a journey by sending a well-equipped party to watch them, and by trading with the Indians along the way at liberal prices to deny the intruders opportunities for trade.[109] The McGillises did not attempt the journey, but Simpson instructed Chief Factor John Swanston at Fort Garry to keep in readiness at all times two fully equipped boats and at least two canoes, with an assortment of essential trading goods, to be sent out to accompany any traders who might start for the Mackenzie.[110]

Although the Company was able to maintain its monopoly prices in the Mackenzie River district, the serious consideration by free traders of a venture into the district indicated the extent to which their competition had grown. During the spring of 1856 the Company paid £8,023.10.2 at Fort Garry for the furs of free traders. The value of furs sold to the Americans cannot be determined so specifically, but it appears to have been almost equal. The largest amounts paid by the Company for furs during the trading season of 1856 were to the following: [111]

| | |
|---|---|
| William McGillis | £540 |
| William McMillan | 335.15 |
| John Dease | 387.4 |
| George Racette | 205.18.6 |

| Arthur Pruden | 426.13 |
| Urbain Delorme | 762 |
| Michael Chartrain | 223.2.6 |
| Pierre Chartrain | 188.13 |
| Antoine Gingras | 624.13.4 |

These were cash sales, like most of the sales in the settlement by 1856, and they further reduced the Company's profits, for in barter transactions the Company could make a profit on the selling price of its goods. Some of the money paid for furs returned to the Company in retail sales at the Company's shops, but much of it was spent at the American establishments on the frontier or carried to St. Paul, which had now replaced St. Peter as the principal American supply center.[112]

By 1856, conditions at Red River caused Simpson to despair for the future of the fur trade. He wrote to John Shepherd, who had succeeded Andrew Colvile as governor:

> The Company's Charter, as far as exclusive right of trade goes, is almost a nullity:—as we are unable to enforce its provisions, it is set at nought by the Americans and their Half-breed allies in the country. . . . I am inclined to think we should do almost as well without it as with it; I therefore beg leave to throw out, as a suggestion for your consideration whether it might not be advisable to make a merit of necessity by offering to Her Majesty's Government the voluntary surrender of the Charter on receiving compensation on some such basis as was allowed to the East India Company.[113]

The hope for compensation from the British government was a forlorn one;[114] in the meantime the problem of the Red River free trade had to be met. The only course that seemed practicable was to attempt to collect furs in the interior districts before the Red River traders could arrive, and to buy any furs they succeeded in acquiring, at rates competitive with the Americans. The basic rule at Fort Garry in the 1850's and 1860's was to buy furs at one-half to two-thirds of the average prices at the latest sales in London. Whenever a trader had a large number of furs for sale, however, the Company's officers made a special bargain, in which their offer was dictated by the prices offered by American competitors. In the surrounding districts, *derouine* parties were kept constantly employed during the winter collecting furs as they were hunted by the Indians.[115] By the application of these principles, the Company was able to realize a small profit on the trade at Red River and to retard the expansion of the free traders into other areas.

Growth of the free trade could be slowed down, but it could not be stopped. Water communication from Red River provided transport in every direction for many miles, and with the development of St. Paul as a supply center the half-breeds were able to acquire much larger trading outfits than when the Company ships and sales shops had been the only source of supply.

The necessity of watching parties of free traders who encroached upon the Company's monopoly in its own chartered territory tried the nerves of the Company's officers. Some of the more resolute were indignant at the pusillanimity that seemed to motivate the Company's directors, and all were concerned at the losses caused by the competition. Among those who believed in a more aggressive policy against the trespassers was Chief Factor George Barnston, who was stationed at Norway House from 1851 to 1858. Barnston had been an employee of the Company since the coalition,[116] and had demonstrated the qualities of resoluteness and activity which made him a useful officer in the frontier trade. He had contended with the Americans at Fort Nez Percés and with the Canadians on the St. Lawrence, and on each occasion he had met the opposition with strong competition. At his post at Norway House Barnston was restive at the Company's failure to take vigorous action. Since Norway House was in the path of the free traders Barnston's attitude was important; he was not likely to accept their encroachment with equanimity.

Barnston was confronted in 1857 with a party led by Andrew G. B. Bannatyne, McDermot's son-in-law, who had been in the Company's service from 1846 to 1851.[117] The traders arrived in the vicinity of Norway House with a boatload of goods. There Bannatyne found consigned to him an additional supply of goods which had just arrived from England by the Company's ship. As Bannatyne loaded the goods into his boat in preparation for a trading expedition, Barnston, angered at this brazen violation of the charter, finally exploded. He issued a warrant for Bannatyne's arrest and sent him in custody to Red River. The rest of the party were allowed to proceed with their goods, since they were natives of Red River.[118]

When Bannatyne arrived at Fort Garry there was consternation among the settlers and among the Company's officers. The Sayer case had demonstrated the Company's inability to prosecute an offender against its monopoly rights. On the advice of Francis G. Johnson, governor of Assiniboia [119] and the Company's local legal adviser, the Company's officers immediately released Bannatyne, who, indignant at his arrest, threatened to take legal action.[120]

The Bannatyne affair occurred at a particularly unpropitious time from the standpoint of the Company's interests. A select committee of the British House of Commons had just completed an investigation of the Company's monopoly during which witnesses had condemned the administration of the settlement as unjust and tyrannical. Though the majority of the committee had not accepted all the indictments as valid, it had recommended the opening of the southern area of Rupert's Land to settlement, and a strong minority had favored even more drastic action against the Company's chartered rights.[121] Simultaneously, agitation for transfer of the Company's territory to Canada had grown in the Canadian Assembly and press. The Company's legal advisers in London concurred with Johnson that the arrest of Bannatyne was illegal and that the Company had recourse only to civil action against any encroachments on its rights of trade.[122]

The overzealous Barnston was transferred from Norway House to Michipicoten on Lake Superior in order to make Red River less accessible to him, and Bannatyne's indignation was apparently soothed by compensation, for he took no action against the Company or against Barnston. If the Sayer trial killed the Company's pretensions to rights of monopoly, the Bannatyne case destroyed all hope of their resurrection. No further efforts were made to discourage opposition by other than economic means.

Since coercion or prosecution of free traders was out of the question, Simpson concerned himself during his last years with improving the Company's techniques of competition. The result was the inauguration in 1859 of shipments of goods by rail from Montreal to St. Paul and thence by steamboat to Red River.[123] By 1862 the governor and committee agreed that this route "must henceforth be regarded as one of the ordinary means of introducing supplies into the chartered territory." [124]

The use of the Montreal–St. Paul route improved the Company's supply system, but there was no way to relieve the Company of the increasing pressure of free traders. The same conditions that made the St. Paul route attractive to the Company made St. Paul the center of the fur trade in northern United States and the primary support for the Red River traders.

The only effective means of preventing free traders from over-running all of Rupert's Land was the policy employed by the Company in areas outside its chartered territory, to outbid its opponents for furs of better quality or to force prices to levels unprofitable for competitors. After all other possibilities had been tried, this principle of competition remained the Company's primary weapon. By 1860 the Company's techniques of competition in southern Rupert's Land were precisely the same as those in Canada. When the Company was reorganized in 1863, the basic frontier policies remained unaltered. The Company's fur trade in Rupert's Land was saved, therefore, not by the exercise of its chartered rights but by reliance upon effective competition against free traders in the frontier districts. The fundamental assets of the Company were its superior knowledge of the fur trade, its reputation for goods of high quality, and its ability and willingness to sustain losses to discourage competitors. The Pelly-Simpson "frontier policies" which had proved their validity in Canada again justified themselves in the heart of the Company's territories.

# 5

# The Western Frontier

THE TERRITORY between the Rocky Mountains and the Pacific
Ocean was, in a sense, all a frontier, for one of its functions was to
provide a cover for the fur territories to the north and northeast;
as population increased in Oregon and later in British Columbia,
this function became increasingly important. But much of the
region was lucrative fur territory in its own right. For the protection of the trade in profitable areas the Company maintained a
policy of active competition on the periphery to discourage actual
and prospective opponents from entering the interior trade. There
were thus four frontiers on the Pacific slope. One faced Russian
America; the second lay along the shores of the Pacific; the third
extended from the southern border of the Oregon country into
California; and the fourth, in what is now eastern Oregon and
Washington and much of Idaho, came to be known as the Snake
country, from the name given to the Indians who inhabited that
area.[1] The present discussion is concerned principally with the
fourth frontier, for it was there that the Company met the most
westerly extension of the American fur trade. In Mexican California no major competition was encountered, and protection was
not a primary consideration in the expeditions into that area. Policies of the Company on the frontiers of Russian America and along
the coast will be discussed in succeeding chapters.[2]

The Hudson's Bay Company assumed control of the transmon-

[1] For notes to chap. 5, see pp. 441–445.

tane West with the hope that the fur trade would be profitable from the Fraser valley northward and the expectation that it would not in the valley of the Columbia. But there were compelling reasons for the retention of trading posts in the Columbia basin. The treaty of 1818 between the United States and Great Britain left sovereignty undefined in the territory between California and Russian America, and settlement was open to citizens of both states. Since actual occupancy would undoubtedly be a weighty consideration in diplomatic deliberations, maintenance of the Columbia trading posts was justified as a bargaining measure. The acquisition of a few thousand square miles of territory for the British Empire was not the objective of the governor and committee; it was the potentialities of the Columbia valley as the frontier for the trading stations to the north which impelled the governor and committee to write to George Simpson on February 27, 1822:

> We understand that hitherto the trade of the Columbia has not been profitable, and from all that we have learnt on the Subject we are not sanguine in our expectations of being able to make it so in future. But if by any improved arrangement the loss can be reduced to a small sum, it is worth a serious consideration, whether it may not be good policy to hold possession of that country, with a view of protecting the more valuable districts to the North of it; and we wish you to direct the attention of the Council to this subject and collect all the information which you can obtain from individuals acquainted with the country.[3]

At the time of its absorption into the Hudson's Bay Company, the North West Company maintained seven posts in the Columbia district—Fort George, originally Astoria, built by Astor's Pacific Fur Company in 1811;[4] Fort Nez Percés, or Walla Walla, built in 1818; Spokane House, in 1810; Flathead House, in 1809; Kootenay (Kootanie) Fort, in 1811; Fort Okanagan, in 1811; and Fort Kamloops (Thompson River), in 1812. All except Kamloops were south of the 49th parallel.

Fort George had been acquired by the North West Company in 1813 by the well-known purchase from Astor's Pacific Fur Company, and had since been continuously under North West control, despite the formal retransfer of the post to American jurisdiction in 1818. Situated south of the Columbia near the coast, it was the

most important establishment on the west coast in 1821. It was
the port for the district, and its trade with the coastal Indians was
substantial. In 1822 the returns of the post included 6,000 beaver.[5]
On his first visit to the Columbia in 1824, during which he was
zealous to promote economy, George Simpson viewed the preten-
tiousness of the post with a jaundiced eye. He described it in his
journal as follows:

> The Establishment of Fort George is a large pile of buildings
> covering about an acre of ground well stockaded and protected by
> Bastions of Blockhouses, having two Eighteen Pounders mounted
> in front and altogether an air or appearance of Grandeur & conse-
> quence which does not become and is not at all suitable to an In-
> dian Trading Post.[6]

Three hundred miles to the east of Fort George was Fort Nez
Percés, situated at the mouth of the Walla Walla River, about
ten miles below the junction of the Snake River with the Columbia. The territory in the immediate vicinity of this post was not
rich in beaver, and the Nez Percé tribe which controlled the area
was more disposed to war than to trade. Simpson complained that
they did "little else than rove about in search of Scalps, plunder
and amusement." The few furs the Company collected were traded
primarily with the Cayuse tribe. In the 1820's the post produced
annual profits ranging from £1,000 to £2,000, but it was not maintained primarily for profits. The Nez Percés were capable of sever-
ing communications along the Columbia; if they were hostile they
could deny the Company's parties entry into the Snake country;
and every year they provided the Company with about 250 horses
which were essential to the trade.[7]

Spokane House, near the junction of the Spokane and Little
Spokane rivers, was the headquarters of the district which contained Fort Kootenay and Flathead House and to which the Snake
country expedition was attached. In 1823–24 the district collected
approximately 9,000 beaver, about half of which were trapped
by the Snake expedition.[8] Fort Okanagan, near the junction of
the Spokane River with the Columbia, and Fort Kamloops on the
Thompson River were maintained as links in the communication
system between New Caledonia and the posts on the Columbia.
Their returns in furs were insignificant.

The seven posts were divided during the last years of the North

West Company's control into four districts—Thompson's River, including Kamloops and Fort Okanagan; Spokane, including Spokane House, Flathead House, and Fort Kootenay; Walla Walla; and Fort George. The Spokane River district, the most easterly in the Columbia valley, was at the time of the coalition the most prolific source of furs in the entire Columbia area, and its furs were of the highest quality.[9]

The ability of these districts to provide returns of 15,000 skins— as they did in the trading season of 1821–22—suggests that the governor and committee's low regard for the Columbia valley's trading potentialities was unwarranted, and that the losses suffered by the North West Company had been caused primarily by bad management. Subsequent profits under an altered system of trading confirm this view. For the conversion of the Columbia from a liability to an asset, credit is usually given to the energizing effects of George Simpson's celebrated visit in 1824–25,[10] and to the administrative ability of his appointee, Chief Factor John McLoughlin. But the improvement was due in part to other factors. The addiction of the tribes in the district to warfare had reduced their capacity to provide furs for the traders, but as they succumbed more and more to the lure of European goods and as their mutual hostility was restrained by the growing influence of the Hudson's Bay traders, returns from the Columbia increased.

An improvement in management began when Simpson and the council of the northern department appointed Chief Factors John Haldane and John Dugald Cameron to the control of the Columbia district and Chief Traders James McMillan and John Lee Lewes to assist them. Haldane and McMillan, ex-Nor'Westers, had previously served on the Columbia, and Cameron, also of the North West Company, had already acquired a justifiable reputation, which he later enhanced, as a canny trader. Lewes, whose career had been exclusively in the service of the Hudson's Bay Company, apparently was appointed to report to Simpson on the condition of the Columbia trade.[11]

Prospects were further improved by a change in the method of supplying the district and disposing of its furs. The North West Company had employed the agency of J. and T. H. Perkins of Boston to transport supplies to the Columbia and to sell the returns in Canton. The system had not been profitable, for Perkins and Company received approximately one-fourth of the proceeds, and the price paid for Columbia beaver in Canton was only $3.50 per skin, well below the prices on the London market.[12] The inauguration in 1822 of a system of supply from England in the Company's ships and the sale of Columbia returns on the European market made possible an increase in profits.

The North West Company had been inefficient in its use of manpower. In the spring of 1821 it was employing 180 men, including clerks and trappers. That autumn the Hudson's Bay Company's northern council sent additional men, and by the end of 1821 there were 220. Of this number 150 received wages or salaries from the Company; the rest were free trappers who received outfits from the Company and sold their returns at specified rates.[13] Including these trappers, the number engaged in the fur trade on the Columbia at that time was approximately one-sixth of the total personnel employed by the Hudson's Bay Company in all North America. On his first visit to the district, Simpson drastically reduced the number of employees and centralized control in John McLoughlin. Both steps contributed to the subsequent increases in profits.

Administrative changes in the Columbia district which made possible higher profits had thus begun before Simpson became personally acquainted with the area, but thoroughgoing reforms were not inaugurated until his first visit. One of the improvements antedating his visit was a new emphasis upon the Snake country. From the time that the Hudson's Bay Company assumed control of the British fur trade in 1821, the governor and committee recognized that the region south of the Columbia River was almost certain to be awarded to the United States in any boundary agreement. Thus it was to the Company's interest to extract a maximum number of furs from this southern section, and the greatest untapped reservoir was the Snake country.

The North West Company had only begun to exploit the Snake country before the coalition. Donald McKenzie, formerly a member of Astor's Pacific Fur Company, led three expeditions between 1818 and 1821 and established the pattern for future excursions. Instead of seeking to trade with the Indians, his freemen and *engagés* trapped furs themselves. Through the use of horses for supply and transport and an emphasis on living off the land, Mc-

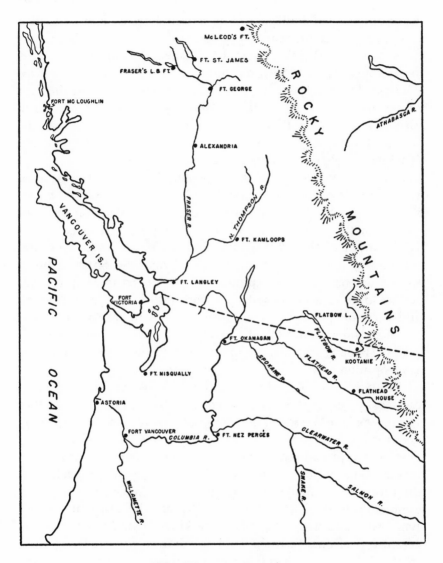

*The Western Frontier*

Kenzie developed a self-sustaining mobile force able to roam over a tremendous extent of territory before returning to its base.

Despite McKenzie's imaginative leadership, however, the returns appear to have been disappointing, though Alexander Ross contended that the ventures had been a great success.[14] At the time of the coalition the North West Company's officers had decided to abandon the Snake River district entirely, concluding that the unfriendliness of the Indians, particularly of the Piegans and Blackfeet, made profits impossible.[15]

Chief Trader John Lee Lewes, whom Simpson had instructed to examine the condition of the Columbia trade, was not convinced. The Company had quieted unfriendly tribes on previous occasions; its posts on the Saskatchewan produced large profits in the midst of the most warlike Indians in all North America. There was no reason, thought Lewes, that the Snake country should not be similarly exploited. He suggested to Simpson that it "has hitherto been looked upon with rather too high a glance," and that the possibility of increased trade in that vicinity was worth consideration.[16] Chief Factors Alexander Kennedy, who replaced Haldane in 1822, and John Dugald Cameron were of the same opinion.[17]

The possibility of profits from the Snake River was further indicated by an 1823 expedition led by Finan McDonald, another veteran ex-Nor'Wester. The McDonald party may be accurately described as a "caretaker" expedition, for one of its primary purposes was to provide employment for freemen, who might in their idleness cause mischief, until a final decision could be reached on the future of the Snake country fur trade.[18] McDonald's men became embroiled with the Piegan tribe, and his assistant, Michel Bourdon,[19] and five other men were killed. Unnerved by the experience, McDonald wrote, "I got Safe home from the Snake Cuntre thank . . . and when that Cuntre will see me agane the Beaver will have Gould Skin."[20] The loss of six men was a regrettable though not an uncommon incident in the fur trade. But what must have impressed Simpson and the governor and committee was that McDonald's party, despite the hostility of the Indians, had brought back over 4,000 skins.[21]

Even before McDonald's party returned, Simpson, on the advice of Cameron and Kennedy, had decided to test the resources of the Snake country by reinstating the expedition as a regular aspect of the Columbia trade. On their suggestion he selected Alexander Ross, whose association with the Oregon country since his arrival with Astor's first party in 1811 seemed to qualify him for the responsibility. Ross had not participated in previous expeditions, having served only at Forts Okanagan and Nez Percés. But he had discussed the characteristics of the Snake country with Donald McKenzie, and a statement he had prepared in the spring of 1823 on the subject of expanding the trade of the area seems to have been a factor in the decision of Simpson and the northern council to employ him as head of the expedition.[22] Peter Skene Ogden was appointed to the charge of Spokane House, the headquarters of the Snake country expedition.

Ross, as events proved, was not an ideal selection for the responsibility of managing a party of ruffian freemen in the midst of a hostile Indian population, but his problems were complicated by a difficulty with which none of his predecessors had had to contend—competition from American trapping parties. Since the days of Astor's Pacific Fur Company, no American fur traders had ventured into the interior of the Oregon country,[23] and the only opposition to British traders was that of hostile Indians. Chittenden was undoubtedly guilty of exaggeration when he contended that "if the Astorian enterprise had succeeded . . . no part of the Pacific coast line would now belong to Great Britain."[24] But certainly the failure of Astor's venture enabled the Hudson's Bay Company to gain a control over the Columbia basin from which it could not easily be dislodged. When opposition to the British traders reappeared, it came from the direction of the Missouri River, and the first contact occurred in the course of Ross's first expedition when his trappers met a group headed by Jedediah S. Smith from General William H. Ashley's company.

After the failure at Astoria, the reopening of American trade with the trans-Mississippi West had been delayed for two reasons. The unremitting enmity of the Blackfeet who controlled the passes caused trappers to concentrate their activities in the less hazardous territories from the three forks of the Missouri eastward. Also, for several years after the War of 1812, little capital was available for exploitation of the Western fur trade. The financial risks seemed to many investors too great for the prospective returns.[25]

By 1822, however, prospects for the fur trade were reviving. Larger returns than those previously brought to the St. Louis market stimulated the investment of capital, and one observer estimated that a thousand men were then engaged in the fur trade of the Missouri and the upper Mississippi. Among the first to enter the mountain trade was General Ashley, whose expeditions in 1825 brought out 8,829 pounds of beaver, worth from $40,000 to $45,000 in St. Louis. These rich returns encouraged others to seek fortune in the Rocky Mountains, but the major opposition to the Hudson's Bay Company during the next five years came from Jedediah Smith, David Jackson, and William P. Sublette, who bought out Ashley in the summer of 1826.[26] These three were experienced mountain men, wise in the ways of survival in a world where an expedition could be ruined by the slightest carelessness or destroyed by unwariness. They were the strongest rivals confronting the Company's expeditions.

The appointment of Ross therefore coincided with a change in the character of the Snake country expedition. Negotiations between Richard Rush, the American minister plenipotentiary, and the British commissioners dragged on from the spring of 1824 until Rush's recall to the United States, and continued after the arrival of his successor, Albert Gallatin, in 1826. As the discussions continued, it became apparent to all concerned that immediate settlement of the boundary question was unlikely. Whether or not the "joint occupation" agreement of 1818 was renewed in 1828, the final decision would unquestionably be influenced by actual occupation. Control of the Snake country thus became of enhanced importance to the Hudson's Bay Company. In addition to the furs it might provide, it was now a frontier area where American competition must be discouraged before it could penetrate into the country farther west. By repelling the Americans in the Snake country, British claims to sole occupancy of Oregon could be preserved and American traders would be prevented from extending their operations into the western Columbia region and thence into the rich fur country of New Caledonia. Simpson foresaw this danger of American penetration when he instructed Cameron and

Kennedy to warn Ross, if he accepted the leadership of the expedition, "against opening a road for the Americans." [27] This condition Ross found it impossible to fulfill.

Ross left Flathead Post with ten Company servants and fifty-four other men, including freemen and Iroquois hunters, perhaps the poorest human material to be found anywhere in the Company's service. For personnel of such doubtful loyalty the officers of the Company should have been at special pains to provide unusually attractive material incentives. But these men were not treated with justice, and for the difficulties faced by Ross and his successor Ogden, George Simpson and the governor and committee must bear much of the responsibility. Each freeman was required to pay for the horses and traps he used in his hunts. To outfit himself properly with four horses and the requisite traps, he had to pay the Company 150 large beaver. The prices charged for other necessities were also so exorbitant that, in Ogden's opinion, it was almost impossible for a man, however industrious, to clear expenses.[28] Even in the absence of competition these men would have been difficult to discipline, and when opposition appeared they might have been expected to desert the Company for better terms.

Ross, anxious to prove his ability, led this dubious band from their base into the valley of the Bitterroot and thence southward as far as the Lemhi River in the present state of Idaho. As he and his party traveled to the Salmon River, Ross exhorted his men to keep alert for hostile Indians, but they demonstrated complete indifference to his leadership and their own safety. While Ross and the main body of his expedition were on the Salmon River, a detachment of his Iroquois trappers who had been hunting the country to the south returned with a story of having been attacked by the Snakes and robbed of the furs they had collected as well as their traps, guns, and horses. With them were seven American trappers led by Jedediah S. Smith. Ross had good cause for his suspicion that they might be spies,[29] and his precaution of doubling the guard to protect his returns from the Americans demonstrated sound judgment.

Unfortunately for Ross's reputation, his subsequent actions were not marked by the same acuity. He may have had little choice but to permit Smith to accompany him to Flathead House, thus helping the American to gain familiarity with the country. But he was indiscreet in boasting to Smith about the rich fur returns of the Snake country. Ross told Smith that during the previous four years the Company's trappers had procured 80,000 beaver, equal to 160,000 pounds of furs. This was a great exaggeration, and certainly stimulated Smith's ardor to exploit the riches for himself and his company. Ross, however, was not alone in his garrulousness, for Ogden also provided Smith with valuable information.

Despite the misfortune that had befallen his Iroquois detachment, Ross brought back to Flathead Post over 4,000 beaver, a slightly larger quantity than his predecessor had obtained. In view of his difficulties, Ross would seem to have had just cause for satisfaction in these returns. But George Simpson did not so regard his accomplishments. While Ross and his men were struggling back through Blackfoot country, Simpson arrived at Spokane House on his first journey to the Columbia, accompanied by Chief Factor John McLoughlin, Chief Traders James McMillan and Peter Skene Ogden, and Thomas McKay, a clerk. During the horseback journey from the junction of the Columbia and Spokane rivers to the post, or perhaps earlier, Simpson must have discussed the Snake expedition with members of his party, for by the time of his arrival at Spokane House he had decided to replace Ross with Ogden as leader of the expedition.[30] On October 29 Simpson wrote to Ross that he had decided to place him in charge of the missionary school at Red River.[31]

Simpson's motives for relieving Ross are not entirely clear. He was probably not yet aware of the assistance Ross had given the Americans, yet he described Ross as "a self-sufficient empty headed man," [32] whose "reports are so full of bombast and marvellous nonsense that it is impossible to get at any information that can be depended on from him." [33] These judgments were unjust to Ross, who was far from incompetent. But, though Simpson's fairness may be questioned, his fundamental thesis was sound. He saw that the importance of the Snake country expedition had been previously underestimated. It had "hitherto been considered as a forlorn hope," whereas with proper management it could produce large profits. Also, the Snake country lay between the Americans and the posts on the Columbia. If the region were trapped so intensively as to eliminate the beaver, the Americans would be less likely to push westward. The Company would be left in undisputed control in Oregon, and the British representatives would possess a strong argument for a boundary at least as far south as the Columbia.[34] Here was the origin of the effort to create a "fur desert."

This policy was not unique for the Snake country. On all its frontiers the Company endeavored to eliminate the supply of fur-bearing animals as rapidly as possible to dissuade competitors from penetrating into the interior of its domain. In this respect the policies Simpson proposed to introduce were essentially the same as those in effect at Red River and Rainy Lake and along the Canadian frontier. What distinguished the Snake country was the association of the political objective of securing a treaty favorable to Great Britain and the Hudson's Bay Company with the economic motives dominant in other areas.

Conceptions of the extent of territory included in the Snake country varied widely. George Simpson, accustomed to thinking in large terms, described it as follows in a dispatch to the governor and committee on March 1, 1829:

> The boundaries of this Country, are by us considered, the Rocky Mountains on the East, and a chain of mountains running nearly parallel with Coast on the West: on the North the 46th parallel of Latitude from the Rocky Mountains till it strikes the South branch of the Columbia near its junction with the Main Stream, and on the South, the Waters of the Rio Colorado.[35]

This was the country of the Snakes and of war parties of Piegans and Blackfeet, a largely uncharted country in which annihilation was the fate of those who lacked vigilance and, indeed, of many who possessed it. For the management of a rowdy, insolent, completely undisciplined mob of trappers, for the conduct of resolute competition against Americans who sought to preëmpt the territory, no better selection could have been made than Peter Skene Ogden.

Ogden had entered the fur trade not through economic necessity but from a love of adventure. His father, Isaac, was a prominent loyalist who had gone to England when British troops evacuated New York and had thereafter been appointed to judicial positions in Canada. Peter's brother Charles was for many years attorney general for Lower Canada and was the first to hold that office in united Canada after 1840.[36] A cousin, William M. Meredith, was secretary of the treasury in the Fillmore administration.[37]

The conventional success to which these family connections could contribute made no appeal to Peter Ogden, and in 1809 or 1810 he entered the service of the North West Company as a clerk. In the years of conflict which followed, Ogden distinguished himself as one of the most active of the Nor'Westers in the prosecution of physical as well as economic conflict. Ross Cox, who saw him in 1817 in the Île-à-la-Crosse district, described him as "humorous, honest, eccentric, law-defying," and as "the terror of the Indians, and the delight of all gay fellows." [38]

In 1818 Ogden was transferred by the North West Company from Île-à-la-Crosse to the Columbia. The cause for his removal seems to have been his alleged violence against Hudson's Bay Company employees, and when the two companies coalesced he was not retained. He was reëmployed, however, after a personal appeal to the governor and committee, who apparently concluded that so energetic a man might be useful in the Columbia trade.[39] Ogden had the reputation of being able to outbrawl, outswear, and outjest any of his subordinates; these were qualities of value in the Snake country. He was of only medium height, but he was massively corpulent, and long after his death Indians remembered his "great obesity." [40]

Ogden possessed another quality equally as important as his physical characteristics—a keen sense of fairness. The knowledge that he would represent their interests to the full extent of his authority was an important factor in the willingness of the freemen in the Snake country to follow him. Coupled with his concern for underlings was a vaulting ambition, an intense craving for recognition and for the material fruits of fame.

In appointing to the management of the Snake country a man whom he believed to be unscrupulous and addicted to violence, Simpson took upon himself a grave responsibility. A collision between Ogden and the Americans might have serious consequences for Anglo-American relations, and Ogden was given no specific instructions on his conduct toward American parties or on the limitations of his area of operations. No person who had been given careful indoctrination could write, as did Ogden in his "Snake Country Report" for 1825–26, "The Snake Country is bounded on the North by the Columbia Waters on the South by the Missourie, on the West by the Spanish Territo[ries] and the East by the Saskatchewan Tribes."[41]

Ogden set out in December, 1824, accompanied by fifty-eight freemen and servants and by Smith's party, which traveled with him until the following March. Two months later occurred one of the most famous incidents in the history of the fur trade. Ogden, extending his search for beaver farther than any of his predecessors had, crossed the 42nd parallel into Mexican territory. This was not the first time a British party had strayed beyond the Oregon territory, but it was unquestionably the most consequential. Shortly after Ogden crossed the boundary, he met a group of American trappers led by Johnson Gardner. Gardner told Ogden's party that they were in American territory and that the freemen were therefore relieved of all obligation to the Hudson's Bay Company. As a result, twenty-three of Ogden's freemen deserted, taking with them their horses and furs.[42] That the entire group did not desert in response to promises of better terms is a rare tribute to the freemen's respect for Ogden. John McLoughlin wrote Simpson that it was more surprising that any remained than that any ran away.[43]

Ogden and the Americans were in Mexican territory west of the Continental Divide. In view of the confusing terrain in that area both may have been under a misapprehension as to their exact location, but Ogden had never made any effort to limit his operations to the Oregon territory. The Company's officers were contemptuous of Mexican authority in California. As Simpson admitted to the governor and committee, the Company followed the example of its American opponents by making no inquiries about the territorial rights of the Mexican republic.[44] Before receiving specific instructions from the governor and committee to respect the American boundary, the officers on the Columbia had taken much the same view of American territory. George Simpson had not observed the frontier line south of Red River before the arrival of the American Fur Company and the customs agents. He would respect the western frontier only when it was prejudicial to the interests of the Hudson's Bay Company to violate it. This was not the view of the governor and committee, who castigated Ogden for having crossed into foreign territory.[45] It was not until after the incident had evoked the displeasure of London headquarters that Simpson instructed McLoughlin that the expedition must under no circumstance cross the Continental Divide.[46] Perhaps the most significant letter in the correspondence on Ogden's alleged violation of the frontier line was one from McLoughlin to Simpson on March 20, 1828. Stung by the reproaches of the governor and committee, McLoughlin protested to Simpson:

> . . . I can only say I find no document here to show that any directions were given not to cross the Eastside of the Mountains by the Gentlemen who outfitted the Snake expedition prior to Mr. Ogden, and he conceived he was right in following the route of the preceding expeditions, since it had been sanctioned by his predecessors, who outfitted it from the Flatheads, indeed as long as the Snake expedition was outfitted from that place in consequence of a very high range of Mountains that runs east and west between the Snake country and the Flatheads people leaving the latter place in the Fall to go to the former must cross to the East side of the Rocky Mountains, proceed South and recross them to get to the Snake Country. . . .[47]

The failure of the Company's officers to demand respect for the American boundary was further demonstrated when Ogden and the remainder of his party, after the encounter with Gardner, crossed the Continental Divide to trap on the east branch of the Jefferson River.[48] In so doing he was not conscious of violating any instructions from the Company, and indeed none had been given.

Despite Ogden's misfortune at the hands of the Americans, he brought back from the Snake country 2,485 large beaver and 1,210 small beaver, with profits estimated by McLoughlin at approximately £2,000.[49] Such returns were an additional incentive to expand the Snake expedition, and Ogden set out on his second journey in November, 1825, with an augmented party and with instructions to stay within the borders of the Oregon country. To prevent a recurrence of desertions, the contracts with the freemen were liberalized. McLoughlin raised the price offered for beaver and lowered the prices of supplies.[50] The policy in effect after 1826 was to sell the freemen supplies for their personal use at the same rates as employees enjoyed—50 per cent above prime cost on all imported goods. Freemen paid only £2 for horses, and when they returned from an expedition the Company took back the implements it had issued, charging them only for those they had lost and for the cost of repairing those they had broken. The Company raised its beaver prices to levels competitive with those of the Americans.[51] Thus service for the Hudson's Bay Company became more attractive than employment by American trappers. Tangible evidence was provided when some of the freemen who had deserted Ogden in 1825 appeared at Flathead Post in the spring of 1828 and delivered their hunts to the officer in charge.[52]

The incident of May, 1825, was not repeated. American trappers had other preoccupations than antagonizing parties of the Hudson's Bay Company, for they found the Indians, particularly the Snakes, decidedly hostile. A total of thirty-two Americans were killed in the trading seasons of 1824–25 and 1825–26.[53]

Ogden led six expeditions, the last in 1829–30, and continued to interpret the instructions of the governor and committee more liberally than they had intended. During his last five expeditions, Ogden led his parties as far south as the Gulf of California[54] and as far east as the Bear River in Utah. In all these he remained west of the Continental Divide, but on his last two journeys he was well within Mexican territory, although he avoided the settlements on the coast. The violations of Mexican territory, also committed with impunity by American traders, elicited no comment from the directors or Governor Simpson so long as they did not lead to conflicts with the Mexican authorities. They also helped to sustain returns from the Snake country as the supply of furs in that district declined. But protection of northern and western Oregon against the Americans remained a fundamental function of the expedition. The Company assumed that, as in other areas of North America, fur traders would precede agricultural settlement, and that, if the fur traders could be driven back, the appearance of the farmer would be delayed.

Simpson expressed the fundamental principles of the expedition in a letter to McLoughlin, July 9, 1827, which embodies the views of the London committee:

> The greatest and best protection we can have from opposition is keeping the country closely hunted as the first step that the American Government will take towards Colonization is through their Indian Traders and if the country becomes exhausted in Fur bearing animals they can have no inducement to proceed thither.
>
> We therefore entreat that no exertions be spared to explore and Trap every part of the country and as the service is both dangerous and laborious we wish our people to be treated with kindness and

liberality, and such prices given for their hunts as will afford them a fair remuneration for their services and their supplies sold in such terms as would convince them that by desertion they would seriously injure their own interests.

The trade of the Coutainais and Flat heads should be closely watched and if the Americans do visit or are likely to visit those Tribes we must endeavour to undersell them and thereby make their Trade unprofitable if we have not sufficient influence with those Indians to attach them to us otherwise.[55]

This plan had been effective on other frontiers against opponents with little capital, such as the American trappers. Without the use of violence, the Company could by these techniques gain dominance on the frontier of the Oregon country.

Although Ogden frequently came into contact with American trappers, at no time did he or his successors come into physical conflict with them. This record would have been more difficult to maintain had Simpson been successful in another of his plans to bulwark the Snake expedition. During the summer of 1826 he conceived the idea that he might relieve the turbulence of the Red River settlement and strengthen the Company's power in the Columbia district by engaging the most energetic half-breeds for service in the Snake country.[56] When he arrived at the settlement in the summer of 1827, he began to organize such a party. To command the group he selected Chief Trader Simon McGillivray, himself a half-breed, and to assist McGillivray he chose Cuthbert Grant. Grant, who had actively supported the Nor'Westers at the massacre of Seven Oaks, had since gained the esteem of the Company as "Warden of the Plains," sworn to uphold order and suppress illicit trade in the district of Assiniboia. His influence among the half-breeds was strong, and he was given the responsibility of recruiting a party of twenty-five "steady fellows" to be employed in "voyaging, hunting, or as required," at £15 a year and a fair price for the furs they collected. It was soon apparent that recruitment on these terms would be difficult, since, as Simpson said, the views of the majority were directed more to horse stealing and Indian warfare than to beaver hunting.[57]

Simpson's willingness to utilize the services of Grant and his fellow half-breeds illustrates a difference in viewpoint between him and the governor and committee. He at no time contemplated or desired aggression upon American parties, but he was prepared to use violence in defense of the Company's rights if incidents such as the Gardner affair were to recur. The governor and committee, fearful of provoking the American government to diplomatic action on behalf of its traders and perhaps to more active interest in the Oregon country, were more cautious. They wrote to Simpson on January 16, 1828:

> If the American Traders settle near our Establishments, they must be opposed, not by violence, which will only be the means of enabling the Traders to obtain the interference of their Government, but by underselling them, which will damp their expectations of profit, and diminish the value which they at present feel upon that trade.[58]

Simpson did not carry out his plan to augment Ogden's forces with Grant and his half-breeds. But the Company could not hope to oust all competition from the Snake country by any method. The best it could hope for was to prevent the competition from becoming entrenched. If by high prices to the Indians and intensive trapping it could make the trade unprofitable to others, the Company could keep the opposition weak and prevent it from penetrating to the Columbia.

Complete extermination of the fur-bearing animals was an objective that the Company could not achieve. But the intensive trapping of the Snake country substantially reduced the fur resources, as illustrated by the numbers of large beaver procured by the Snake expeditions in various years: 1826—2,099; 1830—1,330; 1831—737; 1832—788; 1834—350; 1835—220; 1836—800.[59]

A substantial number of American trappers, despite Blackfoot and Snake hostility and competition from the Snake expedition, continued to venture yearly into the country until the mid-1830's. During the season of 1825–26, Ashley sent about 100 men in small parties to trap in the Snake country.[60] During the season 1830–31, the Company's officers estimated that approximately 140 Americans were in the area; and in 1831–32, about 200.[61] John McLoughlin later estimated that between 1832 and 1838 there had been from 500 to 600 Americans annually in the Snake country.[62] This is probably an exaggeration, particularly for the latter years. Increasingly, trappers who rendezvoused at Green River brought their returns from the east side of the mountains. By 1836 the only American party of significance was that of Nathaniel Wyeth, and he was forced to withdraw during the next year.

The weaknesses of the American trappers were readily apparent to Hudson's Bay Company officers on the Columbia. The majority were outfitted by St. Louis merchants who possessed little capital and who were prone to strike sharp bargains.[63] The trappers in turn felt little loyalty to their employers, and were easily seduced by opposition that offered better terms. Since they were subject to little discipline, American trappers frequently committed outrages against the Indians, which stimulated the hostility of the tribes. Americans usually traveled in smaller parties than the Company's men and were therefore more vulnerable. War parties infrequently attacked Hudson's Bay parties, but they constantly haunted the camps of the Americans, waiting for opportunities to massacre the trappers.[64]

The lack of discipline, inadequacy of capital, and competition among numerous small parties prevented the Americans from becoming a serious threat to the trade of the Columbia. Although they far outnumbered the Hudson's Bay Company's Snake expedition, and indeed, in most years, the entire body of Hudson's Bay employees on the Columbia,[65] they could not compete on equal terms with the organization, capital, knowledge of the fur trade, familiarity with the terrain, and rapport with the Indians possessed by their British rival. The only American enterprise in the area for which the Company had respect was that of Ashley and his successors. When Ashley retired in 1826, he had acquired a fortune of between $50,000 and $80,000, largely from trade in the mountains in competition with the Hudson's Bay Company. This impressive feat, though attempted by others, was not duplicated, but the firm Ashley had established gave the Hudson's Bay Company its most severe competition. In 1826 he sold his interests to Jedediah Smith, David Jackson, and William L. Sublette, all experienced trappers, who continued the trade under the name of Smith, Jackson, and Sublette. After a promising first year, when its returns were valued at $22,690,[66] the firm suffered a series of misfortunes. Most notable was the ambush of Smith's party on the Umpqua River on July 14, 1828, when fifteen of his men were killed.[67] In 1830 Smith, Jackson, and Sublette, facing increased opposition from other American companies in the upper Missouri country, sold their interests to the newly organized Rocky Mountain Fur Company, and turned their attentions toward Sante Fe. There were other compelling reasons for their decision. Profits from the Snake country had dwindled as the supply of furs was reduced, and in the late 1820's the price of furs in the St. Louis market had declined. At the same time trade in the Santa Fe area was productive of increasing profits. Trappers were therefore drawn increasingly to Santa Fe, and Smith, Jackson, and Sublette followed the example of others. They must have left the Snake country with no regrets. During his 1827–28 expedition Ogden had encountered several small parties from this company, all of whom complained of privation, unprofitable hunts, and harassments by the Indians, particularly the Blackfeet.[68]

It was, peculiarly enough, danger from the Blackfeet and the shortage of furs in the Snake country which contributed to the farthest penetration of American competition into the Columbia area since the Hudson's Bay Company had acquired the North West Company's trade. The miseries of the trade in the upper Snake valley led the Americans to consider the possibility of more profitable trade to the west and to the north. One small group of trappers during the winter of 1827–28 traveled to within a few day's march of Fort Walla Walla. The leader wrote Samuel Black that they intended to pay him a visit,[69] but the party apparently changed its course. Other Americans pushed north to the vicinity of Flathead Lake, where they established winter quarters. Two parties encamped in the area, one headed by David Jackson and the other by Joshua Pilcher. The size of Jackson's group is unknown, but Pilcher was in command of nine men. Pilcher had headed the Missouri Fur Company which failed in 1825, and this expedition was his final effort to recoup his fortunes in the fur trade.

A strange competition ensued, with each of the contending American parties professing friendship for the Hudson's Bay Company and each contributing to the ruination of the other. Their competition disrupted the Company's trade with the Flathead Indians for that season, and destroyed all hope of profit for any traders. The Americans became increasingly short of supplies, and before the winter was over they were forced to exchange about one-half of their returns for necessities.[70]

In growing desperation Pilcher proposed to Simpson an alliance with the Hudson's Bay Company, by which the Company would supply him in trading expeditions east of the mountains in the Blackfoot country at the headwaters of the Missouri. The Company would gain little from so unequal an alliance, particularly since the arrangement would violate United States laws. Simpson, seeing that he could use Pilcher's letter to demonstrate the Company's regard for the rights of foreign states,[71] replied: "I do not think it would be reputable in the Hon^ble Hudsons Bay Co^y to make use of indirect means to acquire possession of a Trade to which it has no just claim." [72] He then forwarded the correspondence to the governor and committee for use should the Company's practices be called into question.

In his confidential correspondence with Company officers Simpson assumed a less elevated tone. Recognizing Pilcher's proposal as a symptom of weakness, he instructed Ogden to use every possible means to induce freemen remaining in the Americans' employ to desert, and to acquire every possible skin from American parties. These instructions Ogden carried out during his 1828–29 expedition.[73] In the space of four years, the Americans who had threatened to demoralize the trade of the Columbia had been reduced to such an extremity that Simpson could say with justice that "the Company had nothing to fear" from rival American traders.[74] Although American competition continued thereafter, it was weak and ineffective.

The policies contributing to this result varied in detail from the procedure in Canada and at Red River, but the basic principle was the same—that the trade must be made unprofitable to the opposition even at the risk of loss to the Company. In the Snake country, however, the Company continued to make profits. In 1824 Ross's party, despite all its misfortunes, had produced a £3,700 profit; and Ogden's first three expeditions realized £3,000, £2,000, and £2,500, respectively.[75]

Serious American competition came in 1829, not from the Snake country but from the sea, and Chief Factor John McLoughlin's method of repelling it provoked one of his earliest conflicts with his superiors. Early in the century Yankee sea captains had dominated the fur trade of the Pacific Coast.[76] But the sea-otter trade which had been the major attraction for the American maritime fur trade had declined to small proportions by 1820.[77] The Americans with whom the Hudson's Bay Company had to contend were primarily engaged in trading provisions with California and Russian America and land furs with the Indians of the northwest coast.

Although American vessels entered the Columbia River, no ships challenged the Company's monopoly there before 1829. But it was inevitable that sooner or later an American vessel would sail up the Columbia to trade for furs. Simpson instructed McLoughlin in July, 1827, that, if American ships appeared in the neighborhood of Fort Vancouver, the Company should lower its tariff to whatever level was necessary to secure the bulk of the returns.[78] In March, 1829, the expectation of competition was realized when the *Owhyhee,* commanded by Captain John Dominis of Boston, employed by the firm of Marshall and Wildes, entered the river and anchored off Fort George. Five days later the *Convoy,* employed by the same company, appeared.[79] Dominis immediately began to trade, offering prices for furs far above those the Company had established during its monopoly. He offered guns for six skins,[80] 2½-point blankets for two skins, and other goods at comparably low levels. Before his arrival the tariff at Fort Vancouver had been eighteen skins for a gun and five skins for a blanket. At the time of Dominis' arrival, Simpson was at Fort Vancouver on his second visit to the Columbia, and he and McLoughlin took action to resist the American competition. The tariff was quickly reduced to the level offered by Dominis, and parties were sent out to the surrounding country to buy up furs before the Indians became aware of the attractive American offers. Donald Manson, then a clerk, was appointed to watch Dominis and to report on his movements. Competition forced the price of furs steadily upward until a blanket sold for only one skin.

Despite the severity of competition, the two American vessels remained in the Columbia River until July, 1830, coursing up and down from Fort George to the rapids above Fort Vancouver. When one vessel made occasional voyages along the coast in search of furs or to the Sandwich Islands for supplies, the other remained in the river.

McLoughlin's problems were further complicated when an

American trapper named Bache, formerly in the employ of the Hudson's Bay Company, established opposition headquarters at The Dalles. Bache was married to the daughter of a Nez Percé chief, and his relationship to the Indians in addition to his trading experience in the service of the Company made his competition more serious. To prevent Bache from gaining a foothold, McLoughlin sent James Birnie and three other men to oppose him with instructions to force prices down to a point where he would give up the contest. Nevertheless, Bache's competition attracted Indians from as far away as Forts Okanagan, Colvile, and Walla Walla, and embarrassed the officers at those posts who continued to offer monopoly prices.[81] But the trade did not prove so remunerative as Bache had expected, and he signed an agreement to reënter the Company's service, whereupon he was sent on a trapping expedition with other Company employees.[82]

Employment of an obnoxious competitor in the Company's service was not an uncommon expedient, but buying off an opponent was contrary to the Company's policy, and this was the way McLoughlin tried to rid himself of Dominis. When Dominis first appeared in the spring of 1829, McLoughlin faced a severe shortage of goods caused by the wreck of the supply ship *William and Ann* on the bar at the mouth of the Columbia. Initially, therefore, he was forced to meet the American competition under a serious handicap, which might have justified his deviation from general policy by buying his opponents' goods. But another supply ship, the *Ganymede,* arrived in June and the shortage was relieved. McLoughlin was thus enabled to continue opposition at the low prices that competition made necessary. The loss of the *William and Ann,* however, had emphasized to McLoughlin the uncertainties of his supply system, and in March, 1830, when Dominis expressed a willingness to sell his remaining goods, McLoughlin was receptive. The price Dominis asked was high—$4.00 per blanket, to be paid in beaver at the rate of $4.50 per large beaver. But an arrangement that would add to Dominis' stock of furs was unacceptable to McLoughlin, who suggested that the Company pay for goods suitable for the Columbia trade with boards at the rate of $10 per thousand feet. McLoughlin was aware that such negotiations were contrary to Company policy, but he justified himself on the grounds that a treaty depriving the Company of the Columbia trade might be signed at any time, and that his supplies were so depleted that it was risky to continue competition.[83]

No arrangement was concluded, however, and the Americans left the Columbia in July, bound for China. Dominis and his crews had collected 2,900 land skins, principally otter and beaver.[84] His visit had been expensive to the Hudson's Bay Company but apparently was equally so for his employers, according to an article from the New York *Gazette* sent to McLoughlin in 1832:

> Today arrived the Brig *Owhyhee,* Capt. Dominis, whom we have seen, who informed us that he had passed the best part of Summers, 29 & 30 & the intervening Winter in the Columbia. He represents the Country as delightful, but that the Hudson's Bay Coy. are too well established for citizens of the United States to make any thing in the way of Fur Trade.[85]

McLoughlin's uncertainty about receiving supplies adequate to support prolonged competition undoubtedly justified his offer of boards for Dominis' supplies. Simpson acknowledged the expediency of the proposal, although he took occasion to reëmphasize the view of London headquarters that it was bad policy to buy out opposition.[86] But there was a difference in emphasis between McLoughlin's views and those of the governor and committee. McLoughlin was concerned primarily with the avoidance of loss and, if possible, the achievement of maximum profits at the posts under his control. The directors of the Company, on the other hand, viewed the Columbia district as expendable, an area where profits could be hoped for "but where opposition must be met and defeated, even at the price of loss." The difference in viewpoint was illustrated by McLoughlin's relations with Nathaniel J. Wyeth.

Wyeth appeared at a time when the desirability of continuing the Snake country expedition was under debate. When Ogden relinquished the command to Chief Trader John Work, returns from the Snake country had greatly declined. Work experienced more difficulties in finding beaver than had his predecessor, and although during the next three years he traveled as far south as the San Joaquin River, as far east as the headwaters of the Missouri River,[87] and as far west as the Pacific Coast, between Bodega Bay and Cape Mendocino, his returns were small.[88] The paucity of returns from the Snake country led George Simpson as early as August, 1832, to recommend its abandonment.[89] Work's expedition in 1831–32 was the last to concentrate its activity in that area.[90] Later roving expeditions were directed toward California where there was sufficient beaver to make trade profitable.

By 1832, then, the Company's officers had come to regard the territory between the Rocky Mountains and the Snake River as largely a "fur desert." It was at this time that Nathaniel J. Wyeth with eleven men arrived at Fort Vancouver after a journey across the continent. Wyeth's intention, which he made no effort to conceal, was to establish a base on the Columbia for curing salmon and trading in furs, but his hopes were frustrated by the wreck of his supply vessel en route from Boston to the Columbia. Without goods Wyeth was helpless, and all but two of his men accepted his invitation to withdraw from his employ. During the winter of 1832–33 McLoughlin lodged the party at Fort Vancouver and provided them, at no cost, with the same rations as the Company's employees received.[91] Wyeth was not inclined to give up his plans for trade in the Oregon country as a result of his misfortune, but his observation of the Company's trading methods at Fort Vancouver led him to consider a modification of his original plan. He proposed to McLoughlin that the Company equip him to hunt south of the Columbia. McLoughlin emphatically refused; Wyeth, he said, could go nowhere west of the mountains where the Company's regular employees could not go. The two held no further conversations,[92] but Wyeth was not convinced that such an arrangement with the Company could not be made with mutual advantage.

Wyeth left Vancouver in February, 1833, for Flathead Post, in company with Francis Ermatinger, a clerk, whose mission was to lead one of two small parties into the Snake country to trade with the American trappers for furs.[93] When he arrived at Fort Colvile, Wyeth wrote Simpson an elaboration of his proposal to McLoughlin, but added that he might be able, as an American, to visit parts of the country from which the British were excluded—presumably east of the mountains.[94]

Simpson summarily rejected Wyeth's overture,[95] but, unfortunately for McLoughlin, the ship bearing this news did not reach the Columbia until October, by which time McLoughlin had already made an arrangement with Wyeth. The latter, in accordance with an agreement of the previous summer with the Rocky Mountain Fur Company, had proceeded overland to the rendezvous with his goods. Thomas Fitzpatrick of that company repudiated the contract, however, and Wyeth faced the problem of disposing of his outfit. He decided to make a virtue of necessity by establishing a post, which he named Fort Hall, near the junction of the Snake and Portneuf rivers. Pushing on he arrived at Fort Vancouver in September, 1834. Almost simultaneously his supply ship, the *May Dacre,* arrived after a harrowing voyage, bringing supplies for the salmon trade and machinery for a sawmill.

Wyeth had been at Vancouver only three days when he made a proposal to McLoughlin which was to be the cause of considerable criticism of the chief factor by the governor and committee. He asked the Company not to oppose him in his salmon trade, and to avoid competition in the Snake country by dividing the territory between his enterprise and the Hudson's Bay Company. Both parts of his proposal, particularly the latter, were repugnant to the policies of the Company, which sanctioned permanent division of territory only with a large company capable of enforcing its part of such an arrangement. The governor and committee had authorized Ogden during his expeditions to reach agreement with American opponents on their respective areas of trade in order to avoid violence, but such agreements were intended to be for one season only.[96] Wyeth's proposals were much more extensive. McLoughlin nevertheless entered into negotiations with the American and reached an agreement after a few days. The principal change from Wyeth's original suggestion was in the delimitation of the trade in the Snake country. McLoughlin agreed that the Company would not trade beyond the Grand Ronde River, a tributary of the Snake, except for parties under the leadership of Francis Ermatinger and Thomas McKay, which should continue to have the right to enter the country to the south and west to trade with American trappers, particularly at the Green River rendezvous.[97] McLoughlin further instructed Pierre Pambrun, the clerk in charge at Walla Walla, to assist Wyeth "as far as consistent with our interest and our engagement to Mr. McKay." If Wyeth should find difficulties in transporting supplies to Fort Hall, McLoughlin instructed Pambrun to store the property for him.[98]

This agreement has been ably defended as a politic action on the part of McLoughlin.[99] It can be pointed out that the Company surrendered little of value, for the Grand Ronde country was not rich in furs and the right granted Ermatinger and McKay to trade at the rendezvous preserved the Company's only valuable connection with that country. Trade with the Nez Percé and Flathead Indians remained in the Company's hands, and Wyeth promised not to encroach upon the trade at Fort Vancouver or above the Grand Ronde River. The agreement saved the Company the expense of opposing Wyeth, and the failure of his business by the end of 1836 would seem to vindicate McLoughlin's judgment. These arguments, however, are not entirely satisfying. The wisdom of sacrificing temporary advantage in order to deter future opponents had been repeatedly demonstrated.

The policy adopted toward Wyeth was in striking contrast to the techniques employed against his compatriot, Captain Benjamin L. E. Bonneville. This explorer-trader first appeared in the Oregon country in 1832 when, at the head of a party of 120 men, he crossed the Continental Divide and established winter quarters on the Salmon River. The appearance of "Major Boneyville," as McLoughlin called him, was disturbing. McLoughlin, aware that the Snake country could not sustain such a force, feared that Bonneville's eventual destination might be the Willamette valley where his followers would establish themselves as colonists.[100] For the next three years Bonneville and his party traded and trapped with some success on both sides of the mountains.[101]

No attempt was made to reach an understanding with Bonneville. On the contrary, the orthodox policy of active opposition was followed, and Pambrun's only deviation from that policy was censured by McLoughlin. Pambrun sold Bonneville a roll of tobacco and some dry goods at the prices paid by freemen, and received payment in beaver at freemen's rates. McLoughlin lectured Pambrun for this "injudicious" transaction, explaining "the error he had committed" in trading with the opposition.[102]

The primary difference between the treatment of Wyeth and Bonneville stemmed from McLoughlin's convictions, based on his intimate association with Wyeth, that Wyeth would honorably abide by any agreement into which he entered. McLoughlin believed that an agreement with such a man, in which the Company sacrificed little, was preferable to competition in which, though Wyeth would be ruined, the Company would also suffer losses. The fact remains, however, that McLoughlin, by continuing the arrangement with Wyeth after receiving instructions from the governor and committee, was guilty of violations of discipline which would have wrecked the Company had they been typical of the conduct of officers. Even after receiving McLoughlin's explanations, the governor and committee rightly censured the chief factor and reiterated their convictions on frontier policy in the following statement:

> The only and most effectual mode of relieving ourselves from such sources of annoyance, and of securing to the Company the entire and undisturbed command of the trade is to meet them at all points, to oppose them vigorously in every way, to have our vessels watching them unceasingly, and by underselling them, to prevent their getting any Furs, or if they do get any, at such a cost, as to be productive of loss, instead of profit.
>
> We are aware that such a system of trade, must necessarily involve a certain temporary loss to the Company, but that loss we are willing should be incurred, as the immediate sacrifice will be a saving of means and a source of profit in the long run. And instead of entering into arrangements as in Wyeth's and Bounaville's opposition, from which no reciprocity of advantage can arise, we desire that in cases where we may be interfered with in trade, the most vigorous opposition be observed, as we are determined to become masters of the trade of the Coast, and to retain that of the Columbia River, and the Country to the Northward of it, even should it occasion a sacrifice of money.[103]

One aspect of the McLoughlin-Wyeth contract, the provision for Francis Ermatinger's and Thomas McKay's trading parties, seems worthy of special comment, for it reveals the change that had taken place in the character of the Company's trade in the southern and western Snake country since Work had demonstrated the paucity of its remaining resources. Wyeth's account of his visit to the Green River rendezvous during his journey east in 1833 stimulated McLoughlin to send parties to trade with the American trappers there assembled. In February, 1834, he appointed Francis Ermatinger, who had accompanied Wyeth in 1833 to within a few days' march of the rendezvous, to the command of such a party. McLoughlin authorized Ermatinger to offer $4 per pound for beaver, payable half in dollars in Canada and the other half in goods at prices 150 per cent above prime cost, and to propose, as a first step toward later trade, that the Company sell the trappers up to a total of £1,000 worth of goods.[104] Apparently no detailed records of this expedition survive, but Ermatinger reached the rendezvous and supplied goods to Warren Ferris of the American Fur Company.[105]

A primary function of Ermatinger's reconnoitering expedition was to prepare the way for another party headed by Thomas Mc-Kay, the son of McLoughlin's wife by a previous marriage. McKay's ambition to attain a position of importance in the Company's service had been frustrated, and in 1833 he decided to retire and to become a farmer in the Willamette valley. McLoughlin, however, saw in the prospects for trade at Green River an opportunity for McKay to prosper. He arranged to have the Company supply McKay with goods to carry on the trade, and McKay apparently agreed to deliver to the Company for fixed compensation all the furs he would collect.[106] In order to advance McKay's chances of success McLoughlin made a supplementary arrangement by which McKay could trade beyond the Grand Ronde River, the designated limit of trade for the Company's employees.[107]

During the winter of 1834–35 McKay was in the vicinity of the River Boise, and apparently at that time built a fort on the east side of the Snake River near its confluence with the Boise. The post was initially known as Snake Fort and eventually as Fort Boise. During the seasons of 1835–36 and 1836–37 McKay continued as an independent trader in the Snake country; the two expeditions brought the Company profits of £411 and £997, respectively.[108] McKay apparently produced these returns by trapping and trading with the Indians, for he does not seem to have visited the American rendezvous. McLoughlin instead sent Chief Trader John Mc-Leod, Jr., who visited the camp in 1836 and 1837, to acquire information.[109] The unusual expedient of employing an agent to trade in the Snake country rather than using the Company's employees was not favorably viewed by Simpson. In June, 1836, he tactfully informed McLoughlin that the contract with McKay must be terminated.[110]

McLoughlin's relationship with Wyeth continued cordial while Wyeth remained in the Snake country, for the chief factor considered the contract highly advantageous to the Company. In 1836 he instructed John McLeod to establish a common tariff for Snake Fort and Wyeth's Fort Hall at a level low enough to offer Indians from Walla Walla no inducement to bring their furs there in the hope of higher prices.[111] But before the common tariff could go into effect, Wyeth's enterprise succumbed. When his woes were compounded by disease and death among his men and the loss of his own health, Wyeth decided to retire from the fur business. In December, 1836, he offered to sell his property to the Company, and asked the Company's assistance in transporting home seven Sandwich Islanders, providing passage also for three of his American employees, and supplying goods to the value of £150 with which to pay his debts to his employees.[112] The Company agreed to buy the property and provide the requisite assistance,[113] and in the autumn of 1837 purchased Fort Hall.[114]

The departure of Wyeth coincided with the beginnings of a new kind of American opposition. During the 1820's rumors of impending American settlement on the Willamette had frequently circulated, causing the Company transient alarm, but had always proved to be without foundation. Expeditions like Bonneville's and Wyeth's, however, helped to spread interest in the Oregon country as did the visit of four Nez Percé and Flathead Indians to St. Louis, which was publicized by the religious press as motivated by the thirst of the transmontane Indians for Christianity. Jason Lee, appointed by the Methodist Missionary Board to convert the Flatheads, had crossed the continent with Wyeth in 1834. Lee and his associates found the Willamette valley congenial, their interest in the Flatheads receded, and they settled on the Willamette River near Salem. There they found little scope for missionary work but much for agricultural development. They became the advance agents for American colonization. In the mid-1830's, therefore, the Columbia basin country had ceased to be a frontier of the fur trade and was about to become a frontier of settlement.

For a few years the Company enjoyed a respite from competition. But by the end of the 1830's the "Oregon fever" began to spread among Americans. In 1839 small parties of migrants crossed the plains and the mountains to settle in Oregon. Others followed in 1840; a larger number arrived in 1841, and the tide of immigration steadily increased thereafter. Chief Trader Pambrun, at Walla Walla, in the path of the migration, wrote to Simpson on March 3, 1841: "Emigration from the U.S. hither has become so common & regular that it forms no further a novelty to us. We had several parties again last September some for the Welamatte." [115]

Fort Hall was at a junction point of the route that came to be known as the Oregon Trail and the road to California. Chief Trader Richard Grant, who between 1842 and 1851 was in charge of the Snake country with headquarters at Fort Hall, found an opportunity for profit in the sale of flour, rice, coffee, sugar, and other staples to the immigrants.[116] But he also found that the Americans provided competition for furs that would otherwise have been brought to Fort Hall or Fort Boise. Not only did they occasionally buy beaver, but they created a demand for meat and leather, which made it more profitable for freemen and Indians to hunt antelope than to search for beaver.[117]

The coming of the Mormons contributed first to profit and then to loss for the Snake country outfit. When they arrived in 1847 they eagerly purchased goods from Grant at Fort Hall.[118] By 1850 they not only had ceased to be a market but had become active competitors. They maintained their own well-stocked stores, selling many articles at lower prices than the Company could afford at Fort Vancouver.[119] When Grant left the Snake country in 1851, its prospects for profit were at an end. His successor, a clerk named McArthur, completed its ruination by his incompetence; his desertion in 1854 was an appropriate conclusion to the Snake country trade.[120]

The Company finally abandoned its posts in the Snake country in the summer of 1856, realizing that in Oregon's new era they could serve no useful function. The Snake country was no longer a frontier for the fur trade; its posts no longer produced profit; and American settlers were hostile, particularly after the series of Indian wars between 1850 and 1855 in which the Company's employees were suspected of being sympathetic to the Indians. In 1854, according to an unverified report, postmaster Charles Ogden at Fort Boise had been trading ammunition to Indians, who had used it to murder immigrants; this rumor was used by enemies of the Company to stimulate hostility.[121]

The Company had been successful in its opposition to American fur traders in the Snake country. But the techniques that were so effective against rival traders were of no value against settlers. In Oregon, as elsewhere, the fur trader was forced to withdraw when the agriculturist appeared. The Company remained in Oregon after 1846 primarily because it hoped to sell its posts to the United States government and feared that abandonment might weaken its bargaining position.[122] Profits from the Oregon department after 1846 were increasingly derived from sales to settlers, rather than from the fur trade. In the trading season 1849–50, for example, of a total profit of £35,390, the Fort Vancouver sales shop provided £14,902.[123] But as American goods became more plentiful, the Company's profits declined. In Outfit 1851 the Company suffered a net loss of £6,754; [124] in 1852 there was a profit of £5,-400; [125] and in 1853 the Company lost over £1,200.[126] Losses were more frequent and more impressive than profits thereafter, but the Company retained its posts until 1860 in the hope that its continued occupancy would stimulate the United States to offer a satisfactory purchase price.

The Company's policies in California provide an instructive contrast with those on the Canadian, Red River, and Snake country frontiers. In California, as in Hawaii, where the Company maintained an agency between 1839 and 1859, the sole motivation was profit. There was no need for protection, and the continuation or abandonment of trapping activities was judged upon the area's ability to produce profits. When profits from California declined to a low level, trade was immediately discontinued. This was not the policy in Canada or along the Company's southern frontier, where the Company was willing, and indeed was often required, to bear losses in order to prevent the penetration of opposition into valuable fur territories. In the Snake River area profits alone would not have justified the continuation of trade after 1830. The Company remained because it hoped that the activity of its parties would restrain the westward penetration of American fur traders.

The Company's policies of frontier defense proved eminently sound. They could not prevent the occupation of Oregon by American settlers, but they did confine American fur traders to the Snake country, where competition soon became so unprofitable that the Americans withdrew. They could not prevent Red River traders from disrupting the trade of southern Rupert's Land, but they effectively restrained American fur traders along the border. The Company's frontier policies could not hold back the advance of the Canadian lumbering and agricultural frontiers, but they did retard the extension of competition from Canada across the Laurentian shield into Rupert's Land. The Company could not cope with farmers and lumberers; against those who combined fur trading with farming, lumbering, or shopkeeping it was relatively weak; but against those who depended for their livelihood upon the fur trade, its power was overwhelming.

The Hudson's Bay Company was, therefore, the active force in British North America west of Canada. The expansion of its trading territory as it sought additional profits, and the competitive policies it introduced along the frontiers of this trading area, established the bases for British diplomacy in North America. There was an "Oregon question" because of the trading activities of the North West and Hudson's Bay companies; the Russo-British boundary dispute in northwest America was produced by the rivalry of fur-trading companies. When the interests of the Company and the ambitions of Canada came into conflict, the Company's vested rights became an obstacle whose removal was for over a decade the preoccupation of the Colonial Office and the Canadian government. In its expansion and in its demise the Great Monopoly was an important factor in international politics for almost fifty years.

PART

II

Relations with Russian America

CHAPTER

6

# The Anglo-Russian Treaty

THE HISTORY of North America west of the Rocky Mountains and north of California in the first hundred years of European exploration and occupation is preëminently the history of the fur trade. From the discovery of northwest America by Vitus Bering in 1741 until the arrival of American farmers on the Columbia River almost a century later, a territory of more than a million square miles and its adjacent waters were the unchallenged domain of the trapper and the fur trader. Diplomatic controversy over the area was largely the result of conflict among Russian, British, and American fur traders; the activity of these entrepreneurs was a primary basis for each government's claims and for its knowledge of the terrain.

The fur-trading influence was particularly strong in the motivation of Russian and British political action, for their fur trade was conducted by powerful monopolies—the Russian American Company and the North West Company and, after the amalgamation of 1821, the Hudson's Bay Company—which maintained posts on the mainland or on adjacent islands. The American trade, on the other hand, was carried on, after the demise of John Jacob Astor's Pacific Fur Company, by a large number of petty capitalists. After 1813 it was almost exclusively maritime, with barter conducted on the decks of ships rather than at land bases.[1] American fur traders, therefore, provided neither so strong a basis for terri-

[1] For notes to chap. 6, see pp. 445–448.

torial claims north of the Columbia basin nor so potent an influence on governmental action as did those of Russia or Britain.

The Russian American Company and the Hudson's Bay Company, though alike in their common abhorrence of the petty competitor and in their desire to enjoy unchallenged control over a maximum area of profitable trade at minimum expense, were dissimilar in antecedents and in structural characteristics. These differences influenced the course of their contest for mastery of the fur trade of northwest America. The Russian fur trade was first stimulated by Bering's discovery that the American coast was rich in furs. Particularly valued by the Russians was the fur of the sea otter, the average price of which fluctuated between 100 and 300 rubles, with the best specimens bringing as much as 1,000 rubles,[2] although other furs, notably fur seals, were in great demand.

In the ensuing competition scores of small companies and independent traders were ruined, the herds of fur seals and sea otters were decimated, and the natives were debauched. Among the efficient traders who survived was Gregori Ivanovich Shelekhov, who in 1784 established at Three Saints Bay on Kodiak Island the first permanent Russian trading station in North America. He and his associates, partly through superior acumen and partly through favor of the Imperial court, gradually mastered their competitors until on July 8, 1799, they received from Paul I a charter granting their company, thereafter to be called the Russian American Company, a monopoly for a period of twenty years. By this grant the company not only was guaranteed the exclusive use of all hunting grounds and establishments on the coast of America north of 55° north latitude, but was authorized to extend its control southward into any territory not already occupied by any other state. Within its area of exploitation the company was vested with governmental authority.[3] This system of indirect government was superficially similar to that by which the Hudson's Bay Company exercised authority in Rupert's Land, and indeed may have been patterned after it. But in practice the Russian American Company possessed a very different relationship to the ultimate political authority than its British counterpart, more closely akin to that of the East India Company between the India Act of 1784 and the extinction of its Indian monopoly in 1813.

In 1811 the Russian American Company was placed under the supervision of the Ministry of the Interior, and in 1819 the regulation of the company's activities was transferred to the Ministry of Finance, under whose jurisdiction the company continued for the remainder of its existence. The control exercised by the Ministry of Finance was minute and thorough. The relationship between the company and the government was so intimate as to make the former a quasi-governmental body.[4] The intimacy extended to the local administration of the colonies. The second charter, granted in 1819 and confirmed in September, 1821, required the chief manager to be a captain of the Imperial Navy; other responsible positions in the colonial administration were also occupied by naval officers.[5] The latitude exercised by the company's administration in St. Petersburg was consequently most restricted. The discretion of the officers in America was that of distant subordinates, authorized to make decisions within the framework of the general policy laid down by their superiors, as was true of the Hudson's Bay Company, but governors of the Russian colonies were inclined to take a less exalted view of their authority than Sir George Simpson did of his. The excessive paternalism of the Russian government was almost certainly a factor in the decline of the Russian American Company to the stagnant and unenterprising body it became in its latter years. In 1840, when the deterioration was well advanced, James Douglas recorded the following observations on the character of the company:

> The business of the Russio American Company does not appear to be conducted with system or that degree of well judged economy so necessary in extensive concerns.
> The two establishments I have visited are crowded with men and Officers living in idleness or in employments equally unnecessary and Profitless to the business: the Officers almost all belong to the Imperial service and besides their pay from Government have an allowance from the Company and after 5 years service they return to Europe. . . .
> A decidedly vicious and ill advised feature in the management of this business is the appointment of Naval officers, a class of men ignorant of and by their previous habits of life, the most unqualified to manage commercial undertakings. . . .[6]

Naval officers were in control in 1821, but the spirit of the late Alexander Baranoff, chief manager from 1799 until 1818, had not yet died in the councils of the Russian American Company, and the company was still in its expansionist phase. Baranoff, one of the most active advocates of expansion in the history of North America, had planted a settlement at Sitka in 1799 on the island later to bear his name and, after its destruction by the Indians, had rebuilt it as New Archangel in 1804. This position, at 57° 30' north latitude, was then the most southerly permanent occupation of the Russians on the shores of the North American continent, but Baranoff visualized a far greater empire, embracing a large part of the Pacific littoral of the continent. He established Fort Ross on Bodega Bay, California, in 1812, primarily as a fur-trading center and source of food supplies for the northern colonies, but also as an outpost of Russian power on the west coast; he maintained a station on the Farallones; and he coveted the Hawaiian Islands and built a fort at Honolulu in an abortive effort to establish Russian hegemony.[7] In each instance the primary purpose was trade, but so long as the eastern Pacific remained almost a power vacuum the extension of Russian sovereignty to these areas of economic activity was an increasing possibility.

In 1821 the only significant counterforces in the North Pacific were the British and American fur traders and whalers and the influence they exerted on their respective governments. The fur trade of both nations on the western coast was at first maritime. After the death of Captain James Cook, his ship arrived in Macao at the end of 1779. The crew sold several sea-otter skins in the cargo to the Chinese at prices that stimulated other sailors to envision wealth for themselves in this trade. Despite the crew's efforts to conceal the source of supply, rumors soon circulated that sea otters were in abundance on the northwest coast of America. In 1785 a ship, appropriately named *Sea Otter*, left Macao under the command of the British Captain James Hanna and returned after a five-week sojourn in the area of Nootka Sound with 560 sea-otter skins, which were sold for 20,600 Spanish piastres (approximately $21,000.[8] Such lucrative prices caused others to follow Hanna's example, and the collision between Captain John Meares and the Spanish in 1789 and the resultant Nootka Sound Convention were produced by the growing interest in the fur trade. The ships engaged in the trade were at first predominantly British and American, but with the onset of war between the British and the French the field was left to the Americans.[9] When the British fur trader returned to the coast, he came by land rather than by water. The value of the trade at the height of its profits is indicated by the following statistics of the American trade at Canton, the principal market, from June, 1800, to January, 1803: [10]

| | Sea otters | Value | Sealskins | Value |
|---|---|---|---|---|
| June 11, 1800, to April 27, 1801 | 6,450 | $123,050 | 325,000 | $276,283 |
| May 15, 1801, to June, 1802 | 14,187 | 298,263 | 426,750 | 393,395 |
| June, 1802, to January 9, 1803 | 13,720 | 274,000 | 297,000 | 237,600 |
| Total | 34,357 | $695,313 | 1,048,750 | $907,278 |

The Russian American Company itself between 1797 and 1818 procured 80,271 sea otters and 1,493,626 fur seals,[11] but the competition of American petty traders caused it increasing annoyance. In public protests to the United States government, Russia complained that American captains traded rifles and ammunition to natives in the neighborhood of Russian settlements, thus endangering the lives and property of the company's servants, and debauched the Indians with liquor which they dispensed wholesale. But there were other more material reasons for Russian irritation. Not only did the free traders purchase furs which might otherwise have been bought by the Russians, but their competition forced the company to pay higher prices for furs. As early as 1808 Count Romanzoff proposed to the United States a convention by which American citizens on the northwest coast should trade exclusively with the Russian American Company rather than directly with the Indians; in 1810 the Russian chargé d'affaires in Washington renewed the effort to secure a treaty prohibiting American citizens from trading directly with the natives. Since the chargé d'affaires could not specify the area where his government wanted such restrictions to apply, the question was referred to St. Petersburg. When John Quincy Adams, the American minister, rejected Count Romanzoff's claim to all the northwest coast as far south as the Columbia River, the subject was immediately dropped.[12]

The issue lay dormant until after the Napoleonic Wars, when the Russian American Company attempted to control American competition by restricting the purchase of American goods by the Russian colonies. The decline in the number of sea otters after 1815 lessened the attraction of the Pacific Northwest for the Yankee captains. The Russians hoped that American shipowners, deprived also of revenue from trade with Russian America, would seek other areas of exploitation than the northwest coast.[13] There is no evidence that Russian restrictions had the desired effect; on the contrary, Captain Golovnin, on a trip to Russian America in 1818, when intercourse between the Russian colonists and the Americans was totally prohibited, reported that the depredations of American petty hunters continued to cause grievous vexation to the management of the Russian company.[14] The most impressive effect of the embargo was to reduce the Russian American colonies to extreme distress; they experienced great difficulty in procuring not only articles of trade but even such necessities of life as grain and flour. Shipments from California were inadequate and unreliable, and provisions had to be brought by Russian ships from as far away as Chile.[15] In 1824 the company finally recognized the failure of this effort when, by the Russo-American treaty, it reopened New Archangel to the trade of American vessels.[16]

The claims of the Hudson's Bay Company to a share in the territory west of the mountains rested almost entirely on the activities of the North West Company with which it amalgamated in 1821. Only one party of Hudson's Bay traders, led by Joseph Howse in 1810–11, had ventured across the mountains. Although the expedition was profitable, the hostility of the Indians convinced Howse that no further ventures should be attempted, and the field was left to the Nor'Westers.

The most illustrious British names in western exploration before 1821 were, almost without exception, those of traders of the North West Company, exemplifying the tremendous energy characteristic of the Nor'Westers. Alexander Mackenzie, Simon Fraser, Daniel Harmon, Duncan McGillivray, David Thompson—all represented the dynamism that the company displayed throughout its life. In 1793 Mackenzie journeyed up the Peace River and crossed the height of land at Peace River Pass, whence he traveled southwest by river and portage until he reached the Pacific Ocean at Dean Channel. No action was taken to exploit Mackenzie's discoveries until Simon Fraser in 1805 established a trading post at

McLeod's Fort (McLeod's Lake) near the 55th parallel, just east of the Continental Divide.[17] During the next year he built Fort St. James, south of Stuart Lake, and Fraser's Lake Post on the Stuart (Nechako) River; in 1807 he constructed Fort George at the confluence of the Stuart and Fraser rivers.[18] These posts were the only stations in the vaguely defined district of New Caledonia until 1821, just after the union of the North West and Hudson's Bay companies, when Fort Alexandria was established on the Fraser River below its junction with the Quesnel River.[19]

Through these forts the North West Company had ruled the Fraser country between 51° and 55° north latitude. From them its traders proceeded to adjacent river valleys to the north and to the south. Daniel Harmon traversed the Babine country to the north, and John Stuart reached the upper Columbia on the south. The key to the great river system of British Columbia was thus in the hands of the North West Company. Since the Nor'Westers west of the mountains, like their fellows to the east, traded *en derouine* —outfitting themselves at posts and peddling goods at Indian villages in the adjacent area rather than waiting for the Indians to come to the posts—it is impossible to delineate specifically the area of the company's operations, but clearly the axis of its activity in New Caledonia was north and south rather than toward the ocean. Two conditions seem to have been principally responsible for confining the company to the interior. The river valleys of the area usually led the trader to the north or to the south, and the unfriendly disposition of the coastal Indians provided no inducement for communication to the west.

In 1821 the North West Company had no posts west of the Continental Divide north of 54° 30′, or west of 125° west longitude.[20] At no point were British traders in conflict with those of the Russian American Company, since the Russians had confined their trade to the coast and had not progressed beyond Sitka and its adjacent waters.

When the Russian government renewed the Russian American Company's charter, its immediate intent was to protect the company against the free traders. The most effective means of frustrating American competition was to establish a *cordon sanitaire* around the area of the company's actual and potential operations. This was the intent of the ukase of September 4, 1821, by which the tsar decreed that all islands and waters north of 51° north latitude on the American coast were Russian property and warned all foreigners not to approach within 100 Italian miles of the Russian coast.[21] The objects of the Russian American Company and its government were, therefore, both defensive and expansionist, and this dual purpose was further emphasized when the charter was finally renewed on September 13, 1821. By the revised charter, the sovereignty of Russia was extended to the "shores of northwestern America which have from time immemorial belonged to Russia, commencing from the northern point of the Island of Vancouver, under 51° north latitude to Behring Straits and beyond them." [22] Though the ukase was primarily directed against the Americans,[23] it also struck at the interests of the Hudson's Bay Company. As a result the controversy became a conflict over territorial sovereignty as well as maritime rights.

The Marquis of Londonderry (Castlereagh) received the first intimation of the new Russian pretensions on November 12, 1821, when Baron Nicolay, the tsar's envoy extraordinary to London, presented him with a justification for the exclusion of foreign shipping north of 51°.[24] Neither the maritime nor the territorial claims of the Russians were acceptable to the British Foreign Office, but it was the maritime exclusionist policy that principally worried the British government. The law officers of the Crown were consulted for substantiation of the British position against "this infringement on the rights of commerce and navigation," [25] and the Board of Trade devoted its attention to "squeezing information" from British maritime concerns, principally the whale fisheries, to provide evidence that major British interests would be adversely affected by the decree.[26] But it was apparently not until February, 1822, that the Hudson's Bay Company became aware of the Russian claims, and then through nonofficial channels. Such tardiness of intelligence so important to the Company's interests suggests a deficiency in its liaison with the Foreign Office. Pelly, then deputy governor, endeavored to stimulate closer coöperation by a strong reminder to Londonderry that the Company, which had at the last session of Parliament been vested with control over the trade of the "Indian territories" west of Rupert's Land, expected the protection of the British government against infringement of its interests by any foreign state.[27] From the dispatch of this reminder until the signature of the Russian-British treaty in 1825, the Hudson's Bay Company had no cause to complain of governmental lack of attention to its interests. After the appointment of George Canning as foreign secretary on September 16, 1822, the government pressed the Company's claims with an energy that was most gratifying to Pelly and his fellow directors, though the Company was finally forced to accept a territory of less magnificent extent than it had contended for.

The progress of negotiations on the northwest American boundary must be understood in the context of European diplomacy. To Lord Liverpool's government, the question of the future of a few thousand square miles of barren wilderness was of relatively little moment. The issue was certainly not of such importance to the material interests of Britain as to justify an unyielding position, and both Castlereagh and Canning, like their Russian counterparts, took care to avoid the intrusion of national prestige as an issue in the negotiations.

The maritime aspect of the tsar's decrees involved the more serious question of the right of any state to interdict the use of large sections of the high seas to the commerce of its rivals, and against such pretensions both Castlereagh and Canning were prepared to act strongly. But even the maritime issue was of less urgency than the conflict of foreign policies involved in the Greek insurrection, the revolution in Spain and the threat of French intervention on behalf of "legitimacy," and the prospect of action by France, Russia, and Austria to restore Spanish control over the revolted American colonies. British diplomacy in the Greek rebellion sought to avert the danger of Russian intervention. To manage negotiations in such a way as to secure the coöperation of Russia required the utmost delicacy and finesse, and the British government was not inclined to jeopardize success by an unyielding stand on a peripheral issue.

Within these limits, George Canning was prepared to support the representations of the Hudson's Bay Company and the whalers, "the furry and the finny tribes." [28] With Canning or the government of which he was a member the leaders of the Hudson's Bay Company apparently possessed little personal influence. The circles in which Edward Ellice the Elder moved were inimical to Canning.[29] Yet John Henry Pelly as spokesman for a great commercial enterprise found Canning sympathetic to its interests and energetic in representing them in negotiations with Russia.

The false antithesis drawn by the nineteenth century between the policies of Castlereagh and Canning has been corrected by more recent historical scholarship. But the similarity of their views should not be overstressed. Canning possessed a world outlook not shared by his predecessor. The potentialities of the New World excited his creative imagination. As an energetic advocate of the expansion of British commerce, prestige, and influence, Canning saw in the Americas a fertile field of activity.[30]

Though his attention was directed primarily toward the erst-while Spanish colonies, Canning did not underestimate the prospective importance of the northwest coast. As he wrote to Lord Liverpool in July, 1826, "The trade between the Eastern and Western Hemispheres, direct across the Pacific, is the trade to the world most susceptible of rapid augmentation and improvement." [31] From a man with such a vision, the Hudson's Bay Company as the sole representative of British enterprise in northwest America could expect active support, limited only by the larger considerations of continental European diplomacy.

In that wider setting of diplomacy, it is correct to describe the boundary dispute in northwest America as a conflict between the ambitions of two great fur-trading companies, each eager to seize a maximum area for its present and future operations, and each convinced, with sound justification, that the other contemplated monopoly of the trade of the entire coast from California to the Arctic Ocean. In 1823 Nicholas Garry, deputy governor of the Hudson's Bay Company, described the Russian ukase as a plan to provide the Russian American Company with the land beavers and otters needed by the company in its barter trade with China but not available in numbers in the territory previously claimed by Russia.[32] Although this analysis of Russian motivation was not sufficiently comprehensive and did not consider its defensive aspect, Garry appears to have assessed correctly one of the bases for the Russian action. At about the same time as Garry was penning his observations, Vassili Berg, the Russian historian of the fur trade, published a work describing the China trade in beaver as most profitable for the North West Company and for the Americans, and suggesting that Russia might emulate them. Berg stated:

The principal trade was hitherto in Sea Beavers but as this trade is much diminishing it will be necessary to conduct this business on other and perhaps better principles. This trade must be established in the interior of America. The Hudson's Bay Company existing more than 200 years may serve us an example. They have about 20 different Establishments in the interior of America and dealing with the Natives, they purchase almost incredible quantities of River Beavers and Otters.[33]

Against the Russian thrust, the Hudson's Bay Company and its officers in North America were not content to rely upon representations to the Foreign Office. Since the Russian American Company had not yet established trading stations on the continent proper, the governor and committee thought that the immediate erection of posts by the Hudson's Bay Company in the unoccupied territory would provide a claim that the British government might support. On February 27, 1822, they instructed George Simpson to extend the trading area of the Company as far west and north from the Fraser River as might be practicable and profitable in order "to keep the Russians at a distance." [34] The London headquarters also ordered the Company's officers in the Columbia district to report the number and tonnage of Russian vessels in the disputed area and to discover the location of any fixed establishments of the Russian American Company.[35] In an effort to expand the market for furs from the Pacific Coast and thereby provide a profitable basis for the extension of posts into new areas, the Company attempted to negotiate an agreement with the East India Company modifying the restrictive policy that had forced the North West Company and the Hudson's Bay Company to employ Americans as their representatives in the trade with China. By the proposed arrangement, the Hudson's Bay Company could send a vessel to the Columbia to transport the furs to England, whence they could be transshipped to China in vessels of the East India Company. Although such transport would be expensive, the directors of the Hudson's Bay Company believed that the trade could be profitable to both companies because of the high prices of Russian furs in China.[36] The East India Company consented to make the experiment. In 1824 it agreed to purchase from the Hudson's Bay Company 20,000 beaver skins and 7,000 sea otters for that year and the same quantity for 1825.[37] The profits did not, however, justify the confident predictions of the Hudson's Bay Company, and the arrangement was not continued. After a brief and unremunerative effort to dispose of furs in the China market through American firms, the Hudson's Bay Company also lost interest in trade with the Orient.

Despite the ill success of its venture into China and a depression in the London fur market in the early 1820's, the Company continued its pressure for a boundary that would permit further expansion of the British fur trade and at the same time confine the Russians to the islands they then occupied. Traders under the direction of Chief Factor John Stuart followed the rivers and lakes north and west from the Fraser River. In the summer of 1822 a party under the command of Chief Trader William Brown struck northward from their base at Fort St. James and in October reached the northern end of Babine Lake, north of the 55th parallel set by Tsar Paul in 1799 as the limit of the Russian American Company's jurisdiction, and a few miles south of the Skeena River which flows into Chatham Sound. There Brown constructed a post which he named Fort Kilmaurs in affectionate remembrance of his native parish in Ayrshire, Scotland,[38] but which came to be known generally as Babine Fort. This station was the most northerly and westerly permanent post maintained by the Hudson's Bay Company before 1825.

An attempt to extend trading operations into the Chilcotin country met with less success. The attention of the Company's officers was first directed to this area by the report of George McDougall, who had ventured into the Chilcotin land from Alexandria [39] in January, 1822, and had found an abundance of furs. In July, 1823, the council of the northern department consequently decided to establish a post among the Chilcotin Indians, "say about 150 miles N. West of Frasers River." But the fort was not built until the autumn of 1829 because of an excessively mild winter in 1823–24, unrest among other tribes of New Caledonia, which necessitated strengthening existing establishments, and war between the Chilcotin tribe and Indians between them and the Fraser River.[40]

The erection of only one permanent station in four years might appear to reflect a lack of energy on the part of the Company's North American representatives. Such a conclusion, so easy to draw from a casual examination of the maps or from a twentieth-century journey through the area, would be unjust to Stuart and Brown, the officers in New Caledonia. Between 1821 and 1825 New Caledonia was largely terra incognita. Mackenzie, Thompson, Harmon, Fraser, Stuart, and a few others had penetrated into various sections and the record of their hardships is a monument to human courage and endurance, but beyond their immediate routes virtually nothing was known of this vast territory. Not only did the narrow river valleys crib and confine the explorer-trader, but the Indians often provided an even more formidable barrier. The harmony between Hudson's Bay Company traders and the natives, so noteworthy in contrast to the characteristic conflict between their American counterparts and the Indians, resulted from trust built upon long association. In the 1820's suspicion and hostility greeted the fur trader. The militant coast Indians barred the routes to the ocean, and the interior Indians, even when they initially welcomed traders into their territory, could not be relied upon. The murder in the summer of 1823 of two of the Company's servants at Fort George by Indians of the vicinity caused the temporary abandonment of that post.[41]

To execute the instructions of the governor and committee in the face of such conditions required a far greater number of Company employees in New Caledonia than Governor Simpson and the council of the northern department were disposed to provide. In 1822, when instructions were received to expand north and west, the personnel of the area included two officers, six clerks, two interpreters, and thirty-four men. For the expedition into the Babine country, the council allocated an additional ten men to carry supplies. Until 1825 no further enlargement of the force in New Caledonia was authorized.[42] Such an establishment was barely sufficient to maintain existing posts and was certainly grossly inadequate for an energetic program of expansion into unknown country.

In thus restricting the increase of personnel in the area, Simpson and his council were not violating the intent of their instructions. The governor and committee had advised them to expand north and west as far "as may be practicable, if there appears any reasonable prospect of doing so profitably." [43] But practicability and the potentialities of profit were limited by the obstacles described above, and a further deterrent to expansion of staff was the chronic disaffection of clerks and men of the New Caledonia district against their new masters since the amalgamation of 1821.[44] Until unrest was eliminated, the district could not produce substantial profits and the Company could not penetrate with vigor into new areas.

The objective of the governor and committee—to extend trading posts far to the north and west of the Fraser River—was therefore frustrated by a combination of natural and human opposition. But the London headquarters continued to urge their officers to greater efforts. They particularly wanted a post established on the coast, "as far North as may be practicable," in order to provide an effective argument against Russian claims on the mainland.[45] These hopes could not be realized before conclusion of the treaty, and the Company was forced to rest its case upon less powerful arguments.

The claims of the Company, despite these disappointments, were nevertheless impressive. Its representatives and those of its predecessor, the North West Company, had been the only European explorers of the interior country north of the Columbia system between the coast and the Rocky Mountains; its traders were established north of 55° north latitude and west of 126°. The Fraser country, as well as the area drained by the Mackenzie River immediately to the east of the Continental Divide, was firmly in its hands. The Company had a strong case, and Pelly and his associates presented it effectively. In their importunities to the Foreign Office, they enjoyed an additional advantage—not only did they represent the only British economic interest in the boundary dispute, but they were the sole source of information about the area in question, the locations of the Company's trading stations, and the extent of territory covered by its operations.

From this strategic position, Pelly's influence on the boundary negotiations, though not decisive, was of great weight, and the provisions of the treaty of 1825 give evidence of this fact. The degree to which the final treaty satisfied the desires of the Hudson's Bay Company cannot be determined by comparing its provisions with Pelly's initial demands, which were unquestionably far greater than the Company expected the Russian government to accept. Rather, the treaty should be judged by the degree to which it recognized the substantial interests and aspirations of the Company. The Company's basic objectives were: (1) to secure the right to trade within the Fraser River area and to force back Russian claims at least as far as the boundaries laid down in Tsar Paul's ukase of 1799, in order that a maximum area of expansion would be left to the Company and the Russians would be "kept at a distance"; (2) to secure transit between inland territories and the Pacific Ocean; and (3) to preserve inviolate under Company control the Mackenzie River system, one of the richest fur provinces on the continent. All these, with Canning's energetic support, the Company achieved.

Although the minimum requirements of the Russian American Company, as distinguished from the extreme pretensions of the ukase of 1821, were in conflict with the objectives of the Hudson's Bay Company, they did not appear to provide serious obstacles to agreement. As Baron Tuyll wrote to Count Nesselrode on November 2, 1822:

> . . . supposing it to be impossible to succeed in extending the frontiers of Russia much farther towards the south, it seems that it would be indispensable to have them fixed at least at the fifty-fifth degree of north latitude, or, better still, at the southern point of the archipelago of the Prince of Wales and the Observatory Inlet, which are situated almost under that parallel. Any nearer neighborhood of the English establishments could not fail to be injurious to that of Novo-Archangelsk [Sitka], which is in latitude 57° 3'.[46]

The essential demands of the Russian American Company, therefore, were recognition of Russian sovereignty over the Prince of Wales [Alexander] Archipelago and over a strip of land on the nearby continent sufficiently extensive to prevent the embarrassment of the Russian trade by foreign rivals.[47] The Russian American and Hudson's Bay companies had not by 1821 collided at any point; the boundary dispute between their respective governments concerned the determination of sovereignty over the wilderness between the two companies' areas of influence, a vacuum into which each hoped to expand. The adoption of mutual convenience rather than absolute right as the basis for the boundary negotiations [48] was therefore appropriate.

Throughout the controversy [49] Canning acted in close association with Pelly. He was usually guided by his advice and was always dependent upon him for information. Pelly's facts were undoubtedly as accurate as the knowledge of the governor and committee permitted, but were naturally presented so as to maximize the Company's claims. In his first communication to Canning, on September 25, 1822, Pelly contended that since the North West and Hudson's Bay companies had been the only traders in the whole territory of New Caledonia from the mouth of the Fraser River to about 60° north latitude, the area was rightfully British. That such an argument was misleading Pelly must have recognized, for, as he admitted, no British explorer or trader had ventured into the country west of the mountains and north of 56° 30'.

The governor was inaccurate in giving the locations of trading posts in New Caledonia, and without exception the deviations were favorable to the case of the Hudson's Bay Company. Fraser's Lake he located at 55° north latitude and "about" 127° west longitude, almost one degree of latitude north and more than two degrees of longitude west of its actual position.[50] Such inaccuracies were not the result of deliberate misrepresentations by the Company's officers. Rather, they were the product of reliance upon primitive surveying techniques. The source of Pelly's information on the position of the Company's posts was the journal of Daniel Williams Harmon, the North West Company trader.[51] The failure to correct Harmon's observations, based on rough calculations he had made in 1810, is eloquent testimony to the Company's lack of familiarity with the territory for which it was contending. The Arrowsmith map available to both the Company and the government was generally unreliable in its delineation of the northwest coast. George Simpson on his visit to the Columbia in 1824–25 found it "very erroneous."[52] But in their prosecution of the boundary dispute Canning and his representatives—Wellington at the Congress of Verona and Sir Charles Bagot and his successor, Stratford Canning, at St. Petersburg—depended upon the Company's information, accurate or inaccurate. There was no other source of information on the interior of New Caledonia.

After an exploratory interchange between Wellington and Lieven at the Congress of Verona, over a year passed before the British renewed negotiations on the boundary issue. Their apparent inactivity was no doubt due in part to preoccupation with the more pressing problems of Spain and its colonies and with

the Greek rebellion, but it also reflected Canning's desire to reach
a preliminary understanding with the United States for a joint
approach to Russia on the maritime phase of the dispute. Canning's hopes for such collaboration were based upon the erroneous
assumption, fostered by Secretary of State John Quincy Adams,
that the United States had no territorial pretensions north of 51°
north latitude.[53]

When, on November 17, 1823, the foreign secretary received
word from Bagot in St. Petersburg that the United States emissary
had instructions to press American claims to participate in the division of the territory between the 42nd and 61st parallels,[54] he
suspected that the wily Adams was endeavoring to enhance the
American position on the Pacific by exploiting the Russo-British
territorial controversy.[55] An interview with Richard Rush, American minister to London, confirmed this suspicion. Canning saw
that Adams' objective was to force Britain, by a simultaneous agreement with Russia and the United States, to accept an Anglo-
American boundary favorable to the United States. He therefore
instructed Bagot to pursue the negotiations with the Russians
alone, and sketched alternative boundaries that would be acceptable to Great Britain.[56] Pelly had suggested these boundaries as
satisfactory to the Hudson's Bay Company.

The alternative lines proposed by Pelly through Canning were,
in order of preference: Chatham Strait, the channel between the
island on which Sitka was located and the islands to the east;
Stephen's Passage, which separated the Alexander Archipelago
from the mainland; or, finally, a line giving the Russians a strip
of from 50 to 100 miles of the coast opposite the Alexander Archipelago. In Pelly's last alternative lay the basis for the final agreement.

The extent to which the foreign secretary depended upon the
Hudson's Bay Company for facts and represented the Company's
wishes in his instructions to Bagot may be gauged from the following passage from his letter of January 15, 1824, which was typical
of other communications:

> The most southern establishment of Russia on the northwest
> coast of America is Sitka, which is not laid down in our latest maps
> with sufficient exactness, but which appears by the Russian map
> published in 1807 to be situated, as the inclosed copy of a letter

from Mr. Pelly, chairman of the Hudson's Bay Company, also represents it, in latitude 57° and not (as the map of which a copy was
enclosed to your Excellency indicates) on the continent, but on a
small island of the same name at the mouth of Norfolk Sound; the
larger islands contiguous thereto, forming (what is called by Vancouver) King George's Archipelago are separated from each other
by a strait, called Chatham Strait, and from the mainland by another strait, called Stephen's Strait or passage. Whether the Russians have extended their settlements to these larger islands is not
known, but Mr. Pelly positively avers that they have no settlement
on the mainland, nor any commerce to the eastward of the coast.
He suggests, therefore, either the channel between the islands, or
that between the islands and the mainland, as the most desirable
line of demarcation to the eastward, which being agreed to, the
line to the southward might be drawn so as to comprehend Sitka
and all the Russian settlements upon the island.[57]

Canning, then, was the spokesman of the Hudson's Bay Company to the extent that its demands involved little risk of collision
with the interests of Russia. Count Nesselrode, the Russian foreign minister, and Poletica, who was immediately responsible for
the negotiations in St. Petersburg, viewed the dispute in essentially the same terms. Nesselrode stated to Admiral Nicholas
Mordvinof of the Russian American Company, "Great Britain, on
her part, represents the rights of the Hudson's Bay Company."[58]

Superficially, the negotiations from January, 1824, to February,
1825, consisted of an unyielding representation of the Russian
American Company's position by its government and the gradual
withdrawal of the British government from its extreme pretensions
until it substantially accepted the Russian proposals. In such a
view, the Russo-American convention of April 17, 1824, by which
the United States accepted 54° 40′ north latitude as the northern
boundary of her claims, might seem to be a serious embarrassment to the British negotiators and a contributory factor in their
eventual "surrender" to the Russian case.

This hypothesis bears no relationship to fact. Canning, even
before the news of the Russo-American treaty reached him, had
decided to agree substantially to the Russian proposals. He and
Pelly had concluded that immediate acceptance of these terms
would be preferable to indefinite prolongation of another vexatious boundary controversy.[59] But this was not surrender in the
commonly accepted meaning of the term. The Russian govern-

ment demanded a boundary that would protect the life of its fur trade against a more aggressive, more efficient Hudson's Bay Company. The line Britain contended for represented the extreme pretensions of the Hudson's Bay Company but was in no way related to the Company's security.

The British negotiators, Bagot and later Stratford Canning, were thus able to make concessions with good grace, whereas their Russian counterparts could not do so without risking infringement upon the interests of the Russian American Company. The Russian plenipotentiaries did, however, concede one point, and in so doing seriously undermined the position of their company. They agreed to allow British subjects free access to the interior on all rivers emptying into the ocean through the coastal strip which they desired to establish as Russian territory.[60] Such a concession, as became abundantly evident after the treaty, was an invitation to the Hudson's Bay Company to cut off, by the establishment of interior posts, a substantial portion of the Russian fur trade at its source, since the coast Indians with whom the Russians traded acted as middlemen for the Indians of the interior.

At the time that this concession was offered, the Hudson's Bay Company had displayed no desire to enter the maritime fur trade. Pelly in his letter to Canning of January 8, 1824, had showed no interest in trade along the coast of Russian America.[61] The right of free navigation on the coast was incorporated in the Anglo-Russian convention because it had been secured by the United States negotiators and because the British whaling interests and Sir John Barrow, the ardent promoter of exploration, had exerted pressure.[62]

The Hudson's Bay Company had made no recommendation on this point. But it is perhaps significant of a change in the thinking of the governor and committee that on April 19, 1824, when Pelly gave his formal consent to acceptance of the Russian proposal, he stated that the Company saw no reason to object to it, "as it appears to secure to them a free access to the Sea for the purposes of their trade on the whole Coast to the Eastward of the 139th degree of longitude."[63] Here was a hint of that new orientation of the trade of New Caledonia which during the next decade was to embroil the Hudson's Bay Company with the Russian American Company.

The Anglo-Russian boundary agreement, therefore, though appearing to coincide with the requirements of the Russian negotiators, was a severe blow to the interests of the Russian American Company.[64] By that convention and the Russo-American treaty of 1824, the Russian government completely abdicated the position it had taken in the ukase of 1821 and the objectives it had then sought. Smuggling by Americans, which had been one of the causes of the ukase, now became a legalized trade, at least for the next ten years; the Russian American Company was confined to the islands it had previously claimed and to a narrow strip of the mainland, but the purpose for which the strip had been sought was rendered largely nugatory by the establishment of the Hudson's Bay Company's right to navigate the rivers flowing through it. In the guise of safeguarding the Russian American Company, its government had subverted its position.

The treaty of 1825 suggests that the liaison between Pelly and Canning was more intimate than that between their Russian counterparts, or that the Russian negotiators were lacking in perspicacity. But there is another possible explanation for the Russian failure to represent more adequately the interests of the fur trade. Russia, like Britain, viewed the dispute in the context of European diplomacy; in 1824 she coveted the Balkans, not North America. She was most anxious to avoid irritations that would further jeopardize her primary objectives. Nesselrode emphasized this in a brief lecture to Nicholas Mordvinof of the Russian American Company:

> . . . while endeavoring to protect interests laboriously established, and even secure new advantages by all allowable means, it must not be forgotten that there may exist other most important necessities and interests of State which impose very grave duties on the Government. To you, Sir, as a man acquainted with every branch of the science of government, I consider it superfluous to explain that the greater or smaller utility of desirable acquisitions cannot serve as a guide in political negotiations. What the Ministry of His Imperial Majesty will tenaciously follow is the principle of *right*, and there where it cannot with accuracy be recognized or defended without inordinate sacrifices in its entirety, it is necessary to take into consideration not only the degree of mutual demands, but also the degree of possibility of attaining the objects of the same without any dangerous strain of strength.[65]

Canning's portrayal of himself as a man taxed to the limit of his patience who had with the greatest difficulty prevailed upon the Hudson's Bay Company to accept modifications of its original demands must have been particularly impressive. The Russian envoy to London, Count Lieven, reported Canning's efforts on behalf of Russia in a letter to Nesselrode on June 1, 1824: "I must confess that Canning has exerted himself very faithfully to satisfy us completely, but he had to struggle against a violent opposition on the part of the companies interested." [66]

While Lieven was writing these words, Pelly was expressing his satisfaction with Canning's intention to accept the line of demarcation proposed by the Russian government in a dispatch from Nesselrode to Lieven on April 17, 1824. Pelly's only modification was to suggest that, since neither Russia nor Britain possessed accurate geographical knowledge of the coastal territory, the Russian proposal to fix the boundary at the mountains following the sinuosities of the coast should be changed to provide for a boundary "at the nearest chain of Mountains not exceeding a few leagues of the coast." [67] Canning incorporated this suggestion in his instructions to Bagot on July 12, 1824, when he stipulated that the boundary should be a maximum of ten leagues from the coast. [68]

By April, 1824, Russia and Great Britain had reached substantial accord on the boundary issue. Final agreement was delayed for ten months by disputes over rights of trade and navigation by British subjects on the northwest coast. Britain contended for the rights in perpetuity to trade at Sitka, to navigate along the coast from Portland Channel to 60° north latitude, and under certain conditions to visit Russian territory north of that parallel. The Russian government was willing to concede privileges for only ten years in the area south of 60° and would make no concessions whatsoever north of that parallel. [69] In demanding such concessions, Canning represented the views of the British whaling interests rather than of the Hudson's Bay Company. Pelly advised Canning that in the Company's view the Russian proposals for a treaty were not so substantially different from those of Britain as to justify further controversy. [70] Confronted with a Greek question "full of peril and plague," [71] Canning finally conceded these points to the Russians, but demanded and obtained a deviation in the boundary north of 59° from 139° to 141° west longitude, "the latter being the parallel which falls more directly on Mount Elias." [72] More important, the 141st meridian was further removed from the mouth of the Mackenzie River, which the Hudson's Bay Company wished to maintain as its preserve of trade, although there is no direct evidence that the Company suggested this deviation.

By the treaty signed on February 28, 1825, the boundary between Russian and British America began at the most southern point of Prince of Wales Island, 54° 40′ north latitude, and followed the Portland Canal to its head at 56° north latitude. From that point the line followed the crest of the mountains alleged to be parallel to the coast, except that it was nowhere to be more than ten marine leagues from the coast. At the point where the line intersected the 141st meridian, it was prolonged on that degree to the Arctic Ocean. British subjects were accorded, as Americans had been by the treaty of 1824, the privilege of trade with Sitka for ten years and were permitted to trade in Russian coastal waters south of Mount Saint Elias for the same period. The right to travel to and from the interior through the Russian coastal strip was guaranteed forever to British subjects. The treaty granted the Hudson's Bay Company unchallenged control over the vast interior of New Caledonia and, through provisions for free navigation of rivers flowing to the coast, gave it the means to intercept and undercut the trade of its Russian rivals. With sound basis did the directors of the Russian American Company complain in later years that their government had sacrificed their interests, for it had opened the coastal trade to the legalized attacks of their competitors.

CHAPTER

# 7

# Competition on the Northwest Coast

EVEN BEFORE the signature of the Anglo-Russian convention, the Hudson's Bay Company began to lay plans to utilize prospective Russian concessions. By July, 1824, when the outlines of the prospective agreement had become clear, the Company advised its officers on the Columbia River to prepare themselves for a drastic new departure in the conduct of the fur trade. The governor and committee instructed Chief Factor John Dugald Cameron, in charge at Fort George, to send the supply brig *William and Ann* northward to ascertain whether there were any good roadsteads or harbors in Portland Canal or between that channel and the Columbia, to examine the navigability of the rivers flowing from the interior between Portland Canal and Mount Saint Elias, and to report on the character and number of the Indians inhabiting the coast.[1] The intent of these orders was clear. The Hudson's Bay Company was preparing to enter the contest for control of the maritime fur trade.

The governor and committee made this decision despite the pessimism of their North American officers regarding the possibility of profits from such a venture. The chief factors and chief traders who had been responsible for the trade west of the Rocky Mountains prophesied that the maritime fur trade was doomed to failure. They pointed out that the Russians, though not scrupling to use "such cruel and arbitrary methods as we could not

[1] For notes to chap. 7, see pp. 448–450.

reconcile ourselves to," were barely able to maintain a foothold against the formidable coastal tribes and that their profits were derived mainly from the hunts of the Kodiak Indians, whom they had virtually enslaved. A maritime fur trade was alien to the experience of these officers, and they were therefore certain of its failure.[2] George Simpson at York Factory, on the eve of departure for his first journey to the Columbia, which would provide him with a basis of personal observation for his views, agreed with the council of the northern department that the returns from the northwest coast would not justify the danger and expense of the trade. Yet the expansionist in Simpson struggled against the conclusion that the Company should confine itself to its present area. Before he left York he voiced the hope that British claims to the coast would be confirmed.[3] His subsequent observations in New Caledonia and the Columbia converted him to enthusiastic advocacy of the views of the governor and committee. He wrote from Fort George on March 10, 1825, before the news of the conclusion of the treaty had reached the Columbia:

> The Riches of this Coast and its Interior are certainly worth contending for and if the British government does take that interest in the fur trade which it is wonted to do in every other branch of its widely extended commerce, it must as a matter of course fall into the hands of the Honorable Company and if the business is properly managed and sufficiently extended I make bold to say that it can not only be made to rival but to yield double the profits that any other part of North America does for the amount of capital employed therein but in order to turn it to the best advantage New Caledonia must be tacked to the Dept. and the Coasting Trade must be carried on in junction with the inland business.[4]

In promoting the coastal trade the governor and committee wanted, in addition to immediate profit, nothing less than a monopoly of the entire fur trade between Mount Saint Elias and California, which involved eliminating both Russian and American competition from the entire Pacific slope. But it was against the American petty traders that their efforts were principally directed. The Russian American Company confined itself to the offshore islands, collecting principally sea otters and fur seals, whereas the Hudson's Bay Company's profits were dependent primarily on land pelts, with beaver still the most important single source of revenue. Not only were the American sea captains vexatious to both monopolies but their profits were a continuing attraction for American interest in the Columbia. If the American coasting trade was destroyed, Simpson and the governor and committee believed that the Hudson's Bay Company might be left to the quiet enjoyment of its Columbia trade, and an Anglo-American boundary favorable to the Company's interests more easily won. The Company therefore determined first to oust the Americans from the coast, if possible with the assistance of the Russians, and then to attack the Russian American Company.

The American sea captains had two weaknesses which the Hudson's Bay Company could exploit: since their capital was small, they could not survive serious monetary loss; and they were dependent for profit on trade with the Russians at Sitka and the settlements to the north. The Hudson's Bay Company therefore attacked the Americans both by reducing prices of goods to the coastal Indians below the Americans' cost of supply and by wooing the Russian American Company with offers of supplies at lower prices than the American traders were able to match. The coast would be scoured of furs by a combination of trading posts and trading ships, and the Boston vessels, unable to purchase furs or to sell to the Russians, would be forced to leave the northern Pacific. This was the plan, and the governor and committee proceeded to put it into vigorous execution. To superintend the marine activities the Company in 1826 appointed Æmilius Simpson, a lieutenant of the Royal Navy on half-pay retirement, and a relative of George Simpson. In 1827 Lieutenant Simpson assisted in the erection of Fort Langley at the mouth of the Fraser River, the first link in the chain of posts designed to eliminate American competition. In the summer of 1831, just before his death, he established a post at the mouth of the Nass River. When the post was moved to a more protected position on Dundas Island three years later, it was named Fort Simpson in his memory.[5] In 1833 the Company built Fort McLoughlin on Lama Passage. Within eight years of the convention of 1825, the Hudson's Bay Company had constructed a chain of trading stations, at intervals of approximately 200 miles, from the Columbia River to the southern limits of Russian America. These were reinforced by trading vessels which cruised the intervening coast and swept up furs that might otherwise have fallen into the hands of the Americans. With the *Cadboro,* sent from England in 1827, the *Lama,* bought in the Sandwich Islands in 1832, and the steamer *Beaver,* which arrived on the coast from England in 1836, the Company was able to monopolize the coastal trade south of Russian America. Other vessels, owned or chartered, were employed primarily in transport to and from England.

Destruction of the American trade was made easier by the assistance of the Americans themselves. When the Hudson's Bay Company entered the field, excessive competition among small ventures for a supply of furs inadequate to sustain them all had already resulted in ruination for some shippers and insignificant profits for others.

Though the Yankee captains traded for both sea and land furs, much of their profit had been derived from the sale of sea-otter pelts. The slaughter of these animals had produced a scarcity which increased prices, while the Chinese market for the pelts declined. The American traders were therefore particularly vulnerable when the Hudson's Bay Company began active competition. When Lieutenant Simpson visited California in 1827 to investigate its potentialities for trade, the Russians at Fort Ross informed him that the trade of the coast had been "greatly overdone by the Americans of late years" and that several vessels had been forced to abandon it. Five American vessels of from 200 to 350 tons continued to compete on the coast, but were it not for profits derived from trade with the Russian settlements and from cargoes acquired at Canton in exchange for furs, these ships, too, would be forced to leave.[6] This intelligence indicated that if the Americans were undersold for a few seasons they would quit the contest.

The technique applied, as in all other areas where the Company faced competition, was to attempt to buy the furs of the Indians before the arrival of opposition and to offer prices sufficiently attractive to dissuade the Indians from retaining their furs in the hope of getting better bargains from the Americans. Chief Factor John McLoughlin maintained three price levels in the New Caledonia and Columbia districts. In the protected interior zone the valuation of furs in goods was low; in the coastal zone, when opposition was not actually present, the Indians received a price sufficiently high to encourage them to dispose of their furs rather than withhold them for possible future sale; and when the opposition was actually in the area, the Indians enjoyed the luxury of prices that were exorbitant by the other two standards. The Indians throughout the interior soon became aware of this differential and the traders of the interior posts were forced to bear the brunt of their displeasure. Chief Trader Samuel Black at Fort Walla Walla, an old Nor'Wester who had become one of the most efficient servants of his new masters, was subjected to the menaces of the Nez Percé Indians because he could not adjust his tariff to that in effect nearer the coast; as early as 1829, the first year of active opposition to the American coastal traders, some of his Indians journeyed to Fort Vancouver where they traded sixty skins at the higher tariff.[7] It was difficult for him and his successor George Barnston to explain to the neighboring Indians the intricacies of a trading system that made a blanket worth five skins at Walla Walla worth only one skin at Fort Vancouver.[8] McLoughlin attempted to relieve this embarrassment by directing his clerks to ask five beavers for a blanket when Indians from the interior arrived to trade,[9] but this expedient was apparently not effective. The immediate cause for the high prices at Vancouver in 1829 and 1830 was the arrival in the Columbia of Captain John Dominis of Boston, in charge of the *Owhyhee*.[10]

In general McLoughlin acted upon the fundamental principles set down by the governor and committee for eliminating competition. He gave orthodox instructions to William Ryan, Hudson's Bay ship captain, for a voyage to Nisqually at the base of Puget Sound and to Fort Langley and Fort Simpson. He ordered Ryan to trade at the rate of three skins per 2½-point blanket in the Straits of Juan de Fuca if no opposition were present, and at one skin per blanket if competition should appear.[11] In 1830, when American competition was strong, McLoughlin instructed Lieutenant Simpson to dispose of his goods at 150 per cent advance on invoice price, not an exorbitant increase because of the costs of transportation, in exchange for furs at the following valuations:[12]

| Large beaver | 20/ | Minks | 1/6 |
| Small beaver | 10/ | Musquash | 6*d*. |
| Fishers | 4/ | Land otters large | 10/ |
| Martens | 5/ | Land otters small | 5/ |

| Cross foxes | 11/ | Sea otters small | 40/ |
| Red foxes | 5/ | Large black bear | 10/ |
| Silver foxes | 30/ | Small black bear | 5/ |
| Sea otters large | £6 to £8 | Large brown bear | 10/ |

These rates, higher than those paid in the interior, were set as a standard in the absence of immediate opposition. With competition, prices were adjusted to those offered by the opponent. This system was costly to the Hudson's Bay Company. In 1833, when the Company purchased furs on the coast valued at £13,000, McLoughlin estimated the loss at £2,800. But this was a small price to pay for unchallenged monopoly, and American competition noticeably weakened after 1830. In 1833 there were no American vessels on the coast,[13] and although they appeared sporadically thereafter, sustained opposition had ended.

This end was not achieved solely by matching or undercutting American prices. Ship captains in pursuit of profit were not deterred by moral considerations. The goods that Indians demanded above all others were weapons, ammunition, and liquor, and these were forthcoming. The Hudson's Bay Company, despite the prohibitions of the convention of 1825,[14] also traded in these commodities, for, as Simpson pointed out to the governor and committee, "without these articles we can have no chance of success, we must therefore either abandon the contest altogether, or follow the example of our opponents by the unlimited sale of them to the natives." [15]

As American opposition receded, the tariff was gradually altered and the coastal Indians were weaned from the rich diet they had enjoyed. When the Indians, noting that the prices paid by the trading ship were more attractive than those paid at the forts, withheld their goods for sale to the ship, the differential between the ship and the coastal posts was removed. In 1834 the price of a blanket on the coast had risen to four skins; it gradually increased thereafter, except when opposition forced downward readjustments.[16]

The Russian American Company contributed to the downfall of the American petty traders by closing Russian American territorial waters to them in 1834, at the end of the ten-year term during which trading privileges were permitted by the treaty of 1824.[17] By this action the Russian American Company demonstrated its abhorrence, in common with the Hudson's Bay Company, of all competition within its area of interest, rather than a desire to assist its sister monopoly. The Russian American Company viewed with increasing apprehension the march of the Hudson's Bay Company up the coast, and its belief hardened that the British Company intended not only to eliminate the Americans but to attack the trade of the Russian company itself. Baron Ferdinand Wrangell, governor of the Russian American colonies, watched with dismay the efficiency of the Hudson's Bay Company's operations. He had become convinced by 1832 that encroachment on Russian trade would not be long deferred. He wrote the board of directors:

> Although Mr. [Æmilius] Simpson's sudden death temporarily put a stop to this intention, it is probable that it will not be for long and in a year or two the English will occupy a post there also undoubtedly in prejudice of our commercial relations with the Kolosh. For the excellent quality and abundance of the merchandise of the English constitute an attraction to the Kolosh which we have no means to compete with, and there is no doubt whatever that if the Board of Directors does not find means to supply the colonies with merchandise of such quality and in such quantity as to be able to hold out against the Hudson Bay Company, this company will be in possession of the whole fur trade in northwestern America from Cross Sound or even from a more northern point to the south as far as the coast of California.[18]

The fear that Russian trade would be invaded had not yet matured when the Hudson's Bay Company made its first overtures to the Russians for an agreement by which it would supplant the Americans in trade with the Russian settlements. The earliest suggestion of such an arrangement was apparently made by George Simpson during his first visit to the Columbia in 1824 and 1825,[19] but no further action was taken until Simpson returned to the Columbia in 1828 and 1829. By then the idea had taken more definite form. Simpson now proposed to the governor and committee that the Hudson's Bay Company furnish the Russians with British manufactured goods and with grain, beef, and pork to be produced at the newly established farm at Fort Vancouver, if necessary at prices sufficient to cover only the costs of production and transportation.[20] He instructed Lieutenant Simpson, before the latter set out on his voyage to survey the harbor of Nass, to visit Sitka and to present this proposal, without, of course, specific references to prices.

Upon his arrival at Sitka in September, 1829, Lieutenant Simpson delivered George Simpson's letter to the governor, Captain Peter Chistakoff, who received it in the "most polite manner." Politeness and hospitality cost little and Chistakoff dispensed both in abundance, but commitments to an agreement such as Governor Simpson had proposed were not within his authority.[21] Overtures from London to the board of directors in St. Petersburg [22] met with no more encouragement, but the Russian American Company took the occasion to issue a pointed reminder that the trade in firearms and spirits in which the Hudson's Bay Company was engaged was a violation of the convention of 1825.[23] The coolness of the Russian response could not quell the ebullient enthusiasm of George Simpson, who chose to regard it as an encouragement for further negotiations.[24] But it is apparent that the directors of the Russian American Company had concluded by 1830 that the great threat to the security of their trade was not the American sea captains, vexatious though they were, but the Hudson's Bay Company. For the Russians to aggrandize their British rivals in order to eliminate the American petty traders was akin to invoking the aid of the tiger to destroy wolves. The Hudson's Bay Company desired to maintain friendly relations with the Russian American Company in order to intensify the attack on the American trade, but British plans to control the resources of the coast south of Mount Saint Elias precluded the peaceful coexistence of the two companies except on terms that the Russians in 1830 were unwilling to accept—the withdrawal of their trade from the coastal strip they had won by the treaty of 1825.

While awaiting a reply from St. Petersburg on its proposals for a trade agreement, the Hudson's Bay Company was laying plans to extend its trade into the area of Russian influence. Nass, in British territory but immediately south of the boundary, was in a position to attract natives from the Russian coastal strip, and British command of this harbor would deprive the Americans of one of their richest sources of furs. In consultation with Simpson, who had arrived in London on October 17, 1829, the governor and committee spent the next few days making plans for vigorous prosecution of the coastal trade. On October 28 they instructed McLoughlin to occupy Nass with a force of not less than fifty men to be commanded by Chief Trader Peter Skene Ogden,[25] whose fearless leadership of the Snake country expeditions seemed to qualify him for the task of establishing a post where trouble might be expected from either the natives or the Russians. McLoughlin could not execute these orders until the summer of 1831 because an outbreak of fever on the Columbia in 1830 incapacitated so many of his men that it was difficult to maintain the Company's existing establishments.[26]

The Company had decided to construct a post at Nass on the basis both of American reports that it was the source of most of the land furs acquired by the Americans [27] and of the assumption that the harbor lay at the mouth of the Skeena River, a broad, navigable stream which provided access through its tributary, the Babine, to the trading posts of the interior. The reports were exaggerated and the assumption was false, but the discovery of the error in geography led to a second mistake of more impressive proportions. Lieutenant Simpson, while cruising along the coast during the summer of 1831, deduced that the Babine [Skeena] River entered the sea at the harbor of Stikine within the Russian coastal strip, and was informed, perhaps by American captains, that the Americans collected from 3,000 to 4,000 beaver annually at that place. Here, obviously, was another opportunity to gain profits at the expense of the Americans. Lieutenant Simpson was correct in his observation that Stikine Harbor was located at the mouth of a large, navigable river, but he was incorrect in identifying that stream as the Babine, which actually entered the ocean at Chatham Sound, well within British territory, many miles south of Nass Harbor, and approximately 200 miles in a direct line southeast of Stikine.[28]

On one fact of geography, however, there could be no mistake. The harbor of Stikine lay in Russian territory. But this was no deterrent to the exploitation of its resources by the Hudson's Bay Company, as Governor Simpson pointed out to the governor and committee. The sixth article of the convention of 1825 accorded British subjects the right to navigate all streams that crossed the boundary south of Mount Saint Elias, and the seventh article granted them the privilege for ten years of trading along this section of the coast. The Company could establish a post on the river over ten leagues from the coast, in British territory, and could supply it from the sea by the rights accorded by Article VI. At the same time, by the privileges granted in Article VII, which did not expire until 1835, the Company's ships could trade with the natives along the coast in Russian territory.[29] In this way the Russian American Company would be exposed to superior competition on the coast, and the Hudson's Bay Company could buy many of the land furs directly from the interior Indians instead of indirectly through the coastal Indians, who acted as middlemen. The execution of this plan would, therefore, almost inevitably drive the Russian traders from their own coastal territory.

The Russians suspected that these were the intentions of the Hudson's Bay Company even before the governor and committee decided to carry them out. Lieutenant Simpson, who was apparently more communicative than he was required to be, told Baron Wrangell that he planned to build a post on the Stikine in British territory. Wrangell saw the danger to the Russian American Company, but at first he could discover no legal way of frustrating the plan.[30]

Wrangell's prediction that the death of Lieutenant Simpson would delay the establishment of a post on the Stikine for only a year or two was justified. In fact, Simpson's death does not appear to have deferred the adoption of his plan. On February 1, 1834, the governor and committee instructed McLoughlin to send a party up the Stikine during the course of the summer to build a fort. Their intention was to withdraw from Nass after the Stikine post had been established.[31]

While McLoughlin's instructions were on the way, the chief manager of the Russian American Company's settlements was preparing to prevent their fulfillment. Wrangell knew that he could not halt the plan by economic means alone. But the treaty that gave the Hudson's Bay Company its opportunity also contained an article that Wrangell hoped to utilize to the advantage of the Russian American Company. The second article provided:

> In order to prevent the right of navigating and fishing, exercised upon the ocean by the subjects of the high contracting Parties, from becoming the pretext for an illicit commerce, it is agreed that the subjects of His Britannic Majesty shall not land at any place where there may be a Russian establishment, without the permis-

sion of the Governor or Commandant; and, on the other hand, that Russian subjects shall not land, without permission, at any British establishment, of the Northwest coast.[32]

If a Russian fort could be established at the mouth of the Stikine before the British ships arrived, a pretext might be found in this article for refusing to allow the British to proceed beyond that point. Wrangell was aware that such an interpretation of the treaty strained language to the breaking point and was not justified by the manifest intent of the article, but the threat called for desperate expedients. He wrote to his superiors on April 28, 1834:

> The greatest trouble I have now is the Hudson Bay Company which is allowed by the convention to navigate freely on rivers falling into the sea in our possessions, for it is the region neighboring upon the rivers which furnished us with beavers and not the coast, and I beg of you that should any other convention be signed (the term of the old ones having expired) you should solicit that free navigation on the rivers should at least be limited by the condition that free navigation to the British from the interior to the sea should not be forbidden, while free navigation from the sea up the rivers should be prohibited. Of course it would be best not to allow any navigation whatever, though I think that it will not be possible to manage it. However, this circumstance will depend upon diplomatic transactions and until further instructions *I will hinder the British by force* from sailing up the Stachin river.[33]

That a man of Wrangell's acumen should have interpreted the treaty so erroneously is difficult to believe. The right of navigation on rivers flowing into the interior was not limited to a term of years, as Wrangell undoubtedly knew. But it was convenient for his purposes to appear uninformed, since he had decided that the British must be prevented from using the river. In preparation for what he regarded as an inevitable clash with the British traders, Wrangell sent his assistant, Captain Adolf Etholine, on the brig *Chichagoff* to reconnoiter the waters adjacent to the mouth of the Stikine and to inaugurate trade with the natives. Etholine left Sitka on April 3, 1833, and returned on May 26 with the assurance that the Stikine Indians would welcome a Russian trading station, but with the disturbing news that the Indians had also invited the traders of the Hudson's Bay Company to settle among them. Thereupon Wrangell sent the *Chichagoff*, under the command of Lieutenant Dionysius Zarembo, back to the Stikine in the autumn of 1833 to winter there and to begin construction of a redoubt the next spring as soon as weather permitted.[34]

Zarembo was busy constructing the fort, which was garrisoned by twenty men, when a lookout reported on June 18, 1834, that a British vessel was approaching. It was the brig *Dryad* under the command of Chief Trader Peter Skene Ogden whom McLoughlin had sent to build a fort on the Stikine. The Russian and British accounts of what transpired thereafter are somewhat divergent, the British insisting that Zarembo threatened to use force and Zarembo emphatically denying the allegation. But both agree that Zarembo presented Ogden with a document. This paper as translated for the Hudson's Bay Company contained the following statement:

> In the Year 1834, the 18th of June. On the brig of the Columbia Company of Mr. Ogan at Stakeen—I prohibit to trade with the inhabitants of Stakeen which have their settlements here and accordingly refer to the Convention.—To the Colonies of the Russian American Company, no permission is given to trade. I neither allow to enter the river Stakeen in consequence of the instructions received from Chief Director Baron Wrangel.[35]

Ogden remained in the vicinity of the fort for the next few days in the hope that Zarembo would receive instructions from Sitka to permit the expedition to proceed up the river, but on June 29 dispatches from Sitka confirmed Zarembo in his opposition.[36]

Balked in their primary mission, Ogden and his party turned south. On July 14 the *Dryad* anchored in an inlet in British territory south of the Portland Canal near which, on July 23, the men began to measure the ground for a new Fort Simpson, the old position on the Nass River having proved unsatisfactory. While the fort was under construction, the expedition received additional proof of Russian determination to repel all encroachments into Russian America. On July 30 Ogden sent a small party across the channel to cut spars on the north shore near the Russian settlement of Tongass, but before the British could accomplish their mission they were driven off by employees of the Russian American Company. These actions by subordinates were in strict conformity with the instructions of the chief manager, Baron Wrangell.

As Ogden proceeded north from Fort Simpson toward Sitka to renew his protests against the violation of the treaty at Stikine, he must have known that there was little chance that Wrangell would reverse his policy. Nevertheless, it was useful to the interests of the Hudson's Bay Company that a formal protest be lodged and rejected. When Ogden arrived at Sitka on September 8, 1834, he was greeted politely by Wrangell, who had recently returned from conferences with his board of directors in St. Petersburg. Wrangell, as was his custom, provided gracious hospitality, but his visit to Russia had reinforced his determination to obstruct the Hudson's Bay Company's plans on the Stikine. He repeated to Ogden that the provisions in Article II of the treaty justified the prohibition, particularly since the true object of the British on the Stikine was an attack upon Russian trade.[37]

When Ogden returned to Fort Vancouver in December, 1834, McLoughlin began to formulate the most impressive possible case against the Russian American Company, including a generous estimate of financial losses of £22,150.10.11 caused by the Russian action. When the documents substantiating this claim reached London in October, 1835, Pelly immediately filed a formal protest with the Foreign Office, charging the Russian American Company with violations of Articles VI, VII, and XI of the convention, the last of which prohibited the use of armed force in incidents of this kind. With a strong case, pressed by the aggressive Palmerston as foreign secretary and by Lord Durham as ambassador to St. Petersburg, the Hudson's Bay Company was in an excellent strategic position. The Russian American Company had provided it with an opportunity to press for indemnification through diplomatic channels. At the least, the Hudson's Bay Company could expect to exact some payment from the Russians and to reinforce their right to navigate the rivers flowing through the coastal strip; at the best, it could hope for an agreement with the Russian American Company on its own terms.

Under these circumstances the most effective policy seemed to be to exploit the advantage provided by the *Dryad* incident while extending to the Russian American Company the offer of a friendly and mutually advantageous understanding. While action was being taken against the Russian American Company in St. Petersburg, the Hudson's Bay Company renewed its offers to supply the

Russians with manufactured goods and food "on reasonable terms." The Hudson's Bay Company did not wish to destroy the Russian American Company as it did the American petty traders; it merely desired to eliminate it as a competitor for the trade south of Mount Saint Elias.[38]

The London headquarters therefore instructed McLoughlin to avoid collisions with the Russians and to divert some of the Company's resources, which might have been used in coastal expeditions to the Stikine, to the trade with the Mexican settlements in California. Such a shift in emphasis not only was calculated to reduce Russian irritation, but it cost the Company nothing, for the governor and committee had matured plans to capture the furs of the Stikine by posts supplied from the interior of New Caledonia. Chief Trader John McLeod had recently discovered a river, which he named the Pelly, whose source was west of the headwaters of the east branch of the Liard River. The Company's officers concluded that this stream was the Stikine River. If this assumption was correct, then trade could be conducted on the Stikine from McPherson's River and the interior at less expense than from the coast, since a smaller establishment would be required to trade "with the poor timid Indians of the Interior" than with the quarrelsome inhabitants of the coast. Also, the Indians of the interior, who were the hunters, would sell their furs at cheaper prices than the Stikine middlemen, who were accustomed to the high prices produced by competition.[39] At its meeting in June, 1836, the northern council adopted a resolution to execute the instructions of the governor and committee:

> The Governor and Committee being desirous that a Post should be established as early as possible on Pelly's (supposed) Stikine River falling into the Pacific, for the purpose of intercepting the valuable trade which now finds its way to the Coast and there falls in the hands of the Russians and Americans, It is resolved,—
> 19. That an officer and 6 men be forwarded with Outfit 1837, in order to enable Chief Factor McPherson to establish a post to be called Fort Drew in the summer of 1838 down the river at a distance of at least 200 miles from Dease's Lake.[40]

The river was indeed the Stikine, although the northern council's estimate of the distance was somewhat exaggerated. But the council's intention was clear—to conduct a vigorous campaign for the monopoly of land furs on the northwest coast.

While these plans were being made, Lord Durham was presenting the Hudson's Bay Company's case in St. Petersburg. Although the controversy was spun out for three years, Count Nesselrode in effect accepted the validity of the British case in his first interchange with Durham. In reply to Durham's formal protest, he wrote:

> The matter therein treated, as far as it concerns a difference which has arisen between Russian and British subjects, has already, for that reason only, caused sincere regret to the Imperial Ministry, and this regret is all the deeper because reports arriving here directly on this same affair, are of a nature to confirm the supposition that the authorities of the Russian settlements on the North West Coast of America have on the arrival in those parts of a vessel belonging to the Hudson Bay Company, acted in a manner which is far from the intentions of the Imperial Government and its constant desire to maintain and strengthen the friendly relations now subsisting between the two Powers.[41]

Nesselrode disclaimed the actions of Wrangell and his subordinates as contrary to the provisions of the treaty and promised that there would be no recurrence of such incidents. But, as Wrangell recognized, force or threat of force was the only means of keeping the trade of the coastal strip in Russian hands. Nesselrode refused to accept the British contention that Zarembo had made threats, and argued that Ogden had "yielded less to an absolute necessity than to an excess of prudence"; therefore, the Russian authorities were not liable for damages from whatever losses had been sustained. This, however, was defense of a secondary objective. The main battle had already been lost. When the board of directors of the Russian American Company complained to Nesselrode that his acknowledgment of the violation of Article VI of the treaty had exposed the company to ruin, they were not overstating their case.[42]

For the next two years, Nesselrode used every conceivable argument to avoid acceptance of the claims for damages: the Russians had not threatened; rather, their remarks had been misinterpreted; the fear of the hostile Stikine Indians and not the Russians had prevented Ogden from entering the river; the *Dryad* was larger and stronger than the *Chichagoff*, and Ogden could have forced his way into the river even if the Russians had resisted; the Hudson's Bay Company had previously violated the convention by trading liquor and firearms to the Indians, and should be asked to pay damages rather than receive them.[43]

These evasions irritated the governor and committee, and George Simpson began to hint darkly of imminent war between Great Britain and Russia,[44] but the policy of courting the Russians by offers of trade while pressing them for damages remained unchanged. The reappearance of American competition gave the officers of the Hudson's Bay Company an additional incentive to renew their offers of a trade agreement with the Russians. Two American vessels, the *Peabody* and the *LaGrange*, toured the coast in the summer of 1836 buying furs and forcing up prices, and paying scant regard to two Russian armed vessels which guarded the frontiers of Russian America. The *LaGrange*, under the command of Captain Snow, visited Sitka in the spring of 1836 and sold goods there for $10,000, in bills payable at St. Petersburg.

On being apprised of the presence of these ships, Chief Factor Duncan Finlayson, in immediate charge of the coastal trade, visited Sitka for an interview with the governor, Ivan Kupreanoff, who had succeeded Wrangell the year before. Finlayson repeated the arguments of Lieutenant Simpson and Ogden that the presence of the Americans was obnoxious to the interests of both companies. The Hudson's Bay Company was therefore prepared to supply at moderate cost all goods that the Russians were accustomed to purchase from the Americans. Kupreanoff listened with polite attention and expressed interest in the proposal, but explained that he had no power to exclude the Americans without authorization of the board of directors in St. Petersburg. But the quality of the goods that Finlayson had brought in the *Lama* impressed the governor, and the prices were attractive. Also the prospect of a steady supply of wheat from the Columbia instead of the uncertain supply from California was most alluring. Kupreanoff agreed to write his superiors, and his letter was forwarded to St. Petersburg by the Hudson's Bay Company.[45]

Finlayson's visit to Sitka gave the governor and committee an occasion to renew their offers to trade with the Russian American

Company. They had called McLoughlin to London to explain his accounting of damages in the *Dryad* affair, but by the time he arrived relations between the two companies had entered a new phase. McLoughlin's assistance was now required in the development of a system of supply for the Russian colonies rather than in the substantiation of a bill for damages.

As early as March 7, 1838, George Simpson described the prospects of a trade agreement as "more than probable," [46] though there may have been no definite assurances from St. Petersburg. On August 27, while the diplomatic representatives of Russia and Britain continued to wrangle over damages, Pelly and Simpson arrived in St. Petersburg to confer with the directors of the Russian American Company. But they spoke no Russian, and neither the British chargé d'affaires nor any of the British residents of St. Petersburg could describe the structure of the Russian company or its mode of operations. Pelly stated that "so much involved in mystery are the affairs of that Concern, that none of the English residents in St. Petersburg with whom we had communication could give any distinct information respecting its affairs, altho many of them were Stockholders." [47] Such a deficiency was apparently more remarkable in a nineteenth-century company than in a twentieth-century corporation.

Several days passed before Pelly and Simpson were able to communicate with the directors. Finally, on August 31, they met the board at the company's place of business, and presented a statement of the advantages that the Russian company would gain by a trade agreement. The directors listened with "much attention" and expressed great interest in the proposals, but informed Pelly and Simpson that they could make no decisions until the arrival of Baron Wrangell, who apparently had become the most powerful member of the board. The directors asked that in the meantime Pelly commit his proposals to paper.[48]

During the next six days, the Hudson's Bay Company representatives acquired firsthand information of business methods in tsarist Russia. Pelly and Simpson, accustomed to prompt attention to business, found "the tardy manner" of the Russians most distasteful. Pelly had prepared a letter to the directors on September 1, but six days elapsed, "three of them saints' days or holy days," before he could even get the letter translated into Russian.[49] With such slovenly disregard of efficiency, obviously the Russians could not expect to be successful in life.

Pelly's terms were in the language of one monopolist to another. The business of the northwest coast, he stated, was divided among three parties. Two of them—the Russian American Company and the Hudson's Bay Company—were reliable, established businesses, but it was impossible to come to terms with the American petty traders, "birds of passage" whose identity changed from year to year. Another source of competition was also beginning to manifest itself in "certain residents of the Sandwich Islands who, if not checked, are likely to become troublesome." [50]

To eliminate American competition and to remove all causes of friction between the companies, Pelly proposed that (1) the Russian American Company agree, for a specified term, to buy from the Hudson's Bay Company all goods it customarily bought from the Americans; (2) the two companies confine their trade to their own territories; and (3) the sale of arms, ammunition, and liquor be discontinued on the northwest coast. By such an agreement, the companies would be able to establish a "fair and equitable standard of trade" with the Indians and "to introduce such measures of economy generally in the management of their business as would yield a handsome profit in the shape of savings." [51]

The Russian American Company was disposed to accept the proposals, although Wrangell and his associates attempted to haggle over what Pelly called "fractional niceties" of price, but all opposition ceased when Pelly offered to sell them at Sitka the land furs they desired for the Russian market. By this means they could sell free of duty furs that when imported from foreign countries were either subject to high duties or were excluded altogether.

Here was the basis for the agreement in 1839 by which the Russians leased their coastal strip to the Hudson's Bay Company, for the sole value of that strip, aside from its protection to the adjacent islands, was the land furs it provided. If competition could be ended and if the Hudson's Bay Company would sell these furs to the Russian company, which could resell them at a profit in the protected Russian market, all basis for opposition to a trade agreement was removed. As Wrangell knew, the alternative was ruin for Russian trade on the coastal strip, since the Hudson's Bay

Company could, by establishing posts in British territory on the rivers flowing through the strip, intercept most of the furs before they reached the coastal Indians. In fact, while Pelly was negotiating with the Russians for a treaty of amity, he and Simpson were planning to build a chain of posts along the boundary, beginning with that fort on the Stikine which Ogden had been prevented from establishing three years before. By these posts, Simpson and Pelly agreed, "we may in course of a few years become possessed of the whole trade of our own proper territory, which now forms the principal part of that enjoyed by our Russian neighbours." [52]

When they returned to London, Pelly and Simpson, probably in consultation with McLoughlin, composed instructions to James Douglas to prepare for the establishment of a post in British territory on the Stikine in the summer of 1840. The expedition, to include three ships and 104 officers and men under the command of William Rae, would be in far greater force than Ogden's had been. The Company was prepared to use this power against the Russians if they should again attempt to frustrate the plan, but Douglas was instructed that the project

> should be kept a profound secret, and be known to no one but yourself and the commander of the expedition, until after it has sailed from the Columbia River, as if it obtains publicity, the Russians and the Indians under their influence may concert measures to frustrate our plans, and the service being unpopular, we may moreover have difficulty with our own people in making your preparations, therefore it may be advisable to let it be understood that the object is to establish a Post on Vancouver's Island or some other part of the coast.[53]

As this letter implied, it was not direct Russian resistance that was feared, since the Russian government had repudiated the actions of Wrangell and Zarembo in 1834. Rather, the Company was apprehensive that the Russians might incite the Stikine Indians to attack the expedition. The commander of the expedition, therefore, was to be instructed, should the Indians seem hostile, to entice some of their chiefs on board the ships and detain them as hostages. The name selected for the new post was Fort Durham, in honor of Lord Durham.[54]

The plan was not executed because the consummation of an agreement with the Russian American Company made it unnecessary. Discussion of the lease to the Hudson's Bay Company of the coastal strip south of Cape Spencer had apparently begun during Pelly and Simpson's visit to St. Petersburg, for by the end of November, 1838, Simpson and Wrangell had by correspondence reached substantial agreement on the details of such a contract.[55] They concluded the arrangement on February 6, 1839, in Hamburg.[56] By the provisions of the contract,

1. The Russian American Company leased to the Hudson's Bay Company for ten years from June 1, 1840, the coastal strip on the mainland north to Cape Spencer for an annual rent of 2,000 seasoned land otter skins from the west side of the Rocky Mountains.

2. The Hudson's Bay Company agreed to sell a maximum of 2,000 additional land otter skins from the west side of the mountains at a rate of 23 shillings per skin, and 3,000 from east of the mountains at 32 shillings per skin.

3. The Hudson's Bay Company promised to provide the Russians with supplies of food stuffs for the term of the contract, including wheat, peas, barley, butter, beef, and ham, and agreed to transport from England British manufactured goods desired by the Russian colonies at the rate of £13 per ton.

4. The Russian American Company promised that, in the event of war, the Hudson's Bay Company would be given three months' notice to evacuate goods and other property from the leased territory.

5. The Hudson's Bay Company relinquished its claims to damages for losses incurred in the *Dryad* incident of 1834.[57]

By direct negotiation the two companies thus arrived at a settlement of all disputes and founded an alliance which continued in effect until the cession of Alaska to the United States in 1867. Contrary to the views expressed by a recent Russian writer, there is no reason to suspect that the agreement was dictated by political considerations.[58] Neither the Russian nor the British foreign office seems to have been privy to the discussions until they were well advanced. On December 9, 1838, Count Nesselrode wrote Count Kankreen, the minister of finance, that he had exhausted "all plausible pretexts" for refusing to admit the responsibility of the Russian American Company for violations of the treaty of 1825 in the *Dryad* affair. He suggested to Kankreen that the company should "enter into friendly negotiations with the Hudson's Bay Company for a settlement of the damage claims." [59] These were not the words of a man intimately acquainted with the progress already made by the companies themselves toward settlement of the dispute. The board of directors did not formally ask the government for permission to lease the territory until December 20. Nesselrode was not informed until December 30. The texts of all communications prove that the motivation for agreement was primarily commercial, although Nesselrode saw political advantages in a settlement, both in eliminating an area of friction with Great Britain and in avoiding further pressure by the United States for the reinstatement of American privileges of navigation in the coastal area.[60]

As might be expected from the relationship of the British and Russian companies to their respective governments, the British government was less fully informed of the negotiations than the Russian. It was not until January 4, 1839, that Pelly first intimated to Palmerston that the long-standing diplomatic dispute might be resolved by direct agreement between the companies, and even then the governor gave no hint of the intention to lease the coastal territory.[61] Palmerston, of course, was most willing for the claim to be settled, but warned that the Hudson's Bay Company had no authority "to barter away territorial or other rights of the British Crown." [62] Even after the agreement of February 6, 1839, the Company did not deem it necessary to acquaint the Foreign Office with the terms of the contract. The Hudson's Bay Company thus acquired commercial and quasi-political control over a substantial section of the northwest coast, subject only to the formal sovereignty of Russia, without seeking the sanction of the British government.

# The Pacific Coast Monopoly, 1839-1867

By THE CONTRACT of 1839, the Hudson's Bay Company had finally achieved mastery of the entire coastal trade from Cape Spencer to California. It could now proceed to alter the price structure of the fur trade and to accustom the Indians to more modest returns for their furs.

Even before the agreement, American opposition had virtually ceased. The directors of the Russian American Company, now that Sitka could receive supplies from the Hudson's Bay Company, demonstrated a pleasing willingness to coöperate in preventing the return of the Americans. Free from the dangers of competition either from the Americans or from each other, the monopolies were able to reduce the prices of furs and to end the sale of arms, ammunition, and liquor to the Indians, although distribution of spirits to the coastal Indians was not entirely discontinued until after Simpson and Governor Etholine agreed in 1842 to end the practice.[1] During the summer of 1840, James Douglas and the Russian governor, Ivan Kupreanoff, agreed to introduce a standard tariff for furs on the entire coast in the shortest time compatible with the safety of the posts.[2] The days of luxurious living had ended for the coastal Indians.

[1] For notes to chap. 8, see pp. 451–453.

For such benefits, a rent of 2,000 otter skins might be considered moderate. But the cost was actually even lower, as the following calculations by an officer of the Hudson's Bay Company suggest: [3]

| | | |
|---|---|---|
| 3,000 HB seasoned land otters sold to Russian American Company for term of 10 years from 1840 | 32/ | per skin |
| Average net price HB seasoned land otters 1827–1837 | 26/5 | " " |
| Less insurance, landing, warehouse, and other charges | 1/5 | " " |
| | 25/ | net per skin |
| Advance on average sales of last ten years | 7/ | |
| 2,000 Columbia seasoned land otters sold for term of 10 years from 1840 | 23/ | per skin |
| Average net price Columbia seasoned land otters 1827–1837 | 18/11 | " " |
| Less insurance from Columbia, landing, warehouse, and other charges | 1/5 | " " |
| | 17/6 | net per skin |
| Advance per skin | 5/6 | |
| Rent of Russian territory leased to Company, 2,000 land otters at 17/6 | £1,750 | per year |
| Advanced price on otters sold | 1,600 | " " |
| Reducing rent to | £150 | |

The Russians likewise seemed to have cause for satisfaction. They had ended a serious dispute and had assured themselves a supply of land otters from the coastal strip. All bases for collision between the two companies had apparently been removed, and as a result profits might be expected to rise. Also the Russians were relieved of the expense of maintaining Fort Dionysius, estimated at 12,000 silver rubles (approximately $13,000) per year.[4]

Acquisition of the coastal strip gave the Hudson's Bay Company the monopoly it had sought for almost two decades. Although in the 1840's American whalers annoyed officers of the coastal forts by trading for furs, their activities were not sufficiently extensive or sustained to destroy the monopoly price structure.[5] But the governor and committee and Sir George Simpson were not content to enjoy the profits of monopoly prices. The conclusion of the agreement introduced two new questions of policy. The first, which occasioned the famous feud between Simpson and McLoughlin, was to what extent the end of competition made possible the reduction of trading posts and personnel on the coast. By 1841 Simpson had decided that all the coastal posts could eventually be abandoned except Fort Simpson, which would serve as a supply base, and that the *Beaver* could be used for the collection of furs from the entire northern coastal area. McLoughlin violently and vociferously disagreed.[6]

With the acquisition of trading control over the coastal strip, only two areas remained to be conquered in order to achieve a complete monopoly of the fur trade of the west coast—California and the remainder of Russian America. California had been the object of some interest at least since 1829, when Chief Trader A. R. McLeod had visited the "Buena Ventura" (Sacramento) country. His expedition, however, had brought back few furs, and later expeditions by John Work and Michel Laframboise had not been notably successful. But as the beaver resources of the Snake country were reduced the attention of the Company's officers was directed to the expansion of the California fur trade. Here there was no serious competition for land furs. The Russian American Company had been active in hunting sea otters and the prospect of competition briefly excited the interest of the governor and committee. On a visit to St. Petersburg, however, Simpson learned from Baron Wrangell and his board of directors that profits in this trade had declined because of overhunting and because of the increased costs of acquiring skins. The response of the governor and committee is an interesting commentary on Victorian business ethics. If the sea-otter trade was no more promising than appeared from the reports of the Russian American Company, they informed McLoughlin, "We do not think it would be good policy, or acting in good faith with that Association to interfere with them." [7] The Hudson's Bay Company therefore took no part in the sea-otter trade of California, but concentrated its attention on the area to the north.

In 1840 James Douglas traveled to Sitka aboard the *Beaver* to arrange specific details for the execution of the agreement. In the course of his journey he took possession of Fort Dionysius, hereafter to be known as Stikine, and began building a fort near the entrance to the Taku River.[8] At the time of the agreement of 1839, the governor and committee intended this arrangement of posts to be only temporary. Although the rental was small, the Hudson's Bay Company could not be certain that the Russians would extend the contract beyond the ten years of the lease. Pelly and the committee, in consultation with Simpson, initially conceived the plan of constructing a chain of posts along the coast north to Cross Sound and another line of establishments in the interior within British territory. Such a scheme seemed to possess three advantages. The Company could thereby acquire every fur between the coast and the Rocky Mountains; many of the furs of the interior could be bought directly, and middleman charges paid to the coastal Indians could thus be avoided. Finally, the presence of the interior posts would force the Russians, if they continued the lease, to offer more advantageous terms to the Hudson's Bay Company, or, if the lease should be terminated, would enable the Company to continue to collect the bulk of the furs from the interior. This plan, the Company discovered between 1839 and 1841, was founded on false premises. Exploration disclosed that the country between the coast and the Rocky Mountains was far more thinly populated and much less valuable than originally believed. Also, officers in New Caledonia discovered that communication between the coast Indians and those of the interior was constant and intimate and that it would be difficult to break their trading relationship without great financial sacrifices. The project of occupying the interior country was therefore suspended, to be reinstituted only if the lease was not renewed.[9]

This change of emphasis did not mean an end to expansion on the northwest slope. Rather, trading operations were extended northward. In September, 1839, Simpson instructed Robert Campbell, stationed at Fort Halkett at the fork of the Liard and Smith rivers, to reconnoiter the territory to the northwest. Campbell and a small party proceeded by canoe and on foot into the territory now called the Yukon, where he reached the Pelly River near its headwaters. His examination of the surrounding country convinced him that a trading post could profitably be established, and in the autumn of 1842 he returned to erect a post at Frances Lake, southeast of the Pelly River, and an outpost shanty on the Pelly itself. From this base, Campbell and his associates extended their operations to the north. In 1846 Campbell built a station at "Pelly Banks," as he called the place where he had first reached the Pelly River, and in the summer of 1848 proceeded northward down the river to its junction with the Lewes River. Here he built another post which he named Fort Selkirk.[10]

By the establishment of Fort Selkirk, the Company pressed within 200 miles of the Russian frontier at the 141st meridian. Since the posts of New Caledonia had been extended to the vicinity of those on the lower reaches of the Mackenzie River, little further construction seemed necessary. But in 1846 Governor Simpson and his northern council made a decision that is difficult to reconcile with the Company's promises in the contract of 1839. They decided to extend the trade to the junction of the Porcupine and Yukon rivers where Chief Trader John Bell had found, during an expedition in 1844, that a profitable trade in furs could be sustained. On the basis of this information, they assigned to a young clerk, Alexander H. Murray, the responsibility for erecting a post at that point. Surveying methods in western North America were primitive, but not so unreliable as to leave any doubt that the new post, named Fort Yukon, was well within Russian territory, for the junction of the Yukon and Porcupine rivers was more than five degrees of longitude beyond the boundary. Murray himself was aware that he had been sent into Russian territory. While his men were at work on temporary buildings at the junction in June, 1847, Murray learned from a local chief that the Indians "expected the Russians here soon." Murray's response to this report is enlightening. He declared:

> This was not very agreeable news to me, knowing that we were on their land, but I kept my thoughts to myself, and determined to keep a sharp lookout in case of surprise. Mr. McKenzie and I divided the night watch between us, a rule laid down and strictly adhered to when Indians were with us.[11]

Arrowsmith maps based on information provided by the Company thereafter clearly delineated the courses of the Yukon and Porcupine rivers to their junction, which was correctly drawn well within Russian territory, but Fort Yukon did not appear on the maps. There can be no question that Pelly and Simpson as well as their subordinates were aware that they had invaded Russian territory. But the area occupied by Fort Yukon had been outside the orbit of Russian trading activity. No Russian appeared until 1863. The Hudson's Bay Company had found a profitable trading area unexploited and had occupied it.

Pelly and Simpson, however, rationalized their violations of the agreement by professing ignorance as to the exact location of the fort. In October, 1848, Pelly wrote Simpson that instruments for determining the exact location would be sent, and that if the Russians disputed Murray's right to occupy the area he and the Russian representative should refer the dispute to their respective headquarters.[12] The instructions did not order Murray to withdraw should accurate observations determine that he was in Russian territory; rather they authorized him to remain until the Russians protested his presence. The Russians did not protest. Fort Yukon remained in British hands until after the cession of Alaska to the United States.

Apart from this violation of Russian territory, the Hudson's Bay Company fulfilled to the limit of its abilities the obligations of the lease, and the Russian American Company found little cause for complaint. A committee appointed by the Russian government reported in 1863 that

> During the whole time of the Hudson Bay Company's possession of the piece of ground in question on the strength of this lease, all the obligations which it had taken upon itself were fulfilled promptly and to the letter, and the mutual friendly understanding between the two companies was never interrupted.[13]

This statement must, however, be modified, for the uncertainties of production at Fort Vancouver sometimes prevented the Hudson's Bay Company from fulfilling its contract to supply the Russian colonies with foodstuffs. But both companies found the agreement advantageous and wished to continue it. The directors of the Hudson's Bay Company agreed privately that the contract had been profitable. During Outfit 1843, for example, the Company collected from the coastal strip 3,500 beavers, 2,600 martens, 3,000 minks, 884 land otters, 86 sea otters, 160 foxes, 540 bears, 1,573 deerskins, and smaller numbers of other furs, valued at approximately £8,000. The freight shipped for the Russians from London gave the Hudson's Bay Company a profit of about £4,000 per year, and shipments of grain from Fort Vancouver provided an additional £750 when the Company was able to fulfill the contract.[14] The agreement to sell the Russian American Company otters from the east side of the Rocky Mountains at 32 shillings per skin had not proved profitable because of a scarcity of otters and a rise in prices, but the loss was small in comparison with profits from other phases of the contract, and the Russian American Company showed an accommodating willingness to cancel this provision.

This assessment of the value of the contract was, of course, not presented to the Russian American Company. In his communications with Wrangell Pelly declared that the trade in the leased territory provided little profit even without charging the account with interest or a proportion of the general expenses of the Company. The rent of 2,000 otter skins, he stated, was excessive.[15] Wrangell replied that the agreement must be mutually inconvenient, for his government did not look with favor on the occupation of Russian territory by subjects of another state, and that he had reason to believe his fellow directors would be unwilling to renew the agreement on any terms.[16] Whether either was deluded by the other it is impossible to state, but upon receipt of Wrangell's gloomy letter Pelly hastened to reply that he had been misunderstood, and that despite the lack of profit from the contract, the Hudson's Bay Company wished to continue the arrangement in order to prevent collision between the servants of the companies.[17] The interchange ended, as do most discussions involving mutual advantage, with the negotiation of a new contract. The revised agreement, finally concluded on April 3, 1849, continued the lease for nine years from June 1, 1850.[18]

The revised contract made no provision for the Hudson's Bay Company to supply foodstuffs and manufactured goods or sell land otters to the Russian American Company. The nonrenewal of the foodstuffs contract was occasioned by the unreliability of the supply of grain and butter at Fort Vancouver, but it was doubly fortunate, for the discovery of gold in California so disrupted the economy of Oregon that the Company would have been unable to fulfill the contract.[19]

All the other articles in the first agreement were continued substantially unchanged. Two of the provisions assumed greater importance during the next few years:

> Article 4th.—It is further agreed that in case of rupture between Great Britain and Russia all the transactions for the preceding time between the contracting parties must be fulfilled without contradiction as if their respective nations were in friendly relations.
> Article 5th.—It is further agreed that in case of rupture between Great Britain and Russia during the existence of this agreement,

the Russian American Company shall guarantee and hold harmless the Hudson's Bay Company from all loss and damage arising from such hostilities in so far as to enable the Hudson's Bay Company to evacuate and abandon their possessions or trading stations within the Russian territory quietly and peaceably and to remove their goods, furs, and other property within three months after receiving information of such hostilities or declaration of war. The Hudson's Bay Company is obliged in this case to liquidate with the Russian American Company the payment of the rent of two thousand otter skins till the datum on which the information of the rupture will be received on the spot.[20]

The insertion of these provisions may have merely reflected the recognition that war between Great Britain and Russia was always a possibility, but the negotiators must have been particularly concerned about the disruption of their trade by war both in 1839, when the agreement was first made, and in 1849, when it was renewed. On both occasions Viscount Palmerston, the inveterate foe of Russia, was at the Foreign Office and Anglo-Russian relations had deteriorated to a point where war appeared imminent. After the conclusion of the first agreement, tension was relieved by the fall of the Whig government and its succession by the more pacific ministry of Sir Robert Peel, whose foreign secretary, Lord Aberdeen, devoted himself to the preservation of international harmony at any cost short of the sacrifice of important British interests. But at the time the revised agreement was signed, Russia and Great Britain again viewed each other with enmity and distrust. As Baron Jomini later described it, the "germ" of the Crimean War had been planted. In 1849 Stratford Canning, the ambassador at the Porte, arranged with the Turkish government for the entrance of a British squadron into the Dardanelles, in violation of the Straits Convention of 1841. Although upon the representations of Russia the ships were withdrawn, Canning's action contributed to the Russian attack on Turkey and the consequent Crimean War.[21]

After the outbreak of war between Russia and Turkey and the movement of the British and French fleets into the Black Sea, the directors of the Russian American Company discussed the protection of their commercial interests during the now inevitable war between Great Britain and Russia. They had occasion to recall a conversation between Sir George Simpson and Governor Adolf Etholine during Simpson's visit to Sitka in 1841, which had apparently been reduced to writing for reference in just such an eventuality as was now impending. Simpson had suggested that it was insane for the two companies to attack each other and to destroy each other's trade because of a war fought over issues remote from the interests of either. Such hostilities would, he said, undermine the "principal objects of their existence," the propagation of Christianity and the spreading of morality and civilization among the natives of the northwest coast of North America. The two companies should, therefore, in the interests of these higher objectives, exert their influence with their respective governments to quarantine the northwest coast from the area of conflict.[22]

Simpson's suggestions had particular appeal for the directors of the Russian American Company, since they were convinced that without the protection of a neutrality agreement their colonies in North America would be attacked by British and French squadrons cruising in the Pacific Ocean, and they realized that they might lose their possessions at the conclusion of war. The small naval establishment of the Russian American Company could provide no defense. The land fortifications were effective against Indians but could offer no significant resistance to attack by a maritime power. On the eve of the Crimean War Governor Alexander Rudakov informed the Russian minister in Washington that "all the settlements in the Russian-American colonies have, to be sure, some sort of fortifications, but these may be relied upon to stand up only against savages and are almost useless in the event of real warfare." The headquarters at Sitka was more effectively prepared for defense than any other settlement, but even there resistance could not withstand serious attack.[23]

The Russian company saw in Simpson's suggestion of 1841 a hope that its colonies might be saved.[24] On February 14, 1854, six weeks before the formal British declaration of war, the directors therefore wrote to London. They reminded the governor and committee of the Simpson-Etholine conversations in 1841 and expressed the conviction that if the Hudson's Bay Company could induce the government of Great Britain to quarantine the northwest coast, they could prevail upon the Russian government to do likewise.[25] The belief that the Russian government would consent to such an arrangement was based on more than wishful thinking.

On January 25, 1854, the directors of the Russian American Company were authorized by their Foreign Office to initiate direct negotiations with the Hudson's Bay Company and were assured that the Russian government would accept an agreement involving "the neutrality of the possessions and ships of the two companies." [26]

The Hudson's Bay Company viewed the neutralization of the northwest coast with as much enthusiasm as the Russians. Although British squadrons might ravage the Russian coast, their actions would be of no direct benefit to the Hudson's Bay Company and their victories would be cold comfort if Russian armed vessels descended upon the Company's depot at Victoria, Vancouver Island. The only protection against such forays would be the presence of British cruisers, and the Company could not be certain that no Russian vessels would slip past the British warships. The Company's forts could provide no defense against naval fire, its ships were not adapted for war, and its servants were not organized for military action.[27] Simpson was most alarmed by the fear that Russian armed vessels would seize the Company's ships. The valuable goods of land establishments might be moved inland, out of reach of Russian marauders, but the capture of the Company's two steamers would be ruinous. In March, 1854, before the news of negotiations for a neutrality agreement had reached him, Simpson urged the board of management of the western department to consider, in the event of Russian attacks, a withdrawal of personnel and of the steamships *Beaver* and *Otter* to the haven of the Columbia River, "as we may rely on the neutrality of the Americans at the very least, if not on their support." In any event, the Company's property would be safe from Russian attack if it was removed to the Columbia.[28]

A secondary fear was the prospect that the Indians might be drawn into the conflict and might "gratify their savage passions" by war not only against each other but against the Europeans. Simpson also professed concern lest the disruption of trade cause suffering among the Indians,[29] but it is evident that his fears were dominantly for potential Company losses.

The two companies probably overestimated the capabilities and the intentions of the Russian and British governments. Although the British squadron in Pacific waters had the power to wreak heavy damage upon the Russian settlements, the British government had no evident intention of wresting Russian America from its owners. The eastern Pacific was a backwater of no significance to British policy, and the Russian settlements were too preoccupied with defense to provide a serious threat to the Hudson's Bay Company's establishments.

It was precisely because no national interests would be advanced by offensive operations upon the mainland of North America, and because the interests of British and Russian commerce would be protected, that the two governments were willing to support a neutrality agreement. Arguments against expenditures for colonial purposes, so impressive to exchequer minds like Gladstone's, were doubly cogent at a time when war in the Crimea was draining the treasury and imposing additional burdens on the taxpayer. The British government, whether its foreign secretary was an Aberdeen or a Palmerston, was not prepared to incur expenditures for offensive operations in an area of so little significance as northwest America. When James Douglas, governor of Vancouver Island, heard of the outbreak of war against Russia, he immediately asked the Colonial Office for authority to raise a force of 500 men for defense of the island, and to pay for its arms, equipment, and maintenance with government funds. The response of Great Britain was unequivocal that no funds could be expended for such a purpose, that the rear admiral in Pacific waters would be instructed to visit the island frequently with one or more warships, and that this protection must suffice. When Douglas made his request, the neutrality agreement had already been approved. His fears were therefore largely unjustified, but the tone of the Colonial Office gave no encouragement that it would have provided troops or money for land operations either for the defense of New Caledonia and Vancouver Island or for an attack upon Russian America.[30]

Since Great Britain had no intention of employing any force beyond the squadron already in the Pacific, the proposals of the Hudson's Bay Company were entirely in harmony with the objectives of British policy. The British government was required to make no sacrifices, and was relieved of financial obligations for the defense of Vancouver Island and British possessions on the mainland. On March 22, 1854, the Foreign Office agreed to the neutralization of northwest America, provided that the agreement was confined to the land itself and that the high seas remained an area of conflict. Russian goods and vessels, whether the property of the Russian American Company or not, would thus be liable to capture by allied warships and the coasts and ports would be subject to blockade.[31] Such an agreement allowed Great Britain to use its naval power in the Pacific with virtually no restriction, except for bombardment and spoliation of posts in northwest America, and since no land force was available or projected, no self-denial was involved.

The agreement was less extensive than the Russian American Company had hoped to achieve, but it had the advantage of securing Sitka and other posts in America from enemy attack. The administration of the Russian American colonies had feared that when war came the British would immediately send a force to occupy these posts. The agent of the Russian American Company in California heard that the Hudson's Bay Company was "already taking steps to seize everything it possibly can." He sent this information, which bore no relationship to fact, to the Russian minister in Washington. To protect his company against the impending invasion, the agent negotiated a fictitious contract with a group of Americans, the "American-Russian Company of San Francisco," with whom the Russians had conducted some business. By this agreement the Americans promised to pay $7,000,000 for the cession of Russian America to them. The contract was probably of no legal value, and Edward de Stoeckl, the minister in Washington, after discussions with American politicians, found that

> In spite of their willingness to protect our colonies and their genuine interest in them, they regard it as impossible to prove to the English that the contract is not fictitious and that, in particular, it was drawn up before the war and cannot, therefore, be of any real use.[32]

Rumors that such a contract existed might possibly have reached the British government and reinforced its decision to approve the neutrality agreement, as one writer contends,[33] but Russian efforts to avert an occupation of their American possessions reveal their estimate of British intentions and potentialities. Their fears were exaggerated, but under their assumptions the neutrality agreement was to the advantage of Russia. There is no evidence to support the legend that the British and Russian governments, to advance the commercial interests of two fur-trading companies, cynically flouted their national interests. The Crimean War was not a total war; it was a limited conflict for limited objectives. The commercial interests of the Hudson's Bay and Russian American companies were safeguarded by the neutrality agreement; but neither country was required as a consequence to sacrifice any interests or aspirations.

Both governments scrupulously observed the agreement. Allied warships visited Sitka on one occasion, but only to reconnoiter. The fate that must have befallen the Russian company's North American headquarters had the agreement not been in effect is indicated by the bombardment of Petropavlovsk and of the island of Urup, in the Kurile chain, both of which were outside the quarantined area. On September 2, 1855, two warships, one British and one French, not only subjected the tiny Russian settlement at Urup to naval fire, but seized the furs and papers of the Russian American Company, burned the buildings, and took prisoner the manager of the island and two other men, the only Russians on the island.[34]

The Russians had good reason to congratulate themselves on the neutrality agreement. The tsar publicly commended the Russian American Company for its astuteness,[35] and Stoeckl expressed his satisfaction over a contract that had been "entirely to our benefit, since we were not in a position to attack the English possessions, whereas the English would have been able to seize ours." Stoeckl's explanation of British magnanimity was that rumors of Russian preparations to sell the colonies to the United States had caused Great Britain to sanction the neutrality of the northwest coast in order to prevent such a transfer.[36]

Although Stoeckl's thesis may have some validity, it is doubtful that the British decision would have been different had there been no fear of American purchase. Although Her Majesty's cruisers could have mauled Sitka and seized its goods, the value of such a raid would have been small and the power of Russia to wage war would not have been diminished. With the neutralization of the coast, the security of the Hudson's Bay Company possessions was assured at no cost to Great Britain.

For the Hudson's Bay Company, the neutrality agreement was highly beneficial. Trade along the coast, including the leased territory, continued without interruption. Since the Russians, cut off from their base of supplies by British and French warships, were unable to prosecute their trade on the islands with their accustomed vigor, the coastal trade was brought more firmly under the control of the Hudson's Bay Company. The Company was even able to rent the privilege of cutting ice in the vicinity of Taku to a San Francisco company, and the ice business was carried on without interruption to the end of the war.[37]

The ice contract and the demand of San Francisco for lumber, which was available in abundance on the leased territory, caused the Russians to seek modification of the contract when negotiations began for its renewal. With remarkably little haggling the two companies agreed to renew the lease until January 1, 1862, on the same terms as before, except that the Russian company reserved control over ice, timber, coal, and salt fish, and was thus free to make separate contracts for the exploitation of these commodities.[38]

Sir George Simpson expressed his pleasure at the renewal of the lease and the prolongation of the "good understanding" between the two companies, though he foresaw possible interference with the fur trade by contractors for ice, timber, coal, or fish who might not scrupulously confine themselves to the terms of their concessions.[39] But a far greater threat impended. New Caledonia in 1858 ceased to be a fur-trade preserve. Gold, which had attracted to California the most adventurous and the most turbulent of the world's population, was found in quantity in the Fraser River valley. Within a few months the valleys of the Fraser and its tributaries, hitherto frequented only by fur traders and Indians, were occupied by a mining population of 10,000 men. The end of the fur-trade domination of the northwest coast was at hand, and it was appropriate that the Hudson's Bay Company's license of exclusive trade should expire in the same year that the mainland of western British North America was invaded by those who would make ineffective all attempts to enforce such special privilege. New Caledonia became British Columbia; [40] a new era had begun.

Not only did gold miners disrupt the fur trade of their immediate vicinity, but those who came to enrich themselves by supplying the miners entered any area of trade which gave promise of profit. The fur trade, for so long conducted at monopoly prices, appeared attractive to many of them. Competition, which the Company had eradicated from the northwest coast, now appeared in a new and more virulent form. First British Columbia and then the leased territory of Russian America became the haunts of the petty trader, with the usual results. By July, 1861, the governor and committee had heard from their officers on Vancouver Island that the leased territory had been invaded by petty traders who undersold the Company and sold liquor to the natives. They protested to the Russian American Company that it was the duty of the latter either to protect the trade against such incursions or to lower the rent. The reply was not encouraging. The Russians acknowledged no responsibility since they carried on no trade in the leased territory. They professed to have neither the power nor the means to prevent the invasion of petty traders, but they did promise, if the Hudson's Bay Company notified them of the appearance of a ship engaged illegally in the fur trade, to send a vessel to "take measures of repression." Such police action after the culprit had flown could hardly be effective. Instead of providing aid and comfort, the directors of the Russian American Company proposed only to extend the lease on the same terms to June 1, 1863, a date selected because the question of renewing the charter was under consideration by the tsarist government.[41] The Hudson's Bay Company agreed,[42] thus indicating that competition had not yet become so serious as to eliminate profit, but also providing itself with an opportunity for more mature consideration of measures necessary to meet mounting competition.

Information received during the next year convinced the governor and committee that competition could not be disposed of without serious loss and that the lease had become practically valueless. Not only were petty traders becoming more numerous, but there were reports that Indians, after purchasing blankets and other supplies from the Company, had on occasion sold these goods to petty traders at one-tenth their value in exchange for liquor.[43] The governor and committee therefore informed the Russians that they would not renew the lease.[44]

Their communication had a tone of finality; there was none of the temporizing that had characterized previous suggestions for alteration in the terms of the agreement. To the directors of the Russian American Company, the prospective loss of an annual revenue of £1,500 was depressing, especially since they possessed neither the power nor the inclination to compete with the petty traders whom the more efficient British company could not control. They therefore professed a willingness to do everything within their power to help control the competition.[45] The initial reaction of the Hudson's Bay Company was to reaffirm its intention to give up the lease. During the autumn of 1862, however, the governor and committee received less discouraging information from their Pacific Coast representatives, which led them to believe that retention of the lease might yet be advantageous. They consequently offered to accept a renewal for a one- or two-year period,[46] and the Russian company gladly accepted the longer term.[47]

Reversal of the decision to terminate the lease was motivated by the sharp decline in the production of gold from the river bars where it had first been found and a consequent depression in the fortunes of merchants who had supplied not only the miners but the fur traders. The discovery of gold in the Cariboo Mountains brought a second rush of miners and a temporary return of prosperity to British Columbia, but the petty traders in the leased territory and in British Columbia decreased in numbers and strength. The fur trade of the West again became profitable for the Hudson's Bay Company. Company steamships cruising along the coast during the autumn of 1862 engaged in such a brisk trade that they disposed of all their goods and returned to Victoria for further supplies to satisfy the demand along the Russian frontier. This improvement in the fortunes of the fur trade caused the suspension of plans to evacuate the coastal strip and possibly the entire area of British North America west of the Rocky Mountains.[48]

The fluid state of trade prevented a decision by the governor and committee on the desirability of continued operations on the northwest coast before the cession of Alaska to the United States eliminated the need for further consideration. The lease was renewed for a year in 1865 and again in 1866. But before American acquisition removed the Hudson's Bay Company from the strip north of Stikine, an incident occurred which suggests either that the Russian American Company was ill informed on the intentions of its government or that Russia by the beginning of 1865 had not decided on the future of its North American dominions.

In January, 1865, A. Rutkovski arrived in London as the agent of the Russian American Company, which wanted to replace the short-term lease with a more lasting engagement giving the Hudson's Bay Company full responsibility for police operations against the intrusions of petty traders. There were two alternatives by which this objective could be achieved: sale of the leased territory to the Hudson's Bay Company, or extension of the lease to include the fur trade not only of the mainland but of the adjacent islands. Although Rutkovski implied that the Russian government might consider selling the leased territory to the Hudson's Bay Company, he made no mention of a possible purchase price nor did he provide further details to indicate that such a transfer was seriously proposed.[49] Rutkovski, however, was authorized to offer an enlargement of the lease giving the Hudson's Bay Company a monopoly of the maritime and land fur trade from Stikine to Mount Saint Elias. He proposed that the Hudson's Bay Company pay a rental of £3,000 a year for the privilege of collecting all furs on the coast and islands of Russian America south of Mount Saint Elias. The Russian American Company would retain control of their settlement at Sitka and of the adjacent islands, where they would enjoy exclusive control over the ice and lumber trades and the fisheries. On these islands the Russians would continue the fur trade but only as agents of the Hudson's Bay Company. In all other sections of the leased territory, the British company would assume exclusive privileges of trade except for the sale of ice, which would remain a Russian monopoly.[50]

Such a proposal would have been unhesitatingly accepted had it been made twenty years earlier. But the same uncertainties of the value of the trade which induced the Russians to make such an offer in 1865 prevented the Hudson's Bay Company from accepting. A contract to pay £3,000 rent per year for the five-year lease suggested by Rutkovski was hazardous at a time when there was no assurance of continuing profits. The governor and committee were unwilling to undertake a commitment without further reassurance from their officers on the Pacific Coast, but because of the possibility that profits might yet be made they were not inclined to reject the offer completely. They therefore offered to sign a contract for £2,000 per year on a five-year lease, hoping in this way to keep the negotiations open pending the receipt of additional information from the western department. Since Rutkovski was not authorized to accept any such reduction, he returned to St. Petersburg.[51]

When the tsar in April, 1866, agreed to renew the charter of the Russian American Company until 1886, the directors proposed continuation of the old lease for one year so that discussions might be resumed for an enlarged lease.[52] Before such negotiations could begin, the Russian government had decided to sell the territory to the United States.

The replacement of Russia by the United States as the sovereign power in Alaska had more far-reaching effects for the Hudson's Bay Company than the end of its lease. On the assumption that Russia's commitments in the Anglo-Russian convention of 1825 would be equally binding upon the United States as its successor, the officers of the western department revived with some modifications the project that had produced the Stikine episode in 1835. They sent the steamship *Otter* to the Stikine River with instructions to pass up that stream into British territory to trade with the Indians of the interior.

The Americans, unlike Wrangell, did not threaten force if the British attempted to enter the river. Their technique in 1867 was more subtle, more vexatious, and more effective. Customs officials informed the captain of the *Otter* that, before proceeding up the Stikine, he must first obtain clearance from the headquarters at Sitka. The voyage from Stikine to Sitka involved threading through approximately 360 miles of intricate and dangerous inland waterways, but the harassments of the captain did not end with completion of the journey. At Sitka he was required to pay $150 for lighthouse dues, although there was no lighthouse in the vicinity. Even in Washington Territory, where the Company had suffered embarrassments at the hands of customs officials, no such impositions had been made, and three lighthouses were in operation there.[53]

After the *Otter* had twice paid lighthouse dues for the non-existent lighthouse at Sitka, the Company protested to the British government that the Americans were violating the Anglo-Russian treaty of 1825. The Company was informed that it had no legal case. The United States, wrote the spokesman of the Foreign Office, was bound by the provisions of the treaty only so far as the boundaries of Russian and British territory were concerned. Other concessions made by Russia to Great Britain, including the right of navigation, were no longer in effect.[54] The British government, already embroiled with the United States in the *Alabama* claims controversy, was apparently not inclined to add another subject of dispute by representations against the petty irritations of customs officials in a remote area of the Pacific.

The cession of Alaska to the United States ended a trade which was already deteriorating, and which would probably have soon ceased to be profitable to the Hudson's Bay Company even had the territory remained in Russian hands. Settlement on Vancouver Island and in British Columbia contaminated the fur trade far beyond the agricultural and mining frontiers. Many of the petty traders had suffered losses in 1863 and 1864, and many had been forced to retire, but others came to replace them. Their intrusion into the previous sanctuary of the Hudson's Bay Company under-mined the price structure on which the Company depended for profitable operations on the northwest coast. Even if the United States had not acquired Alaska, it seems likely that the Company, in recognition of the new era of mining and settlement, would have abandoned its lease and withdrawn into the interior.

Territorial expansion of the Hudson's Bay Company was at an end. The new era required more effective government than the Company could provide. The Hudson's Bay and North West companies, by their explorations and trading posts, had laid the basis for British claims to the northwest coast. The amalgamated Company had been the primary pressure group influencing the Foreign Office in its negotiations with other states. Its knowledge of the land was indispensable to the prosecution of the British case in the boundary dispute. British Columbia became British rather than American or Russian largely because of the work of a small number of fur traders and of the capitalists they represented. Pursuit of profits thus resulted in the expansion of British political authority into northwest America.

PART

# III

# The Oregon Question and Its Aftermath

# The Oregon Dispute, 1821-1838

IN THE BOUNDARY NEGOTIATIONS between Britain and Russia, the interests of two fur-trading companies had been the fundamental factor motivating the claims and counterclaims of the diplomats. In the boundary dispute with the United States, the basis for the British case was also the trade of the North West Company and the Hudson's Bay Company on the Pacific Coast. Against the Hudson's Bay Company there was no important American economic interest until settlers arrived in the 1840's. After 1825 American competition from the east was insignificant, and after 1830 American sea captains had ceased to be a menace. Yet the Hudson's Bay Company and the British government were forced to accept defeat in their controversy with the United States.

Obviously, there were elements in the American negotiations which were absent in the dispute with Russia. The influx of settlers was certainly a factor in the final decision, but it cannot entirely explain the insistence of the United States government during the previous quarter century on a boundary no farther south than the 49th parallel. In that insistence, the desire to control the protected waters of Puget Sound was a dominant consideration, for American statesmen from John Quincy Adams to James Buchanan recognized the value of the harbors in the sound for the expansion of American trade in the Pacific. But there was another factor that transcended economics. Protagonists in the United States developed a conviction that "Oregon" must become a part of their country, and that it was rightfully American by what came to be called "manifest destiny." Against such enthusiasm the force of the Hudson's Bay Company was insufficient. In 1846 the location of the Oregon boundary was of great moment in the United States and of relatively little consequence in Great Britain.

The British fur trade determined the conditions of British diplomacy with regard to western America. The Nootka Sound Convention of 1790 had resulted from an altercation between John Meares, a ship captain searching for furs, and Estevan José Martínez, sent by the viceroy of Mexico to assert Spanish authority. The trade of the North West Company was the dominant material interest that Britain sought to protect in the negotiations leading to the convention for "free and open" occupation in 1818. After the coalition of 1821, the Hudson's Bay Company was the most important positive force influencing the British position, as it continued to be until the final decision of 1846. As the dispute continued, however, material interests came to be overlaid with considerations of national pride and prestige.

As a chartered monopoly in an age increasingly devoted to the idea of free trade, the Company was unpopular with most British politicians. Attacks upon its privileges won easy applause in Parliament, but it was nevertheless a British company and those who attacked it as a domestic institution were usually prepared to support it in its conflicts with foreign states. The protection of the Company's rights in Oregon was thus the concern of the British government; and the course of British policy in the boundary dispute cannot be understood without reference to the influence of the Company.

By the retention of its Columbia posts the Company expected to provide British diplomats with their most potent argument for a boundary settlement based upon the line of the Columbia River. The country to the south of the river they assumed would be American. The area of dispute was the land lying between the Columbia River and the 49th parallel. As in the Russian boundary settlement, the Company was not content to play a passive role but utilized all its influence to keep the government stanch on its behalf.

For almost three years after the coalition, the Company showed little interest in the Columbia boundary, for it was preoccupied with the threat of the tsar's ukase of 1821. The United States at first appeared to be a potential ally of Great Britain in prospective negotiations with Russia. Thus agitation by such expansionists as Congressman John Floyd was not initially regarded as foreshadowing any serious attempt by the American government to assert its authority. Perhaps indirectly inspired by Floyd's efforts to arouse the American people, a rumor reached London in the summer of 1822 that a party of 180 persons had left Missouri with the intention of crossing the Rocky Mountains and perhaps of settling on the Columbia, and that the United States government would support American colonization in that area.[1] But when the reports proved unfounded, anxiety subsided.

The attention of the governor and committee was again directed to the southern boundary in the spring of 1824. John Quincy Adams saw in the triangular conflict over the northern boundary of Oregon the opportunity for the United States to extract concessions from Great Britain in exchange for American support. In 1823 he had admitted that the United States had no territorial claims as far north as 51°.[2] Nevertheless, in 1824 he instructed the American minister, Richard Rush, to make a suggestion to Great Britain which he knew would be unacceptable to Canning but which he hoped might produce a "compromise" at the 49th parallel. On April 3, two weeks before the signature of the Russo-American convention, Rush proposed that during the next ten years no settlement be made on the northwest coast of America by citizens of the United States north of 51° or by British subjects either south of 51° or north of 55°.[3]

Canning was not deceived by the American proposal, which he recognized as intended for bargaining purposes. Although there is no direct evidence, he probably consulted with Governor John Henry Pelly before replying, for his response could only have been made after discussion with the Company. Canning was prepared to prosecute the British case even more strenuously against the Americans than against the Russians because he regarded the United States as a nation with ambitions beyond its just claims or its physical power. The overbearing Yankees, he was convinced, must be restrained, and the conviction strengthened his determination to uphold the Company's claims. As he wrote Sir Charles

---

[1] For notes to chap. 9, see pp. 453–454.

Bagot, "We shall have a squabble with the Yankees yet in and about those regions." [4] That quarrel he was not inclined to avoid by territorial concessions. He therefore instructed the British commissioners, William Huskisson and Stratford Canning, to propose precisely the boundary that the Hudson's Bay Company requested:

> . . . the Boundary Line shall be carried due West across the Rocky Mountains, along the forty-ninth Parallel of Latitude, until it strikes the main North-Eastern Branch of the Columbia, designated in the Maps as McGillivray's River, and thence down along the whole of its Course to where it empties itself into the Pacifick Ocean. [5]

This boundary would involve the Company's renunciation of its trade in the Snake country and in the remainder of Oregon south of the Columbia, but the concession was a minor one since the country was being exhausted by trapping parties. As Canning said, the only matters of substantial importance to the Hudson's Bay Company were "the undisputed Possession of the whole Country on the Right Bank of the Upper Columbia, and a free issue for its Produce by the Channel of that River." [6]

The two assumptions on which the Company and Canning based their demands were that possession of the territory between the Columbia River and the 49th parallel was essential to the protection to the fur trade of New Caledonia, and that the Columbia was the only practicable means of communication between the northern posts and the coast. These assumptions remained fundamental to the British case for the next twenty years, and Rush's counterproposal of the 49th parallel as the boundary was consequently unacceptable.

Although the negotiations of 1824 ended in deadlock, the governor and committee expected them to be resumed after Rush had consulted further with his government. They were confident that the resoluteness of Canning would bring the United States to accept the boundary he had proposed. But even under the most favorable settlement they could not hope to retain their posts on the south bank of the river, and at Fort George the Company conducted its trade on the sufferance of the Americans, who could take possession whenever they desired. The London board therefore advised John Dugald Cameron, in charge at Fort George, not to construct new buildings or make extensive repairs, and to find a new situation on the north bank of the river to which the business of the fort might be moved.[7]

The board's decision was based also on George Canning's view that such action was desirable. At an interview with Pelly, probably the same at which the British reply to Rush was discussed, Canning suggested that the British case might be strengthened by voluntary withdrawal from a place rightfully owned by the United States. At the time Canning was under the misapprehension that restitution of the post had taken place in 1815 as a result of the Treaty of Ghent. He later discovered that the decision had been made in 1818 by a cabinet of which he was a member, under conditions that were "absolutely unjustifiable, and will not bear the light of discussion." This, however, did not change his view that the Company should leave Fort George. He wrote to Liverpool:

> . . . it is one thing to give up a settlement which nobody used, and another to abandon half a continent. In truth, though we ought not to have withdrawn, as we did, from Astoria, to withdraw from it was not ill policy. It lies on the south side of the Columbia, to which we are not unwilling to abjure all claim, keeping the north to ourselves. The cession of Astoria was therefore in furtherance of our present proposition. It now makes our present ground stronger by showing how willingly we departed from that part of it which we thought untenable.[8]

On his first journey to the Columbia, George Simpson was given the responsibility of supervising the transfer of the Columbia district headquarters from Fort George to the north bank of the Columbia River.[9] The new location envisaged by the governor and committee was somewhere near the mouth of the Fraser River, from which they hoped that both the New Caledonia and Columbia districts would be supplied.[10] Simpson, however, found the Fraser unnavigable through part of its course, and subsequent investigations, culminating in his second personal survey of the river in 1828, convinced the governor and committee that the Fraser was not a satisfactory means of communication. The functions of Fort George as a trading post, as distinct from its position as a headquarters, could be assumed only by another fort in its immediate vicinity, but on the north bank of the Columbia.

Simpson was given an additional incentive to hasten the abandonment of Fort George when in the summer of 1824 he heard another rumor that the United States government intended to plant a colony at the mouth of the Columbia during the spring and summer of 1825. Such an expedition would certainly take possession of Fort George and, if no alternative trading post had been constructed, would seriously embarrass the Company in its trade on the lower reaches of the Columbia.[11]

There was some basis for these reports of American intentions. In his message to Congress in December, 1824, President Monroe had recommended the establishment of a military post at the mouth of the Columbia or at some other point within the "acknowledged limits of the United States." [12] Congressman Floyd, who required no encouragement to make proposals for the advancement of American claims, immediately introduced a bill providing not only for the establishment of a post but for the creation of an Oregon territory under the United States from the Mexican border to an unspecified northern limit, presumably the Russian frontier at 54° 40'. Floyd's bill actually passed the House of Representatives and received strong support in the Senate.[13]

On his way west in the fall of 1824, Simpson carried with him the conviction that, though Floyd had failed, the resumption of American authority at Fort George could not be long deferred. Shortly after his arrival there in November, he sent Chief Factors McLoughlin and Kennedy upstream to look for a suitable site. They could find no location nearer the sea than Belle Vue Point (so named by Lieutenant William R. Broughton, a member of Vancouver's staff), situated just above the confluence of the Willamette and Columbia rivers. Construction was begun there during the winter of 1824–25. On March 19, 1825, Simpson formally christened the new post Fort Vancouver, to emphasize that the Company's right to occupy the territory rested on Vancouver's discoveries.[14]

Fort Vancouver, although more remote from the ocean than Fort George, possessed the advantage of good soil. The cultivation of crops and the raising of livestock, particularly in remote districts, were highly desirable since transportation of provisions was expensive. This was the sole basis for the beginning of agriculture and stock raising at Fort Vancouver, but the possibility of utilizing such activity as an argument in diplomatic negotiations quickly became apparent to the governor and committee.

Although no Americans appeared, the Company abandoned Fort George on June 7, 1825.[15] The botanist John Scouler, who visited it in September, found it "entirely abandoned by the settlers, and taken possession of by the Indians who are rapidly reducing it to a state of ruin and filth." [16] The post remained deserted until 1829 when, after the ships of Captain Dominis appeared, Simpson and McLoughlin sent a clerk to the old establishment to offer the opposition more direct competition than Fort Vancouver could provide.

The only permanent post south of the boundary line proposed by Canning was Fort Nez Percés, which the governor and committee also wanted removed to the north bank. To the London board, the transfer of a post to the other side of the river must have seemed a simple undertaking. To the officers on the spot, the problem was more complicated. The Nez Percé Indians, whose hunting grounds were south of the river, could not be ignored. When McLoughlin visited Walla Walla in the fall of 1825, he told the Nez Percé chiefs of the Company's intentions, and gained the impression that they would not oppose the transfer.[17] The chiefs, however, changed their minds, and at the end of the winter informed Chief Trader Samuel Black, who was in charge of the post, that it must not be moved. When Black said that he must carry out his orders, the chiefs tried to influence him by proffering him gifts of beaver and horses, and, when that persuasion failed, resorted to threats.[18] Since the trade of the post depended upon the good will of the Nez Percés, it was obviously impolitic to antagonize them. The project was suspended by McLoughlin and was not reopened when the breakdown of negotiations between the United States and Great Britain made unlikely an immediate settlement of the boundary controversy.[19]

The stalemate occurred after Canning, impelled by the Company, had made a further effort to conclude a treaty. Simpson arrived in London in the fall of 1825 for conferences on basic policy with the governor and committee. Among the subjects of importance was the trade of the Columbia district, upon which Simpson could now speak with an authority based upon firsthand observation. The outcome of discussions between Pelly and Simpson was the decision to press Canning to reopen negotiations with the United States.

The claims of the Company and of Great Britain could not be stronger than they were in 1825. The Company's employees were the sole European occupants of the Oregon country; their exclusive control might not long continue; and rumors of American expeditions to the Columbia might at any time become reality. Simpson therefore drafted a letter [20] that embodied the joint conclusions of Pelly and himself. Pelly signed it and sent it to Canning on December 9, 1825. This letter is important, not because it contained significant new information, but because it stimulated Canning to try again to bring the Oregon dispute to a conclusion. The line Pelly now suggested was considerably more favorable to Great Britain than his and Canning's proposal of the year before:

> . . . starting from Lat: 49 at the Rocky Mountains the line ought to be continued Southward along the height of land to the place where Lewis and Clarke crossed the Mountains, said to be in Lat: 46.42 thence westerly along the Lewis's [Snake] River until it falls into the Columbia and thence to the sea, leaving the navigation of both these Rivers free to the subjects of both nations.
>
> This line would leave to America the Trade and possession of an Extensive & valuable country, and would furnish fewer opportunities of Collision between the Traders of the two nations than any other line that could be suggested.[21]

In suggesting a boundary farther south than had ever been seriously proposed by any British statesman, Pelly was unquestionably asking more than he expected to gain, hoping thus to "compromise" for the line he actually wanted. His proposal could be defended by the argument that the Company controlled the trade of some of the territory that would be granted to the United States, as well as of the area assigned to Britain, but he must have recognized that there was no possibility of any American government's accepting a boundary less favorable to it than the one proposed by Canning in 1824.

The aggressive expression of the British case in the Simpson-Pelly letter was well attuned to the mood of George Canning at the end of 1825. In his larger sphere, Canning was as ardent an advocate of the expansion of British trade and influence as were

Pelly and Simpson. But greater zest was added to his acceptance of Pelly's plea by his increasing antipathy to the government of the United States. His old diplomatic adversary John Quincy Adams was now president. Canning had not yet received a copy of Adams' message to Congress in December, 1825, recommending again that a post be established on the Columbia, but the mentality of Adams, so curiously like his own in its assertive nationalism, was repugnant to him. Delay worked on the side of the Americans; Canning resolved to press again the British case while it was at its strongest.

For Canning's purposes the presence of Simpson in London was fortunate, since he possessed greater knowledge of the Columbia area than any other man, with the possible exception of Company officers stationed there. Canning therefore asked Henry U. Addington, permanent undersecretary of state for foreign affairs, to secure from Simpson additional information of value for the British case. After a conference with Simpson on December 30,[22] Addington asked him to provide written answers, "the more matter of fact the better," to a series of questions. The questions and answers indicate the approach Canning hoped to use in his forthcoming negotiations with the United States. The answers revealed that the Columbia River was the only satisfactory means of inland water communication west of the Rocky Mountains, the lands it drained were controlled by the Company, and the fur trade of the district, "yet in its infancy," produced from £30,000 to £40,000 worth of furs every year. Without the control of the Columbia, Simpson contended, the Company "must abandon and curtail their Trade in some parts, and probably be constrained to relinquish it on the West side of the Rocky Mountains altogether." [23]

By April, 1826, Canning felt the British case to be sufficiently well formulated. He requested the American minister, Rufus King, to inform his government of Great Britain's desire to reopen negotiations. Adams accepted the invitation and appointed Albert Gallatin, King's successor, as the American representative.

The subsequent negotiations were foredoomed to failure because of conflicts within the British cabinet. Not only was the ambitious, unorthodox Canning distrusted by the more conservative Tories, but there was a conflict of basic principles which the Oregon dispute served to emphasize. Canning was an economic imperialist in an age when such ideas were increasingly at variance with accepted economic doctrine in Great Britain. Although he was not an advocate of vested monopolies such as the Hudson's Bay Company, he visualized the Company as the representative of a vast general British interest in its prosecution of trade on the Pacific Coast. The issue, as Canning conceived it, was not the preservation of the fur trade, but rather the maintenance of a British colony on the shores of the Pacific which might be an important contributor to trade with the Orient. As he wrote to the prime minister, Lord Liverpool, in an effort to persuade him to support a strong stand on Oregon,

> We cannot yet enter into this trade, on account of the monopoly of the E. I. Cy. But ten years hence that monopoly will cease; and though at that period neither you nor I shall be where we are to answer for our deeds, I should not like to leave my name affixed to any instrument by which England would have foregone the advantages of an immense direct intercourse between China and what may be, if we resolve not to yield them up, her boundless establishments on the N. W. Coast of America.[24]

Canning's arguments did not convince Liverpool, nor, apparently, did they completely convince even the Canningites. William Huskisson, president of the Board of Trade, who usually supported Canning, seems to have been among those who regarded the Oregon controversy as of little consequence to British interests. Huskisson had already struck heavy blows at mercantilist conceptions by loosening the regulations that had promoted a self-contained empire. He, like Canning, was ardently devoted to the expansion of British trade; but, unlike the foreign secretary, he could not agree that the retention of a few thousand square miles of the west coast of America substantially contributed to that end. The appointment of Huskisson as one of the British commissioners to treat with Gallatin was therefore an augury that the British case would be less strongly prosecuted than Canning himself would have desired. In July, 1826, before the negotiations began, Huskisson followed Addington's precedent of addressing a series of questions to the Hudson's Bay Company. Huskisson's questionnaire, unlike Addington's, was concerned with claims based on British priority in exploration and occupation of the disputed territory.[25] Such questions were relevant to the presentation of an effective

British case, but were of little value unless combined with a strong assertion of British rights based upon actual occupation. Huskisson lacked enthusiasm for the latter. He and the other commissioner, Addington, began well enough by offering again Canning's boundary of 1824 and by reaffirming British intentions to protect British interests. But when Gallatin objected that such a boundary would give Britain all the best anchorages on the Pacific Coast, Huskisson offered to assign the United States a detached triangle of territory on the Olympic Peninsula from Gray's Harbor to Juan de Fuca Strait, which provided access to Admiralty Inlet and the Hood Canal. The proposal was unacceptable to Gallatin. The British commissioners in turn rejected the American's proposal of the 49th parallel as the boundary, with the privilege of British navigation on the Columbia should that river or any of its tributaries prove navigable north of that line.

In their boundary offer, Huskisson and Addington went beyond the concessions Canning was personally willing to make, but their actions can be justified as attempts to reach agreement without sacrificing the substantial interests of the Hudson's Bay Company. If Gallatin's report of the conversations with the British negotiators is correct, however, Huskisson undermined the British case by his admissions. He left Gallatin with the impression that the British government had no intention of colonizing the Oregon territory, and that they had "no other immediate object than that of protecting the Northwest [Hudson's Bay] Company in her fur-trade." Huskisson allegedly averred, however, that the Company was of little weight, and the dominant issue was actually British prestige. Gallatin conceived from Huskisson's comments that

National pride prevents any abrupt relinquishment of her pretensions; but Great Britain does not seem indisposed to let the country gradually and silently slide into the hands of the United States, and she is anxious that it should not, in any case, become the cause of a rupture between the two powers.[26]

Such damaging statements by the principal British commissioner could hardly lead to concessions, even had the American plenipotentiary been so inclined. The negotiations were deadlocked, and were finally terminated in August, 1827, by an agreement to prolong the convention of 1818 indefinitely, subject to abrogation by either party on a year's notice.

The renewal of the convention worked to the advantage of the United States. Though it left the Hudson's Bay Company in control of the entire Oregon country, the part that the Company and Canning had offered to the United States was virtually worthless to the fur trade. The Company could not strengthen the bargaining position it occupied in 1825; any change thereafter would be a deterioration. Yet there was no possibility of a solution favorable to the Company even had Canning's views been accepted by the British cabinet. The only means of forcing the United States to accept the line of the Columbia was war, and not even Canning was willing to support the Company to that extent. On the other hand, the only means of speedily ousting the Company from Oregon, as a few American expansionists demanded, was also war, and no responsible American statesman was yet prepared to take such a step. The Oregon question in the 1820's was a minor issue to both Britain and the United States; it became a major issue to the United States in the 1840's. This is the background for the eventual American diplomatic victory.

On the day that the renewal of the "joint occupation" was signed, George Canning died. In that coincidence there was an omen, for any hopes the Hudson's Bay Company might have had for vigorous support of its Oregon claims died with him. No future foreign secretary would prosecute the case of the Company and of Great Britain with the vigor that Canning had displayed. The Oregon question lapsed, to be revived by the outburst of American expansionism in the 1840's which swept James K. Polk into the presidency.

Oregon had been almost forgotten by the politicians; only the Hudson's Bay Company remained preoccupied with the prospects of the territory. The failure of the British negotiators to win the Columbia boundary line was a disappointment to the governor and committee, who had expected the Americans to accept the line and an enclave on the coast as a reasonable division. The prospect of continued stalemate led them to reconsider their Oregon policy. There could be no change in the frontier policy of opposition to American traders whenever they appeared, but the London board decided that it had been a mistake to accept with such alacrity Canning's suggestion that the Company move its posts north of the river. By so doing, they concluded, they had weakened the

British bargaining position. They accordingly sent Simpson the following instructions:

> The Country on the West of the Mountains remaining common to the Americans and us for an indefinite period determinable by a years notice from either Government it becomes an important object to acquire as ample an occupation of the Country and Trade as possible, on the South as well as on the North side of the Columbia River, looking always to the Northern side as falling to our Share on a division, and to secure this, it may be as well to have something to give up on the South, when the final arrangements come to be made.[27]

These were brave words, but the resources the Company was prepared to devote to "occupation" of the Columbia were pitifully small. There were in the employ of the Company on the Columbia only 224 men and 21 officers and clerks, who were needed to staff the posts and to serve on the Snake and southern expeditions,[28] and the northern council provided no substantial reinforcements in response to the governor and committee's suggestion for a more active policy.[29] The post of Walla Walla remained south of the river, and the Company reoccupied Fort George in 1829, but there was no significant increase in trading activity as the result of the governor and committee's decision. A company whose principal objective was profit was not an effective instrument for the occupation of an area the size of the Oregon territory south of the Columbia River, in which no profit could be made. The only new station built by the Company south of the Columbia was Fort Umpqua, constructed in 1832, an insignificant post on the south side of the Umpqua River three miles below the mouth of Elk Creek.[30] The energies of the Company were directed to the expansion of the coasting trade of the northwest coast and intensification of competition with the Russian American Company, rather than to the unprofitable task of occupying southern Oregon. The Company therefore continued to rely upon the same basic policy after 1828 that it had employed previously—to prevent the entry into Oregon of American fur traders by rendering trade unprofitable to them.

The corollary of this policy was that the Company's officers should not provide aid and encouragement to Americans who visited the posts. This principle was increasingly stressed by the

governor and committee, who made McLoughlin's allegedly excessive hospitality to American visitors the occasion for their emphasis. They approved his assistance to Jedediah Smith after the
massacre of Smith's men on Umpqua River, since "all feelings of
self interest must be laid aside when we can relieve or assist our
Fellow creatures." [31] But Wyeth was in no such state of desperation,
and McLoughlin's cordial relationship with him caused the governor and committee to instruct the chief factor to assist no
strangers unless they presented a letter of introduction either from
the governor and committee or from Simpson, or were in such distress that considerations of humanity dictated the provision of aid.
Moreover, the stay of a distressed stranger should be as short as
possible.[32]

McLoughlin did not carry out these instructions, and his continued hospitality to American visitors vexed his superiors. Although he induced the missionary Jason Lee and his associates,
who arrived with Wyeth in 1834, to settle south of the Columbia
on the Willamette River, he did not treat them with the chilly
aloofness recommended by London headquarters. Rather, he gave
them supplies and assistance. Some have discerned in McLoughlin's
actions toward missionaries and later toward settlers an ulterior
motivation. Such critics allege that he was a republican, since he
demonstrated sympathy with the Canadian rebels in 1837, and
was therefore sympathetic to the Americans. This view has no
foundation in fact. McLoughlin's preoccupation was with trade,
not with politics. He was devoted to the enlargement of profits
for his Company and himself, and his actions in Oregon were
dominated by a mercantile motivation. The political overtones
were not apparent to him as they were to the governor and committee. To McLoughlin, it was incredible that his hospitality to
American visitors should in any way affect diplomatic decisions
on the future of Oregon, and the record of the final stages of the
Oregon crisis largely supports his view. But his actions were contrary to the views of the governor and committee and of the British
government, who feared serious political consequences.

Until 1838 the governor and committee had good cause to believe that their basic techniques of opposition to American penetration into Oregon had been sound. Though there were recurrent
rumors of impending American expeditions for settlement along

the Columbia, no large parties had reached Oregon. The assumption that American settlement could be delayed by the discouragement of American fur traders seemed justified. But events of the 1830's destroyed this illusion. The arrival of William A. Slacum on the Columbia in December, 1836, was evidence of a renewed American interest in Oregon. Slacum was sent by Jackson's secretary of state, John Forsyth, to acquire information that might be of value to the United States when negotiations were reopened. To this evidence of governmental activity was added the existence in the Willamette valley of a tiny American agricultural community around the core of missionaries. In 1838 the Willamette settlement numbered twenty-eight adult American males, including ten clergymen; six American women, the wives of missionaries; and twenty-three Canadian freemen, formerly attached to the Company's service. The community was significant not for what it was but for what it might become. As James Douglas declared, these "restless Americans" were an enterprising people, their settlement was annually growing in importance, and if they prospered, their community could exercise "a greater influence than desirable over our affairs." [33]

The disturbing signs of American enterprise convinced the governor and committee that the Company should reëxamine its policies in Oregon. They summoned McLoughlin and Simpson to London for a series of conferences, which took place at the end of 1838. The result was a decision to promote agricultural settlement under Company control north of the Columbia. The agency created to carry out the program was the Puget's Sound Agricultural Company.

# 10

# The Puget's Sound
# Agricultural Company

THE HUDSON'S BAY COMPANY existed primarily for the purpose of making profits for its stockholders; the Company became involved in international disputes because, in pursuit of profit, it desired to expand the area of British North America to the maximum possible extent. Since patriotism can be uninhibited when it is in accord with material self-interest, the governor and committee were undoubtedly sincere in professing patriotic as well as mercantile motives in every question of expansion. The interests of the Hudson's Bay Company, however, were not identical with the interests of the United Kingdom, although the governor and committee were prone to regard them as being so in western North America. This self-delusion was demonstrated when they created the Puget's Sound Agricultural Company. The history of the agricultural company graphically illustrates the defects of a chartered trading monopoly as an instrument for the attainment of political ends.

The pursuit of agriculture as an occupation auxiliary to the fur trade was not in itself an innovation. The London board had long encouraged the Company's officers to raise crops to supply the requirements of the posts, thus reducing consumption of expensive imported food. After the coalition of 1821, Simpson, too, requested the officers to plant crops, much to the gratification of the governor and committee.[1]

The supply of foodstuffs from the immediate locality was of particular importance on the Pacific Coast, since that area was the most remote sector of the Company's trade. When McLoughlin and Kennedy selected Belle Vue Point as the site for Fort Vancouver, an important reason was the evident suitability of the area for agriculture, and one of the first actions of the Company's employees after they moved to the post was to plant 100 barrels of potatoes. They also cultivated one-fourth acre of beans, and three acres of peas.[2] The herds and crops of Fort Vancouver justified McLoughlin and Kennedy's judgment. By the end of 1828, the post had 153 head of cattle, excluding calves, 50 goats, and about 200 hogs. Its residents consumed annually about 6,000 pounds of salted pork, all from its own resources. In the harvest of 1828, Fort Vancouver produced 400 bushels of Indian corn, 1,300 of wheat, 100 of barley, 300 of peas, 100 of oats, and 4,000 of potatoes.[3] It was the productivity of the soil which encouraged Simpson to hope that the post could produce a surplus for barter trade with the Russian American Company, and to make the abortive trade proposal to the Russians in 1829.

Meanwhile the Company became interested in trade with the Hawaiian Islands. Among other commodities the Islands produced hides and tallow, which could be purchased as cargo for the Company's ships on their homeward voyages to England, where there were good prospects of a profitable market for them.[4]

It occurred to McLoughlin and other officers on the Columbia [5] that the plains around Fort Vancouver could sustain large herds of cattle which would provide not only meat for the station but hides and tallow for export. They visualized cattle raising, however, as supplementary to their duties on behalf of the Hudson's Bay Company, and they desired to carry it on as a private venture. On March 10, 1832, they issued a prospectus for a joint-stock company "with the view of opening from the Oragon Country an export trade with England and elsewhere in tallow, beef, hides, horns, &c." This association was to be called "The Oragon Beef & Tallow Company," and was to have a capital of £3,000 in shares of £10 each. With the initial contribution of £5 per share from each of the proprietors, the promoters hoped to buy a herd of 700 to 800 cattle in California and to provide a reserve for operating expenses. They contemplated calling upon the stockholders in 1835 or 1836 for the remaining £5 per share, to be used for the purchase of additional cattle. Thereafter, they expected, no further assessments would be necessary, since the progressive increase in the herds and the sale of the hides and meat would produce ample revenue for operating expenses and substantial profits for the proprietors.[6]

News of McLoughlin's intentions reached the governor and committee in the fall of 1834. Their reaction was instantaneous and negative. But they and Simpson saw in the project an opportunity for the Company to develop cattle raising on a large scale on the banks of the Willamette, at Cowlitz portage, and at other places near the Pacific Coast. For a small outlay, Simpson contended, the Company could reap huge profits, for cattle would multiply on the verdant pastures of Oregon. "In short," he said, "it appears to me to hold out the prospect of becoming an extended and highly profitable branch of trade if taken up by the Company, but in the hands of a Joint Stock Association or Individual, I am decidedly of opinion it would not be found to answer." [7]

The governor and committee were impressed. Here was a potential source of additional revenue to bolster the profits of a sagging fur trade. They consequently approved Simpson's suggestion, subject to the major reservation that the cattle should be pastured north of the Columbia, since the Willamette was certain to fall to the Americans. They instructed McLoughlin to dispatch a competent person to examine Whidbey Island, the land at the head of Puget Sound, and other places that might combine most of the advantages of a good harbor, fertile soil, favorable climate, and plentiful pasture. The frequent visitation of the ague on the marshy plains around Vancouver had been a source of concern to them since the first appearance of the disease in 1826, and they had recommended that another depot be found which would be free of the disease. The new headquarters, they now believed, should be the major cattle-raising establishment as well as the center of the Oregon fur trade.[8] They suggested that McLoughlin purchase 5,000 cows and a proportionate number of bulls. As

Simpson explained, the cost of cattle in California was small—only $3 to $4 a head—and the trouble of driving 5,000 cattle was about the same as that of driving 1,000. He therefore decided that it was preferable to begin on a grand scale at once.[9] Peculiarly, Simpson's endorsement of cattle raising on the Columbia was unaffected by the failure of similar ventures at Red River.

The eagerness of the governor and committee and of Simpson was not transmitted to McLoughlin. His enthusiasm for an independent cattle-raising project was not sustained for a similar venture under Company auspices where his efforts would not result in significant returns for himself. His superiors had given him discretion as to when purchases of cattle should be made. He availed himself of that latitude to the full. It was not necessary to seek an excuse for delay, for the Russians provided him with a justification. In June, 1834, they had demonstrated hostility to the Company by warning Peter Skene Ogden and his expedition away from the Stikine River, when Ogden had been instructed to build a fort upriver in British territory.[10] The attention of the governor and committee was diverted to the north and to the necessary counteraction to force satisfaction from the Russians. They did complain to McLoughlin on January 25, 1837, of his failure to determine the eligibility of Whidbey Island as a prospective depot,[11] but the cattle-raising project was suspended.

Meanwhile, the governor and committee began negotiations with the Colonial Office on a much more important question, whose outcome affected the Company's future policy in Oregon. The license of 1821, which authorized the Company's monopoly west of Rupert's Land, was not scheduled to expire until 1842, but the board decided to seek renewal in 1837. The Whig government of Lord Melbourne held office, but the majority in Parliament was an uneasy coalition of conflicting elements, and the prolonged continuation of a ministry exhausted of constructive ideas seemed highly unlikely. Pelly and his associates were keenly aware of the antagonism toward the Company in Parliament, and knew that the prospects for renewal of the license under a Conservative government were uncertain. In the Whig party, Edward Ellice the Elder was still a powerful force, though he did not hold office; under a Conservative regime his influence would be of less consequence. Further, if the license was not to be renewed, the Company should ascertain this fact in order to prepare for the adjustment to new conditions.

These appear to have been the factors that motivated Pelly in February, 1837, to ask the secretary of state for colonies, Lord Glenelg, to renew the license. To justify his plea, Pelly recited the familiar argument that the Company had transformed the Indian country from a "scene of violence and outrage" to a "state of the most perfect tranquillity, beneficial as well to the Indian population, as to the parties interested and engaged in trade." [12] Competition had debauched the Indians; monopoly had protected them. But Pelly did not content himself with these observations. He declared to Glenelg that the Company intended to extend the cultivation of the soil around Fort Vancouver, to establish an export trade in wool, tallow, and hides, and to encourage the settlement in the Oregon territory of retired servants and "other emigrants under their protection." In this way, said Pelly, "British interests and British influence may be maintained as paramount in this interesting part of the Coast of the Pacific." [13]

The suggestion that the Company intended to promote colonization and to develop a varied trade was well conceived, since the alleged incompatibility of the fur trade with settlement had been one of the bases for parliamentary attacks on the Company. Pelly's appeal was sufficiently impressive to persuade the Committee of the Privy Council for Trade to support the renewal of the license. James Stephen, permanent undersecretary of state for colonies, prevailed upon Lord Glenelg to insist, as a condition for renewal, that the Crown reserve the right to establish colonies of settlement in any part of the Company's territories.[14] Pelly accepted this provision,[15] and another license was issued on May 30, 1838, granting the Company for twenty-one years the exclusive privilege of trade with the Indians west of Rupert's Land. Like the first license, this one specifically provided that the monopoly excluded only other British subjects, and did not affect the right of Americans to trade in the disputed territory.[16]

Pelly's correspondence with the Colonial Office produced a new emphasis in the Company's Oregon policies. Hitherto the Company had considered the Oregon territory as an area of fur trade and as a protection for the trade of New Caledonia. But Pelly had stressed in his request for renewal that the Company intended to promote agriculture and stock raising and to encourage immigration under its auspices. Thereafter the Company's defense of "British paramountcy" would have to be conducted not only by the familiar techniques of the fur trade but by the settlement of British subjects, if Pelly's promises were to be fulfilled.

When the governor and committee summoned Simpson and McLoughlin to confer with them during the summer and fall of 1838, they were thus motivated by two considerations—the necessity of promoting agriculture and stock raising, and the need for reconsidering the Company's policies for the protection of its interests in Oregon against new threats from the United States. The immediate cause of concern was a bill introduced into the Senate by Lewis F. Linn on February 7, 1838, providing for the establishment of territorial government west of the Rocky Mountains north of 42° and for the enforcement of American authority throughout Oregon by sending a military force and erecting a fort on the Columbia.[17] Similar resolutions had been introduced and had failed, but the strong Senate support of Linn's bill alarmed the governor and committee. They were convinced that passage of the bill was not only possible but probable, and that the United States would soon send a man-of-war to the Columbia with troops and supplies.[18]

The apparent likelihood of aggressive American action was both a peril and an opportunity to Simpson and the governor and committee. It was a danger because the Company could not possibly match the resources of the American government; it was an opportunity because the United States might force the conclusion, either by mutual agreement or by war, of a dispute that had continued too long. Simpson's instructions to James Douglas, written on March 8 after the news of Linn's bill had reached London, indicated the line of resistance the Company planned to take. Simpson advised Douglas to take immediate possession of one or two of "the most eligible spots" on the Columbia River at or near the entrance of the Willamette, since actual possession would strengthen claims to rights over the soil and to compensation if the Company was forced to withdraw. At Fort George (Astoria), the Company's employees must retain possession even if ordered to vacate by American officers and must not withdraw until the

Americans had committed some overt act of violence. At Tongue Point, at the entrance to the Columbia, Douglas was instructed to build a small house, to clear and cultivate plots of ground, to erect fences, and to pasture cattle. At Multnomah Island, formed by the two arms of the Willamette and by the Columbia, Douglas was to place an employee under engagement in writing to the Company who would live in a small building, cultivate a few plots of ground, and keep some cattle and pigs.[19] The object of these measures was twofold, to gain possession of the most satisfactory locations for military establishments on the south side of the Columbia below tidewater, and to create a situation likely to precipitate an incident that would force the British government to intervene on behalf of the Company. Linn's bill failed to pass, and the Americans did not come, but the sense of urgency remained in the minds of the Company's directors.

It was in this environment that the London discussions on the expansion of agricultural and pastoral production in Oregon took place. In attendance were Pelly, members of the committee, Simpson, and McLoughlin. McLoughlin, who had conceived the project as a means of enriching himself and now found it appropriated by the Company, must have had difficulty in suppressing his true sentiments. Before he left Fort Vancouver on his way to London, he had written to Douglas:

> I will take this opportunity to state it is my opinion that, though I think individuals who would devote their attention to raising cattle in the Columbia might make a living by it still it is my opinion the Hudsons Bay Company will make nothing by it.[20]

Whether McLoughlin expressed such convictions to the governor and committee is not known; probably he did, since he was forthright by nature and unschooled in dissimulation. But his pessimism did not restrain the enthusiasm of his superiors. The Foreign Office was also favorable to the plan "for political reasons." [21] One obstacle, however, was soon discovered. The Company's legal advisers expressed the opinion that the governor and committee could not, in conformity with the terms of the charter, invest any of the Company's capital in an association formed for agricultural purposes. Such action, they warned, might invalidate the charter.[22] The dilemma was solved by the expedient of creating a satellite enterprise, the Puget's Sound Agricultural Company. The agents of the new company were Pelly, Andrew Colvile, and Simpson, and ownership of stock was confined to the stockholders and officers of the Hudson's Bay Company. Each stockholder in the parent Company could buy one share of stock in the Puget's Sound Agricultural Company for each £300 of stock he held in the Hudson's Bay Company. The authorized capital of the agricultural company was set at £200,000 in £100 shares, with a deposit of 10 per cent to be paid immediately and the remainder to be paid upon later calls. To compensate McLoughlin for the additional responsibility of supervising the affairs of the new company, the governor and committee authorized an annual payment of £500, beginning June 1, 1869, to supplement the regular share of Hudson's Bay Company profits which he received as a chief factor.[23]

The majority of the stockholders displayed little interest in the purchase of shares in the new company. The Earl of Selkirk bought 164 shares, Benjamin Harrison, 56, Andrew Colvile, 11, and the Berens family, 22, but they were all associated with the management of the Company. All the Company's North American officers bought shares, but there is more than a suspicion that they did so because it was expected of them by their superiors rather than because they hoped to make a profit on their investment.[24]

The coolness of the stockholders' response to the invitation to invest can be explained in terms of their conservative suspicion of the prospects of an untried enterprise in a remote part of the world. The determination of the governor and committee to prosecute the project despite the investors' lack of interest cannot be so readily understood. The governing board believed that an agreement concluded on February 6, 1839, with the Russian American Company for the supply to the Russians of wheat, peas, barley, butter, beef, and ham made it likely that an agricultural enterprise in Oregon would yield a small profit. But in negotiating the contract with the Russians the directors had not been guided entirely by the expectation of immediate profit, but also by the desire to exclude American competition from the coast. Similarly, the Puget's Sound Agricultural Company had been organized to perform not only an economic but a political function. The directors of the Hudson's Bay Company believed that by extending agriculture they were strengthening the British claim to Oregon north of the

Columbia. The viewpoint underlying this conviction was expressed by Andrew Colvile in 1841 when he wrote to Simpson:

> It is not easy to judge of it here but I am inclined to think the best policy is to give every encouragement to the settlement of the North side & to secure all the best situations there by such an occupation as will anticipate the plans of the American Missionaries but if it is found that parties cannot be persuaded from preferring the South side to give to all who call themselves British the same or some facilities of stock on shares &c. as on the north side so as to preserve our influence & a friendly communication with the people there whilst the Country remains in its present condition which it may do until that & other points are settled with the States by a war—I fear it must end in that before the two countries will negociate in a way to settle points—during peace one or the other will feel unwilling & so put it off—but at the end of a war the treaty must come to an end & both governments should see the propriety of finally settling points of boundary.[25]

The governing board members were not unanimous in the opinion that war must be the ultimate arbiter, but they believed that physical possession would be an important factor in the boundary decisions of the diplomats whether a settlement was reached by peaceful negotiation or by a postwar treaty. The Puget's Sound Agricultural Company, they hoped, would provide the necessary reinforcement to other British claims to win the boundary of the Columbia River.

The first site selected for the operations of the agricultural company was at Cowlitz portage, between the Cowlitz and Chehalis rivers. There, on instructions from the governor and committee, a party under Chief Trader John Tod during the spring and summer of 1839 plowed 200 acres of land, sowed 275 bushels of wheat, and cleared an additional 135 acres. The Cowlitz plain, although fertile, was of limited extent. The total area available for cultivation was only about 3,000 acres,[26] and an establishment of far greater extent was needed for sheep and cattle raising. The location selected for this purpose was Fort Nisqually, which became the main station of the Puget's Sound Agricultural Company.

Fort Nisqually had been constructed in 1833 with the expectation that it would replace Fort Langley as a primary base for trade north of the Columbia. On instructions from McLoughlin, Archibald McDonald, the officer in charge at Langley, had reconnoitered the southern end of Puget Sound and reported, with some exaggeration, that the soil in the vicinity of the mouth of the Nisqually River was as good as that of Vancouver. But the country unquestionably possessed advantages, for in the level prairies large numbers of cattle could graze, and ships could come in to the shore to discharge their cargo. So impressed was McLoughlin with McDonald's report that he decided to move some of the cattle at Fort Vancouver to Nisqually and to construct a post on the sound.[27] In the summer of 1833, Francis Heron left Fort Vancouver to build the new fort.[28] Heron was not so impressed with the soil as McDonald had been, since he found it sandy and infertile, and his pessimism as to its agricultural prospects was one of the factors in McLoughlin's decision to retain the station at Fort Langley. Fort Nisqually was nevertheless built, though on a less extensive scale than originally intended.[29] Its function as a Hudson's Bay post was thereafter to collect the furs of Indians in the vicinity of Puget Sound, but the suitability of the area for raising cattle led the Company in 1839 to assign Nisqually to the Puget's Sound Agricultural Company as joint owner. The officer in charge thereafter had the responsibility both of collecting furs for the Hudson's Bay Company and of supervising the pastoral activities of the agricultural company.[30] Fort Nisqually became the latter's main station, and Cowlitz Farm remained its only other establishment.

Both stations were well adapted for their purpose. Within two years 4,530 sheep and 1,000 cattle were grazing on the plains around Fort Nisqually, and in 1841 Cowlitz Farm produced about 8,000 bushels of wheat and 4,000 bushels of oats, as well as barley, peas, and potatoes.[31] The Nisqually farm in the same year produced 1,000 bushels of wheat, 300 of oats, 50 of barley, 500 of peas, and 1,000 of potatoes, an excellent result from the relatively poor soil. But the emphasis was on sheep and cattle raising at Nisqually, and on farming at the Cowlitz portage.[32] By 1845 the number of cattle at Nisqually had increased to 2,280 and of sheep to 5,872.[33] An additional 1,000 sheep were pastured at Cowlitz Farm.[34] The cattle and most of the sheep were obtained in California and brought to Oregon both by ship and overland. The Company [35] attempted to improve the breed of sheep by sending merino, Southdown, Cheviot, and Leicester sheep of the best quality from England. But the cattle were dominantly of the breed called "Spanish cattle," scarcely the aristocrats of the bovine family. Their slim, hardy frames provided little meat and they were poor milkers, but they had two outstanding virtues—they were unusually resistant to disease and unusually prolific.

Without settlers, however, the plan of developing the agricultural potentiality of Oregon between the Columbia and the 49th parallel could not succeed. The Company hoped to attract settlers from two sources—the retired servants living in the Willamette valley, and the farming population of Great Britain, particularly Scotland. The idea of transferring the Company's ex-servants north of the Columbia had first been discussed by the governor and committee in 1837, when the bishop of Juliopolis, the head of Roman Catholic missionary work in Rupert's Land, had requested assistance for the passage of two priests across the continent to the Columbia. The request was occasioned by appeals from the French Canadian settlers in the Willamette valley for the services of a priest.[36]

In 1838 the tiny Willamette colony possessed 600 head of cattle, "a good stock of swine," and enough horses for agricultural purposes. One gristmill was in operation, another was being built, and a sawmill had just been completed. In 1836 the settlers had produced a surplus of 1,000 bushels of wheat, all of which was bought by the Hudson's Bay Company. The existence of the settlement had caused no serious difficulty for the fur trade, since it was completely dependent upon Fort Vancouver for supplies, but there were already evidences of future troubles in the restlessness of the Company's employees to escape from the service and to become settlers on the Willamette. As Douglas said:

> The interests of the Colony and Fur Trade will never harmonize, the former can flourish only, through the protection of equal laws, the influence of free trade, the accession of respectable inhabitants, in short by establishing a new order of things, while the fur Trade, must suffer by each innovation.[37]

In the Willamette settlement there was another source of danger beyond the irreconcilability of agriculture and the fur trade—the presence of the American Methodist missionaries headed by Jason Lee. These men, who were emphatically Americans as well as missionaries, might infect the colony with hostility to the Company. The Canadians were friendly to the Company they had served, and the "vagrant Americans" who had settled in the valley were, if not cordial, certainly not hostile. But the Company's officers suspected with reason that the Methodists nourished "secret views, at variance with our interests." The Methodists, unlike most of the Presbyterian missionaries in Oregon, demonstrated a distinct interest in affairs of the flesh as well as those of the spirit. Whereas the Presbyterians pledged themselves not to trade in furs, the Methodists made no such commitments. On the contrary, they were keenly aware of the economic potentialities of the Willamette valley. In journeying to the United States in 1838, Lee was motivated by the twin desires of stimulating American interest in Oregon and of advancing the material welfare of himself and his mission. While in the East, he purchased goods to be sent by ship to Oregon.[38] This news was disturbing to Douglas and to the governor and committee, for the arrival of the goods would force the Company into competition with the Methodists, a contest certain to be harmful to the Company. The Methodists would be able to attract general sympathy in the Willamette and in the United States by "raising the cry of persecution" against the Hudson's Bay Company, and they were certain to stimulate hostility against the Company among the other settlers.[39]

When the Roman Catholic bishop requested aid in transporting the two priests, Lee's intentions had not yet become fully evident. But the governor and committee saw an opportunity to utilize the services of the priests on behalf of the Company. The boundary line would certainly not be drawn so as to include the Willamette settlement in British territory, but if the Canadians of the Willamette could be induced to move north of the river to the Cowlitz plains, they would be removed from possible contamination by the Americans and at the same time would help strengthen British claims north of the river. The governor and committee therefore agreed to give passage for the two priests, provided that they would induce the Willamette freemen to move to the Cowlitz and would promise not to trade in furs and to trade exclusively with· the Company.[40] The bishop of Quebec accepted the conditions and appointed Francis N. Blanchet to the charge of the Oregon mission, to be assisted by Modeste Demers. The two priests left Montreal in May, 1838, and arrived at Fort Vancouver in November. Meanwhile, John McLoughlin had convinced the governor and

committee that the Company's interests would be served by allowing one of the priests to take up residence on the Willamette, for
his presence would serve to counteract the influence of the Methodists.[41] In 1839, consequently, Blanchet was able to establish himself on the Willamette, and Demers remained in charge of the
Cowlitz mission.

The Catholic missionaries were the strongest allies that the Company possessed against the Americans in Oregon. Their influence
was soon demonstrated by the refusal of the Canadians to join with
the Americans in petitioning Congress to assume authority over
Oregon, whereas two earlier petitions had been signed by as many
Canadians as Americans.[42] But not even the priests could convince
the French Canadians that the Cowlitz was more attractive than
the Willamette. Despite the pleas of the missionaries and the Company's officers, the freemen chose to remain in the Willamette
valley.

The Company had no greater success in promoting emigration
from Great Britain itself. Scotland was selected as the principal
source of supply, partly because poverty was an inducement to its
population to emigrate and partly because of the predilection of
Scots influential in the Company for members of their own nation.
Edward "Bear" Ellice of Aberdeenshire was not an unbiased judge
when he informed Sir John Henry Pelly, "The Governor may depend upon it, that he will find English emigrants infinitely inferior to Scotch ones, as far as agriculture is concerned. . . . I
think Governor Simpson [also a Scot] will concur with me in this
opinion." [43]

Neither Scottish nor English emigrants, however, were likely to
be attracted to Oregon under the program initiated by the Hudson's Bay Company. Nowhere is the antithesis between the autoc-
racy of the Company and the freedom necessary for agricultural
settlement in North America more evident than in the efforts of
the Company to promote colonization in Oregon. The governor
and committee were guided in their planning by two considerations: the supply of British settlers must be controlled by the Company in accordance with the number the Puget's Sound Agricultural Company could absorb, and these settlers must remain
subject to the control of the Company since free settlement was
hostile to the interests of the fur trade.

The plans of the Company were outlined by Pelly, Colvile, and Simpson in September, 1839. They expected that by 1841 the agricultural company would possess a stock of about 2,000 cattle and 10,000 sheep. When the supply of animals reached that level, they expected to send "a few respectable farming families" from Great Britain, each to be accompanied by two or three laboring servants. On arrival each family would receive a house, 100 acres of land already cleared, 20 cows, 1 bull, 500 sheep, 8 oxen, 6 horses, and a few hogs, and would be furnished with provisions during the first year of residence. After that the families were expected to maintain themselves. They would be supplied with Indian herdsmen in accordance with their requirements. But the farmer could not gain ownership of the land he tilled. He would lease the land from the Company, which would be entitled to one-half of the increment in his stock and one-half of his agricultural produce.[44] Such a system was alien to North American conditions, yet the governor and committee and even Simpson acted under the delusion that the advantages of their plan would attract large numbers of potential emigrants. Simpson boasted that the Company's arrangements for agricultural settlement were "greatly superior" to those of the various emigration companies attracting settlers to Australia and New Zealand. He wrote to Alexander Christie:

> If people could be made to understand all the advantages which our new and very promising settlement on the Cowlitz River holds forth, thousands would gladly avail themselves of them; but as very few are required from this country at present owing to the pressing applications by our own retiring servants who are desirous of being permitted to settle there, it is not considered expedient to draw the attention of the public at present to that part of the country.[45]

Simpson's assumption that thousands of farmers would apply for passage to Oregon under the Company's program was overly optimistic. As Ellice found in his search for possible emigrants in Scotland, laborers might volunteer since any change would be an improvement over their present condition, but farmers with capital of their own would inspect such a scheme carefully before accepting it.[46] But in any event the opportunity was not presented, since no publicity was given the project, and before the Company was ready to accept applications the course of events in Oregon caused the governor and committee to revise their plans and to seek emigrants from a source closer to the disputed territory.

This decision was motivated by a piece of misinformation provided George Simpson by Jason Lee. On his way from Canada to New York to sail for London, Simpson heard that Lee and a reinforcement of missionaries intended to sail for the Columbia on the *Lausanne* in October. Hoping to acquire knowledge that might be useful to the Company, he saw Lee and received from him the news that 200 persons from Massachusetts intended to leave for Oregon in the summer of 1840.[47] Lee was undoubtedly innocent of any deliberate misrepresentation. The group to which he referred was in all probability the Oregon Provisional Emigration Society, whose officers he had consulted, but the society did not fulfill his expectations.

The Company's own correspondence with the society seemed to confirm Lee's statement that a large American migration was impending. On March 4, 1839, the secretary, the Reverend F. P. Tracy of Lynn, Massachusetts, wrote to Simpson that "a large number of gentlemen" had associated in the society for the purpose of emigration to Oregon and that "several thousands" would soon be on the way, well equipped with all the supplies necessary for settlement. Tracy asked Simpson if the Company would give his group information, assistance, and supplies if they would promise not to engage in the fur trade and to do all in their power to uphold the Company's monopoly. He suggested that the Company might find it doubly advantageous to support his group, since the people of Oregon might decide to establish their own sovereign state, independent of either the United States or Great Britain.[48] Simpson forwarded Tracy's letter to the governor and committee who in turn submitted it to the Colonial Office, which sent it to the Foreign Office. The personnel of the Foreign Office agreed that the establishment of an independent state by the settlers could not be tolerated and that a large-scale migration such as Tracy predicted would be an infringement on the spirit of the conventions of 1818 and 1827, but they had no constructive suggestions to offer on the policy to be adopted should the emigration take place. In the Colonial Office a subordinate advised the colonial secretary, Lord Normanby, that the likelihood of large-scale emigration made it necessary to settle the Oregon dispute as soon as possible. Normanby left the suggestion unanswered. His successor at the Colonial Office, Lord John Russell, decided that the question lay outside his jurisdiction and should be handled by the Foreign Office and the cabinet. All agreed that some action was necessary but that nothing could be done, at least at present.[49]

The Hudson's Bay Company could not afford the luxury of such temporizing. The foreign secretary, Lord Palmerston, engrossed in the affairs of Europe, Turkey, and Mehemet Ali, could not be concerned over the prospective migration of a few hundred Americans to the wilderness of Oregon, but to the Company such a prospect was a matter of serious moment. The governor and committee decided that they must affect a friendly attitude toward the Oregon Provisional Emigration Society, at least until they acquired additional information on its strength and its intentions. The secretary of the Company accordingly wrote to Tracy that, if his association would send an agent to London, the Company would favorably consider reaching an agreement.[50]

The committee members had not changed their view that the Company's interests would not be promoted by agreements with Americans. But they were realistic enough to recognize that they should appear to coöperate with a movement they could not prevent, since their refusal to do so would serve no useful purpose and would arouse enmity. Meanwhile, they must decide on immediate measures to reinforce the Company's claims north of the Columbia River, for the Oregon dispute seemed to be approaching a climax. The activities of Lee and Tracy were not the only symptoms. On December 18, 1839, Senator Linn introduced resolutions reasserting the view that "the title of the United States to the Territory of Oregon is indisputable," requesting the president to give notice of the termination of the conventions of 1818 and 1827, and providing for the extension of American laws over Oregon, and for the dispatch of a military force not only to overawe the Indians but to dominate any "foreign forces" that might be in the territory.[51]

These evidences of American intentions caused the governor and committee to take two actions: first, they attempted to counter the American migration with another movement of British subjects, and second, they appealed to the Foreign Office to recognize its obligation to protect British subjects. The best source of supply, they decided, was the Red River settlement. If the Company could induce a substantial number of Red River residents to migrate to the Cowlitz portage and the Nisqually plains, it would not only strengthen British claims but it would siphon off population from a settlement that was becoming a growing menace to the fur trade of Rupert's Land. A stronger British settlement on the Columbia and a more placid Red River colony with little outlay by the Company—here indeed was a master stroke of policy! On November 15, 1839, Simpson advised Chief Factor Duncan Finlayson to begin a campaign to encourage "steady respectable half breed and other settlers" with small families to migrate to Oregon, and these instructions were repeated by the governor and committee in March, 1840.[52]

This migration, as conceived by the governor and committee, was primarily a political movement, and its direct economic benefit to the Company was of little significance. The governing board explained its objective to McLoughlin, who was not accustomed to think in other than economic terms, in the following language:

> We consider it of the utmost importance for various reasons, but especially in a political point of view to form a large settlement at the Cowlitz portage as early as possible, as the fact of a numerous British agricultural population being actually in possession there would operate strongly in favor of our claims to the territory on the Northern bank of the Columbia River. We are considering therefore whether in due time it may not be expedient to send from this country, occasionally by steam navigation to Panama, agriculturists with their families for the Columbia River, to proceed from Panama to St. Blas by the line of packets that has recently been established, and from St. Blas they might be taken by our own vessels at stated periods.[53]

The projected migration of Europeans via Panama did not take place, but Finlayson began immediately to try to execute his instructions. The first reaction in the Red River settlement to the suggestion of a migration to Oregon was highly encouraging. Finlayson wrote McLoughlin in June, 1840, that the majority of the colony favored such a movement, but whether of themselves or of others he did not make clear. The enthusiasm of prospective migrants was dampened, however, by the Company's conditions for land tenure in Oregon.[54] They could not understand why they could not own the land they occupied rather than leasing it from the Company and assigning half the product of their labor to the Company. Such objections were incomprehensible to the mind of George Simpson. The benefits to a settler from assistance by the Company seemed to him so clear that there could be no argument as to the superiority of the Company's plan over unassisted free settlement. Simpson expressed his views in a dispatch to Finlayson on September 10, 1840:

> You say the people are averse to taking Farms on halves, and suggest that Land should be sold to them as in the United States and Canada. In the present unsettled state of the Boundary question it is impossible for us to effect sales, the sovereignty of the country is not even, as yet, determined, and altho' we have every reason to believe the Columbia River will be the boundary, and that the country situated on the Northern bank of that river will become British territory, still we have no assurance that such will be the case, nor can the Company, in any shape, effect sales of Land on the west side [of] the Mountains. But even if sales could be effected we think it would be preferable for the people to take farms on halves, as already suggested as by so doing, they would be put in possession of certain parcels of Land, part of which will be broken up, houses will be erected for them—stock, such as cattle, sheep, horses &c provided, likewise agricultural implements, without any advance being required from them, in fact the Company is willing to provide them with capital, their proportion of the capital being labour, and the Company looking to be repaid for their advances in the shape of produce, say half the increase of stock and produce of every kind. These terms are more favorable to industrious settlers than any we have yet heard of, either in the United States, Canada, of any of the new Colonies. You may therefore inform such people that allotments will be made to each family of at least 100 acres of land, besides the use of common or pasture lands, parts thereof broken up with the necessary buildings erected for them, and live stock advanced to each family, of a Bull and ten or more cows, 50 to 100 Ewes, with a sufficient number of rams, hogs, Oxen for agricultural purposes, and a few horses; in short, as many of these different stocks as they may be equal to the management of; all valued at low money prices, the expences of erecting the buildings being a charge upon the farm; the cattle valued at £2 a head, the sheep at 10/ a head, horses at 40/ each, and other stock in proportion, a credit given to them from year to year for their increase, produce or returns, at such fair prices as the state of the markets may afford.[55]

The terms offered by the Company were not ungenerous. But they did not provide for one important element in successful North American colonization—the freedom of the settler, his right to own the land he tilled, to sell it if he chose, and to bequeath it to his posterity. The mind of George Simpson could not comprehend the significance of this freedom, which was alien to the traditions of the Company he served. In the limitations of his outlook is reflected the basic weakness that made the Company an ineffective instrument for the promotion of settlement. Paternalism was a poor competitor with free settlement; and significantly, the idea of free colonization of Oregon by British subjects did not occur to either Simpson or the governor and committee. The Company was an organization that existed for an economic purpose, and its political objectives were related to that fundamental purpose. Free settlement, regardless of the nationality of the settlers, was the bane of the fur trade. The Company therefore insisted that all colonization which it promoted be subject to its control. The Company cannot be criticized for failure to act in a manner alien to its being, but it is evident that any colonization project undertaken under its auspices was foredoomed to failure.

The Company's ability to absorb settlers within the requirements of its agricultural program was extremely limited. McLoughlin feared that shiploads of European farmers might be landed on the Columbia before the Puget's Sound Agricultural Company's business had expanded sufficiently to receive them. His concern was unfounded. The governor and committee had no intention of sending any settlers from Great Britain or from Europe until McLoughlin asked for them. Simpson instructed Finlayson to limit the Red River migration to approximately fifty "respectable families," [56] and the governor and committee envisaged an annual migration thereafter to the Cowlitz of between fifteen and twenty families.[57]

Even the modest objective of fifty families for the first migration was difficult to attain. Finlayson was able to report by April, 1841, that between thirty and forty families might be induced to migrate during the summer. But prospective migrants would not consent to leave Red River until after they had had an opportunity to see Simpson in the hope that he might offer more favorable terms than Finlayson had been authorized to make.[58] Even before Simpson's arrival, Finlayson found it necessary on his own responsibility to modify the proposals for land tenure. Not a single family of respectability would consent to go to Oregon if they could expect no more than leases of land and division of profits. Finlayson, in order to secure any commitments at all, had to promise that as soon as the boundary question was settled, with the Columbia River established as the line of demarcation, the Company would sell the land outright. Land tenure was not the only cause for reluctance. There was the natural disinclination to leave familiar surroundings for a long and arduous journey into a territory about which Red River residents knew little, and rumors circulated in the settlement that on the Columbia they would be subject to the harsh discipline of John McLoughlin, whose reputation as a man addicted to violence had spread throughout the Company's territories.[59]

Finlayson with some difficulty reassured the intending emigrants, and when Simpson arrived at Red River on June 9, 1841, he found that 23 families, including 121 men, women, and children, had left a few days previously on the journey to Oregon. At their head Finlayson had placed James Sinclair, a half-breed settler, whose reputation as a keen, active man had already been established. Sinclair had been selected when Alexander Ross of Snake River fame had refused to undertake the responsibility. Most of the emigrants received advances of £9 or £10 to assist them on their journey and after their arrival.[60]

Simpson and his party caught up with and passed the emigrant column between Carlton and Edmonton. The file of carts and horses stretched out for over a mile. Each family had two or three carts in which the women and children rode under awnings erected to protect them from the sun and the rain. On the flanks of the column, herded by men and older boys on horseback, plodded the cattle. The emigrants ranged in age from an old woman of 75 to infants born en route, but the party was composed preponderantly of young families.[61] Two families apparently turned back, for when the column arrived at Fort Vancouver it included only 21 families, totaling 116 persons. McLoughlin sent 14 of the families, including 77 persons, primarily English half-breeds, to Nisqually. The remainder, French Canadians and half-breeds, whose lives had been devoted mainly to buffalo hunting rather than to agriculture, were sent to Cowlitz, since Simpson and McLoughlin considered that their backgrounds did not qualify them as efficient stock raisers.[62]

This accession of population, small as it was, nearly equaled the number of American settlers in Oregon in 1841. On the Willamette at this time there were only 65 American families. In addition there were 61 Canadian retired servants, who were British subjects. The total population in Oregon did not exceed 500, of whom 350 were Canadians. But this was the last migration to Oregon under the auspices of the Hudson's Bay Company before the boundary treaty was signed. Though the governor and committee continued to talk about further transfers from Red River to relieve the pressure on that colony, Simpson and McLoughlin held that no further immigration should be encouraged, at least until there had been opportunity to evaluate the success of the first movement.[63]

They did not have long to wait, for the experiment proved an unqualified failure. The light, sandy soil of Nisqually did not produce good crops and the Red River families were not experienced in tending stock. Scab broke out in the sheep, 500 ewes lost their lambs, and the immigrants soon came to the conclusion that the prospects for success in such a perverse country were slight. In September representatives of the Nisqually group visited McLoughlin to inquire whether, if they remained another year to give the soil a fair trial and then decided to leave, they would be permitted to keep half the increase of their cattle during that period. McLoughlin replied that he had no authority to make such a commitment.[64] But in all probability no assurances could have induced them to stay. By the autumn of 1843 all the Red River families had left for the Willamette. William Fraser Tolmie, in charge at Fort Nisqually, watched their departure with no regrets, since he had found them "insolent and thriftless." [65] Most of the families that had gone to the Cowlitz portage, however, appear to have remained, perhaps because the land was more fertile, but almost certainly in part because they enjoyed the services of a Catholic priest, the Reverend Modeste Demers. No such spiritual guidance was available at Nisqually where the only missionary was the American Methodist, the Reverend J. P. Richmond, M.D., who also found the environment unpleasant and left for home with his family in September, 1842.

The Company's enthusiasm for colonization had been short-lived. Governor Pelly observed, even before the Red River settlers had arrived on the Columbia, that "if we attempt to settle People where they do not like . . . we shall not only have great difficulty, but our labour & money may be thrown away." [66] But Pelly was far away in London and had never visited the Columbia or indeed any other part of the Company's territories. He therefore trusted Simpson's local knowledge, and Simpson was convinced that further increments of population were dangerous to the economic interests of the Hudson's Bay Company. By the spring of 1842 the Company's policy toward assisted emigration, now largely controlled by Simpson, had become one of opposition rather than encouragement. Simpson now viewed every prospective migrant with distrust, whether British or American, a Company employee or a free settler. He wrote to McLoughlin on March 1, 1842:

> The desire throughout the service on both sides [of] the Mountains, for permission to retire & settle as Agriculturists on the shores of the Pacific amounts at present almost to a mania, & if complied with to any material extent, might be attended with serious inconvenience.[67]

Any doubts that the governor and committee may have had as to the wisdom of Simpson's judgment were dispelled when they heard that the Red River settlers had left Nisqually. In decrying the faithlessness of these men who had violated solemn engagements, they were misplacing the responsibility for failure. Their plan had miscarried because they had based it upon unrealistic assumptions. The Company could not have hoped to compete with the flood of migration from the United States which was now beginning, but the characteristics of the Hudson's Bay project made a travesty of its avowed objective.

If the Company had desired to encourage British settlement north of the Columbia River, it could have taken no more effective action than to coöperate with the Roman Catholic Church in establishing missions throughout the territory. Simpson and the majority of the governing board, however, were suspicious of missionaries of any variety. Mission stations in Rupert's Land had been centers for the spread of "bad habits" among the Indians, who had been encouraged to turn from the chase to agricultural pursuits; missionaries' reports to their superiors of alleged maltreatment of the aboriginal population by the Company's officers and of the immoral habits of the Company's employees had frequently caused the Company embarrassment. The Company's officers had good reason to be irritated at the missionaries, who not infrequently displayed intolerance and outright priggishness, but the assistance of Roman Catholic missionaries was essential to any schemes for British settlement. The two reservoirs from which the Company could most easily draw population were the Red River settlement and Canada. In both areas, Roman Catholics comprised a substantial proportion of the population. The sincerity of the London board's protestations of a desire to encourage settlement was tested by their policy toward the Catholic missions, and that policy was one of noncoöperation after their initial assistance to Blanchet and Demers. When the bishop of Juliopolis applied to Simpson for assistance in conveying other clergymen to the Columbia, the governor and committee "after mature deliberation" rejected his request on March 4, 1840,[68] at a time when they were professing their zeal for colonization. Two priests, Jean B. Z. Bolduc and Louis A. Langlois, arrived on the Columbia from Oahu on the Company's ship Cowlitz in 1842, but they paid their passage. McLoughlin, who became a Catholic in 1842, occasionally provided the priests with transportation on the Company's coasting vessels, but in so doing he found it necessary to defend himself for his alleged violation of the Company's policy.[69] McLoughlin's cordiality to the priests was a personal matter, for his instructions from the governor and committee and from Simpson were to provide them only the minimum assistance consistent with humanity.[70] The only significant encouragement from the Company was an annuity of £100 which the council of the northern department placed at Blanchet's disposal in July, 1842.[71]

During his visit to the Columbia in 1841 and 1842, Simpson recommended that the Company provide accommodations for two more priests and six male and two female servants.[72] But within a year Simpson had returned to his earlier view that missionaries were, if not dangerous to the interests of the fur trade, certainly no asset. His reversion became evident in December, 1843, when the bishop of Juliopolis, Joseph-Norbert Provencher, called upon him at his headquarters in Lachine. The bishop wanted to discuss the spiritual condition of the Red River population, but more particularly he hoped to induce Simpson to recommend greater assistance to Roman Catholic missionaries on the Columbia. The Columbia had recently been elevated to the dignity of a bishopric and Blanchet had been designated as its first bishop.[73] Provencher asked whether, in view of the greater importance now attached to Oregon by the Catholic Church, the Company would provide passage to the Columbia on its ships for four nuns and two priests. Since members of the London board had expressed objections to having priests from France sent to Oregon, Provencher assured Simpson that the nuns and priests would be Canadians. Simpson's reply was unenthusiastic. He thought the Company would grant such passage on payment of the usual fare of £75, but that space could probably not be provided until 1845; there was no possibility of transporting priests and nuns across the continent by canoes, since the canoes would be too much encumbered by other passengers.[74] Simpson would undoubtedly have said that the Company's ships were similarly unavailable had it not been that such a position would antagonize the Church hierarchy without serving any useful purpose.

When Blanchet, in Montreal for his consecration in the summer of 1845, requested that the Company provide passage for several nuns and priests, Simpson informed him that he would be "pleased to recommend" that such permission be granted. But he wrote Pelly that he had answered in this way because, if the Company did not provide space, the Jesuits would themselves charter a vessel or would send their missionaries through the United States, and that neither course was desirable. Since the missionaries would reach Oregon by one route or another, he felt it better to appear coöperative.[75]

By 1845 no action of the Company's could have significant effect on the course of events. The Company could not hope to compete with the American emigration now flowing into Oregon. But it had not wholeheartedly promoted British settlement even at a time when American settlers were few and when it seemed that emigration from the United States would, because of public apathy, be no more than a mere trickle. The Company could not promote colonization because its character and purposes were alien to the requirements of agricultural settlement. Its officers never escaped the conviction that the fur trade could survive only in a wilderness environment and that the Company must control the activities of all those who entered the fur-trade domain lest the monopoly be destroyed. Their suspicion of missionaries was based upon the same reasoning.

James Douglas, one of the keenest officers in the Company's employ, had expressed his convictions with force and frankness since his elevation to the chief-factorship in 1839. He looked upon the Company's problems with somewhat broader vision than most of his contemporaries, although he shared their opinion that settlement was the mortal enemy of the fur trade. He told Simpson that the latter had made a serious mistake in 1843 in throwing obstacles in the way of the transportation of Canadian Catholic missionaries to Oregon. Rather, he declared, the Company should have encouraged them by granting them free passage and providing them with all the assistance they required in their labors in the Oregon territory. The cost to the Company would have been a mere trifle; the benefits in good will, great.[76] An advocate of aggressive defense of the Company's interests, Douglas wrote to Simpson:

> When the Legions were recalled from Britain, and other remote possessions, the Roman Empire fell rapidly into decay; with a territory nearly as extensive our dominion would suffer from the same course: there is danger in receding; strength, power and safety are to be found only in a bold advance.[77]

These were the views on which the Company's frontier policies had been and were based. Those policies had been successful along the borders of the Company's trading territory from the Snake country to Canada. But the aggressiveness there displayed was a conventional technique of fur-trade competition. The Company's decision in 1839 to checkmate the Americans by British colonization was an experiment in a very different type of defense, an experiment that was never really attempted. Beyond its abortive effort to send colonists from Red River, the Company did not promote settlement in Oregon; on the contrary, it discouraged immigration, whether British or American. The Puget's Sound Agricultural Company, organized avowedly to promote a political as well as an economic purpose, soon was confined to the latter. A few Englishmen and Scots were sent to Oregon on Company ships to serve as farmers or shepherds, but they came as servants of the Company, not as free settlers.

Even in its commercial aspect the Puget's Sound Agricultural Company was far from a success, thus largely vindicating McLoughlin's prediction that a pastoral venture under the auspices of the Hudson's Bay Company was certain to fail. At Nisqually in 1845 there were 5,872 sheep and 2,280 cattle, not an unimpressive number, but the quality of the stock was low, largely because the supervisory personnel lacked experience in pastoral operations. A shipment of wool and sheepskins to London in 1844 revealed the lack of experience. The expert who examined the consignment of forty-six bales of wool and four bales of sheepskins reported that the wool varied in grade from "fine" to "very coarse" and that the skins varied extremely in quality and size.[78] Simpson thought that the flocks, poor as they were, plagued with scab and cannibalism of mothers on their young, were still more promising than the cattle, which were so wild that it was almost impossible to collect them, and had no value to the Company except as produce of the chase, "like the buffalo on the Saskatchewan." [79] The grain produced at Cowlitz and at Fort Vancouver was not always sufficient to fulfill the terms of the contract with the Russian American Company. As an economic as well as a political undertaking the Puget's Sound Agricultural Company was a failure.

# The Oregon Crisis, 1840-1844

OREGON WAS NOT won for the United States by the pioneers who migrated into the disputed territory before 1846.[1] It was not won by the appeals of Jason Lee, Marcus Whitman, or other missionaries to the American government and public. But the developing "Oregon fever" of which the settlers and missionaries were a manifestation was largely responsible for the American diplomatic victory in the boundary agreement.

The possession of Oregon to at least the 49th parallel became an *idée fixe* in American society, for which the country was ready, if necessary, to fight a war. For support against this strong conviction the Hudson's Bay Company could depend upon British national pride, but not upon British recognition of the importance of Oregon. In retrospect the result appears to have been a foregone conclusion; it was not thus to the officers of the Company who participated in the negotiations. They believed that, since the Company securely held the territory north of the Columbia River, any agreement must recognize its preëminence; they expected that the British government would resist, by violence if necessary, American aggression upon the Company's rights. In these expectations they were not entirely disappointed. They lost their fight for the Columbia River boundary but they won formal American recognition of their special interests in the territory assigned to the United States. Without the continued pressure of the Hudson's Bay Com-

---

[1] For notes to chap. 11, see pp. 456–457.

pany, the controversy would never have assumed the magnitude it did. As Lester Burrell Shippee has stated, "Whatever direct interest Great Britain or her subjects had in Oregon was centered about the Company whose word was law and under whose smile or frown fortunes prospered or languished." [2]

The Oregon dispute resumed its active phase in 1839 when Lewis Linn and his supporters in the United States Senate launched a concerted campaign to force the Van Buren government to support American claims. The resolutions offered by Linn were not essentially novel; similar bills had been introduced by John Floyd more than two decades before. But the environment had changed. In the 1820's American opinion had been apathetic; in 1839, though it was not yet fully aroused, there were evidences of increasing agitation.

Linn not only reiterated the right of the United States to all of Oregon, but he asked that the area be given territorial status and that the laws of the United States be extended over it. Any white male over eighteen years of age would receive 640 acres if he would cultivate and use the tract for five consecutive years. These provisions were in themselves not particularly menacing, but his other resolutions alarmed the Company's governing board. He asked President Van Buren to give notice of the termination of the convention of 1827 and to create a regiment to be sent to the Oregon territory.[3] The news of Linn's resolutions and the evidence of strong support for his appeals reached London in February, 1840, by packet ship from Nova Scotia. Pelly read the report of the proceedings in the Senate, published in the St. John's *Courier* of January 4, 1840. The implications were clear; the Oregon controversy was about to pass into the stage of crisis. Pelly immediately wrote to Palmerston, describing Linn's resolutions and appealing for British protection against American attack:

> Should the United States Government be permitted to carry the measures proposed in those resolutions into effect, they will prove ruinous to the interests of the Hudson's Bay Company in that quarter, likewise to those of the Pugets Sound Agricultural Company, and deprive Great Britain of the only position on the shores of the Pacific, that can be valuable to the country either for colonization or commercial pursuits, while the only safe and commodious harbours on that coast will be in possession of jealous rival powers, giving to them the command of the Northern Pacific, and

in a certain degree that of the China seas, objects of the greatest commercial and political importance to Great Britain.

Under the circumstances I beg respectfully to draw Your Lordship's attention to the important subject in question and to entreat you will be pleased to watch over the interests of the Hudson's Bay Company and the Pugets Sound Agricultural Company in any negotiations that may be in progress connected with the proceedings alluded to.[4]

Pelly's letter was well designed to appeal to the mind of Palmerston. The foreign secretary had already displayed his penchant for the virile foreign policy that made him the epitome of John Bull in the admiring eyes of the masses and an irresponsible blunderer in the view of those who believed that foreign affairs should be conducted with tact and discretion. The twin appeal to British honor and British commerce, Pelly calculated, would evoke a strong response from Palmerston, particularly since the commercial interests allegedly at stake in the Oregon crisis were the trade of the Pacific basin, not merely the fur trade of the Company. Since the resolutions did not pass, Palmerton was not required to take any action, but the British government became aware that the Oregon dispute was reviving. James Stephen at the Colonial Office, to whom Pelly's letter was sent by the Foreign Office for informational purposes, remarked to a colleague, "You will learn from this, that another American boundary question is likely to become the subject of much difficulty." [5]

In this atmosphere of imminent crisis the Foreign Office received from the Admiralty a report, written by Commander Edward Belcher of H.M.S. *Sulphur,* which was highly critical of the Company. One of Belcher's complaints was particularly noted by the government. He accused the Company of assisting American missionaries who, he said, were really agents of the American government devoted to undermining the British position in Oregon. Palmerston sent the report to the Colonial Office with the suggestion that the Company be informed that the employment of American missionaries was dangerous, and Lord John Russell, the colonial secretary, obliged by delivering a lecture to the Company on the necessity of employing British missionaries at the settlements.[6] Russell's criticism, based upon Belcher's misstatements, was unjustified. The Company employed no American missionaries. McLoughlin had received them in a friendly manner and had sold them goods at the same prices charged to the Company's servants. But his policy had been based upon the recognition that refusal to provide them with goods at reasonable prices would serve no useful purpose, since they could receive supplies by their own chartered ships. The Belcher incident reveals the lack of understanding of the Oregon problem displayed by the Foreign Office and the Colonial Office.

The only hope for a settlement favorable to Great Britain was to precipitate a crisis while the Hudson's Bay Company remained in physical control of most of the territory and before the Oregon fever prevented any American government from accepting a boundary south of the 49th parallel. If the issue had been joined while Palmerston was foreign secretary, Great Britain would likely have gone to war rather than sacrifice the line of the Columbia. But Palmerston would not initiate action to force such a crisis; the drift continued, and the increasing flow of emigration from the United States foreshadowed the American victory of 1846. The fall of the Whig government in August, 1841, and the succession of the bellicose Palmerston by the conciliatory Aberdeen made that triumph virtually a certainty.

The increasing militancy in the tiny American colony on the Willamette became evident in February, 1841, when a meeting was held at the Methodist mission under the chairmanship of Jason Lee for the purpose of organizing a government. The Canadians, influenced by Blanchet, refused to coöperate, and Lieutenant Charles Wilkes, commander of the United States exploring expedition then on the Columbia River, advised the leaders of the scheme not to attempt to form a government supported only by a small minority.[7] But this political agitation disturbed James Douglas. Although he was disposed to jest that the agitators must know something about government since "some of these Solons had rubbed shoulders rather closely with the law before now," he did not conceal his concern that the mania for establishing a government might spread. He suggested in a letter to Simpson that the governor might smile at the thought of a tiny group seriously discussing the propriety of organizing a government for Oregon. Douglas did not smile; he knew that they would try again and that their efforts were certain to be harmful to the Company.[8]

As Simpson journeyed down the Columbia River to Vancouver and inspected the American settlements in the summer of 1841, he also was alarmed. He found the missionaries making more rapid progress in the extension of farming than in their ostensible objective of promoting Christianity. The Columbia valley, he declared with some exaggeration, was "studded with missions" on the south side of the river, and the mission of J. P. Richmond at Nisqually was likely to be followed by others north of the Columbia River. Besides the missionaries there were 150 Americans, including 65 adult males, in the Willamette colony.[9]

The measure of Simpson's alarm was his recommendation to the governor and committee that some of the functions of Fort Vancouver be transferred to a more northerly location. The immediate cause for his suggestion was that the ship carrying him from the Columbia to the Hawaiian Islands was delayed for three weeks in crossing the bar at the mouth of the river, but more basic was his fear that the "worthless, lawless characters" from the United States who inhabited the Willamette valley were in too close proximity to the Company's headquarters at Fort Vancouver. He proposed the southern end of Vancouver Island as the location for the new establishment, which would be the center for the coastal trade.[10]

Simpson had a third reason for wanting to remove the Company's headquarters on the Pacific Coast to Vancouver Island. By 1842 he was beginning to entertain doubts that the Company's hopes for the boundary line of the Columbia would be realized. The first tangible evidence that Simpson's optimism had been shaken appeared in his letter to the governor and committee on March 1, 1842:

. . . in the final adjustment of the boundary question, it is more than probable that a line drawn through the Straits of de Fuca till it strikes the mainland South of Whidby's Island, will become the Coast Boundary between Gt. Britain, & the United States, in the Northern Pacific. I say so, because I am of opinion the Government of the United States will insist on having a port on the North West Coast, & that Gt. Britain will, for the sake of peace, accept the Straits of de Fuca as a boundary on the Coast, & thereby give up Puget Sound and Hoods Canal, together with the country situated between those inlets & the lower parts of the Columbia. In that case, I presume the line would be continued from the Southern end of Whidbey's Island, in an easterly direction, till it struck

Lewis River, & following up that River till it struck the Rocky Mountains. It is exceedingly desirable, however, for the British interests in this quarter & for the national honor, that Her Majesty's Government should not submit to such degrading conditions; but I think it is nevertheless well to be prepared for the worst, & under all circumstances I am of opinion that another depot should be established with the least possible delay, and that on the Southern end of Vancouver's Island, such establishment to be the depot of the Coast, & Fort Vancouver that of the interior of the Columbia, including New Caledonia, & for the trapping parties it may be considered advisable to maintain.[11]

Simpson's depression may have been aggravated by his association with Lieutenant Wilkes, whom he met on the Columbia in 1841. Although their relationship was cordial, Wilkes was not communicative about the object of the surveys of coastal waters which members of his expedition were conducting. But through a "very intelligent and confidential" member of the party, Simpson learned that Wilkes intended to advocate that the United States claim the entire Oregon territory between 42° and 54° 40'. Simpson's unnamed informant, however, confided that it was his own intention to recommend a line drawn through the Strait of Juan de Fuca until it struck the mainland south of Whidbey Island and thence across to the Columbia.[12] This was precisely the line, Simpson indicated, which Great Britain might accept.

Such views Simpson would admit privately to his superiors, but in his correspondence intended for the eyes of the Foreign Office no hint of pessimism was evident. In a letter to Pelly written nine days after the private letter to the governor and committee, he stated the conclusions he desired to have transmitted to the government. Britain, he told Pelly, must not consent to a boundary giving the United States any territory north of the Columbia River, since "any boundary North of that stream would deprive Great Britain of the only valuable part of the territory, the country to the Northwards of the Straits of de Fuca not being adapted for agriculture or other purposes connected with Colonization." [13]

It would be a mistake to conclude from Simpson's observations that by 1842 the Company had resigned itself to withdrawal from the Columbia River, for his views were not necessarily those of the governor and committee; it would be a mistake to assume even that the views he expressed in March, 1842, were those he held a year later. Simpson, despite his calculating qualities, often appeared to be a creature of the moment. He not infrequently retracted opinions that he had expressed earlier, and he was not always discreet in the expression of his views. Adam Thom at Fort Garry, who had the opportunity to read Simpson's private letter of March 1, criticized him for committing such speculations to writing. There was no assurance, said Thom, that the letter might not fall into the hands of the United States government and, if it did, "it is not unlikely to be vamped up into a Yankee argument," since the line suggested would be nearly at the 48th parallel, only one degree from the line earlier proposed by the Americans.[14] The governor and committee agreed with Simpson that the depot for the coastal trade should be moved to Vancouver Island, but they appear to have been motivated by the same commercial consideration that had caused them to issue repeated instructions to this effect in the 1830's, that Vancouver Island was more convenient to the coastal trade than Fort Vancouver.[15] The construction of Fort Victoria in 1843 was thus related primarily to an economic purpose.

If the governor and committee had been aware of Aberdeen's low estimate of Oregon, they would have shared Simpson's pessimism. Aberdeen considered the location of the boundary between British North America and the United States of great importance, but the boundary he was preoccupied with was in the Northeast, not the Northwest. He hailed the success of Lord Ashburton in negotiating an agreement with Daniel Webster on the Maine–New Brunswick boundary. Ashburton had authority also to deal with Oregon, but he did not press the issue because he feared that "the settlement of the far more important matter of the North Eastern Boundary should be impeded or exposed to the hazard of failure." When the vexing dispute on the northeast boundary was settled, Aberdeen proposed to deal with the Oregon controversy which, "although not so hazardous," was nevertheless "not without risk to the good understanding between the two countries." [16]

Aberdeen's estimate of the relative importance of the two disputes in 1842 was correct, in terms of both British and American opinion. The Maine–New Brunswick controversy was important to Americans, Canadians, and inhabitants of the maritime colonies. The Oregon dispute was of great significance in 1842 only to the

Hudson's Bay Company, a few American missionaries, and a small group of frenetic American politicians and their supporters. In 1843, and thereafter, Aberdeen's estimates and the generality of British opinion remained unchanged while the possession of Oregon, at least to the 49th parallel, became an object of primary interest to the United States.

Had Daniel Webster been able to settle the Oregon question in accordance with his own views rather than as an officer of a government dependent upon the support of Congress, he might have made a settlement acceptable to the Hudson's Bay Company and to the British government. Webster was a reasonable man. Possession of the harbor of San Francisco Bay and of the territory from the Columbia River to the 36th parallel would have satisfied him. That the territory between 36° and 42° belonged to Mexico was an inconvenience that could be eliminated by joint pressure from Great Britain and the United States.[17]

Failing such an agreement, Webster would probably have been willing to accept a boundary that gave Great Britain most of what the Company desired. He wrote to Everett in 1842:

> It has been suggested that the line of boundary might begin on the sea, or the straits of St. Juan de Fuca, follow up these Straits, give us a harbor at the southwest corner of these island waters, and then continue south striking the river below Vancouver, and then following the river to its intersection with the 49th degree of latitude north.[18]

Webster would have experienced great difficulty in securing the consent of the Senate, even in 1843, to such an agreement, but he retired from office without having taken any formal action to facilitate a settlement. His successors, stimulated by an inflamed public opinion, were not inclined to be so moderate.

The symptoms of the mounting Oregon fever became evident to the British minister in Washington during the summer of 1843. On July 3, a convention of delegates from six states in the Mississippi valley opened in Cincinnati to discuss the most effective means of winning the Oregon territory for the United States. By the end of their three-day meeting, the delegates had adopted a series of resolutions exceedingly hostile to Great Britain. The resolutions affirmed the right of the United States to the Oregon territory from 42° to 54° 40', and advocated increased migration and a protective chain of forts from the Missouri River to the Pacific Ocean. The chairman of the meeting was Richard M. Johnson of Kentucky, who had been vice-president of the United States in the Van Buren administration, and now had hopes that the Democratic party would nominate him for the presidency.[19]

A clearer manifestation of the new enthusiasm was the great increase in migration to Oregon in 1843. The first large migration had taken place in the summer of 1842, when approximately 100 emigrants led by Dr. Elijah White arrived on the Willamette. On the strength of his commission from the United States government as "Sub-Indian Agent West of the Rocky Mountains," White attempted, without success, to act as governor of the American colony and to assume authority over the Indian tribes as far north as New Caledonia. The Company's officers, of course, refused to recognize his authority; but, as Simpson said, White was "an active and very forward presumptious man," [20] and agitation among the American settlers for a provisional government increased after his arrival. White's party, however, was a small one in comparison with the group that reached Oregon in the summer of 1843. The size of this migration has been variously estimated at from 500 to 1,000 men, women, and children. James Douglas, who made an informal and unpublicized census, estimated the total at from 500 to 700; and, since the camp mustered 300 guns, he estimated that 300 must be the number of adult males in the group. The immigrants brought with them 120 wagons and about 1,600 head of neat cattle. Among the settlers there were a few professional men who hoped to receive government appointments, and others were possessed of small means, but the great majority were virtually without capital resources. Douglas was hopeful that many of the Americans, because their funds were inadequate to stock farms, would move to California, as other parties had done, but his hope was dashed when McLoughlin extended credit for the purchase of seeds and equipment. The wisdom of McLoughlin's action can be defended. The immigrants would not have accepted their fate quietly. If forced to extremity, they would have attempted to seize supplies, and the Company could not have successfully resisted a concerted attack. McLoughlin was simply converting necessity into virtue, for many of those who received supplies were thereafter friendly to the Company, in defiance of the rule that "loan oft loses both itself and friend." Whether confining his assistance to food and clothing and encouraging the immigrants to move southward would have reduced the American population remains a moot question. Clearly, by extending credit, McLoughlin knowingly violated Company policy, confident that his knowledge of the local situation justified his action. He could expect little sympathy from Sir George Simpson, from whom he had become alienated, or from the governor and committee, who could not understand the necessity for his violation of instructions. But even his junior colleague, Douglas, who shared his knowledge of local conditions, did not entirely agree as to the wisdom of McLoughlin's actions. Douglas was no sycophant; he defended McLoughlin against other attacks by Simpson. But though he did not directly criticize McLoughlin for extending credit, he did imply strongly that he would have preferred greater emphasis on encouraging immigrants to move on to California.

To Douglas, as to the Company, all Americans, however friendly they might be to the Company's officers, were hostile to its interests. Douglas agreed with John C. Calhoun that, if the question of jurisdiction remained unsettled, an American population in Oregon would decide it eventually in favor of the United States.[21] "The wily old lawyer is correct," said Douglas, "and there can be no doubt of the final success of the plan, if the country remains open a few years longer." Douglas declared to Simpson that, unless Britain took immediate steps to end the dispute, either by peace or by war, the United States would win by default:

> An American population will never willingly submit to British domination, and it would be ruinous and hopeless to enforce obedience, on a disaffected people; our Government would not attempt it, and the consequence will be the accession of a new State to the Union. In that case, then, and supposing the Coast becomes American Territory to the exclusion of other Powers, it is easy to forsee the advantage which the Arms of the Republic will derive from so valuable an acquisition of Territory in any future war with Great Britain. Every sea port will be converted into a naval arsenal, and the Pacific covered with swarms of Privateers, to the destruction of British commerce in those seas. Could England in such a case support navies for the protection of trade, or transport

armies to conquer the country, after it becomes a dependancy of
the United States? Assuredly not: it will therefore be a proof of
wisdom, in our rulers to make Englands rights good, to the last
inch of Territory claimed.[22]

As he watched the Americans arrive Douglas feared that hopes
for a favorable settlement were indeed forlorn. Impressed by the
energy of the Americans, though repelled by their uncouth manners, he wrote Simpson that

> These Yankees are a strange people, admirable in some respects,
> in others detestable.
> The Judge in a ragged coat and slouched hat, is as great a man
> as the Lord Chief Justice of England and the Sheriff is no less
> despotic in his decrees, though he finds it a hard matter to spell
> his own name; and truly a desperate fellow he is who will take no
> refusal. He does not trouble himself about principles, he reasons
> thus "If there are laws, they must be obeyed." I wish we had a few
> of his mettle.[23]

The organization of a provisional government by the Americans
at Champoeg on May 2, 1843, and the adoption on July 5 of a body
of laws based upon the code of Iowa, were further indications that
delay in settling the Oregon question could benefit only the
Americans. Although the Canadians, still held firm by Blanchet in
their loyalty to Britain and the Company, initially refused to join
the government, they were a decreasing proportion of the population. At first the Company's officers also refused to recognize the
provisional government. The dominance of the American population, however, soon forced both the Canadians and the Company
into acceptance of the government's authority. In March, 1844,
the Canadians agreed to join on certain conditions, most important
of which were that they would retain their status as British subjects and that acceptance of the government's authority would not
be interpreted as support for the American assumption of sovereignty.[24] In the summer of 1845, in order to protect the Company's property, McLaughlin in its behalf accepted the provisional
government's jurisdiction, again with the stipulation that the action was without prejudice to the status of the Company or its
employees or to the claims of Great Britain in the Oregon territory.[25]

The Company's officers in Oregon, to a greater degree than the governor and committee or Sir George Simpson, saw in the migrations and in the organization of the provisional government the eventual ruination of the Company's trade in Oregon and the defeat of British political claims. This premonition led Douglas on October 23, 1843, to suggest to Simpson a measure for the protection of the Company's rights in the event that the Americans won a favorable treaty:

> If it should happen . . . that the Columbia is given up, I hope the right of the Hudson's Bay Company to the conditional occupation of their improvements will be respected: the Government of Washington will not venture to deny so trifling a boon, in order to obtain a quiet adjustment of the question. There is no other way of securing our property, it must be done by Treaty or we will be sacrificed. If the question be left to Congress, our doom is sealed, it will be expulsion without benefit of justice. But our property being secured to us by Treaty, we may retain possession of the land, now occupied by our stock and improvements, and turn it to very profitable account hereafter.[26]

Here is the first recorded statement of the principle involved in the "possessory rights" clauses incorporated in the treaty in 1846. The same idea was expressed by Simpson on June 20, 1844, when he advised the governor and committee to use their influence to assure the inclusion of the Company's rights of occupancy in any treaty. But Simpson's suggestion applied primarily to the Willamette Falls property of the Company, whereas Douglas was concerned with the consequences of establishing a boundary north of the Columbia.[27] To Douglas, unquestionably, belongs the credit for originating the demand for recognition of possessory rights which the United States conceded in the treaty and which were to cause continuing dispute thereafter.

Until the end of 1843 only the legislative branch of the United States government participated in the agitation for American sovereignty over the entire Oregon territory. The Hudson's Bay Company had warned the British government of the increasing American fervor for ousting Great Britain from the Pacific Coast, but the Foreign Office had considered it unnecessary to make any representations to the United States so long as resolutions with that objective were defeated in Congress or were unsupported by executive action. Palmerston had taken no action, and Aberdeen, buoyed by Ashburton's success in settling the northeast boundary, was hopeful that the United States would demonstrate the same reasonableness in its negotiations on Oregon that it had shown in the Maine–New Brunswick settlement. Until 1844 Aberdeen therefore gave the representatives of the Hudson's Bay Company no encouragement; Pelly and his associates were not invited to visit the Foreign Office, and the Company exercised no observable influence on Aberdeen's thinking. The foreign secretary thought that the United States, having accepted a compromise on the "important" issue of the northeast boundary, would be similarly inclined with regard to the "less significant" territory of Oregon. He was rudely shocked when at the end of 1843 the executive branch of the United States government began to demonstrate the same demagogic tendencies that members of the Senate and the House of Representatives had previously displayed.

President John Tyler, hopeful of renomination in the election of 1844, saw an opportunity to capitalize on the mounting nationalist preoccupation with Oregon by putting himself at the head of the expansionists. His annual message to Congress on December 5, 1843, was a campaign document. In it he declared that the United States claimed the entire territory from 42° to 54° 40'. Although he expressed the hope that negotiations with Great Britain would be friendly, he left no doubt that he would recommend strong measures if Britain did not accept a treaty favorable to the United States. Immigration to Oregon was increasing, he stated, and a line of military posts should be established to provide protection and assistance for the pioneers.[28]

Aberdeen considered the dispute over a few thousand square miles of wasteland to be of no consequence to the national interest of Great Britain. The appeals of the Hudson's Bay Company did not influence him. In March, 1844, he privately informed the British minister in Washington, Richard Pakenham, that he was personally willing to accept the 49th parallel as the boundary provided that all Vancouver Island was conceded to Britain.[29] Aberdeen, unlike his predecessor in the Foreign Office, had dedicated himself to the preservation of peace, and Oregon was not worth a war. But Aberdeen was not a man to be bullied into accepting an opponent's ultimatum. If the United States intended to use force, or to threaten force, to achieve its objective, Aberdeen would resist and would provide protection for British subjects in Oregon.

Since they were all present or past employees of the Hudson's Bay Company, Aberdeen for the first time held consultations with the governor and committee, not because he believed the Company's interests worth the support of Great Britain, but because he would not be intimidated by the United States.

The evidence that the expansionists were pushing the United States government to an uncompromising demand for the entire Oregon territory prompted Simpson to open correspondence with Pakenham and with the Canadian governor-general, Sir Charles Metcalfe, in the hope of influencing the Foreign Office through them. He first sent them a pamphlet written by Adam Thom, supporting British claims to Oregon and stressing the Company's right to the protection of its interests there. Encouraged by Pakenham's polite response that he would be happy to receive any further information Simpson could provide,[30] Sir George gave the British minister the benefit of his long experience by suggesting a solution of the Oregon problem. He reminded Pakenham that the Foreign Office had consulted him during the negotiations in the 1820's and that, from his visits to the Columbia, he possessed valuable firsthand information. The desire of the United States for a harbor on the Pacific might be met, he advised Pakenham, by conceding a free port either at the southern end of Vancouver Island or on the Strait of Juan de Fuca.[31] Pakenham actually advanced this suggestion of a free port to Secretary of State John C. Calhoun on August 26, 1844, but the source of his instructions was Aberdeen rather than Simpson.[32] It is possible, however, that Simpson's suggestion, transmitted to Aberdeen through Pelly, might have been the basis for the proposal.

Simpson was disposed to follow this recommendation with another. Since the eventual agreement would probably give the United States all of Oregon south of the Columbia, he proposed that the treaty specify the protection of the Company's rights to property in that section of Oregon. The letter was not sent, since Pelly advised Simpson that Pakenham was merely an agent of the Foreign Office and that such suggestions could best be made directly to Lord Aberdeen by the governor and committee.[33] Pakenham, however, continued to call upon Simpson for information, and Simpson continued to provide it. Simpson also enlisted the support of Dr. John Bartlett, editor of the New York *Albion,* to publish articles advocating a settlement along the lines suggested by the Hudson's Bay Company.[34] But the influence of Simpson was thereafter exerted through Pelly upon the Foreign Office rather than directly upon Pakenham.

Concrete evidence that the cabinet would not allow British interests in Oregon to be flouted was provided by the arrival on July 15, 1844, of H.M.S. *Modeste,* an eighteen-gun sloop, under the captaincy of Commander Thomas Baillie. Baillie stayed for three weeks, and visited the Willamette settlement in company with Douglas. Like other British naval officers after him, Baillie did not display as much interest in Oregon as the Company's officers desired. Douglas complained that Baillie and his officers "had more of a taste for a lark than for a 'musty' lecture on politics or the great national interests in question." [35]

The appearance of the *Modeste,* all agreed, had a beneficial effect on the attitude of the Americans in Oregon, who observed that Britain was not unconcerned with the interests of the Hudson's Bay Company. Events in the East, however, had moved toward a new and, as it proved, final crisis. Before Baillie reached the Columbia James K. Polk had been nominated for the presidency by the Democratic party, with a platform providing for the "re-occupation" of Oregon and the "re-annexation" of Texas.

CHAPTER

12

*American Victory, 1844-1846*

INFLUENTIAL BRITISH POLITICIANS regarded the Hudson's Bay Company as the embodiment of those false principles of restrictive trade which must be swept away. The Peel cabinet supported the Company not because they approved of its character but because it was British. As a British enterprise, it could not be abandoned without sacrificing British honor and British prestige. For this reason, protection of the Company's rights assumed an importance far greater than the Company's material influence alone could have made possible.

The bellicosity of James K. Polk made it difficult for any British government to yield concessions to the United States without being attacked by the opposition for craven submission to a display of force. Aberdeen, who was personally willing to accept the 49th parallel as boundary, consequently faced the problem of reaching an agreement without exposing himself and the Peel cabinet to denunciations by the patriotic press and the public. If Polk insisted on British acceptance of an ultimatum, there must be war. Such a war would likely spread. In particular, Peel feared "the fruitful germs of war" in France. The aged Duke of Wellington, whose opinion on military matters was still sought and respected, believed that war with France was probable. War against France at any time could not be taken lightly, but in the 1840's the introduction of steam warships had made the old sailing vessels obsolete, and the power of a French navy composed of steam vessels was a serious threat to Great Britain.[1] Sir Charles Napier, a distinguished naval officer, after seeing a huge French steam warship at a Portsmouth naval display, stated that the Royal Navy possessed no vessels of comparable power. He wrote to his friend Edward Ellice on October 24, 1844:

> I wrote to Peel on the subject some time ago, and I intend seeing him in a few days, and really if something is not done, we ought to rouse the Country, for we certainly are not safe—if we had had war the other day, they might have taken Portsmouth and burnt the Dockyard and every ship there, we had nothing to hinder them but still we are doing little or nothing.[2]

In this environment, a war for Oregon was a fearsome prospect, but Peel and his colleagues were not prepared to accept peace at the price of obvious British surrender. As a distinguished American historian has shown, the agitation for the end of the Corn Laws indirectly contributed to the solution of the dilemma. Peel's advocacy of free trade made possible a tacit understanding with the Whig party on the abolition of the Corn Laws. The government, relieved of much of the fear of Whig attack, could attempt a settlement less favorable to British interests than had been previously proposed by any British government.[3] The Peel cabinet, however, was not a completely free agent; there were limits beyond which no British government could go even in the favorable circumstances of 1846. A patent sacrifice of British interests for the sake of peace would certainly provoke strong protest. Palmerston might not be able to resist the opportunity to play his role as the champion of British honor. Also, there could be no certainty that Polk would accept less than 54° 40', and the British cabinet would make no further concessions than the 49th parallel. Aberdeen, consequently, consulted with the Hudson's Bay Company, first to determine the minimum terms the Company would accept, and second to provide the cabinet with information that would be valuable should Polk prove adamant and war be forced upon Great Britain. It was in this context that the Company influenced British policy in the last stages of the Oregon dispute. In Aberdeen it did not have an aggressive spokesman, as Canning had been. Factors of far greater moment than the Company's welfare dictated the necessity of a settlement; the Company nevertheless played a not unim-

[1] For notes to chap. 12, see pp. 457–460.

portant role in the final Oregon negotiations, for it was the British interest around which considerations of British honor and prestige were centered.

Before the election of Polk, Secretary of State John C. Calhoun had adroitly spun out the negotiations with Pakenham, always protesting his desire for a settlement based upon mutual concessions but never committing himself to any line farther south than the 49th parallel. He convinced Pakenham that he was personally anxious to come to an agreement, but that the Senate would not consent to a treaty less favorable to the United States than Gallatin had been prepared to accept almost twenty years before. On one occasion, Calhoun suggested that he would not object to conceding the free navigation of the Columbia; on another, that he would be willing to concede to Britain all Vancouver Island; but at no time did he express willingness to yield on both points.[4] Calhoun's techniques accorded with his conviction that delay must work to the advantage of the United States. He was undoubtedly correct, but the expansionist spirit admitted of no such delay. This spirit was represented by James K. Polk, and by Henry Williamson.

In mid-February, 1845, Williamson, a recent arrival in Oregon from La Porte County, Indiana, erected near Fort Vancouver a few logs in the form of a hut and posted a notice on a nearby tree that he intended to claim a section of land. As soon as McLoughlin heard of Williamson's action, he had the tree cut down and the logs removed. Williamson, undaunted, returned with a surveyor. After a rancorous controversy in which threats were uttered by both sides Williamson eventually withdrew.[5] But his actions, though disapproved by the provisional government of Oregon, manifested the anti-British sentiment that had swept James K. Polk into the presidency and was much stronger among the immigrants of 1844 and 1845 than it had been among the earlier settlers. Francis Ermatinger of the Company, who resided at the falls of the Willamette, described the migration of 1844 as containing "some of as lawless fellows as ever can curse a countre." "A few more such," he said, "and our business is done, unless, indeed, some power is sent to keep them in check."[6]

The increasing militancy in the United States led the governor and committee to call Sir George Simpson to London for conferences on the Company's policy to meet the emergency. Between

November, 1844, when he arrived, and April, 1845, when he departed, Simpson was dominantly concerned with this question. Aberdeen may have informed Pelly either during this period or earlier that the British government would, if necessary, concede the 49th parallel, for Simpson's discussions with the governor and committee accepted the concession as likely. With this eventuality in view, Simpson, at Pelly's behest, drew up for Aberdeen's consideration a memorandum which was submitted to the Foreign Office on March 29, 1845. Since the memorandum contained the essential provisions for the protection of the Company's interests eventually embodied in the Oregon treaty, it deserves to be quoted *in extenso:*

> Should the present negociations happily result in a partition of the country, the branch of the Columbia called Lewis' River, would be a satisfactory Boundary as regards British interests. But, if that cannot be obtained, the parallel of 49° might be continued as a Boundary line from the Mountains until it strikes the North branch of the Columbia, which, from that point, should be the boundary to the sea. If the 49th parallel be adopted as the Boundary line the whole way from the Mountains to the sea, then it would be indispensable to have Vancouver's Island and the free navigation of the Straits of De Fuca secured to us; as in consequence of the prodigious tideway in Johnston's Straits, it would be impossible for trading ships to reach Frasers River by the Northern Channel.
>
> In such partition of the country, it would, as a matter of course, be necessary that, the Company and British settlers should be secured in their present possessions by a provision in the Treaty; and the free navigation of the Columbia River, as the only practicable communication to the East side of the mountains;—as well as right of way by land (should a practicable route be found) from the Gulf of Georgia to the Columbia should be secured to us. The provision in the Treaty should also secure to us the undisturbed possession of the country now occupied by the Puget Sound Company—the farms on the Cowlitz, in the neighbourhood of Vancouver and on the Multnomah Island; our water privileges on the Willamette River; our posts on the Columbia and Umpqua Rivers and all other establishments now occupied by the Company.[7]

The idea that the treaty should incorporate specific protective provisions was not original with Simpson nor was it first conceived in 1845. When the first large migration of Americans reached the Columbia in 1843, James Douglas had doubted both the Com-

pany's ability to retain control over its possessions and the continued British determination to insist upon the Columbia River
boundary. He had proposed essentially the same means of protection.[8] But Simpson's proposal in 1845 unquestionably brought the
suggestion directly to the attention of the Peel government, for
during the next few days Simpson had the opportunity to express
his views personally to both Peel and Aberdeen. Thereafter they
gave him respectful attention.

The tone of Simpson's correspondence with the British government at this time was not one of quiet resignation. He knew that
Peel and Aberdeen, little as they cared for Oregon, would not
tolerate American aggression. War seemed not improbable, and
Simpson preferred war to the abject surrender of the Company's
interests. In his memorandum of March 29, Sir George proposed
to Aberdeen a plan for the defense of Rupert's Land and Oregon
against American invasion. He recommended the establishment at
Red River of a small force of regular soldiers, to be supplemented
by a company of riflemen drawn from the half-breeds. To protect
British interests in Oregon, he suggested the dispatch of two
steamers and two sailing ships of war with a large body of Marines.
The British government should take possession of Cape Disappointment, at the entrance to the Columbia, and erect a battery
that would command access to the river. The Company would attempt to raise a force of 2,000 men, composed of half-breeds and
Indians from both sides of the Rocky Mountains, for service in
Oregon. This force should be led by officers of the Regular Army.[9]

Simpson's recommendations reached Aberdeen at a time when
the foreign secretary and Sir Robert Peel feared that war with
the United States was imminent. Polk was truculent. His inaugural speech left "little reason to hope for any favorable result of
the existing negotiations," [10] and James Buchanan, considered by
the British government to be among the most violent opponents
of compromise, was secretary of state. The Oregon fever seemed
to have gripped the United States, making rational discussion of
the issue impossible. In preparations for war, Simpson's advice
would be useful, for he possessed intimate knowledge of British
North America. Aberdeen consequently asked Simpson to call on
him and the prime minister at Peel's residence on April 2. At
this meeting and at a later conference with Aberdeen, Simpson

expounded his views on the most effective means of defending western North America. The outcome was that Peel and Aberdeen decided to send one or two engineer officers with Simpson on his annual journey to the interior, on the excuse of enjoying a leave of absence for hunting in the wilds of North America.[11] Since defensive preparations must be related to the possibility of war, Aberdeen instructed Pakenham to transmit to Simpson any information he had on the progress of negotiations.[12] Peel and Aberdeen further authorized Simpson to expend up to £1,000 for the defense of the Company's interests in Oregon. This sum, obviously inadequate for the general strengthening of defenses, was intended to defray the Company's expenses in constructing a fort, ostensibly for purposes of trade but actually to give Britain control over the mouth of the Columbia.[13]

Simpson's influence on British policy in 1845 and 1846 was confined to the area of defense. He had been called upon because Aberdeen and Peel expected in late March, 1845, that Polk's inaugural address meant war. But neither Simpson nor the governor and committee could substantially influence Aberdeen's convictions on Britain's basic policy and on the concessions necessary to maintain peace.

Simpson, whose self-esteem was increased by participation in the shaping of "high policy," [14] was delighted with his new role. After his arrival in Boston, he proceeded to Washington without delay to deliver a confidential dispatch from Aberdeen to Pakenham and to discuss the Oregon crisis with the latter. He learned from Pakenham and "from several influential members of Congress" that Polk's belligerent tone in the inaugural address was not to be taken seriously, that it was intended to satisfy the lunatic fringe of the president's supporters, and that "the most respectable portion of the community" favored an amicable settlement. On his way home to Lachine, he stopped in New York to see Bartlett of the *Albion* to arrange for the publication in American newspapers of facts favorable to the British point of view. When he arrived in Montreal he learned from the governor-general, Lord Metcalfe, that two officers, Lieutenants Henry J. Warre and Mervin Vavasour, had already been appointed to accompany him on his journey westward.[15]

In his association with Warre and Vavasour, Simpson was serving the interests of both the British government and the Hudson's Bay Company. The two functions were not necessarily harmonious. Simpson hoped to use his influence with Warre and Vavasour to strengthen the Company's position at Red River, not only against American attack but against the increasingly restive inhabitants. In his first communication to the two officers, Simpson argued that Rupert's Land could be most effectively defended by establishing British military posts at Red River and on the Kaministikwia River near Fort William, and by maintaining 200 regular troops at Red River as a nucleus for a force of several thousand Indians and half-breeds.[16] These steps would not only help to resist American attack, but would be even more useful in maintaining order at Red River and in counteracting the development of American influence over the Indians of the frontier.[17]

Accompanied by Warre and Vavasour, Simpson arrived at Red River on June 7, 1845. There they remained for a few days, investigating the potentialities for defense. Awaiting them was Chief Factor Peter Skene Ogden, whom Simpson had assigned to guide them to the Columbia. On June 16 Ogden, the officers, a clerk, and six servants left for the Columbia. Their haste was dictated by the report that Lieutenant John C. Frémont had left St. Louis on April 25 for some unknown destination, supposedly the Columbia; Simpson was determined to reach Oregon before Frémont.[18]

Warre and Vavasour's objectives were, of course, cloaked in the disguise of sport and travel, but the dissimulation was not effective. Father de Smet met the party on August 9 near Clark's Fork and, either from remarkable insight or from conversation, discerned the purpose of the expedition. He noted:

> It was neither curiosity nor pleasure that induced these two officers to cross so many desolate regions, and hasten their course towards the mouth of the Columbia. They were invested with orders from their government to take possession of "Cape Disappointment," to hoist the English standard, and erect a fortress for the purpose of securing the entrance of the river, in case of war.[19]

As the party traveled toward the Oregon country, the prospects of peace, which had seemed somewhat improved when Simpson had visited Washington in April, again deteriorated. Pakenham, whose astuteness in the negotiations left much to be desired, had allowed himself to be outmaneuvered by Buchanan. He had re-

jected Buchanan's proposal of July 12 to establish the boundary
at the 49th parallel and to give Britain the right of free ports on
Vancouver Island south of that line. Since the proposal was manifestly unacceptable, Pakenham rejected it instead of referring it
to the British government for instructions.[20] Buchanan thereupon
withdrew his offer and placed the onus for the failure of the negotiations on the British minister.

The news of Pakenham's blunder dismayed Aberdeen. He confided in Lord Stanley, secretary of state for war and colonies, that
war with the United States was "not improbable."[21] But, unlike
Sir Charles Metcalfe in Canada, who believed that in the event
of war Britain should provide a sufficient force to command the
lakes and to strike at the heart of the United States,[22] the British
cabinet agreed that British action must be primarily defensive
and that the main reliance must be on local rather than Imperial
forces. West of Canada these forces were supposed to be subject
to the Hudson's Bay Company, and Stanley proposed that

> . . . it would be very expedient to intrust to the Hudson's Bay
> Company the maintenance of any force which might be requisite
> for the protection of the Country west of the Sault Ste. Marie; and
> I think it would be wise to enter upon a discussion with that
> Company of the terms on which they might be willing to raise,
> organize, and equip such a force.[23]

Stanley felt that if war came it should be conducted as inex-
pensively as possible, and that preparations for war should involve
a minimum drain upon the British exchequer. Peel, confronted
with a national debt of almost £800,000,000, agreed at least with
the latter assumption.[24] The sense of imminent war continued to
the end of the year, and was aggravated when Polk, in his annual
address in December, maintained his aggressive tone. Simpson
wrote his friend Andrew Colvile on December 26, 1845, that "In
this country [Canada], war with the United States is considered
inevitable."[25]

The atmosphere of tension made Warre and Vavasour's early
reports important enough to justify cabinet attention. The party
arrived at Fort Vancouver on August 25, 1845. Two days later
Ogden set out for Cape Disappointment to secure possession of the
cape for Great Britain, one of the principal objects of the mission.
To his dismay he found the cape and all other commanding posi-

tions in the vicinity occupied by American citizens who had broken the soil and erected shacks to strengthen their claims. Simpson had advised Ogden not to attempt to take possession if the land was already held by the Americans. Ogden consequently asked Warre to authorize purchase. After consulting Vavasour, Warre replied that it seemed from Simpson's instructions that the Company intended to take possession of the cape, but he refrained from directly authorizing Ogden to buy the land. After much discussion about authority and the lack of it, Ogden finally decided in February to purchase Cape Disappointment from two Americans, Wheeler and McDaniell, who had valid claims in accordance with the laws of the provisional government. He paid them $1,000 for their claims and spent another $200 for surveyors' fees, registering the claim in his own name.[26]

This interchange probably contributed substantially to Ogden's low estimate of Warre and Vavasour. Warre he found tolerable until the arrival of H.M.S. *Modeste,* after which, said Ogden, Warre assumed an air of importance and sought to bask in the reflected glory of his uncle, Sir Richard Jackson, and his uncle's cook's alleged salary of £500 per year. Vavasour, Ogden declared, was "to the last hour a disagreeable Puppy and at times most disgusting particularly when under the influence of Brandy and Opium—truly a noble specimen of Her Majesty's Forces." [27]

Ogden's estimate of the young men was no doubt unfair. Whatever their defects they did accomplish their objective of reconnoitering the territory and providing accurate information on conditions in Oregon.[28] A similar defense cannot be made for Captain John Gordon, commander of H.M.S. *America* which arrived in Oregon waters in August, 1845. Gordon was the youngest brother of Aberdeen, but apparently had little other claim to exalted station. The *America* had been dispatched to Puget Sound probably on instructions sent by the Admiralty after news of Polk's inaugural address reached England.[29] The story circulated by Roderick Finlayson, that Britain lost Oregon because of Gordon's disgust with salmon that would not rise to a fly, is entertaining but, of course, baseless. Gordon's attitude had no relationship to the final settlement. But his apathy toward the value of Oregon was typical of most of his countrymen. He did not bother to visit Fort Vancouver or the Willamette personally. Instead he sent two young officers, Lieutenant William Peel, son of the prime minister, and a Marine captain named Parke.[30] James Douglas, who accompanied the officers back to Port Discovery where the *America* was anchored, and spent three days on board, reported to Simpson that Gordon "does not think the country worth five straws and is surprised that the Government should take any trouble about it." Gordon advised Douglas that when trespassers squatted upon the Company's claims the dispute should be settled by arbitration, "a very wise plan truly," Douglas sardonically remarked, "to lose everything we had." [31]

The Oregon boundary was not decided on the basis of reports, favorable or unfavorable, from Oregon. Since the spring of 1844 Aberdeen had been prepared to accept the 49th parallel, provided that Great Britain retained all Vancouver Island, and his views remained unchanged to the end of the negotiations. On October 17, 1845, he wrote to Peel:

> If it should ever be possible to effect a settlement between ourselves upon terms, I think the following might perhaps be accepted; and I should be very unwilling to concede more. I would carry the 49th parallel of latitude as the boundary *to the sea* and give to the United States the line of Coast to the South of this degree. This would leave us in possession of the whole of Vancouver's Island, and the northern shore of the entrance into the Straits of John de Fuca. The navigation of the Columbia to its most remote accessible point, should be common to both parties at all times; and all the ports between the Columbia and the 49th parallel, whether on the main land, or in the island, should be Free Ports. I believe that this would give us everything really worth contending for, and it would seem to coincide with the notions of the Hudson's Bay Company who have lately established their principal settlement on Vancouver's Island.[32]

Aberdeen's statement was not accurate as to the Company's motives in establishing Fort Victoria. Construction of the fort implied neither that the Company intended to withdraw from the territory north of the Columbia nor that it had a low regard for the value of that area. Fort Vancouver continued to be the main headquarters, and remained so for three years after conclusion of the treaty. But the establishment of Fort Victoria provided support for Aberdeen's view that a settlement should be made on the basis of the 49th parallel. Peel, although continuing to assert that he would not be influenced by Yankee bluster, appears by the end of 1845 to have been brought to acceptance of Aberdeen's terms. Pelly, who had frequent discussions with Aberdeen late in the year, gained the impression that a settlement based on the 49th parallel was likely. The primary barrier was the belligerence of James K. Polk, for not even Aberdeen was willing to make any concessions to the United States until the American government moderated its tone. Aberdeen professed to see some hope in the truculent message of Polk to Congress in December, 1845. He wrote to Peel:

> With respect to the President's Message, it is in substance very much what I expected; although somewhat more moderate in language. I am glad that he has brought matters to an issue; and whether the Senate adopt his recommendation or not, I cannot doubt that we shall see a reasonable settlement. I have never been afraid of the Oregon question, and feel confident that in the course of the year we shall see it finally settled, either by arbitration or by direct negociation.[33]

By the beginning of January interested parties began to suspect that an agreement on American terms was impending. Edward Ellice, in Paris, wrote his friend Joseph Parkes that "The American question is settled—or is to be settled,"[34] and Ellice's sources of information were usually excellent, although his influence on the Peel government was small. That his statement was not idle speculation may be seen from his observation to Simpson on February 9:

> I am assured that we shall get through the Oregon question without war. The future settlement will be—49—from the mountains to the sea—they giving up the whole of Vancouver Island. The great inconvenience in this, would be in that [sic] Highway of the Columbia River—but you and I know of how little real importance that is—and if the national honor is satisfied—our interests will not be seriously jeopardized. At the same time, I hope friend Pelly is talking of compensation, in these times of compensations and indemnities.[35]

When Archibald Barclay, the Company's secretary, read his copy of the *Times* on January 3, he was convinced that the leading editorial was a feeler sent out by the British government to test public opinion,[36] and in the light of Ellice's statements Barclay's suspicions may well have been correct. The editorial, which appealed for a "reasonable" approach to the Oregon question, contained the following statement:

We think, then, that every purpose both of honour and interest would be answered, if the British Minister, on whom now devolves the duty of making fresh proposals to the Government of the United States, were to renew on his part the offer made to England by Mr. Gallatin in the presidency and under the direction of Mr. Adams. That proposal was to take the 49th degree of north latitude as far as the sea as the boundary line, reserving to Great Britain Vancouver's Island, the harbour of St. Juan de Fuca, and the free navigation of the Columbia. This would be a concession as far as superficial area of ground is concerned. It would leave the United States masters of the greater part of Oregon. But it would secure the principal advantage of the country, the free navigation of the Columbia, to the servants of the Hudson's Bay Company, as well as the harbourage, anchorage, and settlement for English vessels trading with China and our possessions in Australia and New Zealand. It would concede all that the most successful war could acquire—a sovereign but barren dominion; but it would secure all the commercial blessing of an honourable compromise and a rational peace.[37]

The proposed terms offered the Hudson's Bay Company little protection. By 1846 Simpson and the governor and committee agreed that free navigation of the Columbia was of little significance if the boundary was to be the 49th parallel. The concession, as Simpson pointed out, would be important only if the Company retained the territory between the lower reaches of the Columbia and the 49th parallel. The Company did not use the Columbia as a channel to transport merchandise to the east side of the mountains, but merely for expresses and "light travelling." The express from New Caledonia to the east could be sent across New Caledonia to the Peace River, so that no benefit in communications would accrue to the Company by this apparent concession.[38] Simpson therefore contended that the navigation issue was of no importance to any British interest.

It was not the Company, however, which Aberdeen was primarily desirous of conciliating. As Peel's good friend, Edward Everett, pointed out, the right of navigation was an issue of "punctilio," not of substance, since the river had no value as a channel of commerce north of the 49th parallel.[39] But punctilio was important, particularly because national pride would be inflamed by complete and obvious surrender to the arrogant Yankees. The cabinet could not accept less than Gallatin had been willing to concede; Aberdeen therefore insisted on a concession that had little real value.

Aberdeen and Peel were not overly concerned with Oregon in the early part of 1846. The dominant subject then was the prospective repeal of the Corn Laws and its effect upon British society and the Tory party. In foreign relations, the important issues were the Spanish marriage and other European questions.[40] Anglo-American relations were of slight interest to the British public, with the notable exception of the Hudson's Bay Company. Peel, it is true, saw in the repeal of the Corn Laws a means of relieving the Oregon problem. "The admission of Maize," he wrote to Lord Francis Egerton on January 6, 1846, "will I believe go far to promote a settlement of Oregon." [41] In assuming that the benefits of free trade would quiet American nationalism he revealed a lack of understanding of the nationalist mentality.[42]

The foreign secretary waited for the propitious moment to propose his minimum terms of settlement. Richard Croker, the Tory hanger-on, who was on far more intimate terms with the foreign secretary than any director of the Hudson's Bay Company, was apparently used by Aberdeen to help prepare the British public for the approaching surrender.[43] Pakenham's report on February 15, 1846, that the United States had finally rejected the British proposal for arbitration, left no other alternatives if war was to be avoided. Aberdeen's sources of information convinced him that the United States would accept a settlement based on the 49th parallel. Pakenham reported that "there is a certain majority in the Senate in favor of an accommodation of the Oregon question on the principle of equitable partition and compromise." [44] Although Congress passed a joint resolution on April 26, 1846, providing that the required notice be given of the termination of the treaty of 1827, Polk transmitted the notice to Great Britain with words of unwonted courtesy and moderation. Edward Everett, in whose judgment of American opinion both Peel and Aberdeen placed great faith, wrote Peel on April 28 that "the proceedings in the Senate show that there is a large majority friendly to a compromise on the basis of the 49th degree." [45]

Even if Congress, particularly the Senate, was receptive to a settlement on such terms, there could be no assurance that this mood would continue and that the moderate elements could resist the increasing pressure of the extremists. Robert Dale Owen, who in 1844 had introduced into Congress a proposal for an Oregon settlement similar to that now being contemplated by Aberdeen, wrote Peel a letter on March 23, 1846, which may have had some influence in convincing the British government that delay was dangerous. He said:

> I feel confident, that, at this moment, and probably for some weeks to come, the government of the United States would accept an offer on the basis of 49°; and that the Senate would ratify such a treaty, by the necessary two-thirds vote, and nothing to spare. But I doubt whether such a treaty can be either signed or ratified, after three months from this date. I feel absolutely assured, that it will not be, *if the Congress now in Session be suffered to adjourn* (that will probably be in July) leaving the subject in its present open state. Every week, every day, increases the doubt and difficulty. The warmest friends of peace, Mr. Calhoun among the number, admit and lament this. Not one, even of them, dare hint at any compromise south of 49°; and the probability is, that nine out of ten legal voters in the United States, would resent the idea, and consign to political death the statesman who should advocate, or vote for it.[46]

Richard Croker, as self-appointed adviser to Aberdeen, was greatly concerned lest wrangling over such unimportant matters as the rights of navigation on the Columbia prevent the immediate conclusion of a treaty. Croker himself was not a dominant force in the Tory party, but he had a keen sense of the currents of political opinion; his advice, therefore, cannot be disregarded as inconsequential. He wrote to Aberdeen on May 13:

> If you get 49° and the Columbia, you will have done a miracle, but I have no hope of miracles now-a-days, and I shall gladly assent to 49° and half the Straits of Fuca; but, for God's sake, end it; for if anything were to happen to *Louis Philippe,* we should have an American War immediately, and a French one just after, a rebellion in Ireland, real starvation in the manufacturing districts, and a twenty-per-cent complication in the shape of Income Tax,—not pleasant in prospect, and still less so if any portion of the Black Cloud should burst.[47]

These considerations were basic to the cabinet decision authorizing Aberdeen on May 18, 1846, to send Pakenham the dispatch
containing the draft of the treaty as eventually accepted.[48] The influence of the Hudson's Bay Company in this decision, it should
be evident, was extremely small. The Company had no part in
the decision to propose the 49th parallel with Britain retaining
all Vancouver Island. Nor did it insist upon the second article of
the treaty, which provided that the navigation of the Columbia
"shall be free and open to the Hudson's Bay Company, and to all
British Subjects trading with the same." This provision was based
upon Gallatin's proffered concession in 1827 of British rights of
navigation, although his offer had been conditional upon proof
that the river was navigable above 49°.[49]

The contribution of the Hudson's Bay Company to the Oregon
treaty was the inclusion of provisions for the protection of the
rights of the Company and its satellite, the Puget's Sound Agricultural Company. This was Pelly's preoccupation in his conferences with Aberdeen during the early months of 1846. On June 3,
1846, before Aberdeen's offer had become generally known, Pelly
informed Simpson of the prospective provisions of the treaty and
the efforts he had made in the Company's behalf:

> I think we shall consent to continue the Line of the 49° from
> its present Terminus at Rocky Mountains to the Middle of the
> Gulf of Georgia where it divides the Continent from Vancouvers
> Island and from that point keeping the Center till it strikes a
> line drawn through the Center of the Straits of Juan de Fuca if
> this is agreed to; I have been urging that the Hudson's Bay Com.,
> the Puget Sound Association and all British American Subjects
> who are in possession shall be secured in their possessions either
> No. or South of the line (altho the British possessions may be in
> American Territory) of all buildings Posts Lands &c. that they
> occupy at the time of the Treaty (with the Exception that the
> United States have the option of purchasing the possessions of
> the Puget Sound Association at their improved Value, I have sug-
> gested as a price 20 years purchase on the Nett Average profits of
> the Years 1844.5.6)[50] and that the Hudsons Bay Com. and all
> others having possessions in the Oregon [territory] to which the
> Columbia is the nearest way have a right of way by that River
> secured to them. If by this we are allowed to retain Fort Van-
> couver its Lands and Woods, Fort Nes Perces, Fort Okanagan and

Fort Colvile, and there is no restriction as to Trade with the Natives we may yet not be great loosers, and if a Portion of Vancouver Island is given us we may be better off. All this I have asked for, and it has been favourably Entertained, but this is only Entre Nous, I have not mentioned it to any one.[51]

Pelly's emphasis on the obligation of the British government to protect the interests of the two companies was reflected in Articles III and IV of the treaty and in the instructions Aberdeen sent to Pakenham with the draft of the proposed agreement. Since differences in interpretation of these articles were the source of much of the trouble experienced by the Company's officers in Oregon, they should be quoted verbatim:

### Article III

In the future appropriation of the territory south of the forty-ninth parallel of north latitude as provided in the first article of this treaty, the possessory rights of the Hudson's Bay Company, and of all British subjects who may be already in the occupation of land or other property, lawfully acquired within the said territory, shall be respected.

### Article IV

The farms, lands, and other property of every description belonging to the Puget's Sound Agricultural Company, on the north side of the Columbia River, shall be confirmed to the said company. In case, however, the situation of those farms and lands should be considered by the United States to be of public and political importance, and the United States Government should signify a desire to obtain possession of the whole, or of any part thereof, the property so required shall be transferred to the said Government, at a proper valuation, to be agreed upon between the parties.[52]

If those who drafted the treaty had intended to create difficulties for the Hudson's Bay Company they could not have used language better calculated to promote that purpose. Such expressions as "possessory rights," "lawfully acquired," and "belonging to," in a territory where such language was inapplicable before the assumption of American authority, were invitations to American settlers and public officials to harass the Company, and this they proceeded to do.

The interests of the Hudson's Bay Company in Oregon were sacrificed by Aberdeen to the larger interests of Anglo-American harmony. The treaty was signed at a time when Oregon south of 49° was still a source of profit to the Company. The net gain from sales and trade at Fort Vancouver in 1845–46 was £21,263, and the annual average for the seven years ending in 1846 was over £30,000. In addition, the other trading establishments in Oregon produced a net profit of £10,620 in 1845–46, and an average for the seven years of £10,929.[53] The infant Puget's Sound Agricultural Company also showed promise of becoming a profitable undertaking. The profits of the Hudson's Bay Company in Oregon were not large compared to those east of the mountains and were already showing a tendency to decline, but were still substantial enough to justify continued operations. North of the Columbia, the Company's posts were virtually undisturbed. A few Americans had crossed the river, with the largest number, fifteen families, settling in the neighborhood of Fort Nisqually.[54] They were no threat to the Company, and most settlers lived in perfect amity with the Company's officers. But such facts were of no consequence in the determination of the Oregon issue. McLane, who admirably performed his function of reporting to the United States the cross-currents of British society and the mood of the ministry, informed Buchanan as early as December 1, 1845, that an arrangement on the basis of 49° would "prove acceptable to large and important classes in this country—indeed complained of principally by the Hudson's Bay Company and those in its interest." [55]

To Canning, it was sufficient that the Company was British and that the antagonist was the United States; to Palmerston, the Company as an association of British subjects was entitled to the protection of its government. (Had he not promised that "the watchful eye and strong arm of England" would protect any British subject against "injustice and wrong"?) But the spirit of Canning and Palmerston was not evident in Aberdeen. He was not inclined to fight a war for a few thousand square miles of wilderness and the pelts of a few animals. The objections of other members of the cabinet were quieted by apparent guarantees for the protection of British interests in Oregon, and British national pride was salved by the explanation that an "honorable compromise" had been effected. It was no compromise; for Great Britain the Oregon treaty was a surrender.

Shortly after news of the agreement reached England, the Peel government was forced to resign as a result of the furore caused by repeal of the Corn Laws. When Pakenham's letter of August 13, 1846, recording the satisfaction with which the treaty was generally received in the United States, reached England, Palmerston was again in the Foreign Office. His estimate of the treaty was revealed in a note he appended to Pakenham's letter: "It would have been strange if the Americans had not been pleased with an arrangement which gives them everything which they ever really wanted." A clerk added the comment, "Nothing to be done." [56]

Both statements were correct. The United States had won, and Palmerston could not change the result. Far away in Oregon Peter Skene Ogden echoed Palmerson's observation:

> . . . all is ended in giving the Americans all they possibly wished for or required. Far better had they [Peel and Aberdeen] given it at first and then Jonathan would have thanked them for it on the contrary now they boast and laugh at them. . . . Truly may we say "put not your trust in Prime Ministers" thank God Peel is out of power and *long long* may he remain so.[57]

# The Possessory Rights Question, 1846-1869

THE TREATY had been ratified and Oregon south of 49° had become American, but at first the relationship between the Hudson's Bay Company and the settlers seemed basically unchanged. In 1846 the economic interests of the migrant Americans were not yet in serious conflict with those of the Company; on the contrary, the Company's store at Vancouver was an important source of supply for the settlers' necessities. Lieutenant Neil M. Howison of the *Shark*, who was sent by Captain John Sloat of the Pacific squadron of the United States Navy to investigate conditions in Oregon, found little tension between the Americans and the Company. Howison, who was in the Columbia area from July, 1846, to January, 1847, was favorably impressed by the Company's trading practices. Its profits were moderate, and its officers saw plainly that "in the prosperity of others consists their own." The "sudden withdrawal of the Company from Oregon," he believed, "would be forcibly and disadvantageously felt throughout the land." [1]

The relationship between the provisional government and the Company's officers also seemed harmonious. Of the three judges appointed by the government to administer the laws of Vancouver District, north of the Columbia, two were in the employ of the Company—James Douglas and Charles Forrest, the officer in charge

[1] For notes to chap. 13, see pp. 460-464.

of the Cowlitz.[2] The American population in the Willamette area far exceeded the number of British subjects in all Oregon, including the employees of the Company and the Canadian settlers in the Willamette valley.[3] But aside from a few firebrands like Henry Williamson, the Americans showed little disposition to use their dominant position to attack the Company. The Company's officers found the large migration of 1845, which Douglas estimated at 2,600, more "respectable" than those of previous years, by which they meant that the new arrivals were less troublesome to the Company.[4]

This tranquillity could not long endure. Although the Company might follow enlightened trading practices, to the Americans it was nevertheless a "large and powerful moneyed institution, controlled by foreigners in the heart of this young America."[5] American patriots in Oregon would not long continue to view the operations of a foreign monopoly with restraint; sooner or later, unless deterred by the territorial or the federal government, they would seize the Company's property. Peter Skene Ogden, a member of the board of management for the western department with James Douglas,[6] was skeptical even before the treaty was signed that harmony could continue. "So far all is apparently tranquil," he said, "but still we are looked upon with a suspicious eye by one and all."[7]

The first conflict arose over land claims. Emigrants from the United States had come to Oregon for good land, and in the search for choice, unoccupied locations they collided with the Company, which had marked out for itself some of the most desirable acreages. By the Oregon Land Law of 1845, no individual could hold a claim larger than one square mile. In order to protect the Company's rights, McLoughlin and Douglas decided to invest formal title in the Company's land around Fort Vancouver in nine employees. They had the land surveyed and divided into nine claims of one square mile each, which were registered in the recorder's office in September and October, 1845.[8] The nine "owners" then privately signed quitclaims to the Company. The officers in charge at Nisqually and Cowlitz similarly divided the most valuable land in the vicinity. These formal transfers deluded no one as to the real claimant. Encroachments occurred even before the treaty was signed, and at Nisqually it was impossible to find enough Company employees to claim the entire area of pasture for the herds and flocks. In March, 1846, William Fraser Tolmie, at Nisqually, expressed the fear that American squatters would disrupt the operations of the Puget's Sound Agricultural Company by selecting their square miles in the middle of the Company's pasture lands. His fears were soon realized. In 1847 Tolmie notified "one Smith" that he was squatting on land owned by the Puget's Sound Company, but his warnings had no effect. Other squatters did not immediately follow Smith's example, but his successful defiance foreshadowed serious trouble for the company.[9]

Harassment of the Company and its officers was inevitable under the terms of the treaty. Aberdeen in his zeal for an early and amicable settlement had provided the Company with the form of protection without the substance. The clauses safeguarding the Company's rights were not carefully worded, and the two governments made no effort before signing the treaty to reach agreement on their meaning. The second article, granting the right of navigation of the Columbia to the "Hudson's Bay Company, and to all British subjects trading with the same," did not specify whether the right was eternal or whether it expired in 1859, when the Company's license to trade in the territory was scheduled to expire. Both governments recognized the uncertainty, and both skirted the issue. In his conversations with Aberdeen, McLane assumed that the privilege would end in 1859, but he did not express this opinion until after the treaty was signed.[10] On June 12, 1846, the Senate rejected a proposal to put a time limit on the rights of navigation.[11] After the treaty had been signed, Aberdeen declared that he had specifically informed McLane that Britain insisted upon a permanent right to navigate the Columbia and that he had rejected the minister's suggestion to limit the right to a term of years.[12] Either McLane's or Aberdeen's memory was faulty, but regardless of whose version was correct, the disagreement as to interpretation was not resolved.

Polk was of the opinion that the rights of navigation were limited to the term of the license, which he confused with the Company's charter. He labored under the misapprehension that the life of the Company would end when its license expired, and that the navigation rights would thus become extinct. But in June, 1846, no one was disposed to insist on a definition of terms, for such a demand might reopen the controversy and impair the prospects of settlement.[13]

The governor and committee, not concerned at this time over the navigation issue, probably believed that the language was clear. But they thought that the meaning of other articles was open to argument. The first article, which delineated the boundary, placed the line of demarcation between Vancouver Island and the United States at mid-channel of the Strait of Juan de Fuca. But the treaty did not indicate which channel among those formed by the numerous islands was meant. The Company was concerned with the definition of the boundary, since the location of the line was likely to affect its coastal trade to the northwest. The third article, stipulating that the "possessory rights" of the Company, "lawfully acquired," be respected, also provided a basis for conflict, for without definition both expressions were virtually meaningless.

With Palmerston again in the Foreign Office, the Company's governing board was hopeful of vigorous support. Governor Pelly went to see the foreign secretary on July 29, 1846, and expressed the Company's fears that complications would arise unless the provisions of the treaty were more clearly defined. He asked Palmerston to seek American recognition of the claims registered by the Company's officers with the provisional government, and expressed the hope that the United States would purchase the lands of the Puget's Sound Agricultural Company at a fair valuation, as provided for in the treaty. A fair price, Pelly believed, would be from twenty to twenty-five times the net profit for 1845 or 1846, or a minimum of £40,000.[14] He did not suggest that the Hudson's Bay Company would sell its rights in Oregon south of 49°, perhaps because the treaty did not provide for such a sale or because the Company hoped to continue profitable operations there and its land claims, if guaranteed by the United States, would appreciate in value. The Puget's Sound Agricultural Company, on the other hand, could not hope to retain the huge areas of pasturage over which its livestock grazed, and its fortunes were certain to decline.

As to the meaning of the possessory rights guaranteed by the treaty, the officers of the Company could not agree among themselves. Pelly believed that they included the right to cultivate the soil at the Company's establishments, to cut and sell wood growing in the immediate area around the posts, and to trade in furs with natives who visited the posts, but not to send out hunting and trapping parties to places not confirmed as the Company's property.[15] Douglas, also noting the vagueness of the language, correctly predicted that it would cause much difficulty, but both he and Ogden believed that the rights included conduct of the fur trade throughout the Oregon territory. Whatever the interpretation, they did not expect the United States to interfere with the Company's trade until it had established a military force in Oregon sufficient to control the Indians so that Americans scattered throughout the territory would not have to depend upon the protection of the Company's forts. When the United States should decide to apply pressure, Douglas and Ogden feared that the language of the treaty would afford the Company no protection:

> Should there be any disposition on the part of the American Government to impose harrassing restrictions on our trade, a fertile pretext for every species of oppression may be readily found in the 2d Article of the late Treaty, . . . a decitful [sic] clause, in the form of a liberal concession, which substantially leaves the Company subject to the revenue and navigation laws of the United States, and to the heavy import duties, levied to a greater or less extent, on all Goods of British manufacture, whether imported by subjects of Great Britain, or citizens of the United States. If so, the free navigation of the Columbia River, confers no exclusive privilege on the Hudson's Bay Company, as it places them on a perfect equality with any other body of importing merchants.[16]

The judgment of Douglas and Ogden was fully justified, but the federal government did not immediately take any action. The provisional government continued in control until 1849, when the first territorial governor, Joseph Lane, arrived. During these three years, the Company's posts and lands in Oregon were not seriously disturbed. But the governor and committee, Simpson, and the officers in Oregon all agreed that its position would deteriorate. It was therefore in the Company's interests to attempt to dispose of its rights to the United States while its bargaining position was still strong. In August, 1846, Simpson would have been willing to sell the property and rights of the two companies for £100,000—£70,000 to the Hudson's Bay Company and £30,000 to the Puget's Sound Agricultural Company. Pelly would also have accepted this price for all rights and all property except movable goods.[17]

Such negotiations, however, were not likely to be consummated immediately; in the meantime Simpson instructed the board of management (Ogden, Douglas, and Work) to estimate the value of buildings and improvements of the various establishments, including also land under cultivation, and "to take care not to be below the value" of these assets.[18] The estimates they finally submitted to Simpson on May 14, 1847, were perhaps not so generous as Simpson had hoped, but undoubtedly did full justice to the value of the establishments. They valued the buildings and improvements of the two companies in Oregon south of 49° at £87,117.11.9.[19]

These evaluations, which did not include the land, except for Cowlitz Farm, might prove useful should the United States seek to remove the Company by purchasing its assets. Since Palmerston showed no tendency to display his vaunted energy in behalf of the Company, the London board decided to take the initiative itself. As their instrument they naturally chose Sir George Simpson because of his proximity to Washington and his knowledge of North American conditions.

Before the Company attempted to sell its property to the United States, Simpson instructed Douglas and Ogden to regain title for the Company to the land assigned to individual employees. They, however, deemed this move unwise, since Oregon lawyers and most Americans in the territory believed that the treaty granted the Company a right only to its improvements, not to the soil itself. If the quitclaims were returned, they predicted, squatters would overrun the Company's lands; they therefore did not immediately execute Simpson's orders.[20] But Simpson was insistent, and the individuals to whom the land had been assigned retransferred their rights to the Company in 1849 and 1850, but with ill grace. They had performed a service and they had not been paid. Ogden, who had not been compensated for his expenditure for his square mile of land at Cape Disappointment, refused to transfer the title until his £300 was returned.[21] Forbes Barclay demanded either compensation for the 640 acres for which he had accepted responsibility or recognition of his claim.[22] Ogden was eventually paid, but the only satisfaction the other complainants received was a promise that they would be "liberally dealt with" should the Company sell its possessory rights.[23]

The Company did not wait for the return of the quitclaims before seeking to negotiate an agreement with the United States. On November 2, 1846, Pelly instructed Simpson to urge upon Pakenham the importance of settling with the United States the undefined boundary in the Gulf of Georgia and the limits of the possessions of the Hudson's Bay Company and the Puget's Sound Agricultural Company. If the United States government should offer £100,000 for all the rights of the two companies, Pelly advised Simpson to accept it.[24]

Simpson went to Washington in February, 1847, with little hope for a settlement. The expenditures of the Mexican War, he feared, would make the government reluctant to incur any further obligations. His conferences with Pakenham and his observations of American politicians did not increase his optimism. The Polk government, despite its successes in foreign policy, had lost control of Congress. As early as February, 1847, jockeying had begun for the next presidential election, with the Democratic party split into factions, each supporting its favorite candidate rather than the incumbent president. The result was that Polk experienced the greatest difficulty in securing the coöperation of Congress in any of his measures.[25] Even if the executive should be favorable to a settlement, therefore, there could be no certainty that Congress would approve it. While Simpson was pondering these unpleasant realities he was introduced to George N. Sanders, and his optimism returned.

George Sanders was one of a large number of Democratic stalwarts who hung about the edges of Washington politics in the hope of enriching themselves. He was a close friend of Buchanan's and was acquainted with other members of the cabinet. He was imaginative, perhaps to excess; he had extraordinary energy; and he was completely unscrupulous. Simpson, whose estimate of most men was cynical and of American politicians particularly so, found in Sanders a seemingly perfect foil.[26]

Sanders first approached Simpson as the representative of a group of private investors allegedly interested in purchasing the Company's rights with the idea of reselling them to the government at a substantial profit. The scheme was not as well matured as Sanders' enthusiasm at first led Simpson to believe. It involved the formation of a joint-stock company, headed by Captain A. C.

Harris, son-in-law of General Robert A. Armstrong, the United States consul in Liverpool. Harris had secured a contract from the Navy Department to transport mail from Panama to Oregon, and he hoped eventually to monopolize the shipping trade of the Pacific Coast. Sanders proposed that this company buy the possessory rights for $500,000, the minimum price set by Simpson and Pelly. But the purchase was to be conditioned on the Hudson's Bay Company's providing "a large pecuniary" advance for the construction of the mail steamers. Thus Harris, Sanders, and their associates would not be required to expend any money in the purchase of the Company's rights; the expected sale to the government would provide the money for payment and a large profit besides. Simpson could see advantages for Sanders and Harris in this scheme, but none for the Company, and he refused to entertain such a contingent offer. Sanders' associates consequently withdrew, and Sanders then offered himself in a new role as liaison between the Company and the Polk government. He convinced Simpson that his intimacy with key politicians was sufficiently close to make the prospects for a settlement good.

Simpson was not entirely deluded by Sanders. He recognized him as a man of talent and influence but also as one who should "not be trusted too far." Where his interests and those of the Company were in harmony, however, Sanders could be useful. On January 15, 1848, Simpson therefore promised Sanders a $10,-000 commission if he could sell the Company's rights for $500,000.[27] This amount was far short of what Sanders hoped to gain, and he went to London in March, 1848, to seek a more advantageous agreement with the governor and committee.

The result was all Sanders could have hoped for. He signed a contract with Pelly to serve as the Company's agent for one year from April 28, 1848. The Company agreed to accept $410,000 in United States bonds at 5 per cent interest, and to give Sanders 2½ per cent of this amount and all the payment above $410,000.[28] Pelly agreed that the Company's price should be kept secret for the duration of the contract and that Sanders might make as profitable a bargain as possible for himself and his associates. To avoid the dangers of delay, Sanders wanted a representative of the Company, with full power to effect the sale, available in Washington to sign the agreement with the government. Pelly provided Henry Hulse Berens, of the committee, with this authority.

The men through whose help Sanders hoped to succeed were Secretary of State Buchanan and Senators Calhoun, Cass, Crittenden, Hannegan, Houston, and Breese, all of whom had expressed themselves in favor of an immediate agreement to extinguish the Company's Oregon claims. There is no proof that any of this group expected financial gain from their support of such an arrangement, although Sidney Breese of Indiana displayed suspicious enthusiasm for the promotion of Sanders' scheme.[29] Buchanan was privy to Sanders' plans and encouraged him to prosecute them, but there is no evidence that he was guilty of collusion. On the contrary, his insistence that the British government be a party to any agreement requiring the relinquishment of the Company's rights, including navigation of the Columbia, was a serious obstacle. With that reservation, however, Buchanan was prepared to advocate the purchase of the Company's rights in Oregon for $1,000,000, the amount Sanders considered adequate to provide a sufficient profit for himself and his supporters.[30]

Two of the most eminent lawyers in the United States, Richard S. Coxe and Daniel Webster, wrote legal opinions describing the Company's rights in most expansive terms, and Webster added a supplementary opinion that, since the reserved right of navigation related to the Company alone, the Company's relinquishment of it would extinguish it. For these opinions, Sanders paid Webster $5,000 and Coxe an unspecified sum.[31]

Sanders hoped that the Senate would give his project favorable consideration before its adjournment in August, 1848. On August 11, Edward A. Hannegan, chairman of the Foreign Relations Committee, brought the subject before the Senate in secret session, but action was frustrated when an unnamed senator moved that a commission be appointed to ascertain the value of buildings, cattle, and other property. His motion was rejected, but further discussion had to be abandoned, and the subject did not come up again before adjournment.

Simpson joined Berens and Chief Factor Duncan Finlayson in Washington just as the session was being closed. On August 15, he, Berens, Finlayson, and the British chargé d'affaires, John F. Crampton, visited Buchanan at the latter's invitation. Buchanan reiterated that he was personally favorable to the purchase, as were the president, several members of the cabinet, and many influential senators. His desire for a settlement, however, was not based on the value of the Company's possessions or on the wish to remove the Company from Oregon, "as they and their followers would make better subjects than many . . . [American] citizens," but he was anxious to eliminate the treaty provision that gave the Company and British subjects trading with it the right to navigate the Columbia. Though a direct purchase of the Company's rights and interests would virtually eliminate this right, he believed that the only regular procedure would be for the United States and Great Britain to enter into another treaty to sanction the sale. With such a treaty, he said, the Senate would immediately confirm an arrangement, even at a price of $1,000,000. Without it, the Senate would not entertain the proposal.[32]

When Pelly heard about the interview with Buchanan, he had reason to be depressed. He knew that Palmerston was not likely to take an action that might be interpreted as a British withdrawal. Palmerston, preoccupied with defending the prestige of Britain and of himself, could not be expected to defer to the interests of the Hudson's Bay Company. Pelly's fears were confirmed at an interview on September 7 and in subsequent correspondence. The foreign secretary told Pelly that he would not sanction the relinquishment of the navigation rights on the Columbia and that, further, the Hudson's Bay Company could not unilaterally cede the rights, since other British subjects were involved.[33]

Pelly tried every recourse to influence the foreign secretary but without success. He produced the opinions of Webster, Louis McLane, and Josiah Randall that the navigation rights belonged to the Company alone, since the only other British subjects concerned were those trading with the Company. Palmerston's reply ended the discussion. He saw no reason to refer the matter to the Crown's law officers, for to him the meaning of the second article was clear. Obviously, he said, if the Columbia was navigable only to the 49th parallel, and the Company sold its possessions south of that line, the article would be a dead letter. But he believed that it was navigable beyond that point; since the territory north of the line belonged to the British Crown, not to the Company, the British government was not disposed to relinquish the privilege unless the United States would provide some concession in return.[34]

Hopes for early agreement were thus frustrated by the preoccupation of the two governments with a symbol of no substantial value. To Buchanan, the right of navigation was an encroachment on American sovereignty; to Palmerston, it was the sole concession Britain had won in an otherwise humiliating treaty. But even before the Oregon treaty was signed, officers of the Hudson's Bay Company considered the right as of little importance, and immediately after news of the treaty was received in Oregon, Work and Douglas began the search for a route by way of the Fraser River.[35] The brigades were subsequently sent into the interior along the Fraser.[36] Such facts had no weight with Palmerston, who would not be party to any apparent surrender to the United States. The Company had reason to be dissatisfied with the British foreign secretaries of the 1840's. One, in his anxiety to avoid conflict with the United States, sacrificed the Company's interests; the other, by his determination to stand firm, ignored its interests.

Palmerston's uncoöperativeness destroyed any hopes for an agreement. Sanders continued to lobby on his own and the Company's behalf, but in February, 1849, the Senate defeated a resolution for purchase of the Company's property. Only ten senators favored the resolution; the remaining forty either opposed it or wanted to avoid a decision.[37]

Sanders tried again before his contract expired. Incoming President Zachary Taylor appointed Senator John M. Clayton secretary of state. Clayton had not been among the senators whom Sanders had mentioned as friendly, but he manifested a desire for a settlement. Although he had no power to conclude a contract on his own responsibility, he was willing to recommend to Congress the purchase of the possessory rights for $700,000. Accordingly, Daniel Webster, George Evans, and Richard S. Coxe drew up a memorandum as the basis for an agreement. The likelihood of success seemed brightened when Clayton agreed not to insist that the British government participate in the contract and to accept the sale by the Company as constituting for all practical purposes the relinquishment of the right of navigation. No action, however, could be taken until Congress reconvened after its summer recess.[38]

Clayton's words were not matched by his activity. He dallied with the Company for the next year, and had made no effort to bring the matter to a conclusion before he resigned from the cabinet upon the death of Taylor.

Sanders' second failure was doubly serious, for the methods he used compromised the Company in future negotiations with the United States. No longer could it claim that its case was based upon an honest evaluation. The Company allowed the agreement with Sanders to lapse at the end of one year, and so long as Sir John Henry Pelly remained active as governor, it employed no other agents. Pelly had been dubious about a contract contrary to his own sense of business ethics and, if revealed, harmful to the Company's reputation. His successor, Andrew Colvile, was not so squeamish, but the opportunities for agreement under the auspices of future agents never seemed as bright as they had when Sanders was employed.

Between 1846 and 1849 conditions had seemed propitious for a settlement favorable to the Company. Not only were at least some members of the Polk cabinet eager to purchase the Company's rights, but the relationship between the population of Oregon and the Company's officers was generally peaceful. Ogden and Douglas were popular with the great majority of the American settlers, and the esteem in which Ogden was held was further increased by his intervention with the Indians to secure the release of the survivors of the massacre of Whitman and others at the Waiilatpu mission.

During the Cayuse War which followed, this reservoir of good will enabled Douglas and Ogden to resist the importunities of the Americans to join in the war, and may have prevented actual violence against Fort Vancouver. When the commissioners of the Oregon government asked Douglas for a loan to equip the punitive expedition against the Cayuse, he had refused on the basis that he had no authority to commit the Company's funds in this way. Since the Company's store was the principal source of supply for any expedition, Douglas' refusal caused bitterness. It was rumored in Oregon City that the volunteers would help themselves to the Company's goods with or without Douglas' consent. Retired Chief Factor John McLoughlin was informed confidentially by a person close to the expedition that Colonel Cornelius Gilliam, its commander, had said he would "manage ways and means" to get everything he required. Archibald McKinlay brought this disturbing news to Douglas.[39]

Gilliam was the type of American whom Charles Dickens found to be all too common in frontier areas. He was bombastic and swaggering, but he could also be dangerous if the population were hostile to the Company. Douglas, in an effort to avert violence, wrote Governor George Abernethy that he had heard of Gilliam's intentions and that the Company's employees would resist any attempt to seize property at Fort Vancouver. Abernethy replied that Gilliam had assured him there was no plan to use force, but Douglas and Ogden kept the staff at Fort Vancouver in a state of vigilance until Gilliam's band had passed into the interior.[40] Had Ogden and Douglas not been held in high esteem by the provisional government, the ugly rumors might not have been so easily dispelled.[41]

In a community as small as the Willamette colony, which remained the core of Oregon, personalities were of disproportionate importance in determining the relations between the Company and the Americans. Ogden and Douglas both possessed the physical qualities to command respect, they were personable, and they were generous to their friends among the leaders of the American community. The illustrious Joseph L. Meek, marshal of the provisional government and, after 1848, United States marshal, was one of these. Meek was so favorably inclined toward the Company that Douglas suggested that Simpson "use the sponge" with his debts to the Company, which were in excess of $300.[42]

Although Ogden and Douglas could not altogether prevent the growth of American hostility toward "the foreign monopoly," they did retard it.[43] The coöperation between them and the provisional government certainly exercised a restraining influence, for the first serious threats to the Company's claims came, not at Fort Vancouver, but at Fort Nisqually, remote from the center of population. There William F. Tolmie, a competent officer but not of the stature of Douglas or Ogden, was forced to contend with American squatters after 1847. By 1850 ten Americans had occupied land claimed by the Puget's Sound Company, and Tolmie was powerless to resist them by any means more effectual than written notices protesting the encroachments.[44] The protests had no perceptible effect on the settlers, but were intended to serve as a basis for claims when the United States government should decide to purchase the property.

Despite such vexations, the relationship between the Company's employees throughout Oregon and their American neighbors was dominantly harmonious until the provisional government came to an end. Pressure on the Company's claims from land-hungry immigrants was relieved when the discovery of gold in California stripped Oregon of most of its male population and diverted the wagon trains southward.[45] The Company both benefited and suffered from the gold rush. The prices of its goods at Fort Vancouver rose to unprecedented heights, with crowds of buyers eager to purchase. The price of lumber rose from $16 to $65 per thousand feet, delivered at the mill,[46] and the gold of California flowed into Fort Vancouver in gratifying amounts. On the other hand, the Company's servants deserted for California or to other employment in Oregon [47] and the Company was forced to fill the vacancies with Indians. Yet, on balance, the gold discoveries were profitable to the Company. When the first territorial governor of Oregon, Joseph Lane, arrived in March, 1849, Douglas and Ogden had reason for satisfaction with the volume of the Company's business.

The sense of well-being was increased by their confidence in the new governor. Although the provisional government had been dominantly friendly, its influence had declined since the Oregon treaty because of the general expectation that it would shortly be replaced. Lane possessed authority, he had at his disposal a force of 161 regulars,[48] and he evinced a disposition to avoid all difficulties with the Company and to respect its rights as secured by the treaty.[49] Throughout his tenure as governor and during his subsequent representation of Oregon both as congressman and as senator, Lane remained favorably inclined toward the Company, but the basic decisions on American policy toward the Company were made by other and less friendly officials and by individual settlers who ignored the Company's claims.

Between 1846 and 1850 the Company's claims had been generally respected and its trading privileges unrestricted. But between 1850 and 1869, when its claims were finally settled, the Company was subjected to increasing harassment from the federal government and its local representatives and from the squatters. The tactics of local federal officials toward the Company seemed at first to have been motivated by their ignorance and their responsiveness to extreme anti-Company elements among the settlers.

Vexation began with the overzealous application of revenue laws to the goods of the Company. In the spring of 1849, John Adair arrived at Astoria as the first collector of customs. In April, when the Company's bark *Columbia* anchored off Astoria with a cargo of goods, Adair charged duties not only on the goods destined for Fort Vancouver but on those intended for the fur trade north of 49° and for sale to the Company's own employees. His stringent interpretation of the revenue laws was based on inexperience rather than on specific instructions from Washington. When Simpson presented the issue to Secretary of the Treasury William M. Meredith in February, 1850, the latter agreed that the Company's goods destined for the territory north of the boundary should be duty-free and consented to issue instructions that such goods, if in bond, should be allowed to pass without payment of dues.[50]

Early clashes between the Company and local officials were the almost inevitable consequence of the appointment of untrained men to a new customs district. But in 1851 Washington officials first revealed an increasingly rigorous attitude toward the Company's rights. For this development, Oregon's first delegate to Congress, Samuel R. Thurston, was in no small part responsible. Hubert Howe Bancroft has described Thurston as a "scurrilous and unprincipled demagogue" who from his first day in Congress labored unceasingly to undermine the interests of the Hudson's Bay Company and of all who were associated with it.[51] The evidence amply supports this description; but if Thurston was a demagogue, he was an exceedingly able and energetic one. Opposition to the Company was for him not merely a tool of partisan advantage; his hate was genuine, and his fervor increased his power with the ultrapatriots to whom he appealed. It was through Thurston's importunities that the secretary of the treasury in May, 1850, prohibited all direct intercourse between Victoria and Nisqually, requiring all vessels bound for the latter port to visit Astoria for customs inspection,[52] thus adding several days to their journey.

The Company was further harassed by Simpson P. Moses, the first collector of customs at Olympia. Moses appears to have been an unprincipled man, anxious to win popularity with the extreme "patriots" of Puget Sound. He was so regarded not only by the

Company's employees, who might be expected to be less than objective in their opinion, but by Captain Hill of the Steilacoom garrison, who considered him a man of "no principle." [53] Moses' characteristics were evidenced by two incidents. On one occasion, he showed Tolmie a letter he had received from Secretary of State Daniel Webster in which Webster asked him to estimate the value of the Company's possessory rights. With this evidence of his importance, Moses suggested to Tolmie that for a "suitable consideration" he would draw up a petition asking Congress to purchase the Company's rights and would secure signatures throughout the Oregon territory. Tolmie, though at first suspicious about the authenticity of Webster's letter, finally concluded that it was genuine. The letter was indeed genuine, but it was not an indication of Moses' influence, as Moses had led Tolmie to believe, for identical communications had been sent to all federal officers in the Oregon territory. Moses almost certainly was aware of this. [54]

As collector, Moses adopted an anti-Hudson's Bay Company attitude, which was popular with the settlers. His point of view was first indicated in the seizure of the Company's steamer *Beaver* and the brigantine *Mary Dare*. On the evening of November 27, 1851, while Tolmie was absent on business, the two vessels arrived at Nisqually. Chief Factor John Work, with members of his family, and Miss Rose Birnie, a recent arrival from England, landed and spent the night at the fort. Next day, as soon as the steamer had taken on wood, both vessels proceeded to Olympia for customs inspection. Work, and Tolmie, who had returned that morning, were on board the *Beaver*. Miss Birnie and Work's children remained at Nisqually. The ships anchored below Olympia on the evening of November 28, and were boarded by Elwood Evans, the deputy collector of customs, who sealed the hatches. Tolmie was anxious to have the ships cleared immediately, since they were expected to transport livestock from Nisqually to Fort Victoria on their return voyage. Consequently he hurried to Olympia to see Moses as soon as the ships anchored. After a delay occasioned by the week end, Moses informed Tolmie that the *Mary Dare* was confiscated for having on board a package of refined sugar weighing less than 600 pounds, in violation of an act of Congress of March 2, 1799, which stipulated forfeiture of the vessel for such an offense. Moses seized the *Beaver* for entering the port as in ballast when it had no ballast on board. Later, he added as a reason for seizing the *Beaver* the landing of Miss Birnie and the Work family without first clearing through the port of entry.[55]

The captains of both vessels had unquestionably committed technical violations of the law but these lapses were a frivolous pretext for the seizure of the ships. Tolmie appealed to the courts and Moses released the *Beaver* before the hearing. Since the *Mary Dare* had violated a law that authorized seizure, Tolmie's attorney, Samuel B. Marye of Olympia, did not ask for adjudication. Instead he relied on an act of Congress permitting appeals to the secretary of the treasury for the remission of a forfeiture imposed for unwitting violations. His petition was presented to District Judge William Strong, who sent a certified statement of the facts to the Treasury Department. Moses meanwhile released the *Mary Dare* under $13,000 bond. Secretary of the Treasury Thomas Corwin ordered the bond and the 230 pounds of sugar that had been seized returned on the payment by the Company of legal costs. The Company was eventually awarded $1,000 as compensation for its losses in the seizure of the *Beaver*.[56]

This decision in Washington was not accompanied by a change for the better in Oregon; on the contrary, the antagonism of the settlers steadily increased. By the end of 1851 the Company's claims around Fort Vancouver were nearly all occupied by squatters, who might have sought to oust the Company entirely had they not been restrained by the presence of Regular Army forces. The Army in 1850 designated Fort Vancouver and the land immediately around it as a military reservation, and Brevet-Colonel W. W. Loring, the commander of the troops, like other Army officers in Oregon, was friendly to the Company. Such support was desperately needed, for the passage of the Oregon Donation Act of 1850 had stimulated a rush to occupy choice farming locations. The act granted 320 acres to every male occupant of public land who was above the age of eighteen and was a citizen or declared his intention of becoming one before December 1, 1851. A married man was entitled to 640 acres, half of which belonged to his wife. Before the news of passage of the act reached Oregon, the judge of the probate court, acting on the assertions of Senator Thomas Hart Benton and Thurston that the Company had no rights to the land itself, proceeded "to sell every vacant spot between the buildings" at Fort Vancouver. Colonel Loring advised the judge to desist, but the sales continued. Because of the warnings of the military, however, no purchaser attempted to take possession,[57] and the Army shortly after announced that the land had been designated a military reservation.

Nisqually, Cowlitz, and other Company claims had no such protection. By the beginning of 1851 there were at Nisqually twenty-eight alleged trespassers, all duly presented with written notices, and the number increased to fifty by 1853. The bounties of Providence and American citizenship were not restricted, in the eyes of these men, to land. The Company's cattle and sheep were also expropriated. Tolmie and his associates were helpless to resist. The squatters were prepared to use force to maintain their claims, and no redress could be found in the courts, which were sympathetic to the squatters. An incident related by Edward Huggins, in charge of Muck Farm near Nisqually, illustrated the dilemma faced by Company officers at stations situated on arable land:

> On Saturday last, the 1st May 1852, a party composed of Mr. J. B. Chapman, a citizen of America and residing at Steilacoom City, P. Sound, O. T., H. Barnes, E. Dean, and Myself, Englishmen in the employ of the P.S.A. Compy. at Nisqually, were set upon by a Company of Men (Squatters on the Company's lands) armed with double barrelled Guns & Pistols. They desired to know what authority we had for running a line around their claims, and said they had come with the determination of stopping our procceedings, whereupon one of them a Mr. Smith Very fiercely drew a Stake which we had just driven in the Ground and hurled it a long distance off. They were very much embittered against Mr. Chapman, the Surveyor and told him if he would insist in procceeding with the Survey, they would break his Compass and otherwise injure him. Mr. Chapman was compelled to discontinue the Survey.[58]

Until 1853 the vexations suffered by the Company's officers were attributable almost entirely to the actions of local officials, rather than to policy dictated from Washington. But the irritations were serious enough; profits in Oregon, after the excitement of the gold rush subsided, declined to negligible proportions.[59]

There were, however, some encouraging developments. Military officers in Oregon had recommended the purchase of at least the

Fort Vancouver military reservation. Justin Butterfield, the federal land commissioner, had suggested in his annual report of November 26, 1851, that Congress take action for the "prompt, summary and final adjustment" of the Company's claims. Anson Dart, the superintendent of Indian affairs in Oregon, also had strongly advised the government to buy the "possessory rights," arguing that the purchase would benefit the American population because the Company would then withdraw from competition with American traders. Dart's recommendation that negotiations for purchase be conducted in Oregon by representatives of the Company and of the United States [60] was not particularly attractive to the Company, which preferred a more summary settlement of its claims, but his suggestion of immediate purchase was helpful, and might serve as justification for a friendly government to make a settlement. This prospect seemed to be brightened by the appointment of Daniel Webster as secretary of state in July, 1850. Since Webster had written an opinion highly favorable to the Company's interests, the governor and committee were optimistic. For almost two years Webster was unable to devote much attention to the relatively unimportant issue of possessory rights, but in the spring of 1852 he said he was ready to negotiate. The proximate cause of his renewed interest was probably an agreement consummated in March, 1852, between Robert J. Walker and the governor and committee. Walker was to try to sell the possessory rights for $1,000,000 at a commission of 10 per cent. He had been involved in Sanders' earlier negotiations, and it was apparently on Simpson's recommendation that the governor and committee agreed to employ him. The spokesman of the London board on this occasion was the deputy governor, Andrew Colvile, for the governor was in failing health and died a few months later.

Walker seemed an admirable choice. He had been secretary of the treasury in the Polk administration and was thus well known in Washington society. To a man like Simpson, who had a low opinion of American political morality, Walker was particularly well qualified, for he was unscrupulous in his zeal to advance his personal fortunes. Through Walker's agency,[61] speedy progress was made. Webster readily assented to the payment of $1,000,000, but insisted that the agreement be incorporated in a convention between the two governments.[62] Here again was the obstacle that had defeated the Company's efforts during Buchanan's tenure as secretary of state. Any treaty acceptable to the United States must specify relinquishment of the right of navigation on the Columbia; no treaty including such a provision would be acceptable to any British government of the period. But Webster was insistent, and the Company made an effort to gain the consent of the British government.

The cause was hopeless. The Derby ministry, which had come into office in February, 1852, and was destined to be ejected in December, could not be party to any action that might be interpreted as surrender in the United States, for it was a "stop-gap government without a majority and without a policy." Nevertheless, the governor and committee, with $1,000,000 at stake, appointed John Shepherd, the deputy governor, to seek governmental consent. Shepherd, who had been chairman of the board of the East India Company, had presumably acquired a knowledge of practical politics.[63] He was not, however, an intimate of politicians. He called upon Bear Ellice for assistance in presenting the Company's case to the Foreign Office, and through Ellice's brother, Russell, obtained access to Lord Malmesbury.[64] Malmesbury was friendly and expressed solicitude for the Company's welfare, but he was powerless to grant a concession refused by his predecessor Palmerston.

A strong government in a period of tranquillity might have risked attack from the opposition and relinquished the privileges, but the Derby government was weak, and Anglo-American relations were disturbed by the issue of American fishing rights in the waters off British North America. Malmesbury accordingly advised the Company that, since its withdrawal from Oregon would in fact end the right of navigation, no reference to the right was required in any treaty between the United States and Britain, and that for Britain to cede a right that had ceased to exist would place the government in a false position.[65] Whether Webster would have consented to a treaty on such terms must be a matter of surmise, for he died on October 24, 1852. Walker withdrew as the agent of the Company, richer by $21,500 for his unsuccessful effort.[66]

Lack of success with both Sanders and Walker should have convinced the Company that the employment of unscrupulous agents was not good policy. But Simpson clung to the notion that such methods were the only effective means of dealing with American politicians. Sanders might have succeeded with better planning; Walker might have done so with more time. Perhaps the elusive settlement might yet be concluded by more astute or more powerful agents. The group to whom Simpson now confided the negotiations was headed by L. C. Levin, a Philadelphia lawyer, and George M. Dallas, vice-president of the United States in the Polk administration. They undertook to serve the Company for the balance of the commission that the Company had agreed to pay Walker, or $78,500, and arranged to communicate with Simpson through John F. Crampton, the British minister, who had participated in the negotiations during and since Sanders' agency. The legation's courier was to carry confidential communications and pay the commission when the sale was effected. Simpson advised the courier that since the land of Oregon had steadily risen in value the Company should now ask $1,500,000, with the agents' commission to be proportionately increased.[67] Simpson's motive, as he admitted to his intimates, was to make the United States more anxious to "compromise" at $1,000,000.[68]

Simpson assumed that Dallas, a former vice-president, could accomplish what Sanders and Walker had been unable to do. He was disabused of this erroneous expectation during a trip to Washington in October, 1853, when he learned, in an interview with Secretary of State Marcy, that the State Department files contained evidence of Sanders' attempts to bribe senators. Professedly shocked at this information, Simpson assured Marcy that Sanders, though employed as a resident agent, had never been authorized to use bribery and corruption, and that "his conduct had been injudicious and reprehensible." Because of Sanders' perfidy, Simpson promised, the Company would hereafter deal directly with the government rather than through agents. These protestations undoubtedly did not deceive Marcy. But he stated that several other members of the cabinet were favorable to the purchase and would recommend a settlement to Congress if they could be satisfied on two points—the ability of the Company to cede the right of navigation and the fairness of the Company's price.[69]

Marcy, however, had no intention of concluding an immediate agreement. For over a year he took no action, while the federal authorities in Oregon exerted steadily greater pressure on the Company's trade. Finally, Marcy informed Crampton that he would discuss a settlement with Simpson on January 15, 1855. The long delay and the accompanying vexation, Marcy expected, might bring the Company to settle for less than it had previously been willing to accept. He therefore presented Simpson with a virtual ultimatum that $300,000 was the utmost the government would offer the Hudson's Bay and Puget's Sound companies. He held that the rights would cease with the expiration of the Company's license in 1859 and that the extinction of the right of navigation was of no importance. For the sale of four years of occupation, $300,000 was a large sum. In rebuttal, Simpson referred to the opinions of Webster, Coxe, and others which described the Company's rights in more expansive terms. Marcy said the opinions were worthless, since Sanders had obtained them as part of his "lobbying scheme." The final offer, Marcy repeated, was $300,000. This was more than the property was worth, he stated, and the government offered it only to get rid of a troublesome question.[70]

Simpson, his resistance beaten down, did not refuse the offer. Rather he advised Governor Colvile that, if Congress approved the appropriation, the Company should accept.[71] As he left the conference with Marcy, Simpson must have reflected on the unreliability of the Washington "influence peddlers" who had made such fair promises. The Company had expended thousands of dollars and in return had received nothing. The agents had, in fact, been a liability, for evidence of their underhanded dealings had been utilized by Marcy to belittle the value of the Company's property.

When Marcy held his conferences with Simpson, the executive branch had already called the attention of Congress to the desirability of purchasing the Company's rights. In his annual message to Congress in December, 1854, Franklin Pierce stated that he had "reason to believe" that an arrangement could be made "on just terms" for the purchase of the Company's rights, including the navigation of the Columbia, and recommended that Congress make an appropriation for that purpose.[72] A motion to authorize the purchase was introduced in the Senate in March, 1855, but was defeated.[73] Another recommendation by Pierce in December, 1855,[74] met the same fate. The governor and committee would probably have reluctantly accepted $300,000 for their property, although they complained that it was unworthy of a reputable government to utilize hostile feeling toward the Company in order to depreciate the value of its property.

The refusal of the Senate to take favorable action was unfortunate for the Company's employees in Oregon. Squatters, who before 1855 had generally respected the Company's rights to tilled and enclosed lands, now encroached upon these claims as well, aware that the Company was powerless to restrain them. The unfriendly attitude of settlers and public officials, the impossibility of carrying on a profitable trade, and the prospect of a future bleaker than the present all contributed to a mood of black depression. The Indian wars of 1855–56 added to the pessimism, for the Americans suspected the Company's men of complicity with the Indians and of providing them with ammunition. The abandonment of Fort Walla Walla, in the midst of the area of turbulence, on October 16, 1855, by order of the American Indian agent, anticipated the decision of the governor and committee to withdraw because of financial losses. James Sinclair at Walla Walla and Dugald Mactavish, in charge of the Oregon department, attempted to make a virtue of necessity by preparing a claim for compensation against the United States government. They estimated the value of the property abandoned at $67,525.62 and of the ammunition destroyed at $1,104.00; [75] they listed horses at $100 each, when the actual value of horses in the area was from $10 to $50. As Mactavish admitted, prices were set high in order to provide a basis for the claim; the actual loss was only about $8,000.[76] The forwarding of such claims, which were certain to be greatly reduced by government accounting officers, could not relieve the financial burdens imposed by losses from the Oregon department. Simpson complained in January, 1856, that the annual losses from the posts in American territory had reached such proportions that they "sensibly affect the profits of the fur trade as a whole." The maintenance of these posts served only one purpose, the preservation of the Company's claims as a basis for compensation by the United States. The only profitable establishment in American territory in 1854–55 was Fort Colvile and its dependencies at Kootanie and Flathead, and the trade there was disrupted by the Indian wars of 1855–56.[77]

Losses in the Oregon department were further increased by the levies of tax assessors who valued the Company's property much more highly than did their fellow Americans who were contending that the property was "measurably worthless." The contrast is illustrated by the varying estimates of the value of the land around Fort Nisqually. In his report to Marcy in 1854, Governor Isaac I. Stevens estimated the value at $150,000; but the legislature of Washington Territory contended that his valuation was far too high on land of "less value than the same amount . . . in a state of nature." [78] Yet with that mental astigmatism so often evident when interests vary, Washington territorial officials found the land very valuable for tax purposes. The taxes paid at Nisqually in 1855 totaled $6,725.62.[79]

Such a levy on property allegedly almost worthless appears inordinately high, and the conclusion seems inescapable that the taxes were imposed, not only for revenue, but to hasten the departure of the British companies from American territory. Tax assessors valued the Company's property at Fort Vancouver at $112,000 in 1854, and at $197,000 in 1855.[80] The Company continued to pay taxes there until it abandoned the establishment in 1860, but the governor and committee directed Tolmie to refuse payment at Nisqually and Cowlitz after 1858 on the justification that the taxation was discriminatory, since the Company's subsidiary was forced to pay higher rates than American settlers.[81]

Another source of irritation was the federal land office. In 1851, when surveys were begun in Oregon Territory, the land office instructed the surveyor general to draw only township lines in all areas where the Company claimed possessory rights, in order to avoid disputes. But in 1855, ten days after the Senate had rejected a proposal to authorize purchase of the property, the land commissioner revised his instructions. He now ordered the lines extended "up to the actual settlements of the British claimants according to the lawful and proper limits of the same at the date of treaty." [82] Since the Company's officers had not clearly defined their estates prior to conclusion of the treaty, and since there was then no "lawful" authority in Oregon with which to register such claims, disputes between the Company's officers and surveyors were inevitable.

Because of mounting losses and uncertainty as to when, if ever, an agreement could be made, Simpson and the governor and committee decided in 1855 to reduce the Company's staff in the Oregon department to the minimum required to preserve its claims and to move Fort Colvile from American territory to a new site across the border.[83] Fort Shepherd was built just across the border to assume the functions of Fort Colvile, but the Company retained Fort Colvile in American territory until the possessory rights were extinguished. The number of employees, however, was greatly reduced, as at other posts south of 49°. But so long as the United States government continued to be apathetic to an agreement, the maintenance of even a small establishment involved continued loss without advancing the prospect of settlement. The only means of inducing the United States to bargain with the Company, Simpson and the London board concluded, was vigorous intervention by the British government on the Company's behalf. Between 1846 and 1855 the Foreign Office had provided only the most casual assistance; its primary role had been to obstruct the conclusion of a treaty by its refusal to accept the relinquishment of navigation rights on the Columbia River.

While Great Britain was fighting the Crimean War, it was unlikely that the Foreign Office could be induced to make forceful representations to the United States. With the end of hostilities, Governor John Shepherd, Deputy Governor Henry Hulse Berens, and Edward Ellice, Jr., visited the foreign secretary, the Earl of Clarendon, to plead for more active assistance. Pointing to the increasing encroachments of American settlers and the impositions of the tax gatherers, they expressed the hope that Clarendon would seek a speedy settlement on just terms rather than on the arbitrary decision of American officials.[84] Clarendon was sympathetic, and agreed to instruct the British representative in Washington to bring the possessory rights question again to the notice of the United States government. Unfortunately for the Company, it was not the time for effective diplomatic action in the United States. Simpson's good friend, John F. Crampton, was summarily dismissed by Secretary of State Marcy in May, 1856, for violating American neutrality laws by enlisting volunteers for the Crimean War. The irritation of Great Britain at Marcy's action quickly subsided, but Crampton's removal left the legation in charge of a mere secretary, J. Savile Lumley, who could not command the respect accorded a minister. Lumley found what the Company already knew, that the United States government was inclined "to drive a hard bargain," and "to cheapen the purchase to the utmost by depreciating its value." [85] He could not move Marcy to reopen negotiations.

Lord Napier, appointed minister to Washington in 1857, became the Company's most effective diplomatic representative since the signing of the treaty. Crampton had been zealous in promoting the Company's case, but he had done so through the agency of corrupt politicians and influence men. Napier had no personal interest in the settlement of the possessory rights question, but the Company was a British enterprise and as such had a claim upon his services. The prospects for a settlement seemed improved with the election of James Buchanan to the presidency, for Buchanan had earlier expressed support for a purchase at $1,000,000, and his secretary of state, General Lewis Cass, also seemed disposed to negotiate. The Company's optimism was short-lived. The governor and committee set their price at $1,000,000; Cass suggested $300,000, as Marcy had proposed in 1855, and refused to go higher, despite Napier's argument that the assessed value of the property remaining in the Company's hands, excluding that occupied by squatters, was $797,500. [86]

Napier, after repeated representations, finally concluded that the federal government did not really want to purchase the property, that they would not offer a reasonable price, and that if they did it would not be accepted by Congress. [87] Simpson sought to break the deadlock by suggesting to Napier that the Company would probably accept $600,000, [88] and Napier proposed a price of $650,000, but Cass remained adamant. He argued, with considerable force, that if Congress had refused to authorize a payment of $300,000 in 1855, it could hardly be expected to accept a settlement for double that amount two years later. But the most telling blow came, not from Cass, but from George N. Sanders. In July, 1858, for some obscure reason, Sanders showed Napier a copy of the agreement he had made with the Company. Napier was shocked. He had bargained with the United States on the assumption that the lowest offer the Company had previously been willing to accept was $1,000,000, and he now discovered that the Company actually expected to receive only $410,000 in the negotiation in which Sanders was involved.[89] The explanations of Governor Berens and Sir George Simpson did not entirely satisfy Napier, nor did they satisfy the Company's own elder statesman, Edward Ellice, who asked how the Company could now demand more than it had contracted to receive through Sanders.[90] Napier, despite his disillusionment, continued to press for a settlement and seemed to be on the verge of an agreement with Cass for the appointment of a joint commission [91] when he was called home and Lord Lyons, the minister at Florence, replaced him. Another opportunity had been lost, and the Company was now subjected to intensified American pressure, this time from the military authorities who had previously been friendly.

The first serious breach between the Army and the Company resulted from an apparently insignificant dispute. Captain Rufus Ingalls of the Quartermaster Corps sought to have the Company's salmon house on the river at Fort Vancouver removed in order to erect a wharf for government use. Dugald Mactavish, the officer in charge, wanted to postpone his answer until he had conferred with the board of management of the western department. When Ingalls, without waiting for Mactavish's consent, continued his work at the wharf, Mactavish protested.[92] With the approval of his commanding officer, Ingalls then told Mactavish that the military authorities, though not concerned with the extent of the Company's claims, considered that the lands occupied by the military reservation, except for the Company's buildings and enclosures, belonged to the Army.[93]

With the expiration of the Company's license to trade in British Columbia in 1859, a rumor circulated throughout Oregon that Cass had decided that the possessory rights in American territory were automatically extinguished.[94] This position American officials had maintained with varying conviction since 1846. When asked by Lord Lyons to confirm or deny the rumor, Cass replied only that the question was being studied by the American government,[95] but the commanding general of the Oregon department, W. S. Harney, was not so reticent. A stanch believer in "no nonsense" where the British were concerned, Harney had already distinguished himself by seizing disputed San Juan Island, for which he was later recalled. In March, 1860, he informed John Work, then in charge of the Company's business at Fort Vancouver, that "in consequence of the expiration of their charter as a Trading Company on the Coast" the Company's possessory rights had expired, and that the Company should prepare to move from the land, which the Army intended to use.[96] Lyons protested to Cass that "a spoliation so unjust and unprovoked, one in which the rights of a public Company and the stipulations of a Treaty would be alike disregarded, would meet with the steady and determined resistance of Her Majesty's Government." This was the strongest language a British diplomat had used in defense of the Company since 1846, and Cass hastened to disavow Harney's authority to make such a decision.[97]

Before news of the American government's repudiation of Harney reached the Pacific Coast, Alexander Grant Dallas, in charge of the Company's operations west of the Rocky Mountains, had decided that no useful purpose would be served by enduring further vexation and had ordered the Company's personnel to withdraw from Fort Vancouver.[98] Dallas took this step after being convinced that Harney had acted on orders, rather than on his own initiative. The necessary evidence was provided when a staff officer at Fort Vancouver showed James A. Grahame a letter from Secretary of War John B. Floyd to Harney, declaring that the rights of the Hudson's Bay Company had ceased with the end of the license and endorsing Harney's course.[99] Any doubts as to the authenticity of the letter were removed by the publication on December 3, 1860, of the annual report of the secretary of the interior, which stated that "on the expiration of the Charter of the Hudson's Bay Company in 1859, the possessory rights of that Company, under the third article of the treaty, terminated." [100] This suggests that the cabinet had decided to end the issue by confiscating the Company's property, but had been deterred by the strong protests of the British minister. Harney, already in a shadow for his seizure of San Juan Island, was consequently saddled with the responsibility of acting without authority when he had actually been carrying out the instructions of his superiors.

Dallas' haste to withdraw from Fort Vancouver may have been partially motivated by his realization that the trade in the Oregon department could not be profitable. During the last full year of trade, Outfit 1858, the Company made a net gain of £29 from its operations in American territory; there would have been a serious loss had it not been for a profit of £2,085 from the Fort Vancouver sales shop. The fur trade was now completely ruined. Even at Fort Colvile, for many years the only source of substantial profit from furs, the net gain was only £107. In 1859, for the first time, Fort Colvile's enclosures and pasture lands were invaded by squatters, and rival traders increased the expense of procuring furs from the Indians.[101] There was no economic justification for remaining in Oregon and Washington, and Harney's ultimatum gave Dallas the opportunity to dramatize the Company's harassments in the hope of stimulating the British government to more active intervention.

The strong tone adopted by the Foreign Office might have brought the possessory rights issue to an amicable conclusion before Buchanan and Cass left office had it not been for the preoccupation of the American government with the threatened secession of the Southern states. When the Lincoln administration took office, Lyons immediately brought the dispute to the attention of Secretary of State William H. Seward and revived the suggestion considered by Cass and Napier in 1858 that a joint commission be appointed, thus relieving the American government of direct responsibility for deciding on the price to be paid. Lyons, recognizing the disinclination of Congress to vote money for nonessential purchases when it was expending huge sums for the war, did not press Seward to accept this proposal immediately. Finally, in March, 1863, in response to pressure from the Company, Lyons again spoke to Seward and found him desirous of reaching a settlement. Despite his earlier truculence, Seward in 1863 wanted to avoid further complications with Great Britain. The possessory rights question was insignificant in comparison to the great issues of Anglo-American relations, most notable of which was the construction of Confederate warships in Great Britain. No national interest could be served, Seward concluded, by continuing the unnecessary friction in Oregon. As a senator he had earlier expressed sympathy for the Company's case, and in the winter of 1862 he had told John Rose, the Company's Canadian counsel, that he was desirous "on national grounds" of taking the affair out of the "arena of controversy."[102] As an ex-senator, however, Seward realized that to induce Congress to accept such an agreement would require finesse. He told Lyons it would be useless to ask the Senate to approve a convention specifying the amount to be paid. There were only two ways of settling the question, Seward and Lyons agreed—by a joint commission of eminent British and American lawyers or by foreign arbitration. The first alternative was preferable. The governor and committee agreed, provided they were allowed to select the British representatives.[103] On July 1, 1863, Lyons and Seward signed a convention specifying that each country name a commissioner. The two commissioners were in turn to name an umpire or arbitrator to whom the dispute would be referred if they could not agree.[104]

The Company chose Charles D. Day of Montreal, formerly solicitor general of Lower Canada, to plead the British case. The American protagonist was Caleb Cushing, then at the height of his career. On the Company's recommendation, the British government appointed John Rose, a member of the Canadian assembly, as a commissioner. Rose, who had served on several ministries, possessed one of the keenest minds in Canada on financial matters; as the Company's long-time legal counsel he might be expected to favor its case. The United States chose Alexander S. Johnson, of Albany, formerly judge of the Court of Appeals of New York. Since deadlock was not unlikely, the identity of the umpire was of great importance. Governor Head suggested Benjamin R. Curtis because of his acknowledged ability, honesty, and legal knowledge. Curtis, who had retired from the Supreme Court in 1857, was famous for his dissenting opinion in the Dred Scott case. Both commissioners agreed, and in May, 1865, almost two years after the convention was signed, the commission was organized and ready to begin hearings. Four more years elapsed, and fourteen volumes of testimony and arguments were accumulated, before the commission made its decision.[105]

Estimates of the value and extent of the possessory rights, of course, varied widely, and the Americans emphasized the lowest valuations. But perhaps Cushing's most telling argument arose from a transaction not directly related to the issue. In 1869 the Company agreed to sell Canada its chartered rights in all Rupert's Land for £300,000. Cushing argued that if the Company valued so vast a territory at only $1,500,000, the value of its lands south of the 49th parallel must be small. Day admitted that Cushing's argument would reduce the award that the Company could expect. In September, 1869, the commissioners finally announced their award of $450,000 to the Hudson's Bay Company and $200,000 to the Puget's Sound Company for the extinguishment of their rights.

The end was not yet. A bill for payment of the $650,000 passed the House of Representatives in May, 1870, despite the protest of an Ohio congressman that the award was too high and that the United States should not pay until American claims for the depredations of British-built Confederate cruisers had been satisfied. But the act as finally approved by the president in February, 1871, contained a proviso that the companies must pay any taxes they owed in Oregon and Washington. The taxes at issue were those imposed upon Fort Nisqually and Cowlitz Farm, which the Puget's Sound Agricultural Company had been refusing to pay since 1858. The amount claimed, including penalties, was over $61,000.[106] The Department of State, however, chose to ignore the claims of local officials, and the final payment was made in September, 1871, without deductions.[107]

The Hudson's Bay Company had been subjected to twenty-five years of controversy, during most of which it received little support from the British government, largely because the Foreign Office failed to use exact language in defining the rights of the Company and its subsidiary, the Puget's Sound Agricultural Company.[108] In his anxiety to reach a peaceful settlement, the Earl of Aberdeen avoided precise stipulations which might have delayed or prevented the agreement he so earnestly desired. After the treaty was ratified, British statesmen paid scant attention for over a decade to the Company's pleas for assistance in inducing the United States to purchase the possessory rights. Sir George Simpson's cynical estimate of American politics led the Company into a series of abortive dealings with Washington lobbyists, knowledge of which made it more difficult to negotiate an agreement on terms satisfactory to the Company. But it is doubtful whether, if Company representatives had been straightforward with the United States government, the result would have been different. After the death of Daniel Webster, no secretary of state displayed much enthusiasm for the purchase of the possessory rights. Most American officials held the view that, by delay, they could force a dictated settlement and that they might perhaps even acquire the property without compensation, since the Company's license for trade expired in 1859. Without the intervention of the British government, this view might have been correct. The strong support given the Company by the Foreign Office between 1857 and 1863, and the desire of the United States during the Civil War to avoid unnecessary irritations with Great Britain, brought about the final settlement of a dispute in which neither the Company nor its American opponents had appeared to advantage.

Given the inexactitude of the language in the treaty, the mutual hostility of Great Britain and the United States, and the lack of coördination between executive and legislative bodies characteristic of the presidential system, the miserable "possessory rights" conflict between 1846 and 1871 was virtually inevitable. It was the price that had to be paid for Aberdeen's "peace with honor."

# Company Control of
# Vancouver Island, 1847-1865

AFTER THE victory of the United States in the Oregon boundary dispute, the governor and committee were convinced that Americans would encroach on the territory north of the line unless an effective government was immediately established. American settlers, the London board believed, had contributed greatly to the success of the United States in the Oregon negotiations; unless restrained, they might move farther north and thus provide a basis for an American coup in British territory. Particularly vulnerable was Vancouver Island, for Fort Victoria was the center of the Company's coastal trade, and possession of the island was important to the trade of New Caledonia.

At least one member of Lord John Russell's Whig government, which replaced the Peel ministry in 1846, was also disturbed by the prospects of further American expansion west of the Rocky Mountains. Earl Grey, the new colonial secretary, declared on September 16:

> Looking to the encroaching spirit of the U.S. I think it is of importance to strengthen the B[ritis]h hold upon the territory now assigned to us by treaty by encouraging the settlement on it of B[ritis]h subjects; and I am also of opin. that such settlement could only be effected under the auspices of the Hudson's Bay co. wh. I am therefore disposed to encourage.[1]

[1] For notes to chap. 14, see pp. 464–467.

Grey's desire to protect British territory was limited by one important restriction: such support must be provided at minimum expense or, if possible, at no expense whatsoever to the British taxpayer. But colonization would involve levies on the Imperial exchequer unless a private association assumed the responsibility for transporting and governing settlers. Grey believed that the Hudson's Bay Company, because of its long experience in governing of the "Indian territories" and its large resources of capital, was well qualified. He therefore asked his subordinates to consult with Governor John Henry Pelly to determine "what measure may now safely and properly be adopted with a view to establishing more B[ritis]h settlers in this territory." [2]

Grey's desire to have the Hudson's Bay Company undertake the settlement of Vancouver Island is understandable, though his judgment is questionable. The motives of the Company's governing board are not so easily assessed. The Company valued Fort Victoria for its importance to the maritime fur trade; since 1836 the governor and committee had known that coal deposits of undetermined extent and quality existed on the north end of the island.[3] But neither Fort Victoria nor the coal deposits could alone have induced the governor and committee to accept the task of governing Vancouver Island. Fort Victoria could have continued to be the Company's base under the direct jurisdiction of the Crown, and the Company had not been notably successful in ventures alien to the fur trade, like coal mining. The willingness of the governor and committee to become the colonizing agent can be understood only in the context of the "frontier policies" of the Company's fur trade.

The relationship between the fur trade and Vancouver Island has long been recognized, but often misunderstood. The Company has usually been regarded as the cunning monopolist whose profits from the fur trade depended on the exclusion of settlement, and Earl Grey as an unconscious dupe or willing accomplice.[4] This interpretation is based upon two assumptions: that the Company's objective was the maintenance of a fur preserve, and that its professions of willingness to promote colonization were insincere. Each assumption is an oversimplification. Vancouver Island was not important for fur hunting; its furs were scarce and of little value. But it was close to New Caledonia, and thus in Company hands was a protection for the fur trade; in other hands it could be a threat. The governor and committee's desire to acquire control of the island was, therefore, an ideal application of the frontier policies of Pelly and Simpson. But the decision to seek such authority was Pelly's alone, and he insisted upon its value despite the opposition of several of his most influential associates. Simpson was convinced as late as October, 1848, that the assumption of responsibility for Vancouver Island would be of little, if any, benefit to the Company; any attempt to colonize the island from Great Britain was predestined to failure because the soil and climate of Oregon and California offered superior attractions; and the Company would incur odium and expense in a useless undertaking.[5] Archibald Barclay, secretary of the Company, shared Simpson's views. He wrote Simpson on October 13, 1848: "I quite agree with you as to the estimate of Vancr. Island. It is in my view *worthless* as seat for a colony. It is about the last place in the globe to which (were I going to emigrate) I should select as an abode." [6]

Edward Ellice the Elder, to whose views on political questions Pelly was usually inclined to defer, also opposed the Company's colonization of Vancouver Island. So strongly did Ellice object that he appealed directly to Grey, his friend and relative, to reconsider his decision. Grey's reply, "I do not see what we cd. have done better," [7] did not satisfy Ellice, and he remained hostile to the project throughout the period of the Company's responsibility. In September, 1859, he wrote:

I have always thought the Directors wrong, in accepting the grant of the Island from the Govt. & when that transaction was challenged in Parliament as a great boon to the Company, I stated my opinion that it was a most rash undertaking on their part, for the exclusive advantage of the public. Ld. Grey was wiser than the opposition who found fault with his policy. . . . There was no chance or hope of Revenue to defray the expense of such an establishment—& very little of emigrants, for agricultural settlements & Ld. Grey rightly thought that a large & unnecessary expense might be saved by inducing the H. B. Co. to undertake the temporary administration. Their only object in accepting it was to protect their own establishments, which might have been exposed in the then state of the Pacific to the danger of plunder or destruction.[8]

The continued opposition of Ellice, the most influential liaison between the Company and the Whig government, and the initial objections of Simpson, whose opinions on the conduct of the fur trade were usually carefully considered by the London board, suggest that the thesis of the "fur-trade conspiracy" in respect to Vancouver Island cannot be accepted without reservations. To explain the involvement of the Hudson's Bay Company in the colonization of Vancouver Island, it is necessary to examine the motives of two men—Pelly and Grey—who were almost exclusively responsible for the decision.

The initial suggestion that the Company might be used as a vehicle for colonization was apparently made not by Pelly but by Grey. Pelly's first communication to Grey on the subject of Vancouver Island after the conclusion of the Oregon treaty was written on September 7, 1846. Pelly inquired whether the Company's possession of lands around Fort Victoria, which it had occupied prior to ratification of the treaty, would be confirmed.[9] He wanted the British government to recognize the Company's rights north of 49° as the United States had done south of the boundary, but Grey's plan was more broadly conceived. It was in response to Pelly's letter that Grey suggested to his subordinates in the Colonial Office that the Company might be used as an instrument of colonization.

After an interview at the Colonial Office on September 23, Pelly displayed a new interest in colonization under Company auspices.[10] In ensuing months his concept attained greater magnitude until, on March 5, 1847, he made a suggestion of truly imperial proportions, that the Company should receive the grant of all British territory north and west of Rupert's Land. Such a proposal was manifestly unacceptable to James Stephen, the permanent undersecretary, who regarded the Company as the embodiment of monopoly. But even Benjamin Hawes and Earl Grey, though sympathetic to the idea of using the Company as the agency of the Crown in Vancouver Island, were taken aback at Pelly's request, which was quickly refused.[11]

Pelly's motives in seeking such a colossal grant may be determined from the arguments he later employed to convince a skeptical Sir George Simpson of the benefits of Company control over a colonization scheme. Pelly early came to the conclusion that if the Colonial Office did not find the Company a satisfactory agency, it would turn to another joint-stock association. If another company were established with plenary powers in the territory west of the Rocky Mountains, the Company's fur trade and sales shops in New Caledonia would suffer, and Vancouver Island or mainland territory in other hands might well become a base for incursions across the mountains into Rupert's Land.[12] His reasoning was compelling enough to convince other members of the London board, and Simpson himself was forced to admit that "it will unquestionably be more advantageous to the fur trade that it [Vancouver Island] should be in the hands of the Company than of strangers." [13]

It is impossible to determine whether or not a specific alternative proposal first stimulated Pelly's fears, but it is certain that the plans of James Edward Fitzgerald early became the major threat to the Hudson's Bay Company's interests. Fitzgerald was not in himself an influential man. His family, though prosperous Irish gentry, was not powerful in English politics; his position in the antiquities department of the British Museum did not suggest intimacy with the business world; and he at no time offered evidence that he was associated with men of large capital. Fitzgerald was introduced to Benjamin Hawes of the Colonial Office in the spring of 1847 by Anthony Panizzi, principal librarian of the British Museum. An introduction by Panizzi was of no small value, for he was well acquainted with the leaders of the Whig party. But what impressed Hawes most of all was that Fitzgerald had ideas (that they were borrowed from Edward Gibbon Wakefield did not lessen their attraction) and was "very energetic," and his antecedents were "highly respectable." [14]

Hawes suggested that Fitzgerald write the Colonial Office a statement of his plans. The resultant letter, on June 9, 1847, was a faithful reproduction of Wakefield's views on systematic colonization. Fitzgerald proposed the formation of a joint-stock company, to be called the "Company of Colonists of Vancouver's Island." The government of the colony and the management of the company would be vested in shareholders resident on Vancouver Island. The company would use its capital and the proceeds from sales of land to convey young married couples to the colony. It would sell land at a "sufficient price" to ensure a proper balance between land and labor. For each hundred acres of land purchased, six laborers would be sent to the colony.[15] The scheme was favorably received, but Grey and Hawes were not disposed to entertain it seriously until Fitzgerald could demonstrate adequate financial support. Such evidence Fitzgerald did not and probably could not provide, either for his initial project or for another proposal he made in February, 1848, stressing the exploitation of the coal deposits on the island rather than systematic colonization.[16]

Fitzgerald's failure to produce evidence of substantial financial backing is of key importance. The files of the Colonial Office entomb many schemes of varying attractions, consigned to oblivion because there was no evidence that men of standing in the City were willing to invest in them. What is remarkable about Fitzgerald's proposals is not that they were rejected but that they were given such serious consideration. The communications among the staff of the Colonial Office do not support the view that Grey connived with the Hudson's Bay Company in a corrupt bargain. The prime requisite for eligibility as an instrument of colonization on Vancouver Island was capital. The Hudson's Bay Company possessed that capital; Fitzgerald and his friends apparently did not; and no other individuals or groups who did possess it entered the competition. Fitzgerald's effervescence and youthful vitality [17] could not outweigh the resources of capital and experience possessed by the Hudson's Bay Company. On March 13, 1848, therefore, the Colonial Office first notified the governor and committee that it was willing to consider the grant of Vancouver Island to the Company.[18] The final decision, however, was not taken until after the opposition, led by William E. Gladstone, had made severe attacks in Parliament upon the motives of Grey and the Company. The source of much of Gladstone's criticism was James Edward Fitzgerald.

Throughout most of his political career Gladstone was a bitter opponent of the Hudson's Bay Company. To him it was an anachronism, a throwback to the days when restrictive trade practices had been accepted. His mind was shuttered and barred against all testimony favorable to the Company, but he received information prejudicial to its interests with uncritical credulity. The Hudson's Bay Company was a monopoly, and to Gladstone monopolies were per se hostile to the public interest. With ammunition supplied by Fitzgerald,[19] therefore, Gladstone attacked the grant, and Lord Lincoln (later the Duke of Newcastle) and others joined him. Lord Monteagle denounced the grant as "the most lavish, the most inconsiderate, and . . . the most reprehensible ever made by any Colonial Minister." On August 18, 1848, Gladstone's effort to censure the government for assigning the island to the Company was defeated in the House of Commons by a vote of only 76 to 58.[20] The defense of the government's action by Grey's parliamentary undersecretary, Benjamin Hawes, lacked the power shown by the opposition, for he spoke without apparent conviction.[21]

Grey was highly irritated at the attacks of his opponents, particularly of Gladstone, who had "much to answer," [22] but he was nevertheless forced to modify the terms of the grant to reduce parliamentary criticism. He added a provision that the Hudson's Bay Company would sell land on reasonable terms to all who wished to buy and that the revenue derived from sales of land and from royalties on coal and other minerals should be applied, after a deduction of 10 per cent for profit to the Company, to the colonization and improvement of Vancouver Island. If the Crown decided within five years that the Company had not sufficiently exerted itself, the grant could be revoked. With these additions, the royal grant was issued on January 13, 1849, making the Company "the true and absolute lords and proprietors" of Vancouver Island, "in free and common soccage" to the Crown for an annual rent of 7 shillings.[23]

Grey was justified in his resentment against the attacks of Gladstone and others. He considered the Hudson's Bay Company the best qualified agency for the colonization of Vancouver Island. It possessed knowledge based on experience in western North America, a disciplined staff of officers and servants, and large resources of capital, and it had already established agricultural and pastoral operations in Oregon and on Vancouver Island. Moreover, the force of its economic power could render unprofitable the activities of any rival associations or individuals. To the argument that a fur-trading monopoly was constitutionally unable to advance colonization, Grey and his associates in the Colonial Office could reply that the economic interests of the Company on the northwest coast, and in particular on Vancouver Island, were not the same as in the interior areas of North America. In the interior, nature and the interests of the Company both conspired against settlement. But in the comparatively mild climate of the Pacific slope and Vancouver Island, the circumstances were "very different," for the fur trade was of little consequence, and Grey believed that it would be in the interests of the Company to promote settlement and trade.[24]

If Grey was not an accomplice, was he a dupe of the Company? Did the governor and committee seek the grant under a false pretense that they would promote colonization? The conditions the Company imposed for the alienation of land might seem to support an affirmative answer to both questions. The governor and committee agreed that land should be sold at £1 per acre and that no grant should contain less than twenty acres. Purchasers could either provide passage for themselves and their families or have passage provided by the Company "at a reasonable rate." They must also take with them to the island five single men or three married couples for every hundred acres they acquired. All minerals were to belong to the Company, which would compensate the owner of the soil for any damage done to the surface by mining operations. The owner might mine for coal on his own land, provided he paid the Company a royalty of 2/6 per ton.[25] The price of £1 per acre and the requirement of bringing laborers were an almost certain guarantee against colonization of a remote island with unknown potentialities and no market for its products, particularly since settlers could acquire land free, or at a nominal price, in neighboring American territory. But this conclusion does not prove a conspiracy on the part of the governor and committee. A strong case can be made for the contention that both Grey and Pelly were victims of precisely the same delusion as James Edward Fitzgerald—that systematic colonization could be undertaken successfully in such an area as Vancouver Island. No suspicion can be cast on the genuineness of Fitzgerald's zeal for colonization, yet he had proposed that purchasers of land be required to transport six men for each hundred acres. He estimated that passage for these laborers would cost approximately £300, or £3 per acre allotted to their sponsor.[26] The Company's plan to charge £1 per acre and require purchasers of large acreages to bring laborers was no more restrictive than Fitzgerald's, and the price was suggested to the Company by the Colonial Office.

It may be contended with some basis that the governor and committee were sincere in their professions of willingness to colonize. They encouraged Charles Enderby to establish a whaling station on the island because they believed that whaling ships would provide a market for the produce of the island.[27] Governor Pelly displayed interest in colonization of the island not only in letters to the Colonial Office but, more significantly, in private letters to his associates in the Company.

It would be an error, however, to conclude that the Hudson's Bay Company was merely the victim of circumstances beyond its control in the subsequent failure of the colonization effort. The Company must assume some of the responsibility; the unimpressive record of immigration to the island can be explained in part by the Company's inherent assumptions and by the attitudes of its personnel.

Governor Pelly was willing to assume the responsibility for colonization because he feared that otherwise the government would assign the project to another group of entrepreneurs, who might disturb the tranquillity of the nearby fur preserves. Other members of the committee also recognized the danger but reached a different conclusion. At least two, Lord Selkirk and Andrew Colvile, sought the grant with the deliberate design of delaying the colonization of Vancouver Island. Selkirk wrote to Pelly on May 27, 1848:

> I heard incidentally that there are a lot of people who want to go and colonize Vancouvers Island. A man of the name of Fitzgerald who has a place in the British Museum wants to get command of the expedition and expects the thing to be taken up by the Government. I do not know if there is any truth in this story but there is no doubt but there are many people who have got a notion of that country and if they go out they will play the devil.[28]

In order that others would not "play the devil" and that the Company could profit from the coal sales, Selkirk supported the request for the grant, but he at no time showed enthusiasm for immigration to Vancouver Island. Andrew Colvile held similar views. From the onset of Pelly's last long illness in 1850, until 1856, when Colvile died, Colvile was unquestionably the Company's dominant policy-maker, and his views were therefore of decisive importance in the formulation of plans with regard to Vancouver Island.

The idea of unrestricted settlement in any part of the Hudson's Bay Company's area of influence was repugnant to Colvile. Since the Colonial Office had decided to colonize Vancouver Island through a private agency, he agreed with Pelly that the Company must seek control, but he did not want to encourage settlement. The popularity of "systematic colonization" offered a solution to this apparent dilemma. Colvile was convinced that imposing a price on land would certainly deter immigration to Vancouver Island. So long as land was sold for £1 per acre, he informed his confidant Simpson, "You need not be afraid of too many settlers" on the island.[29] After the grant of the island, Colvile believed that the Company could rigidly restrict immigration. Through its subsidiary, the Puget's Sound Agricultural Company, it could produce foodstuffs for its employees and for sale to whalers and coal ships. The coal mines would provide additional revenue.[30] The pattern of the Company's immigration program confirmed Colvile's expectations.

Sir George Simpson, who had at first opposed the Company's assumption of responsibility for colonization, found comfort in Colvile's arguments. He was well aware that the government could revoke the grant if the Company failed within five years to give evidence of effective colonization. But, as Simpson saw it, a delay of even five years would be advantageous to the Company, for the encroachment of settlement into Rupert's Land and the decline in the demand for beaver would soon render the fur trade unprofitable.[31]

In accordance with the dictum that colonies should not be a drain on the Imperial exchequer, Vancouver Island was expected to be self-supporting. The Crown was to appoint the governor and a council of seven, and inhabitants who owned at least twenty acres of land apiece were to elect an assembly. In July, 1849, Grey appointed as the first governor Richard Blanshard, a lawyer, without salary from the British government. The appointment was made with the concurrence of Governor Pelly, who believed that his support of an independent person would refute the charge that the Company intended to keep the settlement subservient to its views.[32] Blanshard's tenure was short and unpleasant. He arrived at Fort Victoria in March, 1850; in November he tendered his resignation and, on news of its acceptance, left the colony in September, 1851. He had expended his private resources in governing a territory composed almost entirely of Hudson's Bay Company employees, who gave their respect to the Company's officers but not to him; he early became convinced that the Company intended to appropriate the best land for itself and had no desire for free settlement; and finally he contracted the ague. He left the island with no regrets.[33] On the recommendation of Pelly, who contended that the governor should be experienced in dealing with Indians, the Colonial Office appointed Chief Factor James Douglas, senior officer of the western department, as Blanshard's successor.[34] During most of the Company's tenure on the island, Douglas attempted to play the double role of Company officer and representative of the Crown.

When the Company undertook the responsibility of colonization in 1849, the times were most unpropitious for settlement. The discovery of gold in California proved so tremendous an attraction that it had temporarily stripped Oregon of most of its population. Within a fortnight after news of the gold strikes reached the Willamette valley, 1,500 men left for California.[35] With such excitement the undeveloped land of Vancouver Island could not hope to compete. In 1850, miners sent out to work in the coal mines at Nanaimo deserted in a body for California.[36] They could hardly have been expected to do otherwise. Their wages of £50 to £60 a year with subsistence, attractive enough in their native Scotland, could not compare with wages being paid in Oregon. Mechanics in Oregon were then receiving $10 to $16 a day, and common laborers, $3 to $5,[37] and even these wages were not sufficient to counteract the lure of California.

Even after the surge of the gold rush was over, the disadvantages of settlement on Vancouver Island remained. Nevertheless, the governor and committee launched a campaign to advertise the immigration scheme. Their prospectus was printed in the London *Times, Daily News,* and *Morning Chronicle,* the Liverpool *Journal,* and other English metropolitan and provincial newspapers. As their agent in Scotland, they appointed John Harthill and Sons of Edinburgh, who were responsible for publishing news of the scheme in Scottish newspapers. The advertisements elicited responses, but not from the farmers they were avowedly designed to attract. Most of those who expressed interest desired employment by the Company in supervisory positions. One perceptive correspondent advised the Company that it could not expect farmers to emigrate until it agreed to send them to the island free of expense.[38] His advice was sound, but it went unheeded.

During the first few years of the Company's tenure, its own schemes provided virtually the only activity in settlement. At Simpson's suggestion, James Douglas marked out twenty square miles of the choicest land in the neighborhood of Fort Victoria for the Company. Before the Oregon treaty was signed, Douglas had described these lands as belonging to the fort, but only about six square miles were actually enclosed, including about two square miles in tillage and four square miles of cattle range. On the advice of the governor and committee, Douglas claimed as a possessory right 3,084 acres actually occupied.[39] They were the best locations on the island, and their possession by the Company was the cause of much hostile comment by Blanshard, by visiting officers of the Royal Navy, and, later, by intending settlers. Rear Admiral Fairfax Moresby, commanding H.M.S. *Portland,* was one of the critics. He wrote from Fort Victoria in July, 1851, that there could be no hope for a flourishing settlement so long as the Company managed the affairs of the island. Moresby protested that the Company charged its own servants 12 shillings per hundredweight for flour but forced naval vessels to pay much higher prices, and that it had appropriated the most desirable land. He added: "There cannot under present circumstances be any expectation of competition, the interests of a Company with exclusive rights of trade being incompatible with the free and liberal reception of an Emigrant community." [40]

The private correspondence between James Douglas and Sir George Simpson revealed that the latter's point of view was precisely in accordance with the one Moresby had ascribed to the Company. In 1849 Douglas, who at first assumed that the Company genuinely desired to promote immigration, recommended an initial shipment of twenty families, totaling about 100 persons. In reply, Simpson cautioned him against the dangers of too ambitious a program:

After reading the description you give of the Southern end of the Island where nearly all the cultivable soil is occupied by the Hudson's Bay and Puget Sound Companies, I was surprised that you should recommend so large an annual immigration as about 100 souls—I think it would be safer to regulate the influx of population by the success of the first efforts now making: all new settlers will require to be maintained for the first year or two, and as the Company cannot be expected to furnish the requisite provisions, you must look to the settlers for the necessary supplies for new comers—: in this way the increase of the population will be proportioned to the capabilities of soil & climate for the support of an agricultural colony. The great danger to be apprehended in a too rapid settlement of the island is that a year of unfavorable crops might occasion scarcity & that would inevitably lead to the immediate abandonment of the colony by the settlers who would seek more genial climes in Oregon or California. I think it might be a profitable speculation to lay out town lots, as you recommend, the only objection being that in a Country where there is not an efficient police or military force, it is far more difficult to maintain good order when the people are collected in villages or towns than when scattered as farmers; our experience at Red River Settlement is sufficient to prove the truth of this.[41]

An accusation of deliberate duplicity would possibly be unfair to Simpson, but it would not be unjust to say that he forced facts into conformity with the interests of the fur trade and exaggerated the hardships resulting from the extension of agriculture into the fur-trade domain. In the guise of solicitude for the welfare of present and future settlers, Simpson wanted to restrict the influx of free farmers to Vancouver Island. Douglas conceded that he had "probably exceeded the mark" in recommending so large an annual immigration.[42]

Such discussions were instructive as to the philosophy of the participants, but the issue of the volume of immigration remained largely academic so long as there were onerous restrictions on the purchase of land. The requirement to transport and maintain five laborers for every hundred acres was even more discouraging to prospective purchasers than the price of land. There was no prospect in the early 1850's that a farmer on Vancouver Island could pay his laborers sufficiently high wages to prevent their desertion for more lucrative employment in the United States. This perversion of the Wakefield conception of systematic colonization was a guarantee against independent colonization. Only three independent purchasers of over 100 acres settled on Vancouver Island during the Company's tenure, and none of them prospered from the investment.[43]

With these minor exceptions, the colonization of Vancouver Island in the years before the Fraser River gold rush was almost entirely under the auspices of the Hudson's Bay Company and the Puget's Sound Agricultural Company. Unlike the Hudson's Bay Company, the Puget's Sound Company made no claims to occupation of land prior to the treaty, and it paid the prescribed £1 per acre for all land it occupied. But for its eventual occupation it marked out from 15,000 to 20,000 acres between Esquimault and Victoria, from which tracts would be purchased as required. No settler could purchase land within this "reserve" without the consent of the company's directors. To Blanshard's and Moresby's complaints that the two companies were monopolizing the best land, Pelly replied that the Hudson's Bay Company was entitled to the land it had improved before the treaty and that the Puget's Sound Agricultural Company required large tracts for its flocks and herds, since the Americans would in all likelihood soon seize its land at Fort Nisqually and Cowlitz Farm.[44] Pelly's argument reflected the assumption that the Company's interest on Vancouver Island was paramount, an attitude that could have little support outside the Company. Even Chief Factor James Douglas agreed privately with Blanshard's contention that the prescription of reserves by the two companies was "injurious to the country," although as a loyal servant he publicly defended the right of preëmption.[45]

The first large contingent of immigrants to Vancouver Island, a group of eighty, mostly miners, arrived on the *Norman Morison* in March, 1850. Their destination was the coal mines at Fort Rupert in the northeast corner of the island. The mines proved to be of little value and the miners were dissatisfied. The center of mining operations was soon shifted to Nanaimo, on the Gulf of Georgia.

The first sizable migration of agricultural settlers began in November, 1850, when 127 passengers sailed from Gravesend for Vancouver Island on the *Tory*, chartered by the Company. Among them were three bailiffs, with their families, each employed to manage a farm for the Puget's Sound Company, seventy-four laborers, nine laborers' wives, and four children of laborers. These men, to be employed by the companies in agricultural or other tasks, were engaged for five years at annual salaries of £17. In addition they were provided with free passage for themselves to the island and, at the expiration of their contracts, back to England. They were lodged and fed by the Company, which also supplied their implements. Such contracts were standard in the fur trade, but the wages were much lower than the prevailing scale paid by American employers on the Pacific Coast.[46] Opinions as to the well-being of the laborers differed widely. Richard Clemens, who saw them a few months after their arrival, commented on the "forlorn, dejected appearance" of these men, all of whom, without exception, complained bitterly of unjust treatment. He alleged that they received a miserable pittance for their work, and quickly spent it for necessities at the Company's store, where prices were exorbitant.[47] Pelly denied the charge of unfair treatment. He contended, with justice, that the men were better nourished than they had been in their homeland. They were fed pork and salmon,[48] and occasionally beef and mutton. They were able to save money, and most of them sent remittances home. In contrast, in Dorsetshire, whence most of the men had come, the average wage of laborers was less than 7/6 per week, which had to cover food, clothing, and all other necessities.[49]

By the ethical standards of the era, Pelly was eminently justified in his attitude. But the standards of contentment in England and on Vancouver Island were very different, and the most impressive evidence of chronic dissatisfaction was the continued desertions of the Company's employees from the island for the fairer field of the United States. The colonization program had sadly degenerated from the optimistic expectations of 1848. Instead of the select agricultural laborers then envisaged, the island received a nondescript group of unskilled workers on the verge of destitution; instead of young married couples, the *Tory* had brought seventy-four laborers and only nine wives. The predictions of critics and of some of the Company's officials that the Company could not promote free settlement seemed to be sustained.

The Company's first report to the Colonial Office on its trusteeship provided further evidence that colonization was progressing very slowly. Governor Colvile stated that from the date of the grant to April 27, 1852, the Company had sold 1,478½ acres to eleven persons and that nineteen others had applied for an additional 2,355 acres. In addition the Puget's Sound Agricultural Company had assumed responsibility for four farms, together covering about 2,500 acres. Colvile did not state, however, that the majority of the purchasers were employees of the Hudson's Bay Company. The following tabulation of emigrants brought to Vancouver Island to work as agricultural laborers, miners, and mechanics for the Company enumerates almost the entire immigration during this period: [50]

|  | Males | Females | Children |
|---|---|---|---|
| 1848 | 21 | 5 | 6 |
| 1849 | 67 | 5 | — |
| 1850 | 99 | 25 | 27 |
| 1851 | 28 | 2 | — |
| 1852 (to April) | 56 | 43 | 51 |
| Total | 271 | 80 | 84 |

Between 1852 and January, 1855, little progress was made. By the latter date, 11,455 acres had been sold; but of this the Hudson's Bay Company had purchased 6,200 acres and the Puget's Sound Agricultural Company, 2,574. There were forty-three "settlers" on the island, but most of them were either past or present officers and clerks of the Company. Since April, 1852, an additional 312 emigrants—146 men, 80 women, and 136 children—had been sent out by the two companies. Two hundred square miles of land had been surveyed and laid out into districts, a road of a proposed length of thirty miles was under construction, and several bridges had been built. A church and three schools had been constructed, and two flour mills and five sawmills were in operation. Although some progress had obviously been made in the colonization of Vancouver Island, it was scarcely enough to support Colvile's contention that the efforts of the Company had been "tolerably successful." [51]

The governor and committee displayed more zeal in promoting their own projects than in promoting free colonization. They were preoccupied with securing miners for coal mines and bailiffs and laborers for Company farms; they made relatively little effort to stimulate the enthusiasm of others over the potentialities of the island. Their views on free settlement were perhaps most impressively displayed in their expenditures for advertising. Between February, 1849, and April, 1852, they spent £344.3.10 for advertisements in Scottish, English, and Irish newspapers; [52] but from October, 1852, to May, 1853, their total disbursement for "advertisements, stamps, and a land deed" was £28 6d.,[53] and advertising expenditures continued to be insignificant for the duration of the Company's tenure.

By their lack of emphasis on free settlement, the governor and committee demonstrated their conviction that independent settlers must necessarily clash with the Company, a viewpoint for which they already had impressive documentation in Oregon and at the Red River settlement. Further evidence of incompatibility was provided on Vancouver Island itself when fifteen residents, styling themselves "the whole body of the independent settlers," delivered a petition to Governor Blanshard in November, 1850. Six of the fifteen were members of the Muir family who had been brought in by the Company as miners, and another, Robert J. Staines, was the Company's chaplain. Their protest expressed the same spirit displayed by settlers in Oregon and at Red River, condemning the Company as a grasping, monopolistic enterprise.[54]

This petition caused no evident reaction in London, but another presented to Parliament in the spring of 1854 caused more consternation in the Company. The petitioners complained that the high price of land and the lack of a proper government prevented settlement. They appealed to Parliament to take the island under Imperial control and to provide governmental institutions that would encourage free settlers to immigrate. Although not intended to be unfriendly to the Company, the petition was based upon a misconception that the government could resume control at the end of five years if the Company did not promote settlement. It was presented by Sir John Pakington in the House of Commons and by Earl Fitzwilliam in the House of Lords, but evoked no response in either house. Parliament, preoccupied with the Crimean War, had no time or energy for complaints from Vancouver Island.[55]

If the petition excited little interest in Parliament, it caused a furore in the Company. Unlike the previous petition, it was signed not only by independent settlers but by Company person-

nel, including Chief Traders William F. Tolmie and Roderick
Finlayson and retired Chief Trader John Tod. The memorial
was composed by the Reverend Robert J. Staines, who had also
been associated with the first memorial. Simpson was furious. He
talked of removing Tolmie and Finlayson to the northern department, presumably to exile them to an isolated station. Lacking
information detrimental to the moral character of Staines, Simpson considered it unwise to remove him from his position. He
predicted, however, that the council of the northern department,
when it heard about Staines's conduct, might refuse to vote him
any further salary and might also terminate the grant for the
school he conducted.[56] The cooler counsel of the governor and
committee restrained Simpson from extreme actions. Simpson,
however, was correct in his assertion that circulation of the petition was damaging to the Company's interests. The petition
reached England, in fact, through the hostility of Charles Fitzwilliam, member of Parliament for Malton and the son of Earl
Fitzwilliam. During a visit to Vancouver Island in March and
April, 1853, Fitzwilliam became convinced that the Company was
smothering the economy of the island. He and Douglas quickly
became mutually antagonistic, allegedly because of Douglas' "want
of civility" toward him.[57] This animosity undoubtedly heightened
Fitzwilliam's activity in presenting the petition to Parliament and
in making subsequent attacks on the Company.

The apathy of Parliament was not shared by the Colonial Office. As the months passed without evidence that the Company
was seriously promoting independent colonization, Grey became
increasingly disillusioned. Reports from Blanshard and from naval
officers strengthened his suspicion that the Company did not in-
tend to carry out its promises. The arguments of the governor and
committee, blaming the unimpressive record on the California
gold rush, the remoteness of the island, and other factors, did not
convince him. On December 20, 1851, Grey had expressed the hope
"that more efficient measures may be taken" for the improvement
of Vancouver Island "than appears hitherto to have been the case,"
for he believed that there would be a large influx of settlers if the
Company provided greater encouragement.[58] Pelly replied sharply
that he did not know what "measures" Grey had in mind and that
the directors would be pleased to entertain suggestions.[59] The

honeymoon between Earl Grey and the Hudson's Bay Company was over.

When a colonial secretary as friendly as Grey was dissatisfied, the Company could expect more severe criticism from officials less favorably disposed. After a brief Tory interlude in 1852, a Liberal government came into power, headed by the Earl of Aberdeen and including Gladstone as chancellor of the exchequer and the Duke of Newcastle as secretary of state for colonies. Two of the Company's most bitter critics were now in key offices. Newcastle began the attack in October, 1853, when he informed the governor and committee that the government was considering the advisability of authorizing freedom of trade with the Indians in the settled parts of Vancouver Island, subject to restrictions on the sale of liquor.[60] He was surprised to hear from Andrew Colvile that "the Company does not claim the right to and has not exercised, any exclusive dealings with the Indians of Vancouver's Island since it became a colony; neither has there been any restriction on the freedom of trade as regards the Indians or any other parties." [61] Colvile's statement was technically correct, for the same result had been accomplished by economic means. Potential competitors were simply smothered by the same methods that proved so effective against petty traders in other areas.

Between 1849 and 1858 the Company's monopoly of trade on Vancouver Island was virtually complete. But its profits were inconsequential. The coal mines did not prove lucrative, trade with the few settlers and with the aboriginal population was insignificant, and the area was of little value to the fur trade. The languishing condition of the island was not exclusively or even primarily the responsibility of the Company. Even the Duke of Newcastle admitted that the remoteness of the island and the superior attractions of the United states were serious obstacles to colonization. Yet the Colonial Office also recognized that the Company would not be an active contributor to colonization in any event, and its influence might retard settlement because it controlled the government as well as the trade of the island. Newcastle took no further action during his first, brief tenure as colonial secretary,[62] but his successor Sir George Grey made the decision that foreshadowed the early extinction of the Company's governmental powers. On April 15, 1855, he reminded the Company that the grant was voidable at the pleasure of the Crown. The Colonial Office, stated Herman Merivale, speaking for Grey, had no wish to prejudge the issue, but there was a basis for doubt that the objectives of the grant had been attained. Merivale therefore asked the governor and committee whether they would surrender the grant voluntarily before the license of trade expired, thus avoiding the possibility of an unpleasant investigation.[63]

Sir George Grey examined the character of the government on Vancouver Island. Since September, 1851, James Douglas had been governor as well as senior chief factor of the Company's western department. These two positions could not be entirely harmonious, and there was reason to suspect that so long as Douglas occupied both, the Company would receive especially favorable treatment at the hands of the government. The Colonial Office, though not yet ready to insist that Douglas choose between the two jobs, had taken note of Fitzwilliam's accusation that the government was controlled by a tight little oligarchy sympathetic to the Company. The law advisers of the Crown provided further basis for concern when they rendered the opinion that the terms of the grant gave the governor and council of Vancouver Island no power to legislate, since that power was vested in the governor, council, and an elected general assembly, which had not yet been called into existence.[64] In February, 1856, the Colonial Office instructed Douglas to call an assembly, and the first one, composed of seven members, met on August 12.[65] The majority were friendly to the Company (four had been employees and a fifth was Douglas' son-in-law), but the establishment of an elected body pointed to the impending dissolution of the Company's control.

To the proposal by the Colonial Office that the Company relinquish its grant, Governor Colvile replied that the committee would make no objection if the Company was reimbursed for its outlay in promoting settlement.[66] Since all the immigrants brought to the island at Company expense had been Company employees, and since government and public works on the island had been supported by land sales, license fees, and other revenues, Colvile's reference to expenditures for colonization was not clear, and the Colonial Office did not ask for an explanation. It was not merely aversion to providing compensation which caused the Colonial Office to lapse into silence. Rather, the impending termination of the license for exclusive trade west of Rupert's Land, and the beginning of Canadian agitation for acquisition of the Company's chartered territory, caused an over-all investigation of the Company's operations.[67]

The select committee of the House of Commons, which met in 1857 to take testimony and to present recommendations, devoted relatively little attention to Vancouver Island, but most witnesses who presented evidence concerning the colony were unfavorable to the Company. They included Richard Blanshard and Charles Fitzwilliam, neither of whom could be expected to present the Company's point of view. The committee recommended termination of the Company's tenure on the island, and the Colonial Office soon resumed correspondence with the governor and committee to achieve that end.

The character of this negotiation was suddenly transformed by the discovery of gold on the Fraser River and the rush of miners, principally from western United States, to the gold fields. The previously empty valley of the Fraser now contained thousands of Europeans, and the turbulence characteristic of gold rushes in California and in Australia seemed likely to appear in British North America. Previous to the gold strikes on the Fraser, there had been gold discoveries in other areas of British territory west of the Rocky Mountains, but none had proved profitable. News of the most promising of these abortive discoveries, on the Queen Charlotte Islands, had excited the cupidity of gold seekers as far away as San Francisco.[68] To forestall American adventurers Douglas sent an expedition of "about forty hands," avowedly to maintain British control over the islands, but also to ensure the Company a monopoly of the gold. Such precautions soon proved unnecessary, for the amount of gold was insignificant; by April, 1852, Ballenden could state that "Queen Charlotte's Island is knocked on the head." [69]

The excitement over the Queen Charlotte Islands discovery was a foretaste of American reaction to the news that gold had been found on the banks of the Thompson River, a tributary of the Fraser. Small quantities of gold had been brought to the Company's posts by Indians since about 1852, but it was the report of large quantities at the mouth of the Thompson in 1857 which caused the rush of 1858, when from 30,000 to 40,000 miners left

the United States for the gold fields.[70] Although a few took the risk
of traveling up the Columbia through lands occupied by hostile
Indians, most of the miners came by ship. Of these the vast majority landed at Victoria, which experienced a tremendous boom.
The officers of the Company at first looked upon the gold discoveries as a magnificent opportunity for profits which would more
than compensate for the declining returns of the fur trade in New
Caledonia. On February 16, 1858, Simpson wrote Dugald Mactavish at Fort Victoria that the Company should immediately and
"thoroughly occupy the field" to keep out strangers from California and elsewhere. Only British subjects would be allowed access. Since existing stores at Victoria would be unable to supply
the demand, he authorized Mactavish to send for goods from California and the Hawaiian Islands.[71] In these instructions Simpson
revealed his monopolistic views and his ignorance of gold rushes.
The company did not possess the power to prevent the influx of
American miners.

The discovery of gold put the dual position of James Douglas to
its first serious test. Could the interests of the Crown and the
Company be reconciled, and, if not, which would he choose? Douglas' decision on December 29, 1857, to require the licensing of all
miners could be justified as loyalty to both Crown and Company.
But his subsequent actions could not be so regarded. He began
negotiations with the Pacific Mail Steamship Company to institute a steamer service from Victoria to the head of navigation on
the Fraser River. The ships would carry only miners who had licenses and only goods belonging to the Hudson's Bay Company.
Further, on May 8, 1858, Douglas issued a proclamation stating
that the Company possessed a monopoly of trade with the Indians
in the territory and warning all violators that they were subject
to punishment by the government of Vancouver Island.[72] Douglas
had demonstrated that his first loyalty was to the Company. The
colonial secretary, Sir Edward Bulwer-Lytton, disallowed Douglas'
proclamation and refused to accept the proposed contract with the
shipping company. He chastised Douglas for using his powers to
benefit the Hudson's Bay Company and reminded him that the
Company's exclusive license extended only to the Indian trade.[73]
Henry Hulse Berens, governor of the Company, interviewed Lyt-

ton and was sufficiently impressed with the vigor of his objections to write privately to Douglas cautioning him against using his office to advance the Company's interest.[74]

Because of the gold rush, the British government passed an act on August 2, 1858, establishing direct rule over the mainland, thereafter to be known as British Columbia,[75] and the Company's rights of exclusive trade within that colony automatically ceased. Douglas was made governor of both the mainland colony and Vancouver Island on condition that he give up all association with the Hudson's Bay and Puget's Sound Agricultural companies. This he did, not only resigning as chief factor and disposing of his interests, but zealously applying the free-trade principles espoused by the British government. By February, 1859, he was already at odds with his son-in-law, Alexander Grant Dallas, whom the governor and committee had sent out to head the board of management of the western department. There followed a long series of disagreements over the Company's land claims, charges for the use of Company steamers, and many other issues, in which Douglas demonstrated a degree of impartiality which to the Company seemed to verge on antipathy.

The Company's rule had ended not only in British Columbia but on Vancouver Island. Merchants swarmed into Victoria to extract gold from successful miners and money from hopeful seekers. A quiet community was transformed into a bustling city. Lots in Victoria which previously had been difficult to sell at £1 per acre now sold for £100 an acre.[76] In 1857, sales of public lands had totaled only 6,303 acres, but the total rose to 30,948 in 1858.[77] Legally the Company remained the governing power, but its authority was gone.

Negotiations for the transfer of legal power began in January, 1858, before news of the effects of the gold discoveries gave an additional impetus to the extinction of the Company's rights. Henry Labouchere, following the recommendations of the select committee, asked the Company to list its colonization expenses as a basis for compensation when the Crown assumed authority. In response, the directors itemized every conceivable expenditure, apparently assuming that the Colonial Office would differentiate between legitimate colonization expenses and ordinary commercial expenses. The total claimed was an impressive £112,810.19,[78] an amount the Company could not possibly obtain, as the governor and committee well knew. For the next four years representatives of the Company and the government haggled over the account. The dispute was finally settled in 1862 by an agreement to pay the Company £57,500,[79] although the final indenture of surrender was not completed until April 3, 1867. The Company surrendered all its rights on Vancouver Island except for some farm acreage and most of the land included in the site of old Fort Victoria.[80]

The Company had been responsible for colonizing Vancouver Island at a time when the island had little appeal for intending emigrants. No British company would have been likely to populate the island between 1850 and 1858, and no enterprise other than the Hudson's Bay Company, with the possible exception of Fitzgerald's anonymous associates, displayed any interest. The British government refused to authorize expenditures from the exchequer for the purpose of keeping Vancouver Island in British hands, and the Company could best assume the responsibility at no expense to the public. It was not until gold had promoted prosperity and provided a basis for a self-supporting colony that Her Majesty's government relieved the Company of its functions. Edward Ellice, Sr., observed that the government had used the Company and then, at the moment the discovery of gold stimulated land sales and offered the prospect of remuneration, had ousted the Company.[81] The responsibility for the impossible conditions of land sales at £1 an acre and of bringing laborers to the island at the landowner's expense rests in the first instance with the government, for the Colonial Office outlined these conditions to the Company. In November, 1859, Robert Lowe, then a rising politician in the Liberal party, wrote his friend Ellice:

> I cannot imagine anything more absurd [than] the policy of the Colonial Office. Of course the HBC was a perfect God-send affording a means at hardly any expense of keeping order in the new Colony. . . . Had the price of land been lowered to the American rate, that object [of colonization] would have been attained and had the hands of the Company been strengthened by every means at the disposal of government, they would have kept as much order as is required between the diggers and the Government.[82]

It is doubtful that the Company, as Lowe contended, could have preserved order in the gold fields, but his allegation that the government gave the Company virtually no support is justified. Between 1850 and 1858, the only energy observable in British North America west of the Rocky Mountains was that of the Hudson's Bay Company. The Company brought in the only settlers and conducted the only important trade. The only significant function performed by the British government was that of destructive critic, for while it condemned the Company for inactivity it failed to provide assistance or constructive advice to promote colonization.

Settlement of Vancouver Island before the discovery of gold on the Fraser River was probably impossible for any colonizing company, and Lord Grey suffered from a strange delusion when he concluded that the Company's experience with settlements at Red River and on the Columbia qualified it for this responsibility. The Company undertook the function for a negative reason; it wanted to keep the island from becoming a base for opposition, either British or American, against its mainland establishments. Its officers could not divest themselves of the belief that settlement was antagonistic to the interests of the fur trade.

Though Sir John Henry Pelly was undoubtedly sincere in expressing a desire to promote British settlement in order to secure the island against incursions from the United States, the Company's directors could not have been expected to rise above the dictates of immediate commercial interests. The traditions of the Company were autocratic, repugnant to the free institutions that settlers in a British colony would inevitably demand. At Red River, in the Oregon territory south of the 49th parallel, and on Vancouver Island, the Company attempted to reconcile itself to the requirements of an agricultural society, and on each occasion it failed. Such failure was probably inherent in the make-up of a fur-trading monopoly.

# IV

# The Last Years of the Monopoly

CHAPTER

# 15

# The Growth of Unrest at
# Red River, 1846-1853

THE RED RIVER COLONY was the anathema of the fur-trade monopoly. Free traders in liaison with American purchasers demoralized the price system in southern Rupert's Land; the Company's efforts to restrict this allegedly illicit trade met resistance in the colony, and protests against its "injustices" reached England, where they were used by the Company's enemies to discredit it. The very existence of the settlement was evidence that agriculture could be carried on with hopes of success in at least part of Rupert's Land, and thus stimulated both Americans and Canadians to search for new land resources in British North America.

Young Governor George Simpson had been prescient when he predicted in 1822 that the settlement would ultimately ruin the trade "unless the Company could establish and enforce its monopoly rights as against the inhabitants." [1] The officers of the fur trade supported Simpson's view. But it was not enough to recognize the problem; the Company required powers of coercion which were beyond its resources, since the expense of maintaining a police force large enough to support the Company's authority would greatly reduce the profits that the force was intended to protect. Between 1821 and 1846 no force was available other than employees engaged in the trade, except for a few useless constables who them-

[1] For notes to chap. 15, see pp. 467–469.

selves required watching. Consequently illicit trade had grown to alarming proportions by the mid-1840's. Seizure of furs was dangerous and, in the opinion of Adam Thom, legal adviser in the settlement, illegal unless the hunter was caught in the act of selling them.[2]

The British government could not be expected to help the Company enforce its trading privileges. No administration of the mid-nineteenth century, regardless of its political coloration, would contribute to colonial expenditure unless a pressing national interest was involved. No such claim could be made for a tiny settlement of no discernible value to British society and isolated in the middle of a vast and reputedly frozen wilderness. Further, the general hostility of the British mercantile community to monopolies made the Company reluctant to draw its affairs to the attention of Parliament.

The governor and committee and Sir George Simpson, therefore, confronted the conundrum of how to exercise authority without possessing power. While they faced this problem, the crisis over the Oregon territory developed, and war between Great Britain and the United States seemed likely, if not inevitable. In this unhappy prospect the Company's directors saw an opportunity. The British government might consent to help the Company defend Red River against American attack, and a military unit sent there for that purpose would also overawe the fractious inhabitants. The idea of asking for troops probably originated with Simpson, for the subtlety of the scheme accorded with his mentality. It was he who first broached the proposal to the foreign secretary, the Earl of Aberdeen.[3]

As Simpson escorted Lieutenants Warre and Vavasour westward from Lachine to Red River he continued to dispense the propaganda that the British national interest required the dispatch of a military force. The Americans, he told the two officers, were forming a cordon of military posts along the frontier from the Great Lakes to the Mississippi, and the British must do likewise.[4] An American military force, Simpson said, might march unchecked into British territory that could easily have been defended at trifling cost to the British taxpayer. But he was also aware that American military posts were centers of influence over the frontier Indians, who showed a tendency to trade in the United States rather than at the Company's posts. British military posts at Fort William and Red River, he believed, would restore respect for British, and Company, authority.[5] This second function of the posts he did not discuss with his officer companions.

Simpson also was granted a sympathetic hearing by Sir Charles Metcalfe, governor-general of Canada. Metcalfe believed that, in order to meet American attack, the British should gain command of the Great Lakes and place at the disposal of their commander in chief in North America from 50,000 to 100,000 men, to make of Great Britain "a greater Continental Power than they are."[6] His proposals were fantastic in the estimation of the Peel ministry, since the maintenance of such a large force in North America would impose an intolerable burden on the British taxpayer, but his desire to enlarge the British forces made him receptive to Simpson's proposals. Metcalfe accordingly recommended to the Colonial Office that British military posts be established along the frontier of Rupert's Land, opposite those built by the United States.[7]

In his consultations with British officials, Simpson was concerned with defense; in his discussions with his superiors, with trade. He warned Henry Hulse Berens in September, 1845, that "without a military post at Red River, I fear the inhabitants of that settlement will run riot and strike a blow at the Fur trade from which its recovery would be very doubtful."[8] The only chance for the dispatch of a military force lay in continued excitement in the United States and Great Britain over the likelihood of war; since negotiations were being actively pursued in Washington for settlement of the controversy, Simpson pleaded with the governor and committee to make their request quickly, while the sense of crisis was still upon the Peel government.[9]

To stimulate the government's sense of urgency, Simpson described for Metcalfe a meeting between United States cavalry and Red River hunters in American territory in August, 1845, in which the American commander had allegedly attempted to seduce the half-breeds from their British allegiance. Simpson alleged that the encounter was not accidental, that the cavalry were under instructions to meet the half-breeds rather than, as was their ostensible purpose, to punish the Sioux who had murdered missionaries. Whether the meeting was planned or not, quite clearly the com-

manding officer of the cavalry unit used the occasion to describe
to the half-breeds the advantages of settlement in the United
States. He informed them that, as British subjects, they had no
right to hunt in American territory, but if they would settle at
Pembina, inside the American boundary, they would be assured
of the benevolent protection of the United States.[10]

The construction of forts and the attempts of American officers
to spread disaffection among British subjects were cited by Simpson and Pelly as evidence of aggressive American intentions toward
Red River. During the winter of 1845–46, Simpson in Montreal
and Pelly in London pressed responsible officials to send a detachment to Red River immediately. Aberdeen was sufficiently impressed by Simpson's warnings to commend the Company's request to the favorable consideration of the Colonial Office.[11] The
colonial secretary, Lord Stanley, in turn requested the Earl of
Cathcart, who because of Metcalfe's resignation had taken on the
administration of the Canadian government in addition to his
duties as commander in chief, to consult with Simpson and to make
recommendations.[12] The letter reached Cathcart's desk on December 22, 1845. President Polk's belligerent message to Congress
earlier in the month had convinced most Canadians that war was
inevitable, and Cathcart agreed to provide between 200 and 300
troops, contingent upon the Company's contributing to their support.[13] Success seemed assured, but just as Pelly and Simpson were
congratulating each other, a new development threw them into a
state of gloom. Lord Stanley resigned as secretary of state for colonies as a result of disagreement with the Peel government's advocacy of repeal of the Corn Laws. In forming a new ministry, after
an abortive Whig effort to form a cabinet, Peel made the worst
possible appointment, from the Company's point of view, to the
colonial-secretaryship—William E. Gladstone. Gladstone had not
yet reached the height of his invective against the monopoly, but
he had already expressed his hostility. In an effort to prevent the
collapse of the plan to send troops, Pelly obtained interviews
with Gladstone on January 27 and February 2, 1846. He was relieved to find that the new colonial secretary showed no disposition to oppose the dispatch of troops. Warre and Vavasour had
recommended that a military unit be stationed at Fort Garry;
Lord Aberdeen and Lord Cathcart had supported the Company's

request; and Gladstone seemed willing to follow their advice. The only undecided issues were the route the troops should take, whether by way of York Factory or by the rivers and lakes from Canada, and the portion of the expense the Company should bear.[14]

The principal basis for the government's decision was not the fear of direct American attack on Red River, but the belief that a detachment from the Regular Army would provide the half-breeds with tangible evidence of British interest, in addition to constituting a nucleus for a force of settlers and Indians. In this way the continued subversion of the Red River hunters by American officers would be prevented, and the community's allegiance to Great Britain secured.[15]

Only one obstacle remained after February, 1846, but it proved the most formidable of all. Though the decision on the desirability of stationing troops at Red River rested with the cabinet, the decision as to the practicality came within the jurisdiction of the Duke of Wellington as commander in chief of Her Majesty's forces. Wellington was obsessed with the conviction that the weakness of the Army on the home island threatened the national security, and he was alarmed at the prospect of dissipating already inadequate forces by assignments to colonial areas. Recognizing the threat to Red River, he was prepared to send a detachment of troops there for one year, but then he wanted them relieved by a unit specially recruited in England. He also insisted that the detachment be sent from England to Red River via Hudson Bay rather than through Canada, because of the difficulty of communication by the latter route.[16]

Wellington's conditions were of little consequence to the governor and committee, who were willing to accept either route provided that troops were sent. But Wellington soon found another objection. After reading Warre and Vavasour's reports, he concluded that the fortifications at Fort Garry were almost useless and that no troops should be sent until works that would resist attack by an organized military force had been constructed. Gladstone, with, one suspects, no regrets, now informed Pelly that the government intended to reconsider the expediency of sending troops.[17] Pelly was shocked. He had understood that the basic decision had already been made and that correspondence with the War Office now related only to details. He protested that Rupert's Land as a

British colony had the same right to British protection as other colonies and that the ministry would be violating its obligations if it now reversed itself.[18] Gladstone, who had shown admirable self-control in his relationship with the Company, dropped his restraint when he read Pelly's observation. He had his undersecretary inform Pelly that

> . . . he [Gladstone] cannot omit to apprise you that he must demur to a doctrine which denies any distinction in regard to the responsibility of Her Majesty's Executive Government where there is so very broad a distinction in regard to its power, as between the Colonies on one hand, and the Territories of a Chartered Proprietary Company on the other and that as he conceives reason & analogy and the very words of the Hudson's Bay Charter point to the establishment of such a distinction, altho' it is happily unnecessary to fix its precise limits particularly at a time when Her Majesty's Government has expressed its willingness to lend the aid of the regular force for the defense of the Territories of the Company and when the Company on its part, had stated its readiness to bearing the expence of rendering the post defensible at which it is proposed to place a detachment.[19]

Despite Gladstone's antipathy to the Company, the cabinet did not reconsider its decision. The War Office agreed to send a force of about 300 regular infantry to Fort Garry by way of Hudson Bay on the understanding that the troops would be relieved the next spring by a local corps of riflemen specifically organized for the purpose of garrisoning Fort Garry.[20] Having agreed to send troops, the War Office was generous. Instead of the promised 300, they sent approximately 400 men from the Sixth Royal Regiment of Foot, with supporting artillery, under the command of Lieutenant Colonel John F. Crofton. Far from being pleased, Simpson was dismayed. For the purpose of overawing the settlers, he considered 200 men sufficient; 400 would impose a strain on the limited food resources of the colony. But the choice was between 400 and none, and Simpson accepted the necessity of providing for them.[21]

The troops left Great Britain in June, before news of American acceptance of Aberdeen's draft of an Oregon treaty reached London. When they arrived at York Factory, the possibility of war had been eliminated. Had the Peel government remained in power after the agreement on Oregon, the troops might well have been recalled, but with the friendly Lord Grey in the Colonial Office, no action was taken by the incoming Whig ministry. Since the threat of American attack was removed, the only excuse for retaining troops in the settlement was the preservation of tranquillity among the inhabitants. That function they performed effectively, and previously unruly settlers now showed respect for the laws. Alexander Ross commented on the change effected by the troops:

> Generally speaking, everything is quiet & orderly. The presence of the red coats has made us draw in our horns like so many snails. The laws are respected, no mob-meetings, no plots, no threats, no illicit smugglers, no fur traders. We begin for the first time, to look upon the property we possess, as our own—protection is written in legible characters. The universal feature of things are becoming changed. Public feeling is reformed, so that I hope ere long, the general feeling throughout Rupert's Land will be, let us all go to Red River. Come my friends, I would say, you are all welcome.[22]

These idyllic conditions did not last. Though the troops remained for two years, twice as long as the government had agreed to maintain them, the quiet they had maintained did not long survive their departure. Nor could the presence of the troops at Fort Garry control the Company's antagonists in England, who began their attacks early in 1847. The occasion for the new outburst against the Company was the receipt in London of a memorial drawn up by Georges-Antoine Belcourt, a Roman Catholic priest in the settlement, and signed by 977 inhabitants in June, 1846, before the arrival of the troops. The memorialists alleged that "from the harsh administration of the Hudson's Bay Company, discontent and misery prevail amongst the Natives of Rupert's Land to an unparalleled extent," and that the Company had "permitted generation after generation of the hapless race consigned to their care to pass their lives in the darkest heathenism." By the impoverishment of the Indians, they contended, the Company had "amassed a princely Revenue" of nearly a quarter of a million pounds sterling per year. Other alleged sins of the Company included the reintroduction of liquor and the imposition of exorbitant prices for goods. The Company's deity, stated the author of the memorial, was gold, "to obtain which they trample down Christianity and benevolence." [23]

The petition contained an element of fact and a mass of exaggeration and falsehoods. Blaming the Company for famine and cannibalism among the Indian tribes was a fantastic misrepresentation, and the allegations as to profits, debauchery of the Indians by liquor, and opposition to the introduction of Christianity were exaggerated. The document was written in excellent French, and it was by no means certain that the "signatories" were fully cognizant of the contents, since, as the petitioners themselves declared, there were few literate Indians or half-breeds in the territory. But the charges could not be brushed aside. The memorial was shrewdly drawn. Emphasizing the misery of the Indians, not of the half-breeds, it was well calculated to have maximum effect on such humanitarian organizations as the Aborigines Protection Society and various missionary societies.

As spokesman in England for the Indians and half-breeds, Alexander K. Isbister proceeded to exploit the sensitivity of the British conscience. Isbister was himself a métis. His father and an uncle, William Kennedy, had been employed by the Company. Isbister was sent to Scotland to be educated, but in 1837 he returned to North America and entered the service of the Company as a clerk in the Mackenzie River district. The life of a fur trader, however, offered little scope for his ambitions, and in 1840 he departed to continue his education in British universities, where he eventually concentrated on the study of medicine. By the summer of 1845 he was seeking a position in which he could use his knowledge. He applied for a post at the University of Aberdeen, the appointment to which rested with the Crown. Recognizing that he could have little hope of success without the support of influential men, he asked Governor Pelly to write a testimonial, and Pelly obliged with the following endorsement: "I hereby certify that Mr. Alexander Isbister was three years in the service of the Hudson's Bay Company, during which period he acted in the capacity of clerk and accountant discharging the duties of his office with the utmost integrity and with great ability." [24]

This certification was not enough to win Isbister the position, and the next year he sought Pelly's help again. Until the summer of 1846, at least, he was friendly enough to the Company to ask the assistance of its governor in his search for employment.[25] But later in the year his attitude changed, and thereafter he devoted himself to destruction of the monopoly. The proximate cause of this impressive transformation in young Isbister was probably his association with James Sinclair, who arrived in London in October, 1846, to ask the governor and committee for additional compensation for freighting he had done for the Company.[26]

After his conversion to antagonism, Isbister attacked the Company with energy and a marked lack of discrimination between facts and falsehoods. In his denunciations he drew not only from his own experience but from the writings of the Reverend Herbert Beaver and Alexander Simpson. Neither of these sources was reliable. Beaver had been the Company's chaplain at Fort Vancouver but had resigned after violent conflict with McLoughlin. He had been shocked by the dissolute character of the Company's officers, living, as he conceived it, in sin with Indian and half-breed women, and friction between him and McLoughlin increased until on one occasion McLoughlin assaulted him.[27] Alexander Simpson, brother of Thomas Simpson, the Arctic explorer, had been a chief trader in the Company's services in the Hawaiian Islands, but had resigned when Governor Simpson transferred him to another position in the northern department.[28]

Isbister cited Beaver's testimony that, of the articles bartered by the Company for furs and other produce, "over half may be classed as useless, one quarter as pernicious (ardent spirits), and the remainder as of doubtful utility." The established range of prices paid the natives for their furs in most districts was outrageously low, Isbister declared, and it was only where competition from American traders was a threat that a more favorable standard of exchange was provided.[29]

Not only were prices extortionate, said Isbister, but none of the profits resulting therefrom were returned to the Indians in the form of services, such as educational facilities. On the contrary, the sale of spirituous liquors had increased after the renewal of the Company's license. His black picture of misery and degradation was greatly overdrawn, but it conformed to the views of leading politicians like Gladstone, Roebuck, and Hume. Earl Grey could not ignore the charge.

Since the government had no regular channel of communication with a wilderness hundreds of miles removed from the centers of settlement, Grey requested Lord Elgin, governor-general of Canada, to obtain information. Grey suggested that the Anglican and Roman Catholic bishops of Canada and the head of the Methodist body might constitute themselves a committee to acquire information from their clergy in Rupert's Land. Elgin might then determine from their reports the truth of Isbister's charges.[30]

A year passed with no reply from Elgin. Finally, after being prodded by Grey, Elgin forwarded his report in June, 1848, and explained his delay. The distance between Red River and Canada, the almost complete lack of intercourse between them, and the "peculiar" character of the Company's jurisdiction made it difficult to obtain sufficient data for a report. From available sources of information, however, he concluded that the Company's government had on the whole been beneficial to the Indians and that the Company was to be commended for its efficiency in a vast and inhospitable territory. Apart from Lieutenant Colonel Crofton, Elgin did not name his informants, but it was evident that he had not leaned heavily on information provided by half-breeds or missionaries. He castigated the complainants for their lack of realism and their overzealousness to elevate a race of inferior culture without sufficient realization of the obstacles:

> It is indeed possible that the progress of the Indians toward civilization may not correspond with the expectations of some of those who are interested in their welfare. But disappointments of this nature are experienced I fear in other quarters as well as in the Territory of the Hudson's Bay Company and persons to whom the trading privileges of the Company are obnoxious may be tempted to ascribe to their rule the existence of evils which it is altogether beyond their power to remedy. There is much reason to fear that if the Trade were thrown open and the Indians left to the mercy of the adventurers who might chance to engage in it, their condition would be greatly deteriorated.[31]

Elgin's opinion could not have been more favorable to the Company had Sir George Simpson written it, and indeed there is reason to suspect that the testimony upon which he based his judgments was biased. Since Crofton was the only source mentioned by name, Elgin probably relied upon him dominantly or even exclusively. Crofton, accompanied by Simpson, had an interview with Elgin in

August, 1847, after he was relieved of his command at Fort Garry and as he was on his way home to a new assignment. Upon his arrival in England he reported to officials of the Colonial Office. As an officer of the Regular Army he might have been expected to present an independent judgment, but apparently he did not. Crofton worked in the closest association with the Company; in return he expected Pelly's assistance in obtaining a more attractive position in the Army. His report to the War Office on the need for sending pensioners to Fort Garry to replace the Sixth Regiment was prepared with Simpson's assistance. When the Colonial Office at Pelly's suggestion, in February, 1848, sent Crofton a statement of Isbister's charges and asked for his comments, he presented the same testimony he had given Elgin and wrote Simpson that "I believe my answers have been satisfactory" to the Company.[32]

Crofton was not a credible witness. But his testimony conformed in all essential particulars to the statement of Major Griffiths, his subordinate, who returned to England from Red River in October, 1848; there is no evidence that Griffiths was tampered with, beyond an allegation by John McLaughlin of Red River that he received a gift of valuable furs upon his departure from the colony.[33]

While the investigation was in progress Isbister was not idle, but he showed little discretion. In July, 1847, he wrote to Alexander Rowand, a Montreal physician who was the half-breed son of Chief Factor John Rowand of the Saskatchewan country. He boasted that he had "literally forced" Earl Grey to grant an inquiry on the charges of the half-breeds, and that Grey, "seemingly afraid to take the matter up himself," had transferred the case to Canada. He sent this information, he told Rowand, so that Canadian sympathizers with the half-breeds could make the cause of Red River as public as possible. "Now is the time or never to overthrow the Company," Isbister wrote to Rowand. He added that if he did not flay Sir George Simpson alive, "my name is not Isbister." [34] Whatever may have been the benefits to Isbister's self-esteem in such statements, the letter would be highly dangerous to the cause he represented if its contents were revealed to those he was attacking. Rowand divulged the contents of the letter to Edward Hopkins, Simpson's secretary, and also read Hopkins a letter from William Kennedy, Isbister's uncle, stating that preparations were being made to stimulate agitation in the Canadian press against the Company. Rowand, "from idleness of disposition, as from self-interest on his father's account," had no desire to become involved, and he transmitted this and subsequent letters to the Company. Simpson in turn provided Elgin with a copy of Isbister's letter, and Elgin sent it to Grey.

Simpson also sought to discredit William Kennedy, who had been a clerk in the Company's service between 1833 and 1846. At Isbister's suggestion, Kennedy inspired attacks on the Company in Canadian newspapers, and wrote Lord Elgin that in obedience to the dictates of God he was compelled to give evidence against the Company he once served. The Satanic motto "pro pelle cutem" (a skin for a pelt), Kennedy lamented, ruled the Company in its relations with the Indians whom it debauched or, in times of scarcity, left to starve.[35] Simpson rebutted Kennedy's charges in the Montreal *Courier,* thus deviating from the Company's policy of refraining from public controversy. More effectively, he demonstrated to Elgin that Kennedy had remained in the service long after the events he mentioned and, after leaving the service, had asked Simpson to give him a twenty-year license to trade on the Labrador coast as an associate of the Company and to advance him £2,000 for this purpose.[36] These facts, Grey wrote Elgin, destroyed "any importance that Kennedy's charges might otherwise have possessed."[37]

Isbister had been consistently outmaneuvered. With the evidence presented to the Colonial Office, Grey and his subordinates could only conclude that the charges had not been substantiated. Grey consequently informed Isbister that the charges were "in part undeserving of credit, in part so unimportant as not to merit inquiry."[38] The Company had won a point, but the victory was a minor one, for the enemies of monopoly in Parliament used the memorial of the Red River settlers as a basis for renewed attacks.

The first wave of denunciations came in August, 1848, in connection with the prospective grant of Vancouver Island to the Hudson's Bay Company. Gladstone, fortified by extensive reading from the writings of Lieutenant Charles Wilkes, Isbister, James Edward Fitzgerald, and others who supplied evidence unfavorable to the Company, presented to a generally sympathetic House of Commons a dramatic picture of a heartless monopoly enslaving

Indians, half-breeds, and its own employees, denying them access to the civilized world, debauching the Indians with liquor in order to eliminate their resistance to exploitation, and excluding from the benighted people the beneficial influences of free trade. He cited Wilkes's statement that Orkney laborers received £17 per year, out of which they were required to pay for their clothing at an 80 per cent advance over English prices, and for a considerable portion of their food. Employees were kept in constant debt to the Company, he alleged, and were thus unable to free themselves from a condition virtually indistinguishable from slavery. Gladstone quoted Isbister to the effect that in 1837, before the Company's license was renewed, 3,800 gallons of spirits had been imported into the Company's territories, whereas 9,000 gallons had been imported in 1845.[39]

In his attack on the Company, Gladstone's fervor dulled his critical faculties. It was true that Orkney laborers received only £17 a year, but, as Sir George Simpson pointed out in a critique of Gladstone's speech, these young men, most of whom had been employed in their late teens, would have found it difficult to procure employment at home at comparable wages. The prices of goods to employees were only 50 per cent higher than English wholesale prices, not 80 per cent, and servants were not required to buy provisions in order to survive, although it was necessary to purchase food to vary a monotonous diet. Isbister's allegation of an enormous increase in the amount of liquor dispensed to the Indians was untrue. The Company's invoices did not indicate a large importation of spirits into the Company's territories during the period in question, and Simpson was correct in his contention that the total was less than 9,000 gallons, most of which was dispensed in frontier districts.[40] Following is an invoice of liquor sent to the lower Red River district, near the American border, for Outfit 1841: [41]

|   |   |   |   |   |
|---|---|---|---|---|
| 2 | Casks | Brandy | 24 Gals. | each |
| 20 | " | Demerara Rum | 24 Gals. | " |
| 30 | " | Spirits | 24 Gals. | " |
| 2 | " | Shrub | 24 Gals. | " |
| 1 | " | Madeira Wine | 23 Gals. | " |
| 1 | " | Port | 29 Gals. | " |

Of this shipment, the bulk of the brandy and the wines was destined for consumption by Company personnel. Consignments of liquor to the Company's posts declined after 1841, and at the time of Isbister's and Gladstone's denunciations were of negligible proportions. The Reverend Peter Jacobs, a missionary in the frontier Lake Superior district, stated on July 2, 1849, that for the last ten years he had not observed the Company selling or giving rum to the Indians of that area. In the Lac la Pluie district, where the Indians enjoyed a strategic position because they controlled the supply of wild rice, they received a little rum as a reward for successful hunts or for the supply of wild rice and dried sturgeon and sturgeon oil. But even there the amount was insignificant. Jacobs stated:

> The average quantity of Spirits that comes into this District [Lac la Pluie] is about four glasses of spirits a year for every Indian in this District and at the rate of two glasses of spirits an Indian gets in the fall, and at the rate of the other glasses he gets in the spring. Consequently there are no Drunkerds here. But all the Indians consider themselves temperance men for when they get their two glasses spirits at [e]very Six months they only feel themselves rightly Tempered.[42]

Pelly answered the charge of debauchery by showing that since 1842 the Company's average annual importation of liquor into all the territories under its control was only 4,396½ gallons, which, if distributed only to employees, would give each man a daily allowance of less than two tablespoonfuls. But the Company had to supply not only employees and Indians, but also the Sixth Regiment at Red River and the pensioners who succeeded them.[43] The charge that the Company contributed to widespread intoxication was therefore unfounded. But general ignorance in England of the true state of affairs in the interior of North America, widespread suspicion of the Hudson's Bay Company, and the reticence of the governor and committee in providing information contributed to the acceptance of misrepresentation of the Company's policies.

Though Grey had dismissed Isbister's charges, he still had to meet the contentions of Gladstone and his supporters that the Company's rights had no legal status. With the concurrence of Pelly, Grey therefore assented to the resolution of the House of Commons in July, 1849, asking for information on the legality of the powers in respect to territory, trade, and government claimed or exercised by the Company under its charter or any other authority.[44] Pelly, who had spent several months preparing an answer to the resolution in collaboration with Edward Ellice the Elder,[45] argued that, although the original title granted by the charter remained a sound basis for the Company's rights, this authority had been supplemented by legislative recognition. The Quebec Act of 1774, for example, had described Quebec as bounded by the territories of the Hudson's Bay Company, and other legislation had recognized the Company's authority.[46] The Company's exposition of its rights was presented by Earl Grey to the attorney general and the solicitor general, who submitted the following conclusion to Grey in January, 1850:

> . . . having regard to the powers in respect of territory, trade, taxation, and government, claimed by the Hudson's Bay Company in the statements furnished to your Lordship by the Chairman of that Company we are of opinion, that the rights so claimed by the Company do properly belong to them.
> Upon this subject we entertain no doubt. . . .[47]

The opinion was, however, based upon an ex parte statement, since the Company's opponents had not been given an opportunity to document their contention that its claims were illegal. The law officers therefore suggested that Isbister could appear as complainant and present his case before either the Judicial Committee of the Privy Council or the Committee of Trade and Plantations. Prosecution of such litigation was out of the question for a man of Isbister's meager resources, and he declined to petition. John McLaughlin of Red River, who was in London in 1850 agitating against the Company, also refused when given the same opportunity. Like Isbister, he realized that he could not compete with the resources of the Hudson's Bay Company. He wrote Earl Grey that he could not at his "own cost and hazard assume the responsibility of prosecuting a great public corporation, who, in such a case, where the very existence of their monopoly of trade is at stake, would naturally resort to every legal subterfuge, entailing an amount of expense which no private individual would be justified in incurring." [48] None of the Company's fervent opponents in Parliament offered to give Isbister or McLaughlin financial assistance.

The law officers' favorable opinion produced a temporary lull in attacks upon the Company in Parliament, but meanwhile a crisis in the government of Red River presaged another and more formidable series of denunciations. The tranquillity of the colony, which was so gratifying to the Company's officers in 1846 and 1847, had been maintained largely by the presence of the Sixth Regiment of Foot. But the British government had restricted its stay to one year. In May, 1847, Earl Grey notified the Company that the detachment would be withdrawn during the summer, because of the original time limitation and because the Company had failed to make Fort Garry defensible against military attack.[49] Pelly and the committee were not alarmed. Red River was quiet, and Grey's notification arrived so late in the spring that it was impossible to evacuate the troops before the summer of 1848. The Company's ships customarily arrived at York Factory, where the troops would embark, in August and had to leave in September, while the weather remained benign, and news could not reach Fort Garry in time for so early a departure.[50] The governor and committee therefore had a year of grace in which to reconsider the means necessary to maintain the Company's position. They soon agreed that a replacement must be found for the Sixth Regiment or the Company's rule would become a nullity.

News of the impending withdrawal of the troops reached Red River at an unpropitious time. It came hard on the heels of reports that Isbister had proved the Company's authority illegal, the British government would soon free the colony from the restraints imposed upon it by the monopoly, and the decision to remove the troops had been made at the insistence of Isbister and his associates.[51] The Company's officers at Fort Garry, Simpson, and the governor and committee foresaw serious consequences if the vacuum created by withdrawal of the troops was not filled. On the advice of Colonel Crofton, Simpson recommended replacement of the Sixth Regiment with one or two companies of the Canadian Rifles, or failing that, employment of two companies of pensioners.[52]

There remained the problem of convincing the government that the interests of British society would be served by the dispatch of military forces. The sending of the Sixth Regiment had been justified by the threat of American attack; now no prospect of war remained. Consequently, when Pelly appealed to Grey in December, 1847, for continued protection, he based his request on the argument that American intriguers were fomenting unrest in the colony and that, unless troops were sent, they would agitate for annexation to the United States.[53] The identification of anti-Company settlers as pro-Americans was a keen stroke, for it associated domestic turbulence with alien influence. But it was a misrepresentation of the facts; except for Simpson's dispatch of October, 1845, reporting the encounter of United States cavalry with Red River hunters, no dispatches from Company officers in North America supported such a contention. Significantly, Simpson's report was the only evidence adduced by Pelly.

Earl Grey seems to have been sufficiently impressed by the evidence or sufficiently friendly to the Company to recommend the dispatch of one or two companies of the Canadian Rifles, but the Duke of Wellington was obdurate. The Company should have no troops, the duke declared, until it fulfilled its promise to build fortifications at Fort Garry.[54] The Company was therefore forced to accept its second choice of a company of pensioners. In January, 1848, Grey introduced Pelly to the secretary of war, Fox Maule, "a very nice accessible man." Pelly requested that 100 married pensioners and their wives, with an average of three children per family, or a total of 500 persons, be sent to Red River in the summer of 1848.[55] The name "pensioners" evoked in the minds of some of the Company's officers visions of the lame, the mutilated, and the superannuated. But the War Office was reassuring. The men who would be sent, stated an officer at the Horse Guards, were among the best soldiers in the service. Some were still in their teens and none beyond their forties; but they had been permitted to retire because they were discontented with the military life or "for other reasons." [56] For this sterling body of men, the government required the Company to pay all travel expenses to Red River, plus a supplementary daily allowance to the rank and file of 1 shilling during the first year and 6 pence during the second. Each officer would receive an annual subsidy of £300 in addition to a daily allowance of 10/6 and a grant of 100 acres. Each soldier would receive a grant of land within two miles of the fort not to exceed twenty acres for a private, thirty for a corporal, and forty for a sergeant; at the end of seven years the land would become the property of the pensioner.[57]

The character of the pensioners was not quite as the War Office had represented it. The first contingent left England on board the transport *General Palmer* in June, 1848. Of the fifty-six men who sailed only forty-two were married. The unit was under the command of Major William B. Caldwell, "a fine tall athletic man of very commanding appearance," who was also appointed by the Company as governor of Assiniboia.[58] The pensioners reached Red River on September 19, but even before then it had become evident that they were far from the elite of the British Army. They were constantly grumbling on the journey from York to Fort Garry, "principally about grub and grog." When they were given pemmican for their rations, some threatened mutiny, for which they received a severe reprimand from Caldwell. A Company officer who accompanied the pensioners to Fort Garry expressed surprise that old soldiers were so insubordinate and their officers were not more rigorous in enforcing discipline.[59] And Chief Factor John Ballenden, after observing the pensioners for three months, predicted that half of them would become burdens on the Company. He thought that a few, perhaps ten, might become good settlers, but he was doubtful even of these.

The soldiers of the Sixth Regiment had overawed the population as the handful of pensioners could not, but they had not eliminated the pressures that caused friction between the settlers and the Company. Indeed, in one way, they intensified the pressures. The presence of over 300 men had stimulated mercantile activity, so that the number of persons who imported goods greatly increased. With the departure of the troops, these importers were left with large stocks of goods which could not be sold in the settlement. The combination of glutted inventories and contempt for the authority of the pensioners encouraged many settlers to resume the fur trade in defiance of the Company, and led the Company's officers in 1849 to the desperate measure of prosecuting Pierre Guillaume Sayer and three others for alleged illicit traffic in furs. The outcome of the trial, which laid bare the Company's weakness and demonstrated its inability to enforce its claim to monopoly, might have been different had the pensioners been an effective military force. But the two officers, Major Caldwell and Captain Foss, were unable to maintain discipline or even to agree between themselves. The inadequacy of the pensioners as a police force was exposed by their conspicuous absence from the Sayer trial, and by Caldwell's admission that they would be unable to maintain the peace if the settlers were roused to violence.[60]

Alexander Ross ascribed the deterioration of order in the settlement in part to the pensioners themselves:

> The political feature of the settlement was never in a worse state, than it is, and has been since the arrival of the blackguard Pensioner squad. Had we been all saints, they would have made us devils like themselves, everything in the way of confidence and good order has been destroyed. If they do not prove the ruin of the Colony, & the downfall of all authority here, it will not be their fault. In bringing the Pensioners here, the Company committed a fatal error. If we required 300 regulars to keep us in order before, we require double that number now! Their introduction was the signal of our troubles.[61]

The moving spirit behind the half-breeds' defiance of the Company's authority, Simpson was convinced, was Father Belcourt. To blame Belcourt exclusively for the incitement of the half-breeds was to exaggerate his influence, but clearly he tried to undermine the Company's authority. In conversations with the settlers and in correspondence with his superiors in the Roman Catholic Church, Belcourt attacked the alleged despotism of the Company's officers at Red River.[62] Some of his letters were published in England, and Gladstone used his statements as evidence of the Company's tyranny. One published letter which Gladstone clipped from a newspaper contained this passage: "What a quantity of infernal secrets are concealed and concentrated in these far countries, where despotic power can operate at ease with a certainty of immunity." [63] To this observation Gladstone wrote a resounding "No!" He marked for reference passages on the stifling effect of the monopoly on the progress of agriculture, and the Company's use of liquor in trade.

Belcourt was a dangerous man, and Simpson was determined to remove him from his position at Red River unless he would give assurances that he would cease his attacks on the Company. Several conferences with the priest apparently convinced Simpson that Belcourt would act with greater moderation, and Simpson was willing to keep him at Red River. But meanwhile Belcourt had procured a transfer to the diocese of Dubuque, and was assigned by the bishop of Dubuque to a mission at Pembina just across the

border in the United States.[64] There he became the leader of disaffected half-breeds who crossed the border to be free of the Company's authority. From the security of American territory, Belcourt
was able to attack the Company more violently than ever. He cor-
responded with the leaders of the half-breeds in Red River, encouraging them to settle on the American side of the frontier.[65]
On March 5, 1849, he wrote J. Louis Riel, father of the leader of
the later Riel Rebellion, that word from London confirmed the
belief that the Company's pretensions to exclusive trading privileges were contrary to law. Riel read Belcourt's letter outside the
church after services on the Sunday preceding the Sayer trial, "with
many additions of his own of a similar character." [66] Although not
physically present, Belcourt thus helped to incite the Red River
settlers at the time of the trial. The fears expressed by the governor and committee in April, 1849, that Belcourt at Pembina
would do more mischief than Belcourt at Red River were fully
realized.[67] A protest to the United States government through the
British minister, John F. Crampton, was unavailing,[68] and Belcourt's activities continued without restriction.

Victory in the Sayer trial encouraged the leaders of the half-
breeds to press further demands on the Company. When Simpson
arrived at Fort Garry in June, 1849, he was presented with a petition for the removal of Adam Thom, the recorder of Rupert's
Land.[69] Thom, as the Company's legal adviser in the settlement,
was particularly unpopular because he was regarded as primarily
responsible for the harassment of free traders. But Thom's functions were advisory, not executive. It was Chief Factor John Ballenden who decided to prosecute Sayer, although Thom apparently
suggested the move and prepared the case. But even though the
responsibility was not his alone, Thom was a convenient target.
He was officious, he paraded his superior learning, and he made no
secret of his contempt for the uncouth residents of Red River.[70]
But Thom's unpopularity was more deeply based. As legal adviser of the Company, his official functions inevitably concentrated
upon him the enmity of the population. He was correct in his
observation that "it is not against Mr. Thom, but against the
Company, that the ultimate aim is directed." [71]

Thom was obnoxious, but he had courage. He ignored threats
of violence upon his person or of the burning of his house and

remained in the settlement, although he agreed to withdraw from the court and from the council of Assiniboia. Finally, after three years of pressure from Simpson, he consented to retire from the service, effective July 1, 1854.[72] Thom's resignation solved no problems for the Company, nor did the replacement of Major Caldwell as president of the council of Assiniboia by Eden Colvile, son of Andrew, in August, 1850, on the demands of the Red River insurgents.[73] Both instances revealed the bankruptcy of the old order.

The collapse of the Company's authority at Red River caused Simpson to become steadily more pessimistic during the last years of his life as to the future of the fur trade. As early as March, 1848, he had predicted that if the settlers were allowed to trade, the Hudson's Bay Company would be ruined within a decade.[74] After the Sayer case, virtually free trade had come to pass. Further, the Company was under attack in Parliament, and the market for beaver was depressed by the competition of silk hats. The officers in the service shared Simpson's pessimism. Donald Ross, in charge of Norway House, wrote to Simpson before the Sayer trial that the Company's directors ought to sell their privileges to the British government while they still could, rather than attempt to stem "a current which it will be impossible to surmount or withstand." Ross stated:

> We can no longer hide from ourselves the fact, that free trade notions and the course of events are making such rapid progress, that the day is certainly not far distant, when ours, the last important British monopoly, will necessarily be swept away like all others, by the force of public opinion, or by the still more undesirable but inevitable course of violence and misrule within the country itself—it would therefore in my humble belief be far better to make a merit of necessity than to await the coming storm, for come it will.[75]

In 1848 Simpson was already inclined to the same opinion, as was Sir John Henry Pelly, governor of the Company. In a private letter to Earl Grey, Pelly hinted that the Company might surrender its property if it were secured a return of 10 per cent on its capital and allowed to retain the same rights of trade as other British subjects.[76] These were essentially the terms then being proposed for the termination of the East India Company's charter.

The suggestion of allowing the Company to trade as a private association, in addition to receiving a guaranteed return, evoked no response from Parliament or the cabinet, and Pelly made no further reference to the Company's willingness to sell its chartered rights. But after Pelly's death Simpson renewed his prediction that, unless the Company negotiated the sale of its property soon, it would have no rights of any value to sell.

At the suggestion of Pelly's successor, Andrew Colvile, Simpson estimated the value of the Company's posts in the chartered territory, Canada, Labrador, the licensed territory, Oregon, and the Hawaiian Islands. He placed the posts in six categories in accordance with their importance to the Company's trade, and evaluated them on the basis of estimated construction and land improvement costs. He estimated the total value of the Company's 140 posts at £408,000. Of this, posts in the licensed territory were valued at £66,500; those in Canada and Newfoundland at £57,500; those in Oregon at £70,500; the three on Vancouver Island at £18,000; and the station at Honolulu at £4,000. The posts in Rupert's Land were valued at £161,500.[77]

Without a prospective purchaser, such a valuation was little more than an intellectual exercise. At the time the British government had no inclination to purchase the Company's rights, and Canada as yet had neither the resources nor the desire to negotiate. But Simpson's eagerness to sell the chartered rights was an early manifestation of his conviction that the prosperous days of the fur-trade monopoly were approaching an end. By 1860 the entire leadership of the Company shared his views, and consequently were receptive to offers for the sale of their property. By 1860, too, Canada had become interested in the agricultural possibilities of southern Rupert's Land, although Canadians demonstrated a distinct disinclination to pay the Company for the transfer of its rights.

## CHAPTER 16

# The Company in British and
# Canadian Politics during the 1850's

WHILE THE AUTHORITY of the Hudson's Bay Company was being
undermined by the inhabitants of Red River, Great Britain evidenced little interest in the affairs of the Company. Most British
politicians, like the population at large, accepted without question
the picture of Rupert's Land as the frost kingdom, where crops
could not grow, a region that should be left to the Indians and
the buffalo, since it was unfit for European settlement. The Company's personnel contributed to this exaggerated view of the rigors
of life in its territories, not so much by their testimony as by their
silence. The few descriptions of the interior were usually associated with Arctic explorations, and it was easy to generalize from
these accounts as to the characteristics of all Rupert's Land. But,
had anyone been actively interested, he could have found bases
for a contrary view from so exalted a source as Sir George Simpson
himself. In his published descriptions of Rupert's Land, Simpson
made no effort to hide the fertility of the soil in several districts.
The following, for example, would not contribute to a negative
view:

> The river which empties Lac La Pluie into the Lake of the
> Woods is, in more than one respect, decidedly the finest stream on
> the whole route. From Fort Frances downwards, a stretch of nearly
> a hundred miles, it is not interrupted by a single impediment,

while yet the current is not strong enough materially to retard an ascending traveller. Nor are the banks less favourable to agriculture than the waters themselves to navigation, resembling, in some measure, those of the Thames near Richmond. From the very brink of the river, there rises a gentle slope of greensward, crowned in many places with a plentiful growth of birch, poplar, beech, elm, and oak. Is it too much for the eye of philanthropy to discern, through the vista of futurity, this noble stream, connecting, as it does, the fertile shores of two spacious lakes, with crowded steamboats on its bosom, and populous towns on its borders? [1]

The governor later had occasion to regret the enthusiasm of the "ghost writer" who composed such passages, when asked by members of the select committee of the House of Commons to reconcile them with his assertion that none of the Company's territories was well adapted for agriculture. His reply that he had described only the river banks, and that the hinterland was unfit for farming, did not convince his questioners.

Canadian agitation against the Company was begun in the late 1840's by two newspapers, the *Globe* and the *North American,* edited respectively by George Brown and William McDougall. Their attention was first directed to Red River by the attacks of Isbister and Kennedy. After this initial stimulus the two editors gradually shifted their emphasis until they became protagonists of Canadian acquisition of Rupert's Land, or the "North West Territories," as they preferred to call it. On November 12, 1850, Brown's *Globe* contained two columns of denunciations of the Company. On that day Stuart Derbishire, Simpson's close friend and informant on Canadian affairs, was in Armour's bookshop in Toronto when Brown came in to ask whether the proprietor had any works on the Hudson's Bay Company. During the conversation, to which Derbishire attuned his ear, Armour stated that Kennedy had received an "awful smashing" in another newspaper, adding that he scarcely ever read attacks on the Company since that time, as they proceeded from persons with ulterior motives. Brown angrily replied that Kennedy's allegations were true, and that the Company should be brought to account for its exploitation of the Indians. He allegedly told Armour that the Company's statistics on liquor importation were correct for only one year, but that the

[1] For notes to chap. 16, see pp. 469–471.

preceding year the quantity had been much greater—Derbishire understood him to say a million hogsheads.[2]

For several years not many Canadians shared Brown's interest in the Red River settlement. In the mid-1850's, however, two significant groups began to demand Canadian annexation of at least part of Rupert's Land. A group of Toronto businessmen, attracted by the reports of fabulous profits from the fur trade, envisioned the creation of a new North West Company which would again make of Canada a great fur center. Canadian claims to Rupert's Land would support their attacks on the Company's monopoly. The other interested Canadians, initially less influential but steadily growing in numbers and power, had no immediate self-interest to promote. They wanted to preserve for Canada the resources of Rupert's Land, fearing that, if action were not taken soon, the territory would cease to be British.[3]

On April 15, 1857, certain members of the first group, who also belonged to the Toronto Chamber of Commerce, petitioned the Canadian government to use "all constitutional means" to destroy the monopoly and incorporate its territories into Canada.[4] Perhaps associated with the petitioners or inspired by them, a party of three young men left Toronto in April for St. Paul, Minnesota. Their leader was one Lonsdell, formerly in the Company's service in the Lac Seul area. Carrying about £600 worth of goods, they avowed their determination to push into the interior of Rupert's Land. The expedition was a fiasco. Simpson, informed by friends in Toronto of the party's strength and intentions, warned his officers along the frontier to watch for Lonsdell's arrival and to buy up furs before his party could acquire them.[5] These precautions proved unnecessary. The group was split by dissension. Lonsdell quarreled with his companions Richardson and Ball, and the two factions did not reach Red River until September. Fortunately for them, goods were then scarce at the Company's store, and they were able to sell their outfit in the settlement.[6] There were rumors during the autumn of 1857 that a Montreal group was planning to organize a large fur company, but it did not materialize.[7]

Rival fur traders were not as potentially dangerous to the Company as the coalition of editors, farmers, and politicians who insisted that Rupert's Land was fertile, Canadian farmers had the

right to cultivate it under the jurisdiction of a Canadian government, and it must soon be transferred to keep it from falling into
American hands. The energy of Americans excited the envy and
reluctant admiration of these Canadians, who compared the relatively slow expansion of Canada's wealth and population with the
tremendous surge of the United States. In 1850 the total population of Minnesota, adjoining the Red River colony, was only 6,077
for a territory larger than the present state, but during the succeeding decade thousands of settlers arrived. Minnesota became a
state in 1858, and by 1860 had a population of over 172,000. An
increasing number of Canadians foresaw that, when the land of
Minnesota was appropriated by farmers, the flow of migration
would continue northward into British territory.[8]

There was reason for alarm. American railroad extension was
rapidly directing emigrants toward Minnesota. By 1856 the Illinois
Central Railway, the first land-grant railroad, was transporting settlers to the Mississippi River at Cairo and East Dubuque. In 1858
Anson Northup launched a steamer bearing his name on the Red
River, and in the same year a railroad was under construction
between the headwaters of the Red River and St. Paul.[9] The Red
River colony was being drawn into the American economy by a
transportation system linking it with the United States. The im-
minence of American absorption of the settlement seemed to be
symbolized by the extension of the United States postal service to
Pembina in 1857.[10]

Constant hammering on the theme of the West by Brown and
others first had a noticeable effect on the Canadian government
in the summer of 1856. In September of that year, Philip Vankoughnet, president of the Executive Council, declared that Canada should stretch across the Hudson's Bay Company lands to the
Pacific and that this vast territory should be bound together by a
railroad passing entirely through British territory. Vankoughnet
was reported to have said: "The charter of the Hudson's Bay Company—no charter—no power could give to a few men exclusive
control over half a continent. That vast extent of territory stretch-
ing from Lake Superior and the Hudson's Bay belonged to Canada
—or must belong to it." [11]

In a minute of January 17, 1857, the council took up the theme
with the assertion that it was the "general sentiment" in Canada

that the colony's western frontier was the Pacific.[12] Proponents of acquisition of the Company's territory argued that the most desirable lands of Canada had been allotted and that, unless new lands were soon made available, agricultural immigrants and the sons of Canadian farmers would be forced to seek their opportunities elsewhere, in particular in the United States. These contentions do not appear to be borne out by the *Parliamentary Book of Statistics* for 1856, which indicated that the government remained in possession of over 155,000,000 acres of disposable lands, whereas only about 7,000,000 acres were under cultivation in all Canada,[13] nor by the report of the commissioner of crown lands for 1857. The distribution of land as indicated in the commissioner's report was as follows: [14]

| Canada West | Acres |
|---|---|
| Vacant surveyed Crown lands | 830,398½ |
| "        "    Clergy   " | 422,944½ |
| "        "    School   " | 139,643¼ |
| Total of disposable surveyed lands | 1,446,976¼ |
| Private lands | 19,388,997¾ |
| Total surveyed lands | 20,835,984 |
| Unsurveyed waste lands of the Crown | 56,770,466 |
| Total area of Canada West within water shed of St. Lawrence and Lakes | 77,606,400 |

| Canada East | |
|---|---|
| Vacant surveyed Crown lands | 4,797,550 |
| "        "    Clergy   " | 487,683½ |
| Total disposable public lands, seigneuries excepted | 5,285,233½ |
| Township lands hitherto alienated | 6,373,597 |
| Extent of seigneuries | 10,678,931 |
| Total surveyed lands | 22,331,761½ |
| Unsurveyed lands | 112,075,039 |
| Total area of Canada East | 134,412,800½ |

Statistics, however, do not provide a true picture of the Canadian land problem in the mid-1850's. Much of the unappropriated land was either unfit for farming or of inferior quality. The frontier of settlement was pushing out to the edges of the Laurentian barrier. Practically all available good arable land was wooded, and many farmers preferred prairie land, which did not require back-breaking labor to bring it into cultivation. But many leading politicians

were not convinced of the urgency of the need. John Rose, the
Company's solicitor in Canada, stated in a letter to Edward Ellice
the Elder:

> If you ever see our Newspapers—you will perceive they are
> clamourous about the Hudson's Bay question—protesting that the
> charter is invalid—that the Land belongs to Canada, & that our
> Legislature must assert its right in a practical form to the Ter-
> ritory: The agitation fortunately has its origin with discharged
> servants of the Coy.—& the statements are exaggerated, & untrue,
> so that the movement is likely to defeat itself,—by alienating
> the support of moderate & reasonable men. I have got one or two
> respectable papers to take a fair view of the question, & to point
> out the impossibility of our governing the country even if we had
> it. It is time enough when our population has no elbow-room
> in our admitted Possessions to look out for others, & if the Ter-
> ritory were given up to us tomorrow we shall have to double our
> revenue & support the necessary military force to protect our
> population from Indian depredations.[15]

Rose's analysis was reasonable, although not entirely objective.
But he did not influence the Canadian protagonists of annexation,
who remained convinced that Canada must have Rupert's Land
both as an area of settlement and as a bridge to the Pacific slope.

Canadian agitation began at a time when Company leaders were
first beginning to suspect that the days of the great fur-trade monopoly were approaching an end. Simpson, who had held this view
since the 1840's, suggested in 1856 to the newly elected governor,
John Shepherd, that it would be wise to sell the Company's rights
before the British government became aware that they were worthless.[16] But Shepherd, whose experience as chairman of the board
of the East India Company had given him some understanding of
the problems of dying monopolies, did not agree. After consulting
the committee, he replied that the illicit traders, although their
competition was irritating, had little capital and would not make
serious inroads into the Company's profits for many years. In any
event, he insisted, it was poor business for the Company to propose the surrender of its charter, for that was tantamount to an
admission that it no longer attached great value to its exclusive
privileges. Instead of resigning itself to early extinction of its
monopoly, Shepherd declared, the Company should assume the
offensive by asking the government to renew the license of ex-

clusive trade and by requesting the War Office to provide troops to maintain order at Red River.[17]

The increasing agitation in Canada during 1856 brought to the fore the issue of renewal of the license. The Colonial Office under Henry Labouchere had no desire for political responsibilities in Rupert's Land. When a petition requesting direct British rule at Red River was presented to Labouchere in July, 1856, the Colonial Office personnel agreed that the establishment of such a government was "simply impossible under present circumstances." [18] But the prospect that Canada might assume both responsibility and expense gave the issue a different aspect. During the summer of 1856 Robert Lowe, vice-president of the Board of Trade, made a tour of Canada to collect information on such fundamental economic factors as railways and disposable public lands. During his journey through Canada West and the western part of the United States, Lowe was accompanied by John Rose, who, as the Company's legal adviser, was keenly interested in Lowe's observations on matters affecting the Company. Lowe volunteered the opinion that Canada should annex Rupert's Land, and undoubtedly would, but that in such event the Company would be entitled to just compensation for the loss of its privileges. This observation Rose duly reported to the governor and committee.[19]

This position was, of course, precisely the one Simpson had hoped the British government could be prevailed upon to adopt. While Lowe was visiting Canada, Edward Ellice the Elder, on behalf of the board, was pressing the government either to accept renewal of the license or to pay the Company for the surrender of its rights. Ellice wrote Labouchere:

> Before you lay the train, or permit Sir E. Head to lay the train, which may set fire to this instrument that has worked so well, both for the governors and the governed, be very sure that you see your way clear to some better substitute that you may accomplish the same object and get rid of the one inconvenience connected with it, our almost if not only remaining monopoly.
>
> I say, lay the train, for any encouragement that you will lend your hands to the destruction or abolition of the Hudson's Bay Company, before you have made up your minds to some other scheme for the administration of the country, will lead to *orders* to you to complete the work.—Do not suppose you can resist or retreat after the first stroke of the axe.

The Hudson's Bay Company are quite willing to dispose of their territory and their establishments. It is a question of a million of money. If either this Government or the Government of Canada wish to take the affair into their own hands I can tell them the cost of the undertaking.—But in my mind, as far as the maintenance of order and peace throughout that vast territory is concerned, that is the smallest part of the question.[20]

The alternatives, as Ellice presented them, were thus the renewal of the license of trade or the abolition of the Company's chartered rights by the payment of £1,000,000 sterling. Neither was likely to be palatable to Canada, since the Canadian government would be expected to provide the compensation. Labouchere suggested to Ellice that perhaps there was a third alternative, the cession to Canada of only those portions of the Company's territory which were suitable for cultivation, with the Company retaining its monopoly rights beyond. Ellice admitted that this might be a subject for discussion.[21] But the increasing attention paid to Red River by the press of Canada, the United States, and Great Britain made it evident that the lack of British policy was becoming increasingly dangerous. A line of action crystallized at a series of conferences in November and December, 1856, between Labouchere and members of the Company's governing board.

At the first meeting, Henry Hulse Berens, Eden Colvile, and Governor Shepherd met with Labouchere. The colonial secretary took pains to say that his preconceived opinions were generally favorable to the Company. He praised its treatment of the Indian population and expressed the view that in the government of Rupert's Land there was no cause for complaint. In fact, said Labouchere, the peculiarities in the conditions of Rupert's Land and in the economy of the fur trade might well make the Company's monopoly an exception to the general rule that free trade best served the public interest.[22]

Labouchere's personal attitude, however, he reminded the group, was not the determining factor in the government's policy. His influence might reduce the severity of governmental action against the monopoly but could not prevent it, if an aroused public opinion, through Parliament, demanded it. Since the agitation in Canada had again brought the Company's affairs to public attention, Parliament would expect an inquiry on the status of the licensed territory and of Rupert's Land. It would be in the interests of both government and Company if the government moved for the appointment of an investigating committee rather than allowing the initiative to come from an opponent of the Company.

The argument was conclusive, and the Company's directors readily agreed that Labouchere should so move at the beginning of the forthcoming parliamentary session. The plan was that a committee of the House of Commons should seek "the most correct and authentic information" on all aspects of the issue, and that Canada and the Company should both present evidence in behalf of their respective cases.[23] On February 5, 1857, in accordance with Labouchere's wishes, the House of Commons appointed a select committee of nineteen members "to consider the State of those British Possessions in North America which are under the Administration of the Hudson's Bay Company, or over which they possess a License to Trade."[24]

The committee included almost equal representations of friends and enemies of the Company. Labouchere, who served as chairman; Lowe; Sir John Pakington, a former secretary of state for war and colonies; and Edward Ellice, Jr., a member of the Company's governing board, were defenders of the Company's record of government. The Company needed strong friends, for the committee included its three outstanding critics in Parliament— Gladstone, John A. Roebuck, and Charles Fitzwilliam.

The committee took testimony from twenty-five witnesses, whose estimates of the Company's record ranged from Simpson's to Alexander K. Isbister's. The dissolution of Parliament in March caused temporary suspension of the hearings, but the committee was reconstituted in May with slight changes in personnel, most notable of which was the inclusion of Alexander Matheson, another director of the Company,[25] as a member. When the select committee made its final report, it had taken evidence totaling 550 pages.[26]

The hearings largely vindicated the Company of the extreme charges regarding its treatment of the Indians. Most witnesses, including Lieutenant Colonel John H. Lefroy, who had spent two years in the territory, and the Right Reverend David Anderson, bishop of Rupert's Land, testified that the Company's rule was beneficial to the Indians, though Anderson wished it would make a greater contribution to their education. Approval of the Company's Indian policies was indicated by the committee's recommendation that the monopoly in the Indian trade be continued in those areas where settlement was impossible.

The opposition was on stronger ground, however, in its basic argument that the Company was antipathetic to colonization. Even supporters of the monopoly agreed that settlement must be permitted and encouraged wherever practicable, and the weakest point of Sir George Simpson's testimony was his attempt to discount the territory's value for agricultural purposes despite his previous assertions to the contrary. Simpson's embarrassment illustrates the wisdom of the observation, "Oh, that mine enemy might write a book!" His glowing accounts of southern Rupert's Land in his *Journey Round the World* arose to plague him, and his attempts to explain them away were less than convincing. The committee recommended that Canada annex portions of the chartered territory for purposes of settlement on the condition that her government open and maintain communications with the areas annexed and provide for their administration. Beyond the mention that the cession should be made on "equitable principles," the committee made no recommendations for compensating the Company for the loss of its land. The report was adopted after spirited opposition from Gladstone, who wished it to be couched in terms less sympathetic to the Company.[27]

The Company's directors could derive some comfort from the moderate tone of the committee's report, but they had no occasion for self-congratulation. From this time until Rupert's Land was finally annexed to Canada in 1869, the Company was continually harassed by the Colonial Office. Peculiarly, the pressure in the early stages came almost exclusively from Great Britain, and the Canadian government manifested relatively little interest. Indeed, one of the few surprises in the testimony before the select committee was the unexpected moderation of the Canadian representatives. Chief Justice William H. Draper, who had been sent by the Canadian Executive Council as an observer, spoke in terms largely complimentary to the Company, although he warned that, unless an effective government was soon established, Rupert's Land was likely to become part of the United States. John Ross, who had been a member of the Canadian government from 1851 to 1856, was even more friendly. Although he expressed the view that Canada should acquire land suitable for agriculture, he commended the Company for its enlightened policy toward the Indians, and asked the committee to recommend continuation of the monopoly in all territories not appropriate for cultivation. "I fear very much," said Ross, "that if the occupation of the Hudson's Bay Company, in what is called the Hudson's Bay Territory, were to cease, our fate in Canada might be just as it is with the Americans in the border settlements of their territory." [28]

A cynic might contend that Draper's and Ross's testimony was influenced by their close association with Sir George Simpson. The governor, at Draper's request, had secured the appointment of the latter's son as an apprentice clerk in the service, although the youth died before he could begin his employment.[29] Ross had frequently received gifts from Simpson, and after his return to Canada informed Simpson's agent Stuart Derbishire that the evidence he had given before the committee was favorable to the Company's interests.[30] An analysis of the Canadian position based on such relationships would be superficial and, at least in respect to Draper, almost certainly untrue. The testimony of Draper and Ross reflected a marked change in the attitude of the Canadian government toward the "Hudson's Bay question," which could not be explained in terms of such influence.

Agitation for the annexation of the Company's lands to Canada had been the special province of George Brown and his supporters. The Macdonald-Cartier government considered it expedient to support the campaign rather than allow Brown and the opposition to claim the credit for being the exclusive spokesmen of the agrarian West, but it had little genuine interest in the annexation of all or part of Rupert's Land. John Rose, who was close to the government although he did not become a member of the cabinet until November, 1857, wrote Simpson in February that the government was sending Draper to England primarily because he wanted to make a trip home to London and his appointment gave a quasi-business character to the trip. He added:

> It is a very fair way to easing off popular clamour here, as I assume the extreme limit of his mission will be to ascertain on what terms the Coy. will give up any Territory required for settlement, & by whom,—Canada or England—the Indemnity is to be

made good. The danger is that Draper will be thought to be *too much* in favour of vested rights. You of course know him.[31]

Until the autumn there were continuing evidences of public interest in the future of the North West Territories. The press, particularly those newspapers opposed to the government, continued to demand action, and mass meetings were held in Toronto and other towns in Canada West. But by October the movement had lost its force. Canadians were then confronting the far more pressing problem of the Panic of 1857.

The financial crisis brought not only bankruptcies and unemployment but a collapse of the land speculation boom which had developed from excessive optimism as to Canada's economic future. The government was now preoccupied with falling revenues and increasing financial burdens caused by the obligations it had incurred to railroad companies and their investors. Brown continued his efforts to sustain interest in the West, but with decreasing effect. Derbishire in Toronto reported to Simpson on October 22 that "the fire of the enemy against the Company slackens." On the next day he wrote Simpson in high glee that the *Globe* had attacked Draper and the government in a violent editorial, and Brown's outburst had caused the Hudson's Bay question to become even more a partisan issue.[32] In truth, the issue seemed dead. The *Canadian News* of London, which was a receiving station for reports from Canada on all matters of public importance and was a strong supporter of Brown's position, stated on October 28, 1857, that the principal and indeed the only topic of interest in Canada was the monetary panic in the United States and its probable influence on Canada. On November 11 the newspaper declared that agitation on the Hudson's Bay question had subsided "for the present," and it did not mention the Company again in leading articles until early in 1858.[33]

After the general election of December, 1857, in which the Macdonald-Cartier coalition was returned to power, the government continued to express its desire to annex the Company's arable lands. The speech from the throne in February, 1858, indicated that the ministry would promote this objective, but there were no immediate evidences of determination to do so.

By the end of 1857 the position of the Hudson's Bay Company appeared to be stronger than it had been before the select committee of the House of Commons began its proceedings. The committee had recommended Canadian annexation of portions of the Company's lands, but its tone had been generally friendly, and it had also proposed continuation of the monopoly in areas outside the districts selected for settlement. Such an arrangement would leave the richest fur districts in the Company's hands. Canadian excitement against the monopoly had died down to the point where Brown was practically a solitary voice in his attacks.

These developments were encouraging to the stockholders and directors, and the Company received an additional boon when troops were sent to Red River. Fear of the spread of American influence in the settlement had given the Company an opportunity on which it capitalized. Labouchere was receptive to the suggestion that a detachment of troops be stationed at Red River, and referred the matter to the War Office for favorable consideration. Since the decision would be based on public necessity rather than on private interest, Shepherd instructed Simpson to write a letter describing the danger of American penetration. Simpson's reply was all that Shepherd could have desired. Graphically he placed the colony of 8,000 persons directly in the path of American migration northward, which he predicted could be stopped at the border only by the presence of a British military force. The United States government was about to form a garrison at Pembina, he declared, and its purpose would not be merely defensive. The United States had a covetous eye on the prairies of the Saskatchewan valley, which formed the most convenient railway route to Oregon and Puget Sound. If Great Britain desired to frustrate American plans, he warned, it must dispatch a wing of a regiment, about 400 men, to Fort Garry.[34]

Simpson did not delude the permanent officials of the Colonial Office, one of whom correctly stated that there was no danger of direct aggression from the United States, and that American policy, if actually concerned with Red River, was probably directed toward influencing the half-breeds rather than toward organizing filibustering expeditions. The purpose of the request, they realized, was protection of the Company's interest against outbreaks by the residents of Red River. Labouchere, however, without elaboration of his reasons, recommended that the troops be sent.[35]

The War Office referred the issue of defending Red River to

Lieutenant General Sir William Eyre, commander of the forces
in Canada. He concluded that the Canadian Rifles Regiment
would be better suited for service in a remote part of North America than a regiment of the line.[36] Accordingly 120 officers and men
of the Canadian Rifles under the command of Major George Seton
left Quebec in June, 1857, for York Factory and arrived at Red
River in October.

The mission of the troops was to protect the frontier against
the Americans; they could not be used by the Company to overawe the settlers. But their presence nevertheless had a chastening
effect on the colony, which before their arrival had been rapidly
moving toward another crisis in its relations with the Company.
The occasion for the new agitation was the arrival from Toronto
in February, 1857, of William Kennedy, who had been strongly
urging annexation of the Red River settlement to Canada. He
visited the colony in order to secure signatures to a petition requesting the Canadian legislature to protect the colonists from the
injustices of Company rule. Kennedy's support came primarily
from the younger adults in the settlement; more mature settlers
tended to regard his projects with diffidence.

A meeting at the Scottish schoolhouse on the evening of March
16 illustrated Kennedy's procedures and the reactions to them.
Upon hearing that the meeting was to be held, the governor of
Assiniboia, Francis G. Johnson, courageously decided to attend in
order to rebut Kennedy's accusations. When Johnson rose to
present his case he was immediately howled down by the younger
members of the audience. They cried that he had no right to be
there since, as governor, he should not be a partisan, and when
he persisted in his efforts to speak the crowd became uproarious.
Only one person ventured to support Johnson's right to speak—
Andrew Bannatyne,[37] who in September was to come into conflict with Chief Factor George Barnston because of his illicit trade
in furs.

Johnson had a better reception at a meeting of French Canadians called by Louis Riel the Elder, who invited him to attend.
When Kennedy had finished his attacks on the Company, Johnson was given an opportunity to speak, and on this occasion he
was not interrupted. From a meeting which Johnson estimated at
about 400, Kennedy gained only 18 signatures to his petition. In

the discussion of Kennedy's proposals at these meetings and in informal gatherings in the settlement, the practical question of annexation to Canada was hardly considered; the only real division was between pro-Company and anti-Company men, with the latter group hoping that in some way Kennedy's activities might further undermine the authority of the Company.[38]

With the arrival of the troops, the agitation against the Company's political authority was temporarily stifled. Although the free traders continued their operations, the governmental authority of the Company was more secure than it had been since the departure of the Sixth Regiment for England nine years before.

With Red River relatively quiet and Canada preoccupied with other problems, the Company's attention was again directed to the course the British government would pursue as a result of the committee's recommendations. Even before the committee's report had been accepted, Labouchere indicated the line of approach he proposed to take. From the law officers of the Crown he learned that the British government, as the grantor of the charter, should not appear as a party to proceedings reviewing its own acts. They recommended that Canada and the Company submit the question of the territory covered by the charter to the Judicial Committee of the Privy Council, and that the committee's decision serve as the basis for an act of Parliament.[39] There was no evident advantage to the governor and committee in such a course. As Shepherd stated to Simpson:

> I would be glad to avoid the resort to the Privy Council, because, however strong we may feel as to the strength and justice of our claims to the territory we have possessed for so many years, the very fact of submitting the extent of them to a judicial tribunal implies that there are not only grounds for an enquiry but doubts as to the legality of our existing possessions.[40]

The governor and committee therefore evaded a definite reply to Labouchere's request,[41] and Labouchere adopted a different approach. To pry the Company loose from what he regarded as its unreasonable opposition to colonization, he threatened to withdraw the Company's exclusive license of trade in the Indian territories. He discussed with Bear Ellice the renewal of the license as the *quid pro quo* for the annexation of Red River to Canada. Ellice retorted that Labouchere was overestimating the importance

of the license to the Company's monopoly, and that the governor
and committee, if pressed by such a threat, would refuse to accept
the arrangement. "The only real use of the License," said Ellice,
"was to enable the H. B. Co. to keep out *the American traders*,"
and, if the license was withheld, the Company would beat its
competition by the methods that had proved so successful in other
areas.⁴²

Ellice's advice, emanating from a man who had been closely associated with the Company for almost forty years, was suspect to
the Colonial Office. Labouchere and his subordinates believed that
the license must be of value to the Company or the governor and
committee would not have been so anxious to renew it. In January, 1858, therefore, the Colonial Office notified the Company
that the government would renew the license for an additional
twenty-one years provided that the Company agreed to certain
conditions: (1) the reservation, as in the existing license, of any
territories formed into colonies; (2) the exception of Vancouver
Island from the license, since it had already been constituted into
a colony; and (3) an agreement by the Company to submit the
question of the boundary to the Judicial Committee of the Privy
Council. With regard to the last proposal, Labouchere acknowledged that Canada might interject the question of the validity of
the charter itself.⁴³

If an amicable settlement could not be reached, Labouchere
stated, he would propose as an alternative condition for renewal
of the license the Company's surrender to the Crown of all lands
that Canada might require for settlement. Canada might annex
such territory after she had established connecting roads or other
lines of communication and had given "satisfactory evidence" of
her ability to govern the territory effectively. To determine satisfactory performance by Canada, the colonial secretary proposed
a board of three commissioners, one each to be nominated by
Canada, the Company, and the British government. The board
would also be authorized to recommend the compensation due the
Company for the loss of its land.⁴⁴

As a fourth condition for renewal of the license, the Company
was requested to authorize the Crown to issue licenses for mining
and fishing, "within limited districts," to British subjects. Within

a day after the receipt of Labouchere's proposals, the Company accepted all the conditions, asking only that Canada guarantee to preserve order in all territories ceded to it, and to prevent "lawless and dishonest adventurers" from infringing on the Company's rights in areas remaining under its control.[45] The reason for the governor and committee's acquiescence is clear. By Labouchere's plan, the Company would probably receive compensation for lands alienated to Canada. The Canadian government would be required to govern the Red River settlement and to restrain the inhabitants from crossing into the territories remaining to the Company. It appeared that Labouchere was about to win for Canada a new frontier without unpleasant litigation or controversy. He was denied that role by two circumstances which converted the Company from acquiescence to surly defiance and opened a dispute lasting for another decade. A change of government brought the Conservative party under the titular leadership of Lord Derby into office and removed Labouchere at the moment of his apparent success, and Canada refused to put aside the demand that the validity of the Company's charter be determined.

Sir Edward Bulwer-Lytton, the famous novelist, assumed his duties as colonial secretary in June, 1858. During his first few months in office, he confided to Sir Frederic Rogers that "I have learnt two great maxims in life, one to write as little as possible, the other to say as little as possible." [46] Bulwer-Lytton's status as a politician would be higher had he heeded his own advice. Lytton was not content to accept Labouchere's conditions for renewal of the trading license. He demanded that the Company submit to the Privy Council not only the boundary issue, but also the validity of the charter. When the Company refused, Lytton declared that, should its obduracy continue, "both Canada and the British Parliament might justly complain of unnecessary delay," and threatened to "take the necessary steps for closing a controversy too long open and for securing a definite decision which is due to the material development of British North America and the requirements of an advancing civilization." In addition, the license for trading in the Indian territory would not under such circumstances be renewed.[47] In vain the Company protested that it had given its consent to Labouchere's conditions and that it was inequitable for Lytton now to make additional demands. The governor and committee therefore refused to accept Lytton's ultimatum that the validity of the charter must be tested.[48]

Lytton, having threatened, now had to act. He had informed the Company that he would take "all necessary steps" to bring the charter under review. He now found, as had Labouchere, that his government could not begin such proceedings and that any action must be initiated by Canada. When Cartier, Alexander T. Galt, and Ross visited England in 1859 to discuss plans for British North American federation, Lytton urged that their government must assume the responsibility for testing the validity of the charter.[49] While awaiting the Canadian government's decision, he notified the Company that its license would not be renewed but that, since the existing license was scheduled to expire in May, the government in the public interest would extend the Company's privileges for one year.[50]

Before dispatching such a letter, Lytton should have pondered the advice of Bear Ellice that the license was of little value and the government should not withdraw the privilege until it was prepared to provide an equally effective alternative system of government. The directors declined the offer of a year's grace with the explanation that acceptance for any period shorter than twenty-one years would merely continue the state of suspense and might, by creating the impression that the Company's powers were approaching an end, paralyze its authority even within the chartered territory. This reply was drawn up only after much consultation among the directors and correspondence with Ellice, for the governor and committee were well aware of the unpopularity of their monopoly and the care with which they must state their case. Their refusal of Lytton's offer bears the marks of this mature consideration, for they presented as effective an exposition of the Company's position as can be found anywhere in its frequent disputes with those who sought to undermine its authority. They informed the Colonial Office that, if the Company's tenure in the Indian territory was not satisfactory, and direct Crown rule would be more effective, such a transfer of jurisdiction should take place immediately; if the monopoly was a barrier to progress in the chartered territory, the obstacle could be removed by just indemnity to the shareholders.[51] Neither suggestion appealed to the colonial secretary. He replied that it was the "general opinion" among lawyers that the monopoly of trade claimed by the Company under its charter was invalid and could be defended only by a distorted interpretation of an "invidious territorial grant." The colonization of British Columbia, Lytton declared, made it impossible for Britain to temporize further, since the security of Canada and British Columbia demanded effective control over the intermediate territories. It was evident, he maintained, that under Company rule such security could not be provided without the assistance of the British government. He informed the directors that, if Canada did not indicate by May 1, 1859, its desire to act against the charter, the British government would itself institute proceedings. Curiously, in contrast to his fulminations against the iniquities of the Company in the earlier passages of his communication, Lytton concluded by offering to extend the trading license in the Indian territory for two years.[52]

The Company's reply was an unqualified rejection of a two-year extension, on the same grounds as their refusal to accept an additional one-year lease. The directors added that, although they were aware that Canada had the right to test the validity of the charter, they were at a loss to understand why the British government should invite her to take such action.[53] By their consistent refusal to accept any compromise on a full twenty-one-year extension of the license, the governor and committee contributed to Lytton's difficulties, for he had rushed ahead with his plans to strip the Company of its authority before he had the assurance of being able to establish an alternative government.[54]

Lytton knew there was no possibility of Parliament's accepting the necessity for expenditures in the Indian country. His only hope for the success of his plans was the coöperation of Canada. If the colony agreed to assume responsibility for the licensed territory and to initiate litigation against the charter, Lytton might yet claim the credit for giving Canada a new West. The correspondence between Lytton and Head during the spring of 1859 amply justified the Company's belief that the Colonial Office and not Canada was the prime mover in the demand for litigation. Lytton repeatedly prodded Head to encourage immediate action by the Canadian government.[55] When the latter informed the colonial secretary on April 4 that Canada had decided to take no action at that time,[56] Lytton's hopes were wrecked, and he did not conceal his exasperation.[57]

The basis for the Canadian refusal, as stated in an address to the queen initiated by Vankoughnet in the Canadian legislature, was that the chartered territory, since it was not part of Canada, was subject to Imperial and not provincial control, should the charter be proved invalid. The legislature agreed that it was imperative to free the fertile belt of Rupert's Land from Company control immediately in order that settlement could begin, but they insisted that only Britain could do it.[58] Canada and Great Britain, it appeared, were both eager to strip the Company of its rights, but each insisted that it was the other's responsibility. George Brown was furious. He fumed in an editorial in his Toronto *Globe:*

> Mr. Vankoughnet's resolutions are bad enough. Mr. Vankoughnet's speech in support of them is worse. The Commissioner of Crown Lands does not leave room to doubt the purposes of the Government, or the scope of the resolutions they have placed before the Legislature. The question, as between Canada and the Hudson's Bay Company, is surrendered in the Company's favour, and for anything which ministers intend to do, the Company may be left in undisputed possession of a territory to which it has no title beyond that conferred by lengthened possession and the opinion of lawyers feed to pronounce in its favour.
>
> .   .   .   .   .   .   .   .   .   .   .
>
> The true explanation of the affair lies in the disposition of the Ministry to play into the hands of the Hudson's Bay Company. . . . The Hudson's Bay monopoly could have no more effectual friends than the Cartier-Macdonald ministry. If they could manage it, the monopoly would flourish through another generation, and the prairie region of British America would remain sacred only to Indians, fur-growers and fur-traders.[59]

Brown was scarcely an unprejudiced judge of the motives of the Cartier-Macdonald government. But he was clearly correct in his assertion that the ministry was not active in the prosecution of Canada's claims to the Northwest.

Since Canada had refused to test the charter, Lytton was now confronted with his threat that the British government would bring the charter before the courts; no such action was undertaken because the law officers had advised against it.[60] He was preparing a bill to facilitate acquisition of portions of the Company's territories for colonization when he was taken ill. He did not have the opportunity to try this expedient, which was essentially what his predecessor Labouchere had proposed, for in June, 1859, the Liberal party under Palmerston returned to power.

Lytton's actions in the controversy with the Company were not those of a skilled negotiator. In attempting to achieve too much, Lytton achieved nothing. On hearing of Lytton's illness, Bear Ellice wrote caustically, "Poor Man, he is not likely to be called upon to find a remedy for the mess he has made of the whole concern." [61]

The only result of Lytton's efforts was termination of the Company's license of exclusive trade on May 30, 1859. His successor, the Duke of Newcastle, introduced a bill for the appointment of magistrates in the territories previously under license, but its passage had no real effect on the Company's position. The Company continued to trade in these territories as it had done before. The governor and committee instructed the Company's officers to refuse commissions as magistrates, since their service in a double capacity would be harmful to the Company's interests. No such offers were made, however, and the British government put forth no real effort to provide for regulation of the territory. Instead, the Company remained the *de facto* ruler until the sale of its chartered rights in 1869. When traders using liquor entered the old licensed territory from British Columbia during the 1860's, Great Britain took no action to apprehend them, although the governor of British Columbia tried to control the traffic. The non-renewal of the license, as Simpson correctly stated, was "a side wind method" of extricating the government from a parliamentary difficulty while leaving the actual state of affairs almost precisely the same.[62]

Yet, in one respect, the Company's position could never again be the same. The end of the license foreshadowed the end of the chartered monopoly. The directors' knowledge that this would not be the last attack predisposed them and the shareholders to sell their holdings under the most favorable terms possible. The return of the Liberal party to power brought no relief, for the new colonial secretary, the Duke of Newcastle, was no more favorably disposed than Lytton. As Lord Lincoln he had been a leader in attacking the grant of Vancouver Island to the Company in 1848, and his basic attitudes had not changed. Though he scoffed at Lytton as a "great Literary Statesman who, like Canning, believed he had created a New World," [63] his policy was akin to that of his predecessor. Like Lytton, Newcastle hoped to open a route of communications through British North America from Atlantic to Pacific. He did not succeed, but his efforts contributed significantly to the sale of the Company to new stockholders in 1863, and to the eventual sale of the proprietary rights to Canada in 1869.

# 17

# Negotiations Leading to the Sale of the Company, 1859-1863

LORD STRATHCONA and Mount Royal, while governor of the Hudson's Bay Company, observed that the explanation of the late settlement of the Canadian prairie provinces in terms of the opposition of a fur-trading monopoly was grossly overdrawn. Colonization, he declared, was dependent upon efficient communications, and no less a society than that under the enlarged Canadian federation could have administered so large a territory or undertaken the construction of the necessary railways.[1] Strathcona's analysis might be somewhat suspect because of his position in the Company and his previous experience as a chief factor. But as a one-time land commissioner for the Company and as a projector of the Canadian Pacific Railway he was especially qualified to assess the importance of communications as a factor in immigration. The opposition of the Hudson's Bay Company to colonization was not so serious a deterrent to the settlement of southern Rupert's Land as were the superior attraction of the American West and the frowning face of nature between Canada and the Hudson's Bay territories. It was not until after the completion of the Canadian Pacific Railway and the exhaustion of free land in the United States that the great migration to the Canadian prairies took place.

[1] For notes to chap. 17, see pp. 471–474.

Red River, as an isolated community approximately 1,000 miles from the settled districts of Canada, held little attraction for the intending emigrant from Great Britain or Canada. During the 1850's the likely source of migration into the Red River settlement and other cultivable portions of Rupert's Land seemed to be not Canada but Minnesota, rapidly filling up and possessing far easier access to these areas.

During the 1850's the relative intimacy of the Red River colony with the United States seemed to be drawing the settlement into the American orbit. Red River traders found their principal markets in the towns of Minnesota, and the development of communications north and south strengthened the connection. By 1851 a postal service was in operation between St. Paul and Pembina, about seventy miles below Fort Garry, with deliveries about once a month, though the service was irregular.[2] Letters from Montreal to St. Paul were received in eight to ten days in summer and in twelve to fourteen days in winter. Service from St. Paul to Pembina was more uncertain, varying from ten days to two months.[3] Communication became much more regular in 1853 when settlers at Red River organized a monthly mail service between Fort Garry and Fort Ripley, Minnesota; in 1857 the United States established a post office at Pembina to supersede the unofficial station previously maintained by Norman Kittson and his associates.[4] The settlement around Fort Garry was drawn still closer to Minnesota when steamship service was inaugurated on the Red River in 1859. James Wickes Taylor, a leading American advocate of annexation of the settlement,[5] wrote in 1860:

"The people of Selkirk fully appreciate the advantages of communication with the Mississippi River and Lake Superior through the State of Minnesota. They are anxious for the utmost facilities of trade and intercourse. The navigation of the Red River by a steamboat during the summer of 1859, was universally recognized as marking a new era in their annals. This public sentiment was pithily expressed by the remark, 'In 1851, the Governor of Minnesota visited us; in 1859 comes a Steamboat, and ten years more will bring the Railroad.' "[6]

The raw energy of the people of Minnesota evoked mixed disdain, envy, and admiration in British and Canadian visitors. After a visit to St. Paul in 1858, Bear Ellice declared that "it would be sheer skepticism to doubt the practicability of any scheme invented by the brains, and to be executed by the energy and ingenuity of Yankee Heads." [7] Many Canadians, notably George Brown, agreed with him and feared the consequences of continued Canadian failure to promote communications with the Red River settlement, but little was done by the Canadian government throughout the 1850's. The inhabitants of the settlement continued to depend upon the service provided by the Hudson's Bay Company as the only alternative to the route through the United States. The Company dispatched mail by two routes. A packet was sent to York Factory each summer and returned with the mail delivered by the annual ship. The more frequent service was by the rivers and lakes route to Canada. Letters were sent by Company canoes to Canada four or five times a year. But the only regular packets were those in the spring and winter; the rest were dispatched as the urgency of communication required.[8]

The first evidence of governmental interest in the establishment of regular service through British North America came not from Canada but from Great Britain. The British General Post Office in 1849 instructed the deputy postmaster general in Canada, Thomas A. Stayner, to report on the practicability of postal communication between Canada and the Hudson's Bay territories, and Stayner referred the question to Sir George Simpson.[9] Simpson recommended that a post office be established at each of the Company's posts on the line of communication from Sault Ste. Marie to Red River, since the posts, located at strategic points for commercial purposes, would provide the postal service with the certainty of obtaining couriers, provisions, dogs, sleds, and other necessities. Simpson recommended that the mail be carried once a month while there was open water and once every two months in winter. He proposed that for £603 a year the Company would convey six mails in the summer and three in winter to and from Red River and the Sault.[10] Beyond a polite acknowledgment, the British Post Office apparently took no further notice of the scheme.

Interest in the establishment of communications between Canada and Red River was revived by three not unrelated developments: the railway boom of the 1850's, the discovery of gold on the Fraser River and rumors of similar discoveries on the

Saskatchewan, and quickening Canadian interest in the annexation of Red River. Agitation for the acquisition of the Northwest Territories was initially promoted by the agrarian interests of western Canada. But when news of the Fraser River gold rush reached Canada and England, railway interests joined in the demand for annexation of the territories and, of course, for adequate communications with returns guaranteed by the British or Canadian government.

The first action occurred in 1857, when the Canadian legislature, in expectation that the select committee of the House of Commons would recommend the annexation of all or part of the Hudson's Bay Company's territories to Canada, dispatched an expedition under George Gladman, a former Company employee, to explore the country between Canada and Red River, and appropriated £5,000 for the opening up of communications. Gladman's party, which included Henry Youle Hind, a geologist, and Samuel J. Dawson, an engineer, left Toronto in July, 1857, and arrived in Red River in September. Their first contact with the Canadian shield around Lake Superior did not produce optimism as to the adequacy of the sum voted by the Canadian legislature for road construction. One of the surveyors privately expressed the opinion that a road might be constructed from Lake Superior to Red River for about £200,000, but that Canada lacked the resources to finance the construction of a commercial route able to compete with railway communication through the United States.[11] The survey was continued in 1858, when a group under Professor Hind explored the region west of Lake Winnipeg and Red River and another party under Dawson examined the land to the east. Dawson reported that construction of an adequate road between Lake Superior and Red River would probably cost £50,000.[12] Even this amount was too much to be seriously considered by a weak Canadian government, already suffering grave financial difficulties, and the legislature did not authorize Dawson and Hind to continue their explorations.

The energy for opening communications to the west which disturbed the Company did not emanate from governments, either British or Canadian, but from private interests on both sides of the Atlantic who saw possibilities for profit in the construction of railway facilities to Red River and beyond, to the Pacific Coast.

The scheme of transcontinental railway communications through British North America was probably first publicized by Major Robert Carmichael-Smyth in 1848, when he advocated the construction of a railway from Halifax to the mouth of the Fraser River. He elaborated upon his plan for transcontinental communication in a pamphlet addressed to the consideration of Governor Pelly of the Hudson's Bay Company.[13] In 1851 Allan McDonell of Toronto, an inveterate foe of the Company and a close friend of William Kennedy, sought from the Canadian legislature a charter of incorporation for the Lake Superior and Pacific Railway Company. His request was refused on the plea that "the claims of the Indian tribes had first to be adjusted." [14] The sincerity of McDonell's interest in promoting a transcontinental railway through the Indian country and over the Rocky Mountains to the empty valleys of British Columbia is open to serious question. By applying for authorization from the Canadian government, he ignored the claims of the Hudson's Bay Company and thus contributed to the campaign that he, Kennedy, and Isbister were waging against the Company. In 1852 Captain Millington H. Synge and Alexander Douell both proposed a transcontinental railway.[15] Their projects had two characteristics in common: they ignored the chartered rights of the Hudson's Bay Company and they were proposed by men with little capital at their disposal.

With the news of the Fraser River gold discoveries and with the publicity given the agricultural possibilities of southern Rupert's Land by the proceedings of the select committee of 1857, discussion on railway construction entered a new phase as men of experience and capital displayed interest for the first time. Sir Cusack P. Roney, secretary of the Grand Trunk Railway, expressed a desire to determine the practicability of carrying passengers across the continent by his railroad in coöperation with other transportation agencies which might exist or be organized to the westward. The North West Transportation, Navigation, and Railway Company, headed by William McD. Dawson, brother of Samuel Dawson, came into being at the same time. The company apparently originated in discussions among William Kennedy, Allan McDonell, and Dawson on a seemingly unrelated subject—the organization of a new North West Company, with headquarters in Toronto, to challenge the Hudson's Bay Company's monopoly. The railway company was incorporated by an act of the Canadian legislature which received the royal assent on August 16, 1858. It was authorized to have a capital of £100,000 in 20,000 shares, with power to increase that capital. The purpose of the company as stated in its charter was to "build roads, tramways, railways, or canals between navigable water," and "to improve or render navigable water courses or channels of water communication from any place or places on the shores of Lake Superior to any point in the interior, or between any navigable waters within the limits of Canada." [16] The promoters hoped to expand the company's operation so as to transport immigrants to the headwaters of the Saskatchewan and thence over the Rocky Mountains to the gold diggings of British Columbia.

The avowed objective of the North West Transportation Company was to open communication facilities through Rupert's Land without seeking the Hudson's Bay Company's consent, but Simpson and the London board suspected an ulterior purpose. Their suspicion was increased by William Kennedy and Allan McDonell's association with the scheme, and they became even more fearful when the transportation company secured a contract from the Canadian government for carrying mail to Red River, at $1,000 a trip, and placed Kennedy in charge. A steamer was put into service between Collingwood on Georgian Bay and Fort William on Lake Superior, to make three trips a month during the season of navigation. From Fort William the mail was carried by the Pigeon River and Grand Portage route to Red River. But the hope of Dawson and his associates to establish a regular system of mail delivery which would effectively compete with that provided by the United States was doomed to disappointment.

The steamer made its first voyage in mid-July, 1858. The quantity of mail it carried was not impressive. Simpson was informed by his officers at Red River that the total was only fourteen letters and a few newspapers. Because of rumors that the Hudson's Bay Company would oppose the transport of the mails by force, Kennedy and the officers of the steamer were armed with revolvers. Their precautions were unnecessary. Simpson, anxious to avoid intensification of Canadian animosity, instructed his officers to assist the mail parties, and their courtesy was acknowledged by the captain of the steamer and by other persons who made the first trip to Fort William.[17]

The mail delivery scheme was defeated primarily by the unreliability of the service. Most Red River settlers were opposed to it, since their letters from Canada ran the risk of being forwarded by this uncertain means rather than through the United States by way of St. Paul and Pembina.[18] Reluctance to send letters via the transportation company was evidenced by the small packages it transported. Simpson, whose sources of information were usually reliable, reported that letters sent from Red River to Toronto in May, 1859, cost the government £100 apiece. If this information was correct, the mail delivery contained only two letters. Even allowing for a slight exaggeration in this report, the mail contract was extremely expensive to the Canadian government. The delivery of mailbags became more and more irregular, and the Canadian public lost interest in the scheme. To test the efficiency of the Canadian service, Simpson sent two letters from Red River on October 12, 1858, addressed to Lachine, one by way of the United States and the other by the Canadian route. The letter sent through the United States arrived on November 10; the letter carried by the North West Transportation Company arrived on March 2.[19]

In the spring of 1859, Simpson, acting on the advice of Governor Berens, and assuming that Canadian agitation over Red River had died down sufficiently, ordered the Company's officers to provide no further assistance to the mail company. The consequences were soon evident. The mail parties, unacquainted with the routes, suffered severely. In December, 1859, one of the mail canoes arrived at Michipicoten with the occupants in a starving condition. Chief Factor George Barnston in humanity gave them a few provisions to enable them to survive, but informed them that no more help would be forthcoming.[20] The preference of Red River settlers for the American route, the mail parties' ignorance of the terrain, the general inefficiency of the company's management, and the opposition of the Hudson's Bay Company caused the project to be suspended in 1860.

Had the opening of communications with Red River been dependent upon Canadian activity alone, the Hudson's Bay Company would have had little reason for anxiety prior to the federation of Canada in 1867. By 1860 the only Canadian accomplishment was a track cut between Red River and Lake of the Woods by Samuel Dawson's exploring expedition of 1857, and it was rapidly being obliterated by undergrowth. The awakening of English interest, however, instilled new energy into the project of transcontinental communication, and initiated a series of negotiations culminating in the sale of the Hudson's Bay Company in 1863.

English participation began with the organization of a company that had no apparent relationship to a transcontinental route—the Halifax and Quebec Railway Company, whose stated objectives were no more ambitious than its title implied. But among the subscribers were men whose imaginations ran far beyond a railroad joining the maritime colonies with Canada. They included Viscount Bury, Sir Allan MacNab, Samuel Cunard, Joseph Nelson, George Grenfell Glyn, and Charles W. W. Fitzwilliam.[21] Fitzwilliam had established himself as a leading proponent of the colonization of the Hudson's Bay territories. Glyn was a partner in the great private banking house of Glyn, Mills and Company, with Baring Brothers a leading creditor of the Grand Trunk Railway which was in serious financial difficulties. Samuel Cunard had talked of the need for communications with the Pacific, and Joseph Nelson and Sir Allan MacNab were soon to show a like concern. But the man who probably first stimulated the others was Viscount Bury.

Bury had come to Canada as civil secretary to Governor Head, and served in that capacity from December, 1854, to January, 1856. He also acted as superintendent general for Indian affairs. When he returned to England, he carried with him an intense conviction of the future importance of British North America to the safety of the British possessions in Asia, particularly India. Bury believed that the only safe access to India was around the Cape of Good Hope, since the route across the Isthmus of Suez could easily be blocked by hostile powers. But if a railway and telegraph were constructed across North America, the Empire would possess means of communication invulnerable to the threats of Russia or of France. The problems of building such facilities, he insisted, were much exaggerated in the minds of most observers. The only serious obstacle was the Rocky Mountains, and they presented no insuperable difficulties. Water communication was even more easily provided. Ships could already reach the head of Lake Superior from the ocean. All that now remained was to improve the streams flowing into Lake Winnipeg, and to overcome the rapids of the Saskatchewan by three miles of canal. A lift of between 800 and 900 feet would carry boats over the Rocky Mountains, and the Columbia would complete the water communication to the sea. Bury's imagination thus easily dissolved barriers that future construction engineers found very real.

Some of the bond- and stockholders of the Grank Trunk Railway looked upon the intercolonial railway project between the maritime colonies and Canada as the possible salvation of the great railway network in which their funds were tied up. They consequently gave the Halifax and Quebec Railway Company their support, contingent upon its success in securing subsidies from the Imperial and colonial governments. The promoters immediately sought a grant of £60,000 from the British government to match a hoped-for subsidy of the same amount from the governments of Canada, New Brunswick, and Nova Scotia. A delegation from the company met with Bulwer-Lytton in June, 1858. Among the group were the Marquis of Bath, Judge Thomas C. Haliburton of Nova Scotia, Sir Francis Bond Head, Samuel Cunard, Joseph Nelson, and nineteen members of Parliament, including Bury, George Grenfell Glyn, Roebuck, and Bear Ellice.[22] These impressive personages would have been welcomed had they come merely to seek governmental blessing for their project. But no British government of the 1850's and 1860's, whether Liberal or Conservative, was willing to grant public money for colonial purposes, and the delegation could not gain the support of the Colonial Office. The rejection caused the death of the Halifax and Quebec Railway Company, or, rather, its absorption into the grander scheme of a transcontinental railway, which the projectors hoped might have greater prospects of winning financial assistance from the British and colonial governments.

In the winter of 1858–59, Viscount Bury visited Canada and the maritime colonies,[23] and during his travels he apparently discussed railway matters with William Dawson. When Dawson came to England at the beginning of 1859 to seek additional capital for his

North West Transportation Company, Bury was his liaison with British capitalists, and either during Bury's Canadian visit or immediately after Dawson's arrival in England, Bury became a member of that company's board of directors. Bury probably introduced Dawson to Robert Benson of the London investment house of the same name. Through Benson, the company applied to the treasury for a subsidy for the conveyance of mail from the Atlantic to the Pacific. If the subsidy was granted, Dawson promised to associate himself with English capitalists to expedite the completion of the mail project, which he predicted would lead to the construction of a great railway system across British North America. As usual, the treasury and the Colonial Office were favorably disposed, but not to the extent of recommending expenditures.[24]

Even without promise of a subsidy, Benson entered into negotiations with London capitalists, and in March an amalgamated company of English and Canadian investors was organized. The direction of the North West Transit Company was to be in London but there was to be an executive management in Canada under the control of the London board. The English shareholders included Bury, MacNab, and Fitzwilliam in addition to Benson, Pascoe Charles Glyn, and others of lesser significance. Glyn, a younger brother of George Grenfell Glyn, was at this time associated with Messrs. Robert Benson rather than with his family's banking establishment. The first directors of the transit company were MacNab, Bury, and Henry Carr Glyn,[25] who also had no connection with the management of the family bank. The purposes of the North West Transit Company, like those of the Halifax and Quebec Railway Company, were linked with the Grand Trunk, but there is no evidence that the management of the Grand Trunk system or its English bondholders—Glyn, Mills and Baring Brothers—had assisted in the promotion of either enterprise.

In the summer of 1859 Pascoe Glyn and Nathaniel Clayton secured from Sir George Simpson letters of introduction to Chief Factor William Mactavish at Fort Garry and to J. C. Burbank, the Hudson's Bay Company agent at St. Paul, to aid them in exploring the transit company's prospective route from Canada to Red River. Simpson privately explained that he coöperated because he expected Glyn and Clayton's report of the difficulties in the way of transportation to dampen the enthusiasm of the English capitalists interested in the project.[26] The report may have had the expected effect, but a far more important deterrent was the continuing reluctance of the British government to guarantee investments or provide subsidies for colonial purposes, without which no prudent capitalist would invest in such an enterprise.

Other communications schemes for British North America in 1859 offered greater prospects for safe and adequate returns. Perry McDonough Collins planned a transcontinental telegraph line to join at Bering Strait with another to be built from Russia through Siberia, thus providing world communications without the necessity of crossing large bodies of water. The proposal won the support of the Russian, British, Canadian, and American governments during the next few years, and construction was well advanced in 1866, when the successful laying of the Atlantic cable caused the project to be discontinued.[27] The Atlantic Telegraph Company was also organized in 1859 with the promise of a guarantee of 8 per cent from the British government so long as the cable it proposed to lay was in working order.[28] Cables and telegraphs could be justified as important for Imperial purposes, but railroads and other transportation systems, of benefit primarily to the areas they served, were not so easily accepted by Gladstone and other economy-minded British politicians as deserving of financial subsidy.[29]

The Palmerston cabinet, however, contained one member upon whom the promoters of British North American railways could rely for at least moral support, the Duke of Newcastle. From the time of his appointment as colonial secretary in the summer of 1859, Newcastle sought to promote settlement in the interior of British North America. He envisioned flourishing agricultural communities in districts once inhabited only by Indians and fur traders. To him there seemed to be no serious natural obstacles to the realization of his dream, and the readiness of British financiers to invest in railways was a means to its fulfillment. There were, however, severe limitations. Canada, which had seemed so zealous for the annexation of parts of Rupert's Land in 1857, showed little interest in 1859, and Gladstone kept the keys to the Imperial treasury. Newcastle early came to the conclusion, therefore, that the settlements he hoped to create must, at least initially, be established as crown colonies, at minimum expense to the Imperial government.

Another obstacle was the chartered rights of the Hudson's Bay Company. Newcastle believed that Lytton had mishandled the negotiations with the Company and that the most effective approach was the one suggested by Labouchere. There was, however, one basic change that he deemed necessary. Labouchere had intended the areas for settlement to be annexed to Canada; Newcastle believed they must be made into a crown colony. He submitted a bill incorporating his ideas for the administration of the Red River and Saskatchewan districts to Governor Berens for the Company's reactions in May, 1860. The bill provided that, within five years of its passage, the Company should surrender the Red River and Saskatchewan districts to the Crown, and that it might later relinquish other territories at the discretion of the Crown. After passage of the act, the government might acquire land from the Company for the purpose of constructing railroads, canals, or other communications facilities.[30]

These provisions were no more objectionable to the Company than Labouchere's proposals, but on one essential point Newcastle's bill was completely unsatisfactory. It provided that the Company be compensated for losses in only the following categories: all immovable improvements, such as forts and buildings, roads, and bridges, and cultivation of land; livestock or other chattels which the Company could not move without loss; and financial losses arising from the end of a monopoly which the Company could prove it had enjoyed in the annexed districts. The amount of compensation was to be determined by two arbitrators, one appointed by the government and the other by the Company. There was no provision for payment for the Company's loss of its chartered rights in the territory affected; indeed, the proposed legislation merely recognized these rights as claims that had not been established.

By avoiding payment for the fee-simple rights, the British government could make land available to settlers at minimum expense to itself. Further, all revenues from land sales would be paid to the British government until the expenses incurred in compensating the Company had been reimbursed. The bill also provided that the Crown by executive action could determine the boundaries of Rupert's Land. This attempt to acquire new farm lands "on the cheap" by skirting the issue of the Company's rights was certain to evoke opposition from the governor and committee. After three weeks of consultation with his colleagues, Berens replied that the Company would not be a party to its own confiscation. He proposed instead that the bill explicitly recognize the Company's title to lands granted by the charter, and that the Company take part in the determination of the boundaries.[31] There was thus a substantial difference between the views of Newcastle and Berens, and the session of Parliament came to an end before any progress could be made toward a settlement.

In June, 1860, while Parliament was in recess, Newcastle, perhaps to make the Company more amenable to his suggestions, announced his intention of relieving the detachment of the Royal Canadian Rifle Regiment at Fort Garry.[32] Berens protested in vain that the troops were serving an Imperial purpose by maintaining order in a district adjacent to the United States.[33] The decision remained, but because instructions could not be sent to Red River in time to permit the removal of the troops that year, their departure was delayed until the spring of 1861.

The Company's refusal to agree to Newcastle's bill vexed the colonial secretary, particularly because his advisers counseled him against precipitately stripping the Company of its property. T. W. C. Murdoch, the land commissioner, stated that the bill as originally drafted would cause the government "no end of trouble" in the matter of compensation, and that in his opinion the government should not take any action at all. "Do what you will," warned Murdoch, "if you buy Red River from the Company it will only be for the benefit of American citizens, who will be able to push you out whenever they wish—as some day they probably will wish." Red River, he pointed out, was militarily indefensible, for American troops could cross the border with ease, whereas British troops would have to be sent through Hudson Bay, which was closed over half the year.[34] The parliamentary undersecretary, Chichester Fortescue, and the permanent undersecretary, Frederic Rogers, did not entirely endorse Murdoch's pessimistic conclusions, but they both dissented from Newcastle's reluctance to give explicit recognition to the Company's chartered rights. Rogers warned that the government was taking a false position and was exciting justifiable hostility by refusing to recognize what its own law officers had declared an "undoubted right." [35] Murdoch came away from an interview with Berens and the Company's legal adviser, Joseph Maynard, with the impression that they were more concerned about the recognition of the chartered rights than about the amount of compensation for the arable portions of Rupert's Land, and that they might dispose of the latter for between £10,000 and £20,000. In addition, however, the Company would be able to claim compensation for the money they had paid Lord Selkirk for the district of Assiniboia and for improvements there, which would involve several hundred thousand pounds. If the government was disposed to buy all the Company's chartered rights, Berens suggested, a fair valuation was £1,500,000, or twenty times the net annual income of £75,000. [36]

Newcastle disagreed with his subordinates. He knew that the ministry and Parliament would be most reluctant to support appropriations for the purchase of all or part of the Company's rights. He also considered explicit governmental recognition of these rights unwise, for discoveries of gold or other valuable resources might give the chartered territories immense value. [37]

The debate within the Colonial Office continued for six months, from February to July, 1861, without a final decision on what action, if any, should be taken. Meanwhile another session of Parliament had come to an end, and consideration of the proposed legislation was again delayed.

The progress of events at Red River, however, could not be overlooked. Newcastle heard in September, 1861, that gold in substantial quantities had been discovered on the upper waters of the North Saskatchewan River by a party of California miners. Although the report was exaggerated, there could be no certainty that it would not be followed by genuine news of rich gold strikes which would cause a rush to the chartered territory like that into the Fraser River valley. If Great Britain was not to lose the territory by default, an effective government must be established and adequate communications must be provided. The uncertain state of Anglo-American relations as a result of the American Civil War gave additional emphasis to the latter need.

Recognition of these facts, and further impressive evidence

later in 1861 of the inadequacy of British communications with Canada,[38] made Newcastle more receptive to the plans of British capitalists for the construction of an intercolonial railroad and for a transportation system from Canada to the West. Newcastle thus came into intimate contact with the British North American Association and, in particular, with Edward Watkin.

The British North American Association brought together a variety of interests which faced the common problem of persuading the British government that railroads and other transportation facilities in British North America served a significant Imperial function. The Grand Trunk Railway bondholders and stockholders, the advocates of an intercolonial railway, the North West Transit Company, and the governments of Canada and the maritime colonies all had this common objective. The immediate origin of this union of interests and of the emergence of Edward Watkin as a liaison between the capitalists and the Colonial Office was an interview between a deputation of London financiers and the Duke of Newcastle on June 14, 1861. The group requested the government to offer its support and, in particular, its financial assistance, to the intercolonial railway project. Their ideas accorded with Newcastle's own hopes for a British railway system from sea to sea. But he knew that, unless a large and influential body presented the proposals to the government and carefully delineated the details, including the assistance the British North American colonies would provide, there could be no prospect of winning the sanction of Gladstone.

Newcastle's expression of these views seems to have contributed to the formal organization of the British North American Association at London Tavern on January 30, 1862. At this "exceedingly important and influential meeting," according to the *Canadian News*, it was explained that the purposes of the organization were to promote communication between British and British North American capitalists and to diffuse information in Britain on Canada and the maritime colonies.[39] The real object of the association, however, was to influence the government to provide financial support for the projected intercolonial railway. Robert Wigram Crawford, chairman of the meeting, was M.P. for the City of London and a director of the Bank of England. Joseph Nelson, of the stillborn Halifax and Quebec Railway Company, became secretary of the association. Also present were Robert Benson of the North West Transit Company; Thomas Baring and George Carr Glyn, the leading bondholders of the Grand Trunk Railway; William Newmarch of Glyn, Mills and Company; William Chapman of Herries, Farquhar and Company, private bankers; and Arthur Kinnaird of Ransom, Bouverie, and Company, private bankers. Practically all the investment houses in the City of London and all those with British North American interests were represented at this and subsequent meetings of the British North American Association. Philip Vankoughnet, whom Canada had sent to press the intercolonial project on the home government, also attended. One of the committee appointed by the association to carry on negotiations with the Imperial government on behalf of the intercolonial railway was Edward W. Watkin.

Watkin's relationship to the purchase of the Hudson's Bay Company in 1863 and to the maneuvers that contributed to the federation of the British North American colonies is well known, largely as a result of his self-advertisement in his autobiographical *Canada and the States*. Watkin was a promoter of the type so familiar in the United States in the last half of the nineteenth century. His schemes were grandly conceived, and his persuasiveness was convincing, particularly when he was able to use the great financial names with whom he associated himself. When George Grenfell Glyn and Thomas Baring selected Watkin, then the general manager of the Manchester, Sheffield, and Lincolnshire Railway, to shore up the tottering structure of the Grand Trunk Railway, they paid tribute to his talents, but they could not have realized that his appointment would give a new direction to the railway negotiations. Nor, in all likelihood, could he.

Watkin was appointed in the summer of 1861, after the inconclusive meeting between the advocates of the intercolonial railway and the Duke of Newcastle, but before the formal organization of the British North American Association. His instructions were to investigate the maladies of the Grand Trunk, without making any other than necessary changes, and to act as a liaison with the various governments in the promotion of any plans upon which the directors might agree until a permanent reorganization could be effected.[40] The intentions of Glyn and Baring did not extend beyond the internal reorganization of the Grand Trunk Railway, but

Watkin's ideas were much more broadly conceived. In February, 1861, he had written an article for the *Illustrated London News* advocating a transcontinental railway, and he was convinced that the salvation of the Grand Trunk Railway lay, not in the relatively modest changes envisaged by his employers, but in a daring program of railway construction from the Atlantic to the Pacific. On July 17, 1861, before departing for North America on the business of the Grand Trunk, he visited a kindred spirit, the Duke of Newcastle. Like Watkin, Newcastle was a man of imagination; and, like Watkin, he could not himself summon the capital to make his dream reality. Watkin was dependent upon the support of the Barings and the Glyns, who would be likely to look askance at his grandiose schemes; Newcastle could grant no subsidies to such a venture without the support of Gladstone, who was also likely to be unreceptive. The two agreed that, though the intercolonial railway was the "preliminary necessity," the union of all parts of British North America into one great colony was the grand objective, and a necessary condition of such a union would be a railway to the Pacific. Newcastle authorized Watkin to tell any interested parties in Canada and elsewhere that the Colonial Office would pay part of the cost of the surveys for these railways, and assured Watkin of his cordial assistance.[41]

Watkin helped to arrange the conferences with Canadian and maritime representatives which resulted in their decision on September 30, 1861, to send delegates to London to seek aid for the intercolonial railway. He may also have encouraged the Canadian government to display a new interest in the West. But Watkin's contributions were those of an arranger, for the colonial governments were convinced of the necessity of action in these directions by more fundamental factors. The continued tension between the United States and Great Britain, reports of new gold strikes in the Saskatchewan district, and the obvious inclination of the citizens of Minnesota to expand northward accentuated Canadian fears that the Americans would appropriate the fertile prairies of southern Rupert's Land. Canada was not yet financially strong enough to annex and administer the territories herself, but perhaps Great Britain could be prevailed upon to recognize the threat and to assume the necessary burden. These were the thoughts that undoubtedly inspired the Canadian Executive Council on March 7,

1862, to propose that Great Britain establish a crown colony in the Saskatchewan territory. Members of the council had read a report from the commissioner of crown lands which pointed out that, although the Imperial Parliament had passed an act in 1859 for the organization of the Saskatchewan Territory, no action had been taken. The commissioner argued that,

> Considering the excited State of Affairs in the United States, the numbers who have been disturbed in the pursuits in which they were engaged when the War broke out, the large floating population seeking locations all over the Continent, and the difficulty which may hereafter arise in dealing with squatters, and especially foreigners, who may have settled themselves in the Country, he considers it desirable & recommends that the subject be brought under the Notice of the Imperial Government.[42]

Since the proposal involved no cost to Canada, the Executive Council strongly endorsed this recommendation, which Lord Monck, the governor-general, forwarded to Newcastle. But the act to which the commissioner referred [43] had been passed to provide for the administration of the territories previously licensed to the Hudson's Bay Company, not to authorize the erection of a crown colony in the Saskatchewan country or at Red River, which were within the Company's chartered territory. The Executive Council also underestimated the aversion of the British government to additional financial responsibilities in the interests of British North America. Even for Vancouver Island and British Columbia, where the long coast lines offered facilities for naval stations and where, in the Fraser River valley, there were valuable gold fields, the treasury disputed with the Colonial Office over every £1,000 of suggested expenditure. As T. F. Elliot of the Colonial Office said, it was "very unpleasant to have to meet Parliament with the Estimates for these Settlements." If this was the attitude toward colonies with manifest advantages, there could be no hope for sympathy from the treasury or Parliament for a proposal to create a crown colony "buried in the middle of the American Continent, and surrounded by nothing but dwindling hordes of wandering Savages and perishing herds of wild animals." [44] The Colonial Office was not interested in administering a colony for the benefit of Canada, which showed no inclination to pay even part of the cost.

Another Canadian proposal, in this instance to the Hudson's

Bay Company, had more effect, although the results were not as the Canadian government had intended. On April 15, 1862, Charles Alleyn, secretary to the Canadian government, suggested to Alexander Grant Dallas, Simpson's successor as governor of Rupert's Land, that the Company might coöperate in the construction of a proposed post road and telegraph line from Canada to British Columbia. Canada would be responsible for the construction of communications to the height of land west of Lake Superior, and the Company was to undertake the job through the chartered territory. Unless communications were constructed soon, Alleyn warned, American "adventurers" would swarm into the territory. British rule in the territory would become a nullity, and "the Key of the Trade to British Columbia, and ultimately China [would] have been surrendered to our rivals." [45]

Alleyn's communication was inspired by a series of conversations between Dallas and Georges Étienne Cartier, the leader of the government and of the French Canadian wing of the Conservative party. Each saw in the proposal for communications through British North America advantages for himself and the interests he represented. Cartier had been accused by the *Globe* and other critics of opposing, with other French Canadians, the annexation of the Northwest Territories for fear of giving the British of Canada West an undue preponderance in the assembly. This accusation he denied, but he did not share the Clear Grits' zeal for western extension. French and British members of the Cartier-Macdonald government agreed that Canada did not possess the financial strength to undertake litigation against the Company's charter and then, if unsuccessful, as seemed likely, to pay the Company for the loss of its territory. Even if Canada could win the land without payment, she would still have to administer the new territory and construct communications, burdens she could not assume in addition to providing subsidies for the intercolonial railway and paying for the militia she would have to raise upon the imminent departure of Imperial troops. The cabinet nevertheless wished to demonstrate interest in the West in some dramatic and economical fashion, to counter assertions that only the Clear Grits were concerned with the welfare of the Western farmer. A proposal for the construction of a telegraph line and postal road could win cheap popularity, especially since negotiations with the Company and the British government would require time, and Canada would not be committed to any expense beyond its own borders.[46]

Dallas, on the other hand, saw advantages for the Company in the proposal. Dallas shared the pessimism of the late Sir George Simpson with regard to the future of the fur trade. Gold strikes on the Saskatchewan, the formation of companies to provide transportation to the West, and aggressive American intentions seemed to presage early dissolution of the monopoly. Unless the Company sold its rights soon, it would have no rights to sell. The Company could not offer its property to Canada or to Great Britain lest it demonstrate eagerness and thus discount the value. But if Canada were to make the first move and the Company were to appear reluctant to sell, the British government might offer a substantial sum to prevent the loss of the territory to the United States. As Dallas told old Bear Ellice, "I do not mind playing into his [Cartier's] hands so long as it suits our own game." [47]

Dallas therefore replied to Alleyn that the Company could not coöperate with the Canadian proposal, for it had no source of revenue for such a project. Further, he declared, the Red River and Saskatchewan districts, although not in themselves rich furproducing areas, were nevertheless of great value, for they were the sources from which the Company procured its main supplies of winter food. Settlement of the territory would consequently be ruinous to the Company, for it would disrupt the trade of the northern posts through the inability of their personnel to secure food.[48]

Dallas thus implied that, to open up the Saskatchewan and Red River districts, the British government should buy the Company's rights to the entire chartered territory. It was a shrewd scheme, but it had two serious defects. First, Dallas overestimated the fear that this correspondence would engender in the British government and underestimated its resistance to expenditure. Second, by engaging in the correspondence, he had usurped the prerogatives of the governor and committee. The news of his indiscretion opened a violent controversy within the Company, with the directors at odds with each other over the line the Company should take and in agreement only that Dallas should be chastised.

Governor Berens felt that Dallas had played into the hands of the "wily Canadian diplomatists" by his discussions with Cartier.

The Canadian and the British governments, he said, wanted control of the Saskatchewan and Red River without payment to the Company.[49] The governor attempted to undo the alleged damage that Dallas had done by pointing out to the Colonial Office that Canada had talked of communications to the West before and had failed to achieve any practical results. The Company, he stated, was not willing to make any outlay for such schemes. If Canada or Great Britain wanted the territory, the Company remained willing to part with it for reasonable compensation. In the meantime, the governor of Assiniboia had instructions to grant land to settlers on "easy conditions" without any restriction as to the Company's rights of trade.[50]

Bear Ellice objected to Dallas' interchange with Cartier for a different reason. The old man held that Dallas had put the Company in a false position by appearing to oppose settlement in the valleys of the Red River and the Saskatchewan because it would disrupt the fur trade. The Company, he told his friend John Rose, had no right or desire to prevent the occupation of a single acre that could be cultivated, but it was entitled to fair compensation. Further, if Canada desired to open negotiations affecting the Company, the correspondence should be carried on with the secretary of state for colonies, since the Company had neither the power nor the desire to act as an independent state.[51] Aside from insubordination, the principal issues between Dallas and the London board were the effect of the sale of the Saskatchewan and Red River districts on the fur trade of the rest of Rupert's Land, and the degree of urgency to negotiate a sale. Dallas contended that the Saskatchewan was the key to the entire fur trade. Once it was lost all was lost. Free traders and settlers would pour in, and the Company would be left with the shadow of its rights without the substance. The Company must seek compensation immediately.[52] The majority of the board were not convinced that the loss of the Saskatchewan meant the end of the fur trade, nor did they foresee immediate loss of their property.

The directors could not know that their differences with Dallas were actually a tempest in a teapot, since at the time neither the British nor the Canadian government could consider the purchase of the Company's property. The staff of the Colonial Office, except for the Duke of Newcastle, believed that Great Britain should take no action whatsoever. T. F. Elliot, the senior clerk, regarded all transcontinental communications projects, either of roads or of telegraph lines, across an empty land to be "premature and visionary." "They strike me," he said, "as specimens of a fallacy which is very common to the American Continent, a morbid anxiety to anticipate the future." Fortescue, the parliamentary undersecretary, considering the position of the Company unassailable, believed that the only way to open the country for settlement was to buy the Company out. Since purchase by the British government was out of the question, Canada must be the source of the necessary funds. But as the Duke of Newcastle pointed out, Canada could not bear any such burden.[53]

Newcastle, however, could discern one ray of hope. Canada had offered to build a road and telegraph to the borders of Rupert's Land. Berens had said that the Company would not invest its money in such a project, but he had expressed no opposition to others employing their capital for it. Perhaps a group of British financiers might be prevailed upon to undertake the responsibility. The recently organized British North American Association was the logical group to approach, and Newcastle's fellow enthusiast for transcontinental communications, Edward W. Watkin, was the man to promote the scheme. The bait was Colonial Office support for a subsidy to the intercolonial railway. Here was the background for the well-known application of July 5, 1862, by Thomas Baring, George Carr Glyn, and other financiers for assistance in the construction of a road and telegraph line across British North America. Since they were aware that Parliament would not vote money, they asked for land grants as a subsidy.[54] The signatories to the request, besides Baring and Glyn, were the latter's son, George Grenfell Glyn; Robert Wigram Crawford, chairman of the British North American Association; William Chapman; and Kirkman Daniel Hodgson, a partner in Baring Brothers and also a member of the committee of the Hudson's Bay Company. All were members of the British North American Association; all except Crawford were London directors of the Grand Trunk Railway; and all were promoters of the intercolonial railway. But, as Hodgson's participation in the group suggests, they were not hostile to the interests of the Hudson's Bay Company. Rather, as Hodgson confided to Berens, the object of the Grand Trunk Railway bond-

holders was to obtain grants of land for the completion of a railway from Halifax to Quebec, and they had "not the remotest intention" of asking for land within the territories of the Hudson's
Bay Company.[55]

Old Edward Ellice considered it incredible that a sober businessman like Thomas Baring was genuinely interested in this wild
speculation, and voiced the suspicion that Baring's name must
have been used "without sufficient authority." [56] Ellice was in
error, but he was not far from the truth. Baring allowed Watkin
to use his name only with the utmost reluctance. As Watkin admitted, Baring was not sanguine as to the success of the telegraph
scheme. He told Watkin that "if the Duke wants these great efforts
made he must make them on behalf of the Government; he must
not leave private persons to take the risk of Imperial work." [57] The
Pacific road and telegraph project was primarily the scheme of the
Duke of Newcastle and Edward Watkin, not of the Grand Trunk
Railway. The possessors of the "weighty names" that so impressed
the personnel of the Colonial Office were led to participate by the
hope of Imperial grants and subsidies for the project of primary
interest to them—the intercolonial railway.

Newcastle had now achieved the first step in his program of
building communications facilities without expenditure by the
Imperial government. The next move was to bring the Hudson's
Bay Company and the telegraph promoters together. He therefore
asked Berens whether the Company would be willing to grant a
strip of land across its territory to a company that "men of such
position and character" as Baring and the Glyns might form, and
he advised Baring that the Colonial Office would provide its good
offices and the financiers should communicate directly with the
Hudson's Bay Company.

The directors of the Hudson's Bay Company were in a difficult
position. They were anxious to avoid allegations that the Company was an impediment to progress. If the road was built, however, it would facilitate the spread of free trade and settlement.
The governor and committee resolved to take the risk. On August 11, 1862, Berens informed Newcastle that the Company was
ready to coöperate, if it did not have to advance any capital, and
would grant such land as might reasonably be required for effecting the proposed communications, if the telegraph company gave

adequate security for completion of the project.[58] Even the most rabid critic of the Hudson's Bay Company thus could not complain of its lack of coöperativeness.

The directors' decision had been influenced by Hodgson's assurance that Baring and the other financiers were not eager to build the facilities across the continent. The scheme might be shelved, or, if it was begun, might fail as had other projects for western transportation. Indeed, there was a current example of the hazards of such projects in the troubles besetting the British Columbia Overland Transit Company. This enterprise had been organized in London in 1862 by a group of questionable integrity. Its purpose was to carry passengers from Great Britain to the gold diggings of British Columbia by way of the Saskatchewan. The promoters promised to carry passengers across the Atlantic and through British territory in five weeks at a cost of £42 per person, and indicated that stations had been established at convenient distances along the way where travelers could secure food and other necessities at moderate prices. A group of thirty-two emigrants left Glasgow at the beginning of June, 1862, under the auspices of the transit company.[59] A month later Governor Monck of Canada received a telegram from a man named Collingwood, one of the emigrants. They had been stranded at St. Paul, Minnesota, since there were no facilities for their transportation through Rupert's Land and the bills they had been furnished by the company for their passage were unsalable.[60] The failure of the Overland Transit Company, the prosecution of its secretary, and the flight of its chief promoter, a Colonel Sleigh, did not daunt the Duke of Newcastle. Rather it convinced him that transcontinental communications could be built only by a group with large capital and a carefully planned project.

Contrary to Newcastle's assumptions, a qualified group willing to assume the responsibility did not exist. Thomas Baring, who had been cool to the scheme from its inception, became convinced that he was being used as a cat's-paw by the Duke of Newcastle against the Hudson's Bay Company and that the venture was basically unsound. Despite Watkin's frantic efforts to prevail on Baring at least to allow his name to be used in connection with the venture, Baring refused. George Carr Glyn, who was more favorable to the project, also withdrew on November 5, 1862, when

he found that Baring was not interested, although George Grenfell Glyn continued the family's association thereafter.[61]

The duke remained in ignorance of these defections of "weighty
men" supporting the telegraph route, for Watkin dared not tell
him. Newcastle therefore continued to act as a liaison between
"Baring's group" and the Company. Since the Company had
offered to grant a right of way, the width of such a strip became of
paramount importance, and he questioned the directors about
it.[62] Newcastle's inquiry seemed to envisage a strip of substantial
proportions rather than a narrow right of way, and confirmed the
directors' suspicion that Newcastle wanted large sections of Rupert's Land. "There is no doubt," Berens told the younger Ellice,
"that the Duke wants us to give up a Territory which he may offer
to any Company as an inducement for them to undertake the making of a Road. I really think it is quite preposterous to make such
a demand upon us." [63] Berens, however, merely told Newcastle
that he could not determine the size of the grant until he knew
more about the route.[64]

The result of this interchange was an interview between Berens
and Newcastle on November 17 or 18 when the duke revealed that
the promoters would require substantial amounts of land. According to Watkin's later report, Berens lost his self-control and burst
out with the protest that such a grant would "sequester our very
tap-root" and "let in all kinds of people to squat and settle and
frighten away the fur-bearing animals they don't hunt and kill."
"If these gentlemen are so patriotic," Watkin quoted Berens as
saying, "why don't they buy us out?" When Newcastle inquired
the price at which the Company would sell, Berens placed it at
about £1,500,000.[65] The psychological moment had arrived. The
government had taken the initiative and Berens could name his
price without risking depreciation through later bargaining.

The valuation was not made on the spur of the moment. It was
the amount Berens had suggested to T. W. C. Murdoch in 1861.[66]
Newcastle had repeated this price to the House of Lords on July 4,
1862,[67] and he and Watkin had discussed the possible purchase of
the Company at the same valuation. But to extract from Parliament such a sum for such a purpose would be difficult, if not impossible. As Newcastle wrote to Watkin on August 14, 1862, "I
admire your *larger views,* and have some tolerably large ones on

this matter of my own, but I fear purchase of this great territory is just now impracticable." [68]

Berens' suggestion that the Company would be willing to sell its rights presented Watkin with two alternatives. He could continue to prosecute the original scheme of construction in the hope that the governments of Great Britain and Canada would be generous with land grants and the Hudson's Bay Company would offer more than a mere right of way. Failing that, he could seek support from financiers for the purchase of the Company in the hope that Imperial and Canadian subsidies for communications and settlement would be forthcoming.

While Newcastle was in communication with Berens, Watkin was in Canada discussing the renewal of the colony's proposals for an intercolonial railway with members of the government. Perhaps in part as a result of his urging, the Canadian cabinet agreed to send another deputation to London to press, in concert with representatives from Nova Scotia and New Brunswick, for an Imperial guarantee in the construction of the intercolonial railway and also to advocate a railway or road to the Pacific.[69] Louis V. Sicotte and William P. Howland were sent by the government of John Sandfield Macdonald, which had ousted the Cartier-Macdonald ministry in May, 1862. Before the delegates arrived in England, Newcastle was forewarned of future difficulties. In a memorandum of October 12, the Canadian Executive Council attempted to shift to the British government the primary responsibility for financing both the intercolonial railway and the telegraph project. Members of the council asserted that in agreeing to send delegates to London they had been "influenced in a high degree by the understanding of the value which in the judgment of the Imperial Government attaches to the Railway as a means of strengthening the defensive power of the Province as an integral part of the British Empire." [70]

The bland assertion that Canada was willing to coöperate in an Imperial project was intolerable to Newcastle. The project had originated with Canada and the maritime provinces, he told Howland and Sicotte, and the primary responsibility must continue to be theirs.[71] This difference of opinion between Canada and Great Britain was basic to the eventual breakdown of negotiations on the intercolonial railway,[72] but there seemed to be no such disagreement about the western transit line. The Canadians and Newcastle were in substantial agreement as to the loads their respective governments should assume. The major obstacle seemed to be the Hudson's Bay Company.

Watkin's group and the governor and committee first met face to face on December 1, 1862. Watkin was accompanied by George Grenfell Glyn, Henry Glyn, and Newmarch, with the significant additions of Henry Wollaston Blake, a member of the British North American Association and a director of the Bank of England, and Robert Benson. Through the association of Benson, Watkin amalgamated his objectives with those of the North West Transit Company. Berens, Eden Colvile, and George Lyall represented the Hudson's Bay Company. It was a chilly interview. Berens, who had convinced himself that "the Transit Company are determined to annihilate us," informed the visitors that the Hudson's Bay Company would give only the actual site of the road and telegraph, and, if the prospective company wanted more, they could buy the entire chartered territory for £1,500,000.[73]

So long as adequate guarantees from the British and Canadian delegates were in prospect, Watkin and his group put aside the larger issue of purchasing the Company and concentrated on the more moderate objective of securing land grants in Canada and British Columbia and guaranteed returns from these colonies and from the Imperial government. For a short time, the prospects for the success of the telegraph and road project seemed good. At a series of conferences with Watkin and his associates early in December, 1862, Howland and Sicotte indicated that Canada would guarantee interest at 4 per cent on a third of the investment of £500,000, if the governments of Great Britain and British Columbia would make equal guarantees. If the British government refused to subscribe, and proposed instead that British Columbia assume a larger share, Howland and Sicotte stated that Canada would probably guarantee interest on half of the investment, or £10,000.[74] Newcastle could not promise that the cabinet would endorse a British guarantee of interest, but he encouraged Watkin by promising to support such a guarantee.[75]

Watkin was kept dangling for two months, but while he waited anxiously for the decisions of the British and Canadian governments, he was not entirely idle. At a meeting of the British North

American Association on January 21, 1863, he proposed a resolution supporting the "completion of a line across the British portion of the continent, from the Atlantic to the Pacific," as "a necessity of the times." The resolution was unanimously adopted.[76] Such votes cost no money.

Watkin's influence can also be vaguely discerned in a petition drawn up at Red River at this time. Since the withdrawal of the Canadian Rifles, agitation at Red River had steadily increased. Petitions were constantly being circulated in the colony. One of these, like the rest titled a "Memorial of the People of Red River," was circulated by James Ross, coeditor of the Nor'Wester, in January, 1863. The petitioners appealed for the construction of a telegraph and road across British North America. The petition was supposedly presented to a large "public meeting," and Sandford Fleming, the Canadian railway engineer, was appointed to carry the memorial to the Duke of Newcastle. An unfriendly critic, Joseph James Hargrave, contended that only Ross and his coeditor, William Coldwell, had attended the meeting, and that less than twenty persons knew of its deliberations prior to their publication in the Nor'Wester.[77] Dallas, denying that there was any meeting at all, claimed that the petition had originated in a fee of $100 paid by Fleming to Ross.[78] Whatever the truth of these allegations, Fleming's association with the petition lends credence to the suspicion that railway interests represented by Watkin were involved in its circulation. Fleming, who was soon to be appointed chief engineer for the intercolonial railway, was an intimate of Watkin's and shared his views on the nature of transcontinental communication. Fleming did not arrive in England until June, 1863, too late to influence the British government's decision with regard to the subsidy. Even without the support of Ross's petition, however, Watkin was optimistic about the eventual government decision. The Canadian ministry agreed on February 9 to place a request for $50,000, or 4 per cent on half of the proposed capital, in the estimates for the forthcoming session, to promote postal and telegraphic communications with British Columbia.[79]

Watkin's hopes were rudely jolted when he learned unofficially from Newcastle on February 20 that the British cabinet would not sanction a subsidy for the Atlantic and Pacific Transit and Telegraph Company, as the enterprise was now called, because

Gladstone, chancellor of the exchequer, opposed it. Gladstone insisted that a subsidy for a land telegraph would set an undesirable precedent. The case for subsidies in aid of submarine cables was stronger, but even here the demands on the treasury had been so great that the cabinet had decided to limit its support to the cable between Britain and India. The chancellor dismissed the subject with the observation, "I do not think the House of Commons as at present minded would assent to such a vote if it was proposed, as I trust it will not be." [80]

Watkin was not so easily defeated as to accept Gladstone's opposition as final. He argued that Gladstone misunderstood the purpose of the communications system. It was not merely to stretch a wire across the continent, but to open up 2,000 miles of British territory by roads and by river and lake navigation. But his most telling point was a political one directed at the Duke of Newcastle. Watkin, who knew Newcastle's views on empire perhaps better than any other man, believed that the duke's advocacy of a crown colony for southern Rupert's Land was not based merely on the realization that Canada was unable to assume the responsibility, but upon the view that the territory belonged to Great Britain and not to Canada and that Canadian extension into it should be resisted. Watkin pointed out that the maps prepared by the Canadian government after the surveys of Dawson and Hind represented the whole of Rupert's Land as Canadian, with "Canada" printed in large letters across the entire area. Watkin's letter is a remarkable document which deserves to be quoted at length:

> Assuming that this country is to be thus opened up at the risk of Canada and British Columbia only, the Canadians will not willingly tolerate any subsequent control over the territory or the enterprize on the part of the British Government. The country will be settled by them, and under their special and exclusive direction, and all the control which ought to be exercised from home will, as it seems to me, be lost.
> Canada will then have *taken possession,* and Great Britain will be regarded as having given it up—whereas if the fact of British ownership and control be practically recognized by accepting the Canadian proposal now, all future aggrandisement of Canada will be avoided.
> But, is it the interest of this country that the Hudson's Bay territory should become a mere extension of Canada? and if not,

the handing over of the task of colonization to Canada must be, in every way, injurious.

But besides, as the prospect has essentially Imperial purposes will not the avoidance of the really petty assistance asked for be looked upon illnaturedly? Will it not damage, where otherwise help might be given to, the Intercolonial?

And, in fine, should Imperial grasp be lost over this beginning of a greater route? [81]

The effect of this communication on Newcastle is not known, but Gladstone was not influenced by it. He replied that he could not agree that, by granting a colony or a private association the power to construct a telegraph, the British government would abandon either in theory or practice any territorial rights which it would be expedient for it to exercise.[82] Watkin was finally forced to admit that he could gain no financial assistance from the Imperial government. He had one last suggestion. He proposed to Newcastle that the government grant his company, in lieu of the subsidy, a portion of the Athabaska country previously licensed to the Hudson's Bay Company. The suggestion was congenial to Newcastle, since it involved no Imperial expenditure.[83]

While awaiting replies to this application and to the requests for subsidies from Canada and British Columbia, Watkin turned to the subject of the possible purchase of the Hudson's Bay Company. Since there was no hope of liberal land grants from the present directors, and since Newcastle's continued interest in the creation of a crown colony indicated that the British government would accept responsibility for administering the territory, Watkin opened active negotiations with the Company in February, 1863. In anticipation of his overtures, the governor and committee had instructed the Company's accountant, Edward Roberts, to prepare a valuation of its entire property, and of the arable territory alone should the prospective purchaser want only that part. Not surprisingly, Roberts estimated the value of the chartered rights in Rupert's Land at £1,500,000. Property outside the chartered territory he valued at £491,748, including land on Vancouver Island, in British Columbia, and in Canada, and the possessory rights in Oregon.[84] The entire assets of the Company were thus, he calculated, worth almost £2,000,000.

Watkin met with the Company's solicitor, Joseph Maynard, on

February 24, 1863, and, as usual, talked in large terms. He and his friends, he said, would have no difficulty in raising the required funds but they must first examine the books to be satisfied that the Company was worth the purchase price.[85] Such a suggestion was completely unacceptable to the governor and committee. They had always guarded the Company's secrets from prying eyes, and they saw no reason to make an exception even for a prospective purchaser. Should the negotiations fail, Watkin and his associates would possess information that could be used to the embarrassment of the Company. They finally compromised by agreeing to let him see abstracts of the accounts, but insisted that he inspect them at Hudson's Bay House. On May 13, after the usual haggling, Watkin finally accepted the Company's terms of sale. The entire stock of the Company was to be sold for £1,500,000, the bulk of it delivered within two months of the agreement, and most of the remainder within four months. Watkin also promised that the new company would respect the rights of the old officers and servants.[86]

Watkin was on the eve of attaining his goal. All that stood between him and the long-desired control over the Hudson's Bay Company was £1,500,000. But that was a substantial amount, especially since the governor and committee demanded cash.

Watkin had considered the formation of two companies—a fur company and a land company. The fur company would pay the interest on £800,000 for the Hudson's Bay Company's trading rights and stations, and the land company would pay the interest on £700,000 for the fertile area of southern Rupert's Land. One-fourth of this land would be given to the Imperial government for the formation of a crown colony, to be called Hysperia. The government in return would lend the £1,500,000 necessary to purchase the stock of the Hudson's Bay Company. The plan was discarded when Gladstone refused to agree to any such loan.[87]

The promoter had carried the negotiations as far as he could. The men of capital with whom he had been associated now had to determine the course of action. Watkin states in his book that "after a short, but anxious delay," the Duke of Newcastle told him that any purchase must be made entirely with private resources, but that "all sorts of moral support" would be available.[88] This decision should not have been surprising, since it was consistent with the government's general policy.

The principal backers of the transcontinental scheme and the purchase of the Company were now revealed. They were George Grenfell Glyn and Robert Benson, particularly the former. Glyn and Benson were convinced that both the telegraph project and the purchase of the Company offered good investment opportunities, especially since Watkin had persuaded them that the projects were sponsored by the Duke of Newcastle and the British government would assist the communications company either through subsidies or land grants.[89] Whether they ever intended to control the new Company themselves, or merely to act as brokers in the formation of a company with a colonization program, is not clear. Certainly after the governor and committee insisted on a cash payment of £1,500,000, they promoted the second objective. Neither the purchase of the Company nor the telegraph scheme was a Grand Trunk project, as has often been suggested, although its promoters hoped to make the telegraph line and road a success by coöperating with the Grand Trunk Railway.

Glyn and Benson were not willing to assume the job of raising the necessary money themselves. They agreed that the purchase of the Company should be undertaken by a large number of capitalists, and the logical agency was the International Financial Society, in which both were interested. At Glyn's suggestion,[90] Watkin turned to the society to finance the purchase, and it appointed Richard Potter as its representative to assist in the final negotiations.

The conjunction of the organization of the International Financial Society with the purchase of the Hudson's Bay Company, and the participation of Robert Benson, president of the society, in the purchase negotiations, have created the general misapprehension that the society was organized for the purpose of buying the Company. There is no foundation for this belief. The society was organized on May 11, 1863, to make investments throughout the world. In the words of the articles of association, its objectives were "the undertaking, assisting, and participating in financial, commercial, and industrial operations and undertakings, both in England and abroad, and both singly and in connection with other persons, firms, companies, and corporations."[91] The nominal capital was £3,000,000 in 150,000 shares. Practically every important banking firm in the City of London was represented, most notably

Robert Benson and Company, Glyn, Mills and Company, Samuel Dobree and Sons, Frederick Huth and Company, George Peabody and Company, Frühling and Goschen, and Sterns Brothers. The outstanding exception was Baring Brothers, although James Stewart Hodgson, Kirkman's brother, who in 1866 also became a partner in Baring Brothers, was a subscriber.[92]

The purchase of the Hudson's Bay Company was one of two undertakings assumed by the International Financial Society in its first two weeks of existence; the other was the flotation of shares for the Egyptian Commercial and Trading Company. Between 1863 and 1866 the society enjoyed great success, and its shares sold at a premium. It suffered reverses in the financial panic of 1866 and thereafter declined to relative insignificance.

After the intervention of the International Financial Society, arrangements were quickly concluded between Watkin and Potter and the governor and committee. The agreement was finally completed on June 15, 1863, and the particulars were essentially the same as those to which Watkin had assented in May. The society agreed to purchase all the stock at the rate of £300 for each £100, and the governor and committee agreed to sell the stock belonging to them and to use their influence to secure the consent of other stockholders.[93] No effort was made to poll the entire body of stockholders, and none was necessary, since the directors controlled the preponderance of the stock. Although a few proprietors displayed a reluctance to sell, most of them recognized a bargain and disposed of their holdings immediately.

Those who had most reason to feel slighted were the chief factors and traders. Since their careers and their past and present interests were tied to the fur trade, they could not be expected to look with favor upon the promotion of land settlement which might injure that trade. They had been recognized as "wintering partners" in the amalgamation of 1821, yet the negotiations were undertaken without their knowledge and came to their attention through the devious channels of rumor. In January, 1863, six active and retired chief factors led by George Barnston wrote the governor and committee that they had heard of negotiations between the Imperial government and the Company with a view to opening Rupert's Land to settlement, and that the only remaining issue was the amount of indemnity.[94] They were, of course, mis-

informed, but the board's reply that "there is not the least probability" of the surrender of the charter [95] is difficult to reconcile
with the fact that negotiations had been initiated for the sale of
the Company. The resentment of the "wintering partners" on the
news of the purchase is understandable. As Joseph J. Hargrave
wrote, they heard the news with "a feeling of stupefaction quickly
succeeded by one of deep indignation." [96] Well might they be
angry and fearful, for the closed secretive body they had served
had been replaced by a great financial association. Shares in the
new Company were sold in the open market, and Rupert's Land
seemed to be on the eve of a new era which held out a bleak prospect for the officers of the fur trade. The *Canadian News,* which for
six years had been campaigning for the colonization of Rupert's
Land, hailed the news of the purchase and quoted with satisfaction a statement in a New York newspaper that the old Company
had "died of the railroad and the steamboat." [97]

Such obituaries were premature, but advocates of colonization
seemed to have cause for satisfaction in the backing and direction
of the new Company. At the suggestion of the Duke of Newcastle,
the International Financial Society selected Sir Edmund Head
as governor of the reorganized Company. Richard Potter, Daniel
Meinertzhagen, James S. Hodgson, and J. H. W. Schröder represented the London financial community. Eden Colvile and George
Lyall, members of the old committee, were reëlected to the new
board to provide continuity, and Curtis Miranda Lampson, who
had begun his career as an American fur merchant but had migrated to London and become a British subject in 1848, was added
to improve the efficiency of the fur trade. Old Edward Ellice, who
thought the colonization scheme an unsound venture for the creation of a "Newcastle Utopia" which would banish distance, climate, Indians, and all other impediments to settlement,[98] reluctantly admitted that the directors represented "a most respectable
and powerful association" and that Lampson, though an American,
was "one of the most acute, and intelligent men in the City." [99]

At a general court of the new stockholders, which was actually
attended only by Colvile, Lyall, Richard Wilson Pelly, and the
Company's secretaries, William G. Smith and Thomas Fraser, the
stock for the new Company was set at £2,000,000.[100] Thus the
stock of the old Company, which had been bought for triple its

nominal value, was quadrupled in price. In anticipation of the general court's action, the International Financial Society at the end of June issued a prospectus to investors, offering the new stock for sale in the open market.

In the promises of the prospectus lay the causes for much dissension between directors and shareholders during the next six years. The prospectus contained the following statement:

> Consistently with these objects [the fur trade], the outlying estates and valuable farms will be realized where the land is not required for the use of the Company. The Southern District will be opened to European colonization under a liberal and systematic scheme of land settlement. . . . Possessing a staff of factors and officers who are distributed in small centers of civilization over the territory, the Company can, without creating new and costly establishments, inaugurate a new policy of colonization, and at the same time dispose of mining grants.[101]

This statement, issued with the sanction of the new Company's directors, clearly seems to misrepresent the potentialities of land sales under private auspices in a region virtually without means of communication except for lakes and rivers. It ignored the problems of government which would inevitably arise in agricultural and mining communities. It failed to consider the enormous expenses that had wrecked so many other colonization companies. Although it is true that an advertisement designed to sell stock should not emphasize the hazards of the purchase, the prospectus nevertheless overstressed the Company's prospects for immediate profits. When expectations of quick, profitable land sales proved unjustified, the protests of the shareholders that they had been duped were difficult to answer.

That sober businessmen like the majority of the shareholders should have invested in the stock of the Company without sufficient investigation of its ability to fulfill its promises can be explained in part by the speculative mania that gripped England in 1863. The availability of excess capital and the eagerness of its possessors to invest in enterprises promising large returns made it possible for the International Financial Society to dispose of the shares with little difficulty.

The society received handsome compensation for its services. The committee it selected to head the new Company stipulated,

as a condition of their acceptance, that the society contribute
£200,000 to the new Company as working capital; this sum was
paid over, but the society received a gross profit of almost £300,000
on its venture.[102] After organization of the new Company, the
society continued to hold a large amount of stock. On March 1,
1864, it held 17,140 shares with a par value of £342,800.[103] Its representative at stockholders' meetings consequently could speak
with considerable power. But the society did not dominate the new
Company. Control was widely distributed among more than 1,700
shareholders. Unlike the proprietors of the old Company, who
were usually represented at the meetings of the general court only
by the governor and committee, the shareholders of the new Company were frequently critical of the directors and the meetings
of the general court were often stormy. The society gradually disposed of its Hudson's Bay holdings and by June, 1867, held only
3,000 shares,[104] and its influence over the Company had dwindled
to relative insignificance.

The six years between the sale of the old fur-trade monopoly in
1863 and the transfer of the proprietary rights to Canada were
marked by frustrations for all parties concerned. The shareholders
denounced the directors for their failure to carry out the promises
of the prospectus; the directors repeated the same accusations as
the old governor and committee that the British and Canadian
governments wanted to steal their land; the British and Canadian
governments exhorted each other to bring about a settlement; and
the press denounced the Company as a barrier to progress. Contrary to the general expectations in the summer of 1863 that a new
era had dawned, the old problems continued in very much the
same form. One factor had changed. The Company's stock had
quadrupled in value, and the price required to purchase the Company's rights had consequently increased.

CHAPTER

# 18

# The End of the Monopoly

BETWEEN 1863 AND 1869 the Hudson's Bay Company engaged in a strange triangular conflict with the British and Canadian governments over southern Rupert's Land, and after 1865 the United States was an increasingly interested observer. Each of the three parties was acutely aware of the weakness of its position, but none seemed able to make concessions that would break the deadlock.

The governor and committee were confident that the charter was a valid instrument, but without governmental assistance the land was of no value except as a base of operations for the fur trade. Yet the price of the Company's stock had been based to a large extent on the promise of immediate land sales. Shareholders expected speedy remuneration from some or all of the following sources, which the Company's accountants valued at more than a million pounds: (1) Rupert's Land, including agricultural land, mineral rights, and the forts and buildings of the territory; (2) lands and trading posts in Canada and British Columbia and on Vancouver Island; (3) claims against the United States under the treaty of 1846.[1] Each of these assets was highly speculative in character, and the value of the holdings in Rupert's Land was completely dependent on the construction of communications facilities and establishment of a governmental authority adequate to maintain order. Neither, contrary to the assurances contained in the prospectus, was within the powers of the Company.

[1] For notes to chap. 18, see pp. 474–477.

A succession of four colonial secretaries between 1863 and 1869 expressed a desire to open the chartered territory to colonization and to institute effective government. Each of these officials, after consulting the law officers of the Crown, concluded that the Company's charter was probably legal and that it would be undesirable to challenge its validity. But all agreed that the purchase of the Company's rights, if any was to be made, must be at no expense to the British exchequer.

The desire of Canadian governments for the acquisition of Rupert's Land fluctuated during these years. In 1864, when George Brown joined the Canadian cabinet to promote federation, the government adopted his policy of annexation of the Northwest Territories. After he left the coalition in 1866, the ardor of the ministry varied in intensity. But until the end of the negotiations, when fear of American intentions toward the chartered territory became extreme, Canadians agreed that Great Britain, not Canada, should compensate the Company, since Canada was serving an Imperial purpose.

The directors of the Company took part in two major interrelated negotiations with the British and Canadian governments, and each caused them acute frustration. The greater project was the realization of profits from land; the lesser, the establishment of a telegraph line.

With the organization of the new Company, the interests of Watkin's Atlantic and Pacific Telegraph and Transit Company were merged with those of the Hudson's Bay Company, in which Watkin was a stockholder. Although his holdings were substantial,[2] he and his friends did not control the Hudson's Bay Company. Nevertheless, during the first few months he regarded it as his creation, and therefore as an instrument for the promotion of his communications project.

The governor and committee wanted to facilitate the same project, but under their direction, not Watkin's. A conflict of wills was inevitable. For a short time, however, the directors and Watkin coöperated in the common purpose. In July, 1863, the board sent him to Red River to report on the settlement and the neighboring territory, the prospects for colonization, and the steps necessary for construction of the telegraph. En route Watkin communicated with members of the government of John Sandfield

Macdonald, which was precariously in power, and with the supporters of John A. Macdonald and Cartier who might soon return to office. Watkin found that both Sandfield Macdonald and the Macdonald-Cartier group were apathetic to the annexation of Rupert's Land and preferred that Great Britain create a crown colony in its arable areas. This view, he reported, was general also among the Catholics of Lower Canada. George Brown and the Clear Grits were the only politicians who favored acquisition of the territory by Canada.[3] This was useful information, and if Watkin had contented himself with performing the functions of a reporter his relationship with the governor and committee would have continued cordial.

Watkin, however, had not come to Canada merely to gather information. Eager to begin the construction of his telegraph, he negotiated an agreement with O. S. Wood of the Montreal Telegraph Company. The engagement provided that the Montreal company construct the line from Halifax to Sault Ste. Marie before October 1, 1865, and that the Hudson's Bay Company complete the line from Fort Langley to Fort Garry and thence to the United States boundary near Pembina by October 15. The Hudson's Bay Company would also arrange for construction between Fort Garry and Sault Ste. Marie if the Canadian government gave adequate financial assistance. If it did not, the two sections of the telegraph would connect with American lines. By a second agreement, Watkin authorized Wood to construct the telegraph from Fort Garry to Jasper House at the Hudson's Bay Company's expense. These engagements were subject to approval by the directors of the two companies.[4] Watkin was in a hurry, however, and transatlantic communications were painfully slow. Proceeding therefore as if the agreement were ratified, he placed a conditional order for telegraph wire and authorized Wood to leave for the interior immediately. This assumption of authority was too flagrant for the governor and committee to tolerate, and Head reminded Watkin that the control of the Company was in London and that the board could not consent to move so rapidly as Watkin desired.[5]

Despite their pique at Watkin, the board finally agreed to begin construction of the line. In the spring of 1864 they sent John Rae, a retired chief factor justly famed for his Arctic explorations, to survey the route of the telegraph from Fort Garry to the Pacific Ocean. Since they expected construction to begin in the spring of 1865, they completed the purchase of the telegraph wire. Over seventy tons of wire were sent to the Red River settlement, sixty tons to Victoria, and another large shipment to York Factory.[6]

The governor and committee would have been well advised to move more slowly, for even before Rae set out on his survey, the Canadian government had undermined the project. In February, 1864, the cabinet of John Sandfield Macdonald and Antoine A. Dorion, on the eve of being ousted, decided to throw overboard the program of western communications to which Howland and Sicotte had agreed. Their excuse was that the Atlantic and Pacific Telegraph and Transit Company now proposed to build a telegraph but made no mention of a road. Also, they objected to the Hudson's Bay Company's proposal to divide the land into sections and, as soon as telegraphic communication was established in each section, to have the colonies participating in the agreement guarantee the telegraph company a rate of profit on the capital expended. Canada might thus be called upon to pay interest on the cost of sections of a telegraph line wholly outside its territory and having no connection with any line in Canada. Further, the cabinet requested that the British government take immediate steps to settle the boundary between Canada and the Hudson's Bay territories.[7]

The Canadian government was correct in saying that proposals since December, 1862, had mentioned only a telegraph. But there was no basis for the assertion that the Hudson's Bay Company had given up the road-building project. The ministers wanted a pretext to break off negotiations that would cost the already overburdened treasury additional expense, and found their excuse in the omission of any mention of a road. Watkin protested that he had explained to the Canadian ministry in July and August, 1863, that the telegraph would be accompanied by a road,[8] but the Canadians had already withdrawn. Since Canada refused to cooperate, British Columbia also took no action. The telegraph project was dead, and tons of wire were left unused at Victoria, Red River, and York Factory.

By renewing the suggestion that the boundary be determined, Canada returned to Draper's contention before the select committee of 1857 that central British America belonged to Canada as the heir of France, since France had been the rightful owner before 1763. This argument, as the personnel of the Colonial Office realized, was weak, and no Canadian government actually pressed the issue. The cabinet's action was merely a reaffirmation of Canada's desire to acquire a new West without substantial expenditure, and contributed nothing to the settlement of the future of Rupert's Land.

The directors of the Company expected little from Canada. Their reliance was on the good will and assistance of Newcastle and the British government. Watkin had convinced them, as apparently he had convinced himself, that the duke would offer all aid short of levies on the treasury. Consequently, on August 28, 1863, they passed the following resolution:

"Resolved that the time has come when in the opinion of this Committee it is expedient that the authority, executive and judicial, over the Red River Settlement and the South Western portion of Rupert's Land should be vested in officers deriving such authority directly from the Crown and exercising it in the name of her Majesty. . . ." [9]

The first official response seemed encouraging. Newcastle reiterated his willingness to give favorable consideration to any specific proposal the Hudson's Bay Company might make.[10] For several months, both Head and Newcastle professed optimism as to the prospects of an early agreement. They believed they could reach an arrangement whereby payments to the Company would come from land revenues rather than from the Imperial exchequer. This was the basis on which Head made the new Company's first specific proposal on November 11, 1863. He suggested that the Company retain ownership in fee simple of half the lands in the prospective crown colony, and that the other half should be transferred to the Crown, each half to be of equal value for cultivation. This proposal was subject to the following conditions:

1) The Company would have the sole right to erect the telegraph through the territory, and would guarantee to complete it in five years. The governments of British Columbia and Canada would pledge themselves to subsidize the project on the basis of the arrangement suggested in the discussions with Howland in December, 1862. The Company would construct a road beside the telegraph. Land one mile in width along the road would belong

to the Company, and would be considered as part of its half of the land of the colony. In constructing the telegraph, the Company would be entitled to use wood and other materials from ungranted land.

2) The Crown would possess the exclusive right to grant licenses for mining, on the condition that it paid the Company one-third of the receipts from all fees derived from the mines.

The area the governor and committee proposed to transfer was the southern part of Rupert's Land. The specific northern limits of the territory to be constituted a crown colony would be either the Saskatchewan itself or a line from the Rocky Mountains through Edmonton House and Cumberland House, down the Saskatchewan to Lake Winnipeg. From the mouth of the Winnipeg River, where it entered the lake, the line could run eastward to the Canadian boundary. This was the area that became known conventionally as the "fertile belt."

Head concluded with the following observation, intended to emphasize the liberality of the Company's offer:

> While suggesting a plan which involves the cession of the Company's right of property over one-half of a vast tract of British North America the Committee simply ask that the Crown will exercise on British soil, in favor of British subjects that amount of controul and protection which the Queen's prerogative can alone afford—a protection in other cases, at least, deemed perfectly consistent with the unimpaired enjoyment of existing rights of private property, and which in fact, is commonly thought to be directed specially to the maintenance of those very rights against wrong or violence of any kind.[11]

Head's arguments did not please Newcastle. Rather, they demonstrated to him that the new board had been infected with the philosophy of the old one. Like Pelly, Ellice, and Berens, Head was now contending that the government had an obligation to protect the rights of a private trading company. This position Newcastle had rejected in his earlier debates with Berens, and he repudiated Head's contention with equal emphasis.[12] His counter-proposal was that the Company surrender its territorial rights in the fertile belt to the Crown, and that the government pay the Company 1 shilling per acre for all land sold, payment to cease when the aggregate receipts reached £150,000, or at the expiration of fifty years. In addition, the Company would be entitled to one-fourth of the money received by the government from licenses from gold mines or from export duties, until the aggregate paid the Company from this source reached £100,000, or for fifty years.[13]

These conditions were far short of the Company's demands, particularly since the £100,000 maximum to be paid from gold-mine revenue was highly speculative. The directors of the Company discreetly kept their correspondence with the Colonial Office confidential, but it is possible to visualize an emotional explosion from the shareholders had they heard the suggestion that they accept a loss of several hundred thousand pounds on their investment.

Since the Colonial Office and the governor and committee, in assessing the price the Company should receive, were in distinct conflict, there was no possibility that agreement could be reached by mere argument. The only way to a settlement was for one side or the other to abandon its position out of desperation. The conflict became increasingly a war of nerves. Each side was well aware of the hopes and fears of its opponents, and sought to exploit the weaknesses of the other parties while attempting to conceal its own. The Canadian suggestion that southern Rupert's Land belonged to Canada as the heir of France offered an opportunity which the Colonial Office seized to make the Company more amenable. After notifying the governor and committee of Newcastle's proposal, Fortescue, almost as a postscript, stated that Canada contemplated the assertion of a claim to the fertile belt and that ". . . it must of course be understood that the above suggestions are made on the supposition that the cession by the Company will place Her Majesty's Government in possession of an indisputable title to the Territory ceded by them." [14]

The Company's reaction was not what the Colonial Office had intended. Not only did Head reply, as expected, that the Company's title was sound, but he notified Fortescue that the appearance of the Canadian claim had caused the Company to defer construction of the telegraph, as it was undesirable to expend capital for construction in an area that was the subject of litigation.[15] Since the Colonial Office considered the Canadian claim worthless,[16] and since Newcastle was anxious to see the telegraph line erected, Head's response was particularly effective. Fortescue assured the governor that there had been no intention to cast doubt on the validity of the Company's claim and that the government was prepared to accept the Company as rightful owner of the land west of the Mississippi River, to which the negotiation primarily referred. Further, Newcastle promised that on the completion of a road and telegraph from the Canadian boundary to the border of British Columbia, the land adjacent to the line would be granted to the Company at the rate of one square mile for every lineal mile of road and telegraph construction.[17]

Though the threat of litigation had misfired, the government's refusal to establish a crown colony except on its own conditions effectively prevented any returns at all from the sale of land. But the Company was not without a lever to use against the government. If the Company could not colonize, neither could the government, and Newcastle had made one of his primary objectives the opening of the interior of British North America. Further, if delay was prolonged, there might be no land for British emigrants to settle, for it might be appropriated by the United States. Emphasis on the inability of the Company to defend its territory against penetration by American farmers and miners was, of course, a two-edged weapon, since the Company's interests would be affected as much as the British government's. But Head and his associates were of the opinion that the government was more concerned about the possible loss of the territory than the Company, and they shaped their strategy accordingly.

The first opportunity to use the American threat as an incentive to British governmental action came with the wars between the Sioux and American troops in Minnesota. During the autumn of 1863, Sioux fleeing from the cavalry crossed into Rupert's Land and encamped near Red River. The Company's personnel were powerless to remove them, and the United States was insistent either that Great Britain provide sufficient forces to prevent the Indians from violating the neutrality of British territory, or that American troops be permitted to pursue them into Rupert's Land.[18]

Alexander Grant Dallas, governor of Rupert's Land, agreed to allow the officer in command of the American cavalry unit to follow the Sioux across the border. His acquiescence, given without the consent of either the governor and committee or the Imperial government, was a clear demonstration of the Company's complete inability to cope with the problem of maintaining order along the international frontier.[19] The Montreal *Evening Telegraph* heatedly protested:

> It is hardly possible to conceive that the Governor of Red River would have assumed so great a responsiblity without instructions from the Imperial Government; yet what can we think of a Government which on the demands of a foreign power [s]trips itself of the highest attribute of sovereignty, abandons the hitherto sacred right of asylum, virtually hauls down the British flag in the Indian Territory, and allows the armed forces of another nation to pursue and murder with its connivance, the miserable remnants of tribes which have placed themselves under the guardianship of our honor.[20]

There was much justification for the newspaper's denunciation. The Company's government was no government at all around the Red River settlement. This fact was evident, but the solution was more difficult to discern. Head sought to capitalize on the Company's weakness. He argued that in the absence of military assistance it would be impossible for the Hudson's Bay Company to restrain the Indians and that international complications would result unless an effective government was soon established. Further, he pointed out, if the Sioux preyed upon the inhabitants of Red River, the population of that community would look to the United States for protection.[21]

The picture of a helpless population seeking the assistance of the United States against the Indians was overdrawn, for the Red River hunters were well able to take care of themselves, but the prospect of the spread of American influence and of disputes arising from violations of British territory by the Sioux nevertheless caused anxiety in the Colonial Office. The personnel of the Colonial Office privately admitted that some action must be taken, but they all agreed that the treasury and Parliament would not easily be convinced that the national interest required the expenditure of government funds for the purchase of the Company's rights. In this dilemma some of Newcastle's advisers began to look wistfully to Canadian annexation as a possible solution. Elliot declared that he could conceive of no place less desirable as a colony than this settlement in the heart of the American continent. Red River should logically be part of Canada, he said, and it was unfortunate that the Canadians should be so lukewarm.[22] To the end of his tenure, however, Newcastle showed no desire to promote Canadian annexation, nor, so long as Canada refused to admit the Company's rights, did the governor and committee.

Head was confronted with the problem of steering between the extremes of antagonizing the shareholders by asking too little and of discouraging the Colonial Office by asking too much. On April 13, 1864, he attempted to break the deadlock by offering to accept Newcastle's proposal, provided the government would raise the maximum amount to which the Company would be entitled to £1,000,000.[23] Newcastle did not have the opportunity to reply. He had been in ill health for months, and a few days after the letter was received, he resigned. Edward Cardwell was appointed as his successor.

Cardwell, like Newcastle, was determined to sweep away the anachronism of the chartered monopoly. But, unlike the duke, he regarded the establishment of a crown colony under any terms as impracticable. If Rupert's Land was to remain British, Cardwell soon convinced himself, it must be annexed to Canada. His first response to Head's offer of a settlement indicated that negotiations thereafter would take a different course, for he told the governor and committee that he must consult the Canadian government before giving a definite answer.[24] He wanted the Canadian government to declare its interest in assuming control over the Red River settlement and to send a representative to participate in further negotiations with the Hudson's Bay Company.[25]

Cardwell's inquiry arrived in Canada at a propitious time. The political deadlock that had prevented effective action by the Canadian ministry had been broken when George Brown had put aside his personal and political differences with John A. Macdonald to join a Taché-Macdonald ministry to work for Canadian federation. The presence of Brown in the cabinet was certain to stimulate the government's interest in the West. Until after the Quebec conference in October, however, the Canadian government could not reply to Cardwell, since the decisions on confederation at Quebec would have considerable bearing on the future of the western territories. The delegates to the conference at Quebec did not explicitly agree to support the annexation of Red River, but they did resolve that communications with the Northwest Territories should be promoted "at the earliest possible period," and James Ross of the *Nor'Wester* attended the conference as the unofficial representative for Red River.[26]

Finally on November 11 the cabinet discussed the policy that Canada should pursue toward the Hudson's Bay territories. The decision was a disappointment to the Colonial Office. The Canadian government reaffirmed its desire to acquire the Red River settlement, but again insisted that Great Britain must assume the expense of compensating the Company, since the Imperial government was responsible for the Company's privileged position.[27]

The Canadian ministry appointed Brown to confer further with Cardwell, and he arrived in London in December, 1864. Brown was a poor selection. His editorials in the Toronto *Globe* had heaped abuse upon the Company and had stressed the illegality of its claims to exercise political control over Rupert's Land. This was the line that Brown adopted in his discussions with Cardwell; and, as might be expected, he accomplished nothing. He dismissed Head's suggestion that the Company be paid up to a maximum of £1,000,000 from land sales as utterly untenable. Even if the charter were valid, he asserted, all Rupert's Land was not worth £1,000,000. The entire landed property of the Company was valued in the Company's own balance sheets at little more than this amount, and he had heard that the American government had offered to pay $1,000,000 for the extinction of the Oregon possessory rights alone, but that the Company had rejected the offer in expectation of receiving a much larger sum.[28] If his information was correct, he contended, the fertile belt should be valued at only a small proportion of £1,000,000. But this matter was for the British government to decide, said Brown. He was merely offering friendly advice, since his government could assume no responsibility for making any payment whatsoever.[29]

Brown's talks with Cardwell were cut short by the Christmas holidays, after which he returned to Canada for the opening of the legislature. Conferences between the two governments were suspended until April, 1865, when a four-man delegation from Canada, composed of Brown, Macdonald, Cartier, and Galt, arrived in London to discuss confederation and related questions. The ensuing conferences led to an agreement in June between

Cardwell and the Canadians that the whole of Rupert's Land would be transferred to Canada "subject to such rights as the Hudson's Bay Company might be able to establish," and that compensation, "if any," would be made by Canada with a loan guaranteed by the Imperial government.[30]

The decision to drop the objective of establishing a crown colony and instead to promote the annexation of the territory to Canada was made by Cardwell in consultation with Gladstone. They disregarded the advice of the permanent undersecretary, Frederic Rogers, that an agreement with the Company on the general lines proposed by Newcastle might soon be reached, and that transfer of the negotiations to Canada would delay a settlement.[31]

At no time during these discussions was the Company, the legal possessor of the territory,[32] consulted as to its views. The only official information the governor and committee received from the time Cardwell became colonial secretary until he reached an agreement with Canada a year later was a bald statement in December, 1864, that Cardwell was in communication with Brown. Enclosed was a copy of the Canadian cabinet's statement of November on the subject of the Red River settlement. This was cavalier treatment, and it was an indignant group of shareholders who were informed by the directors that the Colonial Office would entertain no further proposals and that the Company must negotiate with Canada.[33]

The shareholders, who had invested with rosy expectations of large returns, were not content to wait for possible compensation in the indefinite future. An increasingly vocal group began to complain that the directors were, if not incompetent, at least lacking in zeal for colonization.[34] More and more vehemently they charged that the failure of the governor and committee to state, in the prospectus of 1863, the difficulties in the way of settlement in Rupert's Land made them party to a fraud. The directors could not meet such attacks effectively, for although they all knew that the Company would be ruined if it attempted colonization at its own risk and cost, they were reluctant to state their opinion explicitly for fear of spreading discouragement as to the Company's future.[35]

The agreement between Cardwell and the Canadians, giving Canada the exclusive right to negotiate with the Company, accentuated the pressure on the governor and committee, for the colony showed no inclination to consider compensation. Criticism by the shareholders and continued Canadian refusal to negotiate probably were responsible for a most unusual correspondence at the beginning of 1866. In January Alexander McEwen wrote the Company a brief, two-sentence letter of inquiry, whose contents were of great importance. He asked simply "on behalf of self and friends" whether the Hudson's Bay Company was able and willing to dispose of its cultivable territory to "a party of Anglo-American Capitalists" who desired to colonize the area "on a system similar to that now in operation in the United States in respect to the organization of Territories and States." [36] The directors replied immediately that they would consider favorably any proposal for the purchase of land for colonization. Since Rupert's Land was a British possession, they stated, the concurrence of the British government would be necessary but there was no reason to expect that the Crown would object to the arrangement.[37]

This was indeed a strange interchange. By the agreement of June, 1865, the Colonial Office had in effect denied the Company the right to sell to any other agency than the government of Canada. Yet, despite this prohibition, the Company's directors expressed confidence that the British government would not oppose the sale to a syndicate of British and American investors. The personnel of the Colonial Office expressed some suspicion that the offer was not genuine, for as W. E. Forster said, the Company surely "cannot suppose they will be allowed to sell British Territory to aliens." [38] Cartier and McDougall of the Canadian government were more explicit. They stated flatly that McEwen's ventures "were not merely encouraged but suggested and concocted by prominent members of the Company, for the purpose of producing an impression on the Government, and with a view not to colonization but to negotiation and the Stock Market." [39]

These suspicions were probably justified, although the specific background of the McEwen letter is unknown. McEwen himself remains a mysterious figure. He was a Glasgow financier who in 1865 or 1866 opened an office in Nicholas Lane in the City of London. He was not a shareholder in the Hudson's Bay Company, but he had an interest in North American investments. Most important, he was a director of the Grand Trunk Railway Company, and undoubtedly in that capacity came into close association with

Edward Watkin, whose irritation at the continued stalemate had
steadily grown. He was probably the same Alexander McEwen who
invested in Canadian copper mines during the 1860's and 1870's.
If so, he entered bankruptcy proceedings later in 1866 and allegedly, upon being called to give evidence as to the mysterious
disappearance and reappearance of his private letter book, stated
on oath that in order to recover the book he had consulted a clair-
voyant.[40] Although the Colonial Office concluded from McEwen's
letter that the group he represented was dominated by Americans,
the identity of his associates was never revealed, and the existence
of any such group is doubtful.

The McEwen letter was precisely the type that the impatient
shareholders would have desired. An increasingly large number
of proprietors were disaffected by the failure of the directors either
to begin colonization directly or to sell the landed property. The
suggestion that a group, including Americans, was willing to make
the purchase was calculated to produce a reaction from the Canadians.

As the governor and committee undoubtedly expected, the
Colonial Office refused to authorize the sale because Cardwell had
already decided that negotiations must be undertaken between
the Company and Canada, and because, "until this engagement
shall have been disposed of, it will be necessary for Her Majesty's
Government to keep it in view in any steps which they may be
called upon to take in the matter." [41] The hope of the directors that
Canada might be stimulated to action was vain. On June 22, 1866,
the Canadian cabinet finally stated its position regarding the proposed purchase of land by McEwen and his associates. Its memorandum is probably the clearest and most concise summary of the
Canadian argument in a dispute too often characterized, particularly on the Canadian side, by invective and abuse.

The cabinet reaffirmed its contention that the fertile belt was
not part of the territory granted to the Company by the charter of
1670, and that, even if it were, there were serious objections to the
sale to McEwen. "Canadian experience," the ministers agreed,
"has shown that sales of large tracts of land to individuals, or
Commercial Corporations, have operated prejudicially to the best
interests of the province and retarded, rather than promoted, its
settlement and progress." [42]

In its memorandum the Canadian cabinet at last explained its failure to open negotiations with the Company. In 1866 the dominant question in Canada was the proposed confederation of the British North American colonies. Canada deemed it improper to begin negotiations until after the consummation of confederation, since the other prospective provinces would share the responsibility for fulfillment of any agreement. The explanation seemed to imply that Canada expected the Hudson's Bay Company to be compensated, and maintained the position that Rupert's Land should be transferred without cost for bargaining purposes only. In any event, the cabinet requested the support of the Imperial government in "discountenancing and preventing any such sales of any portion of the territory as is now applied for." [43] This support the Colonial Office had already provided.

The position of the Colonial Office is difficult to rationalize except in terms of the conviction that possession of the territory was essential to the success of the proposed federation, and that any action by which Great Britain could promote that end, short of payment to the Company from the British treasury, was justified. Though Canada had refused to recognize the Company's rights to the territory, the law officers of the Crown had upheld the Company's claims, and Cardwell did not dispute their validity. Yet the Imperial authorities, without consulting the Company, had entered into an agreement with Canada for the transfer of the Company's territory, with the provision that compensation, "if any," would be paid under Imperial guarantee. Such an agreement afforded the Company no protection, and the governor and committee had to wait until Canada decided to initiate action.

A large and powerful group of shareholders, including Edward Watkin, Junius S. Morgan, and George Peabody, would not accept continued inaction. On January 8, 1866, ten days before McEwen wrote his letter, some of them, including Watkin, asked the Company's secretary for permission to use the hall at Hudson's Bay House for a conference on colonization of the Company's territory. When denied this privilege, they selected London Tavern as their meeting place. On January 24, approximately 150 persons assembled for the discussion, of whom at least 130 were shareholders, almost 10 per cent of the entire number of proprietors.[44] One shareholder, James A. Dodds, delivered an address which must have lifted the flagging spirits of his auditors. Their property was worth not merely £2,000,000, said Dodds, but far more. Within fifteen years the growth of population in surrounding areas would increase the value of the fertile belt to at least £3,200,000. If the Company sold its proprietary rights over the entire territory, the loss of the trade could be calculated at £1,570,000. The entire value of the property was thus about £5,000,000. If Great Britain refused to erect a crown colony—he made no mention of Canada—Dodds proposed that the Company begin immediate colonization, which he insisted it was well able to do with its own resources. His confident dismissal of all obstacles is illustrated by the following passage:

> ". . . we have admittedly the right as proprietors to exercise very large governing powers, and during the transition period we could have little difficulty, with our forts and establishments, and with the hardiest and most skilful and self-reliant staff of factors and agents that the world ever saw, to maintain order, peace, and regularity amongst the first hive of population. We must not start at straws, and hum and haw, but act like men who, by God's providence, have a continent grown up on their hands." [45]

As the wrecks of numerous colonization companies in North America and elsewhere testified, the job of populating a wilderness was more hazardous than Dodds was willing to admit. But his hearers were swept off their feet. They unanimously adopted a resolution that the Company should accept not less than £5,000,000 for its rights, and, if this amount was not offered, should itself begin colonization.[46] The same group met again in May, 1866, and passed two more resolutions, one asking that immediate steps be taken to institute colonization, and the other protesting against the reported intention of the British government to assign the Company's lands to Canada. The shareholders appointed a deputation, including Lionel N. Bonar, Dodds, and Lieutenant Colonel Millington Synge, to discuss their demands with the committee. This group in itself represented 1,235 shares, or one-eighth of the total number held by the public.[47]

The governor and committee, now squeezed into a position where they could no longer maneuver, were forced to meet the attack of the disgruntled shareholders head on. The clash came at a meeting of the general court on July 5, 1866. Dodds repeated his charges that the directors lacked courage and energy, and that with more vital leadership the Company could reap large returns. Watkin vented his disappointment at the failure of the governor and committee to build the telegraph that he had promoted with such energy. Its construction, he said, should not be delayed until negotiations with the governments concerned had been completed; rather, the line should be built immediately so that the directors could send and obtain information quickly. To force the issue, the dissidents introduced the following resolution:

> That the Hudson's Bay Company having been rearranged in 1863 with the expressed object of opening to European colonization a large area of the territory under a liberal and systematic scheme of land settlement, the interests of the company demand the accomplishment of that object without any further delay, and that the directors be requested to take into their earliest and most serious consideration the best means of effecting that object; and that a committee of shareholders be appointed to confer with them upon that subject.[48]

The resolution, although couched in the most respectful terms, was clearly an appeal for a vote of no confidence in the governor and committee, and Head and his fellow directors so interpreted it. Head argued that the zealousness of the opposition had outrun its judgment. He said it was one thing to have the power of making law and enforcing rights, but quite another to render that power effective. Unless the laws of the country had the assent of the Crown, the Company could not rely upon the British courts to uphold them. As an illustration, he cited one experience when the Company had sold 736 acres of land but had not been paid because a dispute arose and the Company had been unable to enforce its rights in the courts of England. As to the Company's establishing its own courts in the territory, it might be difficult to convince Englishmen that the Company could be plaintiff and judge at the same time.[49] A mail ballot on the resolution upheld the directors: 122 stockholders, possessing 5,308 shares, voted in favor of immediate colonization; 496, possessing 53,942 shares, voted in the negative.[50]

The significance of the vote is not the decisive defeat of the resolution, but its support by one-fifth of the voting shareholders despite pressure from the directors, who made the issue one of confidence in the Company's management, and despite recognized obstacles to immediate colonization. The directors won a vote of confidence, but they had learned that a substantial proportion of the stockholders, much higher than 20 per cent, were impatient for a return on an investment of £2,000,000, and that the impatience was growing.

Though the returns from the fur trade averaged in excess of 4 per cent, the profit was much less than the shareholders had been led to expect when the Company reorganized in 1863. As discontent became more pronounced, the directors became more importunate in their communications with the Colonial Office. It was with some asperity that Head asked the Colonial Office in March, 1866, whether Canada had been given an option of indefinite duration.[51] Whether or not the option was indefinite— and the evidence is that there was no time limit on Canadian action—the settlement of the future of Rupert's Land could not be long deferred. American allusions to a northern "manifest destiny" for the United States seemed a prelude to more positive action.

American expansionism was stimulated by the covetousness of residents of Minnesota and the Dakota and Montana territories for the rich land across the border and the possible mineral wealth awaiting exploitation, and by irritation at the use of the Company's territory as a refuge by Indians at war with the United States. The spokesman for the western annexationists was James W. Taylor, special agent of the Treasury Department in the Minnesota area from 1859 to 1869. Taylor had been appointed primarily to report on trade and communications between the United States and the Hudson's Bay territories, but he took a more exalted view of his functions. His objective was annexation of the territories to the United States, and he used his office to promote that aim.

He was presented with an opportunity to stimulate political action when in March, 1866, the House of Representatives passed a resolution requesting a report on commercial relations with British America, and the secretary of the treasury assigned him the responsibility for its preparation. His report was far more than an analysis of commercial relations; it was a plea for annexation of all British North America. He embodied his proposal in a draft bill entitled "An Act for the admission of the States of Nova Scotia, New Brunswick, Canada East, and Canada West, and for the organization of the territories of Selkirk, Saskatchewan, and Columbia." He proposed to pay the Hudson's Bay Company $10,-000,000 for the surrender of its claims.[52] Taylor's proposal had particular appeal to Congress because of the general opinion, confirmed by numerous surveys, that the most feasible route for a transcontinental railway lay through British North America.

Taylor's bill was introduced in the House of Representatives in July, 1866, by Nathaniel P. Banks, chairman of the Committee on Foreign Relations, but was withdrawn on the advice of Secretary of State Seward that it would needlessly complicate relations with Great Britain. The withdrawal of the bill did not eliminate the fear of aggressive American intentions toward Rupert's Land. On the contrary, Taylor's report suggested that official action might be unnecessary to achieve his ends. The following passage was cited by the governor and committee as evidence that, unless Canada or Great Britain acted quickly, the territory would be Americanized:

". . . in 1865, the American territory of Montana adjoins the region which excited the enthusiasm of De Smet. Its population of 25,000, to be increased during 1866, to 50,000, have been drawn to the sources of the Missouri, by discoveries of gold and silver mines close to the international border, and rumors of gulches and ledges in the Saskatchewan District, yielding even greater prizes to the prospector, are already rife, and will soon precipitate a strong, active and enterprising people into the spacious void. What is called 'Americanization' of the Red River settlements has been slow, although sure, since the era of steam navigation, but the Americanization of the Saskatchewan will rush suddenly and soon from the camps of treasure-seekers in Montana." [53]

The news of the annexation bill reached London just after a change of government had brought into office the Conservative ministry of the Earl of Derby, and the Earl of Carnarvon had succeeded Cardwell as colonial secretary. Carnarvon, like his predecessor, desired to promote Canadian federation, and he and Cardwell reached an agreement by which the question would not become a party issue.[54] Carnarvon was not bound to follow Cardwell's policy with regard to Rupert's Land, but his inclination was to agree that the territory should belong to Canada. During his few months in office Carnarvon took no action to break the deadlock between Canada and the Company, since he was preoccupied with arranging the details of confederation. But the American gestures toward Red River alarmed him, though some of his advisers professed unconcern as to whether the United States took the territory. Sir Frederic Rogers frankly expressed the wish that either Canada or the United States would take the territory,[55] for in its present undefended condition it was a source of international irritation, and its remoteness made it indefensible by British troops. C. B. Adderley, the parliamentary undersecretary, held a similar view. In Adderley's opinion, no British or Canadian action could stop the influx of the Americans into Rupert's Land, "nor should we attempt to bar the progress of mankind in occupying the earth." Congress, he realized, would be far more generous in expenditures for communications than the British treasury. He therefore viewed the future of interior British America, whatever it might be, with equanimity. "All we can do," he said, "is to promote Confederation—& to expedite the settlement of territory beyond." [56]

The reports from the British minister to Washington, Frederick W. A. Bruce, that further delay in providing adequate communications with the West might lose Rupert's Land and British Columbia to the British Empire thus produced no apprehension in either Rogers or Adderley. In January, 1867, Bruce warned that, if Britain did not try at least to provide an adequate government over the Hudson's Bay territories, "the desire of the U.S. to drive their British rivals off the continent will be powerfully reinforced by the material interests of the North West which will be enlisted in favor of conquest or annexation." [57] Carnarvon was impressed with the urgency of Bruce's appeal, and the subject was apparently discussed, but the British government could take no effective action without large expenditures. Not even the Derby-Disraeli government was willing to recommend levies on the treasury for the protection of Rupert's Land, and it apparently decided to trust to fate that the Canadian federation about to be formed could annex the territory before an Anglo-American crisis developed over the inadequacy of the Company's government in Rupert's Land.

Bruce's warnings were given additional emphasis when the American minister to London, Charles Francis Adams, protested to the Foreign Office on April 13, 1867, that Indians who had "committed outrages" in American territory were still finding a haven in Rupert's Land. The specific cause of the protest was the attacks of Indians in the Dakota and Montana territories on emigrant trains along the road that ran west about 100 miles south of the boundary. On the appearance of American cavalry the Indians escaped across the line. Since the Company was unable to act against them, Adams conveyed a proposal from Seward that American troops be allowed to pursue hostile Indians for a "reasonable distance" into British territory. Seward's request was most embarrassing to the Colonial Office. The law officers of the Crown had held that it was lawful to authorize the pursuit of Indians into British territory, but that such pursuit would not justify their arrest for violations of American municipal law. Further, to accord such a privilege to the United States would be a humiliating confession that Great Britain was not willing to assume its proper obligations as a sovereign power. Nevertheless, as T. F. Elliot said, it might be "more expedient than inexpedient" to grant permission.[58]

When Adams' protest reached the Colonial Office, Carnarvon had resigned and had been replaced by the Duke of Buckingham and Chandos. Canadian federation had already become a reality with the passage of the British North America Act, although the new dominion would not come into existence until July 1. Buckingham took the convenient view that the primary responsibility for policing the territory must rest with the Hudson's Bay Company and with Canada as the heir apparent. Accordingly he asked the Company what action, if any, it proposed to take to prevent further use of its territory as a refuge.[59] As expected, the Company replied that it could do nothing, and these incidents were additional evidence that the Crown must provide protection.[60] But on June 21, Head sent the Colonial Office a communication which kept the government from making any use of the Company's confession of weakness. He enclosed an Arrowsmith map showing the boundary between the United States and the Hudson's Bay territories. North of Montana Territory, Head pointed out, streams flowed southward, not toward Hudson Bay. The land above the 49th parallel drained by these streams was therefore not under the jurisdiction of the Hudson's Bay Company, but was subject to control by the British government. Responsibility for the Indian problem in that sector thus rested with the Colonial Office.[61] This fact was unpleasant, but the government did not provide troops to police the area. Canada was expected to undertake the responsibility when, with the assistance of the Colonial Office, it should come to terms with the Company.

Meanwhile, knowledge that the Canadians had been given the prescriptive right to Rupert's Land caused further unrest in the Red River settlement. A small group headed by Dr. John Schultz, who had become editor and proprietor of the settlement's only newspaper, the *Nor'Wester*, constituted itself a spokesman for the settlement in seeking union with Canada. A smaller group loudly demanded annexation to the United States, but the majority preferred either to be ruled as a crown colony or to continue in their present status. Against these contending elements the council of Assiniboia was completely ineffectual.

The helplessness of the Company was illustrated by its experience with Thomas Spence. Spence was a self-important Canadian surveyor who was ambitious for the distinction of bringing Red River into the Canadian federation. In August, 1866, just before setting out from Montreal to Red River, he wrote Carnarvon for a statement of the Company's powers and of the government's intentions with regard to the future of the colony.[62] The communication inflated Spence's self-esteem, for it was dignified by a reply. His first public appearance at Red River took place in December, when he convened a meeting in the courtroom to prepare a memorial to the Imperial government asking for union with a "Grand Confederation of British North America." When the purpose of the meeting was made public, the American party led by George Emmerling, nicknamed "Dutch George," expressed an interest in attending. What took place thereafter is a matter of dispute. Spence's opponents alleged that he held his meeting several hours early, a charge he vehemently denied. But both sides agreed that only he and four others attended; they passed the resolutions for annexation to Canada unanimously, and then dispersed.[63] A memorial to the queen was circulated on the basis of the resolutions, asking for the immediate creation of a crown colony with a view to eventual annexation by Canada, subject to the approval of the Red River community, and for a detachment of troops to protect the settlement against the Indian menace. This document, signed by eighty-four men, most of whom were English or Scottish half-breeds, was forwarded to the Colonial Office by the lieutenant governor of Canada, Sir John Michel.[64]

In the spring of 1867 Spence moved from Red River to the settlement of Portage la Prairie, about eighty miles up the Assiniboine River from Fort Garry. There, in January, 1868, at a meeting Spence said was attended by 400 settlers, a government of "Manitoba" was created, with Spence as president of the council, and the boundaries of the new British dependency were delineated.[65] In notifying Angus Morrison of this action, Spence explained that it had been necessitated by the failure of the Imperial government to provide protection, and warned that, should Canada not recognize the government or annex the dependency to the new dominion within six months, the people would ask the United States for recognition and eventual annexation. Spence sent another announcement, couched in less threatening terms, to the secretary of state for foreign affairs. Meanwhile his government began collecting taxes and tried, without success, to impose a duty on the Company's imports into the territory.[66] These comic-opera proceedings demonstrated that Rupert's Land was in a state of anarchy. Spence's purposes had apparently been to draw attention to himself and to dramatize the need for immediate action by the British and Canadian governments. These ends he accomplished, though his government disintegrated after a warning from the Colonial Office that it had no authority to impose any form of coercive power, including taxes, and that if he continued to assert such authority he would incur "grave responsibilities." [67]

Despite the urgent need for effective government, the opening of discussions with the Company had to await Canadian federation. Within two months after the Dominion of Canada came into existence, the Duke of Buckingham urged the governor-general, Viscount Monck, to press the Canadian government to begin negotiations with the Company, for, he said, "The question of the Hudson's Bay Territory is rapidly becoming urgent, and if delayed much longer may give rise to political difficulty. No time should, therefore, be lost in deciding on the course of action to be pursued by Canada." [68]

Buckingham's admonition was based upon the recognition that

the course Canada desired to pursue would lead to no conclusion. Canada could not possess Rupert's Land without compensating the Company, nor could it expect the British government to assume the financial obligations. In April, 1867, the delegates from Canada and the maritime colonies had reminded the Colonial Office that Article 146 of the British North America Act provided for the admission of Rupert's Land to Canada, and had asked that the territory be directly annexed to Canada rather than formed into a crown colony.[69] This definite assertion that Rupert's Land should be part of the new dominion without passing through the transitional phase of Imperial control marked an advance from previous Canadian positions, but it did not suggest how the new dominion proposed to acquire the territory. No such statement of policy could be made until after the first government of the Dominion of Canada had been formed. But the implication was that Great Britain should immediately assign the territory to Canada, and that the Company's right to compensation should be decided later. This, Buckingham and his advisers suspected, would be illegal, and their belief was confirmed by the law officers of the Crown, who advised that Britain could not establish a government in Rupert's Land without the Company's consent and without an act of Parliament. They added:

We think, that though the Power of Parliament would extend to the establishment of a Government in the Hudson's Bay territories, which might be supported by local taxation, it is a question deserving of much consideration whether it would be advisable to exercise that power by passing an Act against the wish of the Company, while the Charter continues to exist. Such an Act would, as we conceive, of necessity, indirectly at least, repeal or materially interfere with, many of the privileges granted to, and which have been exercised by the Company under their Charter, and give rise to a conflict of powers and jurisdictions which would be attended with much inconvenience. We think that there would be much difficulty created by the existence of the Charter, to putting into execution the powers of the 140th [146th] section of the British American Act, 1867, assuming that the Hudson's Bay Company were adverse to the Union. We think that this difficulty will necessarily exist, even though the proprietary rights were interfered with as little as possible.[70]

The appeal of the British North American delegates for the Crown's summary assignment of Rupert's Land to Canada could not be reconciled with this advice. But in December, 1867, before the law officers delivered their opinion, the dominion government of John A. Macdonald reaffirmed the position taken by the delegates in April, that the Crown should issue an order in council for annexation of the territory. The Canadians argued that the transfer should not be delayed by negotiations or correspondence "with private or third parties whose position, opinions and claims have heretofore embarrassed both Governments in dealing with this question." Such delay, they asserted, might involve serious consequences, since the westward advance of mining and agricultural settlement and "the avowed policy of the Washington Government to acquire territory from other powers by purchase or otherwise" necessitated immediate action. To emphasize the urgency of their request, they asked for a reply by cable.[71]

The Canadian resolutions reached the Colonial Office at about the same time as the opinion of the law officers, and the two communications strengthened the conviction of Buckingham and his staff that the Canadians would not progress toward their objectives without more guidance and, perhaps, pressure from London. As Sir Frederic Rogers pointed out, the suggestion that the Company should not be consulted in the disposition of its property was equivalent to stating that "in appropriating other people's property time should not be lost by allowing them an opportunity of saying anything on the subject." [72] The threat that the United States or its citizens might in some way gain control over Rupert's Land, the Colonial Office agreed, remained serious, although the Senate's rejection of Seward's treaty for the purchase of St. Thomas and St. John in the Danish West Indies was an encouraging sign that a reaction against expansion had begun to set in.

Clearly, Canada and the Hudson's Bay Company could not be brought together if the British government restricted itself to the role of referee. In the estimation of the Colonial Office, the Company overvalued its property and Canada dismissed the Company's rights too lightly. If the Canadian proposal was accepted, Buckingham was convinced the Company would get short shrift. Canadian courts would not be likely to support the Company's claims, and before the tardy processes of appeal to the Privy Council had been completed, emigrants would have swarmed over the Company's lands, and its rights would be extinct. "The people who had expelled the bears and wolves, and turned the wilderness into fields, would laugh to scorn any demands for payment from a Company sitting in Fenchurch street." [73] If Buckingham informed Canada that the Crown would agree to its acquisition of Rupert's Land only on condition that it recognized the validity of the charter, however, he would be acting with undue favoritism to the Company. Buckingham concluded that he must adopt a course that avoided both extremes. Also, he must find a solution that involved no charges upon the British government or upon Canada. But first he must prepare the two parties for negotiation. To this end he sent a copy of the Canadian resolutions to the Company and a copy of the law officers' opinion to the Canadian government. The Company, of course, was not favored with the legal arguments supporting its claims.

The major question remained as to what proposal the British government could make which both Canada and the Company might be brought to accept. Buckingham decided that the best prospect for a settlement lay in a modified version of the proposals made by the Duke of Newcastle in 1864 for compensating the Company from money derived from land sales. Buckingham's first plan was for the Imperial government to reach an agreement with the Company for the sale of its proprietary rights to the Crown, and then to transfer jurisdiction to Canada subject to the stipulations of the agreement.[74] There was a serious defect in his scheme, as his colleagues in the cabinet pointed out. If Canada refused to accept the terms, the British government might be left with the responsibility of governing an unwanted crown colony. The plan was therefore modified to provide that Canada must be a partner to any agreement.

Discussion within the Colonial Office proceeded during the first months of 1868 at a leisurely pace, too slowly for the governor and committee or for the Canadian government. The Company's directors, berated by the stockholders for failing to realize returns on land sales, were particularly anxious for evidence that the future of Rupert's Land was under active consideration. Their increasing frustration with the British government for its continued inactivity had been demonstrated by their reaction to McEwen's proposals of January, 1866. It was demonstrated again in their eagerness to negotiate with James Walker later in the same year.

Walker was a Yorkshireman of large ideas who professed to have the support of Lord Milton, the explorer, and other wealthy persons for the establishment of a colonizing company.[75] In October, 1866, Walker proposed that the Company sell the fertile belt to him and his associates for £1,000,000, the nonarable parts of Rupert's Land to remain the property of the Hudson's Bay Company.[76] The directors, though recognizing that Walker's offer came under the same strictures as McEwen's, apparently concluded that the knowledge that the Company's property was in demand might cause the Canadians to negotiate. They informed Walker that, should the British government free the Company from its restrictions, they would be ready to consider an offer, although they would not pledge themselves in advance to accept £1,000,000.[77]

The directors' estimation of Walker's potentialities was highly exaggerated. In May, 1867, he inquired as to the price at which he could buy land in Rupert's Land. The Company secretary, probably visualizing the sale of a large tract, asked Walker how much land he desired. When Walker replied that he wanted only 100 or 200 acres, he ceased to interest the governor and committee.[78]

The frustration over continued stalemate, which had caused the governor and committee to treat with McEwen and with Walker, steadily increased as months passed. By February, 1868, the vexation had become so acute that the directors sent Sir Curtis Lampson, the deputy governor, to see Buckingham. Lampson accused the British government of being a party to injustice by its assignment of Rupert's Land to Canada, and argued that it was morally bound to protect the interests of the Company by intervening to break the deadlock. This was precisely what the colonial secretary hoped to do, and Lampson was receptive to his proposal to seek a settlement on the basis of Newcastle's plan.[79]

Lampson's visit was an encouraging indication that the Company might accept a more moderate amount for its land than it had previously been willing to consider. But there remained the more difficult task of inducing the Canadian government to agree to a plan requiring substantial payments to the Company. The Macdonald government had to recognize the crosscurrents of Canadian society and had to avoid any arrangement that would alienate important elements in the Conservative party. The Western farmers, to whom George Brown's *Globe* sought in particular to appeal, might be antagonistic to a government that seemed to lack zeal for the opening of the West, and Macdonald was not the man to concede such a talking point to the opposition Liberal party.

Macdonald and the British Canadian members of his cabinet needed no convincing that Rupert's Land was important to the dominion. Canada, they realized, could not hope to achieve national stability unless it possessed this territory. The French Canadians, however, had their doubts. Before the establishment of the federation, most French Canadian politicians had been either cool or antagonistic to the acquisition of the Northwest Territories. They feared that Brown and the Clear Grits were plotting to institute representation by population, which would swamp the French Canadians and endanger their institutions.[80] The protection afforded Quebec by the British North America Act quieted the fears of domination by a British majority, but did not dispel them. By 1867 Sir George Cartier, leader of the French in the Conservative party, had come to accept the desirability of acquisition in the national interest, but he supported it with less ardor than some of his colleagues, notably William McDougall, for whom annexation of the West had been a major objective for almost twenty years. On one point all factions were agreed. The acquisition of Rupert's Land would cost money. Not even Brown believed that the validity of the Company's rights to Rupert's Land could be successfully challenged.[81] But until federation was completed, Canada could make no financial commitment. In the meantime, the Company's price might be reduced by prolonged Canadian refusal to offer any payment whatsoever. It was a risky game, as the Macdonald cabinet realized, for the United States might steal the prize, but the state of the Canadian treasury before and immediately after federation dictated that the gamble must be taken.

Through private advice from Governor-General Monck, Buckingham was aware of the Canadian tactics, but he hoped that his plan for payments from land revenues might be acceptable, since it would forestall direct levies on the Canadian treasury. But when he asked Monck how the Macdonald government would react, he received a discouraging reply. Monck contended that payment of royalties from land sales would be impossible, since the land could be settled only by free grants such as the United States provided by the Homestead Act. Reserves of land to the Company would therefore impede settlement and create irritation between the Company and the inhabitants.[82]

Buckingham nevertheless determined to try for an agreement on the basis he had proposed. Two steps were involved. The law officers had advised in January, 1868, that an act of Parliament must be passed before the Crown could assume direct control over Rupert's Land, and the consent of the Company must be secured before any transfer of authority was made. Buckingham therefore prepared a bill by which the Crown could assign the territory to Canada after an arrangement satisfactory to the parties concerned had been reached. This legislation, the Rupert's Land Act,[83] became law without difficulty on July 31, 1868. It authorized the British government to assign Rupert's Land and the territories between it and British Columbia to the Dominion of Canada on request of the Canadian Parliament. But British approval was conditional upon agreement between the Company and Canada on the terms of transfer. Passage of the act thus merely removed a legal obstacle to the annexation of Rupert's Land to Canada. The fundamental problem remained.

When the Colonial Office inquired what terms the Company would accept on the basis of Newcastle's plan of compensation for land and mineral rights, the response indicated that years of attrition had not shrunk the directors' estimate of the value of their property. The Earl of Kimberley, Head's successor as governor, stated that Newcastle's proposals had extended only to the surrender of the fertile belt, whereas Buckingham wanted to extinguish the Company's rights in all Rupert's Land. For the surrender of the entire territory, Kimberley proposed the following terms:

1) The Company would retain its posts and stations with an area of 6,000 acres around each, except in the Red River settlement, where no reservation of land would be claimed.

2) The Company would receive 1 shilling for each acre within the chartered territory disposed of by the government. It would also be entitled to one-fourth of the revenue derived by the government from gold or silver mines. The total amount of compensation from both sources would not exceed £1,000,000.

3) Canada would confirm all titles to land alienated by the Company at Red River and elsewhere.

4) For every 50,000 acres granted or sold by the government, the Company might select a free grant of 5,000 acres.

5) No taxes would be imposed on any uncultivated land belonging to the Company, and no exceptional taxes would be imposed on the Company's other lands or on the Company's servants.

6) Canada would buy from the Company all the materials shipped to the West for construction of a telegraph. The payment would include the cost price and expenses incurred, with interest.

7) Until the £1,000,000 had been paid, no tariff would be imposed on furs exported by the Company, and no duties would be levied on articles imported by the Company into that part of the transferred territories outside the fertile belt.

8) The boundary between Canada and Rupert's Land would be defined before the cession was completed.[84]

These terms were more than Buckingham was willing to support. In particular he objected to the proposal that the Company select the free grants of land it would receive, and to its special exemptions from taxation.[85] But the duke had been sufficiently impressed by the law officers' opinions to refrain from outright rejection of the proposals. The Toronto *Globe,* always on the alert for evidences of collusion between government and vested interests, received the erroneous information that Buckingham had decided to support the Company's offer, and in a series of editorials poured abuse upon his head. This agreement, it screamed, was "preposterous," "outrageous," "a source of great joy to speculators and capitalists" who held the Company's stock. The duke had become the mouthpiece of the Company, the *Globe* alleged, and there were dark implications of scandalous connivance.[86] The *Globe's* alarm was unjustified. The Company's offer had been made, not as an ultimatum, but as a basis for bargaining; the British government had not endorsed the terms; and the Canadian government had no intention of accepting them. The Macdonald cabinet sent Cartier and McDougall to London to negotiate with the Company, authorizing them to arrange for the admission of the Northwest Territories to the Dominion of Canada, either with or without Rupert's Land. Any agreement on compensation was to be subject to the approval of the Canadian cabinet.[87]

Arriving in London in October, the delegates had a few exploratory interviews with Buckingham, but McDougall became ill and the discussions were suspended. Before McDougall recovered, Buckingham decided to use Kimberley's terms, with substantial modifications, as the basis for an offer to the Company. Buckingham's recommendations were as follows:

1) The amount of land to be retained by the Company around its posts would vary with the value of the land. The maximum in any area would be 6,000 acres; in the fertile belt it would be 3,000 acres for principal posts and 500 acres for minor stations.

2) The Company would receive one-fourth of all money paid the government for land. For free grants made for other than public purposes, the Company would receive 3 pence per acre. The Canadian government would also pay one-fourth of the sums received for gold or silver licenses or leases. The maximum that the Company could receive from all sources would be £1,000,000.

3) The Imperial government would confirm all titles to land that had been alienated by the Company at Red River or elsewhere.

4) The Company would have the right to select five lots of not less than 200 acres each in each township, on payment of surveying costs.

5) The boundary between Canada and Rupert's Land would be defined.

6) No wild lands would be taxed until they were surveyed and marked.

7) When the payment of £1,000,000 had been completed, either from land revenues or directly from the Canadian treasury, the Company's right to select township lots would cease, although it would retain those it already possessed.[88]

Before either the Company or the Canadian delegates could voice their reactions to these terms, the Derby-Disraeli government was ousted from office and the Liberal party returned to power. The Company's old bête noire, Gladstone, became prime minister, and Lord Granville was the new colonial secretary. With the change of administrations, Sir Stafford Northcote, who had been successively president of the Board of Trade and secretary of state for India in the Conservative ministry, replaced Kimberley as governor of the Company. Northcote thus had to play the peculiar role of judging whether the terms proposed by a cabinet of which he had been a member were advantageous to the Company. In his new capacity he deemed the terms inadequate, suggesting instead either acceptance of a substantial part of Kimberley's plan or Canadian purchase of the territory for cash or by the delivery of bonds.[89]

The rejection of Buckingham's proposal freed his successor from any commitment to support his terms. Granville was now a free agent from whom the Company could expect little sympathy. But Granville and the other members of the Gladstone cabinet recognized that immediate action was necessary. In the first place, the admission of British Columbia into the Dominion of Canada was contingent upon Canadian acquisition of the intervening territory. Buckingham had informed the government of British Columbia in November, 1867, that this was a necessary condition, and Granville agreed.[90] Second, Granville realized that the Company's rights to Rupert's Land could not be ignored, and that some compensation must be paid. Finally, the danger of conflict with the United States dictated the establishment of a strong government.[91]

Before issuing an ultimatum, however, Granville gave Canada and the Company a final opportunity to state their terms. In reply, Cartier and McDougall reiterated the Canadian position that the Company had no rights to the southern part of Rupert's Land, and attacked the Company in such violent terms that Northcote was moved to protest against "this transatlantic style of writing." Canada's major charge was that the Company had taken no action to relieve distress at Red River. Locusts had destroyed the crops in 1868. The people were in danger of starvation, the Canadian delegates declared, and, because the Company had done nothing, the Canadian Parliament had appropriated $20,000 to build a road from Lake of the Woods to Fort Garry over which provisions could be hauled to the settlement. No government representing the interests of its people could do otherwise, they stated, but the Company was unable or unwilling to provide even minimum assistance to a starving population.[92] The accusation of indifference to human suffering was unjust. The Company had provided relief, both by direct grants and by subscription funds raised under its auspices.

Accusations and counteraccusations between the Company and the Canadians served no useful purpose. The Canadian delegates, however, had a concrete proposal. The Company's claims had a nuisance value, since a prolonged lawsuit would have to precede their legal rejection. To avoid this unpleasant contingency, the dominion would offer a maximum of £106,000, and, if the Company refused, the Imperial government should transfer the territory to Canada, "subject to the rights of the Company." No effort was made to define this phrase, and it is interesting to speculate as to what agency McDougall and Cartier had in mind as the final authority to determine the Company's rights.[93] The Company's counterproposal, which proved to be its last before it was forced to accept a dictated settlement, was the creation of a crown colony on the basis suggested by Newcastle, or, failing that, the establishment by the Company of a government that would meet British requirements for effective control.[94] Neither suggestion was acceptable to the Gladstone administration, since both were directly contrary to the Imperial objective of relaxing home authority and establishing a strong, transcontinental British North America.

By the beginning of March, 1869, Granville had decided that a settlement could be reached only by imposing terms upon the contestants. On March 9 he issued what was in effect an ultimatum to the Company and Canada. His terms were essentially those that were finally accepted: payment of £300,000 and reservation to the Company of its posts and one-twentieth of the fertile belt, which Granville defined as the land bounded on the south by the United States, on the west by the Rocky Mountains, on the north by the north branch of the Saskatchewan, and on the east by Lake Winnipeg, Lake of the Woods, and the waters connecting them. In addition, Canada was to purchase the materials that the Company had stored for the unrealized telegraph at cost price, including transport charges but not interest, and subject to deductions for deterioration.[95]

In the event that the Company refused, Granville said its claims would be submitted to the Judicial Committee of the Privy Council. The nature of his pressure on the Canadians is not indicated in his correspondence, but there were two levers he could apply. If the case before the Privy Council was decided in favor of the Company, which was likely, Canada might be forced to pay a much higher price for the property. Also, the "no-transfer" agreement that Cardwell had imposed upon the Company might be withdrawn. Cartier accepted Granville's terms with alacrity, but McDougall, who had been hopeful that Canada might acquire Rupert's Land without expenditure, was loath to agree. Finally, after several days of resistance, he acceded to Granville's proposal.[96] He had no alternative, for Granville's terms would cost Canada less than any others previously advanced by the Colonial Office. Even the Toronto *Globe,* which had denounced Buckingham as a tool of the Company and had consistently maintained that Canada should pay nothing, expressed pleasure at the moderation of Granville's terms. He "takes the tone of an umpire," declared the *Globe*'s editorialist, "and we can discover no leaning to the Company's side." [97]

The Company accepted with far greater reluctance. In conferences with the colonial secretary, Governor Northcote had been impressed with the necessity of immediate submission, and finally agreed to support the terms. But it was a difficult task to convince either the directors or the proprietors that the proposals did not mean virtual confiscation. When Northcote read Granville's ultimatum to the committee, he opened a stormy controversy. All the directors agreed that the terms were unjust, and three of them, Richard Potter, Edward W. T. Hamilton, and George Lyall, argued that the Company should defy Granville rather than accept a pittance for its claims. Not only was the cash sum insufficient, they protested, but the tariffs that Canada would impose on the Company's imports would eliminate any profits the Company might make on the transaction. The Company would pay out £15,-000 per year for customs duties, and, in addition, would have to pay taxes. These charges would soon neutralize any advantages to be gained by accepting £300,000. Sir Curtis Lampson, the deputy governor, and two members of the committee, Eden Colvile and James S. Hodgson,[98] agreed to support Granville's terms, subject to certain modifications. The principal reservations were that Canada should lay no export duty on furs, and that the Company should receive one-tenth instead of one-twentieth of the fertile belt.[99]

Since Granville had stressed that his terms were not subject to argument, but that details could be discussed between the Canadian delegates and the Company, the only course open to the board was to treat these changes as matters of detail. Cartier and McDougall did not regard the doubling of the Company's allotment of land as a detail, and so informed the directors. They also pointed out that tariffs on exports were not imposed by Canada, but they refused to commit future Canadian Parliaments by a promise never to impose duties on furs.[100] There was no more room for negotiation. At a meeting on March 20, 1869, the majority of the committee voted to accept Granville's terms. Hamilton and Potter did not attend, and Lyall registered a final protest,[101] but the decision had been made.

The question arises as to why the directors, if they believed that the Company's claims to Rupert's Land were sound, did not defy the Imperial government. The answer is threefold. Although a favorable verdict by the courts was likely, litigation was certain to be prolonged and expensive. Second, although the validity of the charter might be upheld, the boundaries would remain in doubt and their definition would cause further delay and expense. Finally, even if the judgment was entirely in the Company's favor, the land would be of little value without a substantial outlay for the development of transportation and communications facilities, and the expenditure might be fruitless unless the government of the territory was strong enough to support the Company's exclusive privileges.

To an objective judge, as to the majority of directors, these considerations would seem to be compelling reasons for acceptance of the Imperial ultimatum. But the Company shareholders were not detached observers, and it was not to be expected that they would accept the settlement in good grace. At a meeting of the general court on March 25, 1869, Northcote formally proposed the acceptance of Granville's terms. The reaction was instantaneous and violent. In the ensuing tumult, amidst cries of "Treachery!" Northcote attempted to defend the decision. Opponents of the settlement, far more vocal than its supporters, shouted that the terms were confiscatory, and that tariff charges would wipe out all the profits. These were the protests of disillusioned men who since 1863 had hoped for a bounteous repast and were now served a thin gruel. Time was required to adjust to the inevitable, and the meeting was adjourned, to reconvene on April 9.[102] After a stormy three hours, the recommendation of the governor and committee was accepted by what the recording secretary called an immense majority; he later defined it as "at least two to one." The recorder added to the minutes of this historic session an unprecedented statement of his own views: "The result would have been otherwise had the long-expected but never realized cooperation of an Anglo-American Colonization Society been forthcoming, or had the opposition suggested even partial retention of the dividends for the purpose of ultimate colonization." [103]

The validity of this interpretation is doubtful, since it appears evident that the Company could not resist the combined pressure of the Imperial and Canadian governments, and could not undertake a colonization program alone. But the secretary's concluding statement is more difficult to dispute: "The argument of the minority was the more cogent, but the reasoning of the Chairman, as the event proved, was found to be most convincing." [104]

The Canadian Parliament approved the terms without serious opposition, and December 1, 1869, was set as the effective date of the transfer.[105] But the end was not yet. Among the population of Red River, which had been left out of consideration, were some disquieted half-breeds led by Louis Riel. Fearful of their future under Canadian rule, they organized an insurrection to resist the destiny assigned to them.[106] Against whom were they in rebellion? Canada insisted the Company must assume responsibility for suppressing Riel and his followers, and refused to accept the transfer until tranquillity was restored. The governor and committee insisted that, since Canada had asked for the surrender of the territory on December 1, 1869, and the Company had agreed, all that remained to complete the transaction was formal action by the British government. In the meantime, they contended, the British government, which temporarily exercised authority over Rupert's Land, had at least some responsibility for the restoration of order. In the midst of this confusion, each party hurled recriminations against the other. Deputy Governor Lampson alleged that "the present unfortunate condition of affairs at Red River has been brought about entirely by the want of judgment on the part of Canadian authorities in attempting to take possession of and survey the land previous to any proclamation or announcement on the part of the Imperial Government." [107]

The Toronto *Globe,* which had previously expressed tender concern for the welfare of the Red River half-breeds, now adopted a different tone:

> For a handful of half castes in this way to claim authority over almost the third of a continent is a big thing but the days of such pretensions are over, and though they were not, these men are

not of the stuff nor are they in the position to make such pretensions good.

. . . That country is bound to be occupied, and at no distant day, by thousands and millions of industrious cultivators, and the few foolish persons who are now thinking to stop the way are no wiser, and will be no more successful, than Mrs. Partington in her well-known effort to brush back the Atlantic tide with a mop and pail.[108]

For a time Granville considered using Imperial authority in Rupert's Land for one year to establish order, after which Canada would accept control. But, as Granville knew, this was a highly dangerous expedient, to be adopted only as an extreme measure, since the British government might be left in charge if Canada should decide against assuming control. He and Gladstone also discussed the possibility of holding a plebiscite at Red River to ascertain the wishes of the inhabitants as to their political future.[109] Here, too, there was a risk, for the inhabitants might vote against annexation by Canada. Fortunately, neither measure was necessary, for delegates from Red River reached an agreement with the Canadian government, embodied in the Manitoba Act. The rebellion, if that it ever was, collapsed on May 11, 1870. The Company received payment from Sir John Rose as the Canadian representative, and on July 15, 1870, Rupert's Land officially became part of the Dominion of Canada.[110]

The Riel Rebellion was, in a sense, an appropriate conclusion to the life of the chartered monopoly. Both the proprietary Company and the half-breeds who supported Riel were victims of a civilization to which they could not be reconciled. Canadian interests dictated that Rupert's Land must be traversed by the railroad, joining the eastern parts of the dominion with British Columbia; its fertile acres must be open to settlement by Canadian farmers; its possession was essential if Canada was to become a strong nation. Thus the fur-trade monopoly and the free Red River hunters with whom it contended both became casualties in the advance of an agricultural-industrial society.

The Hudson's Bay Company continued to be an important factor in the economy of the Canadian West after the loss of its proprietary powers. Contrary to the fears of many of its stockholders, the agreement of 1869 was a highly profitable one, at least for those whose families retained their shares for the next two generations. The rush of settlers to the West in the twentieth century brought the Company millions of dollars of revenue from land sales. The increase of population also brought additional profits to the Company's department stores and sales shops, and the fur trade belied the pessimism of Sir George Simpson and others by continuing to provide substantial revenues. But the days of the Great Monopoly were done. No longer was the Company a factor in international politics, either as an active force or as an obstacle. During the years after its amalgamation with the North West Company, the great Hudson's Bay Company made a substantial contribution to the expansion of the British Empire. As the heir of the North West Company, it was the sole British interest on the Pacific slope, and its influence was evident in two boundary negotiations. When the agricultural frontier reached the international boundary in Minnesota and Dakota, it became obvious to the Company, as to other interested parties, that the fur-trade monopoly over 1,400,000 square miles [111] could not long continue. The sale in 1863 to a group with avowed colonizing objectives was based on the recognition that the empire of furs must give way to the farmer. In turn, the sale of the proprietary rights to Canada was dictated by the admission that such colonization could not be successfully undertaken under private auspices.

The urgency that American expansionist tendencies gave to the final negotiations caused the Company to be attacked as a barrier to settlement—the "Stop-the-Way Company." This charge was unjustified. Although it was true that the stockholders' insistence on compensation delayed Canadian acquisition of Rupert's Land, settlement of the prairies would not have begun earlier had the negotiations been less prolonged. Canada annexed the territory almost as soon as it was able to assume the responsibility for effective government, and the settlement of the West did not take place until the exhaustion of the American frontier turned agricultural emigration toward Canada. The proprietary Company performed an important function for Canada and the British Empire; that it did so for motives of profit does not lessen the magnitude of the achievement.

*Notes*

# ABBREVIATIONS

A.B.T.   Proceedings of the Alaskan Boundary Tribunal
H.B.A.   Hudson's Bay Archives
H.B.S.   Hudson's Bay Record Society
P.A.C.   Public Archives of Canada
P.R.O.   Public Record Office

# NOTES

## Chapter 1

[1] The exact date of birth of the North West Company is a matter of dispute. There were references to a "North West Company" as early as 1776, and a formidable association of fur traders formed in 1779 used the same name. The company was reorganized in 1784. During the next three years, the North West Company was locked in a struggle with Gregory, McLeod, and Company. The amalgamation of the two rivals in 1787 gave the North West Company far greater strength in its competition with the Hudson's Bay Company. No adequate history of the North West Company has been written because of the paucity of information. Gordon Charles Davidson, *The North West Company* (Berkeley: University of California Press, 1918), although the product of assiduous research, is nevertheless far from a definitive work. The most satisfactory account is the introduction to W. Stewart Wallace, ed., *Documents Relating to the North West Company* (Toronto: Champlain Society, 1934). Most of my statements about the North West Company are based upon this source.

[2] The dynamic qualities of the North West Company have conventionally been contrasted with the lethargy of its Hudson's Bay rival, which has been described as "asleep by the Frozen Sea" while the Nor'Westers appropriated the trade of the interior. This legend has been grossly exaggerated. Recent publications of the Hudson's Bay Record Society have done much to correct the misinterpretation. See, for example, Richard Glover's introductions to E. E. Rich and A. M. Johnson, eds., *Cumberland House Journals and Inland Journals, 1775–82, First Series, 1775–79* (London, 1951), and *Second Series, 1779–82* (London: 1952), Hudson's Bay Record Society (hereafter referred to as H.B.S.), Vols. XIV and XV.

[3] For further details, see the bibliography in *Canadian Historical Review* (Mar., 1932), 45–50. Also see E. E. Rich, ed., *Colin Robertson's Correspondence Book, September 1817 to September 1822* (London: Hudson's Bay Record Society, 1939); Arthur S. Morton, *A History of the Canadian West to 1870–71* (London: T. Nelson & Sons, [1939]), pp. 508–622.

[4] Coltman to Sherbrooke, May 14, 1818, confidential, encl. in Sherbrooke to Bathurst, May 16, 1818, C.O. 42/181, P.R.O.

[5] Selkirk to Governor and Committee (hereafter referred to as Gov. and Comm.), Feb. 14, 1818, A-10/2, Hudson's Bay Archives (hereafter referred to as H.B.A.).

[6] Profits, which between 1690 and 1800 had ranged from 60 to 70 per cent of the original subscribed capital stock, were greatly reduced between 1800 and 1821. North West Company competition reduced dividends to 4 per cent between 1800 and 1808; no dividends were declared between 1808 and 1814; between 1814 and 1821, dividends of 4 per cent were again paid annually. A-42/3, H.B.A.; Pelly to Lords of Committee of Privy Council for Trade, Feb. 7, 1838. A-8/2, H.B.A. See Douglas MacKay, *The Honourable Company* (London: Cassell, 1937), App. D, pp. 374–377.

[7] I must dissent from the contention of Morton, *op. cit.*, p. 617, that Selkirk could soon have adapted himself to union with the North West Company.

[8] Goulburn's interest in this report is indicated in a memorandum, Whittam, Journal Office, House of Commons, to Goulburn, Jan. 21, 1820, C.O. 42/186, P.R.O.

⁹ John Montgomery to Goulburn, Jan. 29, 1820, C.O. 42/186, P.R.O.; Gov. and Comm. to Williams, May 25, 1820, A-6/19, H.B.A.

¹⁰ Croker to Goulburn, Sept. 8, 1829, in Louis J. Jennings, ed., *The Correspondence and Diaries of . . . John Wilson Croker* (3 vols.; London: J. Murray, 1884), I, 147.

¹¹ Testimony of Ellice in *Report of the Select Committee of the House of Commons on the Hudson's Bay Company . . .* (London: 1857), p. 323. In 1863, shortly before his death, Ellice wrote John Rose: "I made this Hudson's Bay Co.—by the union of the Canada and the English Fur Companies in 1818." Ellice to Rose, June 9, 1863, in Ellice Papers, National Library of Scotland. Microfilm copy in Library, University of California, Los Angeles, from Public Archives of Canada.

¹² For a good short account of the background of the union, see John P. Pritchett, *The Red River Valley, 1811–1849* (New Haven: Yale University Press, 1942), pp. 215–222. In my opinion the explanation of Goulburn's conduct in terms of Ellice's influence is unproved and is almost certainly an oversimplification. The allegations that Ellice controlled Goulburn rest upon the parallelism of their views and the statements of Selkirk and other protagonists of the Hudson's Bay Company. But Goulburn's attitude can also be at least partially explained in terms of the hostility toward the Hudson's Bay Company evidenced then and later by other members of the British government and of Parliament. Such a prejudice would have made Goulburn more willing to accept the North West Company's case.

¹³ Wallace, *op. cit.*, pp. 29–30.

¹⁴ There are many accounts of the "diplomacy" of the amalgamation. See, for example, Morton, *op. cit.*, pp. 614 ff.

¹⁵ 1 & 2 Geo. IV, cap. 66, July 2, 1821, in Hudson's Bay Company, *Charters, Statutes, Orders in Council &c. Relating to the Hudson's Bay Company* (London: Hudson's Bay Company, 1931), pp. 93–102.

¹⁶ Royal License, Dec. 5, 1821, *ibid.*, p. 217.

¹⁷ The unwillingness of the British government to incur expense in the administration of Rupert's Land is indicated by its refusal to appoint justices of the peace for the Indian territories. See Pelly to Bathurst, May 21, 1822, A-8/1; Minutes of General Court, May 29, 1822, A-2/3; and Bathurst to Berens, May 31, 1822, A-8/1, all in H.B.A.

¹⁸ Gov. and Comm. to Williams, Feb. 27, 1822, A-6/20; Gov. and Comm. to Simpson, Feb. 27, 1822, D-5/1, A-6/20, all in H.B.A. The boundaries of the departments varied from time to time in accordance with the requirements of the trade.

¹⁹ R. Harvey Fleming, ed., *Minutes of Council Northern Department of Rupert Land, 1821–31* (London: 1940), H.B.S., III, xiii.

²⁰ Simpson to Berens, July 23, 1859, private, D-4/84a, H.B.A.

²¹ Douglas to Gov. and Comm., Oct. 18, 1838, B-223b/21, H.B.A.

²² Ogden to Simpson, Mar. 10, 1849, private, D-5/24, H.B.A.

²³ New Caledonia constituted the interior of the present province of British Columbia.

## Chapter 2

¹ For a published statement of capital and dividends, see Douglas MacKay, *The Honourable Company* (London: Cassell, 1937), Apps. D, E, pp. 374–383. At the time of the coalition the parties agreed to provide equal shares of capital and to divide profits equally. This arrangement remained in effect for three years.

² Isbister to Alexander Rowand, July 3, 1847, encl. in Simpson to Gov. and Comm., Nov. 16, 1848, A-12/4, H.B.A.

³ Profits were substantial but far from the rumored princely returns. Dividends ranged from 4 to 25 per cent between 1821 and 1863:

| | | | |
|---|---|---|---|
| 1821— 4 | 1825—10 | 1829—20 | 1833—16 |
| 1822— 4 | 1826—10 | 1830—20 | 1834—10 |
| 1823— 4 | 1827—10 | 1831—20 | 1835—15 |
| 1824— 4 | 1828—20 | 1832—20 | 1836—23 |

| 1837—10 | 1844—10 | 1851—10 | 1858—10 |
|---------|---------|---------|---------|
| 1838—25 | 1845—15 | 1852—10 | 1859—10 |
| 1839—23 | 1846—10 | 1853—10 | 1860—15 |
| 1840—15 | 1847—10 | 1854—10 | 1861—10 |
| 1841—15 | 1848—10 | 1855—10 | 1862—10 |
| 1842—15 | 1849—10 | 1856—10 | 1863—11 |
| 1843—10 | 1850—10 | 1857—10 |         |

The dividends were increased by stock bonuses. The capitalization of £400,000 established in 1825 was augmented without outlay by the proprietors to £440,000 in 1850, £462,000 in 1852, and £500,000 in 1854. A-42/3–7, H.B.A. See also MacKay, *op. cit.*, pp. 377–379.

⁴ This information is derived from a biographical sketch in E. E. Rich, ed., *The Letters of John McLoughlin from Fort Vancouver to the Governor and Committee, Second Series, 1839–44* (London: 1943), H.B.S., VI, 399–401. See also Reginald Saw, "Sir John H. Pelly, Bart.," *British Columbia Historical Quarterly*, XIII (Jan., 1949), 23–32.

⁵ At the same time Simpson was granted his knighthood. The occasion for the award of these honors was the Company's participation in the arrangements for the Dease-Simpson Arctic expedition of 1837–1839, although Pelly was awarded his baronetcy upon the much broader basis of distinguished service to the Company.

⁶ This statement is based upon an analysis of private letters in H.B.A. written by Pelly and other members of the board. See, for example, two letters from Halkett to Pelly, undated [1820?], A-10/2, which indicate that Pelly dominated the committee's negotiations with the Colonial Office in the last stages of the dispute with the North West Company. Berens, after his retirement as governor, continued as a member of the committee.

⁷ Pelly to Simpson, Dec. 1, 1841, D-5/6, H.B.A.

⁸ Pelly to Simpson, Sept. 29, 1842, D-5/7, H.B.A. In this letter, which dealt entirely with Company business, Pelly declared that his health had been "completely restored."

⁹ Colvile to Simpson, Dec. 20, 1850, private; Barclay to Simpson, Dec. 20, 1850, private and confidential, both in D-5/29, H.B.A.

¹⁰ McDonell to Simpson, July 24, 1852, D-5/34, H.B.A.

¹¹ Arthur S. Morton, *Sir George Simpson* (Toronto: Binfords, 1944), p. 66, declares: "Andrew Colvile was, to all appearance, the most potent influence on the Board from 1810 on to the union, and, though the evidence is less patent thereafter, right through to the end of his life." I do not entirely agree with this estimate of Colvile's influence after 1821, although his authority was undeniably great.

¹² Toronto *Globe*, May 1, 1868, p. 2.

¹³ For further information on Ellice, see my article, "Edward 'Bear' Ellice," *The Beaver*, Outfit 285 (Summer, 1954), 26–29.

¹⁴ The correspondence between Simpson and Williams grew steadily more hostile between 1821 and 1826. For a good illustration of their relationship, see Simpson's "Remarks on certain paragraphs in Governor Williams Despatch of 11th September, 1825 . . . ," Nov. 4, 1825, D-4/7, H.B.A.

¹⁵ See, for example, Simpson to Pelly, Dec. 1, 1843, D-4/63, H.B.A. No attempt is made here to provide more than a sketch of Simpson's character as governor. There is no satisfactory biography of him. The best is Morton, *op. cit.*, but even this is far from being a good portrait.

¹⁶ Pelly to Simpson, Mar. 2, 1846, D-5/16, H.B.A.

¹⁷ E. O. S. Scholefield and F. W. Howay, *British Columbia from the Earliest Times to the Present* (Vancouver: S. J. Clarke Publishing Company, 1914), pp. 341–342.

¹⁸ Simpson employed Stuart Derbishire, the king's printer, on the Company's business in Canada. There is evidence in the Company files that Simpson bribed Sir Francis Hincks and John Ross, which should not be surprising in view of the moral tone of Canadian politics in the 1850's. For example, in an effort to secure an

ocean mail contract in which he and Hugh Allan were interested (unconnected with the Hudson's Bay Company), Simpson first offered to "adduce 1,000 weighty arguments," to be given to "A and B," for every year of the contract. Later he offered "to produce 10,000 golden reasons" for the mail contract and a tugboat contract. Simpson to Derbishire, Feb. 27, 1854, private, and Mar. 4, 1854, confidential, both in D-4/82, H.B.A. From internal evidence in these letters and from other letters in this file and in D-5/43 and D-5/45, it is clear that "A" and "B" were Hincks and Ross.

¹⁹ Derbishire to Simpson, May 12, 1852, D-5/33, H.B.A. The frequent dispatch of buffalo tongues to politicians caused one of them to express the fear that he might be accused of taking bribes. Derbishire replied that Sir George "only pleaded . . . [his] cause with many tongues." Derbishire to Simpson, July 23, 1852, D-5/34, H.B.A.

²⁰ "Estate of Sir George Simpson, Minutes of the Proceedings of the Executors," D-6/3, H.B.A.

²¹ Morton, *op. cit.*, p. 3, says that Simpson was born in 1787. The *Dictionary of National Biography* gives his date of birth as 1792. The date recorded on his tombstone in Montreal is 1787.

²² Charles R. Dodd, *The Peerage, Baronetage, and Knightage, of Great Britain and Ireland* (London, 1844). Dodd asked Simpson to provide additional information, but Simpson ignored the request. The complete entry is as follows: "SIMPSON, Knt. Bachel. Creat. 1841. Sir George Simpson, Governor of the Hudson's Bay Company's settlements. Residence—New Grove House, Bromley."

²³ This was the agreement with George N. Sanders, who was to use his influence to sell the Company's Oregon property to the United States. See John S. Galbraith, "George N. Sanders, 'Influence Man' for the Hudson's Bay Company," *Oregon Historical Quarterly*, LIII (Sept., 1952), 159–176. See also pp. 257–259 of this book.

²⁴ There were 1,565 contractual employees, including officers, in the employ of the Company in North America in 1845. This total is derived by adding the abstracts of accounts from the various departments: B-239g/25, Northern Department, including Columbia and New Caledonia; B-135g/20, Southern Department; and B-134g/20, Montreal Department, all in H.B.A.

²⁵ Memorandum by Edward Roberts, Mar. 19, 1837, encl. in Pelly to Smith, Mar. 20, 1837, A-10/4, H.B.A. By "Canadians" Roberts meant French Canadian employees who might or might not be of mixed blood.

²⁶ The reports were not entirely baseless. Although both the Company and George Simpson discouraged corporal punishment, there is abundant evidence that laborers, particularly in remote areas, were physically punished. On several occasions Simpson had to caution officers against such methods. As Andrew Colvile wrote Simpson in regard to reports of harsh discipline by John McLoughlin, "That long rope of the Doctor's is an ugly matter—but those cases will occur in countries where there is no practical legal jurisdiction." Colvile to Simpson, Sept. 20, 1841, D-5/6, H.B.A. Simpson wrote Donald Manson in New Caledonia, "You must really put a check upon the 'club law' which prevails in your district." Simpson to Manson, June 19, 1853, D-4/73, H.B.A.

²⁷ The annual wages of an average common laborer were gradually increased from about £12 in the 1820's to £22 sterling in 1860. The wages of certain other categories increased even less. In 1828, maximum wages of boatbuilders were set at £30 per year. An advertisement by the Company in 1858 offered the same wage. Annual salaries of clerks were usually between £75 and £100, but clerks had the additional inducement of possible commissions as chief traders or chief factors entitled to a share in the profits. The average annual payment to a chief factor between 1821 and 1833 was £762.3.4. This was a larger return than the salary of the Company's secretary, as the secretary indignantly pointed out. Smith to Pelly, July 21, 1835, A-10/2, H.B.A. The information on wages is partially derived from the following sources: Minutes of Council, Northern Department, July 10, 1828, D-4/92; Gov. and Comm. to Simpson, Apr. 14, 1859, D-5/49; Simpson to Ogden, Mar. 25, 1859, D-4/78, all in H.B.A. Servants paid for purchases from the Company's stores at prices 50 per cent above

price cost, a moderate advance. Despite reasonable prices, some impecunious employees went into debt to the Company, but there is no evidence that the Company deliberately encouraged the contracting of debts as a means of retaining employees in its service. When the northern council in 1848 attempted to raise prices as a counteraction to increased wages, the governor and committee disapproved. They also disapproved charging Sandwich Island laborers, who received £30 per year, 140 per cent increases on invoice prices when European laborers, who received £17, were charged only a 50 per cent increase. Gov. and Comm. to Simpson, Apr. 4, 1849, A-6/28, H.B.A.

²³ This is the most common spelling of Ogden's middle name.

## Chapter 3

¹ Simpson to Gov. and Comm., Oct. 8, 1827, D-4/14, H.B.A. The statements on population are derived from two sources: Robert Gourlay, *Statistical Account of Upper Canada* (2 vols.; London: Simpkin & Marshall, 1822); *Census of Canada, 1870–71* (5 vols.; Ottawa, 1876). Volumes IV and V of the latter contain summaries of the censuses of New France and Canada from 1665 to 1871, but the information is not explicit as to the distribution of the population, particularly in the frontier districts. Reports from officers at the Company's posts are consequently more helpful for unsettled areas than the statistics of the government. Statistics on population hereafter in this chapter are derived from the census reports.

² Simpson to Gov. and Comm., Mar. 15, 1827, D-4/15, H.B.A.

³ Halifax currency was one of the three basic units of money in British North America. The relative values were: £100 sterling = £120 Halifax currency = £108 Canadian sterling. The correspondence of the officers of the Hudson's Bay Company does not always specify the type of pound in which payment was made, but whenever possible I shall indicate the unit of value.

⁴ *In the Privy Council. In the Matter of the Boundary Between the Dominion of Canada and the Colony of Newfoundland in the Labrador Peninsula* (12 vols.; London: [1926]), VII, 3119.

⁵ Copy of lease, Oct. 1, 1822, E-20/1, H.B.A.

⁶ Simpson to William Smith, Nov. 20, 1826, D-4/13, H.B.A.

⁷ J. F. La Rocque, Portneuf, to McGillivrays, Thain, and Co., Jan. 26, 1826, D-4/119; Simpson to Gov. and Comm., Apr. 26, 1826, D-4/7; Simpson to Smith, Nov. 20, 1826, D-4/13, all in H.B.A.

⁸ For a detailed account of these incidents, see James Keith to Simpson, Apr. 13, 1831, D-4/125, H.B.A.

⁹ The firm of Boyden and Lampson bought the lease in 1827 from James McDouall, who had acquired it from Goudie. James Keith to Smith, Sept. 8, 1827, D-5/2, H.B.A.

¹⁰ Smith to James Keith, Aug. 20, 1830, A-6/22, H.B.A.

¹¹ Simpson to Bewley, July 1, 1831, D-4/18, H.B.A.

¹² Smith to Keith, June 22, July 6, Oct. 22, 1831, all in A-6/22, H.B.A.

¹³ Simpson to Gov. and Comm., Aug. 26, 1830, D-4/97, H.B.A.

¹⁴ Simpson to Gov. and Comm., Aug. 15, 1822, D-4/85, H.B.A.

¹⁵ Report of St. Maurice District, by Cuthbert Cumming, Feb. 24, 1831, B-230e/1; Simpson to Keith, July 2, 1831, D-4/18, both in H.B.A.

¹⁶ Keith to Simpson, Apr. 25, 1835, D-4/127, H.B.A.

¹⁷ Simpson to Gov. and Comm., Aug. 16, 1836, D-4/104, H.B.A.

¹⁸ Simpson to Gov. and Comm., Sept. 24, 1839, D-4/107; Sept. 10, 1845, D-4/67; John McLeod to Simpson, Mar. 28, 1844, D-5/10; Oct. 20, 1845, D-5/15; Simpson to Gov. and Comm., Nov. 20, 1846, D-4/68, all in H.B.A.

¹⁹ Simpson to Gov. and Comm., Dec. 11, 1847, D-4/69, H.B.A.

²⁰ Simpson to Gov. and Comm., Nov. 20, 1846, D-4/68; Dec. 11, 1847, D-4/69, both in H.B.A.

[21] Gov. and Comm. to Simpson, Apr. 16, 1858, A-6/33; McNaughton to Simpson, Jan. 3, 1858, D-5/46; Nov. 11, Dec. 7, 1858, D-5/47, all in H.B.A.

[22] Siveright, Fort Coulonge, to Simpson, Apr. 26, 1827, D-4/120; Simpson to Gov. and Comm., Oct. 8, 1827, D-4/14, both in H.B.A.

[23] Siveright to Simpson, Apr. 29, 1831, D-4/125, H.B.A.

[24] Simpson to Gov. and Comm., June 20, 1841, D-4/58, H.B.A.

[25] Simpson to Gov. and Comm., June 21, 1843, D-4/62, H.B.A. The 1843 depression in the timber trade was attributed to British alterations in duties on timber which increased competition with Canadian timber by foreign states, particularly in the Baltic area.

[26] Simpson to Gov. and Comm., Dec. 11, 1847, D-4/69, H.B.A.

[27] Simpson to Smith, Mar. 10, 1855, D-4/75; Taylor to Simpson, Apr. 4, 1855, D-5/40, both in H.B.A.

[28] Dallas to Fraser, Sept. 4, 1863; Hopkins to Dallas, Dec. 20, 1863, confidential, both in D-8/1, H.B.A.

[29] Dallas to Fraser, Sept. 4, 1863, D-8/1; Fraser to Dallas, Oct. 7, 1863, A-6/38, both in H.B.A.

[30] Simpson to Gov. and Comm., Oct. 16, 1826, D-4/12, H.B.A. A "pack" or a "piece" was ninety pounds of goods.

[31] The conflict between the Company and the lumbermen at Lake Timiskaming is described in a large number of letters. See, for example, Simpson to Keith, Apr. 23, 1840, D-4/25; Simpson to Gov. and Comm., June 20, 1841, D-4/58; Aug. 8, 1844, D-4/66; and Simpson to Siveright, Feb. 23, 1844, D-4/63, all in H.B.A.

[32] Simpson to Gov. and Comm., Sept. 10, 1845, D-4/67, H.B.A.

[33] Smith to Hopkins, Nov. 20, 1867, A-6/41, H.B.A.

[34] Hector McKenzie to Simpson, Aug. 27, 1858, D-5/47, H.B.A.

[35] Simpson to Gov. and Comm., July 5, 1851, D-4/72, H.B.A.

[36] John W. Simpson to Simpson, June 1, 1857, D-5/43, H.B.A.

[37] Simpson hired one competitor, James Bangs, and placed him in charge of a Company post. At the end of three years, Bangs, having recruited his finances and become intimately acquainted with the Company's methods, returned to competition with renewed vigor. McKenzie to Fraser, Mar. 26, 1866, private, A-10/65, H.B.A.

[38] Hopkins to Dallas, Dec. 20, 1863, confidential, D-8/1, H.B.A.

[39] Simpson to William Patton, Apr. 19, 1837, D-4/23, H.B.A.

[40] Gov. and Comm. to Finlayson, Mar. 4, 1840, A-6/25, H.B.A.

[41] Simpson to Samuel Walcott, Civil Secretary, Sept. 21, 1837, D-4/23, H.B.A.

[42] Labouchere to Pelly, Apr. 22, 1839, A-8/2, H.B.A.

[43] Memorandum [by Simpson], Apr. 3, 1838, D-4/23, H.B.A.

[44] Report of Committee of Executive Council, Lower Canada, June 26, 1839, encl. in Stephen to Pelly, Sept. 16, 1839, A-8/2, H.B.A.

[45] Stephen to Pelly, June 24, 1841; Pelly to Russell, June 30, 1841, both in A-8/3, H.B.A.

[46] Barnston to Simpson, Apr. 18, 1844, D-5/11, H.B.A.

[47] Gov. and Comm. to Simpson, Apr. 7, 1847, A-6/27, H.B.A.

[48] L. V. Sicotte, Commissioner of Crown Lands, to Simpson, Mar. 19, 1858, D-5/46; Simpson to Smith, Aug. 14, 1858, D-4/78, both in H.B.A.

[49] *Canadian News* (London), June 9, 1858.

[50] The entire returns of the King's Posts from all sources of revenue brought the Company in Outfit 1852 a profit of £63; in 1853, a profit of £313; in 1854, a loss of £218; in 1855, a loss of £1,100; and in 1856, a loss of £2,054. Simpson to Smith, Aug. 14, 1858, D-4/78, H.B.A. The posts were a constant source of loss thereafter. In 1862 the net loss was $10,968. Fraser to Hopkins, Dec. 6, 1862, A-6/37, H.B.A.

[51] McBean to Simpson, Jan. 8, 1827, D-5/2, H.B.A.

[52] Simpson to Gov. and Comm., Sept. 5, 1827, D-4/14, H.B.A.

[53] Gov. and Comm. to Thain, Mar. 29, 1823; Smith to Haldane, Mar. 13, 1824, both in A-6/20, H.B.A.

[54] Williams to Gov. and Comm., Sept. 18, 1824, D-1/10, H.B.A.

[55] Simpson to Gov. and Comm., July 18, 1831, D-4/18, H.B.A.

[56] Simpson to Gov. and Comm., Aug. 12, 1839, D-4/107; Simpson to Keith, Mar. 1, 1840, D-4/25, both in H.B.A.

[57] Gov. and Comm. to Finlayson, Mar. 4, 1840, A-6/25, H.B.A.

[58] Simpson to W. Simpson, Oct. 10, 1859, D-4/79; Simpson to Barnston, Oct. 11, 1859, D-5/50, both in H.B.A.

[59] Watt to Simpson, Apr. 4, 1859, D-5/49, H.B.A.

[60] Simpson to Gov. and Comm., Aug. 8, 1844, D-4/66; Sept. 10, 1845, D-4/67; Simpson to Crooks, Mar. 7, 1848, D-4/69, all in H.B.A.

[61] Simpson to Crooks, Mar. 7, 1848, D-4/69, H.B.A.

[62] Simpson to Gov. and Comm., July 25, 1857, D-4/77; Simpson to Fraser, Oct. 30, 1858, D-4/78, both in H.B.A.

[63] Simpson to R. T. Pennefather, Supt. Gen., Indian Dept., July 28, 1856, D-4/76a, H.B.A.

[64] Watt to Simpson, Apr. 4, 1859, D-5/49, H.B.A.

[65] Simpson to Ballenden, Nov. 25, 1843, D-4/63, H.B.A.

[66] John Swanston to Simpson, Jan. 10, 1845, D-5/13, H.B.A.

[67] Ballenden to Simpson, July 14, 1845, D-5/14, H.B.A.

[68] Higginson to Simpson, Apr. 2, 1846, D-5/17, H.B.A.

[69] Simpson to Hincks, Dec. 24, 1849, D-4/70, H.B.A.

[70] Buchanan to Simpson, Aug. 25, Sept. 11, 1850; Robinson to Simpson, Sept. 23, 1850, all in D-5/28; Simpson to Barclay, Sept. 23, 1850, D-4/71, all in H.B.A.

[71] Gov. and Comm. to Simpson, Apr. 14, 1859, A-6/34, H.B.A. The officer in charge of the district at this time was Donald A. Smith, later to attain fame and the honor of a peerage as Lord Strathcona and Mount Royal.

[72] "Result of Trade, Montreal Department, Outfit 1862," D-8/1, H.B.A.

[73] For reiterations of this policy after Simpson's death in 1860, see Fraser to William Mactavish, Jan. 10, 1861, A-6/36, and Gov. and Comm. to Dallas, Apr. 16, 1862, A-6/37, both in H.B.A.

[74] Fraser to Hopkins, Mar. 2, 1865, A-6/39, H.B.A.

## Chapter 4

[1] There are many excellent detailed accounts of the Red River colony. Among them are two by former Hudson's Bay Company employees who were residents of the settlement: Joseph J. Hargrave, *Red River* (Montreal: J. Lovell, 1871), and Alexander Ross, *The Red River Settlement: Its Rise, Progress, and Present State* (London: Smith, Elder, 1856). Among scholarly works on the subject are John P. Pritchett, *The Red River Valley, 1811–1849* (New Haven: Yale University Press, 1942), and sections of Arthur S. Morton, *A History of the Canadian West to 1870–71* (London: T. Nelson & Sons, [1939]). For an account of the Selkirk period, see Chester Martin, *Lord Selkirk's Work in Canada* (Oxford: Clarendon Press, 1916).

[2] Simpson to Gov. and Comm., June 5, 1824, D-4/8, H.B.A. The figure for population in 1824 is a rough estimate. The population in 1831 was 2,417. E. H. Oliver, ed., *The Canadian North-West* (2 vols.; Ottawa: Government Printing Bureau, 1914), I, 267.

[3] Locusts appeared in the summers of 1818 and 1819, when they virtually wiped out the crops. They reappeared in 1820, though in a less severe attack. Then, apparently affected by a blight, they did not return to Red River until 1857. In 1826 a great flood devastated the settlement.

[4] Simpson to Gov. and Comm., June 5, 1824, D-4/8, H.B.A.

[5] Simpson to Gov. and Comm., June 23, 1823, D-4/86, H.B.A.

[6] Simpson to Gov. and Comm., Aug. 31, 1825, D-4/7, H.B.A.

[7] Simpson to Gov. and Comm., July 25, 1827, D-4/14, H.B.A.

[8] McDermot to Simpson, Feb. 28, 1827, D-4/120, H.B.A.

⁹ Gov. and Comm. to Simpson, Mar. 12, 1827, A-6/21, H.B.A.

¹⁰ Simpson to Gov. and Comm., June 30, 1829, D-4/96, H.B.A.

¹¹ For discussions of Astor and the American Fur Company, see Hiram M. Chittenden, *The American Fur Trade of the Far West* (3 vols.; New York: F. P. Harper, 1902), *passim*, and Kenneth W. Porter, *John Jacob Astor—Business Man* (2 vols.; Cambridge, Mass.: Harvard University Press, 1931).

¹² J. Ward Ruckman, "Ramsay Crooks and the Fur Trade of the Northwest," *Minnesota History*, VII (Mar., 1926), 20, 22.

¹³ Simpson to Gov. and Comm., June 23, 1823, D-4/86, H.B.A.

¹⁴ Simpson to McLoughlin, Dec. 22, 1823, D-4/3, H.B.A.

¹⁵ Simpson to Gov. and Comm., Aug. 31, 1825, D-4/7, H.B.A.

¹⁶ McLoughlin to Gov., Chief Factors, and Chief Traders, Jan. 6, 1823, D-4/117, H.B.A.

¹⁷ McLoughlin to Simpson, Feb. 26, 1823, *ibid.*

¹⁸ *Ibid.* There is no evidence that the governor and committee were aware that their officers had been trading south of the border, except for the negative facts that in 1824 Simpson felt it necessary to assure them that the boundary was scrupulously respected (Simpson to Gov. and Comm., Aug. 10, 1824, D-4/3, H.B.A.), and that in 1827 they warned their traders to stay within British territory (Gov. and Comm. to Simpson, Mar. 12, 1827, A-6/21, H.B.A.). In these instructions they had in mind possible violations not only near Red River but in the Snake River country of the West.

¹⁹ Although parts of the boundary between Lake Superior and Lake of the Woods continued to be in dispute until 1842, there was never any serious objection to the Rainy River as a dividing line. The Hudson's Bay Company was particularly concerned that the portages in the water communication to Lake of the Woods should be kept open. The commissioners appointed by the British government represented the Company's case. R. Wilmot Horton to Pelly, Oct. 21, 1824; Garry to Bathurst, Oct. 30, 1824; Pelly to Canning, Nov. 24, 1824, all in A-8/1, H.B.A., and other documents in the same source show close collaboration between the Company and the Crown in the boundary discussions growing out of the Treaty of Ghent.

²⁰ Simpson to Gov. and Comm., June 23, 1823, D-4/86, H.B.A.

²¹ Simpson to Gov. and Comm., Aug. 31, 1825, D-4/7, H.B.A.

²² Porter, *op. cit.*, II, 817–818.

²³ "Substance of Remarks made by Mr. Aitkin, the Gentleman Superintending the Affairs of the American Fur Company at Fond du Lac, to A. Bethune, August 1829," D-5/3, H.B.A. Bethune states that Aitkin, although unwilling to write a formal proposal himself, had read Bethune's notes and declared them to be correct.

²⁴ The contents of this letter are summarized in Smith to W. B. Astor, Mar. 3, 1830, A-6/22, H.B.A.

²⁵ Smith to Astor, Mar. 3, 1830, *ibid.*

²⁶ Simpson to Gov. and Comm., July 18, 1831, D-4/98, H.B.A.

²⁷ Aitkin to Cameron, Sept. 4, 1830, D-4/125, H.B.A.

²⁸ Simpson to Gov. and Comm., July 18, 1831, D-4/98, H.B.A.

²⁹ *Ibid.*

³⁰ *Ibid.*

³¹ Ruckman, *op. cit.*, p. 25.

³² Possibly Alexis La Rose, a long-time trader in the district. See Reuben G. Thwaites, "The Fur-Trade in Wisconsin—1812–1825," *Collections of the State Historical Society of Wisconsin*, XX (Madison, 1911), 186.

³³ Simpson to Gov. and Comm., Aug. 10, 1832, D-4/99, H.B.A.

³⁴ Gov. and Comm. to Simpson, Mar. 1, 1833, A-6/22, H.B.A.

³⁵ Simpson to Aitkin, July 2, 1834, D-4/20; Minutes of Temporary Council, Northern Department, Commencing July 1, 1834, resolution 50, B-239k/2, both in H.B.A. The two men seem to have met at Red River on March 21, 1833, before the governor and committee's letter could possibly have reached Simpson.

[36] Gov. and Comm. to Simpson, June 7, 1833, A-6/22, H.B.A.

[37] Simpson to Aitkin, July 2, 1834, D-4/20, H.B.A.

[38] Simpson to Gov. and Comm., July 21, 1834, D-4/100, H.B.A.

[39] Simpson to Gov. and Comm., July 8, 1839, D-4/106, H.B.A.

[40] Simpson to Gov. and Comm., June 20, 1841, D-4/58, H.B.A.

[41] Simpson to Aitkin, Sept. 8, 1836, D-4/22, H.B.A.

[42] Simpson to Crooks, Nov. 15, 1837, A-6/24, H.B.A.

[43] Simpson to Crooks, Oct. 1, 1839, D-4/25, H.B.A.

[44] Simpson to Gov. and Comm., Sept. 27, 1847, D-4/69, H.B.A.

[45] Simpson to Crooks, May 25, 1840, and encl., Simpson to Allan McDonell, May 25, 1840, D-4/25; Minutes of Council, Northern Department, Beginning June 18, 1840, resolutions 44, 45, B-239k/2, both in H.B.A.

[46] Simpson to Gov. and Comm., Apr. 20, 1841, D-4/108, H.B.A.

[47] Simpson to George Keith, Sept. 18, 1840, D-4/25; Simpson to Gov. and Comm., Apr. 20, 1841, D-4/108; Smith to Crooks, Nov. 19, 1841, A-6/25, all in H.B.A.

[48] When Astor retired from the American Fur Company in 1834, the stock of the northern department was purchased by a group of seven associates headed by Crooks. The new organization retained the name "American Fur Company," and Crooks was elected president. What had been the western department was sold to Pratte, Chouteau and Company of St. Louis. See Chittenden, *op. cit.*, I, 363–365.

[49] Ruckman, *op. cit.*, pp. 27–30.

[50] Clarence W. Rife, "Norman W. Kittson, a Fur-Trader at Pembina," *Minnesota History*, VI (Sept., 1925), 225–231.

[51] Among these are George F. G. Stanley, *The Birth of Western Canada* (London: Longmans, Green, 1936), and Pritchett, *op. cit.* See also Morton, *op. cit.*, particularly pp. 643–668, 870–909. Also, consult Marcel Giraud, *Le Métis Canadien* (Paris: 1945). See Ross, *op. cit.*, and Hargrave, *op. cit.*, for the best contemporary or near-contemporary accounts.

[52] Simpson to Gov. and Comm., Aug. 31 [Sept. 1?], 1825, D-4/7, H.B.A.

[53] Simpson to Gov. and Comm., July 10, 1828, D-4/92, H.B.A.

[54] Livia Appel and Theodore C. Blegen, "Official Encouragement of Immigration during the Territorial Period," *Minnesota History Bulletin*, V (Aug., 1923), 167.

[55] H. G. Gunn, "The Fight for Free Trade in Rupert's Land," *Proceedings of the Mississippi Valley Historical Association*, IV (1910–1911), 80.

[56] Simpson to Gov. and Comm., June 20, 1844, D-4/65, H.B.A.

[57] Gov. and Comm. to Simpson, Mar. 1, 1841, A-6/25, H.B.A.

[58] Simpson to Gov. and Comm., June 20, 1844, D-4/65, H.B.A.; Sinclair to Christie, Aug. 25, 1845, cited in Chester Martin, "The Hudson's Bay Company's Monopoly of the Fur Trade at the Red River Settlement, 1821–1850," *Proceedings of the Mississippi Valley Historical Association*, VII (1913–1914), 262.

[59] Simpson to Gov. and Comm., June 20, 1844, D-4/65, H.B.A.

[60] Notice by Christie, Dec. 7, 1844, B-235/4, H.B.A.

[61] Christie to Simpson, Dec. 31, 1844, D-5/12, H.B.A.

[62] Thom to Simpson, Mar. 10, 1845, D-5/13, H.B.A. This order for seizure was made despite Thom's advice that such action might be illegal. Christie to Simpson, Dec. 27, 1844, D-5/12, H.B.A.

[63] Christie to Simpson, Apr. 16, 1845, D-5/13, H.B.A.

[64] The questionnaire and Christie's reply are included in a list of papers sent by the governor and committee to Simpson, Nov. 6, 1845, D-5/15, H.B.A.

[65] Simpson to Pelly, Oct. 24, 1845, D-4/67, H.B.A.

[66] Christie to Simpson, Apr. 16, 1845, D-5/13, H.B.A.

[67] Thom to Simpson, Jan. 2, 1845, *ibid.*

[68] Christie to Simpson, Dec. 27, 1844, D-5/12; Apr. 16, 1845, D-5/13, both in H.B.A.

[69] Simpson to Crooks, July 10, 1845, D-4/67, H.B.A.

[70] Christie to Simpson, Aug. 26, 1845, D-5/14, H.B.A.

[71] Simpson to Borup, July 3, 1845, D-4/67, H.B.A. Ramsay Crooks had authorized Simpson to make the request.

[72] Crooks to Simpson, Nov. 21, 1845, D-5/15, H.B.A.

[73] Christie to Simpson, Jan. 1, 1846, D-5/16, H.B.A.

[74] Rife, *op. cit.*, p. 235.

[75] Simpson to Barclay, May 24, 1846, D-4/68, H.B.A.

[76] Simpson to Crooks, Dec. 8, 1845, D-4/67; Simpson to Barclay, May 24, 1846, D-4/68, both in H.B.A.

[77] Rife, *op. cit.*, p. 235.

[78] Simpson to Gov. and Comm., July 24, 1846, D-4/68, H.B.A.

[79] Simpson to Barclay, Dec. 24, 1846, confidential, A-12/3, H.B.A.

[80] Sinclair to Pelly, Oct. 13, 1846, A-10/22; Gov. and Comm. to Simpson, Apr. 14, 1847, confidential, D-5/19, both in H.B.A.

[81] Sinclair was employed to escort emigrants from Red River to the Columbia, and then was placed in charge of Walla Walla. This was his second such journey. The first was in 1841.

[82] Borup to Crooks, July 30, 1846, encl. in Crooks to Simpson, Dec. 8, 1846, D-5/18, H.B.A.

[83] For a discussion of troops at Red River, see chap. 15, pp. 312–317 and *passim*.

[84] Minutes of Council, Northern Department, Beginning June 10, 1844, resolution 49, B-239k/2, H.B.A. For a description of the currency at Red River, see Hargrave, *op. cit.*, pp. 179–180.

[85] Pelly to Simpson, Apr. 3, 1846, private, D-5/17, H.B.A.

[86] Pelly to Simpson, Feb. 3, 1846, private, D-5/16, H.B.A.

[87] Pelly to Simpson, Sept. 17, 1845, D-5/15, H.B.A.

[88] Pelly to Simpson, Apr. 3, 1846, private, D-5/17, H.B.A.

[89] Christie to Simpson, Dec. 31, 1845, D-5/15, H.B.A.

[90] Simpson commented on this fact in a letter to Barclay, Mar. 26, 1846, continued on Mar. 27, D-4/67, H.B.A.

[91] A. Ross to Donald Ross, Aug. 6, 1849, AB 40 R732, Provincial Archives, British Columbia. For further discussion of the pensioners, see chap. 15, pp. 327–329.

[92] There are many accounts of the Sayer trial. Simpson described it in a letter to the governor and committee, June 30, 1849, D-4/70, H.B.A. Among the published accounts that provide a detailed description are Ross, *op. cit.*, pp. 372 ff.; Stanley, *op. cit.*, pp. 47 ff.; Morton, *op. cit.*, pp. 814–816; and Pritchett, *op. cit.*, pp. 261–263.

[93] Simpson to Corcoran, Apr. 20, 1846, D-4/67, H.B.A.

[94] Rowand to Simpson, Dec. 28, 1848, private, D-5/23, H.B.A.

[95] Rife, *op. cit.*, pp. 230–231.

[96] Christie to Simpson, Aug. 26, 1845, private, D-5/14, H.B.A. The post was so close to the line that a later survey placed it in American territory.

[97] Simpson to Gov. and Comm., June 18, 1846, D-4/68, H.B.A.

[98] Simpson to Gov. and Comm., June 24, 1848, D-4/69, H.B.A.

[99] W. Sinclair to Simpson, Dec. 10, 1851, D-5/32, H.B.A.

[100] Simpson to Gov. and Comm., June 26, 1856, D-4/76a, H.B.A.

[101] Rife, *op. cit.*, pp. 249–250. Kittson later became an agent for the Hudson's Bay Company in the transport of its goods through Minnesota. He died a prosperous man, but his wealth apparently came from real estate in St. Paul rather than from his fur-trading activities.

[102] Sinclair to Simpson, Nov. 1, 1853, D-5/38; Simpson to Sinclair, Dec. 20, 1853, D-4/82; Simpson to Smith, Feb. 17, 1855, D-4/75, all in H.B.A.

[103] Barclay to Simpson, Apr. 15, 1853, A-6/30, H.B.A.

[104] Simpson to Colvile, Dec. 23, 1854, confidential, D-4/83, H.B.A.

[105] William Christie to Gov. in Chief, Chief Factors, and Chief Traders, Feb. 1, 1856, D-5/41, H.B.A.

[106] Simpson to Colvile, June 28, 1855, confidential, D-4/83, H.B.A.

[107] Simpson to Swanston, June 26, 1856, D-4/76a, H.B.A.

[108] Simpson to Gov. and Comm., June 26, 1856, *ibid.*
[109] Simpson to Swanston, June 26, 1856, *ibid.*
[110] Simpson to Swanston, Dec. 4, 1856, *ibid.*
[111] Simpson to Gov. and Comm., June 26, 1856, *ibid.*
[112] *Ibid.*
[113] Simpson to Shepherd, Aug. 2, 1856, confidential, A-7/2, H.B.A.
[114] For discussion of the Company's relations with the British government during this period, see chap. 16, pp. 333-354.
[115] Simpson to Gov. and Comm., June 24, 1858, D-4/78, H.B.A.
[116] Barnston joined the North West Company as an apprentice clerk in 1820 and after the coalition was employed by the Hudson's Bay Company as a clerk.
[117] Bannatyne to Simpson, Nov. 2, 1846, D-5/18, H.B.A. Information on Bannatyne's service was supplied by Miss A. M. Johnson, archivist, H.B.C.
[118] Barnston to Simpson, Sept. 28, 29, 1857, both in D-5/44, H.B.A. Bannatyne was a native of the Orkney Islands.
[119] Johnson was appointed governor of Assiniboia by a commission dated November 26, 1855. Dep. Gov. & Comm. to Simpson, Apr. 17, 1856, A-6/32, H.B.A.
[120] Simpson to Smith, Dec. 7, 1857, D-4/77, H.B.A.
[121] For a discussion of these proceedings, see chap. 16, pp. 341-342.
[122] Crowder and Maynard to Smith, Dec. 29, 1857, A-10/42, H.B.A.
[123] Fraser to Simpson, Oct. 28, 1859, A-6/34, H.B.A. A small consignment was sent by two routes in 1858 to test their respective merits. Carts were used to carry the 1859 shipment from St. Paul to Red River. This primitive form of transportation was replaced the next year by a steamboat which carried the goods on the Red River.
[124] Gov. and Comm. to Dallas, Apr. 16, 1862, A-6/37, H.B.A.

## Chapter 5

[1] Father Pierre de Smet believed that these Indians were called Snakes "because in their poverty they are reduced like reptiles to the condition of digging in the ground and seeking nourishment from roots."
[2] See chap. 7 on relations with Russian America, and chaps. 9-11 on the Oregon controversy.
[3] Gov. and Comm. to Simpson, Feb. 27, 1822, A-6/20, H.B.A., printed in H.B.S., III, 302.
[4] The Nor'Westers purchased Astoria in 1813. The sale was made under threat of seizure either by British warships or by the employees of the North West Company. Since the Treaty of Ghent provided for restoration of all places taken by either side during the war, the United States successfully contended that Astoria should be restored to the United States. Title was finally transferred in 1818 at a ceremony in which the American flag was hoisted, but the North West Company remained in actual possession, and its successor, the Hudson's Bay Company, retained control until after the Oregon treaty of 1846. For a description of the ceremony in 1818, see T. C. Elliott, "The Surrender at Astoria in 1818," *Oregon Historical Quarterly*, XIX (Dec., 1918), 271-282.
[5] Simpson to Gov. and Comm., Mar. 1, 1829, D-4/93, H.B.A., printed in H.B.S., X, 67.
[6] Frederick Merk, *Fur Trade and Empire* (Cambridge, Mass.: Harvard University Press, 1931), p. 85.
[7] H.B.S., X, 44.
[8] Merk, *op. cit.*, p. 44.
[9] Lewes to Simpson, Apr. 2, 1822, D-4/116, H.B.A.
[10] See Merk, *op. cit.*, for the journal Simpson kept during his visit.
[11] H.B.S., IV, xv. Haldane was replaced by Chief Factor Alexander Kennedy in 1822.

[12] James Keith to Gov. and Comm., Feb. 12, 1822, A-10/2, H.B.A.

[13] *Ibid.*

[14] Alexander Ross, *The Fur Hunters of the Far West* (2 vols.; London: Smith, Elder, 1855), I, 184, 212–214.

[15] Keith to Gov. and Comm., Feb. 12, 1822, A-10/2, H.B.A.

[16] Lewes to Simpson, Apr. 2, 1822, D-4/116, H.B.A.

[17] Simpson to Chief Factors of Columbia River District, July 12, 1823, D-4/2, H.B.A.

[18] Ross, *op. cit.*, II, 2. A previous caretaker expedition had been sent out under Michel Bourdon in 1822.

[19] Bourdon's name is also spelled Bordoe, Bourdeau, and Le Bourdeau.

[20] McDonald to J. G. McTavish, Apr. 5, 1824, B-239c/1, H.B.A., quoted in H.B.S., III, 53n. For a brief description of the encounter, see Simpson to Gov. and Comm., Aug. 10, 1824, D-4/3, H.B.A.

[21] E. E. Rich, ed., *Peter Skene Ogden's Snake Country Journals* (London: 1950), H.B.S., XIII, xxxvii.

[22] Ross, *op. cit.*, II, 2. Simpson engaged Ross for a three-year term at £120 per year. Simpson to Ross, July 12, 1823, D-4/1, H.B.A.

[23] American ships continued to trade along the coast.

[24] Hiram M. Chittenden, *The American Fur Trade of the Far West* (3 vols.; New York: F. P. Harper, 1902), I, 227.

[25] Harrison C. Dale, *The Ashley-Smith Explorations and the Discovery of a Central Route to the Pacific, 1822–1829* (Cleveland: Clark, 1918), pp. 55–56, 68.

[26] Dale L. Morgan, *Jedediah Smith* (Indianapolis: Bobbs-Merrill, 1953), p. 189 and *passim*. This is the best account of the American fur trade in the Rocky Mountains during the 1820's. Smith, Jackson, and Sublette sold out to the Rocky Mountain Fur Company in 1830.

[27] Simpson to Chief Factors of Columbia River District, July 12, 1823, D-4/2, H.B.A.

[28] Ogden to Gov., Chief Factors & Chief Traders, Oct. 10, 1826, D-4/120, H.B.A. See also McLoughlin to Simpson, Mar. 20, 1827, *ibid.*

[29] Alexander Ross, "Journal of the Snake River Expedition, 1824," *Oregon Historical Quarterly*, XIV (Dec., 1913), 366–388.

[30] Merk, *op. cit.*, p. 43. They traveled by horseback because the Spokane River was not navigable at that season.

[31] Simpson to Ross, Oct. 29, 1824, D-4/7, H.B.A. Simpson wrote Ross two letters on this date, the first informing him of his transfer to Red River and the second acknowledging the arrival of an express from him.

[32] Simpson to Gov. and Comm., Mar. 10, 1825, D-4/7, H.B.A.

[33] Merk, *op. cit.*, p. 46.

[34] Simpson to Gov. and Comm., Mar. 10, 1825, D-4/7, H.B.A.

[35] Simpson to Gov. and Comm., Mar. 1, 1829, D-4/93, 95, H.B.A., printed in E. E. Rich, ed., *Simpson's 1828 Journey to the Columbia* (London: 1947), H.B.S., X, 52.

[36] *Quebec Chronicle*, quoted in *Canadian News*, Apr. 5, 1866, p. 215.

[37] Ogden to Simpson, private, Jan. 27, 1851, D-5/30, H.B.A. For details of Ogden's antecedents, see T. C. Elliott, "Peter Skene Ogden, Fur Trader," in *Oregon Historical Quarterly*, XI (Sept., 1910), 229–278. Most of the information here presented on Ogden is derived from this source.

[38] Ross Cox, *Adventures on the Columbia River* (2 vols.; London: H. Colburn and R. Bentley, 1831), II, 244.

[39] H.B.S., III, 53. Samuel Black, who had shared in the odium surrounding Ogden, was reinstated at the same time and sent west of the Rocky Mountains.

[40] Adrien G. Morice, *The History of the Northern Interior of British Columbia* (Toronto: Lane, 1904), p. 168.

[41] H.B.S., XIII, 262.

[42] See *ibid.* for an extended account. Morgan, *op. cit.*, pp. 148–153, also describes the incident. There is some doubt as to the exact number of deserters. Ogden's account differs from that of his subordinate, Kittson. In June, 1825, Ogden gave the total number as twenty-one. H.B.S., IV, 298.

[43] McLoughlin to Simpson, Mar. 20, 1827, D-4/120, H.B.A.

[44] Simpson to Gov. and Comm., Mar. 1, 1829, D-4/93, H.B.A.

[45] Gov. and Comm. to Simpson, June 2, 1826, A-6/21, H.B.A.

[46] Simpson to McLoughlin, July 10, 1826, D-4/13, H.B.A.

[47] McLoughlin to Simpson, Mar. 20, 1828, D-4/121, H.B.A.

[48] H.B.S., XIII, 67. It was at this time that Ogden wrote a letter headed "East Fork, Missouri." But as Lewis A. McArthur and Robert W. Sawyer point out in their excellent commentary in this volume, Ogden was actually on the east branch of the west fork of the Missouri, which is called the Jefferson. He had previously crossed the divide when Jedediah Smith was traveling with him.

[49] McLoughlin to Simpson, Mar. 20, 1827, D-4/120, H.B.A., printed in H.B.S., XIII, 257.

[50] McLoughlin to Simpson, Mar. 20, 1827, D-4/120, H.B.A. This is not the same letter as the above.

[51] McLoughlin to Work, July 22, 1828, B-223b/4, H.B.A.

[52] Simpson to Gov. and Comm., Mar. 1, 1829, D-4/93, H.B.A.

[53] This was an estimate Ogden made in a letter to Gov., Chief Factors & Chief Traders, Oct. 10, 1826, D-4/120, H.B.A.

[54] See Alice B. Maloney, "Peter Skene Ogden's Trapping Expedition to the Gulf of California, 1829–30," *California Historical Society Quarterly*, XIX (Dec., 1940), 308–316. For journals of other expeditions, see *Oregon Historical Quarterly*, X, XI (1909, 1910), as corrected in H.B.S., XIII.

[55] Simpson to McLoughlin, July 9, 1827, D-4/90, H.B.A.

[56] Simpson to McLoughlin, July 10, 1826, D-4/13, H.B.A.

[57] Simpson to McLoughlin, July 9, 1827, D-4/90, H.B.A.

[58] Gov. and Comm. to Simpson, Jan. 16, 1828, A-6/21, H.B.A.

[59] "Fort Vancouver, Fur Trade Returns Columbia District & New Caledonia, 1825–27," AB20 V3, Provincial Archives, British Columbia. The figures after 1830 exclude the expeditions to California, which were separately listed.

[60] Simpson to Gov. and Comm., Mar. 1, 1829, D-4/93, H.B.A. This estimate by the Company's officers is probably close to the actual number. See Chittenden, *op. cit.*, I, chap. xvi, p. 264 and *passim*. See also Dale, *op. cit.*, p. 156.

[61] Simpson to Gov. and Comm., Aug. 10, 1832, D-4/99, H.B.A.

[62] McLoughlin, "An Account of his relations with the Americans, 1825–45," P-A 155, Bancroft Library.

[63] These questionable practices were not confined to small enterprises. The American Fur Company was also accused with some justification of swindling its employees.

[64] Simpson to Gov. and Comm., Mar. 1, 1829, D-4/93, H.B.A.

[65] In 1829 the total number of Hudson's Bay employees in the entire Columbia district, excluding officers, was 224. Simpson to McLoughlin, Mar. 15, 1829, D-4/16, H.B.A.

[66] Morgan, *op. cit.*, p. 233. The Company's officers reported that the Americans had collected between 4,000 and 6,000 beaver. This estimate was not far wrong. Simpson to Gov. and Comm., Mar. 1, 1829, D-4/93, H.B.A.

[67] See Morgan, *op. cit.*, chap. 13, for an account of the Umpqua massacre.

[68] See "Peter Skene Ogden Journal, 1827–28," *Oregon Historical Quarterly*, XI (Dec., 1910), 361–379. Some of the parties Ogden met were composed of free trappers. Their plight was similar.

[69] McLoughlin to Black, Mar. 22, 1828, B-223b/3, H.B.A.

[70] Simpson to Gov. and Comm., Mar. 1, 1829, D-4/93, H.B.A.; Morgan, *op. cit.*, p. 299. Simpson said Pilcher was accompanied by a clerk and forty trappers.

[71] *Ibid.*

[72] Simpson to Pilcher, Feb. 18, 1829, in Merk, *op. cit.*, pp. 307–308.

[73] See "Journal, 1828–29," in *Oregon Historical Quarterly*, XI (Dec., 1910), 382.

[74] Simpson to Gov. and Comm., Mar. 1, 1829, D-4/93, H.B.A.

[75] *Ibid.*

[76] For a more extended discussion of the Hudson's Bay Company's competition with the Americans along the Pacific Coast, see chap. 7, pp. 136–140.

[77] The standard work on this subject is Adele Ogden, *The California Sea Otter Trade* (Berkeley and Los Angeles: University of California Press, 1941).

[78] Simpson to McLoughlin, July 9, 1827, D-4/90, H.B.A.

[79] Simpson to Gov. and Comm., Mar. 1 (cont. Mar. 24), 1829, D-4/94, H.B.A., printed in H.B.S., X, 103. For detailed accounts of Dominis on the Columbia, see Samuel E. Morison, "New England and the Opening of the Columbia River Salmon Trade, 1830," *Oregon Historical Quarterly*, XXVIII (June, 1927), 111–132; F. W. Howay, "Brig Owhyhee in the Columbia, 1829–30," *ibid.*, XXXV (Mar., 1934), 10–21.

[80] A "skin" was the skin of a full-grown beaver in prime condition, which was the standard of trade.

[81] For elaboration on this point see chap. 7, pp. 139–140.

[82] McLoughlin to Black, Sept. 23, 1829, B-223b/5; Simpson to Gov. and Comm., Aug. 26, 1830, D-4/97, both in H.B.A.

[83] McLoughlin to Simpson, Mar. 20, 1830, D-4/123, H.B.A.

[84] Morison, *op. cit.*, p. 122.

[85] McLoughlin to Ogden, Oct. 5, 1832, B-223b/8, H.B.A., printed in H.B.S., IV, 315–316.

[86] Simpson to McLoughlin, July 30, 1830, D-4/17, H.B.A.

[87] During his 1831–32 expedition Work crossed the Continental Divide. In so doing he was, unlike Ogden, acting contrary to specific instructions. Simpson to Gov. and Comm., Aug. 10, 1832, D-4/99, H.B.A. For Work's account of this expedition, see William S. Lewis and Paul C. Phillips, eds., *The Journal of John Work* (Cleveland: Clark, 1923).

[88] For a summary of Work's expeditions, see H.B.S., IV, 356–358.

[89] Simpson to Gov. and Comm., Aug. 10, 1832, D-4/99, H.B.A.

[90] Consult Lewis and Phillips, *op. cit.*

[91] McLoughlin to Simpson, Mar. 20, 1833, D-5/4, H.B.A.

[92] McLoughlin to Simpson, Mar. 18, 1834, D-4/126, H.B.A.

[93] Ermatinger was to have charge of four men who would proceed from Flathead Post. The other party, headed by François Payette, was to set out from Walla Walla and join Ermatinger at Salmon River. McLoughlin to Simpson, Mar. 20, 1833, D-5/4, H.B.A. These parties were not Snake River expeditions in the old sense, since their primary purpose was trading with the Americans rather than trapping.

[94] "The Correspondence and Journals of Captain Nathaniel J. Wyeth, 1831–6," in F. G. Young, ed., *Sources of the History of Oregon* (Eugene: 1899), I, lxxii.

[95] Simpson to Wyeth, Nov. 28, 1833, A-6/22, H.B.A.

[96] Gov. and Comm. to Simpson, Mar. 12, 1827, in Merk, *op. cit.*, pp. 286–287.

[97] McLoughlin to Pambrun, Oct. 10, 1834; McLoughlin to McKay, Oct. 4, 1834, private and confidential, both in B-223b/10, H.B.A.

[98] McLoughlin to Pambrun, Oct. 13, 1834, *ibid.*

[99] W. Kaye Lamb, in H.B.S., IV, cviii–cxi.

[100] McLoughlin to Simpson, Mar. 20, 1833, D-5/4, H.B.A. The size of the party is McLoughlin's estimate. Bonneville stated that he had 121 men. Wyeth, who saw Bonneville in 1833, said that he had 80 men. All the figures may be correct, for there were undoubtedly desertions during the winter of 1832–33.

[101] McLoughlin to Finlayson, Apr. 6, 1834, B-223b/10, H.B.A.

[102] McLoughlin to Gov. and Comm., Oct. 31, 1837, B-223b/17, H.B.A., printed in H.B.S., IV, 195–196.

[103] Gov. and Comm. to McLoughlin, Jan. 25, 1837, A-6/24, H.B.A.

[104] McLoughlin to Ermatinger, Feb. 1, 1834, B-223b/10, H.B.A.
[105] McLoughlin to Gov. and Comm., Sept. 30, 1835, B-223b/11, printed in H.B.S., IV, 142.
[106] McLoughlin to McKay, Oct. 4, 1834, private and confidential, B-223b/10, H.B.A.
[107] McLoughlin to Pambrun, Oct. 10, 1834, *ibid.*
[108] H.B.S., IV, 349.
[109] *Ibid.*, pp. 208–210.
[110] *Ibid.*, p. 349.
[111] McLeod's Instructions, May 7, 1836, B-223b/12, H.B.A.
[112] Wyeth to Gov. and Comm., Dec. 5, 1836, A-10/3, H.B.A.
[113] Smith to Wyeth, Jan. 11, 1837, A-6/24, H.B.A.
[114] Douglas to Simpson, Mar. 18, 1838, printed in H.B.S., IV, 279.
[115] Pambrun to Simpson, Mar. 3, 1841, D-5/6, H.B.A.
[116] Grant to Simpson, Mar. 15, 1844, private, D-5/10, H.B.A.
[117] Grant to Simpson, Jan. 2, 1846, private, D-5/16, H.B.A.
[118] Grant to Simpson, Dec. 31, 1847, D-5/20; Simpson to Grant, June 30, 1849, D-4/70, both in H.B.A.
[119] Grant to Simpson, Jan. 31, 1851, D-5/30, H.B.A.
[120] Ogden and Mactavish to Simpson and Council of Northern Dept., Apr. 12, 1854, D-5/39; Simpson to Board of Management, Oregon Dept., June 28, 1854, D-4/74, both in H.B.A.
[121] Mactavish to Barclay, Oct. 6, 1854, B-223b/41, H.B.A.
[122] See chap. 13.
[123] "Comparative Statement of Result of Trade in Columbia District, Outfits 1849 and 1850," A-12/5, H.B.A.
[124] E. Colvile to Gov. and Comm., July 21, 1852, A-12/6, H.B.A.
[125] Simpson to Board of Management, June 18, 1853, D-4/73, H.B.A.
[126] Ogden and Mactavish to Simpson and Council of Northern Dept., Apr. 12, 1854, D-5/39, H.B.A.

## Chapter 6

[1] An exception to this generalization, which does not relate to negotiations involving Russia, is the operations of American trappers in the Snake country, discussed in chapter 5.

[2] S. B. Okun, *The Russian-American Company,* trans. Carl Ginsburg (Cambridge, Mass.: Harvard University Press, 1951), p. 57. A ruble of the coinage of 1801 was worth approximately 65 cents.

[3] A translation of the charter is contained in Alaskan Boundary Tribunal, *Proceedings* (7 vols.; Washington: 1904), U.S. 58th Cong., 2d sess., S. Doc. 162, II, 23–24. This document will hereafter be cited as A.B.T.

[4] Okun, *op. cit.,* p. 98.

[5] Ivan Petroff, "The Management and Personnel of the Russian American Company from its Beginning to its Dissolution," MS P-K 23, Bancroft Library.

[6] James Douglas, "Diary of a trip to the Northwest Coast," entry of Apr. [May] 28, 1840, AB 40/D 75.2, Provincial Archives of British Columbia.

[7] See Clarence L. Andrews, "Russian Plans for American Dominion," *Washington Historical Quarterly,* XVIII (Apr., 1927), 83–92. For a discussion of Russian activity at Fort Ross, see *The Russians in California,* California State Historical Society Special Publication no. 7 (San Francisco: 1933).

[8] Vassili Berg, "Chronological History of the Discovery of the Aleutian Islands or the Achievements of Russia's Merchants, with an additional Historical Review of the Fur Trade" (St. Petersburg: 1823), trans. Ivan Petroff, pp. 148–149, MS P-K 7, Bancroft Library.

[9] F. W. Howay, W. N. Sage, and H. F. Angus, *British Columbia and the United States* (Toronto: Ryerson Press, 1942), p. 6. The authors provide the following

statistics indicating the number of vessels engaged in the trade between 1785 and 1815, counting no vessel twice:

|  | British | American |
|---|---|---|
| 1785–1794 | 25 | 15 |
| 1795–1804 | 9 | 50 |
| 1805–1814 | 3 | 40 |

[10] Timothy Pitkin, A Statistical View of the Commerce of the United States of America (New Haven: Durrie & Peck, 1835), p. 251.

[11] Okun, op. cit., p. 58.

[12] J. C. Hildt, Early Diplomatic Negotiations of the United States with Russia (Baltimore: Johns Hopkins Press, 1906), pp. 158–159.

[13] P. Tikhmeneff, "Historical Review of the Origin of the Russian American Company," Part I, pp. 367 ff., MS P-K 1, Bancroft Library.

[14] Letter of Captain Golovnin, dated only 1818, in "Report of the Committee on Organization of the Russian American Colonies" (St. Petersburg: 1863), MS P-K 6, Bancroft Library.

[15] Tikhmeneff, op. cit., Part I, p. 383.

[16] Vassili Berg, "Historical Review of the Russian American Company from 1799 to 1863, compiled by the Department of Imperial Archives," MS P-K 4, Bancroft Library. According to the account in "Report of the Committee on Organization of the Russian American Colonies," the Russian American Company in its own interest supported this provision in the treaty.

[17] J. D. Rogers, "Canada. Geographical," in Charles P. Lucas, ed., A Historical Geography of the British Colonies (6 vols.; Oxford: 1888–1911), Vol. V, Part III, p. 263; Howay, Sage, and Angus, op. cit., p. 68; Simpson to Gov. and Comm., Mar. 1, 1829, printed in H.B.S., X, 1–119.

[18] Rogers, op. cit.; Howay, Sage, and Angus, op. cit.; Simpson to Gov. and Comm., Mar. 1, 1829, printed in H.B.S., X, 1–119. Simpson states that Fort St. James and Fraser's Lake were constructed in 1805. Fort George should not be confused with the post on the Columbia at Astoria, which was renamed Fort George after its purchase by the North West Company.

[19] Howay, Sage, and Angus, op. cit., p. 68; Simpson to Gov. and Comm., Mar. 1, 1829, printed in H.B.S., X, 1–119. Simpson gave the date of establishment as 1820. Alexandria was established in September, 1821, before news of the coalition reached New Caledonia. Its construction should therefore be attributed to the North West Company, not to the Hudson's Bay Company. The boundaries of New Caledonia were never clearly defined. Adrien G. Morice, The History of the Northern Interior of British Columbia (Toronto: Lane, 1904), p. 1, describes it as "that immense tract of land lying between the Coast Range and the Rocky Mountains from 51° to 57° of latitude north," but no description as to territorial extent is entirely satisfactory.

[20] Though McLeod's Fort was located at 55° north latitude it was east of the Continental Divide. Governor Simpson stated to the governor and committee on July 31, 1822, D-4/85, H.B.A., that "some of the posts of New Caledonia" extended as far north as latitude 55° and as far west as longitude 125°. This statement is correct, but New Caledonia included territory both east and west of the divide.

[21] See A.B.T., II, 25–26, for a translation of the ukase.

[22] See ibid., pp. 26–28, for a translation of the charter.

[23] A.B.T., Vol. I, Part II, pp. 63–64; Nicolay to Londonderry, Oct. 31/Nov. 12, 1821, in A.B.T., II, 96.

[24] Nicolay to Londonderry, Oct. 31/Nov. 12, 1821, in A.B.T., II, 95–96.

[25] Christopher Robinson, King's Advocate, to Londonderry, Nov. 20, 1821; Stowell to Melville, Dec. 26, 1821, both in ibid., pp. 102–103.

[26] Thomas Lock, Board of Trade, to Foreign Office, Jan. 7, 1822, ibid., pp. 103–104.

[27] Pelly to Londonderry, Mar. 27, 1822, A-8/1, H.B.A., also in A.B.T., II, 106–107.

[28] Josceline Bagot, *George Canning and His Friends* (2 vols.; London: Murray, 1909), II, 266.

[29] George M. Trevelyan, *Lord Grey of the Reform Bill* (New York: Longmans, Green, 1920), pp. 374–375; Harold Temperley, *The Foreign Policy of Canning, 1822–1827* (London: G. Bell and Sons, 1925), p. 32. For a good account of Canning's political position when he became foreign secretary in 1822, see A. Aspinall, "The Canningite Party," *Transactions of the Royal Historical Society*, 4th series, XVII (London: 1934), 177–226.

[30] Memorandum for the Cabinet, circulated about Nov. 15, 1822, in Edward J. Stapleton, ed., *Some Official Correspondence of George Canning* (2 vols.; London: 1887), II, 48.

[31] Canning to Liverpool, July 7, 1826, *ibid.*, pp. 73–74.

[32] Garry to John Lock, East India Company, [July ?], 1823, A-7/1, H.B.A.

[33] Extract from Berg, "Chronological History of the Discovery of the Aleutian Islands . . . ," F-29/2, H.B.A.

[34] Gov. and Comm. to Simpson, Feb. 27, 1822, in H.B.S., III, 303.

[35] Gov. and Comm. to John Haldane and John Dugald Cameron, Chief Factors in Charge of Columbia District, Sept. 4, 1822, in H.B.S., III, 335.

[36] Garry to Lock, [July ?], 1823, and draft, Garry to Lock, July 15, 1823, A-7/1, H.B.A. The latter was not sent. In 1822–23, the agents of the Hudson's Bay Company in China obtained an average price of 50 shillings for beavers and otters. The Russian American Company was forced to transport furs destined for China overland from St. Petersburg to Kiachta. The Hudson's Bay Company contended that the East India Company could purchase beavers and otters in England at from 18 to 27 shillings and make a profit in the China market. Additional incentive for the Hudson's Bay Company to make such an agreement was the exclusion of foreign furs from the Russian market in 1822 and a decline in the price of beaver in London.

[37] Gov. and Comm. to Simpson, Mar. 12, June 2, 1824, both in A-6/20, H.B.A.

[38] H.B.S., III, 42n.

[39] McDougall to Stuart, Jan. 18, 1822, B-188b/1, H.B.A. For this and the rest of the information in this paragraph I am principally indebted to Miss A. M. Johnson, archivist of the Hudson's Bay Company.

[40] H.B.S., III, 45, 75, and *passim*.

[41] Simpson to Gov. and Comm., Aug. 10, 1824, H.B.S., III, 107 and n.

[42] H.B.S., III, 17, 45, 75.

[43] Gov. and Comm. to Simpson, Feb. 27, 1822, A-6/20, H.B.A.

[44] H.B.S., III, 75–76.

[45] Gov. and Comm. to Simpson, Mar. 12, 1824, A-6/20, H.B.A.

[46] Tuyll to Nesselrode, Oct. 21/Nov. 2, 1822, A.B.T., II, 113.

[47] Poletica to Nesselrode, Nov. 3, 1823, *ibid.*, pp. 137–140.

[48] Lieven to Canning, Jan. 19/31, 1823, *ibid.*, p. 118.

[49] For details, see the Alaskan Boundary Tribunal's seven volumes of *Proceedings*, which remains the most exhaustive account.

[50] Pelly to Canning, Sept. 25, 1822, A.B.T., II, 109–110. The latitudes and longitudes given by Pelly, with the correct positions indicated in parentheses, are: Stuart's Lake, 54° 30′ N. lat., 125° W. long. (54° 26′ N. lat., 124° 15′ W. long.); McLeod's Lake, 55° N. lat., 124° W. long. (55° N. lat., 123° 1′ W. long.); Fraser's Lake, 55° N. lat., 127° W. long. (54° 5′ N. lat., 124° 30′ W. long.).

[51] Daniel Williams Harmon, *A Journal of Voyages and Travels in the Interior of North America* (New York: A. S. Barnes, 1903), pp. 157, 158, 160, 161, 162.

[52] Frederick Merk, *Fur Trade and Empire* (Cambridge, Mass.: Harvard University Press, 1931), p. 113. The map produced by Aaron Arrowsmith in 1795–96 and revised in accordance with information supplied to the Arrowsmiths from the reports of Hudson's Bay Company officers in the field was in general use from 1821 to 1825. No basically new edition appeared until 1832.

[53] Canning to Bagot, Jan. 15, 1824, F.O. 65/141, P.R.O. Adams' desire to act co-operatively with Britain, since the United States had no territorial pretensions north of 51° north latitude, was conveyed in a dispatch, S. Canning to G. Canning, May 3, 1823, A.B.T., II, 120–121.

[54] Bagot to Canning, Oct. 17/29, 1823, confidential, A.B.T., II, 129–130.

[55] For a discussion of Adams' diplomacy in this dispute see Samuel Flagg Bemis, *John Quincy Adams and the Foundations of American Foreign Policy* (New York: Knopf, 1949), pp. 516–517.

[56] Canning to Bagot, Jan. 15, 1824, A.B.T., II, 145.

[57] *Ibid.*

[58] Nesselrode to Mordvinof, Apr. 11, 1824, A.B.T., II, 180.

[59] Canning to Bagot, Apr. 20, 1824, private, in Bagot, *op. cit.*, II, 232–233.

[60] Counterdraft by Russian plenipotentiaries, Feb. 12/24, 1824, encl. in Bagot to Canning, Mar. 17/29, 1824, A.B.T., II, 158.

[61] Pelly to Canning, Jan. 8, 1824, *ibid.*, pp. 149–150.

[62] Canning to Bagot, July 29, 1824, in Bagot, *op. cit.*, II, 266. Sir John Barrow, though officially holding the unimpressive title of second secretary to the Admiralty, was a powerful force in geographical and scientific discovery, and was heard with respect by British politicians. He founded the Royal Geographical Society in 1830. The names of Point Barrow, Cape Barrow, and Barrow Strait are monuments to his interest in Arctic exploration. Barrow was in close communication with William E. Parry and John Franklin. Parry in the spring of 1824 was making ready to sail on another attempt to force a passage through the Arctic, and Franklin was planning to continue in 1825–26 the exploration of the north coast of America from the Coppermine River west to Icy Cape. Restrictions on the navigation of the coast and of Bering Straits would have blocked their plans, and Barrow pro-tested. Franklin to Barrow, Nov. 26, 1823, in *Certain Correspondence of the Foreign Office and of the Hudson's Bay Company* (Ottawa: 1899), Confidential, Part I, pp. 3–6.

[63] Pelly to Canning, Apr. 19, 1824, A-8/1, H.B.A.

[64] For another exposition of this view, see Okun, *op. cit.*, p. 86.

[65] Nesselrode to Mordvinof, Apr. 11, 1824, A.B.T., II, 180.

[66] Lieven to Nesselrode, May 21/June 2, 1824, *ibid.*

[67] Pelly to Canning, Apr. 19, 1824, A-8/1, H.B.A.

[68] Canning to Bagot, July 12, 1824, A.B.T., II, 181.

[69] Bagot to Canning, Aug. 12, 1824, *ibid.*, pp. 190–192.

[70] Pelly to Canning, Oct. 20, 1824, A-8/1, H.B.A.

[71] Canning to Liverpool, Oct. 17, 1824, in Stapleton, *op. cit.*, I, 177.

[72] G. Canning to S. Canning, Dec. 8, 1824, A.B.T., II, 211.

## Chapter 7

[1] Gov. and Comm. to J. D. Cameron, July 22, 1824, private and confidential, A-6/21, H.B.A.

[2] Simpson to Gov. and Comm., Aug. 10, 1824, D-4/3, H.B.A. The conflict over the maritime fur trade, though in a somewhat different form, was one of the major elements in the later famous feud between Simpson and McLoughlin. See W. Kaye Lamb's introduction to E. E. Rich, ed., *The Letters of John McLoughlin from Fort Vancouver to the Governor and Committee, Second Series, 1839–44* (London: 1943), H.B.S., VI.

[3] Simpson to Gov. and Comm., Aug. 10, 1824, D-4/3, H.B.A.

[4] Simpson to Gov. and Comm., Mar. 10, 1825, D-4/7, H.B.A. See his "Report" in Frederick Merk, *Fur Trade and Empire* (Cambridge, Mass.: Harvard University Press, 1931), p. 72, for a similar observation.

[5] For a short biography of Simpson, see H.B.S., III, 455–456.

[6] George Simpson to Gov. and Comm., Mar. 1, 1829, H.B.S., X, 73 ff.

7 McLoughlin to Black, Aug. 29, 1830 [1829], Mar. 20, 1830, both in B-223b/5, H.B.A.

8 A "skin" is the skin of a full-grown beaver in prime condition, and the value of other peltries was based upon this standard.

9 McLoughlin to Barnston, Nov. 30, 1830, B-223b/6, H.B.A.

10 For further information on the competition with Dominis, see chap. 5, pp. 99–101.

11 McLoughlin to Ryan, May 16, 1833, B-223b/9, H.B.A.

12 McLoughlin to Lt. Simpson, July 7, 1830, B-223b/6, H.B.A.

13 McLoughlin to Manson, Dec. 20, 1834, B-223b/10, H.B.A.

14 Article IX, printed in George Davidson, *The Alaska Boundary* (San Francisco: Alaska Packers Association, 1903), pp. 82–83.

15 Simpson to Gov. and Comm., Aug. 10, 1832, D-4/99, H.B.A.

16 McLoughlin to Yale, May 17, 1834, B-223b/10, H.B.A.

17 For correspondence on the termination of this trading privilege, see A.B.T., II, 232–250.

18 Wrangell to Directors, H.B.C., May 6, 1832, *ibid.*, pp. 264–265.

19 Simpson's "Journal," in Merk, *op. cit.*, p. 86. His suggestion was endorsed by the governor and committee in a letter to Simpson, Feb. 23, 1826, A-6/21, H.B.A.

20 Simpson to Gov. and Comm., Mar. 1, 1829, H.B.S., X, 85, 101.

21 Lt. Simpson to McLoughlin, Oct. 1, 1829, D-4/123, H.B.A. Governor Simpson's letter to the governor of the Russian American colonies, dated March 20, 1829, is in D-4/16, H.B.A.

22 W. Smith, Secretary to H.B.C., to Chief Manager and Directors, R.A.C., Dec. 16, 1829, A.B.T., II, 260–261.

23 A. Severin, Director, R.A.C., to Igor F. Kankreen, Min. of Finance, Feb. 27, 1830, *ibid.*, p. 262.

24 Simpson to Gov. and Comm., Aug. 26, 1830, D-4/97, H.B.A.

25 Gov. and Comm. to McLoughlin, Oct. 28, 1829, A-6/22, H.B.A.

26 For an account of these outbreaks of the fever, which appears to have been a form of malaria, see H.B.S., IV, *passim.*

27 Lieutenant Simpson first heard of the importance of Nass from a conversation with the masters of two American vessels whom he met during a voyage in 1827.

28 George Simpson to Gov. and Comm., Aug. 10, 1832, D-4/99, H.B.A. Arrowsmith maps published as late as 1863 are greatly in error in depicting the course of rivers on this section of the coast. On these maps the Babine is merged with the Simpson (Nass) River, and the Skeena River is nowhere in evidence.

29 Simpson to Gov. and Comm., Aug. 10, 1832, D-4/99, H.B.A.

30 Wrangell to Board of Directors, R.A.C., May 6, 1832, A.B.T., II, 264–265.

31 Gov. and Comm. to McLoughlin, Feb. 1, 1834, A-6/22, H.B.A. The London headquarters at this time believed that only three coastal establishments would be necessary north of the Columbia—Stikine, a post to be constructed on Millbank Sound (Fort McLoughlin), and another on Puget Sound to replace Fort Langley— with a steam vessel plying the coast between them. The forts were built, and the steamer *Beaver* arrived on the coast in March, 1836, but Langley was not abandoned.

32 Translation in A.B.T., II, 15.

33 Italics mine. Wrangell to Board of Directors, R.A.C., Apr. 28, 1834, A.B.T., II, 266–267.

34 *Ibid.* The redoubt, completed on August 26, 1834, was named Fort Dionysius by order of Wrangell.

35 Document in F-29/2, H.B.A.

36 See Ogden's "Report," H.B.S., IV, 317–322.

37 The Tongass incident is described in entry of July 30, 1834, "Notes and Extracts from Journal of the Hudson's Bay Company at Fort Simpson, 1834–37," MS P-C 23, Bancroft Library. For the visit to Sitka, see Wrangell to Ogden, Sept. 19, 1834, F-29/2, H.B.A. The Stikine incident is described in greater detail in Donald

C. Davidson, "Relations of the Hudson's Bay Company with the Russian American Company on the Northwest Coast, 1829–1867," *British Columbia Historical Quarterly*, V (Jan., 1941), 37–46. A Russian version is contained in P. Tikhmeneff, "Historical Review of the Origin of the Russian American Company . . . ," Part I, pp. 278–281, MS P-K 1, Bancroft Library.

[38] For a statement of this policy, see Gov. and Comm. to McLoughlin, Aug. 28, 1835, A-6/23, H.B.A.

[39] Gov. and Comm. to McLoughlin, Dec. 8, 1835, *ibid.*

[40] E. H. Oliver, ed., *The Canadian North-West* (2 vols.; Ottawa: Government Printing Bureau, 1914), II, 727, quoted in H.B.S., IV, cvi. The name "Fort Drew," bestowed in honor of a member of the committee, had been assigned to the post Ogden had been instructed to build during his Stikine expedition.

[41] Nesselrode to Durham, Dec. 21, 1835, A.B.T., II, 287–288.

[42] Board of Directors, R.A.C., to Dept. of Trade and Manufactures, Jan. 3, 1836, *ibid.*, pp. 289–290.

[43] For Nesselrode's communications to Durham on this subject, see *ibid.*, pp. 287 ff.

[44] Simpson to McLoughlin, June 28, 1836, D-4/22, H.B.A.

[45] Finlayson to McLoughlin, Sept. 29, 1836, B-223b/12, H.B.A.

[46] Simpson to Gentlemen Chief Factors and Chief Traders of Columbia and New Caledonia Dept., Mar. 7, 1838, D-4/23, H.B.A.

[47] "Report" of J. H. Pelly, 1838, F-29/2, H.B.A.

[48] *Ibid.*

[49] *Ibid.*

[50] Pelly to Directors, R.A.C., Sept. 1, 1838, encl. in Pelly's "Report," 1838, *ibid.* Of the "residents of the Sandwich Islands" to whom Pelly referred, the most important was French and Company of Oahu, which traded supplies with the Russians at Sitka. In 1838 they were not in active competition in the fur trade, but the Hudson's Bay Company feared that experience on the northwest coast might attract them into the competition. See Finlayson to McLoughlin, Sept. 29, 1836, B-223b/12, H.B.A.

[51] Pelly to Directors, R.A.C., Sept. 1, 1838, encl. in Pelly's "Report," 1838, F-29/2, H.B.A.

[52] Pelly's "Report," 1838, *ibid.*

[53] Gov. and Comm. to Douglas, Oct. 31, 1838, private and confidential, A-6/24, H.B.A.

[54] *Ibid.*

[55] Simpson to Wrangell, Nov. 27, 1838, D-4/25, H.B.A.

[56] When Simpson reached Berlin, the city originally selected, Wrangell had not yet arrived. He therefore went on to Hamburg to meet the Russian representative. Simpson to Gov. and Comm., Feb. 20, 1839, D-4/25, H.B.A.

[57] Photostat of agreement, F-29/2, H.B.A.; the agreement is printed in A.B.T., III, 209–212.

[58] S. B. Okun, *The Russian-American Company*, trans. Carl Ginsburg (Cambridge, Mass.: Harvard University Press, 1951), pp. 218–219. Okun contends that the lease was not based on commercial considerations, but was an attempt by the Russian government to remove a possible cause of irritation with Great Britain. Both the author's chronology and his reasoning are badly distorted. He states that "precisely" at the time of the Simpson-Wrangell negotiations, "between August 1839 and July 1840," the Russian ambassador was in London in an effort to promote an understanding on the Straits question. But, as has been pointed out, the companies had reached substantial agreement by November, 1838.

[59] Nesselrode to Kankreen, Dec. 9, 1838, A.B.T., II, 307–308.

[60] Directors, R.A.C., to Kankreen, Dec. 20, 1839 [1838], *ibid.*, pp. 210–211; Nesselrode to Kankreen, Jan. 4, 1839, *ibid.*, p. 312.

[61] Pelly to Palmerston, Jan. 4, 1839, A-8/2, H.B.A.

[62] J. Backhouse to Pelly, Jan. 17, 1839, *ibid.*

## Chapter 8

[1] Simpson to Gov. and Comm., July 8, 1839, D-4/106, H.B.A.; George Simpson, *Narrative of a Journey Round the World* (2 vols.; London: H. Colburn, 1847), II, 206; Memorandum by Simpson and Etholine, May 13, 1842, F-29/2, H.B.A.

[2] Douglas to McLoughlin, Oct. 1, 1840, B-223b/28, H.B.A. A uniform tariff was finally established by Governors Simpson and Etholine on May 17, 1842, when Simpson visited Sitka during his voyage around the world. A copy of the agreement is in D-5/7, H.B.A.

[3] Memorandum, undated [1839?], F-29/2, H.B.A. The "Landing, warehouse and other charges" are deducted because they would be avoided by direct shipments from the Columbia to Sitka.

[4] Extract from P. Tikhmeneff, "Historical Review of the Origin of the Russian American Company," Part I, pp. 264–270, in A.B.T., II, 315.

[5] George Simpson, *op. cit.*, II, 92–94, comments on the presence of a large number of American whalers in the North Pacific. John Work at Fort Simpson reported that whalers had been trading in furs in 1843 and 1844. Work to Ermatinger, Feb. 6, 1844, AB40/Er 62.4, Provincial Archives of British Columbia.

[6] See W. Kaye Lamb's introduction in E. E. Rich, ed., *The Letters of John McLoughlin from Fort Vancouver to the Governor and Committee, Second Series, 1839–44* (London: 1943), H.B.S., VI, xv and *passim*.

[7] Gov. and Comm. to McLoughlin, Aug, 19, 1840, A-6/25, H.B.A.

[8] Douglas to McLoughlin, Oct. 1, 1840, B-223b/28, H.B.A. The post, though officially known as Fort Durham, was usually called Fort Taku. It was originally to be built at the mouth of the Taku River, but because no suitable location could be found there, it was placed on the coast about fifteen miles south of the entrance, in a position given by Simpson as 58° 4′ north latitude and 133° 45′ west longitude. Simpson to Gov. and Comm., Nov. 25, 1841, D-4/59, H.B.A. For a description of the building of Taku, see James Douglas, "Diary of a trip to the Northwest Coast," AB 40/D 75.2, Provincial Archives of British Columbia. Taku was ordered established on the assumptions that large quantities of furs could be collected there and the river provided access to the interior. During his visit in 1842 Simpson found neither assumption to be justified, and the post was abandoned in 1843. See Simpson's "Remarks on existing agreement between the Hudson's Bay Company and Russian-American Company," Oct. 30, 1844, D-4/66, A-12/2, H.B.A. McLoughlin, most reluctantly, complied. News of the abandonment of Taku is contained in McLoughlin to Gov. and Comm., Aug. 2, 1843, H.B.S., VI, 109.

[9] The discovery that the fur resources of the territory between the Rocky Mountains and the Pacific Coast had been exaggerated was a principal reason for Simpson's suggestion that all northern posts except Fort Simpson be abandoned, the returns to be collected by the *Beaver*.

[10] For a description of Campbell's explorations, see C. Parnell, "Campbell of the Yukon," *The Beaver*, Outfit 273 (June, Sept., Dec., 1942). A transcript of Campbell's journal is in the Provincial Archives of British Columbia.

[11] Clifford Wilson, "Founding Fort Yukon," *The Beaver*, Outfit 278 (June, 1947), 40.

[12] Pelly to Simpson, Oct. 27, 1848, D-5/23, H.B.A.

[13] Ivan Petroff, trans., "Report of the Committee on Organization of the Russian American Colonies" (St. Petersburg: 1863), MS P-K 6, Bancroft Library.

[14] Simpson, "Remarks," Oct. 30, 1844, D-4/66, A-12/2, H.B.A.

[15] Pelly to Wrangell, Oct. 22, 1847, A-10/23, H.B.A.

[16] Wrangell to Pelly, private, Oct. 28/Nov. 10, 1847, A-10/23, H.B.A.

[17] Draft, Pelly to Wrangell, private, Dec. 3, 1847, *ibid.* Further communications between Pelly and Wrangell on the subject of renewal of the contract will be found in A-10/23 and A-10/24, H.B.A.

[18] "Agreement . . . Renewing (with Certain Modifications) the Agreement between

the Two Companies of the 6th February, 1839," A.B.T., III, 213–214. The agreement ran for nine years rather than ten because Pelly wanted the lease and the
royal grant of exclusive trade to the Hudson's Bay Company west of Rupert's Land
to expire together; in the event that the grant was not renewed the value of the
lease would be reduced. Pelly to Simpson, private, Mar. 10, 1848, D-5/21, H.B.A.

[19] Ogden and Douglas to Simpson, Mar. 14, 1849, D-5/24, H.B.A.

[20] Agreement of 1849, A.B.T., III, 214.

[21] For a full discussion of the diplomacy leading to the Crimean War, see Vernon
J. Puryear, England, Russia, and the Straits Question, 1844–1856 (Berkeley: University of California Press, 1931).

[22] W. Politkowski et al. to Directors, H.B.C., Feb. 2/14, 1854, encl. in A. Colvile to
Clarendon, Feb. 28, 1854, A-8/19, H.B.A.

[23] S. B. Okun, The Russian-American Company, trans. Carl Ginsburg (Cambridge,
Mass.: Harvard University Press, 1951), p. 234.

[24] Petroff, "Report of the Committee on Organization of the Russian American
Colonies," MS P-K 6, Bancroft Library.

[25] Politkowski et al. to Directors, H.B.C., Feb. 2/14, 1854, encl. in Colvile to
Clarendon, Feb. 28, 1854, A-8/19, H.B.A. Hubert Howe Bancroft states that as
soon as war between Great Britain and Russia became certain, representatives of
the two companies met in London to discuss "the exigencies of the case." History
of Alaska, 1730–1885 (San Francisco: A. L. Bancroft & Company, 1886). Okun, op. cit.,
p. 225, follows Bancroft with no further documentation. I have found no evidence
that any such meetings were held. On the contrary, the correspondence between the
two companies indicates that the first approach was made by the Russian American
Company in the above letter.

[26] Okun, op. cit., pp. 235–236.

[27] Colvile to Clarendon, Feb. 28, 1854, A-8/19, H.B.A.

[28] Simpson to Board of Management, Western Dept., Mar. 29, 1854, D-4/74, H.B.A.

[29] Simpson to Barclay, Apr. 1, 1854, ibid.

[30] Barclay to Peel, Sept. 5, 1854; Manley to Shepherd, Aug. 31, 1854, both in
A-8/7, H.B.A. For other evidences of Colonial Office opposition to expenditures for
colonial purposes at this time, the reader should examine the background of the
Sand River Convention of 1852 and the Bloemfontein Convention of 1854, by which
Great Britain sought to reduce its liabilities in South Africa.

[31] Addington to Colvile, Mar. 22, 1854, A-8/19, H.B.A. The Russians accepted
this definition by letter, Politkowski to Directors, H.B.C., Apr. 5/17, 1854, ibid.

[32] Okun, op. cit., pp. 237–240.

[33] Ibid., p. 241.

[34] Petroff, "Report of the Committee on Organization of the Russian American
Colonies," MS P-K 6, Bancroft Library; Okun, op. cit., p. 241; Bancroft, op. cit.,
p. 571; Etholine et al. to Directors, H.B.C., Feb. 7/19, 1857, A-10/41, H.B.A.

[35] Petroff, "Report of the Committee on Organization of the Russian American
Colonies," MS P-K 6, Bancroft Library.

[36] Okun, op. cit., p. 241.

[37] Simpson to Work, Mar. 28, 1854; same to same, private, Sept. 9, 1854, both
in D-4/74, H.B.A.; Simpson to McNeill, Jan. 28, 1855, D-4/76, H.B.A.

[38] Etholine to Directors, H.B.C., Nov. 27/Dec. 9, 1858, A-10/44; Berens to Directors,
R.A.C., Dec. 28, 1858, F-29/2, both in H.B.A.

[39] Simpson to Fraser, Jan. 24, 1859, D-4/78, H.B.A.

[40] "An Act to provide for the Government of British Columbia," 21 & 22 Vic.,
cap. 99 (1858). The name was changed from New Caledonia to British Columbia
to avoid confusion with the French colony in the South Pacific.

[41] L. Klupfell to Directors, H.B.C., July 13/25, 1861, A-10/50, H.B.A.

[42] Extract, Berens to Directors, R.A.C., Aug. 6, 1861, F-29/2, H.B.A.

[43] Extract, Fraser to Directors, R.A.C., July 11, 1862, ibid.

[44] Gov. and Comm. to Dallas, Apr. 16, 1862, A-6/37; extract, Fraser to Directors, R.A.C., June 3, 1862, F-29/2, both in H.B.A.

[45] Tabenkoff to Gov. and Comm., June 11/23, 1862, A-10/51, H.B.A.

[46] Extract, Fraser to Directors, R.A.C., July 11, Nov. 25, 1862, both in F-29/2, H.B.A.

[47] Tabenkoff to Gov. and Comm., Feb. 25/Mar. 8, 1863, A-10/53, H.B.A.

[48] Gov. and Comm. to Dallas, Apr. 15, 1863, A-6/38, H.B.A.

[49] Extract, Fraser to Directors, R.A.C., May 3, 1865; extract, Minutes of Gov. and Comm., May 29, 1866, both in F-29/2; Tabenkoff to Gov. and Comm., May 4/16, 1866, A-10/66, all in H.B.A.

[50] Memorandum by A. Rutkovski, Jan. 14/26, 1865, F-29/2, H.B.A.

[51] Fraser to Tolmie, confidential, Feb. 18, 1865, A-6/29, H.B.A.

[52] The Hudson's Bay Company proposed a three-year extension of the existing lease in January, 1867, and the Russian American Company accepted, but upon application to the Russian government for sanction was informed of the impending cession. Fraser to Directors, R.A.C., Jan. 26, 1867, A-6/41; Tabenkoff to Gov. and Comm., Feb. 1/13, 1867, A-10/69; Tabenkoff to Gov. and Comm., Apr. 8/20, 1867, all in H.B.A. In 1866 a California company attempted to replace the Hudson's Bay Company as lessee by proposing a twenty-five-year contract on terms more favorable to Russia than those in the Hudson's Bay Company lease. See extract from speech of Sen. Charles Sumner, A.B.T., II, 331–333.

[53] Kimberley to Elliot, June 11, 1868, and encl., Tolmie to Smith, Apr. 29, 1868, A-8/12, H.B.A.

[54] Adderley to Kimberley, July 4, 1868, *ibid.* American policy was somewhat liberalized after the Treaty of Washington was ratified.

## Chapter 9

[1] Gov. and Comm. to Haldane and Cameron, Sept. 4, 1822, A-6/20, H.B.A. For a discussion of Congressman Floyd see Verne Blue, "The Oregon Question—1818–1828," *Oregon Historical Quarterly*, XXIII (Sept., 1922), 193–219.

[2] S. Canning to G. Canning, May 3, 1823, F.O. 5/176, P.R.O. For a discussion of Adams' Oregon diplomacy see Samuel Flagg Bemis, *John Quincy Adams and the Foundations of American Foreign Policy* (New York: Knopf, 1949).

[3] "Proposals of American Plenipotentiary . . . April 3, 1824," in "Papers Relative to the Negociation between Great Britain and the United States, concerning the North-Western Boundary in America," private (for the Cabinet), encl. in Canning to Peel, June 21, 1826, Peel Papers, Addtl. MSS 40,611, British Museum.

[4] Canning to Bagot, July 9, 1824, private, in Josceline Bagot, *George Canning and His Friends* (2 vols.; London: Murray, 1909), I, 266. See also Canning to Liverpool, July 7, 1826, in Edward J. Stapleton, ed., *Some Official Correspondence of George Canning* (2 vols.; London: 1887), II, 73.

[5] Canning to British Commissioners, May 31, 1824, in "Papers relative to the Negociation between Great Britain and the United States. . . ."

[6] *Ibid.*

[7] Gov. and Comm. to Simpson, June 2, 1824, A-6/20; Gov. and Comm. to Cameron, July 22, 1824, private and confidential, A-6/21, both in H.B.A.

[8] Canning to Liverpool, July 7, 1826, in Stapleton, *op. cit.*, II, 73.

[9] For Simpson's journal of this visit, see Frederick Merk, *Fur Trade and Empire* (Cambridge, Mass.: Harvard University Press, 1931).

[10] Simpson to McLoughlin, Apr. 10, 1825, D-4/7, H.B.A.

[11] Simpson to Gov. and Comm., Aug. 10, 1824, D-4/3, H.B.A.

[12] J. D. Richardson, *A Compilation of the Messages and Papers of the Presidents* (10 vols.; Washington: U.S. Govt. Printing Office, 1896–1899), II, 262.

[13] Frederick Merk, *Albert Gallatin and the Oregon Problem* (Cambridge, Mass.: Harvard University Press, 1950), p. 71.

[14] Simpson to Gov. and Comm., June 21, 1825, D-4/7, H.B.A.

[15] H.B.S., IV, 5.

[16] John Scouler, "Journal of a Voyage to N.W. America," *Oregon Historical Quarterly*, VI (Sept., 1905), 277.

[17] H.B.S., IV, 26.

[18] Black to McLoughlin, Mar. 23, 1826, B-223b/2, H.B.A.

[19] Gov. and Comm. to Simpson, Mar. 12, 1827, A-6/21, H.B.A.

[20] The draft, Simpson to Canning, Dec. 9, 1825, D-4/7, H.B.A., is virtually a duplicate of Pelly to Canning, Dec. 9, 1825, A-13/1, H.B.A.

[21] Pelly to Canning, Dec. 9, 1825, A-13/1, H.B.A., printed in Merk, *Fur Trade and Empire*, pp. 257–260.

[22] Addington to Simpson, Dec. 29, 1825, A-13/1, H.B.A.

[23] The questions and answers are printed in Merk, *Fur Trade and Empire*, p. 261.

[24] Canning to Liverpool, July 7, 1826, in Stapleton, *op. cit.*, II, 74.

[25] Pelly to Huskisson, July 25, 1826, "Oregon Book, Queries by Mr. Huskisson, July 1826," A-13/1, H.B.A.

[26] Hubert Howe Bancroft, *History of the Northwest Coast* (2 vols.; San Francisco: A. L. Bancroft & Company, 1884), II, 381–382.

[27] Gov. and Comm. to Simpson, Jan. 16, 1828, A-6/21, H.B.A.

[28] Simpson to McLoughlin, Mar. 15, 1829, D-4/16, H.B.A.

[29] In June, 1829, the northern department authorized the employment of an additional forty-two men in the combined districts of the Columbia and New Caledonia, but they were apparently sent for purposes of the trade rather than politics. H.B.S., III, 244.

[30] Bancroft, *op. cit.*, II, 521.

[31] Gov. and Comm. to McLoughlin, Oct. 28, 1829, A-6/22, H.B.A.

[32] Gov. and Comm. to McLoughlin, Jan. 25, 1837, A-6/24, H.B.A.

[33] Douglas to Gov. and Comm., Oct. 18, 1838, B-223b/21, H.B.A.

## Chapter 10

[1] See, for example, Gov. and Comm. to Simpson, Jan. 16, 1828, A-6/21, H.B.A.

[2] McLoughlin to Simpson, June 20, 1825, B-223b/1, H.B.A.

[3] H.B.S., X, 69.

[4] Gov. and Comm. to Simpson, Feb. 29, 1832, A-6/22, H.B.A.

[5] E. H. Oliver, ed., *The Canadian North-West* (2 vols.; Ottawa: Government Printing Bureau, 1914), I, 54, states that Archibald McDonald first suggested the idea of raising flocks and herds on the Pacific Coast. But Oliver says that McDonald's suggestion was made in 1833, one year after the first proposals were made, and that the site he proposed was the Sacramento River.

[6] Prospectus, Mar. 10, 1832, encl. to Gov. and Comm., Aug. 27, 1834, D-4/100, H.B.A.

[7] Simpson to Gov. and Comm., Aug. 27, 1834, *ibid.*

[8] Gov. and Comm. to McLoughlin, Dec. 10, 1834, A-6/23, H.B.A.

[9] Simpson to McLoughlin, June 5, 1835, D-4/21, H.B.A.

[10] See chap. 7, pp. 146–147.

[11] Gov. and Comm. to McLoughlin, Jan. 25, 1837, A-6/24, H.B.A.

[12] The expressions are Simpson's in Simpson to Pelly, Feb. 1, 1837, encl. in Pelly to Glenelg, Feb. 10, 1837, A-8/2, H.B.A.

[13] Pelly to Glenelg, Feb. 10, 1837, *ibid.*

[14] Stephen to Le Marchant, July 25, 1837, C.O. 43/86, P.R.O.

[15] Pelly to Stephen, Oct. 25, 1837, A-13/1, H.B.A.

[16] Royal License, May 30, 1838, quoted in Hudson's Bay Company, *Charters, Statutes, Orders in Council &c. Relating to the Hudson's Bay Company* (London: Hudson's Bay Company, 1931), p. 219.

[17] Hubert Howe Bancroft, *History of Oregon* (2 vols.; San Francisco: History Company, 1886–1888), I, 370.

[18] Simpson to Douglas, Mar. 8, 1838, D-4/23, H.B.A.

[19] *Ibid.*

[20] McLoughlin to Douglas, Mar., 1838, B-223b/18, H.B.A.

[21] Gov. and Comm. to Simpson, Mar. 20, 1839, A-6/25, H.B.A.

[22] Opinion of Edward Jacob and William G. Polson, undated, A-10/16, H.B.A.

[23] Minutes of Committee, Feb. 27, 1839, A-1/61; Pelly, Colvile, and Simpson to shareholders, June 1, 1839, F-12/1, both in H.B.A.

[24] Pelly, Colvile, and Simpson to shareholders, June 1, 1839; List of shareholders, both in F-12/1, H.B.A.

[25] Colvile to Simpson, Sept. 20, 1841, D-5/6, H.B.A.

[26] McLoughlin to Pelly, Colvile, and Simpson, Mar. 20, 1840, F-12/1, H.B.A. In 1839, half of the acreage was already occupied by the Roman Catholic mission and by private settlers, ex-servants of the Company, so that only about 1,500 acres were available for a Company farm. Farming was begun by the Company in 1838, and the establishment was transferred to the agricultural company in 1839.

[27] McLoughlin to Simpson, Mar. 20, 1833, D-5/4, H.B.A.

[28] McLoughlin to Heron, June 18, 1833, B-223b/9, H.B.A.

[29] McLoughlin to Heron, July 20, 1833, *ibid.*

[30] Pelly, Colvile, and Simpson to McLoughlin, Sept. 14, 1839, F-11/1, H.B.A.

[31] Simpson to Gov. and Comm., Nov. 25, 1841, D-4/59, H.B.A.

[32] Simpson to Pelly and Colvile, Nov. 25, 1841, *ibid.*

[33] "Account of Horned Cattle at Nisqually," "Account of Sheep at Nisqually," both in Soliday Collection, Huntington Library, San Marino, California.

[34] Joseph Schafer, ed., "Documents Relating to Warre and Vavasour's Military Reconnaissance in Oregon, 1845–6," *Oregon Historical Quarterly*, X (Mar., 1919), 60.

[35] "The Company" means the Hudson's Bay Company, for although the Puget's Sound Agricultural Company was legally separate, complete control was exercised by the governing board of the parent Company.

[36] Bancroft, *op. cit.*, I, 315.

[37] Douglas to Gov. and Comm., Oct. 18, 1838, B-223b/21, H.B.A.

[38] Bancroft, *op. cit.*, I, 169 ff.

[39] Douglas to Gov. and Comm., Oct. 18, 1838, B-223b/21, H.B.A.

[40] Gov. and Comm. to Douglas, Nov. 15, 1837, A-6/24, H.B.A.

[41] Gov. and Comm. to Douglas, Oct. 31, 1838, A-6/25, H.B.A. McLoughlin was not yet a Roman Catholic himself. He joined the Church in 1842.

[42] Bancroft, *op. cit.*, I, 321.

[43] Ellice to [Pelly?], Aug. 25, 1839, F-12/1, H.B.A.

[44] Pelly, Colvile, and Simpson to McLoughlin, Sept. 14, 1839, F-11/1, H.B.A.

[45] Simpson to Christie, Apr. 15, 1840, D-4/58, H.B.A.

[46] Ellice to [Pelly?], Aug. 25, 1839, F-12/1, H.B.A.

[47] Simpson to D. Finlayson, Nov. 15, 1839, D-4/25, H.B.A.

[48] Tracy to the Principal Officer of the Hudson's Bay Company, Mar. 4, 1839, D-4/106, H.B.A.

[49] W. Fox Strangways, F.O., to James Stephen, C.O., Aug. 12, 1839, and attached memoranda, C.O. 6/13, P.R.O.

[50] Smith to Tracy, June 13, 1839, A-6/25, H.B.A.

[51] Pelly received the news of Linn's resolutions in an extract from the St. John's *Courier* of Jan. 4, 1840; Pelly to Palmerston, Feb. 26, 1840, A-8/2, H.B.A.

[52] Gov. and Comm. to Finlayson, Mar. 4, 1840, A-6/25, H.B.A.

[53] Gov. and Comm. to McLoughlin, Aug. 19, 1840, *ibid.*

[54] Finlayson to McLoughlin, June 27, 1840, B-235b/2, H.B.A.

[55] Simpson to Finlayson, Sept. 10, 1840, D-4/25, H.B.A.

[56] Simpson to Finlayson, Sept. 10, 1840; Simpson to McLoughlin, Sept. 11, 1840, both in D-4/25, H.B.A.

⁵⁷ Gov. and Comm. to Simpson, Mar. 1, 1841, A-6/25, H.B.A.
⁵⁸ Simpson to Gov. and Comm., Apr. 20, 1841, D-4/108, H.B.A.
⁵⁹ Finlayson to Simpson, May 1, 1841, D-5/6, H.B.A.
⁶⁰ *Ibid.;* Simpson to Gov. and Comm., June 20, 1841, D-4/58, H.B.A. Only twenty heads of families are listed on the agreement signed by the emigrants on May 31, 1841. They were François Jacques, Julien Bernier, Baptiste Oreille, Pierre Larocque, Pierre St. Germain, John Spence, Henry Buxton, Gonzague Zastre, William Flett, Charley McKay, James Birston, John Cunningham, Alexander Birston, Archibald Spence, François Gagnon, Joseph Klyne, James Flett, and John Tate. "Copy of Agreement," in Simpson to Smith, Mar. 11, 1855, A-12/7, H.B.A.
⁶¹ George Simpson, *Narrative of a Journey Round the World* (2 vols.; London: H. Colburn, 1847), I, 89–90.
⁶² Simpson to Gov. and Comm., Nov. 25, 1841, D-4/59, H.B.A.
⁶³ *Ibid.*
⁶⁴ McLoughlin to Pelly, Colvile, Simpson, Oct. 31, 1842, F-12/1, H.B.A.
⁶⁵ Tolmie to Simpson, Oct. 14, 1843, D-5/9, H.B.A.
⁶⁶ Pelly to Simpson, Aug. 28, 1841, D-5/6, H.B.A.
⁶⁷ Simpson to McLoughlin, Mar. 1, 1842, D-4/60, H.B.A.
⁶⁸ Gov. and Comm. to Finlayson, Mar. 4, 1840, A-6/25, H.B.A.
⁶⁹ McLoughlin to Gov. and Comm., Nov. 18, 1843, H.B.S., X, 166–167.
⁷⁰ For a description of the activities of some of these missionaries, see William N. Bischoff, *The Jesuits in Old Oregon* (Caldwell, Idaho: Caxton Printers, 1945).
⁷¹ Finlayson to McLoughlin, July 9, 1842, B-235b/2, H.B.A.
⁷² Smith to James Keith, July 18, 1842, A-6/26, H.B.A.
⁷³ Blanchet was not consecrated as bishop until July 25, 1845, when the ceremony was performed in Montreal.
⁷⁴ Simpson to Gov. and Comm., Dec. 7, 1843, A-12/2, H.B.A.
⁷⁵ Simpson to Bishop of Draza and Vicar Apostolic of Oregon, July 31, 1845; Simpson to Pelly, July 31, 1845, both in D-4/67, H.B.A.
⁷⁶ Douglas to Simpson, Mar. 5, 1845, D-5/13, H.B.A.
⁷⁷ Douglas to Simpson, Apr. 4, 1845, private, *ibid.*
⁷⁸ Daniel Hazard to Agents, P.S.A.C., July 5, 1844, Soliday Collection.
⁷⁹ Simpson to Tolmie, June 19, 1845, D-4/67, H.B.A.

## Chapter 11

¹ Frederick Merk has effectively demonstrated this in "The Oregon Pioneers and the Boundary," *American Historical Review*, XXIX (July, 1924), 681–699.
² Lester Burrell Shippee, "The Federal Relations of Oregon," *Oregon Historical Quarterly*, XIX (Sept., 1918), 216.
³ *Congressional Globe*, 26th Cong., 1st sess., p. 60. A later substitute resolution, proffered on March 31, 1840, provided for the establishment of a line of military posts from Fort Leavenworth to the Rocky Mountains, and for the grant of 1,000 acres to each white male over eighteen after the boundary was settled. *Ibid.*, p. 296.
⁴ Pelly to Palmerston, Feb. 26, 1840, A-8/2, H.B.A.
⁵ Note, Stephen to R. Vernon Smith, Mar. 4, 1840, appended to Backhouse, F.O., to Stephen, Mar. 2, 1840, and encl., Pelly to Palmerston, Feb. 26, 1840, C.O. 6/14, P.R.O. The other boundary question to which Stephen referred was the dispute over the line between Maine and New Brunswick.
⁶ Backhouse to Stephen, May 4, 1840, and encls., C.O. 6/14, P.R.O.; Smith to Pelly, May 13, 1840, A-8/2, H.B.A.; Pelly to Russell, May 18, 1840, C.O. 6/14, P.R.O.
⁷ For details, see Hubert Howe Bancroft, *History of Oregon* (2 vols.; San Francisco: History Company, 1886–1888), I, 292 ff.
⁸ Douglas to Simpson, Aug. 24, 1841, private, D-5/6, H.B.A.
⁹ Simpson to Gov. and Comm., Nov. 25, 1841, D-4/59, H.B.A. This letter lists all the missionaries resident in Oregon in 1841 and locates their missions.

¹⁰ Simpson to Gov. and Comm., Mar. 1, 1842, D-4/60, H.B.A.

¹¹ *Ibid.*

¹² Simpson to Pelly, Mar. 10, 1842, D-4/60, H.B.A.

¹³ *Ibid.*

¹⁴ Thom to Simpson, Aug. 8, 1842, D-5/7, H.B.A.

¹⁵ Gov. and Comm. to McLoughlin, Dec. 31, 1842, A-6/26, H.B.A.

¹⁶ Aberdeen to Fox, Oct. 18, 1842, F.O. 5/376, P.R.O. For a better discussion of the negotiations, see Frederick Merk, "The Oregon Question in the Webster-Ashburton Negotiations," *Mississippi Valley Historical Review*, XLIII (Dec., 1956), 379–404.

¹⁷ Richard W. Van Alstyne, "International Rivalries in the Pacific Northwest," *Oregon Historical Quarterly*, XLVI (Sept., 1945), 205. Webster's scheme is described in Fox to Aberdeen, Feb. 24, 1843, F.O. 5/391, P.R.O. Webster had informed him, said Fox, that Ashburton supported the plan, but he added, "I did not learn from Mr. Webster, what reason he had for expecting that the Mexican Government would consent to the proposed Cession of Territory."

¹⁸ Webster to Everett, Nov. 28, 1842, in Fletcher Webster, ed., *The Writings and Speeches of Daniel Webster, Private Correspondence* (2 vols.; Boston: Little, Brown, 1857), II, 154.

¹⁹ Baltimore *Sun*, July 12, 1843, encl. in Fox to Aberdeen, July 28, 1843, F.O. 5/392, P.R.O.

²⁰ Simpson to Gov. and Comm., June 21, 1843, D-4/62, H.B.A.

²¹ In the session of 1842–43, Calhoun opposed Linn's bill which, after passing the Senate, 24 to 22, was defeated in the House. He based his objections on the ground that the bill was a violation of the treaty of 1827, but he agreed with Linn as to the objective.

²² Douglas to Simpson, Oct. 23, 1843, private, D-5/9, H.B.A.

²³ Douglas to Simpson, Mar. 18, 1844, D-5/10, H.B.A.

²⁴ See R. C. Clark, "How British and American Subjects Unite in a Common Government for Oregon Territory in 1844," *Oregon Historical Quarterly*, XIII (June, 1912), 140–159. See also H.B.S., VII, 3.

²⁵ McLoughlin to Gov. and Comm., Aug. 30, Nov. 20, 1845, H.B.S., VII, 94–95, 97–99, and letters following in same volume.

²⁶ Douglas to Simpson, Oct. 23, 1843, private, D-5/9, H.B.A.

²⁷ Simpson to Gov. and Comm., June 20, 1844, D-4/65, H.B.A.

²⁸ J. D. Richardson, *A Compilation of the Messages and Papers of the Presidents* (Washington: U.S. Govt. Printing Office, 1896–1899), IV, 257–272.

²⁹ Aberdeen to Pakenham, Mar. 4, 1844, Aberdeen MSS, cited in Frederick Merk, "The British Corn Crisis and the Oregon Treaty," *Agricultural History*, VIII (July, 1934), 119.

³⁰ Simpson to Pakenham, Mar. 28, 1844, D-4/64; Pakenham to Simpson, Apr. 9, 1844, D-5/11, both in H.B.A.

³¹ Simpson to Pakenham, Apr. 17, 1844, D-4/64, H.B.A.

³² Pakenham to Aberdeen, Aug. 29, 1844, F.O. 5/407, P.R.O.

³³ Simpson to Pakenham, 1844, encl. in Simpson to Gov. and Comm., June 20, 1844, D-4/65; Pelly to Simpson, Aug. 16, 1844, D-5/12, both in H.B.A.

³⁴ Bartlett had first come to Simpson's attention by publishing complimentary statements on Simpson's assistance to the Hawaiian Kingdom in its efforts to remain independent. Simpson to Bartlett, July 28, 1843, D-4/62, H.B.A. Bartlett continued in the service of the Company, for which he expected to be paid. He received some small compensation, though not so much as he desired.

³⁵ Douglas to Simpson, Mar. 5, 1845, H.B.S., VII, 180.

*Chapter 12*

¹ See John S. Galbraith, "France as a Factor in the Oregon Negotiations," *Pacific Northwest Quarterly*, XLIV (Apr., 1953), 69–73.

[2] Napier to Ellice, Oct. 24, 1844, Ellice Papers, Reel 40, P.A.C. The prospect of war with France was not so serious in 1844 or 1845 as it had been in 1842, when the British missionary, George Pritchard, was expelled from Tahiti. But the fear of French intervention in an Anglo-American conflict remained. British statesmen and military and naval officers were more concerned about possible attacks on British ports than about an invasion of the proportions necessary to conquer the island. For a later statement of this fear, see James Fergusson, *The Peril of Portsmouth; or, French Fleets and English Forts* (London: 1852).

[3] Frederick Merk, "The British Corn Crisis and the Oregon Treaty," *Agricultural History*, VIII (July, 1934). See also, by the same author, "British Party Politics and the Oregon Treaty," *American Historical Review*, XXXVII (July, 1932), 653–677; and Henry S. Commager, "England and the Oregon Treaty of 1846," *Oregon Historical Quarterly*, XXVIII (Mar., 1927), 18–38. For a good summary of the literature and points of view on the Oregon question, see Richard W. Van Alstyne, "International Rivalries in the Pacific Northwest," *Oregon Historical Quarterly*, XLVI (Sept., 1945), 185–218.

[4] Pakenham to Aberdeen, Sept. 28, 1844, confidential, F.O. 5/408, P.R.O.

[5] McLoughlin and Douglas to the Citizens of Oregon, [Mar., 1845]; McLoughlin to Exec. Committee of Oregon, Mar. 11, 1845; Russell, Stewart, Exec. Comm. of Oregon to McLoughlin, Mar. 21, 1845, all in B-223b/32, H.B.A. For a more detailed account, see Hubert Howe Bancroft, *History of Oregon* (2 vols.; San Francisco: History Company, 1886–1888), I, 459–460.

[6] Ermatinger to Simpson, Mar. 26, 1845, D-5/13, H.B.A.

[7] Simpson to Aberdeen, Mar. 29, 1845, D-4/66, H.B.A.

[8] See chap. 11, p. 228.

[9] Simpson to Aberdeen, Mar. 29, 1845, D-4/66, H.B.A.

[10] Aberdeen to Pakenham, Apr. 6, 1845, F.O. 5/423, P.R.O.

[11] H. U. Addington, F.O., to Simpson, Apr. 1, 1845, D-5/13, H.B.A.; Addington to Stephen, Apr. 3, 1845, confidential, W.O. 1/553, P.R.O.; Simpson to Pelly, Apr. 4, 1845, confidential, D-4/66, H.B.A.; Simpson to Metcalfe, Apr. 22, 1845, *ibid.* The original intention was to send an officer or two from England, but upon the recommendation of Lord Fitzroy Somerset at the Horse Guards, the government asked Sir Richard Jackson, commander of British forces in Canada, to make the appointment. Aberdeen to Peel, Apr. 3, 1845, Peel Papers, Addtl. MSS 40,455, British Museum.

[12] Aberdeen to Pakenham, Apr. 3, 1845, confidential, F.O. 5/423, P.R.O.

[13] Simpson to Pelly, Apr. 4, 1845, confidential, D-4/66; Simpson to Pelly, May 4, 1845, confidential, D-4/67, both in H.B.A.

[14] He had previously participated in diplomatic negotiations on behalf of the Hawaiian Kingdom after Lord George Paulet's abortive seizure of the Islands.

[15] Simpson to Pelly, May 4, 1845, confidential, A-12/2, H.B.A.

[16] Simpson to Warre and Vavasour, May 30, 1845, confidential, D-4/67, H.B.A.

[17] Simpson stressed the benefit to the Company's control over the Indians in a letter to Pelly, July 8, 1845, confidential, *ibid.*

[18] Simpson to Ogden, May 30, 1845, confidential, *ibid.* Simpson stated that they arrived at Red River on June 5. Simpson to Metcalfe, July 9, 1845, encl. in Metcalfe to Stanley, July 25, 1845, secret, W.O. 1/552, P.R.O. Frémont was actually on the way to California, not Oregon.

[19] P. J. de Smet, *Oregon Missions and Travels over the Rocky Mountains in 1845–46* (New York: E. Dunigan, 1847), p. 113.

[20] Pakenham to Aberdeen, July 29, 1845, F.O. 5/427, P.R.O.

[21] Stanley to Peel, Sept. 1, 1845, private, Peel Papers, Addtl. MSS 40,468.

[22] Metcalfe to Stanley, July 4, 1845, confidential, W.O. 1/552, P.R.O.

[23] Memorandum by Stanley, Sept. 1, 1845, Peel Papers, Addtl. MSS 40,468.

[24] Peel to Stanley, Sept. 5, 1845, Peel Papers, Addtl. MSS 40,468.

[25] Simpson to Colvile, Dec. 26, 1845, D-4/67, H.B.A.

²⁶ This correspondence is in A-12/2, H.B.A. See also Warre and Vavasour to Metcalfe, Nov. 1, 1845, W.O. 1/552, P.R.O.

²⁷ Ogden to Simpson, Apr. 4, 1846, private, D-5/17, H.B.A. On April 17, 1847, Warre wrote Simpson that his and Vavasour's report might have been better if there had been "unanimity between my coadjutor and myself." D-5/19, H.B.A.

²⁸ Joseph Schafer, ed., "Documents Relative to Warre and Vavasour's Military Reconnaissance in Oregon, 1845–6," *Oregon Historical Quarterly*, X (Mar., 1919), 1–99. Their original report on Oregon is in W.O. 1/552, P.R.O.

²⁹ Aberdeen to Pakenham, Apr. 6, 1845, F.O. 5/423, P.R.O.

³⁰ See Leslie M. Scott, ed., "Report of Lieutenant Peel on Oregon in 1845–46," *Oregon Historical Quarterly*, XXIX (Mar., 1928), 55–60. The story of Gordon's disgust with Oregon salmon is not apocryphal. William F. Tolmie, who accompanied him to the fishing spots around Fort Nisqually, told of Gordon's disappointment. The Nisqually River was too muddy for fly fishing, and the Chute River provided only trout. The captain caught several trout in the Chute, "but having killed salmon in almost every Scottish stream from the Ness to the Tweed, he lightly esteemed such sport." Tolmie to Simpson, Mar. 12, 1846, D-5/16, H.B.A.

³¹ Douglas to Simpson, Mar. 20, 1846, private, D-5/16, H.B.A. See also McLoughlin to Gov. and Comm., Nov. 20, 1845, H.B.S., VII, 146–147.

³² Aberdeen to Peel, Oct. 17, 1845, Peel Papers, quoted in Frederick Merk, "The Oregon Pioneers and the Boundary," *American Historical Review*, XXIX (July, 1924), 698–699.

³³ Aberdeen to Peel, Dec. 28, 1845, Peel Papers, Addtl. MSS 40,455.

³⁴ Ellice to Parkes, Jan. 5, 1846, private, Ellice Papers, Reel 29, P.A.C.

³⁵ Ellice to Simpson, Feb. 1, 1846, D-5/16, H.B.A.

³⁶ Barclay to Simpson, Jan. 3, 1846, *ibid.*

³⁷ London *Times*, Jan. 3, 1846, p. 4. Other newspapers had previously made the same suggestion. The London *Examiner*, April 25, 1845, proposed an agreement based upon the 49th parallel, with all Vancouver Island assigned to Great Britain. The *Edinburgh Review*, July, 1845, made the same appeal. The significance of the *Times* editorial lay not in the novelty of its proposals but in its alleged inspiration by the British government.

³⁸ Simpson to Pelly, Feb. 24, 1846, confidential, D-4/67; Simpson to Pelly, Apr. 29, 1846, D-4/68, both in H.B.A.

³⁹ Everett to Peel, Apr. 28, 1846, Peel Papers, Addtl. MSS 40,590.

⁴⁰ In his correspondence with Aberdeen and others in early 1846, Peel showed concern over the Spanish marriage, but very little over Oregon. For the issue over the Spanish marriage, see A. W. Ward and G. P. Gooch, eds., *The Cambridge History of British Foreign Policy, 1783–1919* (3 vols.; New York: Macmillan, 1922–1923), II, 185 ff.

⁴¹ Peel to Egerton, Jan. 6, 1846, secret, Peel Papers, Addtl. MSS 40,582.

⁴² On this point, see Lester Burrell Shippee, "The Federal Relations of Oregon," *Oregon Historical Quarterly*, XX (June, 1919), 177.

⁴³ See, for example, Croker to Aberdeen, Mar. 21, 1846, in Robert C. Clark, *History of the Willamette Valley, Oregon* (2 vols.; Chicago: S. J. Clarke Publishing Company, 1927), I, 856. It is not unlikely that the knowledge of Ellice and others in January, 1846, as to cabinet intentions may have come directly or indirectly from Croker, who was not notably discreet.

⁴⁴ Pakenham to Aberdeen, Feb. 26, 1846, confidential, F.O. 115/92, P.R.O.

⁴⁵ Everett to Peel, Apr. 28, 1846, Peel Papers, Addtl. MSS 40,590.

⁴⁶ Owen to Peel, Mar. 23, Apr. 25, 1846, Peel Papers, Addtl. MSS 40,588. Owen came to London in April to urge Peel to act immediately. Since Peel was engrossed in the Corn Laws fight he was unable to see Owen, and assigned the responsibility to the undersecretary, H. U. Addington.

⁴⁷ Croker to Aberdeen, May 13, 1846, in Clark, *op. cit.*, I, 859.

⁴⁸ Aberdeen to Pakenham, May 18, 1846, no. 19, F.O. 115/91, P.R.O.

⁴⁹ McLane to Buchanan, July 3, 1846, in David Hunter Miller, *Treaties and Other International Acts of the United States of America* (8 vols.; Washington: U.S. Govt. Printing Office, 1931), V, 83.

⁵⁰ Simpson would have been willing in August, 1846, to accept £50,000 for relinquishing the Company's rights in Oregon, though Pelly thought the amount too low. Simpson to Pelly, Aug. 18, 1846, confidential, D-4/68, H.B.A.

⁵¹ Pelly to Simpson, June 3, 1846, D-5/17, H.B.A. In A-13/11, H.B.A., there is a document, "Heads of Treaty or Convention," signed by Pelly. It was apparently written after the receipt in Britain of the president's announcement that the United States intended to terminate the convention of 1827. Only one proposed article is specified—the division of the territory at 49°, Vancouver Island to be British. The other articles, Pelly stated, should be "as suggested in my letter," but the letter in question could not be located either in the Hudson's Bay Archives or in the Foreign Office papers.

⁵² William M. Malloy, *Treaties, Conventions, International Acts, Protocols and Agreements between the United States of America and Other Powers, 1776–1909* (2 vols.; Washington: U.S. Govt. Printing Office, 1910), I, 657–658.

⁵³ Clark, *op. cit.*, I, 861.

⁵⁴ Tolmie to Simpson, Mar. 12, 1846, D-5/16, H.B.A.

⁵⁵ McLane to Buchanan, Dec. 1, 1845, in S. Doc. 489, 29th Cong., 1st sess.

⁵⁶ Note by Palmerston, Oct. 16, 1846, F.O. 5/450, P.R.O. Pakenham to Palmerston, Aug. 13, 1846, to which the note refers, is in F.O. 115/92, P.R.O.

⁵⁷ Ogden to Simpson, Mar. 15, 1847, D-5/19, H.B.A.

## Chapter 13

¹ Neil M. Howison, "Report of Lieutenant Neil M. Howison on Oregon, 1846," *Oregon Historical Quarterly*, XIV (Mar., 1913), 38. The report is reprinted from 30th Cong., 1st sess., H. Misc. Doc. 29. Howison intended to leave in September but his ship was wrecked on the Columbia bar. He chartered the *Cadboro* from the Company and was again ready to sail on November 1, but unfavorable weather forced him to remain anchored in Baker's Bay until January 18, 1847.

² The third was Michael T. Simmons, an American who had settled in the Nisqually area. The name "Vancouver" was accepted by the provisional government despite strong opposition from its members and from the American community at large, for it seemed to imply recognition of British rights on the north bank of the Columbia. See McLoughlin to Gov. and Comm., Nov. 20, 1845, H.B.S., VII, 106.

³ The population of Oregon in 1846 has been variously estimated; it was probably about 6,000, of whom more than 5,000 were Americans. See Robert C. Clark, *History of the Willamette Valley, Oregon* (2 vols.; Chicago: S. J. Clarke Publishing Company, 1927), I, 434–435.

⁴ Douglas to Simpson, Mar. 20, 1846, D-5/16, H.B.A.

⁵ The phrase is Howison's. Howison, *op. cit.*, p. 38.

⁶ McLoughlin, after a bitter controversy with Simpson, formally retired from active service by letter to Simpson on March 20, 1846, D-5/16, H.B.A. John Work became the third member of the board on McLoughlin's retirement.

⁷ Ogden to Simpson, Mar. 20, 1846, private and confidential, D-5/16, H.B.A.

⁸ McLoughlin to Gov. and Comm., Nov. 20, 1845, H.B.S., VII, 108. The individuals to whom the claims were assigned were James Douglas, chief factor; Francis Ermatinger, chief trader; Richard Lane, James Grahame, and Thomas Lowe, clerks; Forbes Barclay, surgeon and clerk; William Bruce, gardener; Edward Spencer, apprentice; and John McPhail, shepherd.

⁹ *British and American Joint Commission for the Final Settlement of the Claims of the Hudson's Bay and Puget's Sound Agricultural Companies* (14 vols.; Mon-

treal and Washington: 1865–1869), vol. 13, *Arguments on behalf of United States,* p. 30. "Smith" was apparently Lyon A. Smith, who continued to plague Tolmie in ensuing years.

[10] McLane to Buchanan, July 3, 1846, in David Hunter Miller, *Treaties and Other International Acts of the United States of America* (8 vols.; Washington: U.S. Govt. Printing Office, 1931), V, 83.

[11] *Ibid.*, p. 7.

[12] *Ibid.*, pp. 85–86.

[13] Milo M. Quaife, ed., *The Diary of James K. Polk* (4 vols.; Chicago: A. C. McClurg, 1910), I, 452.

[14] Pelly to Palmerston, July 30, 1846, A-8/14, H.B.A. The net profits of the P.S.A.C. were £2,220 in 1845, and £1,733 in 1846. Pelly to Simpson, Jan. 4, 1847, private, D-5/19, H.B.A.

[15] Pelly to Simpson, Nov. 2, 1846, private and confidential, A-5/18, H.B.A.

[16] Douglas to Barclay, Apr. 29, 1847, A-11/70; Ogden and Douglas to Gov. and Comm., Sept. 20, 1847, B-223b/36, both in H.B.A.

[17] Simpson to Pelly, Aug. 18, 1846, confidential, D-4/68; Pelly to Simpson, Nov. 2, 1846, private and confidential, D-5/18, both in H.B.A.

[18] Simpson to Ogden, Douglas, and Work, Aug. 4, 1846, confidential, D-4/68, H.B.A.

[19] Ogden and Douglas to Simpson, Mar. 19, 1847, D-5/19, H.B.A.

[20] Douglas and Ogden to Simpson, Mar. 16, 1848, D-5/21, H.B.A.

[21] Ogden to Simpson, Mar. 16, 1850, D-5/27, H.B.A.

[22] A. Barclay to Ogden, Oct. 31, 1853, A-12/7, H.B.A.

[23] Simpson to A. Barclay, Jan. 21, 1854, *ibid.*

[24] Pelly to Simpson, Nov. 2, 1846, private and confidential, D-5/18, H.B.A.

[25] Quaife, *op. cit.*, I, 371.

[26] Unless otherwise indicated, the following information on the Company's relations with Sanders is taken from John S. Galbraith, "George N. Sanders, 'Influence Man' for the Hudson's Bay Company," *Oregon Historical Quarterly*, LIII (Sept., 1952), 159–176. Another account of Sanders' lobbying activities, differing in some details, is provided by Miller, *op. cit.*, VIII, 1003 ff. For another side of Sanders' career, see Merle Curti, "George N. Sanders, Patriot of the Fifties," *South Atlantic Quarterly*, XXVIII (Jan., 1928), 78–87. Sanders' activities as a Confederate agent in the Civil War were important enough to make President Johnson offer $25,000 for his capture. The resulting attempt to kidnap Sanders from his residence in Montreal was a bizarre episode in a life that, if unproductive, was never dull.

[27] Simpson to Sanders, Jan. 15, 1848, D-4/69, H.B.A. At this time Simpson himself would have been willing to accept $250,000 for the property of the two companies. Simpson to Pelly, Feb. 7, 1849, *ibid.*

[28] "Memorandum of Agreement," Apr. 28, 1848, A-37/27, H.B.A.

[29] See Quaife, *op. cit.*, IV, 301.

[30] "Report" of H. H. Berens, A-10/24, H.B.A. Berens kept a diary of occurrences during his stay in Washington. John F. Crampton, the British chargé d'affaires, informed Berens that Buchanan was willing to support this price.

[31] Simpson to Pelly, Aug. 15, 1848, private and confidential, D-4/70, H.B.A.

[32] Simpson, "Notes of a Conversation at an interview with Mr. Buchanan," Aug. 15, 1848; Simpson to Pelly, Aug. 24, 1848, both in D-4/70, H.B.A. Berens' "Report," A-10/24, H.B.A., agrees with Simpson's version.

[33] Pelly to Palmerston, Sept. 11, 1848, A-8/14, H.B.A.

[34] Addington to Pelly, Sept. 18, 1848, *ibid.*

[35] Douglas to Gov. and Comm., Sept. 20, 1847, B-223b/36, H.B.A.

[36] Douglas and Work to Gov. and Comm., Nov. 6, 1847, *ibid.*

[37] Simpson to Pelly, Feb. 16, 23, 1849, confidential, both in D-4/70, H.B.A.

[38] The correspondence involving Clayton is contained largely in A-12/4 and D-4/70 and 71, H.B.A.

[39] Douglas and Ogden to Simpson, Mar. 16, 1848, and encls., D-5/21, H.B.A.

[40] *Ibid.*

[41] Hubert Howe Bancroft, *History of Oregon* (2 vols.; San Francisco: History Company, 1886–1888), I, 675, states that Douglas eventually "advanced the means to equip and put in the field the first company of Oregon riflemen, at a cost of about a thousand dollars." There is no citation to support this statement. If Douglas did so—and it is likely that he did—he made the advance from his own resources, for he at no time requested authority from the Company or notified his superiors of any such action.

[42] Douglas to Simpson, Mar. 12, 1849, private, D-5/24, H.B.A.

[43] For some exceptions to the general tranquillity, see Howard T. Burnham, "Government Grants and Patents in Vancouver, Washington," *Oregon Historical Quarterly*, XLVIII (June, 1947), 7–44.

[44] Copies of these notices are preserved in the Soliday Collection, Huntington Library.

[45] On October 1, 1848, little more than a month after news of the gold discoveries reached the Columbia, Ogden informed the governor and committee that 2,000 settlers had already left for the Sacramento area. Ogden to Gov. and Comm., B-223b/38, H.B.A. On September 15, 1849, he reported that the immigration to Oregon was small for that year, not exceeding 200, but that not less than 20,000 emigrants had passed Fort Hall on the way to California. Ogden to Simpson, Sept. 15, 1849, private, D-5/26, H.B.A.

[46] Douglas to Simpson, Sept. 22, 1849, private, D-5/26, H.B.A.

[47] Unskilled laborers received from $5 to $10 a day in the Willamette valley in 1849. Ogden to Simpson, Oct. 15, 1849, private, D-5/26, H.B.A. Sailors demanded and received $150 a month. McNeill to Simpson, Sept. 28, 1849, *ibid.*

[48] Frances Fuller Victor, "The First Oregon Cavalry," *Oregon Historical Quarterly*, III (June, 1902), 123.

[49] Douglas to Simpson, Sept. 22, 1849, private, D-5/26, H.B.A.

[50] Simpson to Pelly, Mar. 10, 1850, confidential, D-4/71, H.B.A.

[51] Bancroft, *op. cit.*, II, 115, 118.

[52] Douglas to Simpson, Oct. 15, 1850, private, D-5/29, H.B.A.; Meredith to Adair, May 30, 1850, encl. in Pelly to Palmerston, Dec. 5, 1850, A-8/14, H.B.A. Nisqually was made a collection district early in 1851, but apparently at the request of Michael T. Simmons, a prominent farmer and merchant, rather than for the convenience of the Hudson's Bay Company.

[53] Douglas to Simpson, Feb. 11, 1852, D-5/33, H.B.A.

[54] Tolmie to Simpson, Nov. 15, 1852; Ballenden to Simpson, Dec. 1, 1852, both in D-5/35, H.B.A.

[55] Tolmie to Barclay, Dec. 25, 1851, B-223b/39, H.B.A.

[56] Marye to Tolmie, Jan. 23, 1852, Soliday Collection; Smith to Mactavish, Oct. 22, 1855, A-6/31, H.B.A.

[57] Ogden to Simpson, Oct. 17, 1850, D-5/29, H.B.A.

[58] Memorandum by Huggins, Soliday Collection.

[59] The total profits from Oregon south of 49° in 1850–51 were £14,814. In 1851–52, the district suffered a net loss of £6,754. The sharp drop was caused partly by changes in accounting procedures, but the actual loss was serious. E. Colvile to Gov. and Comm., July 21, 1852, A-12/6, H.B.A. The trade west of the mountains was divided into two departments—the western and the Oregon. The western department was north of 49° and the Oregon department south of that line. One reason for the division was the Company's hope that it could sell its rights in Oregon and withdraw.

[60] 32d Cong., 1st sess., S. Ex. Doc. 1, pt. 3, pp. 7, 473–474; Ogden to Simpson, Mar. 22, 1852, D-5/33, H.B.A.

[61] Simpson later declared that Fletcher Webster was also an intermediary with his father, but his name does not appear in correspondence at the time of the negotiations. Simpson to Shepherd, Mar. 20, 1858, D-4/84a, H.B.A.

[62] A draft convention is published in Miller, *op. cit.*, VIII, 1022–1023.

[63] Shepherd was elected to the committee of the Hudson's Bay Company in 1850; he was elevated to the deputy-governorship upon Colvile's election as governor; and he became governor in 1856 when Colvile died. He resigned in 1858 and resumed his position as a member of the committee.

[64] Shepherd to Ellice, Jr., Aug. 27, 1852; Shepherd to Ellice, Sr., Sept. 6, 1852, both in Ellice Papers, Reel 28, P.A.C.

[65] Stanley to A. Colvile, Nov. 6, 1852, A-8/18, H.B.A.

[66] This was the amount advanced him by the Company. Simpson to Colvile, Oct. 22, 1853, D-4/82, H.B.A.

[67] Simpson to A. Colvile, Aug. 13, 1853, *ibid.*

[68] Simpson to Eden Colvile, Sept. 26, 1853, *ibid.*

[69] Simpson to A. Colvile, Oct. 22, 1853, confidential, *ibid.*

[70] Simpson to Crampton, Dec. 30, 1854, D-4/75, H.B.A. The sum was based on the value of the property as estimated by Governor Isaac I. Stevens of Washington Territory.

[71] Simpson to Colvile, Jan. 20, 1855, D-4/83, H.B.A.

[72] J. D. Richardson, *A Compilation of the Messages and Papers of the Presidents* (Washington: U.S. Govt. Printing Office, 1896–1899), IV, 2811.

[73] *Congressional Globe*, 33d Cong., 2d sess., pp. 1093–1094.

[74] Richardson, *op. cit.*, IV, 2866–2867.

[75] Mactavish to Simpson, Mar. 26, 1856, D-5/41, H.B.A.

[76] Simpson to Eden Colvile, Feb. 23, 1856, D-4/83, H.B.A.

[77] Simpson to Board of Management, Western Department, Jan. 29, 1856, D-4/75, H.B.A. The Flathead post of this period was built in 1847, sixty miles east of the old Flathead post. The Company consequently had no "possessory rights" at the new post. See Albert J. Partoll, "Fort Connah: A Frontier Trading Post, 1847–1871," *Pacific Northwest Quarterly*, XXX (Oct., 1939), 399–415.

[78] Memorial of Legislative Assembly, passed Mar. 23, 1854, in *Journal of the Council of the Territory of Washington*, 1st sess., 1854 (Olympia: 1855), p. 184.

[79] Tax records in Soliday Collection.

[80] Dugald Mactavish to Simpson, Aug. 4, 1855, D-5/40, H.B.A.

[81] Smith to Day, Mar. 21, 1868, A-6/42, H.B.A.

[82] John Wilson to James Tilton, Mar. 12, 1855, in *Journal of the Council of the Territory of Washington*, 3d sess., 1855–56 (Olympia: 1856), p. 199.

[83] Simpson to Dugald Mactavish, Jan. 29, 1856, D-4/76; Simpson to Board of Management, Western Department, Jan. 29, 1856, D-4/75, both in H.B.A.

[84] Shepherd to Clarendon, May 13, 1856, A-8/19, H.B.A.

[85] Lumley to Simpson, Aug. 14, 1856, encl. in Simpson to Shepherd, Aug. 23, 1856, confidential, A-7/2, H.B.A.

[86] Shepherd to Simpson, Oct. 9, 1857, private, D-5/45; Napier to Clarendon, Nov. 9, 1857, A-7/2; Napier to Cass, Nov. 4, 1857, A-7/2, all in H.B.A.

[87] Napier to Simpson, Jan. 3, 1858, D-5/46, H.B.A.

[88] Simpson to Napier, Jan. 11, 1858, D-4/77, H.B.A.

[89] Napier to Malmesbury, July 27, 1858, encl. in Fitzgerald to Shepherd, Aug. 18, 1858, A-8/19, H.B.A.

[90] Ellice to Berens, Sept. 14, 1858, D-4/84a, H.B.A. The provisions of the agreement had previously been unknown to Ellice and to most of the governing board. Only Pelly, who had died, and Simpson had known them.

[91] Hammond to Shepherd, Aug. 9, 1858, A-8/19, H.B.A.

[92] Mactavish to Simpson, Sept. 17, 1857, D-5/44, H.B.A.

[93] Mactavish to Simpson, Oct. 3, 1857, and encls., D-5/45, H.B.A.

[94] Grahame to Fraser, July 22, 1859, A-11/71, H.B.A.

[95] Hammond to Berens, Feb. 13, 1860, A-8/20, H.B.A.

[96] Pleasanton to Work, Mar. 3, 1860, encl. in Berens to Russell, May 3, 1860, *ibid.*

[97] Lyons to Cass, May 25, 1860; Cass to Lyons, June 7, 1860, both in *ibid*.

[98] Dallas had previously been a member of the London board. He had been authorized to take this action, but the governor and committee had requested him to wait until one final representation was made to the secretary of state. Dallas, convinced that no benefit would arise from such delay, chose to act immediately. Fraser to Dallas, June 23, 1860, A-6/35; Fraser to Russell, Aug. 22, 1860, A-8/20, both in H.B.A.

[99] Memorandum by Grahame, July 2, 1860, encl. in Berens to Russell, Oct. 17, 1860, A-8/20, H.B.A.

[100] "Annual Report of the Secretary of the Interior," Dec. 3, 1860, encl. in Berens to Russell, Feb. 7, 1861, *ibid*.

[101] James A. Grahame to Simpson, July 4, 1859, A-11/71, H.B.A.

[102] Rose to Berens, May 11, 1863, A-10/54, H.B.A.

[103] Berens to Russell, Feb. 19, 1863; Hammond to Berens, Apr. 10, 1863, confidential, and encl., Lyons to Russell, Mar. 24, 1863; Berens to Russell, Apr. 28, 1863, all in A-8/20, H.B.A.

[104] Layard to Head, July 27, 1863, *ibid*. Ratifications were exchanged on March 3, 1864.

[105] *British and American Joint Commission for the Final Settlement of the Claims of the Hudson's Bay and Puget's Sound Agricultural Companies* (14 vols.; Montreal and Washington: 1865–1869).

[106] Hammond to Secretaries, H.B.C. & P.S.A.C., June 8, 1871, A-8/21, H.B.A.

[107] Hammond to Secretary, H.B.C., Sept. 13, 1871, *ibid*.

[108] This inexactitude also caused a dispute over the boundary line in the Strait of Juan de Fuca. Hamilton Fish alleged that, before the treaty of 1846 was negotiated, the Americans had agreed to its provisions on the basis of an "honorable understanding" that the Haro channel was to be the boundary, but that Aberdeen at Pelly's suggestion caused the article to be framed in ambiguous language. Northcote to Gladstone, Mar. 17, 1871, Gladstone Papers, Addtl. MSS 44,217, British Museum. If this was true, and there is no evidence at my disposal to support it, the article was the only one seriously affected by Pelly's advice.

## Chapter 14

[1] Note by Grey, Sept. 16, on Pelly to Grey, Sept. 7, 1846, C.O. 305/1, P.R.O.

[2] *Ibid*.

[3] Duncan Finlayson to McLoughlin, Sept. 29, 1836, B-223b/12, H.B.A.

[4] For an early expression of this view, see Matthew Macfie, *Vancouver Island and British Columbia* (London: Longman, Green, Longman, Roberts & Green, 1865), p. 2. One of the first to dissent from the generally accepted view was W. Kaye Lamb, "The Governorship of Richard Blanshard," *British Columbia Historical Quarterly*, XIV (Jan.–Apr., 1950), 18.

[5] Simpson expressed his opposition in a letter to Pelly, October 3, 1848, confidential, D-4/70, H.B.A., and in a private letter to Archibald Barclay, September 7, 1848, the contents of which are indicated in Barclay to Simpson, Oct. 13, 1848, private, D-5/23, H.B.A.

[6] Barclay to Simpson, Oct. 13, 1848, private, D-5/23, H.B.A.

[7] Grey to Ellice, Sept. 23, 1848, Ellice Papers, Reel 35, P.A.C.

[8] Ellice to A. G. Dallas, Ellice Papers, Reel 28.

[9] Pelly to Grey, Sept. 7, 1846, C.O. 305/1, P.R.O.

[10] Hawes to Pelly, Oct. 3, 1846, *ibid*.

[11] Pelly to Grey, Mar. 5, 1847, and notes thereto, *ibid*. The opposition of James Stephen and much of the correspondence between Pelly and the Colonial Office are amply described by Paul Knaplund, "James Stephen on Granting Vancouver Island to the Hudson's Bay Company, 1846–1848," *British Columbia Historical Quar-*

*terly,* IX (Oct., 1945), 259–271. No effort will therefore be made here to describe in detail the negotiations during this period.

[12] Pelly to Simpson, Oct. 27, 1848, private, D-5/23, H.B.A.

[13] Simpson to Pelly, Nov. 22, 1848, D-4/70, H.B.A.

[14] Note by Hawes on Fitzgerald to Hawes, June 9, 1847, C.O. 305/1, P.R.O.

[15] Fitzgerald to Hawes, June 9, 1847, *ibid.* This letter is printed in *Report of the Provincial Archives Department,* 1913, in *Sessional Papers, British Columbia,* Session 1914, II, V54–62.

[16] For a more detailed discussion of Fitzgerald's proposals and his subsequent conflict with the Company, see my article, "Fitzgerald versus the Hudson's Bay Company: the Founding of Vancouver Island," *British Columbia Historical Quarterly,* XVI (July–Oct., 1952), 191–207. Some of the material in this chapter is extracted from that article.

[17] Fitzgerald was twenty-nine years old when he made his first proposal in 1847.

[18] Merivale to Pelly, Mar. 13, 1848, A-8/4, H.B.A.

[19] For the Fitzgerald-Gladstone correspondence see Paul Knaplund, "Letters from James Edward Fitzgerald to W. E. Gladstone Concerning Vancouver Island and the Hudson's Bay Company, 1848–1850," *British Columbia Historical Quarterly,* XIII (Jan., 1949), 1–21. Fitzgerald soon left for New Zealand, where he became a prominent citizen.

[20] *Parliamentary Debates,* 3d ser., CI, 467, 474, 304–305.

[21] Hawes on one occasion stated privately: "I do not believe that the H. B. Co. would enter the Colonization of Vancouvers Island with any large & liberal views." Note by Hawes on Dundas to Hawes, May 30, 1848, C.O. 305/1, P.R.O.

[22] Grey to Ellice, Sept. 23, 1848, Ellice Papers, Reel 35.

[23] Hawes to Pelly, Sept. 4, 1848, A-8/4, H.B.A.; Royal Grant, Letters Patent, Jan. 13, 1849, A-37/1, H.B.A.

[24] Confidential Print, Vancouver's Island, printed at Foreign Office, Mar., 1849, apparently for cabinet use, C.O. 305/1, P.R.O. This statement is reprinted in *Report of the Provincial Archives Department,* 1913, pp. V70–73.

[25] Resolution of Committee, Jan. 24, 1849, A-1/66, H.B.A. Printed prospectus in Gladstone Papers, Addtl. MSS 44,566, British Museum. It may be significant that the only comments written by Gladstone on the prospectus were the questions, "any surveys made? Choice of land?"

[26] Fitzgerald to Hawes, June 9, 1847, in *Report of the Provincial Archives Department,* 1913, pp. V54–62.

[27] A. Colvile to Simpson, Apr. 6, 1849, D-5/25, H.B.A. Enderby first approached Pelly in April, 1848, and was informed that the Company, if it received the grant, would look with favor on the use of Vancouver Island by whaling vessels. Enderby's failure to establish the station was the result of circumstances unrelated to the Hudson's Bay Company.

[28] Selkirk to Pelly, May 27, 1848, A-10/24, H.B.A.

[29] Colvile to Simpson, Mar. 8, 1850, D-5/27, H.B.A.

[30] Colvile to Simpson, Apr. 6, 1849, D-5/25, H.B.A.

[31] Simpson to Pelly, Oct. 25, 1848, D-4/70, H.B.A.

[32] Pelly to Simpson, Sept. 7, 1849, private, D-5/26, H.B.A. Pelly stated that Blanshard's appointment "was with my entire concurrence, indeed recommendation." He would have preferred Douglas, but recognized that such an appointment might arouse further criticism.

[33] See Lamb, *op. cit.,* pp. 1–40.

[34] Hawes to Pelly, Apr. 30, 1851, A-8/6, H.B.A.

[35] Ogden to Simpson, Nov. 10, 1848, D-5/23, H.B.A.

[36] Barclay to Douglas, Nov. 15, 1850, A-6/28, H.B.A.

[37] Douglas to Simpson, June 7, 1850, D-5/28, H.B.A.

[38] L. F. Brannhardt to Barclay, Aug. 23, 1850, A-10/28, H.B.A. Correspondence on the advertisements is contained in A-10/27 and 28.

[39] Arthur S. Morton, *A History of the Canadian West to 1870–71* (London: T. Nelson & Sons, [1939]), p. 754.

[40] Report of Moresby, July 3, 1851, encl. in Hawes to Pelly, Nov. 3, 1851, A-8/6, H.B.A.

[41] Simpson to Douglas, Feb. 20, 1850, private, D-4/71, H.B.A.

[42] Douglas to Simpson, June 7, 1850, private, D-5/28, H.B.A.

[43] One of them, James Cooper, was a financial success, but he made his fortune from the sale of liquor in Victoria rather than from the land. The unhappy fate of overoptimistic landlords is illustrated by Captain W. Colquhoun Grant, the first person to buy a large acreage on the island. For a description of Grant's unsuccessful venture, see Morton, *op. cit.*, p. 758.

[44] Pelly to Grey, Nov. 7, 1851, A-8/6, H.B.A.

[45] Douglas to Simpson, May 21, 1851, D-5/30, H.B.A.

[46] Barclay to Douglas, Nov. 5, 1850; Barclay to Simpson, Nov. 8, 1850, both in A-6/28; Pelly to Grey, Jan. 14, 1852, A-8/6, all in H.B.A.

[47] Statement by Richard Clemens, undated, in Moresby to Admiralty, July 7, 1851, encl. in Frederick Peel to Pelly, Dec. 20, 1851, A-8/6, H.B.A.

[48] The regularity with which salmon was served was a standing complaint among the Company's employees on Vancouver Island and in British Columbia.

[49] Pelly to Grey, Jan. 14, 1852, A-8/6, H.B.A.

[50] A. Colvile to Pakington, Nov. 24, 1852, A-8/7, H.B.A.

[51] A. Colvile to Russell, June 9, 1855, *ibid.*

[52] A. Colvile to Pakington, Nov. 24, 1852, *ibid.*

[53] A. Colvile to Russell, June 9, 1855, *ibid.*

[54] Walter N. Sage, *Sir James Douglas and British Columbia* (Toronto: University of Toronto Press, 1930), p. 168.

[55] *Parliamentary Debates,* 3d ser., CXXXI, 550–551; CXXXIII, 1356–1357.

[56] Simpson to A. Colvile, Nov. 4, 1853, D-4/82, H.B.A.

[57] Simpson to A. Colvile, Sept. 3, 1853, *ibid.* Fitzwilliam described his visit in testimony before the Select Committee of the House of Commons on the Hudson's Bay Company in 1857. See the *Report of the Select Committee . . .* (London: 1857), p. 114.

[58] Frederick Peel to Pelly, Dec. 20, 1851, A-8/6, H.B.A.

[59] Pelly to Grey, Jan. 14, 1852, *ibid.*

[60] Merivale to Barclay, Oct. 27, 1853, A-8/7, H.B.A.

[61] A. Colvile to Newcastle, Nov. 8, 1853, *ibid.*

[62] Newcastle served from December 28, 1852, to June 12, 1854. He assumed the direction of the War Office when it was separated from the Colonial Office.

[63] Merivale to Gov., H.B.C., Apr. 5, 1855, A-7/2, H.B.A.

[64] *Ibid.*

[65] Sage, *op. cit.*, pp. 188–191.

[66] Colvile to Merivale, Apr. 16, 1855, A-7/2, H.B.A.

[67] Labouchere to Head, Dec. 4, 1856, in Governor General's Correspondence, 50, P.A.C.

[68] McNeill to Douglas, Nov. 20, 1851, encl. in Pelly to Pakington, Mar. 26, 1852; Ballenden to Pelly, Feb. 3, 1852, encl. in Pelly to Pakington, Apr. 3, 1852, both in A-8/6, H.B.A.

[69] Ballenden to Tolmie, Apr. 23, 1852, in Soliday Collection.

[70] Hubert Howe Bancroft, *History of British Columbia, 1792–1887* (San Francisco: History Company, 1887), pp. 348–349.

[71] Simpson to Mactavish, Feb. 16, 1858, D-4/77, H.B.A.

[72] Sage, *op. cit.*, pp. 206 ff.

[73] *Ibid.*, p. 214.

[74] Berens to Douglas, July 16, 1858, A-7/2, H.B.A.

[75] 21 & 22 Vic., cap. 99.

[76] R. C. Mayne, *Four Years in British Columbia and Vancouver Island* (London: 1862), quoted in Sage, *op. cit.,* p. 215.

[77] Douglas to Fraser, Nov. 25, 1858, in Berens to Lytton, Feb. 21, 1859, A-8/9, H.B.A.

[78] Shepherd to Labouchere, Feb. 24, 1858, A-8/6, H.B.A.

[79] The government paid the Company £25,000 in 1861, and authorized the remaining £32,500 in 1862.

[80] Indenture, Apr. 3, 1867, in Hudson's Bay Company, *Charters, Statutes, Orders in Council &c. Relating to the Hudson's Bay Company* (London: Hudson's Bay Company, 1931), pp. 223–225.

[81] Ellice to Dallas, Sept. 14, 1859, Ellice Papers, Reel 28.

[82] Lowe to Ellice, Nov., 1859, Ellice Papers, Reel 37.

## *Chapter 15*

[1] Simpson to Colvile, May 20, 1822, Selkirk Transcripts, vol. 24, H.B.A.

[2] Thom to Simpson, Jan. 2, 1845, confidential, D-5/13, H.B.A.

[3] Memorandum, Simpson to Aberdeen, Mar. 29, 1845, D-4/66, H.B.A.

[4] Simpson to Warre and Vavasour, May 30, 1845, confidential, D-4/67, H.B.A.

[5] Simpson to Pelly, July 8, 1845, confidential, *ibid.*

[6] Metcalfe to Stanley, July 4, 1845, confidential, W.O. 1/552, P.R.O.

[7] Simpson to Metcalfe, July 9, 1845, D-4/67, H.B.A.; Metcalfe to Stanley, July 26, 1845, W.O. 1/552, P.R.O.; Simpson to Pelly, Aug. 1, 1845, confidential, D-4/67, H.B.A.

[8] Simpson to Berens, Sept. 12, 1845, private, D-4/67, H.B.A.

[9] Simpson to Pelly, Oct. 24, 1845, *ibid.*

[10] Simpson to Gov. and Comm., Nov. 11, 1845, *ibid.;* Simpson to Gov. and Comm., Oct. 28, 1845, encl. in Addington to Hope, Nov. 27, 1845, W.O. 1/553, P.R.O.

[11] Addington to Hope, Nov. 27, 1845, W.O. 1/553, P.R.O.

[12] Stanley to Cathcart, Dec. 3, 1845, secret, *ibid.*

[13] Simpson to Gov. and Comm., Dec. 24, 1845, confidential, D-4/67, H.B.A.

[14] Pelly to Herbert, Jan. 31, 1846; Herbert to Pelly, Jan. 31, Feb. 2, 1846, all in A-8/3, H.B.A.

[15] See, for example, Herbert to Pelly, Feb. 2, 1846, *ibid.*

[16] Wellington to Gladstone, Mar. 28, 1846, W.O. 1/555, P.R.O. Wellington was also opposed to the recruitment of troops in the colonies to serve locally, presumably because he feared that such military forces might be used against the mother country in the event of rebellion.

[17] Gladstone to Pelly, Apr. 17, 1846 (two letters), A-8/3, H.B.A.

[18] Pelly to Gladstone, Apr. 24, 1846, *ibid.*

[19] Lyttelton to Pelly, Apr. 28, 1846, *ibid.*

[20] Minute 361, North America (Military), July 7, [1846], by P. S[mith], W.O. 1/551, P.R.O.

[21] Simpson to Gov. and Comm., July 23, 1846, D-4/68, H.B.A. When the troops left for home in the spring of 1848, there were 15 officers, 18 sergeants, 6 drummers, and 301 rank and file. Grey to Pelly, Mar. 11, 1848, A-8/4, H.B.A.

[22] A. Ross to D. Ross, Aug. 9, 1847, AB40/R732, B.C. Archives.

[23] Memorial to the Right Honourable Secretary of State for the Colonies, encl. in Isbister to Grey, Feb. 17, 1847, A-13/3, H.B.A.

[24] Isbister to Pelly, undated, recd. July 14, 1845, A-10/20, H.B.A.; certificate by Pelly, July 24, 1845, A-5/15, H.B.A.

[25] Isbister to Pelly, Mar. 10, June 9, 1846, both in A-10/21, H.B.A.

[26] See chap. 4, pp. 65–66.

[27] See H.B.S., IV, cxvii ff.

[28] For a brief biography of Alexander Simpson, see H.B.S., VI, 404–406.

[29] Isbister to Grey, Mar. 5, 1847, encl. in Hawes to Pelly, Mar. 18, 1847, A-13/3, H.B.A.

[30] Grey to Elgin, June 4, 1847, Governor General's Correspondence, 50, P.A.C.

[31] Elgin to Grey, June 6, 1848, in G. 12, vol. 65, Dispatches from Cathcart and Elgin, P.A.C.

[32] Pelly to Simpson, Sept. 3, 1847, private; Crofton to Simpson, Sept. 18, Nov. 15, 1847, all in D-5/20; Crofton to Simpson, Mar. 1, 1848, D-5/21, all in H.B.A.

[33] McLaughlin to Grey, Jan. 16, 1850, encl. in Merivale to Pelly, Jan. 31, 1850, A-8/6, H.B.A.

[34] Isbister to Rowand, July 3, 1847, encl. in Simpson to Gov. and Comm., Nov. 16, 1848, A-12/4, H.B.A.

[35] Kennedy to Elgin, Oct. [?], Oct. 24, Nov. 6, 1848, encls. in Elgin to Grey, Nov. 10, 1848, A-13/3, H.B.A.

[36] Encls. in Elgin to Grey, Nov. 10, 1848, *ibid.*

[37] Grey to Elgin, Dec. 29, 1848, encl. in Merivale to Pelly, Jan. 17, 1849, A-13/4, H.B.A.

[38] Grey to Isbister, Jan. 23, 1849, encl. in Hawes to Pelly, Jan. 23, 1849, *ibid.*

[39] *Parliamentary Debates,* 3d ser., CI, 282.

[40] Sir George Simpson, "Observations on Speeches in the House of Lords and House of Commons . . . ," Mar. 28, 1849, A-12/4, H.B.A.

[41] Store Invoice York Factory, 1840–41, B-239dd/21, H.B.A. Further information on shipments is contained in A-25 series, H.B.A.

[42] Statement by Peter Jacobs, July 2, 1849, D-5/25, H.B.A.

[43] Pelly to Grey, Mar. 19, 1850, A-8/6, H.B.A. This statement was in answer to a charge by the United States government that the Company was furnishing large quantities of liquor to Indians on the frontier.

[44] Merivale to Pelly, Aug. 23, 1849, A-8/4, H.B.A.

[45] Pelly to Ellice, Feb. 17, 1849, A-10/26, H.B.A.

[46] Pelly referred to 14 George III, cap. 83; 1 & 2 George IV, cap. 66; 6 Anne, cap. 37; 18 George II, cap. 17. Pelly to Grey, Sept. 13, 1849, A-8/4, H.B.A. Interestingly, he did not mention the act passed in 1690 (2 William and Mary, cap. 23), which confirmed the rights granted by the charter for a period of seven years and was not renewed.

[47] Sir John Jervis and Sir John Romilly, Atty Gen. & Solicitor Gen., to Earl Grey, Jan., 1850, *Accounts and Papers,* 1850, no. 542.

[48] Isbister to Grey, Mar. 9, 1850; McLaughlin to Grey, Apr. 13, 1850, *ibid.*

[49] Grey to Pelly, May 24, 1847, A-8/4, H.B.A.

[50] Pelly to Grey, May 27, 1847, *ibid.*

[51] Christie to Simpson, private, Sept. 28, Oct. 2, 1847, both in D-5/20, H.B.A.

[52] Simpson to Pelly, Oct. 11, 1847, confidential, D-4/69, H.B.A.

[53] Pelly to Grey, Dec. 2, 1847, A-8/4, H.B.A.

[54] Barclay to Simpson, Dec. 3, 1847, D-5/20, H.B.A.

[55] Pelly to Simpson, Jan. 28, 1848, D-5/21, H.B.A.

[56] Barclay to Simpson, Feb. 11, 1848, private, *ibid.*

[57] Pelly to Simpson, Mar. 10, 1848, private, *ibid.;* Grey to Pelly, Mar. 11, 1848, A-8/4, H.B.A.

[58] Pelly to Simpson, May 26, 1848, D-5/22; Gov. and Comm. to Simpson, June 3, 1848, A-6/27, both in H.B.A. Fourteen pensioners were to have joined the transport at Cork, but were left behind when the Admiralty insisted that the *General Palmer* sail without delay. Caldwell to Simpson, Nov. 29, 1848, D-5/23, H.B.A. These or another fourteen pensioners arrived later, for the pensioner corps numbered seventy in the spring of 1851. Pelly to Grey, Apr. 23, 1851, A-8/6, H.B.A.

[59] W. Sinclair to Simpson, Sept. 20, 1848, D-5/22, H.B.A.

[60] For further description of the Sayer case, see Arthur S. Morton, *A History of the Canadian West to 1870–71* (London: T. Nelson & Sons, [1939]), pp. 814–816; George F. G. Stanley, *The Birth of Western Canada* (London: Longmans, Green,

1936), p. 47; or Alexander Ross, *The Red River Settlement: Its Rise, Progress, and Present State* (London: Smith, Elder, 1856), pp. 372 ff.

[61] A. Ross to D. Ross, Aug. 6, 1849, AB 40/R732, B.C. Provincial Archives.

[62] Belcourt to Simpson, Feb. 11, 1848, D-5/21, H.B.A.

[63] Belcourt to "My Dear Sir" [Isbister?], Mar. 22, 1848, clipping from *Colonial Intelligencer and Aborigines Friend*, Gladstone Papers, Addtl. MSS 44,565, British Museum.

[64] Joseph, Archbishop of Quebec, to Simpson, Mar. 11, 1848, D-5/21, H.B.A. For further details on the Belcourt-Simpson controversy, see James M. Reardon, *Georges Anthony Belcourt* (St. Paul: North Central Publishing Co., 1955), pp. 79–90.

[65] Belcourt to Paschal Berland, June 11, 1849, A-12/4, H.B.A.

[66] Belcourt to Riel, Mar. 5, 1849, *ibid.*

[67] Gov. and Comm. to Simpson, Apr. 4, 1849, A-6/28, H.B.A.

[68] Caldwell to Crampton, Aug. 2, 1849, D-4/70, H.B.A. The letter was written by Simpson and signed by Caldwell.

[69] James Sinclair to Simpson, Jan. 14, 1849, D-5/25, H.B.A. The petition is dated June 2, 1849, and was signed by William McMillan, Louis Rielle [Riel], Pascal Berlin [Berland], Baptiste Faigan, Baptiste Larocque, Antoine Moreau [Morin], Louis Letendre, Soloman Armelin [Amelin], and Urbain de Lorme. All except Faigan, Larocque, and Letendre also were signatories of the "Complaints of the People," presented to the court at Red River during the Sayer trial, demanding that all prosecution for trading in furs be suspended. A-12/4, H.B.A.

[70] Thom was educated at King's College, Aberdeen. He was a Montreal barrister when he was offered the job of recorder of Rupert's Land in 1838. Simpson to Thom, Jan. 5, 1838, D-4/23, H.B.A. He contributed to the section on municipal institutions in the Durham Report. For further information, see E. H. Oliver, ed., *The Canadian North-West* (2 vols.; Ottawa: Government Printing Bureau, 1914), I, 64. In a letter to Shepherd, September 27, 1856, confidential, Simpson stated that Thom advised Ballenden to prosecute Sayer. A-7/2, H.B.A.

[71] Thom to Simpson, June 1, 1851, D-5/30, H.B.A. This is also the view of Alexander Ross. See Ross, *op. cit.*, pp. 224, 378.

[72] Memorandum, Simpson to John Black, July 2, 1853, D-4/73, H.B.A.

[73] Young Colvile was appointed governor of Rupert's Land in 1850, with headquarters at Red River, avowedly to relieve the aging Simpson of some of his responsibilities, but apparently to be trained as Simpson's successor. For discussion of Colvile's supersedure of Caldwell, see Pelly to Grey, Nov. 22, 1850, A-8/6, H.B.A.

[74] Simpson to Pelly, Mar. 1, 1848, confidential, D-4/69, H.B.A.

[75] D. Ross to Simpson, Aug. 21, 1848, private and confidential, D-5/22, H.B.A.

[76] Pelly to Grey, Mar. 4, 1848, A-8/4, H.B.A.

[77] Simpson to A. Colvile, Dec. 24, 1852, confidential, A-12/6, H.B.A.

## Chapter 16

[1] George Simpson, *Narrative of a Journey Round the World* (2 vols.; London: H. Colburn, 1847), I, 45–46.

[2] Derbishire to Simpson, Nov. 13, 1850, D-5/29, H.B.A.

[3] These two groups are described by Chief Justice William H. Draper of Canada in his testimony before the select committee of 1857. See *Report of the Select Committee of the House of Commons on the Hudson's Bay Company . . .* (London: 1857), pp. 216–217.

[4] *Journals of the Legislative Council,* 1857, XV, 191.

[5] Simpson to Swanston, May 14, 1857, confidential, D-4/76a, H.B.A.

[6] Simpson to W. G. Smith, Oct. 19, 1857, D-4/77, H.B.A.

[7] J. L. McDougall to Simpson, [Sept. 22, 1857], D-5/44, H.B.A.

[8] An expression of this alarm is contained in Minute of Council, Jan. 17, 1857, in *Journals of the Legislative Assembly,* 1857, XV, App. 17.

⁹ 37th Cong., 2d sess., H. Ex. Doc. 146, p. 6.

¹⁰ William Smith, *The History of the Post Office in British North America, 1639–1870* (Cambridge: University Press, 1920), p. 319.

¹¹ *Canadian News* (London), Oct. 15, 1856.

¹² *Journals of the Legislative Assembly,* 1857, XV, App. 17.

¹³ Derbishire to Simpson, [Feb. 25, 1857], D-5/43, H.B.A.

¹⁴ *Canadian News,* Apr. 28, 1858.

¹⁵ Rose to Ellice, Dec. 15, 1856, Ellice Papers, Reel 34, P.A.C. For an account of the growing need for fertile land, see A. R. M. Lower, "The Assault on the Laurentian Barrier, 1850–1870," *Canadian Historical Review,* X (Dec., 1929), 294–307.

¹⁶ Simpson to Shepherd, Aug. 2, 1856, confidential, A-7/2, H.B.A.

¹⁷ Shepherd to Simpson, Sept. 1, 1856, private, D-5/42, H.B.A.

¹⁸ Petition to Labouchere, July 4, 1856, C.O. 42/606, P.R.O.

¹⁹ Simpson to Shepherd, Sept. 27, 1856, confidential, A-12/8, H.B.A. Lowe proposed that the Canadian government build a railway and that, as compensation, Rupert's Land be annexed to Canada. The correspondence does not make clear the source from which he expected the Company to be paid. See D. G. G. Kerr, *Sir Edmund Head* (Toronto, 1954), pp. 151–156.

²⁰ Ellice to Labouchere, Sept. 30, 1856, A-7/2, H.B.A.

²¹ Ellice to Labouchere, Oct. 1, 1856, *ibid.*

²² Shepherd to Simpson, Nov. 21, 1856, private and confidential, D-5/42, H.B.A.

²³ *Ibid.*

²⁴ *Report of the Select Committee . . . ,* p. 2.

²⁵ Matheson became a member of the Company's committee on December 1, 1852. A-1/68, H.B.A. He was a friend of Edward Ellice, Jr., who had recommended him for the position. Matheson to Ellice, Jr., Aug. 24, 1852, Ellice Papers, Reel 28.

²⁶ For a more extensive summary of the select committee's proceedings, see Douglas MacKay, *The Honourable Company* (London: Cassell, 1937), chap. xvi, pp. 286 ff.

²⁷ *Report of the Select Committee . . . ,* pp. iii–iv.

²⁸ *Ibid.,* p. 2.

²⁹ Simpson to Draper, Mar. 16, Apr. 4, July 24, 1850, all in D-4/71, H.B.A.

³⁰ Derbishire to Simpson, Apr. 30, 1857, D-5/43, H.B.A.

³¹ Rose to Simpson, Feb. 9, 1857, *ibid.*

³² Derbishire to Simpson, Oct. 22, 23, 1857, D-5/45, H.B.A. The editorial appeared in the Toronto *Globe,* Oct. 23, 1857.

³³ *Canadian News,* Oct. 28, 1857, p. 581; Nov. 11, 1857, p. 597.

³⁴ Simpson to Shepherd, Jan. 6, 1857, A-7/2, H.B.A.

³⁵ Notes on Shepherd to Labouchere, Mar. 16, 1857, C.O. 6/23, P.R.O.

³⁶ Simpson to Shepherd, Jan. 17, 1857, D-4/76a, H.B.A.

³⁷ Johnson to Simpson, Apr. 9, 1857, confidential, D-5/43, H.B.A.

³⁸ *Ibid.*

³⁹ Labouchere to Chairman, H.B.C., July 15, 1857, A-7/2, H.B.A.

⁴⁰ Shepherd to Simpson, Aug. 21, 1857, D-5/44. Simpson disagreed with Shepherd's conclusion, contending that the Company had nothing to lose by such a course, since the Canadians already refused to admit its right to compensation, and a favorable decision would compel the Canadian government to provide such payment. Simpson to Shepherd, Sept. 12, 1857, D-4/84a, H.B.A.

⁴¹ Shepherd to Labouchere, July 18, 1857, A-7/2, H.B.A.

⁴² Ellice to Rose, Sept. 6, 1857, Ellice Papers, Reel 34.

⁴³ Merivale to Shepherd, Jan. 20, 1858, A-8/8, H.B.A.

⁴⁴ *Ibid.*

⁴⁵ Shepherd to Labouchere, Jan. 21, 1858, A-8/8, H.B.A.

⁴⁶ T. H. S. Escott, *Edward Bulwer* (London: Routledge, 1910), p. 303.

⁴⁷ Carnarvon to Berens, Nov. 3, 1858, A-8/9, H.B.A.

⁴⁸ Berens to Lytton, Nov. 10, 1858, *ibid.*

⁴⁹ Lytton to Head, Feb. 11, 1859, in Governor General's Correspondence, 50, P.A.C.

[50] Carnarvon to Berens, Jan. 28, 1859, A-8/9, H.B.A.

[51] Berens to Lytton, Feb. 8, 1859, *ibid*. Also in Governor General's Correspondence, 50, P.A.C.

[52] Merivale to Berens, Mar. 9, 1859, A-8/9, H.B.A.

[53] Berens to Lytton, Mar. 15, 1859, *ibid*.

[54] Herman Merivale told Governor Berens that the proposal for a two-year extension was his, not Lytton's, and that Lytton and Lord Carnarvon, the parliamentary undersecretary, were "very antagonistic" to the Company. Berens to Ellice, Sr., Jan. 12, 1859, A-10/69, H.B.A.

[55] Lytton to Head, Feb. 11, Mar. 10, 18, 1859, Governor General's Correspondence, 50, P.A.C.

[56] Head to Lytton, Apr. 4, 1859, *ibid*.

[57] Lytton to Head, May 13, 1859, *ibid*.

[58] Joint address of Canadian legislature to Queen, *ibid*.

[59] Toronto *Globe*, Apr. 19, 1859.

[60] Attorney-General and Solicitor-General to Lytton, Dec. 10, 1858, Governor General's Correspondence, 50, P.A.C. It should be observed that Lytton had received this communication prior to making his threat to take action against the Company.

[61] Ellice to Rose, May 6, [1859], Ellice Papers, Reel 34.

[62] Simpson to Ellice, Sr., Sept. 23, 1859, *ibid*., Reel 2.

[63] Newcastle to Ellice, Oct. 31, 1859, *ibid*., Reel 28.

## Chapter 17

[1] Roderick G. MacBeth, *The Making of the Canadian West* (Toronto: Briggs, 1898), p. 13.

[2] Simpson to Kittson, Oct. 16, 1851, D-4/72, H.B.A.

[3] Simpson to Gilbert F. Griffin, July 12, 1852, D-4/73, H.B.A.

[4] Joseph J. Hargrave, *Red River* (Montreal: J. Lovell, 1871), p. 100.

[5] For a discussion of Taylor, see Theodore C. Blegen, "James Wickes Taylor: A Biographical Sketch," *Minnesota History Bulletin*, I (Nov., 1915), 153–219.

[6] *Ibid*., p. 168.

[7] Ellice to Berens, Sept. 14, 1858, D-4/84a, H.B.A.

[8] Simpson to Griffin, July 12, 1852, D-4/73, H.B.A. Duncan Finlayson stated in 1847 that a mail service had been established between Sault Ste. Marie and Red River, with packets departing from each place every other month. Finlayson to D. Ross, Dec. 18, 1847, AB40/F492, B.C. Provincial Archives. Hargrave, *op. cit.*, p. 99, erroneously states that packets were dispatched only twice a year.

[9] Stayner to Simpson, Apr. 2, 1849, D-5/24, H.B.A. Simpson suspected that the idea of postal communication originated with Isbister's friends. Simpson to Gov. and Comm., Apr. 11, 1849, *ibid*.

[10] Simpson to Stayner, Apr. 5, 11, 1849, D-4/70, H.B.A. This amount would pay only for letters. If newspapers and pamphlets were carried the total charges would be £783.

[11] Johnson to Simpson, Sept. 9, 1857, D-5/44, H.B.A.

[12] Reginald G. Trotter, *Canadian Federation. Its Origins and Achievement* (London: J. M. Dent and Sons, 1924), p. 251. This is one of numerous accounts of Hind's and Dawson's explorations.

[13] *Ibid*., p. 257; Robert Carmichael-Smyth, *The Proposed British Colonial Atlantic and Pacific Railway Communication* (London: 1849).

[14] Trotter, *op. cit.*, p. 258.

[15] Millington H. Synge, "Proposal for a Rapid Communication with the Pacific and the East via British North America," *Journal of the Royal Geographical Society of London*, 22 (1852), 174–200; Alexander Douell, *A Project for Opening a North-West Passage between the Atlantic and Pacific Oceans by Means of a Railway on British Territory* (London: 1852).

[16] Records of North West Transit Company, no. 1501, Companies Registration Office, Bush House, London.

[17] Simpson to Gov. and Comm., July 21, 1858, D-4/78, H.B.A.

[18] Hargrave, *op. cit.*, p. 143.

[19] Simpson to Ellice, Sr., Mar. 19, 1859, D-4/84a, H.B.A.

[20] Barnston to Simpson, Dec. 5, 1859, D-5/50, H.B.A.

[21] "Memorandum of Association," no. 1238, Companies Registration Office, Bush House.

[22] Petition to Sec. of State for Colonies, June, 1858, C.O. 6/30, P.R.O.

[23] *Canadian News*, Jan. 19, 1859.

[24] George A. Hamilton, Treasury, to Merivale, C.O., Feb. 12, 1859, and encls., C.O. 6/30, P.R.O. The mail project itself did not include construction of a transcontinental railway.

[25] "Memorandum of Association," North West Transit Company, registered Apr. 2, 1859, no. 1501, Companies Registration Office, Bush House.

[26] Simpson to Mactavish, July 28, 1859, D-4/79, H.B.A.

[27] See John S. Galbraith, "Perry Collins at the Colonial Office," *British Columbia Historical Quarterly*, XVII (July–Oct., 1953), 207–214.

[28] Lampson to Berens, July 19, 1859, A-10/46, H.B.A.

[29] The history of attempts to gain British subsidies for intercolonial and other railways cannot be traced here. See Trotter, *op. cit.*, pp. 143 ff. and *passim*; Gilbert P. de T. Glazebrook, *A History of Transportation in Canada* (Toronto: Ryerson Press, 1938); Oscar D. Skelton, *The Railway Builders* (Toronto and Glasgow: Brook & Company, 1920).

[30] C. Fortescue to Berens, May 5, 1860, A-8/9, H.B.A.

[31] Berens to Newcastle, May 30, 1860, *ibid.*

[32] Fortescue to Berens, June 21, 1860, A-8/10, H.B.A.

[33] Berens to Newcastle, July 12, 1860, *ibid.*

[34] Murdoch to Elliot, Feb. 21, 186[1], C.O. 6/33, P.R.O.

[35] Notes by Rogers and Fortescue on *ibid.*

[36] Memorandum, Murdoch to Elliot, Feb. 21, 1861, encl. in *ibid.*

[37] Note by Newcastle, July 12, 1861, on *ibid.*

[38] After the Trent affair, British troops for the Canadian garrisons had to be taken from Halifax to their stations by sleigh.

[39] *Canadian News*, Jan. 30, 1862.

[40] *Ibid.*, July 17, 1861.

[41] Edward W. Watkin, *Canada and the States, Recollections, 1851 to 1886* (London: Ward Lock and Company, [1887]), pp. 64–65. For further information on Watkin and the railway negotiations, see Trotter, *op. cit.*, pp. 178 ff., and Elaine A. Mitchell, "Edward Watkin and the Buying-Out of the Hudson's Bay Company," *Canadian Historical Review*, XXXIV (Sept., 1953), 219–244.

[42] Report of Committee, Executive Council, Mar. 7, 1862, encl. in Monck to Newcastle, Mar. 8, 1862, C.O. 42/633, P.R.O.

[43] 22 & 23 Vic., cap. 26.

[44] Note by Elliot, Apr. 5, 1862, on Monck to Newcastle, Mar. 8, 1862, C.O. 42/633, P.R.O.

[45] Alleyn to Dallas, Apr. 15, 1862, in *Accounts and Papers*, 1864, no. 402.

[46] Dallas to Ellice, Sr., Apr. 22, 1862, Ellice Papers, Reel 2, P.A.C. Ellice introduced Dallas to Cartier.

[47] *Ibid.*

[48] Dallas to Alleyn, Apr. 16, 1862, in *Accounts and Papers*, 1864, no. 402.

[49] Berens to Dallas, May 23, 1862, private and confidential, D-8/1, A-7/3, H.B.A.

[50] Berens to Newcastle, May 19, 1862, C.O. 42/636, P.R.O.

[51] Ellice to Rose, May 13, 1862, private, Ellice Papers, Reel 34.

[52] Extract, Dallas to Berens, Oct. 14, 1862; Dallas to Ellice, Jr., Oct. 18, 1862, both in *ibid.*, Reel 41.

[53] Notes by Elliot, Fortescue, and Newcastle, on Berens to Newcastle, May 19, 1862, C.O. 42/636, P.R.O.

[54] Thomas Baring and others to Newcastle, July 5, 1862, in *Accounts and Papers*, 1863, no. 438.

[55] Berens to Ellice, Jr., Aug. 1, 1862, A-7/3, H.B.A.

[56] Ellice to Rose, Dec. 7, 1862, private, Ellice Papers, Reel 34.

[57] Watkin, *op. cit.*, p. 124.

[58] Berens to Newcastle, Aug. 1, 1862, A-8/10, H.B.A.

[59] *Canadian News*, June 6, 1862.

[60] Monck to Newcastle, July 9, 1862, C.O. 42/633, P.R.O.

[61] For a more detailed account of Baring's correspondence with Watkin, see Mitchell, *op. cit.*, pp. 233–237.

[62] Rogers to Berens, Aug. 20, 1862, A-8/10, H.B.A.

[63] Berens to Ellice, Jr., Aug. 29, 1862, private, A-10/52, H.B.A.

[64] Berens to Newcastle, Sept. 5, 1862, *ibid.*

[65] Watkin, *op. cit.*, p. 120. The interview was set for November 17. Berens to Newcastle, Nov. 16, 1862, A-8/10, H.B.A. But Elliot, in a letter to Berens, Nov. 21, 1862, *ibid.*, referred to the interview as taking place on the 18th. This was unquestionably the interview to which Watkin refers, for Elliot's letter mentioned the suggested purchase of the entire property.

[66] See p. 368.

[67] *Parliamentary Debates*, 3d ser., CLXVII, 1409.

[68] Newcastle to Watkin, Aug. 14, 1862, in Watkin, *op. cit.*, p. 129.

[69] Monck to Newcastle, Sept. 12, 1862, and encls., C.O. 42/635, P.R.O.

[70] Report of Council, Oct. 22, 1862, encl. in Monck to Newcastle, Nov. 5, 1862, *ibid.*

[71] Note by Newcastle on Monck to Newcastle, Nov. 5, 1862, *ibid.*

[72] See Trotter, *op. cit.*, pp. 198–201.

[73] Watkin, *op. cit.*, p. 125; Berens to Dallas, Dec. 5, 1862, private and confidential, D-8/1, H.B.A.

[74] Correspondence in *Accounts and Papers*, 1863, no. 438.

[75] Note on Watkin to Newcastle, Dec. 27, 1862, C.O. 6/34, P.R.O.

[76] *Canadian News*, Jan. 22, 1863.

[77] Hargrave, *op. cit.*, p. 312.

[78] Dallas to Head, Jan. 28, 1864, encl. in Head to Rogers, Mar. 8, 1864, C.O. 6/39, P.R.O.

[79] Monck to Newcastle, Feb. 27, 1863, in *Accounts and Papers*, 1864, no. 402.

[80] Gladstone to Newcastle, Feb. 16, 1863, Gladstone Papers, Addtl. MSS 44,263, British Museum.

[81] Watkin to Newcastle, Mar. 4, 1863, *ibid.*

[82] Gladstone to Newcastle, Mar. 6, 1863, *ibid.*

[83] Watkin to Newcastle, Mar. 27, 1863; Newcastle to Watkin, Mar. 27, Apr. 7, 1863, in Watkin, *op. cit.*, pp. 113, 111, 132.

[84] Fraser to [Ellice, Jr. ?], Jan. 7, 1863, and Statement of Assets, in Ellice Papers, Reel 41.

[85] Maynard to Fraser, Feb. 24, 1863, A-10/53, H.B.A.

[86] Watkin to Berens, May 13, 1863, F-27/1, H.B.A.

[87] Watkin, *op. cit.*, pp. 121–123.

[88] *Ibid.*, p. 127.

[89] George G. Glyn to Charles R. Drake, May 23, 1863, in George G. Glyn, "Private Letter Book," no. 1, Glyn, Mills and Company.

[90] Glyn to Potter, June 26, 1863, *ibid.*

[91] "Memorandum of Association of the International Financial Society Ltd.," 415c, Companies Registration Office, Bush House.

[92] *Ibid.*; *Bankers Magazine*, XXIII (July, 1863), 518–519. Information on Hodgson was supplied by personnel of Baring Brothers. Of some interest is an anonymously

written pamphlet, *The Hudson's Bay Company. What is it?* (London: 1864). The author must have been close to the negotiators, for he was able to trace the progress of the negotiations with remarkable accuracy, although he was badly misinformed on some points.

[93] Minutes of Committee, June 15, 1863, A-1/75, H.B.A.

[94] Barnston *et al.* to Gov. and Comm., Jan. 28, 1863, A-10/53, H.B.A., printed in Canada, *Sessional Papers*, VII, 1st sess., 1867–68, no. 19.

[95] Gov. and Comm. to Robert S. Miles *et al.*, Feb. 27, 1863, printed in *ibid.*

[96] Hargrave, *op. cit.*, pp. 298–299.

[97] *Canadian News*, Nov. 5, 1863.

[98] Ellice, Sr., to Rose, June 9, 1863, Ellice Papers, Reel 34.

[99] Ellice, Sr. to Rose, June 24, 1863, private, *ibid.*

[100] General Court, July 2, 1863, A-2/3, H.B.A.

[101] "Prospectus of the Hudson's Bay Company," 1863, H.B.A.

[102] Heath to Gov. and Directors, H.B.C., July 29, 1863, F-27/1; Head to Benson, Aug. 27, 1863, A-7/4, both in H.B.A. A dispute also arose as to whether the society or the Company was entitled to the £12,500 in unissued stock possessed by the old Company, now valued at £50,000. The controversy ended on November 12, 1863, in victory for the governor and committee. Minutes of International Financial Society, Nov. 12, 1863, in I.F.S. Offices, London. Head to Dobree, Nov. 11, 1863, A-7/4; Dobree to Head, Nov. 13, 1863, F-27/1, both in H.B.A.

[103] "First Report of the Directors to be submitted at 1st General Meeting of the International Financial Society," Mar. 1, 1864, in I.F.S. Offices, London.

[104] The sales of shares are recorded in the minutes of the society.

## Chapter 18

[1] Hudson's Bay Company, *Report of the Governor and Committee to the Shareholders*, June 21, 1864 (London: 1864).

[2] He bought 1,250 shares, with a par value of £25,000. F-28/1, H.B.A.

[3] Edward W. Watkin, *Canada and the States, Recollections, 1851 to 1886* (London: Ward Lock and Company, [1887]), p. 180.

[4] *Ibid.*, pp. 174–176.

[5] Head to Watkin, Aug. 18, 25, 1863, D-7/4, H.B.A.

[6] The considerable correspondence on the wire is contained largely in A-7/4 and A-6/39, H.B.A. Rae's reports on his surveys are in E-15/12, H.B.A.

[7] Monck to Newcastle, Feb. 19, 1864, *Accounts and Papers*, 1864, no. 402.

[8] Watkin to Fortescue, Mar. 17, 1864, encl. in Watkin to Fraser, Mar. 17, 1864, A-8/1, H.B.A.

[9] Head to Newcastle, Aug. 28, 1863, C.O. 6/38, P.R.O.

[10] Note by Newcastle, Sept. 15, 1863, *ibid.*

[11] Head to Rogers, Nov. 11, 1863, *ibid.*

[12] Notes by Newcastle, n.d., *ibid.*

[13] Fortescue to Head, Mar. 11, 1864, A-8/11, H.B.A. Newcastle originally proposed that the Company receive only 6 pence per acre for the land sold, but this was revised in the official letter.

[14] *Ibid.*

[15] Head to Fortescue, Mar. 15, 1864, C.O. 6/39, P.R.O.

[16] Note by Rogers, Mar. 21, 1864, *ibid.*

[17] Fortescue to Head, Apr. 5, 1864, A-8/11, H.B.A.

[18] Seward to Lyons, Feb. 2, 1864, encl. in Layard to Under-Secretary of State, C.O., Feb. 29, 1864, C.O. 6/39, P.R.O.

[19] Head to Fortescue, Apr. 28, 1864, and encls., C.O. 6/39, P.R.O., printed in *H. C. Papers*, 1864, no. 401. The Americans did not avail themselves of the privilege Dallas accorded them.

[20] Montreal *Evening Telegraph*, Apr. 13, 1864.

[21] Head to Rogers, Feb. 5, 1864, C.O. 6/39, P.R.O., printed in *H. C. Papers*, 1864, no. 401.

[22] Note by Elliot, Feb. 13, 1864, on Head to Rogers, Feb. 5, 1864, C.O. 6/39, P.R.O.

[23] Head to Fortescue, Apr. 13, 1864, *ibid.*, printed in *H. C. Papers*, 1869, no. 440.

[24] Rogers to Head, June 6, 1864, A-8/11, H.B.A. This letter is based on a draft of Cardwell's, C.O. 6/39, P.R.O.

[25] British North American Association, *Confederation of the British North-American Provinces* (London: 1865).

[26] Cardwell to Monck, July 1, 1864, *Accounts and Papers*, 1864, no. 550.

[27] Report, Nov. 11, 1864, encl. in Monck to Newcastle, Nov. 12, 1864, C.O. 42/642, P.R.O.

[28] Brown was seriously in error in this description of the Oregon negotiations. See chap. 13.

[29] Brown to Gov. Gen. in Council, encl. in Monck to Cardwell, Mar. 28, 1865, C.O. 42/648, P.R.O.

[30] *Papers Relating to the Conferences which have taken place between Her Majesty's Government and a Deputation from the Executive Council of Canada . . .*, presented to Parliament, June 19, 1865 (London: 1865).

[31] Note by Rogers, July 24, 1867, on Smith to Elliot, July 12, 1867, C.O. 6/42, P.R.O.

[32] Cardwell stated in the House of Commons on May 29, 1865, that the government "could not honourably dispute the rights of the Hudson's Bay Company, under their charter." *Parliamentary Debates*, 3d ser., CLXXIX (1865), 997.

[33] Hudson's Bay Company, *Report of the Governor and Committee to the Shareholders*, June 27, 1865 (London: 1865).

[34] London *Times*, June 21, 1865, p. 12; June 24, 1865, p. 10.

[35] For a statement of this dilemma, see Edward Hamilton to Head, Mar. 15, 1866, A-10/65, H.B.A. Hamilton was one of the directors.

[36] McEwen to Head, Jan. 18, 1866, *ibid.*

[37] Fraser to McEwen, Jan. 24, 1866, A-8/1, H.B.A.

[38] Note by Forster, Feb. 10, 1866, on Head to Elliot, Feb. 6, 1866, C.O. 6/41, P.R.O.

[39] Cartier and McDougall to Rogers, Feb. 8, 1869, confidential, A-8/12, H.B.A.

[40] J. Thomson Duncan to Editor, *North British Daily Mail*, July, 1872, in correspondence on Consolidated Copper Company of Canada Limited, Campbell Papers, Ontario Provincial Archives.

[41] Forster to Head, Feb. 20, 1866, Canada, *Sessional Papers*, VII, 1st sess., 1867–68, no. 19.

[42] Copy of Report of Committee of Canadian Executive Council, June 22, 1866, encl. in Monck to Cardwell, June 23, 1866, *ibid.* For further discussion of the Canadian side of the negotiations, see Arthur S. Morton, *A History of the Canadian West to 1870–71* (London: T. Nelson & Sons, [1939]), chap. x, particularly pp. 839–852.

[43] Copy of Report of Committee of Canadian Executive Council, June 22, 1866.

[44] There were 1,787 shareholders in December, 1868, and the number in 1866 would have been approximately the same. Northcote to Smith, Feb. 26, 1869, A-10/77, H.B.A.

[45] James A. Dodds, *The Hudson's Bay Company, its Position and Prospects* (London: 1866), pp. 56–57.

[46] *Ibid.*, p. 64.

[47] Bonar to Sec., H.B.C., May 12, 1866, A-10/66; note, undated [apparently May, 1866], A-10/55, both in H.B.A.

[48] Hudson's Bay Company, *Minutes of Meeting of General Court*, July 5, 1866 (London: 1866).

[49] *Ibid.*

⁵⁰ The replies are in A-46/1, H.B.A. The results were presented in Hudson's Bay Company, *Report of the Governor and Committee to the Shareholders,* Nov. 20, 1866 (London: 1866).

⁵¹ Head to Forster, Mar. 1, 1866, A-8/11, H.B.A.

⁵² Theodore C. Blegen, "James Wickes Taylor: A Biographical Sketch," *Minnesota History Bulletin,* I (Nov., 1915), 178–179.

⁵³ Report of Secretary of Treasury, June 12, 1866, encl. in Head to Rogers, July 17, 1866, A-8/1, H.B.A.

⁵⁴ The Cardwell-Carnarvon correspondence on this subject is contained in the Cardwell Papers, P.R.O. 30/48/40.

⁵⁵ Note by Rogers, on Head to Rogers, July 17, 1866, C.O. 6/41, P.R.O.

⁵⁶ Note by Adderley, Jan. 30, 1867, on Egerton to Rogers, Jan. 28, 1867, confidential, C.O. 6/42, P.R.O.

⁵⁷ Bruce to Stanley, Jan. 12, 1867, encl. in Egerton to Rogers, Jan. 28, 1867, confidential, *ibid.*

⁵⁸ Note by Elliot on memorandum, "Relations with the United States on the Frontier of the Hudson's Bay Territory," Apr. 16, 1867, *ibid.*

⁵⁹ Elliot to Head, Apr. 20, 1867, A-8/11, H.B.A.

⁶⁰ Head to Elliot, Apr. 24, 1867, C.O. 6/42, P.R.O.

⁶¹ Head to Elliot, June 22, 1867, *ibid.* Upon the advice of the law officers, the British government decided to refuse the United States the right to send troops north of the boundary.

⁶² Spence to Carnarvon, Aug. 13, 1866, C.O. 6/41, P.R.O.

⁶³ Joseph J. Hargrave, *Red River* (Montreal: J. Lovell, 1871), p. 402.

⁶⁴ Michel to Carnarvon, Feb. 11, 1867, C.O. 42/662, P.R.O.

⁶⁵ Mactavish to Smith, Feb. 24, 1868, A-12/45, H.B.A.

⁶⁶ Lampson to Rogers, Apr. 22, 1868, A-8/12, H.B.A.

⁶⁷ Morton, *op. cit.,* p. 865.

⁶⁸ Buckingham to Monck, Aug. 23, 1867, Canada, *Sessional Papers,* VII, 1st sess., 1867–68, no. 19.

⁶⁹ Macdonald to Buckingham, Apr. 6, 1867, C.O. 6/42, P.R.O.

⁷⁰ Law Officers (John B. Karslake, C. J. Selwyn, Travers Twiss) to Buckingham, Jan. 6, 1868, C.O. 6/43, P.R.O.

⁷¹ Report of Committee of Privy Council of Canada, Dec. 28, 1867, encl. in Monck to Buckingham, Jan. 1, 1868, H.C. 440, 1869; joint address of Senate and House of Commons, Dec. 16, 17, 1867, encl. in Monck to Buckingham, Dec. 21, 1867, C.O. 42/664, P.R.O.

⁷² Note by Rogers on Monck to Buckingham, Jan. 1, 1868, C.O. 42/667, P.R.O.

⁷³ "Pending Questions about the Hudson's Bay Territory," confidential print, Jan. 25, 1868, Stowe Papers, H.B.A.

⁷⁴ *Ibid.*

⁷⁵ Walker to Carnarvon, Sept. 13, 1866, C.O. 42/661, P.R.O.

⁷⁶ Walker to Fraser, Oct. 8, 1866, and encl., A-10/68, H.B.A.

⁷⁷ Minutes of Committee, Oct. 16, 1866, A-1/78; Fraser to Walker, Oct. 18, 1866, A-5/32, both in H.B.A.

⁷⁸ Walker to Fraser, May 28, 1867, A-10/70; Smith to Walker, June 5, 1867, A-5/32; Walker to Smith, June 7, 1867, A-10/70; Smith to Walker, June 12, 1867, A-5/32, all in H.B.A.

⁷⁹ Minutes of interview between Lampson and Buckingham, Feb. 5, 1868, Stowe Papers, H.B.A.

⁸⁰ Their fears had some foundation. The *Globe* admitted that "with the Northwest opened up and added to Canada, the demand for representation by numbers would soon be irresistible." Toronto *Globe,* Jan. 3, 1865.

⁸¹ See his remarks in the Legislative Assembly, Sept. 18, 1865, as reported in the *Globe* of the same date.

⁸² Telegram, Monck to Buckingham, undated [Mar., 1868], in Stowe Papers, H.B.A.

[83] 31 & 32 Vic., cap. 105.

[84] Kimberley to Adderley, May 13, 1868, A-8/12, H.B.A.

[85] Adderley to Kimberley, Dec. 1, 1868, *ibid.*

[86] Toronto *Globe*, May 29, June 4, 6, 1868, *et seqq.*

[87] Monck to Buckingham, Oct. 2, 1868, and encls., C.O. 42/671, P.R.O.

[88] Adderley to Kimberley, Dec. 1, 1868, A-8/12, H.B.A.

[89] Northcote to Rogers, Jan. 13, 1869, *ibid.*

[90] Note on draft ltr., Granville to Seymour, June 2, 1869, C.O. 42/675, P.R.O.

[91] Rogers to Northcote, Mar. 9, 1869, A-8/12, H.B.A.

[92] Rogers to Lampson, Jan. 28, 1869, *ibid.*

[93] Cartier and McDougall to Rogers, Feb. 8, 1869, encl. in Rogers to Northcote, Feb. 22, 1869, *ibid.*

[94] Northcote to Rogers, Feb. 26, 1869, *ibid.*

[95] Rogers to Northcote, Mar. 9, 1869, *ibid.*

[96] Granville to Gladstone, Mar. 11, 1869, Gladstone Papers, Addtl. MSS 44,166, British Museum.

[97] Toronto *Globe*, Apr. 2, 1869.

[98] Daniel Meinertzhagen and John S. W. Schröder, the other two members of the committee, were not present.

[99] Minutes of Committee, Mar. 12, 20, 1869, A-1/80, H.B.A.

[100] Encls. in Northcote to Rogers, Mar. 22, 1869, A-8/12, H.B.A.

[101] Minutes of Committee, Mar. 20, 1869, A-1/80, H.B.A. Northcote, Lampson, Colvile, and Lyall were present.

[102] Hudson's Bay Company, *Minutes of Meeting of Hudson's Bay General Court*, Mar. 24, 1869 (London: 1869).

[103] *Ibid.*, Apr. 9, 1869.

[104] *Ibid.*

[105] Young to Granville, Aug. 25, 1869, encl. in Rogers to Northcote, Sept. 15, 1869, A-8/12, H.B.A. The date was originally set as October 1, but was advanced to December to allow more time to complete financial and other arrangements.

[106] For an account of the background and course of the Riel Rebellion, see George F. G. Stanley, *The Birth of Western Canada* (London: Longmans, Green, 1936).

[107] Lampson to Rogers, Nov. 29, 1869, private, A-13/17, H.B.A.

[108] Toronto *Globe*, Nov. 17, 1869.

[109] Granville to [Rogers?], Mar. 6, 1870; Gladstone to Granville, Mar. 6, 1870, both in Granville Papers, P.R.O. 30/29/57.

[110] Order in Council, June 23, 1870.

[111] This was the approximate area of Rupert's Land.

# BIBLIOGRAPHY

## MANUSCRIPT SOURCES

Hudson's Bay Archives. The following series were of major importance:
A-1: London Minute Books, Governor and Committee.
A-2: London Minute Books, General Court and Proprietors.
A-6: London Correspondence Outwards.
A-8, 13: London Correspondence with the Imperial Government.
A-10: London Inward Correspondence.
B-223b: Fort Vancouver Correspondence Books.
D-4, 5, 6: Simpson's Correspondence Books.
Stowe Papers.
Public Record Office
Series C.O. 6, 42, 43, 305; F.O. 5, 65, 93, 115; W.O. 1.
30/48. Cardwell Papers.
30/29. Granville Papers.
British Museum
Gladstone Papers.
Peel Papers.
Companies Registration Office, London
Halifax and Quebec Railway Company.
International Financial Society.
North West Transit Company.
Bancroft Library
Berg, Vassili. Chronological History of the Discovery of the Aleutian Islands.
St. Petersburg, 1823. Translated by Ivan Petroff.
———. Historical Review of the Russian American Company from 1799 to 1863.
Translated by Ivan Petroff.
McLoughlin, John. Remarks . . . on Messrs. Warre's and Vavasour's Report.
Material for the History of the Russian Settlements on the Shores of the Eastern
Ocean. St. Petersburg, 1861. Translated by Ivan Petroff.
Odell, Mrs. W. H. Biography of Samuel R. Thurston.
Petroff, Ivan. The Management and Personnel of the Russian American Com-
pany from its Beginning to its Dissolution. San Francisco, 1877.
Report of the Committee on Organization of the Russian American Colonies.
St. Petersburg, 1863. Translated by Ivan Petroff.
Tikhmeneff, P. Historical Review of the Origin of the Russian American Com-
pany and its doings up to the present time. St. Petersburg, 1861.
Provincial Archives, British Columbia
Douglas, James. Diary of a trip to California.
———. Diary of a trip to the Northwest Coast.
Ermatinger Papers, 1826–1843 (transcripts).
Finlayson Papers.
Fort Vancouver Fur Trade Returns.
Ross Papers.
Tolmie, William F. Letterbook, April, 1844–September, 1874.
Other Archives

Ellice Papers, National Library of Scotland. Microfilm copies in Public Archives of Canada and in Library of the University of California, Los Angeles.
Governor General's Correspondence, Public Archives of Canada.
Minutes, 1863–1866, International Financial Society.
Private Correspondence, 1863–64, Baring Brothers, London.
Soliday Collection, Huntington Library, San Marino, California.
Transcripts from London MSS, Glyn, Mills and Company.

## OFFICIAL AND SEMIOFFICIAL PUBLICATIONS

Alaskan Boundary Tribunal. *Proceedings.* Washington: 1904. U.S. 58th Cong., 2d sess., S. Doc. 162. 7 vols.
*British and American Joint Commission for the Final Settlement of the Claims of the Hudson's Bay and Puget's Sound Agricultural Companies.* Montreal and Washington: 1865–1869. 14 vols.
Canada. *Certain Correspondence of the Foreign Office and of the Hudson's Bay Company.* Ottawa: 1899.
———. Parliament. *Sessional Papers,* 1867–68.
Great Britain. *Accounts and Papers.* 1850, no. 542. 1863, no. 438. 1864, nos. 402, 530, 550.
———. *In the Privy Council. In the Matter of the Boundary Between the Dominion of Canada and the Colony of Newfoundland in the Labrador Peninsula.* London: [1926]. 12 vols.
———. Parliament. *Debates,* 1847–1869. London.
———. ———. *Report of the Select Committee of the House of Commons on the Hudson's Bay Company.* . . . London: 1857.
Malloy, William M. *Treaties, Conventions, International Acts, Protocols and Agreements between the United States of America and Other Powers, 1776–1909.* Washington: U.S. Govt. Printing Office, 1910. 2 vols.
Miller, David Hunter. *Treaties and Other International Acts of the United States of America.* Washington: U.S. Govt. Printing Office, 1931. 8 vols.
Moore, John Bassett. *History and Digest of the International Arbitrations to which the United States has been a Party.* Washington: U.S. Govt. Printing Office, 1898. 6 vols.
Oliver, E. H., ed. *The Canadian North-West.* Ottawa: Government Printing Bureau, 1914. 2 vols.
Richardson, J. D. *A Compilation of the Messages and Papers of the Presidents.* Washington: U.S. Govt. Printing Office, 1896–1899. 10 vols.
United States. Congress. *Congressional Globe,* 1830–1856. Washington.
Washington Territory. Council. *Journals,* 1854, 1855–56. Olympia.

## BOOKS

Adam, G. Mercer. *The Canadian North-West.* Toronto: Rose Publishing Company, 1885.
Adams, Randolph G. *A History of the Foreign Policy of the United States.* New York: Macmillan, 1924.
Andrews, C. L. *Sitka.* Caldwell, Idaho: Caxton Printers, 1945.
Bagot, Josceline. *George Canning and His Friends.* London: Murray, 1909. 2 vols.
Balfour, Frances. *The Life of George Fourth Earl of Aberdeen.* London: Hodder and Stoughton, [1922]. 2 vols.
Bancroft, Hubert Howe. *History of Alaska, 1730–1885.* San Francisco: A. L. Bancroft & Company, 1886.
———. *History of British Columbia, 1792–1887.* San Francisco: History Company, 1887.
———. *History of the Northwest Coast.* Vol. II, 1800–1846. San Francisco: A. L. Bancroft & Company, 1884.

————. *History of Oregon.* San Francisco: History Company, 1886–1888. 2 vols.

————. *History of Washington, Idaho, and Montana.* San Francisco: History Company, 1890.

Begg, Alexander (1839–1897). *The Great Canadian North West.* Montreal: J. Lovell & Son, 1881.

Begg, Alexander (1825–1905). *History of British Columbia from its Earliest Discovery to the Present Time.* Toronto: W. Briggs, 1894.

Bemis, Samuel Flagg. *John Quincy Adams and the Foundations of American Foreign Policy.* New York: Knopf, 1949.

Bischoff, William N. *The Jesuits in Old Oregon.* Caldwell, Idaho: Caxton Printers, 1945.

Bulwer, Henry L. *The Life of Henry John Temple, Viscount Palmerston.* London: R. Bentley, 1870. 3 vols.

California State Historical Society. *The Russians in California.* San Francisco: The Society, 1933.

Chittenden, Hiram M. *The American Fur Trade of the Far West.* New York: F. P. Harper, 1902. 3 vols.

Clark, Robert C. *History of the Willamette Valley, Oregon.* Chicago: S. J. Clarke Publishing Company, 1927. 2 vols.

Coues, Elliott, ed. *Forty Years a Fur Trader on the Upper Missouri.* New York: F. P. Harper, 1898. 2 vols.

Cox, Ross. *Adventures on the Columbia River.* London: H. Colburn and R. Bentley, 1831. 2 vols.

Creighton, Donald G. *John A. Macdonald.* Toronto: Macmillan, 1952.

Dale, Harrison C. *The Ashley-Smith Explorations and the Discovery of a Central Route to the Pacific, 1822–1829.* Cleveland: Clark, 1918.

Davidson, George. *The Alaska Boundary.* San Francisco: Alaska Packers Association, 1903.

Davidson, Gordon Charles, *The North West Company.* Berkeley: University of California Press, 1918.

Escott, T. H. S. *Edward Bulwer.* London: Routledge, 1910.

Fleming, R. Harvey, ed. *Minutes of Council Northern Department of Rupert Land, 1821–31.* London: Hudson's Bay Record Society, 1940.

Fulford, Roger. *Glyn's 1753–1953.* London: Macmillan, 1953.

Glazebrook, Gilbert P. de T. *A History of Transportation in Canada.* Toronto: Ryerson Press, 1938.

Gourlay, Robert. *Statistical Account of Upper Canada.* London: Simpkin & Marshall, 1822. 2 vols.

Greenhow, Robert. *The History of Oregon and California.* London: J. Murray, 1844.

Hargrave, Joseph J. *Red River.* Montreal: J. Lovell, 1871.

Harmon, Daniel Williams. *A Journal of Voyages and Travels in the Interior of North America.* New York: A. S. Barnes, 1903.

Hildt, J. C. *Early Diplomatic Negotiations of the United States with Russia.* Johns Hopkins University Studies in Historical and Political Science, Vol. XXIV, nos. 5, 6. Baltimore: Johns Hopkins Press, 1906.

Howay, F. W., W. N. Sage, and H. F. Angus. *British Columbia and the United States.* Toronto: Ryerson Press, 1942.

Hudson's Bay Company. *Charters, Statutes, Orders in Council &c. Relating to the Hudson's Bay Company.* London: Hudson's Bay Company, 1931.

————. *Proceedings of the General Court of Proprietors, 1860–1869.* London.

————. *Reports of the Governor and Committee to the Shareholders, 1863–1869.* London.

Innis, Harold A. *The Fur Trade in Canada.* New Haven: Yale University Press, 1930.

Irving, Washington. *The Adventures of Captain Bonneville, U.S.A.* New York: [1837].

Jennings, Louis J., ed. *The Correspondence and Diaries of . . . John Wilson Croker*. London: J. Murray, 1884. 3 vols.

Kerr, D. G. G. *Sir Edmund Head*. Toronto: University of Toronto Press, 1954.

Labouchere, Henry. *Canada West and the Hudson's Bay Company*. London: 1856.

Lewis, William S., and Paul C. Phillips, eds. *The Journal of John Work*. Cleveland: Clark, 1923.

MacBeth, Roderick G. *The Making of the Canadian West*. Toronto: Briggs, 1898.

Macfie, Matthew. *Vancouver Island and British Columbia*. London: Longman, Green, Longman, Roberts & Green, 1865.

MacKay, Douglas. *The Honourable Company*. London: Cassell, 1937.

Marshall, William I. *Acquisition of Oregon and the Long Suppressed Evidence about Marcus Whitman*. Seattle: Lowman & Hanford, 1911. 2 vols.

Martin, Archer. *The Hudson's Bay Company's Land Tenures*. London: W. Clowes and Sons, 1898.

Martin, Chester. *Lord Selkirk's Work in Canada*. Oxford: Clarendon Press, 1916.

Maxwell, Herbert, ed. *The Creevey Papers*. New York: Dutton, 1904. 2 vols.

Merk, Frederick. *Albert Gallatin and the Oregon Problem*. Cambridge, Mass.: Harvard University Press, 1950.

———. *Fur Trade and Empire*. Cambridge, Mass.: Harvard University Press, 1931.

Morgan, Dale L. *Jedediah Smith*. Indianapolis: Bobbs-Merrill, 1953.

Morice, Adrien G. *The History of the Northern Interior of British Columbia*. Toronto: Lane, 1904.

Morison, Samuel E. *The Maritime History of Massachusetts, 1783–1860*. Cambridge, Mass.: Houghton Mifflin, 1921.

Morton, Arthur S. *A History of the Canadian West to 1870–71*. London: T. Nelson & Sons, [1939].

———. *Sir George Simpson*. Toronto: Binfords, 1944.

New, Chester. *Lord Durham*. Oxford: Clarendon, 1929.

Ogden, Adele. *The California Sea Otter Trade, 1784–1848*. Berkeley and Los Angeles: University of California Press, 1941.

Okun, S. B. *The Russian-American Company*. Translated by Carl Ginsburg. Cambridge, Mass.: Harvard University Press, 1951.

Petrie, Charles. *George Canning*. London: Eyre & Spottiswoode, 1946.

Pitkin, Timothy. *A Statistical View of the Commerce of the United States of America*. New Haven: Durrie & Peck, 1835.

Porter, Kenneth W. *John Jacob Astor—Business Man*. Cambridge, Mass.: Harvard University Press, 1931. 2 vols.

Pritchett, John P. *The Red River Valley, 1811–1849*. New Haven: Yale University Press, 1942.

Puryear, Vernon J. *England, Russia, and the Straits Question, 1844–1856*. Berkeley: University of California Press, 1931.

Quaife, Milo M. *The Diary of James K. Polk*. Chicago: A. C. McClurg, 1910. 4 vols.

Reardon, James M. *Georges Anthony Belcourt*. St. Paul: North Central Publishing Company, 1955.

Rich, E. E., ed. *Colin Robertson's Correspondence Book, September 1817 to September 1822*. London: Hudson's Bay Record Society, 1939.

———. *The Letters of John McLoughlin from Fort Vancouver to the Governor and Committee, First Series, 1825–38*. London: Hudson's Bay Record Society, 1941.

———. *The Letters of John McLoughlin from Fort Vancouver to the Governor and Committee, Second Series, 1839–44*. London: Hudson's Bay Record Society, 1943.

———. *The Letters of John McLoughlin from Fort Vancouver to the Governor and Committee, Third Series, 1844–46*. London: Hudson's Bay Record Society, 1944.

———. *Peter Skene Ogden's Snake Country Journals*. London: Hudson's Bay Record Society, 1950.

———. *Simpson's 1828 Journey to the Columbia*. London: Hudson's Bay Record Society, 1947.

Rich, E. E., and A. M. Johnson, eds. *Cumberland House Journals and Inland Journals, 1775–82. First Series, 1775–79.* London: Hudson's Bay Record Society, 1951.
———. ———. *Second Series, 1779–82.* London: Hudson's Bay Record Society, 1952.
Ross, Alexander. *Adventures of the First Settlers on the Oregon or Columbia River.* Edited by Milo M. Quaife. Chicago: R. R. Donnelly & Sons, 1923.
———. *The Fur Hunters of the Far West.* London: Smith, Elder, 1855. 2 vols.
———. *The Red River Settlement: Its Rise, Progress, and Present State.* London: Smith, Elder, 1856.
Sage, Walter N. *Sir James Douglas and British Columbia.* Toronto: University of Toronto Press, 1930.
Scholefield, E. O. S., and F. W. Howay. *British Columbia from the Earliest Times to the Present.* Vancouver: S. J. Clarke Publishing Company, 1914.
Shortridge, Wilson Porter. *The Transition of a Typical Frontier.* Menasha: George Banta, [1922].
Simpson, George. *Narrative of a Journey Round the World.* London: H. Colburn, 1847. 2 vols.
Skelton, Oscar D. *The Railway Builders.* Toronto and Glasgow: Brook & Company, 1920.
Smet, P. J. de. *Oregon Missions and Travels over the Rocky Mountains in 1845–46.* New York: E. Dunigan, 1847.
Smith, William. *The History of the Post Office in British North America, 1639–1870.* Cambridge: University Press, 1920.
Snowden, Clinton A. *A History of Washington.* New York: Century History Company, 1909. 4 vols.
Stanley, George F. G. *The Birth of Western Canada.* London: Longmans, Green, 1936.
Stapleton, Augustus G. *The Political Life of the Right Honourable George Canning.* London: Longman, Rees, Orme, Brown and Green, 1831. 3 vols.
———. *George Canning and his Times.* London: J. W. Parker and Son, 1859.
Stapleton, Edward J., ed. *Some Official Correspondence of George Canning.* London: 1887. 2 vols.
Temperley, Harold. *The Foreign Policy of Canning, 1822–1827.* London: G. Bell and Sons, 1925.
Thwaites, Reuben Gold, ed., *Collections of the State Historical Society of Wisconsin.* Vol. XIX. Madison: The Society, 1910.
Townsend, John K. *Narrative of a Journey across the Rocky Mountains.* Philadelphia: H. Perkins, 1839.
Trevelyan, George M. *Lord Grey of the Reform Bill.* New York: Longmans, Green, 1920.
Trotter, Reginald G. *Canadian Federation. Its Origins and Achievement.* London: J. M. Dent and Sons, 1924.
Wallace, W. Stewart, ed. *Documents Relating to the North West Company.* Toronto: Champlain Society, 1934.
Ward, A. W., and G. P. Gooch, eds. *The Cambridge History of British Foreign Policy, 1783–1919.* New York: Macmillan, 1922–1923. 3 vols.
Watkin, Edward W. *Canada and the States, Recollections, 1851 to 1886.* London: Ward Lock and Company, [1887].
Webster, Fletcher, ed. *The Writings and Speeches of Daniel Webster, Private Correspondence.* Boston: Little, Brown, 1857. 2 vols.
Winther, Oscar O. *The Great Northwest.* New York: Knopf, 1950.

## PAMPHLETS

British North American Association. *Confederation of the British North-American Provinces.* London: 1865.
Dodds, James A. *The Hudson's Bay Company, its Position and Prospects.* London: 1866.
Douell, Alexander. *A Project for Opening a North-West Passage between the At-*

lantic and Pacific Oceans by Means of a Railway on British Territory. London: 1852.

Fergusson, James. The Peril of Portsmouth; or, French Fleets and English Forts. London: 1852.

Fitzgerald, James E. An Examination of the Charter and Proceedings of the Hudson's Bay Company with Reference to the Grant of Vancouver's Island. London: 1849.

———. Vancouver's Island. Reprinted from Colonial Magazine (Oct., 1848). London: 1848.

———. Vancouver's Island, The Hudson's Bay Company, and the Government. London: 1848.

The Hudson's Bay Company. What is it? London: 1864.

Isbister, Alexander K. A Proposal for a New Penal Settlement, in connexion with the Colonization of the Uninhabited Districts of British North America. London: 1850.

Kernaghan, W. Hudson's Bay and Red River Settlement. London: [1857].

Memorial of the People of Red River to the British and Canadian Governments. Submitted to Canadian government by Sandford Fleming. Quebec: 1863.

Simpson, Alexander. The Oregon Territory. Claims Thereto of England and America Considered; its Condition and Prospects. London: 1846.

Synge, Millington H. The Country v. The Company. London: 1861.

## ARTICLES

"American Fur Company Employees—1818–1819," in Reuben G. Thwaites, ed. Collections of the State Historical Society of Wisconsin, XII (Madison: 1892).

Andrews, Clarence L. "Russian Plans for American Dominion," Washington Historical Quarterly, XVIII (Apr., 1927), 83–92.

Appel, Livia, and Theodore C. Blegen. "Official Encouragement of Immigration during the Territorial Period," Minnesota History Bulletin, V (Aug., 1923), 167–171.

Aspinall, A. "The Canningite Party," Transactions of the Royal Historical Society, 4th series, XVII (London: 1934), 177–226.

The Bankers Magazine. Vols. XXI–XXIII. London: 1861–1863.

The Beaver. 1920–1953.

Blegen, Theodore C. "James Wickes Taylor: A Biographical Sketch," Minnesota History Bulletin, I (Nov., 1915), 153–219.

Blue, Verne. "The Oregon Question—1818–1828," Oregon Historical Quarterly, XXIII (Sept., 1922), 193–219.

Buck, Solon J. "The Story of the Grand Portage," Minnesota History Bulletin, V (Feb., 1923), 14–28.

Clark, R. C. "How British and American Subjects Unite in a Common Government for Oregon Territory in 1844," Oregon Historical Quarterly, XIII (June, 1912), 140–159.

Commager, Henry S. "England and the Oregon Treaty of 1846," Oregon Historical Quarterly, XXVIII (Mar., 1927), 18–38.

"The Correspondence and Journals of Captain Nathaniel J. Wyeth, 1831–6," in F. G. Young, ed., Sources of the History of Oregon. Eugene: 1899. Vol. I, nos. 3–6.

Curti, Merle. "George N. Sanders, Patriot of the Fifties," South Atlantic Quarterly, XXVIII (Jan., 1928), 78–87.

Davidson, Donald C. "Relations of the Hudson's Bay Company with the Russian American Company on the Northwest Coast, 1829–1867," British Columbia Historical Quarterly, V (Jan., 1941), 37–46.

Elliott, T. C. "Peter Skene Ogden, Fur Trader." Oregon Historical Quarterly, XI (Sept., 1910), 229–278.

———. "The Surrender at Astoria in 1818," Oregon Historical Quarterly, XIX (Dec., 1918), 271–282.

Fitzgerald, James E. "Vancouver's Island—The New Colony," *Colonial Magazine,* XIV (Aug., 1848).

Galbraith, John S. "Edward 'Bear' Ellice," *The Beaver,* Outfit 285 (Summer, 1954), 26–29.

———. "Fitzgerald versus the Hudson's Bay Company: the Founding of Vancouver Island," *British Columbia Historical Quarterly,* XVI (July–Oct., 1952), 191–207.

———. "France as a Factor in the Oregon Negotiations," *Pacific Northwest Quarterly,* XLIV (Apr., 1953), 69–73.

———. "George N. Sanders, 'Influence Man' for the Hudson's Bay Company," *Oregon Historical Quarterly,* LIII (Sept., 1952), 159–176.

———. "Perry Collins at the Colonial Office," *British Columbia Historical Quarterly,* XVII (July–Oct., 1953), 207–214.

Garry, Francis N. A., ed. "Diary of Nicholas Garry, deputy-governor of the Hudson's Bay Company from 1822–35: a detailed narrative of his travels in the North-West Territories of North America in 1821," in *Transactions of the Royal Society of Canada,* 2d series, VI (1900), Sec. II, 73–204.

Gunn, H. G. "The Fight for Free Trade in Rupert's Land," *Proceedings of the Mississippi Valley Historical Association,* IV (1910–1911), 73–90.

Heilbron, Bertha L., ed. "Isaac I. Stevens and the Pacific Railroad Survey of 1853," *Minnesota History,* VII (June, 1926), 127–149.

Howay, F. W. "Brig Owhyhee in the Columbia, 1829–30," *Oregon Historical Quarterly,* XXXV (Mar., 1934), 10–21.

Howison, Neil M. "Report of Lieutenant Neil M. Howison on Oregon, 1846," *Oregon Historical Quarterly,* XIV (Mar., 1913), 1–60.

Knaplund, Paul. "James Stephen on Granting Vancouver Island to the Hudson's Bay Company, 1846–1848," *British Columbia Historical Quarterly,* IX (Oct., 1945), 259–271.

———. "Letters from James Edward Fitzgerald to W. E. Gladstone Concerning Vancouver Island and the Hudson's Bay Company, 1848–1850," *British Columbia Historical Quarterly,* XIII (Jan., 1949), 1–21.

Lamb, W. Kaye. "The Governorship of Richard Blanshard," *British Columbia Historical Quarterly,* XIV (Jan.–Apr., 1950), 1–40.

Listenfelt, Hattie. "The Hudson Bay Company and the Red River Trade," in O. G. Libby, ed., *Collections of the State Historical Society of North Dakota,* IV (1913), 235–337.

Long, Dorothy E. T. "The Elusive Mr. Ellice," *Canadian Historical Review,* XXIII (Mar., 1942), 42–57.

Longstaff, F. V., and W. Kaye Lamb. "The Royal Navy on the Northwest Coast, 1813–1850," *British Columbia Historical Quarterly,* IX (Jan., 1945), 1–24; (Apr., 1945), 113–128.

Lower, A. R. M. "The Assault on the Laurentian Barrier, 1850–1870," *Canadian Historical Review,* X (Dec., 1929), 294–307.

Maloney, Alice B. "Peter Skene Ogden's Trapping Expedition to the Gulf of California, 1829–30," *California Historical Society Quarterly,* XIX (Dec., 1940), 308–316.

Martin, Chester. "The Hudson's Bay Company's Monopoly of the Fur Trade at the Red River Settlement, 1821–1850," *Proceedings of the Mississippi Valley Historical Association,* VII (1913–1914), 254–265.

Merk, Frederick. "The British Corn Crisis and the Oregon Treaty," *Agricultural History,* VIII (July, 1934), 95–123.

———. "British Party Politics and the Oregon Treaty," *American Historical Review,* XXXVII (July, 1932), 653–677.

———. "The Oregon Pioneers and the Boundary," *American Historical Review,* XXIX (July, 1924), 681–699.

———. "The Oregon Question in the Webster-Ashburton Negotiations," *Mississippi Valley Historical Review,* XLIII (Dec., 1956), 379–404.

Mitchell, Elaine A. "Edward Watkin and the Buying-Out of the Hudson's Bay Company," *Canadian Historical Review*, XXXIV (Sept., 1953), 219–244.

Morison, Samuel E. "New England and the Opening of the Columbia River Salmon Trade, 1830," *Oregon Historical Quarterly*, XXVIII (June, 1927), 111–132.

Partoll, Albert J. "Fort Connah: A Frontier Trading Post, 1847–1871," *Pacific Northwest Quarterly*, XXX (Oct., 1939), 399–415.

Pritchett, John P. "Some Red River Fur-Trade Activities," *Minnesota History Bulletin*, V (May, 1924), 401–423.

Quaife, Milo M. "An Experiment of the Fathers in State Socialism," *Wisconsin Magazine of History*, III (Mar., 1920), 277–290.

"Regular Trappers," *Household Words* (June 14, 1854), 471–476.

Rife, Clarence W. "Norman W. Kittson, a Fur-Trader at Pembina," *Minnesota History*, VI (Sept., 1925), 225–252.

Rogers, J. D. "Canada Geographical," *in* Charles P. Lucas, ed., *A Historical Geography of the British Colonies*, Vol. V, Part III. Oxford: 1909.

Ross, Alexander. "Journal of the Snake River Expedition, 1824," *Oregon Historical Quarterly*, XIV (Dec., 1913), 366–388.

Ross, Frank E. "The Retreat of the Hudson's Bay Company in the Pacific Northwest," *Canadian Historical Review*, XVIII (Sept., 1937), 262–280.

Ruckman, J. Ward. "Ramsay Crooks and the Fur Trade of the Northwest," *Minnesota History*, VII (Mar., 1926), 18–31.

Saw, Reginald. "Sir John H. Pelly, Bart.," *British Columbia Historical Quarterly*, XIII (Jan., 1949), 23–32.

Schafer, Joseph, ed. "Documents Relative to Warre and Vavasour's Military Reconnaissance in Oregon, 1845–6," *Oregon Historical Quarterly*, X (Mar., 1919), 1–99.

Scott, Leslie M. "Influence of American Settlement upon the Oregon Boundary Treaty of 1846," *Oregon Historical Quarterly*, XXIX (Mar., 1928), 1–19.

———. "Report of Lieutenant Peel on Oregon in 1845–46," *Oregon Historical Quarterly*, XXIX (Mar., 1928), 51–76.

Scouler, John. "Journal of a Voyage to N.W. America," *Oregon Historical Quarterly*, VI (Sept., 1905), 276–287.

Shippee, Lester Burrell. "The Federal Relations of Oregon," *Oregon Historical Quarterly*, XIX (June, 1918), 89–133; (Sept., 1918), 189–230; (Dec., 1918), 283–331; XX (June, 1919), 173–218; (Sept., 1919), 261–295.

Smith, Alice E. "Daniel Whitney, Pioneer Wisconsin Businessman," *Wisconsin Magazine of History*, XXIV (Mar., 1941), 283–304.

Stacey, C. P. "The Hudson's Bay Company and Anglo-American Rivalries During the Oregon Dispute," *Canadian Historical Review*, XVIII (Sept., 1937), 281–306.

"The Stop the Way Company," *Household Words*, no. 198 (Jan. 7, 1854), 449–454.

"The Story of a Dead Monopoly," *Cornhill Magazine*, XXII (Aug., 1870).

Synge, Millington H. "Proposal for a Rapid Communication with the Pacific and the East via British North America," *Journal of the Royal Geographical Society of London*, 22 (1852), 174–200.

Thwaites, Reuben G. "The Fur-Trade in Wisconsin—1812–1825," *Collections of the State Historical Society of Wisconsin*, XX (Madison, 1911), 1–395.

Van Alstyne, Richard W. "International Rivalries in the Pacific Northwest," *Oregon Historical Quarterly*, XLVI (Sept., 1945), 185–218.

Victor, Frances Fuller. "The First Oregon Cavalry," *Oregon Historical Quarterly*, III (June, 1902), 123–163.

Warre, Henry, M. Vavasour, *et al.* "Secret Mission of Warre and Vavasour," *Washington Historical Quarterly*, III (Apr., 1912), 131–153.

Winchell, Alexander N. "Minnesota's Northern Boundary," *Collections of the Minnesota Historical Society*, VIII (St. Paul, 1898), 185–212.

NEWSPAPERS

*British Colonist* (Victoria), 1859–1860.
*Canadian News,* 1856–1870.
London *Times,* 1856–1869.
Montreal *Herald,* 1865–1866.
Toronto *Globe,* 1856–1870.
Victoria *Gazette,* 1859.

# INDEX